A COLLECTION OF CULTURAL LECTURES

History of Civilization and Ideology

BOOK-I

A COLLECTION OF CULTURAL LECTURES

History of Civilization and Ideology

BOOK-I

Wang Dongyue

A Collection of Cultural Lectures (I)

First Edition

Translated by Bridgemind
www.Bridge-Minds.com

ISBN: 978-1-955779-38-8 (Paper back)
ISBN: 978-1-955779-10-4 (eBook)

Printed in the United States of America

Contents

Book I

4. Overview of the Western Philosophy (II)....................339

5. Cultural Origin of Confucianism............................431

6. Legalism and Social Implementation of National Culture 555

Preface

The class that we never had in the past ......

It is really amazing. This is my personal feeling in learning about Professor Wang Dongyue's thoughts in recent years.

I am not qualified to write a preface for the collection of Professor Wang Dongyue's lectures in any way. But as an ordinary student, I can tell my own experience with this course, with Dongyue' thoughts and the Professor in person.

It was a coincidence for me to walk into Professor Wang's classroom and learn about his thought.

As early as 2015 I bought two books, *The Joy of Fish* and *A Unified Theory of Evolution* after I listened to an audio program called *Logical Thinking*. After a brief reading of the books, I was surprised to find that they were extraordinary. At that time, I didn't know that the author was still alive, let alone the fact that he was lecturing a workshop. Once I went to Fuzhou for a business meeting; when it was over, I wandered around a local street called Sanfang Qixiang and saw a poster of Professor Wang Dongyue's coming lectures in a bookstore called *Useless Space*. I was happy with the information about Wang Dongyue, so I left my phone number with the bookstore owner and asked him to inform me when the event was near ......

After I returned to Beijing, I soon attended a 3-day course on Real Estate held at a local university called Hundun. During breakfast time I chatted with a student in the dining hall; I casually asked her which course she was attending. She told me that she was in a 12-day course on philosophy, so I asked her who was the lecturer? She said it was Professor Wang Dongyue.

"Wang DongYue?!" I exclaimed in shock that I almost dropped

my knife and fork because I did not expect that I got so close to him at the time.

"You say Wang Dongyue?" I asked again unbelievably.

"Yes, shall I introduce you to our class?" she confirmed it friendly.

In less than an hour, I changed my early registered course and became a student at *Dongyue Learning Workshop*. From then on, I began to learn the idea of "weakening compensation"......

Most people in my generation built up our knowledge structure in our high school years. In addition to Chinese, Mathematics, English, Science, Chemistry, Politics, and History the test-education, we did numerous tests or examinations. We had singing competitions in spring and summer; we also participated in various sports in autumn and winter, or after-school competitions of all kinds ...... those years were really filled with plentiful activities, thereby making us feel that we knew almost anything.

After I graduated from college, I started my business activities. I read books in my spare time and I believed I knew quite a lot. But what is knowledge? How can we sort knowledge into ideas? How can we decide on an idea as a correct worldview, and use it to guide our activities? These seemingly useless but fundamentally important questions flash in my mind occasionally when I read relevant articles, but I had never seriously considered them until I met Professor Wang and attended his 12-day course of philosophy......

Many of my fellow friends, after listening to Professor Wang's lectures, feel shocked by his huge amount of knowledgeable information, and it is true.

Science became the major movement in modern times, it develops quickly by virtue of *sub-disciplines and logical exploration,* which constitutes the basic paradigm of our national education, resulting in our people being *narrow subject informed* rather than *integrated* in terms of comprehensive knowledge. It is true that many people are quite *knowledgeable in their special fields,* but they know very little outside their professions. Human knowledge advances rapidly with information increasing greatly, which makes sub-discipline education the only way to learn knowledge. In the 1960s, Bertalanffy mentioned in the preface of *General Systems Theory* that we should shift from "sub-disciplinary knowledge" to "cross-cutting knowledge". In recent years, many cutting-edge scientific institutions, like the Santa Fe Institute, began to adopt a multidisciplinary approach to the study of science. It is clear that people with coherent and integrated knowledge have better cognitive discernment. As Professor Wang said, "If you want to really understand something, you can't just be inside it, you have to stand away from it, or to be above it, so that you can see the whole picture." I believe this statement is also true for *knowledge* as a whole. In contrast, our education is absolutely dominated by subjects, by sub-disciplines, or rather, by fragmentary knowledge, thus we have no idea of what integrated *knowledge* is at all.

In this series of lectures, with the 13.8 billion years of space-time scale as the overall background, Professor Wang discussed the causes of occurrence of human cognition, combined with his extensive knowledge. He discussed various cultural issues with numerous concrete examples, leading us to explore the motives of human civilization and to compare the cultural difference between East and West in philosophy, theology, and science, which provides us a cross-reference for our knowledge structure indeed.

The expansion of knowledge alone does not fully reflect the charm of this course. It is the deep philosophical thought that makes the solid trunk of the lectures, which supports the branches bearing the fruit of knowledge. It is precisely a philosophical sorting of *knowledge* and inquiry of the *direction of knowledge* that made these lectures fascinating.

The 12-day course of philosophy also reveals the meaning of another layer.

In the modern era, the process of human thought has been in a pattern that science advances upward colorfully, but philosophy declines in silence, especially since the Vienna School of logical positivism. Stephen Hawking even said at the beginning of his posthumous work *The Grand Design* that "philosophy is dead". But in this 12-day course, we can really feel the fascination of philosophy. This is not a study of a particular philosopher or school of thought, but rather a study of the whole history of philosophy — as many said, philosophy is the foresight of science!

Philosophy is a game for the few, but the issues discussed in philosophy lay deep at the bottom that concerns the ordinary lives of the most. In Professor Wang's words, "human civilization and their overall actions have to follow the thought channel of thinkers." Unfortunately, in the whole process of our education, we pursue the actual value of practical things, rather than those abstract questions. The lack of education in philosophy has deprived us of the perspective of human thought as a whole and the capability that enable us to reflect on our own thoughts. This course takes cultural and civilizational phenomena as the entrance, leading us to explore the significance of *reflecting on thought itself* so that we change our habitual way of thinking from *seeking answers* to *exploring questions,* which will benefit us in terms of deep thinking.

In the classroom, Professor Wang often says, "If you understand this meaning, then you get somewhat closer to the core of the class."

What is this meaning? — It refers to the *principle of weakening compensation!*

Unlike other previous classes of philosophy, which were mostly based on the history of philosophy or the philosophical thought of a particular philosopher, the structural frame of this 12-day course is built on a logical model of philosophical worldview by Professor Wang with his dedication more than 20 years.

The existence of this underlying idea makes this course like a magic show. Many a time when the lecture came to a crux, Professor Wang made a very little dissection of the previous ideas — like a skillful butcher dissecting a cow with the least movement of a knife before the cow is completely dismantled to flesh and bones — the obscurity of puzzles in human thought history at once became thoroughly clarified......, leaving the audience fascinated.

If anyone is interested in the profound connotation of this principle of weakening compensation, he can read the book *A Unified Theory of Evolution,* and he will see its fascinating reasoning.

Nevertheless, the first barrier to learning philosophy lies in the understanding language of philosophy.

Philosophical thought is far-reaching in scope, with logical reflection on nearly all phenomena universally, and it has to be in three consistencies (self-consistency, other consistency, and continuous consistency). This requires a precise language to express that is beyond our daily language; so, philosophers try hard with it without exceptions. Leibniz said that philosophy should have its own linguistic symbols; Heidegger simply created *Dasein* or *Anwesen* to express his unique concepts of philosophy; Wittgenstein actually considered philosophy to be the misuse of language, thus completely rejecting philosophy in the traditional sense and announced the end of philosophical activity ......

We know that *reading is beneficial*, but for books of philosophy, *reading becomes a hard nut*. Therefore, many people who attempt philosophy end up with the same conclusion — a book of philosophy is harder than learning a language.

Since Professor Wang constructed in *A Unified Theory of Evolution* a completely new logical system of worldview, this book certainly has its own unique terminology. It also contains a lot of references and criticisms of the major ideas of previous philosophy in history. All this surely blocks beginners. Therefore, this 12-day course is a very helpful step of preparation for this difficult philosophical tome.

I was amazed when I proofread the manuscript of this class recording. This lecture series was almost free of redundant words and repetitions, and the statements were all consistent, so I only need to work on punctuation, typos, and special terms, and I hardly had to deal with semantic collation. This superb narration is stuffed with the East-West cultural comparison as the skeleton, taking the familiar Eastern hundred schools of thought, Buddhism, *I-Ching*, Chinese medicine, etc. as the cutting-in points, making reflections of respective criticisms of Western philosophy, scientific thought, and important doctrines as the clue, with the principle of weakening compensation as the analytic tool, screens nearly all aspects of the human cultural history. Therefore, with a little effort in going through the series of lectures, one can build a staircase to reach this great book *A Unified Theory of Evolution*, or even reach the tomes of other philosophers, convenient going further in terms of philosophical thought.

In addition to these brain benefits, the reshaping of concepts and the humanistic care latent in these lectures are perhaps the fundamental reason why this class attracts so many students.

First, the *concept of knowledge* is reshaped. We are not unfamiliar with the concept of *knowledge* itself. The endless quarrels and repeated entanglements of *material, the mind, agnosticism, and semantic confusion* in philosophy for so long a time have led to the increasingly indistinct situation of philosophy itself; in science, the further division and investigation on major issues like *motion, space-time, quantum physics, gene heredity, social configuration,* and *methodology,* etc. really bring us more uncertain information. In contrast, Professor Wang's 12-day course talks about *empirical,* the *proof and falsification* of knowledge, and how the *logical principles of three consistencies* work in the *coupling of mental perceptual attributes* so that the *concept of right and wrong* is eliminated and the *idea of truth-seeking* is replaced by the practical *survival-seeking.* This is a major shift in the view of *knowledge.*

Second, the *view of history* is reshaped. *Who made the history*? The answer to this proposition reflects the understanding of the driving force behind human history. For a long time, we have been educated with the dialectical argument of whether *people make history* or *heroes make history.* As Liang Qichao said, "History is the sum of human activities," so *people* constitute the absolute main part of history or even the whole of it. Therefore, the *making of history* becomes a conspicuous and natural arrogance. However, Professor Wang's *determinism of the structure of being survival* (which is different from Darwin's theory of biological evolution) removes this veil and reveals the underlying fact that *all things sustain in transmutation,* including humans, which is perfectly expressed in that "human nature is the blossom of all-natural things, and humanity is the continuation of the natural evolution". This raised a major shift in our *view of history.*

Third, the *worldview* is reshaped. The establishment of a *world view* is for the development of human thought, which pulls human society and civilization to a high level on the one side, and causes the collapse of human natural status on the other. Philosophy itself is declining, while science is delving into the narrower subdivision, having no time to deal with any grand propositions. In this class, Professor Wang starts by *tracing the cultural origin of East and West,* then builds up step by step till the last two days the new existential criteria of *degree of being, degree of compensation,* and *threshold of subsistence,* providing the *principle of weakening compensation* as a new coordinate for the world view. The major conclusion is that the *survival effect is in inverse proportion to survival capacity, instead of seeking truth all beings live to seek survival,* and *subjective attributes coupled with the objective attribute,* all have a direct impact on our basic cognitive logic, quite different from almost all the doctrines we are familiar with, including Darwin's *evolutionary theory of biology.* This is a major shift in our *worldview.*

Fourth, the *social view* is reshaped. Since the enlightenment of civilization, except for a few sages like Laozi, most human doctrines are based on the *positive aggression* of emotional orientation in the *promotion of civilization,* with the *Renaissance* in particular. Now the proposed logical system of *one-way declination of the degree of revealing* the opposite tone. Although the *progressive doctrine* characterized by the *increasing degree of compensation* still prevails, the foreboding of the future crisis of human existence casts a shadow on every individual and every nation as well, thereby repositioning the meaning of human beings and human society. This is a major shift in our *society's view.*

The reshapes of the above four basic views of *knowledge, history, world,* and *society* render us so much an impact that our concept of *human superiority* is no longer solid; instead, we began to realize the deep existential crisis behind the flourishing civilization, such that we must transcend the individual, nation, and country to establish a worldview of the whole humanity. This is the perspective of humanity as a whole that this 12-day course renders us.

The knowledgeable information, the new concepts, and the way of thought in these lectures certainly set up a perspective and an idea that we never had in the past; but it is the quiet pursuit of the origin of knowledge and the ultimate concern for the destiny of humanity contained in each lecture that makes the backbone of this course.

It has been more than a year since Professor Wang Dongyue closed the pulpit. Whenever I find myself indecisive in the mundane life, or need to argue the reason, or feel tired, pieces of Professor Wang's statements will well up in my mind, and his steady, smooth and low charming voice will ring in my ears .... learn to look at things through the presentments, learn to avoid falling into various entanglements. I believe many fellow friends of the workshop will miss that voice and that classroom as much as I do ......

As a student of that 12-day course, I would like to thank Li Shanyou and Zeng Xingye, who organized the workshop, and arranged the video of the lectures so that it can be spread to more people; thank the monitor Xinran for her dedication to the class.

I would also thank Zhao Mei, the wife of the Professor, for her good care and assistance to Professor Wang, which makes the 12-day course possible.

Sincerely thanks to Professor Wang Dongyue!

Sun Danlin
January 30, 2020

Speech at Opening Ceremony

This is my last time to give lectures.

First of all, it is necessary to state that this is a purely cultural and ideological class, so you should not seek practicality. A philosopher must be very lonely when he is alive, so if any of you want to follow me, he will be in vain; my doctrine may not be accepted by people until after I pass away, but by that time you will be old, so I am afraid you will not see its afterglow. So, you listening to my lectures is much ado about nothing, especially it is not easy. This course will be a little bit deeper, whether it is about Chinese culture or Western philosophy, as well as my philosophical system on the last day of the class, I will not lecture them in the usual way; I will try to give you a little bit of new ideas, so this class is a bit hard to listen to, or rather, it is not very interesting. I hope that you will not listen to this class with a utilitarian mind, so that you can listen to this class to get a taste of it.

Let me give you an example, Schrödinger, one of the founding figures of quantum mechanics, who said in a lecture entitled Science and Humanism that science is generally thought to be useful, and that people respect science and pursue it just because it can bring great productivity, make people's lives more comfortable, more powerful, and so on. This, he says, is the greatest slander of science. True science is first of all an expression of the human spirit, it is exactly the same as archaeology, linguistics, aesthetics and other such seemingly useless studies, it is the sublimation of the human spirit, rather than something practical. If you see science as a practical thing, you are indeed devaluing it, or you simply do not understand what science as a cultural phenomenon is all about. Think about it, if this is so with science, let alone the fact that we are talking about something that is not directly related to science, but is entirely about the origins of the history of human civilization, about the relationship between the history of ideas and the history of civilization, and then about what drives it, what its ultimate direction is, and how it shapes our personality and our society. We are discussing these issues, and it certainly has nothing to do with practicality.

In general, the less you seek practicality in the learning process, the more you will be able to solidify the foundation at the bottom of your spirit. If you seek practicality, you will inevitably keep floating yourself at the shallowest level. Therefore, I suggest that even if some of the things we talk seem to have a little practicality, or have practicality in your association, you should mainly concentrate on the non-practical level of spiritual foundation, so that you may slightly gain some vision of the distance, that is the only value of this course.

Furthermore, I hope that you will follow this course step by step, that is, according to the arrangement of this course, preferably no absence in between, because this lecture series is somehow logically connected.

The first class is on *The Origins of Eastern and Western Cultures*, which is actually about the factors that contributed to the origin of human civilization; so, it is a foundation for the subsequent courses.

Then we will talk about "Laozi", which is the highest end of East- ern thought. The reason we put "Laozi" on the second day is that our next class will be *An Overview of the Foundations of Western Philosophy*, that is, we will bring out the high end of Western philosophy, so that we will have a clear contrast between the high ends of Eastern and Western thought.

Next, we will slowly move on the topics like Confucius, Legalism, *I-Ching*, Buddhism, etc. in order.

In addition to the National cultures, we will have a special session on *Philosophy of Human Body*, and we will also talk about *The Decline of National Culture*, which actually previews or foreshadows the decline of Western culture.

Finally, we will discuss Trends and Crises of Human Civilization, a serious and urgent topic. The idea is based on the philosophicalprinciple presented in the book *A Unified Theory of Evolution*, although it could only be an outline explained in class.

I have to make a statement here that even though I always try to dig as deep as possible when I teach in class, you must understand that these lectures are still superficial things. What does it mean? When I was writing the philosophy book *A Unified Theory of Evolution*, I never accommodated my thought to the reader, and I only pursue the rigorous expression of ideas. But it is absolutely not feasible for me to do so with these lectures, although I strive to have a certain profundity, coherence, logic, I also have to let the audience to be interested. Since I have to take care of the audience, I need to lift up something quite deep to the intuitive level to interpretate at the surface. This poses a big problem, which is to superficialize and vulgarize the profound idea. Therefore, I must emphasize that you will not see the content of my lectures when you read my book. The content of my lectures is the common knowledge of human beings, not my original knowledge, and I only use my thoughts to link it up and elaborate it. I write my book only with my own insight, and I will never write about any discovery that does not belong to me. Therefore, writing a book is the implementation of an original opinion, while doing a lecture is a summary of human culture. And since lectures have to accommodate the audience, they cannot help but running on a superficial, intuitive level, so I would emphasize the reading of the original texts if you want to understand something in depth. Even so, it will be quite difficult for you to listen. For example, if we talk about Laozi, I hope you will read *Daodejing* before we have the class; for example, if we talk about An *Overview of the Foundations of Western Philosophy*, that lecture is rather difficult, even if I only talk about the most superficial part, it is still a challenge. If you can read some books on the history of Western philosophy and do a little bit of pre-reading, you may find the class more interesting.

Another thing, our course, which is taught continuously, is about 80 credit hours in total. As you know, a selective course in university is usually given only 40 hours, that is, two hours per week, one selective course at the end of each semester, so our course is about 80 hours, which is equivalent to a heavy-loaded selective course, that is, equivalent to a systematic course. I hope that you will not focus on the knowledge, though the content of my lectures may be characterized by a large amount of knowledge, but rather on ideas, that is, on how we human beings have developed throughout the history of civilization and how we have unfolded the models and sequences of ideas.

In my past lectures, I kept repeating that human civilization moves on the passage of ideas of thinkers, rather than in the objective world. You know, all animals live in the objective world, but they don't create civilization. So, all the power of human beings comes from ideas; but there are very a few people who have the ability to create ideas. Our lecture will focus on the process of unfolding the ideas of the most famous thinkers from the East to the West in the history of mankind. What do you listen to in this course? Listen to how the basic drive of human civilization operates at the level of human thought, which is the most important connotation that you ought to focus on.

In fact, all of our education in school years of elementary, secondary, and university is for utilitarian purposes, for exams, for advancement in school or for job hunting, etc. In other words, we seldom have any pure, non-utilitarian, purposeless training of the mind and inquiry during our education.

So, this time, I want you to follow me on a journey of mind-training and exploration. This is the most powerful thing that actually shapes the whole model of human existence. It might be something unique to listen to the course in such a detailed way. Along with my thought sequence, along with the thought sequence of the thinkers who previously built the foundation of the entire human civilization, you will start your own thought training and spiritual reshaping. If you can achieve this result, you will gain tremendously.

Lastly, these classes will be relatively dull, because the idea is never flashy, it is never claptrap, and it is never consciously making itself shining. I will discuss how the ideas work in as plain as possible. We are after logical rigor and profound thoughts, and we are after these things, so this course will not be flashy or give you much pleasure. The final conclusion of this course may be a great disappointment to you, because it will tell you that the future fate of human beings is surprisingly a particularly troublesome pattern, and that the future trend of human civilization is, by and large, a groping process with a very limited future and a future full of darkness.

I hope you will attend these lectures with a contemplative and reflective attitude, and with a different interest in pursuit of the insightfulness. There will be nothing inspirational, exciting or encouraging in this course; instead, you may feel some sort of pessimistic mood. This is why Aristotle said that the greatest art of mankind must be the art of tragedy. Why is tragedy the highest form of artistic expression? It is because it reflects the destiny of mankind itself in the most profound way. That is to say, the destiny of humanity contains great tragedy, and this is where the infectious power of tragic art lies. So, when a thought is not conspicuous, not exciting, but in a sad, very deep silent search, it obviously does not fit our daily life aspirations; but it may express some potential decisive element that you must not lose in the inquiry and exploration of humanity's future, because it may affect your fate and even the fate of your kind.

March 9, 2018

Origins of Eastern and Western Cultures and Civilizations

Preamble

Today we are going to talk about the origins of Eastern and Western cultures and civilizations, which is the most basic one of all the 12-day course. I suggest that you audience proceed it step by step, without skipping classes or interruptions, because there is an internal logical continuity between the whole course. Until the last day of the course, I will give a philosophical statement and summary.

I will start with a basic description on this course.

Our aim in this lecture series is to elaborate on the dynamics and direction of the occurrence and evolution of human civilization as a whole. A considerable part of this course is the national culture section, but one must not interpret it as that the national culture is the focus. The reason why we lay a relatively heavier weight on national culture section is that:

First, with national culture as the baseline, we would have a better sense of intimacy in discussing the entire sequence and trend of human civilization development.

Second, we really need to make up ground in this area.

Third, it is easiest to follow this thread to start a discussion of the overall development of human civilization as a whole.

Once again, I emphasize that there is no practicality in this lesson, and we will only discuss Dao part in this lesson. As you know, traditional Chinese culture has been distinguishing between Dao (theory) and Shu (Technique) since ancient times, so let me explain the difference between the two in a different way: Technique refers to you can control and dominate something; the so-called Dao is to explore what controls and dominates you, that is, what controls and dominates human beings. This is the purpose of our lecture series.

Chinese civilization is the only civilization in the world that has continued in one lineage until today. We are all familiar with ancient civilizations like ancient Egypt, ancient Babylon, ancient India, ancient Persia, ancient Greece, ancient Maya, ancient Aztecs, all these ancient civilizations in the world, either discontinued or extinct. Like Ancient Egypt, Ancient India, Ancient Greece, Ancient Persia, even the human race has been replaced. Only the Chinese civilization and its traditional cultural lineage continues to this day. Therefore, it is of immense value.

Let's take a look at what makes this thread of Chinese civilization a baseline for rectifying the total vision of human civilization. It is composed of the following five factors.

First, Chinese civilization has best preserved the grassroots ideological connotations of the primitive period of human civilization.

What does this passage mean? If you go to Egypt now, to Syria and Iraq in the two rivers region, to India, to Greece or Rome, you can still see a large number of ancient artifacts. However, at the beginning of human civilization in the ancient times, the only country that has preserved its sequence of ideas and documents intact is China. Moreover, because China has been using the most primitive hieroglyphic writing of mankind, it is like a safe in which the most primitive and lowest thoughts of mankind were locked, thus leaving a precious heritage.

Moreover, one significant feature of the traditional Chinese culture is that it is even more ancient than ancient Western culture. For what we see now in Western culture has gone through three stages: the theological stage, the philosophical stage, and the scientific stage since modern times. But Chinese culture has preserved intact that part of its thought and culture before the theological stage, which we call pre-theological culture. So we can say that the whole cultural history of mankind has gone through not three stages, but four stages. And the only original specimen we can find in that initial stage is the traditional Chinese culture. (What does that mean? We'll expand on it step by step later in the course.)

Secondly, Chinese traditional culture and its Chinese civilization is the most typical and refined agricultural civilization of mankind, and it has thus become one of the most important specimens for our examination of the history of human civilization.

Due to the closed landscape of East Asia, it avoided ethnic disturbances and cultural conflicts until the Middle Ages, thus allowing the Chinese to refine the primitive agricultural civilization and its ideological lineage for thousands of years, thus forming the most refined and typical cultural specimen sequence of agrarian civilization in the world.

Third, the excessive refinement of this agricultural civilization system has made its transition to an industrial and commercial civilization extremely difficult in modern times, which has led to a violent clash between the type of civilization that represents agricultural civilization in modern China and the type of civilization that represents industrial and commercial civilization in the West.

This conflict process was so serious that we had a humiliating 100-year history in modern times, so much so that at the beginning of the last century, in 1916, Chinese literati advocated the total abandonment of Chinese culture, with the slogan "Down with Confucianism! " We cannot blame those people today because it was a movement to save the country, but the result was that the nation has since discarded almost all of its traditional culture.

This brings us to the requirement of a remedial lesson on this content today, and this is one of the reasons why we lay more weight on national cultural component in this course. And we all need to know that this conflict had reduced us to such a point that one of the most civilized countries in the world in ancient times came to modern times, and it was actually considered a region of barbarism by Western civilization. Our own inferiority to such an extent that in the Republican era, a Western-style walking stick was called a civilization stick, which means that everything we do is not civilized enough, our culture is in complete decline, our culture is reduced to the extent that we despise it ourselves.

This process inspired the fourth feature below, that is, we started to learn to transform, a journey that the Chinese have done more profoundly.

As you know, the Opium War in 1840 marked the complete

decline of Chinese culture, after which the Chinese began to learn from the West, initially called the Foreign Affairs Movement. This foreign affairs movement was summed up in a phrase called "learning the superior techniques of the barbarians to subdue the barbarians later", that is, learning the superior techniques of the West to achieve the purpose of subduing the Westerners. For this reason, our initial learning was superficial and perfunctory.

By 1894, the Sino-Japanese naval battle, the fact of China's disastrous defeat powerfully sounded the alarm to the people of the country. It is important to know that the Meiji Restoration of Japan only occurred in 1868, only 26 years to 1894. It took so short a period for a small country to defeat the Chinese Empire, the country of its teacher; then in the early 20th century, Japan defeated the mighty Russia, which woke up the Chinese astoundingly.

It is not enough for us to learn from the West only the scientific and technological aspects of the West. Japan's Meiji Restoration was successful because they put forward the slogan of leaving Asia and entering Europe, abandoning the Chinese culture altogether and studying the West honestly. After the first Sino-Japanese War, the famous movement of Hundred Days Reform was launched in China, which actually required China to learn from the West comprehensively, including the corresponding transformation of its social and political institutions. The Chinese thus began the process of systematic study of the West, so much so that what we call scholars or outstanding cultural figures of the Republican period were in fact masters in various disciplines who introduced Western culture into China in the most profound way, rather than true cultural builders. The reason they actually became the cultural giants of the Republican period in China is that China was hungered and thirsted to learn from the West, which in a way shows how badly our culture has declined, so much so that we had to Westernize it all, today we have been totally assimilated into Western culture.

Since ancient times, only we assimilated others, but we have never been assimilated by others? But today we are basically assimilated by others in our cultural system. Think about it, from elementary school, secondary school, to university, all the courses you study, except Chinese language, are almost all Western studies. What we put on our head and wear on our body and feet today is also all Western stuff. The writing we use today is still hieroglyphic, but it is completely symbolized. The essays we write today are all

European style, knowing that the real ancient Chinese language, i.e., literary language, has no grammatical and logical structure, and it never even uses logical symbols like punctuation. The articles we write today have a subject, a predicate, and an object, which is typical of the logical system of Western languages.

Because of this reason, we have thrown away all our traditional culture.

But we have also gained an advantage in that we have since learned from the West most humbly, so humbly to the point of obsequious to foreigners. If we can make up this lesson of our traditional culture today, please consider whether we have a major advantage: we learn the culture of all mankind with an open mind, which gives us a powerful bouncing power for the future.

Today the West is very proud of itself because almost all of its cultural contributions for the last 1000 years have been theirs, which makes them disdainful of learning from the cultures and civilizations of other peoples. But we should know that in the late Middle Ages and even in modern times, the West used to study the East enthusiastically, or at least looked up to it, which made them surpass us quickly. Therefore, our recent study of the West must give us an important advantage for the future. This is number four.

Number five, we are currently the fastest growing nation in the world and the most radical in the way we behave. We are somehow more Western than the West, and so we have saved ourselves, and so we will be at the forefront of human civilization, and it allows us to look directly into the future of humanity. We are facing an uncertain future from now on, knowing that in recent times our orientation has always been the backdrop of Western culture.

For the five reasons mentioned above, we can sort out the whole process of human civilization very effectively by pulling the thread of Chinese culture. Moreover, I will constantly compare Eastern and Western cultures in my lectures. The reason for the focus on East and West cultures is that among the hundreds of ancient civilizations in the world, East and West cultures and civilizations are the most polarizing.

What does this phrase mean? It is that they have the most extreme expression of civilized character. But here also brings a problem, that is, the East and West are extremely incompatible with each other.

As you know, only twice in the history of Chinese civilization has a foreign culture invaded China.

The first time was in the middle of the Eastern Han Dynasty when Indian Buddhism was introduced into China. It quietly merged with Chinese culture, so much so that when we talk about national culture today, Confucianism, Buddhism and Daoism, it actually occupies one foot of the tripod.

The second foreign cultural invasion was the Opium War in 1840. More than 170 years have passed since then, but we still cannot find the interface between the Eastern and Western cultures.

What does it mean? It shows that these two civilizations are extremely incompatible. Although the industrial and commercial civilization grew out of the agricultural civilization, it is very difficult for a refined, purely agricultural civilization to find a mutual docking point, a compatibility point, and a point of ideological convergence when it is confronted with a more violent and foreign industrial and commercial civilization.

This has led to a situation in which Chinese politicians, economists, social activists, and even literary scholars have all been in the throes of cultural, behavioral, ideological, and even personality fragmentation, consciously or unconsciously, for the last hundred years of modern times.

Then, the purpose of this deeper examination of the overall trend of Eastern and Western cultures and human civilization as a whole is to address the question of the future of human civilization with a broader vision and a more forward-looking impulse. This is the focus of this series of classes. I will elaborate on it as follows.

What kind of new culture do we need to reorganize? The subtext is that if we are at the forefront of human civilization, that is, if we are out of the old and in the mist, then where are we prepared to go? What are the risks we face? What will we gain? Do we still have a future and a profit?

The whole question can be summarized in this statement: What future form of civilization must we build in order for humanity to continue to survive?

Please note that only by focusing closely on these questions as the central axis, you can listen to these lectures with interest and you will understand the deeper meaning.

Migration of Homo Sapiens: Occurrence of Human Civilization

In order to explain the origins of human civilization, we must first start with anthropology.

We are all familiar with the fact that we humans evolved gradually from the southern anthropoid 16 million years ago. In the past, academics believed that modern humans in different regions of the earth evolved gradually from Homo erectus, which had existed for 3 to 5 million years in different regions of the earth. For example, Europeans believe that they are descended from local Neanderthals, and Chinese believe that we are descended from Beijing Zhoukoudian apes, Shaanxi Lantian apes, and Yunnan Yuanmou apes. However, at the end of the last century, biologists and anthropologists discovered that the existing human being on earth, let's give it a special term, modern Homo sapiens, only evolved from the reproduction of a certain female or a certain race of women 140,000 years ago, which is the famous mitochondrial Eve theory.

Let me explain this terminology. Christianity believes that the originators of humanity were Adam and Eve, created by God, and that Eve is the name of the female originator of humanity. Since the earliest occurrence of modern Homo sapiens is explored here, the name Eve is borrowed.

What is a mitochondrion? The cytoplasm of eukaryotic cells contains an organelle called a mitochondrion. In the past, mitochondria were thought to be nothing more than a structure for cellular energy metabolism. However, in the second half of the last century, biologists discovered that mitochondria also contain a set of genes (DNA, deoxyribonucleic acid). This set of genes is only passed from mother to daughter and from daughter to granddaughter. In other words, this set of genes is expressed in a very pure way. What does this statement mean? It is important to know that the genes inside our cell nucleus are interfered by genes from both sexes in each generation of inheritance, which means that 50% of the genes are passed down from the father and 50% from the mother. Then each generation has at least 50% genetic interference rate in genetic recombination. However, mitochondrial genes are expressed very purely and are only passed down the female lineage. Thus, studying this set of genes, (as well as) studying the deformation or mutation of this set of genes, it is possible to clearly gauge the timing and origin of the occurrence of modern Homo sapiens on Earth.

How do we know this? There is a term in biology called mutation frequency, which means that there is a constant relationship between the number of mutations that occur in a group of genes. For example, if N mutations occur per 100,000 genes per year, it is a constant number. If we know the mutation frequency and we can find the original reference line of this set of genes, then we can determine when this set of genes occurred on Earth.

The mitochondrial genes of all humans have been investigated according to a technique that reveals all humans are descended from a single female or a particular ethnic group 140,000 years ago, called the mitochondrial Eve theory. This theory is a powerful reversal of our past belief that modern humans have been around for more than 3 million years, and it has met with widespread opposition in the humanities. A famous professor of biology at Fudan University in Shanghai named Jin Li was also highly skeptical of this theory at first. So he began to study the Y-gene.

Let me explain the Y gene: the genes inside the nucleus of our human cells are distributed on 46 chromosomes, two of which are called sex chromosomes, female sex chromosome XX and male sex chromosome XY. Please pay attention to this Y gene, which is also only passed from father to son and from son to grandson. In other words, the Y gene is also inherited without interference from maternal genes. People first read what the Y chromosome is, it is the X chromosome with a broken leg. What does that mean? In the 3.8 billion years of biological history, there were only females and no males in the early days. Males occurred around the palaeogeological Cambrian era, which is 570 million years ago when males occurred. In ancient times, biological reproduction was called solitary reproduction, including cell division, which is purely female reproduction. The so-called Y chromosome, that is, the X chromosome broke a leg, which is why the vitality of women so far is much higher than that of men, that is, in harsh environments, women's survival tolerance than men, and the average life expectancy of women has been higher than that of men.

Professor Jin Li traced the Y gene, and since the Y gene is also purely expressed, he took a large number of specimens of the Y gene for testing among all ethnic groups in the world. The results of the census among all human races also showed that the Y gene could only be traced back to between 79,000 and 31,000 years. This again proves that modern Homo sapiens on Earth is less than 200,000 years old. This theory has now gained widespread attention and recognition in the academic community because of the strength of its evidence.

That is, we Chinese are not descendants of the Zhoukoudian apes in Beijing, who all became extinct as Homo erectus 70,000 or 30,000 years ago. This study has not been carried out in depth in other regions, including Asia. Only European scholars have studied the molecular biology between European Homo erectus, or Neanderthal, and modern Homo sapiens in slight depth. Europe today retains less than 3% of the modern Homo sapiens lineage and roughly slightly more than 1% or so of the genetic remains of Homo erectus. The results of the study suggest that Homo erectus was essentially completely wiped out, about 30,000 to 25,000 years ago.

The causes of the extinction are so complex that we cannot expand on them in this class today. We will only slightly mention the more significant elements that can be examined so far, which may be related to the eruption of a volcano called Toba in this part of Indonesia 75,000 years ago. Today that place forms Lake Toba, that is, from a mountain to a depression.

As you know, there have been five biological extinctions in history, two of which were related to the mass eruptions of volcanoes, followed by ash blocking the atmosphere and solar radiation, resulting in a "volcanic winter" and the subsequent mass extinction of plants and animals. Therefore, the eruption of the Toba volcano 75,000 years ago may have been an important factor in the extinction of Homo erectus. Of course, this is only one of the factors, not excluding the conflict and killing of Homo sapiens against Homo erectus, and more factors have not been explored yet.

Where did the origin of human civilization begin to occur? Let's look at the following map, which is called the Migration Roadmap of Modern Homo Sapiens. Please pay attention to this map, it is a migration map of ancient ancestors with the help of molecular biology, that is, genetic theory, gene sequencing, as well as a series of disciplines such as paleoanthropology, archaeology and other comprehensive research.

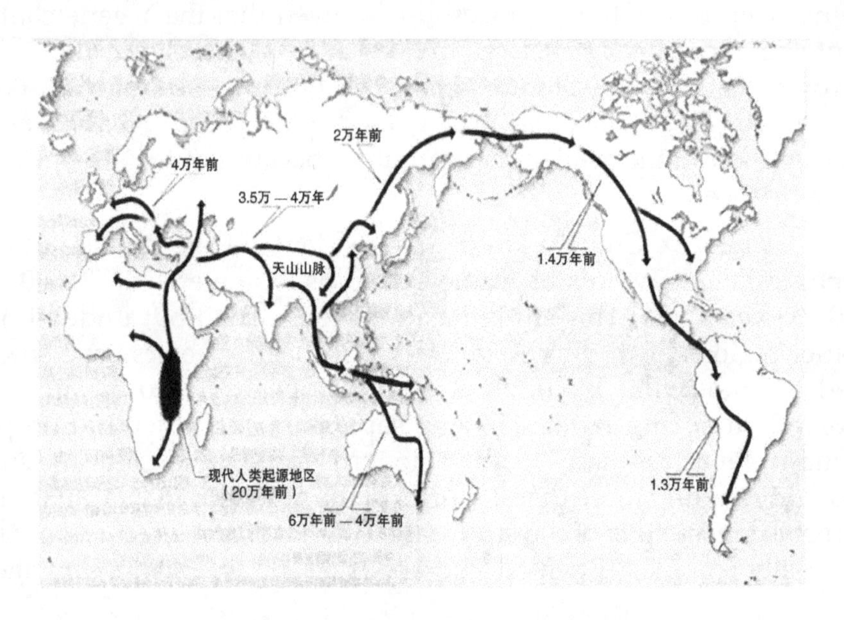

The migration route of modern Homo sapiens

The migration began in the Great Rift Valley of East Africa and took place about 90,000 years ago.

Let's define the concept of migration first, so-called migration refers to the survival and reproduction of a group of people in a place, as population increases, the local means of livelihood is not enough to support the local people, so a small number of them move forward tens of kilometers to settle down again, and then the population of the newly settled people in the place continues to grow, the local means of livelihood is not enough to support the local people, so a small number of them move forward again tens of kilometers. Then the population of the newly settled people in the place continues to grow, the local means of subsistence is again insufficient to support the local people, so a small number of them move forward again tens of kilometers, we call this slow process as migration.

The migration of modern Homo sapiens started from East Africa, and in the early days they were completely blind. 90,000 years ago, they progressed south into South Africa and went to a dead end. Another group of them moved northward, arriving in the Nile

Valley of North Africa about 60,000 years ago. Because of the early migration and settlement of modern Homo sapiens to North Africa, the ancient Egyptian civilization is the most primitive and earliest occurrence of the first crop of civilizations in human history.

Let me give you an example. Hieroglyphic writing in ancient Egypt happened 5500 years ago, while Chinese oracle bone writing only took shape 3300 years ago, a difference of more than 2000 years. What am I trying to illustrate? The echelon of human civilization occurring on Earth correlates with the time of migration and settlement of modern Homo sapiens.

So you should remember the relationship between the time and place of migration and settlement that I will talk about below.

Of course, a problem occurs here, the north-central region of Africa is now distributed in the largest piece of desert on earth, that is, the Great Sahara Desert. It is very difficult for modern people to pass through it, how did the ancient people cross it? You know from the ancient geology, the Sahara Desert was created 15,000 years ago, until 10,500 years ago to fully formed. In other words, when modern Homo sapiens migrated 60,000 years ago, there was no Sahara Desert in Africa.

Modern Homo sapiens continued to migrate from the Nile Valley in North Africa, crossing the narrow passage between the Mediterranean Sea and the Red Sea, where the Suez Canal is located today, to reach the Two Rivers Valley in the Middle East about 50,000 years ago, thus creating the Sumerian, ancient Babylonian and Assyrian civilizations. The modern Homo sapiens that reached the Two Rivers region then reached Europe about 40,000 years ago through the passage between the Caucasus Mountains and the Black Sea and the Mediterranean Sea; another group of people migrated eastward from the Middle East and crossed the narrow passage between the northern foothills of the Tianshan Mountains and the southern foothills of the Altai Mountains, which we today call the Eurasian Continental Bridge, into East Asia, about 35,000 years ago.

Another ethnic group that migrated eastward southward into the Indian subcontinent and then entered East Asia through the southeastern coast of China; this ethnic group is M122 on Professor Jin Li's male genetic marker; an ethnic group that entered China from the Tianshan Mountains, is M175 on his male genetic marker; these two paths form the basis of the Chinese ethnic lineage.

Then, East Asians continued to migrate along the west coast of the Pacific Ocean, making their way northward, eventually arriving in the Americas about 14,000 years ago through the shallow Arctic Sea region, known today as the Bering Strait. Because modern Homo sapiens migrated to the Americas rather late, the occurrence of civilization in the Americas was relatively weak, and it occurred only on a small scale in the central Americas and the Andes region of South America and the Inca Mountains region.

Of course, there is a problem here, namely the Bering Strait, which is very difficult for us to cross today, how did the ancient people cross it? It is important to know that the last ice age on Earth was called the Quaternary Ice Age, which did not recede until 12,000 years ago. During the Quaternary Ice Age, the average temperature of the Earth was much lower than now, the thickness of the polar ice caps was more than a thousand meters higher than now, and more than two-thirds of the Earth's continents were covered by ice, so the sea level was 60 to 130 meters lower than today. And the Arctic region was a shallow sea area, the average depth of seawater was only 40-50 meters, that is, during the Quaternary Ice Age, the Arctic periphery was completely land, exposed above sea level. Therefore, this place was not called the Bering Strait, but the Bering Land Bridge. This is the reason why modern Homo sapiens were able to pass through the Bering Strait without any problems.

Let's look at the group of ancient ancestors to eastward southward. They actually arrived in New Guinea and Australia 40,000 years ago. Please note that this time is even earlier than the group arrival in East Asia, because it was extremely difficult to reach East Asia and China over the Pamir Plateau, while the journey to this place was smooth. Today we see that Southeast Asia is all sea area, but during the Quaternary Ice Age, this part of Southeast Asia was all continents, and only two trenches separated it from Australia. Therefore, the ancient ancestors came to Australia earlier.

Until the Westerners invaded Australia in the seventeenth and eighteenth centuries, civilization in Australia had not yet occurred and the local indigenous people were still in an uncivilized state. So a problem occurs here, as I said earlier, that the gradient of human civilization on earth occurred in relation to the time of migration and settlement of modern Homo sapiens. So, modern Homo sapiens migrated to South Africa 90,000 years ago, and modern Homo sapiens migrated to Australia and New Guinea 40,000 years ago, so they migrated and settled very early, why couldn't civilization happen smoothly?

It is evident that there is another major factor influencing the generation and development of human civilization, that is, the conditions of communication.

It was only after the end of the Quaternary Ice Age that human agrarian civilization began to develop. However, in the main continent of Eurasia and Africa, where civilization took place, the Sahara Desert appeared around the end of the Quaternary Ice Age, which led to the blockage of communication channel between the South African region and the main northward civilization. Furthermore, the sea level rose after the end of the Quaternary Ice Age, so Southeast Asia was plunged into a vast ocean, which also cut off the local inhabitants of Australia and New Guinea from the main continent of Asian and European civilizations. This is an important reason why the civilizations of these very early settlements could not be generated in time.

Why are we talking about the topic of the migration of modern Homo sapiens? It is because we must explore the ethnographic reasons for the occurrence of civilization.

One may note that when we generally mention civilization, it is difficult to imagine that the same human being could have produced such a significant divide between primitive cultures and civilizations, given the vastly different qualities and types of civilization differentiation. This leads to the temptation to explore the roots and causes of civilization and cultural qualities with a tendency to focus on the intellectual differences of different human races, thus causing serious misinformation.

In the last century, a famous Western scholar named Max Weber once devoted himself to exploring why the capitalist system occurred only among the white race in Europe and America, and no other civilized region anywhere else would spontaneously produce such a civilized system. Mr. Weber's research concluded that it had to do with the Protestant Christian ethic. But he makes a statement in his book, saying that I, as a cultural scholar, can only pursue it to this depth, and that strictly speaking, its deeper level involves ethnical differences, i.e., the creation of different cultures and civilizational forms because of the differences in the intelligence of human races. He said that the deeper part of the subject would have to be left to ethnographers and neurophysiologists.

We should know that it is not only Max Weber who holds this view. We Chinese actually unconsciously hold this view. We philosophically believe that the development of anything needs to have both internal and external causes. We believe that internal causes are the basis for what happens, and external causes are the conditions for what happens. If you hold this view, then of course you also believe that the differences in human civilization are the result of differences in ethnographic states of intelligence.

But after we look at this migration map, we will have a whole new consideration of this issue. I would like to start by defining ethnography. What we usually call ethnography is called cultural ethnography, for example, when we say that there are 56 different ethnic groups or many minorities in China, this is a cultural classification of ethnography.

The human species I am going to talk about is a biological species. Biologically speaking, there is only one species of human being, which is the species Homo sapiens. It is divided into three major subspecies, which are: black Africans, also known as the Negro race; white Europeans, also known as the Caucasian race; and between the Caucasian race and the Negro race, the other races with moderate skin color, including us Chinese, known as the Mongolian race.

Let me clarify that we are called Mongolian because Genghis Khan led the Mongolian armies to the edge of Europe in the 13th century, which caused a major impact and threat to European civilization, so much so that Europeans thought that all the yellow scourge were Mongols, which is the origin of the term Mongolian race. This is the origin of the term Mongolian race.

So let's see below how these three major human subspecies were formed.

40,000 years ago, the African Black Negroid race migrated to Europe. Please note this map, this region of Europe is at a comparable latitude to northeast China, and central and northern Europe are even higher than northeast China's latitude. The amount of light is greatly reduced in areas with high latitudes. Then, black

Africans migrate to Europe, their children will die on a large scale because of a disease called rickets, which is commonly known as chondromalacia.

Why is this so? It is because we humans have a layer of cholesterol distributed under the skin, which is converted to 7-dehydrocholesterol by the action of ultraviolet radiation from the sun, and 7-dehydrocholesterol is the precursor of vitamin D. Vitamin D is essential for calcium metabolism, so blacks who migrated to Europe had children with chondromalacia due to impaired vitamin D production, resulting in mass mortality (in ancient times synthetic vitamin supplementation was not possible). Only a very few children whose skin was whitened due to a genetic mutation were survived by natural selection. I would like to draw your attention to the concept of natural selection, which is the most important word to understand if you want to pass through Darwin's doctrine.

Let's look again, the African Black Negro race migrated to the alpine region with low amount of light - Europe, and his adults will again be eliminated by natural selection due to a disease on a large scale, the name of this disease is called pulmonary heart disease. We are all familiar with the fact that in the northeast, people used to be prone to a disease called chronic bronchitis, because the cold and dry air would cause severe damage to the bronchial lining and alveolar cells, so the patient would cough incessantly, and the cough would cause the chest pressure to increase, and the increased chest pressure would cause the alveoli to burst, and then the capillaries distributed over the alveoli would break. The blood discharged from the right ventricle oxidizes through the lungs into the left ventricle, and the blood discharged from the left ventricle nourishes all tissue cells throughout the body, and we call the latter the great circulation. However, we should know that the circulating blood volume of the great circulation is exactly equal to that of the small circulation that goes from the right ventricle through the lungs into the left ventricle. If the alveoli rupture, the capillaries on the alveoli break, the small circulation channel is blocked, and the beat-to-beat pressure of the right ventricle increases, which eventually leads to the attenuation of the right ventricle function, thus causing the failure of both heart and lung organs. This is called pulmonary heart disease, and the mortality rate is extremely high.

At the dawn of ancient civilization, the fourth ice age had just ended and the temperature was much colder than today, plus people did not stay indoors at that time, but mainly hunted outdoors, so the Black Negro race that migrated to Europe had a high rate of pulmonary heart disease in adults. This caused them to fall into death again on a large scale, with only a very few surviving by natural selection due to a genetic mutation that caused their noses to become taller.

Why does a taller nose create some kind of survival advantage in alpine regions? It is because the nose becomes taller and the nasal ducts become longer, which plays a role in warming and humidifying the air. This is the reason why the European Caucasian race finally became white-skinned and high-nosed.

Please understand what I am saying, I am saying that it is simply impossible for humans to undergo significant changes or major mutations in biological traits and intellectual states in just 40,000 years. Because biologists have long studied clearly, any biological trait or any biological state of intelligence to change significantly, must be accumulated after millions of years or even tens of millions of years of genetic mutations to achieve. In a short period of 40,000 years, human beings can only undergo a slight change in the epidermis, which is not enough to form a huge difference in the human race, much less the possibility of forming a difference in intelligence.

Let's look back, why black Africans could maintain the basic physical appearance and skin color of the Negro race, because this place in Africa is around the equator, the sun's ultraviolet radiation is too strong, so they are distributed under the skin thick melanin to block ultraviolet damage to the subcutaneous tissue. Because of the hot and humid air in that place, all Africans have low noses.

The Mongolian race, including us Chinese, has been distributed in the mid-latitudes for 40,000 years due to its survival area, which has moderate amount of light and moderate humidity and heat, so our skin color and nose height is between the Negroid and Caucasian races.

To summarize, there are only three major biological subspecies of human beings on the earth, and it is almost impossible that any important differences in their physical traits and intellectual states could have occurred in just 40,000 years of migration. Therefore, it is obvious that we cannot use ethnographic intellectual states or differences to find the origin of civilizations and the reasons for their differences. So we must look for other reasons.

Natural Prescription of Procession of Civilization

Before exploring the main influences on the origin of human civilization, we discuss below a little some general topics, or clarify some basic historical misconceptions.

As we all know, the advent of human beings, if we count from Homo erectus in the past, has been divided into Paleolithic and Neolithic in the past historiography. The Paleolithic is the time when humans used and made stone tools, which lasted for a million years or even two or three million years, and it is regarded as the eve of human civilization.

However, there is actually a major misconception that only humans are capable of using and making tools, as previously believed by academics. This view has been overturned by contemporary biological research.

We know today that a large number of ancient lower and middle classes creatures could already use tools. For example, the aquatic creature sea otter, it will lift the stone to smash open the mussel shell.

A bird called a dodo, for example, could actually break down a branch, break off a forked twig, trim it into a strip of wood of the right thickness and length, and then use it to pull insects out of a hole in a tree, and this tool was carried by it for a long time and never left its body, which is obviously an extraordinary skill in making and using tools, and it was just a bird. In the case of primates such as apes and monkeys, modern biologists have found that they also have superior tool-making skills, including the use of specific shaped stone tools to crack open nuts, and even the use of wooden ladders to probe for fruit from high places. It is clear that the use and manufacture of tools as a unique characteristic of human civilization is not valid.

What do I mean by this passage? I want to tell you one thing: there is no leap in nature. Our human civilization has actually occurred gradually in an extended sequence of biological evolutionary processes. We cannot find the boundary point of the origin of civilization; we can only draw a line artificially, or even unjustifiably, to make it the starting point of civilization that arrogant human beings think they are.

In general, what is usually called the epoch of human civilization began with the Neolithic, which occurred about 12,000 years ago. This time of the Neolithic era coincides with the end of the Fourth Ice Age, and it shows how significant the natural factors were in influencing the occurrence of human civilization. It was only after the end of the Quaternary Ice Age that the phenomenon of large rivers resumed on the Earth's continents, that is, the rivers that had been mostly frozen for 2.5 million years began to reappear on the Earth's continents.

The phenomenon of the Great River constitutes the natural infrastructure for the occurrence of agricultural civilization. What am I emphasizing? I am emphasizing that the occurrence of human civilization has always been defined by natural processes. There are three major features of the Neolithic that indicate the dawn of human civilization unfolding, which are the domestication of animals, the cultivation of plants and the production of pottery.

We will briefly explain these three aspects below.

First of all, we should know that in the ancient times of our Chinese people, its civilization mainly took place in the Yellow River Basin. Therefore, the agricultural civilization started by our ancient Chinese ancestors, the only crop it mainly cultivated was grain millet, that is, the yellow rice and millet grown in the north. It was cultivated from green bristlegrass, the weed with a large spike on its head, which can be found all over the north-central region of China.

Things like wheat and barley are not native agricultural products of China; it was gradually brought to China from the two rivers of the West along the migration routes of the ancient ancestors. Things like corn, potatoes, peanuts, and tobacco, especially the extremely productive crops like corn and potatoes, it was cultivated by the Native Americans and brought to Eurasia by colonists like Columbus around 1500 AD. This was the main reason why China's population, which historically did not exceed 90 million people until the mid-Ming Dynasty, skyrocketed to hundreds of millions after the mid-Ming Dynasty.

What am I trying to say here? I am trying to say that human agricultural civilization did not progress the same, but grew in response to the constraints of various local natural resources and the efforts to connect and interact with them.

We discuss a small question below: Why did agricultural civilization happen to mankind?

It is a common misconception that agricultural civilization is a selective product of the stretching of our human intelligence. Please remember that this argument is not entirely valid. Please see the point, I am emphasizing one important thing: human civilization is not the result of autonomous human choice and design out of thin air; human civilization is a completely natural and spontaneous process.

I'll give you an example of why agricultural civilization happened because of the emergence of a new cortex of the brain in humans and even apes, humans have a little something more than apes, which is the prefrontal cortex. The neuronal cells above the cerebral cortex were over-differentiated and over-functional, so it had to lose some of its basic functions, otherwise the bioenergy of such cells would not be sufficient to sustain the normal survival of that cellular tissue.

This leads to two serious defects in brain cells.

First, it actually lacks the ability to regenerate. As you know, if any of our body cells are damaged, such as your epidermis is cut, it has the ability to regenerate, the epithelial cells proliferate will cover the wound and grow together as it is. However, our brain cells completely lose the ability to regenerate, once they die out, they cannot regenerate, only scar tissue grows in. This is why brain tissue damage caused by cerebral hemorrhage and cerebral thrombosis, resulting in damage such as hemiplegia, has a very low degree of recoverability, and even a slight recovery is not due to neuronal regeneration, but must rely on peripheral brain tissue function to compensate.

The over functioning of human cortical cells also presents a second and more serious problem, it can actually only use glucose or called carbohydrates as a source of energy metabolism. All cells, includingsinglecells3.8billionyearsagoalltheway toourhumancells today, can metabolize material energy with the help of three energy sources, which are proteins, fats and glucose-based carbohydrates.

Let me explain why we call glucose a carbohydrate. Because a glucose molecule is made up of 6 carbon, 12 hydrogen and 6 oxygen, while water is made up of 2 hydrogen and 1 oxygen. 12 hydrogens plus 6 oxygen equals 6 water molecules, plus 6 carbon atoms, which are called carbohydrates.

All cells can achieve energy metabolism with the help of three major substances: fat, protein and carbohydrate, but brain cells can only use glucose, and it actually loses the function of obtaining energy from fat and protein metabolism.

As you know apes, including hominids gorillas and chimpanzees, they are omnivores and according to biologists, they have to eat more than 300 kinds of fruits and berries. Why do apes like fruits in particular? It is because fruits contain more carbohydrates. But fruit has a serious problem, it grows with the seasons, and it simply cannot be stored and will rot away quickly. This is the reason why apes are particularly fond of carbohydrate-rich food, but have to establish an omnivorous range of predation.

The human cerebral cortex is more developed and it can hardly be without carbohydrates for a moment, so what to do? There is only one way to get carbohydrates from grass seeds.

The trouble is that grass seeds are so tiny that no large animal in the world can get energy from grass seeds, only birds, pheasants, etc. can get energy from grass seeds. So, how difficult it is for humans to cultivate the tiny grass seeds into a staple food.

Think about it, grass seed particles are usually smaller than millet, so why does it contain carbohydrates? It only needs a nucleus for gene transfer, and the nucleus is only visible when you magnify it 1000 times under a microscope. And the reason why grass seed can be seen with the naked eye is because it is wrapped with a layer of carbohydrates on the outside. Why does it need a layer of carbohydrates wrapped around it? It is because any plant growth, its energy is obtained by photosynthesis after the opening of the leaves, before it does not germinate, it takes what energy to germinate? This is the reason why grass seeds are wrapped with a layer of energy material. For humans to extract the carbohydrates contained around grass seeds, i.e., starch, as a staple food, is actually a high natural compulsion or physiological compulsion. That is to say, if this food material is not found, our survival will be greatly threatened and brain development will be retarded. Thus, the onset of agricultural civilization is not the result of our choice and design.

The ancients had no idea that grass seeds were cultivated into grain, what exactly was contained in this stuff. It was an entirely slow and spontaneous process made possible by inexplicable internal needs, an unconscious extension of human behavior to obtain meat sources, i.e., proteins and fats, during hunting and carbohydrates during gathering.

In this process, the larger grains of grass seeds collected, people specifically named it grass plant, collected it back, at first directly eaten, and later found by chance that the seeds spilled around the tribe can grow in patches, and later found that it can be gradually expanded by artificial selection and artificial cultivation This is the process of spontaneous development of agricultural civilization in a long period of time without prior planning.

Again, I emphasize that human civilization is not the result of human choice and design; it is entirely a natural process, a biological compulsion.

Please think again, why did we move from an agricultural civilization to an industrial and commercial civilization, and there was never a second way? This shows that industrial and commercial civilization is also not our active choice or our prior planning, it is still a natural process. What is the so-called agricultural civilization? It is the limited access to resources, that is, the access to resources tied to the limited land. What is an industrial and commercial civilization? It is a trans-regional access to resources, that is, it has a greater spatial and temporal scope of access to resources for survival and a greater total volume of transactions. This is why it necessarily replace agricultural civilization, and this is the path of its spontaneous expansion. As always, this is not the result of our choice and design.

That human civilization is a natural process, just as man himself is a natural product, which is the most important concept to keep in mind. For all of our previous studies of human history and the history of civilization it has been expressed that human civilization and its development process is a uniquely human intellectual choice and a subjective mode of existence created by human beings themselves. This view is a major misconception.

In retrospect, human agricultural civilization actually took the larger herbal seeds of the herbal family and gave them another name, note that this is a completely artificial name, grass family. Humans eventually cultivated and expanded these plants into food.

The distribution of grasses is extremely uneven. For example, in the northern part of the two river basins, there is an area known to historians as the Fertile Crescent, a fertile land in the shape of a crescent, where about 33 of the 56 natural grasses occur in this one place alone. This is the reason why the two rivers region, Mesopotamia, became the most abundant and mature species cultivation base in the early years of human agricultural civilization.

Many scholars want to use this to prove that human civilization evolved purely by chance. However, I would like to argue that this shows that human civilization is strictly limited by natural processes.

Let me give you a few examples. The reason why the first legume cultivated by humans in the two river basins was chickpeas is that all legumes, when their seeds are ripe, their pods must open immediately, thus spreading the seeds wrapped in them in time, otherwise the species would inevitably become extinct. Only a very few chickpeas do not open their pods when the endosperm is ripe, and because of this, the beans were not scattered all over the ground so humans could gather to pick up them. Because of this small difference, the origin of the legume crop and the beginning of human cultivation of legume food began.

Another example is almonds. All fruit cores are inedible, you may try biting into an apple seed, if you do not believe it. It is important to know that most of the kernels are poisonous. The reason the fruit grows very sweet is to attract animals to eat it. The kernel is not easily digested in the animal's stomach and intestines and is excreted in the feces, thus helping it to sow its seeds. If the animal can chew and destroy the seeds as well, then the fruit species would become extinct. Therefore, the kernels in almost all fruits are poisonous and inedible, and if you eat them, you get a bitter taste in your mouth. Only almonds undergo a very small amount of mutation, and some of its kernels are actually sweet. So, humans would plant this sweet kernel of wild apricot in the early years, for apricot is too small to eat, plant it just to collect its kernel to use as a breeding object.

I say this to prove that the process of human cultivation of a certain species, it may look like an artificial selection; but in fact the idea of selection is not valid, it is actually a mandatory receiving of natural products or natural processes.

Such examples abound. For example, Papua New Guinea, as I mentioned earlier, although primitive humans settled in the place early, because of the long distance, blocking communication, their civilization was delayed. When modern Europeans came to that place, they found that local residents were in a barbaric state of existence, basically uncivilized; but they had an amazing ability to catch bats flying at high speed in the air at night, and they capture bats with high precision by making up a fine net and spreading it out to wait. This is what the civilized people of Eurasia could not do back then, why? It was because these Pacific islands of New Guinea had no other foodstuffs high in protein, and no natural species rich in protein to cultivate. The main crop cultivated in that place was called taro, which was so low in protein that it forced the locals to find a source of protein in their meat diet. So they spontaneously developed an extremely high skill in obtaining bat meat sources, although they were not enlightened as a whole.

There is another example but quite strange. As you know, rice is believed to be developed by the southerners in the Yangtze River region of China, the tribe of male genetic marker M122 that I mentioned earlier. The earliest archaeological discovery of rice was the carbonized rice from the Hemudu site in Yuyao, Zhejiang Province, which was cultivated from wild rice straw by the southern people of China about 7,000 years ago. We used to think that this was the earliest birthplace of rice. However, some years ago, in a place called Jiahu Village in Luohe area in southern Henan Province, a more primitive archaeological site was discovered, and carbonized rice was actually found from 8,000 years ago. What does this mean? It means that rice is still the earliest crop cultivated by the civilized people in the Yellow River Basin. But why did it not become the staple food of the Central Plains ancestors, and eventually became a basic food source only in the south? It is because the protein content of rice is too low.

We should know that the average grain we cultivated has a

protein content of about 11% or more, such as wheat, its protein content is 11% to 14%. Whereas humans cannot bear less than 8% of the minimum protein supply in their own food, rice has a protein content of only about 4%. This leads to the problem of protein scarcity, if rice alone is used as a food source, which would cause serious liver damage and physical developmental disorders, so the people of the Yellow River Basin had to give up rice, though rice was first cultivated crop in north.

Then why in the south of China rice could be used as a staple food? In fact, the reason is very simple, because there are rivers and lakes everywhere in the south, the so-called the land of fish and rice, people eat rice at the same time they could always get fish and shrimp as meat, thus replenishing their lack of protein, so rice could flourish in the south.

What am I talking about here? I am talking about how all civilizational processes express our articulated relationship with nature and how the intrinsic requirements of our own biological existence constitute the nodes of the origin of civilization.

Please note that I use a term to call the overall matching of this external natural structure and natural association with our internal physiological evolutionary structure and the spontaneous mobilization progress of intelligence, the survival structure.

I draw your attention to the meaning of this special term, which is in no way the ordinary meaning of human terms such as productivity or relations of production, but a purely naturalistic term. Establishing this concept is the key to our understanding of the origins of civilization.

In a book titled *Guns, Germs and Steel: The Fate of Human Society*, renowned American scholar Jared Diamond mentions that there are a total of 148 large phytophagous species in the world that are available to humans as candidates for artificial domestication.

First of all, note that phytophagous animals are also what we usually call herbivores. Why do we humans always domesticate large herbivorous animals as our meat source? The answer is because herbivores are the least expensive to raise.

Let's think about it, assuming that herbivores eat 10 pounds of grass to get 1 pound of meat source, carnivores have to eat 10 pounds of meat from herbivores again to increase the weight of 1 pound of meat. Then, if humans use carnivorous animals as their own food, which equals the cost to expand more than 10 times. This is the reason that most humans breed cattle, sheep, pigs, etc. are herbivorous or omnivorous animals.

Among the wild strains of large phytophagous animals domesticated by humans only 14 of the 148 have been selected, and their distribution regions are uneven. For example, wild cattle mainly occurred in Southwest Asia, North Africa and India; goats and sheep mainly came from the two rivers; wild horses mainly came from Central Asia and Ukraine; donkeys came from Egypt; wild boars, buffaloes and small animal chickens are products of East Asia, probably the first domesticated by the Chinese; yaks came from Tibet; only large herbivores alpacas remain in the Americas so far; we can see that there are differences in their natural distribution states around the world.

So why do humans breed different herbivores in different regions? It is because the process of human civilization is a completely natural and spontaneous articulation process. I always emphasize this point because when many scholars discuss this issue, they would argue that human civilization was episodic and that it was the chance opportunities brought about by the natural physical conditions in various regions that contributed to the occurrence of civilization. They come to the exact opposite conclusion from me, they think that human civilization is an accidental phenomenon or a synthesis of accidental phenomena.

Please see what I am emphasizing. If our civilization must interface with nature, if the process of our civilization's interface with nature is an involuntary and spontaneous process, then, instead of indicating that our civilization is episodic, it is more powerful evidence that human civilization is a non-selective process of natural articulation.

Let me give you an example. The Americas is a place where modern Homo sapiens only migrated 14,000 years ago, but by that time the locals behavioral ability or state of intelligence development of humans was already relatively high. Although these people had just arrived in the Americas, they had already mastered the ability to hunt using long distance shooting tools such as projectiles and bows and arrows, so they soon shot up all the large phytophagous animals on the American continent in a very short time, eventually leaving only the alpacas in the deep mountains of South America.

One serious consequence of this was that on November 16, 1532, a Spaniard named Francisco Pizarro, leading a cavalry force of only 168 men who straddled war horses and carried muskets, faced 80,000 legions of the Inca Empire and actually defeated them. Why did such a disparity in combat power occur? It was because the legions of Inca Empire had never seen war houses running before, with its riders carrying guns firing from afar, they were believed warriors from heaven. The 80,000 troops were scattered and King Atahualpa was captured, and the Inca Empire fell.

What does this mean? A natural process with some kind of abnormal break in the middle can cause poor articulation and hidden cracks in the evolution of civilization, which shows how closely the initial stage of civilization requires a degree of alignment with nature.

We look next at the early domestication of dogs by humans as domesticated animals to assist hunting. We look back today and think that this should have been a very stupid choice. Because in the face of large carnivores, the dog's fighting ability is very poor, such as encountering wolf, encountering tiger or lion or bear, these animals as long as they roar, the dog would be scared straight back, how could it become the most effective hunting assistant?

Humans should have domesticated the cheetah, because cheetah is fierce in nature, and the fastest runner, selecting it as a hunting assistant is the most reasonable, but why people did not want to domesticate the cheetah? In fact, the reason is ridiculous, because the cheetah species, its courtship process is too complicated. Male cheetahs usually have to run a hundred kilometers or even 200 kilometers to court females, and it may take 3 months to complete the courtship process. So in captivity, cheetahs have no way to breed. So humans had to use that lousy dog as a hunting assistant. What does this mean? It means that as long as you can't connect with a certain natural property, civilization can't be a budding point of growth here.

Let me give you another example, humans have domesticated horses, but we have never seen any people riding on zebras. In fact, the reason why zebras, which were everywhere in Eurasia in the early years, could never be domesticated by humans is again because of a very small reason, that is, although zebras are very docile like horses, but in the process of captive breeding, if a zebra bites you in anger, it will not let you go. This led to men who kept zebras eventually have to give up the chore of domesticating them. Such a small obstacle is enough to cause the failure of zebra breeding.

There are numerous examples, such as why humans have bred sheep and goats, but never domesticated antelope? It is because the antelope is too sensitive and fragile in temperament, so in captivity, the slightest shock will scare the herd. As we all know, animals in captivity are inevitably disturbed, and if they are easily startled, it will lead to mass abortion of pregnant females. For such a small reason, the antelope has never been domesticated by humans.

What am I talking about? I am emphasizing that human civilization appears to be a process of artificial selection, but in fact selection is not valid, it is merely a continuation of natural qualities and natural processes. I will repeat, please remember one basic natural principle: human civilization is not the result of arbitrary human choices and autonomous designs, but on the contrary, it is a completely natural or spontaneous process of physical evolution.

Primitive Social Structure of Civilization

The unfolding process of human civilization is entirely a natural or spontaneous process that includes the sum of natural environmental evolutionary conditions and the human evolutionary sequence itself. We refer to this homogeneous, intrinsically unified and integrated natural physical evolutionary process as a civilizational or human phenomenon, specifically as the survival structure of the Homo sapiens species lineage. (Note: It is essentially the same as the survival structure or natural ecological structure of other biological species, and it is even the same as the existence or evolutionary trend of inorganic substances, and it is closely connected with each other without any break, and each object and species only differs in the running phase of natural evolution.)

So to what extent is this natural process or these natural conditions limiting us?

Here is another example. Some cultural scholars have found that when human civilization occurred in the early days, it could initially spread only in the latitudinal upward direction. As you can see, the main occurrence zone of human primitive civilization is in Eurasia and Africa, which is roughly distributed in the mid-latitudes, including the subtropical and sub-cold regions, that is, it spread in a latitudinal horizontal axis. In other regions of the earth, where the earth's continental plates form a longitudinal row, they cannot become the lush development area of primitive civilization.

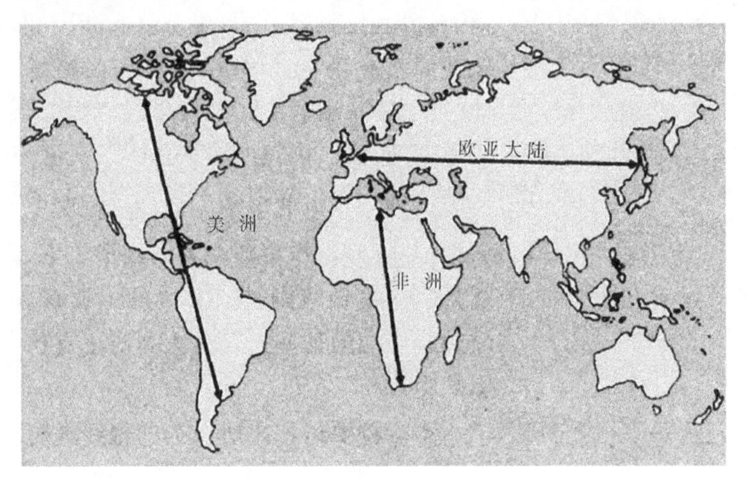

Why is it so? It is because the natural climate and physical conditions of the latitudinal distribution are relatively uniform, so the primitive agricultural and pastoral civilization of mankind at this stage of living on the sky, is more convenient to spread in the latitudinal upward conditions, and there is no obstacle. Think about it, like the African continent, the American continent, because it is the longitudinal distribution of the north-south longitudinal trend, the longitudinal upward running with the change of latitude, the climate and rainfall conditions will change dramatically. Therefore, at the stage of agricultural and pastoral civilization, its spreading process is severely obstructed.

Such a small natural factor actually became a natural prescriptive element of early human civilization that was limited in its development and distribution. We can thus see how significant the decisive influence of the natural situation on human civilization.

We will now discuss another issue, how human social organization and social structure occur. When we speak of society, we cannot help but think that society refers only to human society and that human society is a product of the construction and invention of a highly intellectualized human being. But this is completely wrong.

First of all, I would like to emphasize that human society is not created by humans; human society grows out of animal society. When society entered the developmental stage of quasi-intelligent animal, how did it form a complex system of social structures? It is generally believed that this is the product of human intelligent design and human autonomous planning, but in fact it is still a natural and spontaneous process.

We should know that the primitive human society is called kinship society, it is completely no different from the animal blood society. At that time, the average number of people in a social group was only about 30 to 80, which was a very low group size. And only after the onset of agricultural and pastoral civilization, the population grew massively. Why did this happen? It is because the crop we produce on each acre of land, converted into energy that can be used by the human body, is roughly equivalent to 260 times the amount of energy you get from letting the acre of land grow grass, then the animals eat the grass, and then you go hunting animals. Note this quantitative difference, that means once the agricultural civilization occurred, the population then skyrocketed by more than a hundred times, which is a completely spontaneous process.

Mankind did not expect such a result in advance, it is necessary to know that all biological stocks and community states are limited by their resource availability. So once the agricultural civilization happened, the population will grow a hundredfold, what would it bring about? People would have to keep cultivating the wasteland and destroying the surrounding natural vegetation, so that the arable land can be expanded to accommodate the increase of population. The expansion of arable land and the further increase of population then further created a sense of urgency to reclaim the wasteland. This led to a rapid geographical expansion of agricultural civilization, which led to the gradual erosion and even complete destruction of the previously wooded environment and hunting conditions, resulting in the final degradation of mankind into a bad agricultural civilization.

I say bad because once agricultural civilization occurred, a series of major human disasters began to befall. In the early years, when mankind, like all animals, obtained its means of subsistence directly from nature, it never experienced mass starvation, that is, famine did not occur. Because the population was very small at that time, people could gather plants in summer and autumn, and hunt in winter. In contrast, once agricultural civilization occurred, the conditions of human labor immediately deteriorated. Humans are simply upright animals, and agricultural civilization forced farmers to bend down and plow. The young Israeli historian Harari, author of *A Brief History of Mankind*, was ingenious in suggesting that "agricultural civilization was the beginning of the human catastrophe," which was indeed a profound insight that led mankind to enter into a state of extreme drudgery in an anti-physiological way to survive. Not only that, as they had to expand their farming range more and more, the possibility of relying on hunting to obtain food sources was completely lost. Then, once entering the year of famine, the crop yield is drastically reduced, and there is immediately a mass famine, as a result of which a large number of people inevitably fall into the miserable situation of starvation. Such phenomenon of famine is never seen in any animals.

Not only that, with the increase of agricultural production, people could reasonably reserve some food for their families during the good year. However, the social hierarchy was formed, the powerful government system emerged, and the surplus food you could store in the good year was levied by the cruel taxation in the social organization, so the man-made disaster was added to it, and famine occurred as usual. It expresses the hideous face of human civilized society from the very beginning of its presentation.

Why does the seemingly complex social organization of humans occur? I said earlier that it is in no way the result of human design planning, but is a completely spontaneous process. Let me give you an example of the element uranium, the thing that human used to build the atomic bomb, which is the last of the natural elements, element number 92. Generally speaking, the more post-derivative and the more terminal the existence, the less stable it is. So, if you accumulate pure uranium into a pile volume, as soon as it reaches some mass threshold boundary, it will automatically undergo a neutron bombardment fission reaction. Because, when the accumulated volume is small, the neutrons that are emitted from itself will hit outside the volume; if the accumulated volume is large, then the neutrons that hit will eject back when they hit other nuclei, and so immediately a chain of multiplying neutron bombardment effects will be continuously triggered within the volume. Thus, the neutron bombardment fission reaction of a pure element of uranium, as long as the volume is of an order of magnitude, will occur automatically, as a purely natural process.

The same is true for human society. Social structure and organization are born when the population keeps on skyrocketing without human control. It has nothing to do with human wisdom or human subjective design beforehand.

There are at least four factors that lead to this inevitable outcome.

First, when the population skyrockets, the probability of interpersonal conflict between each two people will be greatly increased. Some scholars calculate that if a community, such as a clan tribe of only 20 people, then the permutation of its clashes between each two people is up to 190 times; but when the population increases to 2,000 people, the probability of clashes between each two in the population will actually rise to as many as 1.99 million times. In other words, the population has only increased 100 times, while the possibility of conflict has increased 10,000 times. What does this mean? It means that once the number of population reproduction increases to a certain level, the inherent regulating mechanism is forced to arise, which is the germination of social organization.

Second, as the population increases, it becomes much more difficult to make decisions together. In *Chronicle of Zuo* it records a saying that "the previous kings ruled by procedure of official discussion". What does this mean? It means that the patriarch in a clan society solved social problems by gathering all the adults in the group, such as 30 or 50 people, together and discussing the problems together. But when the population reaches thousands, tens of thousands, or even hundreds of thousands or millions, can people still sit together and collectively negotiate for all the problems of different sizes? This uncontrollable process of population explosion inevitably requires an organizational structure and a centralized management system to occur.

Third, the division of labor is bound to emerge as the number of the population increases. Because the equal labor of people cannot satisfy the civilized way of human existence. The division of labor emerges as a secondary division while the population soars. Once the division of labor emerges, social disorder increases, thus forcing contractual rules and subsequent legal system to arise automatically.

Fourth, with the development of agricultural civilization, the territories of the formerly separate communities had to expand and form neighboring relationships, so the chance of clan conflicts increased greatly. Moreover, as the number of people in a social group rose, the handling of external conflicts could not be given to the whole population to discuss in time, so the army and the chain of command occurred accordingly. The organizational structure of human society was gradually formed, and it was all a natural evolutionary process after the population had risen to a certain spontaneous group size.

This is the same as the physical changes triggered by the aforementioned pure uranium elemental volume.

Let's look at another issue, which is the difference between China and the West in judging the good and bad of governmental organization systems. It is important to know that in ancient times there was no government. The primitive clan society was a blood kinship society, so why was there a need of government in the family management within the blood? Why was there a need for oppression through violence? Only when civilization developed to a certain level, or when the population grew to a certain level, did governmental organizations emerge accordingly.

Westerners call the organization of government *a gangster system of rule*. Notice what they mean: government must be made up of the worst people, because if they are not bad people, there is no way to govern human beings in a violent way. The basic concept of the West, since its primitive culture, is human evil. So it asks: who can embody the human evil? Ordinary people are scattered, and they can't be evil even if they want to be; those who can really embody human evil to the extreme must be the organized people.

Who has an organization? The government, political parties and the military. So the highest authority in the West is the parliament, the legislature. The first law it enacts is called a constitution. The so-called constitution is the law that specifically controls the government, political parties and the military, which are the organized people. Why does the entire legislative process lay control the government in the first place? It is because the government can express human evil to the extreme. Therefore, the West has always considered the government to be thieves and gangsters, and the most important thing for all people is to monitor the government. This is the major difference between Western culture and Chinese culture.

Where is the point of origin of this distinction? Back in ancient times in China it was the opposite, it was believed that the government in human society was initially composed of the most benevolent and virtuous people. Please note that East and West are extremely incompatible, and one of the manifestations of this, as I mentioned earlier, is that these two cultures are always opposite. If you want to understand Eastern culture, you have to seek the answer at the opposite of that conclusion deduced by Western culture, and vice versa.

There is a reason why the traditional culture of Eastern China believes that the earliest human organizational system, government system, and power system must be composed of the kindest and most moral people, so much so that Confucius called them saints. Because if you go back, in the most primitive stage, who was the manager of human society? It was the elder of the blood group, and he must have been the one who had the deepest care for his blood offspring in order to become the patriarch. So of course he was the most virtuous person, and they eventually developed into the governmental organization of mankind.

Although once it develops into a governmental organization, it has its own unique group interests, it deteriorates and becomes degenerate. Its origin was born from the starting point of goodness and high morality. I say this to tell you that the reason why Eastern and Western cultures differ in their views on the most fundamental point is that there was a gap between the antient horizons of Eastern and Western cultures. Eastern culture is the intact preservation of the most primitive culture of mankind, so its vision stretches back far more farther. This is why Confucius and Mencius advocated human goodness, while when history developed to the time of Han Feizi, his view began to converge with Westerners' and advocated human evil. Please understand the meaning of this passage: the great value of Chinese culture is that it is endowed with a deeper vision of civilizational grassroots search.

Once the government occurs, it must have the following four conditions or initiatives in order for this control organization to operate effectively: first, it must disarm the civilian population, but only arm the upper management group, which is the monopoly of violence that acts on the individual; second, it must take wealth by trickery, such as using taxation to concentrate economic resources in its own hands. This is called economic monopoly, only then it will have the ability to control and organize the material basis of the system; third, if it has such authority, it will be able to launch the regulation or suppression of various social disputes, which is called power monopoly, the origin of politics. Fourth, any ruling class must misinterpret even the ideology and culture of the lower strata of the people as the mainstream ideology conducive to government rule, that is, any human culture, its manifest and mainstream expression must be distorted and used by the ruling class. This is called ideological monopoly.

So we see, once a powerful governing body comes into existence, it does four things, all of which look like egregious acts. But if it doesn't have such an ability, if it is not this kind of operation, the social control system can never be built, and this is the reason why Westerners see the government as a gangster management system. It is inevitably concluded after the formation of the government to be viewed in reverse. The Chinese, on the other hand, began to trace the source of the sage management system before the government was formed, thus forming an opposite concept.

I want to emphasize that we have been assimilated into Western culture today. Why did we historically assimilate others in the past but not now? It is because before the Western invasion of China in the Opium War, the Chinese agrarian civilization had only faced the nomadic civilization. The population of nomadic civilization was low. As I said, the amount of energy available to the human body from growing food on one acre of land is 260 times more than the amount of energy obtained from letting grass grow on the land and then hunting animals, which led to the very thin population of nomadic civilization. Therefore, its social structure must be very simple.

Since social structure is a natural product of population density, once nomadic civilization invaded China, it had to face a more complex social structure, and it had only one way left, which was to be assimilated by the natural social structure facilitated by the high population density of the agricultural civilization, that is the reason why we have always assimilated others. Those we assimilated were nothing more than nomadic civilizers. However, since industrial and commercial civilization is the way to cross over and expand the resources obtained from the limited area of agriculture, it is the necessary way for human history to develop, so once the industrial and commercial civilization comes, we immediately lose the ability to assimilate others, and instead we were assimilated by others. This is the key to understand the concept of cultural assimilation.

We speak of human civilization as occurring gradually with the migration process of modern Homo sapiens, so much so that the timing of migration and settlement had an impact on the gradation of human civilization occurring. We say today that agropastoral civilization occurred 10,000 years ago, but in reality, the factors we have to probe today may have to stretch back dozens of thousands of years further.

What is the basis for this statement? Linguists discovered long ago that the languages of all the species on earth have an intrinsic homology of pronunciation. For example, the word *sheep* in the Indo-European language family is pronounced *owis;* in Lithuanian and Indian Sanskrit, *avis;* in Latin, *ovis;* in Spanish, *oveja;* in Russian *ovtas;* in Greek, *ows;* in Irish, *oi,* and English is *owis,* which is pronounced basically the same. In addition, there are more than 2,000 other words with this homonymic feature, such as *horse, wheel, brother, eyes* and so on. On the contrary, all the words used in modern times, such as gun, artillery, are different even among European countries, such as *fusil* in French and *ruzhyo* in Russian, etc. What does this mean? It means that the languages of early mankind did not occur separately in each place, but were gradually developed during the tens of thousands of years of primitive human migration, before each of them took shape separately.

Some scholars have studied that the pronunciation of words in Taiwan, the Philippines, Indonesia, and the Polynesian Islands in the south-central Pacific Ocean are very similar, and they are called Primitive southern island languages. It is because the ancestors who migrated to the south drifted with the waterways or land ways along the coasts of East and Southeast Asia, so their most primitive words, such as *bird, pig, dog, rice, ear, hair,* and *canoe* with outboard floating material (a flat boat with multiple crossbars on both sides of the boat to slow down the rocking or capsizing in the waves), *sails, fish fences, turtles, octopus, clam,* etc., their pronunciations are very similar. This indicates that the entire East Central and South Pacific region was also homologous during the development of sub-civilizations.

Let me give you another example. The Yellow Emperor of China is called Xuan Yuan, which is a very strange phenomenon. Because the word Xuan Yuan was used to describe a partial component of a vehicle, and the Yellow Emperor lived about 4600 years ago, before the Chinese built vehicles. How could he used this word Xuan Yuan, which was impossible, and it must be a term appeared only after vehicles were introduced to China. Therefore, the Yellow Emperor was called Xuan Yuan, the name must be given to the Yellow Emperor by later generations. The origin of this term is suspicious. Why do you call him Xuan Yuan? He is exactly the same image as the ancient Greek god of war Ares, the ancient Greek god of war Ares was driving a chariot in the sky, so the Chinese Yellow Emperor, his name is also called Xuan Yuan, is it out of the mythological era of the distant West? It seems to require a separate examination.

Noah of the West came from the well-known Noah Ark. The story comes from the *Old Testament* in West Asia, and the name *Noah* is pronounced very similarly to the Chinese name for the ancestor *Nuwa*. In other words, the Chinese deified legend of *Nuwa* and Noah are probably the same phonetic variation.

These aspects are the result of linguistic scholars' research, and we do not know for sure, but if there is a little bit of truth, it proves that the process of civilization transmission in the early years of mankind was expanding on the channel of modern Homo sapiens migration, and it is the expression of the original process of globalization of human civilization.

We have given a brief explanation of the origin of agriculture and animal husbandry, and we will talk a little about pottery, because pottery is the first non-natural artificial material created by human beings. Before pottery, including agriculture, pastoralism, wood and stone tools, human beings used natural materials. Pottery was made through clay and water mixture and then fire it to achieve, because it is the first artificial material created by man, so it is extremely striking in the early development of human civilization.

What is the main thing you see when you visit ancient sites? the pottery! Pottery had a major impact on human civilization later because firing pottery was a remarkable improvement in human skill with fire. We talked earlier about the occurrence of tools, which could not be a definitive indicator of human civilization, because many lower and intermediate class animals were using tools as well. But the use of fire is, indeed, a uniquely human ability. Early human use of fire can only be piled into campfires, and the way of campfires was not possible to burn pottery, because the temperature of campfires is generally only about 400 to 500 degrees Celsius, while the fire temperature needed to burn pottery to be more than 700 to 800 degrees. Please note that the fire temperature of firing porcelain to be more than 1200 degrees Celsius. So when man made pottery, how did he do it? He had to make the fire in the kiln to burn, so that the fire temperature can be raised to 800 degrees or more. The pottery burning process trained the human ability to grasp the fire, thus laying the foundation for mankind's later Bronze Age and Iron Age. As you know, the melting point of copper is 1083.4 degrees Celsius, the melting point of iron is 1535 degrees Celsius. The firing of pottery in kiln in the early years of mankind made it possible to improve mankind's skills with fire, thus paving the way for the development of later civilizations. Some scholars found that there is a color pottery belt of 10,000 kilometers from the sides of Mediterranean Sea, the earliest settlement of human civilization, to the Eastern Asia area.

What does it mean? That is, the invention and production of pottery was probably not reached by modern Homo sapiens in different parts of the earth, but was spread along the migration route of civilization. This is because it was found that in this 10,000 km pottery belt, all the water pattern on pottery was painted with a jagged pattern, and all the animal body parts were painted with a diagonal line as a grid, so the animal squatted in the middle. These unified graphics show that the occurrence of human pottery is a flowing differentiation process, rather than a multi-source breeding process.

Majiayao painted pottery

Painted pottery at the site of Half Slop

Pottery from the Site of Longshan Culture

So we can see, pottery excavated in Qinghai's Majiayao site, its shape and color is quite ancient; and to the Half slop site of Shaanxi, and Yangshao sites of Henan, you will see more bright colors, more complex shape, the painting on pottery even appeared some kind of philosophical interest in the pursuit of life and death; and then to Shandong Longshan culture sites, the pottery shape is more complex, and even appeared pure black pottery. The difficulty of making this pottery is very high. In short, from west to east, the development process of colored pottery shows a gradual complication, vivid, skill level gradually sublimated process, which implies its flow route. Of course, there are many opposing voices and evidences in the academic circles now, for example, in Gansu Dadiwan site, exquisite colored pottery of 8000 years ago was found, and some scholars even think that the Qinghai Majiayao colored pottery was a skill of production returned from the Central Plains. Of course, we cannot draw definite conclusions about these things today, but the argument about the 10,000-kilometer pottery belt is valid to some extent, because it is consistent with the migration route of modern Homo sapiens and the flow of human civilization.

Let's discuss one issue here: everyone today holds the progressive theory. What does that mean? We think that whatever is progressive is good, whatever is primitive and backward is bad, so that today progressive and advanced have become positive words, and primitive or backward have become derogatory terms. However, we must know that the concept of progressive theory is a recent import from the West, the tone of traditional Chinese culture is the opposite, not progressivism, but conservatism.

Let me give you an example, Confucius said that he "recount but not to write, believe in and love ancient times, suppose myself like old Peng". What does he mean by "recount but not to write"? I only recount what has gone before me, never innovate or create, this is called "recount but not to write." What does he mean by "believe in and love ancient times"? I only believe in and love the things of the ancients, but I resent innovations and inventions of the present generation, this is called believe in and love the past. He even compared himself to the old-fashioned Pengzu of the Shang Dynasty, and seemed to feel quite honored with it.

Let me give you an example of a two-wheeled carriage from the ruins of Yinxu, Anyang, Henan Province. This two-wheeled carriage was so well established once it appeared that we have found no precedent for its transitional progress in domestic archaeology. As I mentioned earlier, the earliest domestication of horses was probably by the ancestors of southern Central Asia, including the Ukraine; according to historians, the earliest invention of wheels and vehicles was probably by the ancient Babylonians. Then this vehicle appears to be very perfect once it arrives in China, what does it mean? It means that this vehicle was not invented by the Chinese, but was introduced into China from the west, and this is the only explanation for it.

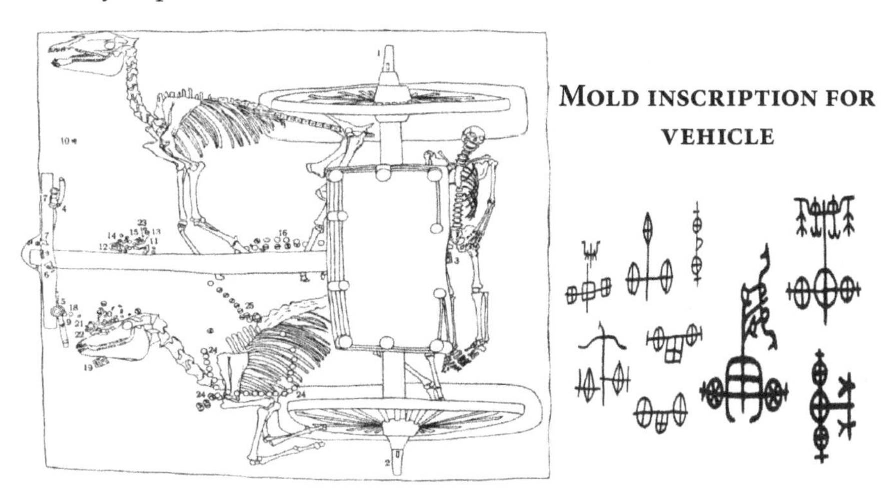

Mold inscription for vehicle

Look closely at this cart, it uses an axle through two wheels. An axle through two wheels of the vehicle, there must be a problem, that is, the wheel speed of both sides is always the same , then the vehicle in turning the corner, the outer wheel speed must be greater than the inner wheel, so this vehicle can only run fast straight but slow down at turning, it cannot be fast turning. So, the Chinese actually used this two-wheeled carriage until around the Republic Revolution (1911). The four-wheeled carriage was invented by the West in the late Middle Ages or even in the late Roman Empire. There is a great difficulty in inventing the four-wheeled carriage, which cannot use two axles wearing four wheels, because if the wheels on both sides of the four-wheeled carriage always have the same speed, it can't even turn at slow speed. Therefore, the invention of the four-wheeled carriage has a premise, it must be separated at the middle of the axle, with a design of gears to recombine, so that the wheels on both sides of the speed is not the same, which is the car today under the big bulge called the differential, but at that time it had not the capacity to drive. The invention of the four-wheeled carriage created the predecessor of the modern automobile chassis.

When I talk about this, you must think that I am slandering Chinese culture, saying Chinese culture does not like innovation, even the old carriage is used all the time till lately. Let me make a statement here: I do not talk about good and bad, but only about what it is. Because to speak of good and bad is a biased evaluation from a different standpoint and with emotional judgment. You can only understand the essence and content of a culture if you understand the reason why it happens and how it works. The Chinese do not innovate because the tone of their culture has always been conservative. We feel today that conservatism must be very problematic, but in fact we have to rethink this issue. If we want to start from the ancient civilization of mankind, if we want to take the traditional Chinese culture, which is closer to us, as the main clue, then when you listen to my class, you must first knock off the progressivism, or at least vacate the progressivism from your mind for a while, so that you can listen to the subsequent threads of thought in this course and you can understand the basic qualities of traditional Chinese culture.

And there is a more important question: on what basis do you think that what is advanced is good and what is backward is bad? How do you know that what is advanced is not the worst thing? No one has really examined this question in depth, and all people are just following the majority based on their intuition, thus creating the mainstream global ideology that pervades the East and the West today. What is the nature of progressivism and conservatism in this topic? We'll talk about that in tomorrow's Laozi class. I repeat, when listening to the history of ancient human civilizations and traditional Chinese culture, please first abandon the notion of progressivism.

Formative Mechanism of Primitive Human Civilization

We have only scratched the surface of some basic issues and explained them in a piecemeal manner.

We will now move on to the topic of how the divergence and evolution of human civilization was formed, since the migration of Homo sapiens could not cause ethnic differences and intellectual differences. In other words, the topic of the formation mechanism of human primitive civilization needs to be investigated.

To illustrate this, let's start with a bit digression. As you know, there are billions of species of living things. When we say everything today, we are mainly talking about living things. Because there are less than 10 million inorganic species, while there are more than 10 billion species of living things, if we include the extinct part. It is surprising that such a large number of biological differentiations is derived from the evolution of a single species of single-celled organism 3.8 billion years ago.

So, how do new species form? Biologists have found that it requires at least two conditions: the first is called geographic isolation, and the second is called reproductive isolation.

Let me first explain what geographic isolation is. In the early years of the Earth, the original continent was called Pangaea, or the Central Continent. If a genetic mutation occurs in one member of a population of animals or organisms, and there is no geographic isolation, this mutated gene will be spread and diluted throughout the population by means of group intercourse, i.e., reproductive inheritance. In this way, new species can never be formed. Therefore, the formation of new species must be predicated on geographical isolation. In other words, the same species that lived in the central continent, with the continental plate drifting into different latitudes of the Earth 200 million years ago, entered into different natural weather conditions, that is, into different directions of natural selection. The accumulation of their genetic mutations in different geographical environments is what caused the formation of new species. This is the first condition, called geographical isolation.

The second condition is reproductive isolation. What does it mean? It is originally belongs to the same species, and then with the continental plate drift into a different geographical environment, finally evolved into different species, if at this time to regroup them together, but each other cannot occur normal sexual behavior, cannot be normal mating, or cannot produce offspring with normal reproductive capacity, we call this phenomenon reproductive isolation.

Let me give you an example, for instance donkeys and horses are two species. Although they are both equid, according to the family, genus and species, they are two species at the level of species.

Why? Because although donkeys and horses can mate normally, the resulting offspring, mules, do not have the ability to reproduce normally, that is, they are reproductively isolated from each other, and are therefore biologically defined as two species.

What do I want to explain in this paragraph? It is to tell you that since human civilization is a natural process, since it is a spontaneous process, it also has two natural constraints, that is, the differentiation of human civilization also requires two major conditions: the first is called geographical isolation; the second is called communication isolation.

We use Eastern and Western civilizations as examples below.

Western civilization is generally referred to as the Greek and Hebrew civilizations by the academic community. The two civilizations concern the ancient Greece and Hebrew. We are all familiar with the fact that ancient Greece was the spark of Western civilization. Then why do we mention the Hebrews? It is because the Western civilization after the A.D. era is also called Christian civilization. Christianity is nothing but a variant of Judaism, and the Bible today is divided into two parts: the Old Testament and the New Testament. The so-called Old Testament is the Jewish text; the so-called New Testament is the Christian text. In those days, a group of non-Jews who believed in Judaism were expelled from Judaism because they did not oppose the Roman Empire's oppression of the Jews of Israel, and then a new, deformed Judaism was spread among the non-Jews, which is Christianity. This is why some people used to call Western civilization the Greek and Hebrew civilizations.

What do we call Chinese civilization? It's called the civilization of Yellow Earth and the Yellow River. Let's look at the Chinese Eastern civilization first. The so-called Yellow Earth, we have to look at a phenomenon, in the upper reaches of the Yellow River in China, that is, in north of Shaanxi and Shanxi, is the distribution of a soil layer thickness of nearly hundred meters or even several hundred meters of loess plateau. This is a very strange phenomenon that geologists are baffled by, because the average thickness of the earth's soil is only 0.5 meters, that is, only half a meter thick, but why there is a thick soil in the upper reaches of the Yellow River so bizarre loess plateau in China?

To clarify this issue, we must first go back to the initial state of the primitive Earth. 4.5 to 4.6 billion years ago, the primitive Earth was formed by the fusion of several planets of different sizes in the Earth's orbit in the solar system; in addition, the Earth's case or crust, was extremely unstable in far ancient times, and the mantle material was constantly overflowing to the surface through volcanic eruptions. As a result, the primitive Earth was almost entirely a molten soft ball. Because it was a fluid, semi-solid celestial body, it swung itself into a ball as it rotated. If it had started out as a hard rocky object, it would have been irregularly shaped like an asteroid.

And one more thing we should know is that the water hydrogen dioxygen in the earth does not exactly happen on earth. Because hydrogen is the number one element on the periodic table of chemical elements and it is extremely stable, it cannot be oxidized on a large scale under Earth conditions. Water on Earth originally came from extraterrestrial impact planets, and the water carried in their rocks formed part of the source of Earth's water. Some scholars have found that crushing and distillation of primitive rock formations or alien meteorites can yield water from the rock in roughly the same proportion as surface water; this, together with the continuous smashing of asteroids, especially comets with ice nuclei, into the Earth over a long period of time thereafter, is a second source of Earth's water.

The temperature of the Earth's surface reached over 1,000 degrees Celsius in primitive times, and water simply could not remain on Earth in a liquid state. It dissolved in the atmosphere in a gaseous state for millions of years. Why didn't these water molecules drift into space? It is because the Earth's mass and gravity are large enough. It is important to know that there was once water on the Moon and Mars, but because of their small mass and insufficient gravity, these water molecules were lost to space, which is the reason why there is no liquid water on the Moon and Mars today.

As the temperature of the Earth's crust and surface gradually drops, the water distributed in the atmosphere in a gaseous state begins to condense at high altitudes, creating the torrential rain that we cannot imagine today falling to the ground. Then, it is vaporized again by the extremely high temperature of the ground and rises into the sky. This repeatedly rained down for 60,000 to 600,000 years or more to cool the earth's crust. Can we imagine what the primitive Earth was like at this time? It had no land at all and was completely encased by the oceans, a complete ball of water. It was not until the palaeogeological Silurian era, 430 million years ago, that the highest point of the crustal uplift rose above sea level - the central continent emerged. Please imagine again what the central continent looked like at this time. Not only was there no soil, no sand, and even no rocks on it, it was a complete crustal rock layer. It is a complete crustal rock layer. The direct sunlight heats it up, and the sudden rainfall cools it down, and under the heat expansion and cold contraction, it first cracks into rock pieces, then crumbles into gravel, and finally winds up sand and soil.

Soil weathering has two channels: first, the physical channel, which is the thermal expansion and contraction effect that I just mentioned. Second, the chemical channel. What does it mean? You should know that the atmosphere of the original earth is called the reducing atmosphere. Our atmosphere today, called the oxidizing atmosphere. Today's atmosphere contains about 21% oxygen, but in the original era, the Earth's atmosphere contains less than 0.1% oxygen, that is, less than 1/210 of the present, while the carbon dioxide content is now tens of thousands of times or even tens of thousands of times more. Once the rain falls, water and carbon dioxide combined, immediately forming a weak carbonic acid. Therefore, the rainfall process in ancient times was all acid rain. Acid rain acts on the surface of the rock layer, causing it to erode and weather, which is the second cause of the soil.

This is the reason why the average soil thickness of the earth is only half a meter thick. Because the rock layer below half a meter thick soil can no longer be heated by the sun, the physical weathering effect of thermal expansion and contraction disappears; similarly, the rock layer below half a meter thick soil can no longer be soaked by acid rain, so the chemical weathering effect also disappears.

Why, then, is there a loess plateau in the middle and upper reaches of the Yellow River with a soil thickness of hundreds of meters? Two things must be mentioned.

First, 30 million years ago the South Asian subcontinent, which is the Indian continental plate, began to collide with the main Eurasian continent and gradually rose to more than six or seven thousand meters by 2.5 million years ago. It effectively blocked the warm and humid airflow from the Indian Ocean, making the dry and high-pressure airflow from the north to ravage the earth, thus rolling the superficial soil layer of northwestern China all the way to the middle and upper reaches of the Yellow River, which is why you will see the Great Gobi Beach when you go to the Hexi Corridor, to Xinjiang, to the western part of Inner Mongolia today. The so-called Gobi beach is a bare area of debris without soil cover. This is the main cause of the thick accumulation of loess in the middle and upper reaches of the Yellow River.

Second, the trade wind. The so-called trade wind, meteorology refers to the wind with certainty, that is, this wind blows according to a fixed wind channel throughout the year. The formation of the trade wind has two sources: first, the equatorial region of the direct sun, the air is heated and upward ascension, and eventually fall at the poles of the Earth, thus forming the first fixed wind channel on Earth; second, the rotation of the Earth from west to east, the rotation of the Earth's entity, inevitably produce some degree of disturbance to the atmospheric flow, coupled with the ground temperature difference and other multiple effects, thus forming the second fixed wind channel on Earth; these two fixed winds combined to constitutes the trade winds on the Earth. The combined forces of these two fixed wind paths form the Earth's trade winds. The trade winds carry the finest dust in the 0.5-meter-thick soil on the Earth's surface and wrap it up in the atmosphere. Any fluid eventually forms turbulence, and the center of the turbulence forms a typhoon cyclone, just like a typhoon eye in the middle of a typhoon. The typhoon cyclone of the trade winds happens to hang in the middle and upper reaches of the Yellow River in China, and it allows those finest soil particles wrapped up in it to settle here continuously, which is the second reason why the Loess Plateau was formed.

It is clear from this that the Loess Plateau must be made up of the finest layers of soil. It inevitably poses a problem of soil erosion once the rain falls. Therefore, soil erosion on the Loess Plateau is not something that happens only today, but has been the norm since it was first formed. Once it rains, the rainwater, wrapped in sediment, mixed into countless small streams, which eventually merge into a big river, which is the Yellow River.

The Yellow River is wrapped in a large amount of fine sediment, flowing all the way east to the Central Plains, where the river suddenly slows down and the sediment begins to settle. Why?

Please look at the topographical map of China first, all rivers in China run eastward. If you go to Europe, you will see that its rivers flow in a chaotic direction and flow in all directions. Why? Because the topography of China is high in the west and low in the east, it has several landmark steps, but if you take the Yellow River as a perspective, then the Central Plains and Henan can be counted as an important node, that is, the steepness of the terrain west of the Central Plains is extremely high, and the inclination of the ground level east of the Central Plains is significantly lower. As a result, when the Yellow River reached the Central Plains, its flow suddenly slowed down, its channel widened considerably, and the sediment began to settle. Before the civilization of East Asia, that is, before human beings built dikes on both sides of the Yellow River, according to ancient geologists, the Yellow River had at least six major diversions. In just 2,000 years after the end of the Fourth ice age, a small alluvial plain was created in China; it took more than 8,000 years to expand this plain into the present-day North China Plain. What is the total amount of sediment brought by this alluvial sedimentation process? I will give you a data, in ancient times, China's Shandong Province was completely shallow sea bed, Taishan Mountain was just an island in China's offshore, that is, about 10,000 years, the alluvial sediment of the Yellow River actually brought China a whole Shandong Province, plus the eastern part of Hebei Province. As I said earlier, the Yellow River's turbulent flow is made up of the finest soil particles, and the Central Plains that it first washed out constitute one of the three major bases on earth where mankind could start primitive farming.

Let me first explain what is meant by primitive farming? The earliest human agricultural civilization may have occurred around 10,000 years ago, when it was still in the Neolithic era, that is, the only tool in the hands of people was just a stone with a sharp edge, at most tied to a wooden stick in the back, all by human power to plough the land. It is important to know that oxen plowing technology did not become popular until 3000 years ago, 8000 to 10000 years ago, man did not have any animal power to work with.

With a stone to plough the raw land, it simply could not be carried out on general land. There were only three pieces of soft and fertile lands on earth suitable for primitive farming: first, the Nile Delta, where the ancient Egyptian civilization took place. As the Nile River flows through the desert of northern Africa, weather in that place is only divided as the rainy season and the dry season, in the rainy season, the land on both sides of the river was flooded, farmers had to flee into the desert to avoid water damage. In the dry season, the riverbed narrowed, the two banks exposed, the Nile brought in from central Africa volcanic ash and humus, sedimented in the River bed, making it extremely fertile and soft natural land. In this way, ancient Egyptian farmers returned to the banks of the Nile every year during the dry season to cultivate the land again. Since they had to measure the land again every year, they tied the rope into knots by unit length and used the rope to measure the land in bends, thus creating the earliest geometry and mathematics of mankind. This situation was recorded by Herodotus, the ancient Greek historian in his book *History*.

The second primitive farming base on earth occurred in the two river basins of the Middle East. By two rivers, we mean the Euphrates and Tigris rivers. These two rivers form an arc that eventually flows into the Gulf. This area forms shallow swamps in the rainy season and becomes the most fertile land with the most humus in the dry season. This led to the creation of the Sumerian, ancient Babylonian and Assyrian civilizations.

The third original farming base on the earth is the Central Plains in China. By now, you should understand that the Chinese agricultural civilization is one of the real original agricultural civilizations on the earth. The only real original agricultural civilizations are in the three pieces of land mentioned above. The agricultural civilization of India is most likely to be transmitted from the west, because botanists can't find the 56 species of related species of big grass plants in India. The ancient Greek civilization was also a secondary civilization. The Chinese agricultural civilization was primary and early, with extremely deep roots.

A question occurs here. After the Middle Ages, the highest agricultural output in China was not in the Yellow River basin, but in the Yangtze River basin. We can still see the names of two counties in the Jiangsu area of the Yangtze River basin today, one is called Taicang and the other is Changshu. The so-called Taicang means a big granary; the so-called Changshu means that the grain grown in this place is always in a mature state, so it is called Changshu.

But why do we not regard the agricultural civilization that took place in the land of fish and rice in Jiangnan as the origin of Chinese agricultural civilization? This brings us to the famous British historian Toynbee. When he studied the history of world civilizations in the first half of the 20th century, Toynbee found that there were at least 600 civilization settlements in ancient times, and that human civilizations must have occurred in places where natural conditions were neither too good nor too bad. Natural conditions were too poor for humans to live in, civilization certainly could not happen, it is easy to understand. But why couldn't a place with too good natural conditions be the birthplace of agricultural civilization?

Let's just look at Jiangnan, southeast region of China. We must first of all know that before the occurrence of human agricultural civilization, the human way of life and all animals are no different, called picking and hunting way of life. As I mentioned earlier, gathering plants and hunting animals is to enjoy what the nature produces. This is the Eden Paradise mentioned in the *Old Testament* of the Christian religion, which says that mankind and all animals lived in the Garden of Eden, provided for by God. Later, when man was tempted by the serpent to eat the forbidden fruit of wisdom, which God did not allow him to eat, he became knowledgeable and shameful, and was expelled from the Garden of Eden by God, and from then on, he worked hard all his life only to get enough to survive. What does it mean? It means that before man was civilized, all he enjoyed were the ready-made means of living in nature. What is the so-called human civilization? It means that nature no longer provides human beings with the means of subsistence directly, and all the means of subsistence for human beings must be prepared by human beings themselves, so it is called the Paradise Lost. We know that what we eat, wear, and use today are all man-made things. Food is cultivated by humans, even fruits such as apples, pears, etc., in the original wild state, may not be as big as a date today, now they are all the products of artificial cultivation.

Remember, civilization began as a disaster against human nature, or rather against the human body's upright physiology of toil and torture. Those who were able to escape civilization were considered the lucky ones at that time. More importantly, the ancients only had a stone axe in their hands. Today give you a steel axe to let you cut down a very thick tree, you won't cut it down in ten days or even a half month. Even if you cut down the tree, you have to get the tree root out of the earth, so that the soil could be used. But if you use stone tools to dig out a tree root, you won't complete it within a month or two. If an acre of land grow three or five trees, you can't finish it in six months. Even if you could reclaim a few acres of land, it still could not grow crops, because the surrounding trees were too high, blocking the sun light, it still could grow grass. This is the reason why places with too good natural conditions could not be the birthplace of agricultural civilization.

We now look back at Europe. As I said earlier, the Caucasians migrated to Europe 40,000 years ago, and the modern Homo sapiens who ascended the Pamir Plateau eastward into East Asia delayed 5,000 years, coming to settle in the Central Plains about 35,000 years ago, so it is reasonable to say that China's agricultural civilization should lag behind the West. But before the Middle Ages, China's agricultural civilization has been far more advanced than Europe, becoming the only counter-example in the history of human civilization, why? Some Western biologists found that 3000 years ago, Europe was full of large dense forests, mainly spruce, which were all over Central and Western Europe.

As I said earlier, the latitude of Europe is almost similar to that of northeast China, and northern Europe is much higher than the latitude of northeast China, then why would it have natural weather conditions similar to those in Jiangnan, China? This brings us to know the warm current of Mexican Gulf.

At the end of the fourth ice age 12,000 years ago, rivers appeared on the earth and ocean currents appeared in the oceans. The largest ocean current on Earth is the Mexican Gulf Current. It leaves the Gulf of Mexico and passes through the equatorial region of the Atlantic Ocean, where it is heated by direct sunlight, raising its temperature by more than 8 degrees Celsius. How large is this ocean current? It is actually 40 times the runoff of all rivers on Earth combined. Such a large flow of water is heated to over 20 degrees Celsius by direct solar radiation, and then releases heat in the North Atlantic Ocean, eventually flowing into Iceland and disappear in the Arctic, which is called the Gulf Stream.

For this reason, after the end of the Fourth ice age, the temperature and rainfall conditions in Western Europe and even central Europe are close to the Yangtze River basin in south China, which makes the region extremely rich vegetation, making it extremely difficult for the Caucasian species that migrated to Europe to develop agricultural civilization. This is why all the ancient civilizations in Europe took place in the desolate southern Europe, the ancient Greek civilization and the ancient Roman civilization were all in the southern Europe near the Mediterranean region, and here is the reason.

Now look back at the Central Plain. The Central Plain is one of the typical primitive farming bases. Please think about it, what kind of way of labor is in agricultural civilization? As I said earlier, once it had a population explosion, it had to continue to reclaim the land, and the area of farmland kept increasing, which made it gradually and completely lost the woodland resources for hunting and survival. Land is a limited natural resource, but the population is multiplying, the consequence of which must be the ongoing shortage of living materials and natural resources. People had to work collectively, diligently and intensively on each acre of land in order to crop enough for food. This natural structure, this survival structure, led to the emergence of Chinese culture, which does not care about individual rights and freedom, but about harmony, cooperation, internal coordination, ethical social relations, and even the formation of close blood ties that do not loose, and this was the origin of Chinese culture. This culture was not designed by anyone in advance, nor was it invented by anyone subjectively.

We said earlier that Western civilization refers to Greek and Hebrew civilizations, which is an inaccurate in concept. It is better for us to call it a circum-Mediterranean civilization.

To understand this civilization, you first have to better understand the Mediterranean Sea. The Mediterranean Sea is a narrow seaway sandwiched between the continents of Europe, Asia and Africa, with calm winds and waves. It allowed the inhabitants around the Mediterranean Sea to use a canoe to cross the Mediterranean Sea in the ancient times, 5,000 to 6,000 years ago. What was a canoe? It is not what we call a boat now, the boat is invented only after the Middle Ages, it has to plan the wooden board extremely fine, the seam is extremely tight, in order to make a boat, which the ancient ancestors simply could not do. The ancients could only cut down a big tree, cut off the two ends, and then saw through the thickest part from the middle, and then hollow out half of it, which is called a canoe. This kind of canoe in any wind and waves in the current is easy to capsize, but could be used only in the Mediterranean Sea, which is like an inner lake, and became a convenient waterway traffic. Why is the origin of the Mediterranean civilization gathered in Greece? Because the southern side of the Greek peninsula is the Aegean Sea, which is distributed with thousands of small islands, just like a chessboard. If you ever travelled in that place, sitting on the boat you could always see islands in the horizon not far away, which makes the sailing fear of navigation process greatly reduced.

The people around the Mediterranean Sea were thus able to cross the Mediterranean Sea for extensive exchanges as far back as 5,000 or 6,000 years ago. The entire Mediterranean rim thus became the only open area on the planet that could nurture a primitive and diverse civilization. Sea or water transportation has been the most important transportation channel for mankind since ancient times, and it is still the least expensive and most voluminous mode of transportation. Let me give you an example, Yangzhou. Why has Yangzhou been the economic capital of China for nearly a thousand years? It is the equivalent of making the great Shanghai, which is only a century old, last for a thousand years. The reason for this was that when Emperor Yang of Sui Dynasty dug the Grand Canal, it connected the two largest water systems in East Asia, the Yangtze and the Yellow River. Yangzhou was the hub of the Grand Canal, and the place became an economic boom in ancient China. It was only in the mid to late 19th century that Yangzhou somewhat declined, due to the blockage of canal transportation by the Taiping Heavenly Kingdom, which meant that canal transportation had to be changed to sea transportation, and to the rise of modern railroads.

What am I talking about? I'm talking about how much water conditions have contributed to human civilization. The Mediterranean Sea provided a channel of communication between the three continents of Europe, Asia and Africa in the ancient times, and it has a unique and open landscape, which was why it became unique.

Let's look at Greece specifically. It is a place with a rocky landscape and poor soil. Before 600 B.C., the population of Greece was so small that the local food production could barely feed the local people. After 600 B.C., as the population soared, the local food production could not feed the local people, and the exploitable agricultural land resources were exhausted, which forced the ancient Greeks to enter into commerce and industry very early to make a living. They made olive oil from the local olives and wine from the local grapes, and developed other handicrafts in large quantities. Then they crossed the Mediterranean Sea to ancient Egypt in North Africa and ancient Babylon in the Near East in exchange for food. This was the beginning and germination of the civilization of industry and commerce started by mankind on a large scale and systematically.

To make a living by industry and commerce, you have to make fantastically crafted goods. If you produce goods that the ancient Egyptians and ancient Babylonians could make, how could you trade with their most vital resource for survival - food. This forced the ancient Greeks to build a corresponding spirit of innovation and a culture of innovation.

Business activities were extremely risky as they had to cross the mountains, other city-states or even primitive tribes. Therefore, a merchant could never travel long distances with his family. He must have left his family in ancient Greece, for example, in Athens, and ventured into business alone or with a few partners, thus creating the spirit of adventure and freedom in their primitive culture.

Business operations rely on an exchange of equals. Even when I go to North Africa, to the Near East, I particularly despise the counterpart person, but the moment I have a material exchange with him, I must consider him as an equal trading partner. This creates the concept of equality and the spirit of contract that goes with it.

Aren't these subliminal qualities the root level of Western culture? It is necessary to emphasize once again that Western culture, like Eastern culture, is not the product of the design and planning of any few people or wise men, but is entirely the product of natural geographical features and natural physical conditions.

Inherent Survival Provisions of Civilizational Differentiation

At this point, we have to revise the concept of culture. When scholars and some educated people talk about culture, they always refer to it as something fancy, such as chess, music, calligraphy, painting, poetry, songs, arts, and so on. This is like someone pointing at the waves of the ocean and saying that waves are the ocean. But it is definitely wrong, because waves are only a few meters high on the surface of the ocean, while the deepest part of the ocean is more than 10,000 meters, the deep ocean without any waves, is the main body of the ocean.

So what exactly is human culture? Obviously, it is not these fancy things. Because human civilization occurred around 10,000 years ago, when there was no writing at all, how could *culture* be chess, music, calligraphy, painting, poetry, songs and arts?

Therefore, I will give another definition of *culture* here: Culture is the sum of the survival behaviors and consciousness systems of intelligent animals such as humans in the face of their living environment and living conditions. In ordinary words, it means that human beings, as a species with a certain degree of brain development, their survival behaviors and responses system is called *culture,* which is the origin and root of *culture.*

Therefore, please remember that all human subsistence is called cultural subsistence. Therefore, culture is never something above subsistence, but the base of subsistence, or human subsistence itself, which is the essence of culture. This is how you can understand where the power of culture lies.

Since ancient times, we in China have emphasized agriculture and suppressed commerce and industry. As early as the Spring and Autumn Period, till the middle of the Qing Dynasty, for thousands of years, the Chinese people were divided into classes of scholar, farmer, worker and merchant, with merchants as the lowest social status. How low was it? In the Ming and Qing Dynasties, merchants were the richest and their descendants were the best educated and most studied, but they were not allowed to take the imperial examinations for official careers, which meant that they were not allowed to change their social status from the lowest class as untouchable.

Why is the social status of Chinese merchants traditionally so low? Let me tell you an allusion. According to the Strategies of the Warring States, Lü Buwei was so smart and capable that he took over his family's business when he was a young man, and later he became so wealthy that he made the business of Lü's merchant society all over the states in East Asia. After making a good deal of fortune in his middle age, he once returned home to discuss with his father the idea of changing his career. The record of their dialogue was this: farming has a profit of ten times, jewelry business has profit of hundred times, while politics has profit of countless times. Here we put aside the topic of politics, see what the first two sentences mean. In ancient times, the Yellow River basin only had one crop a year. Reclamation of wasteland, sowing ten pounds of seeds, produce a hundred pounds of grain, the year is considered high-yielding fields, which is called farming has ten times profit. The so-called business has hundred times profit, not that one time business profit is much higher, but it refers to the turnover of capital many times a year, and by the end of the year, the profit of business is much greater than farming.

Please think what a situation would have emerged if China had not adopted the state policy of emphasizing agriculture and suppressing commerce since ancient times. It is important to know that China is a fully enclosed landscape. First, see the map of East Asia, China's north is desert, steppe and even alpine tundra Siberia; China's west is the Pamir Plateau; southwest is the Qinghai-Tibet Plateau - the roof of the world; south is the Yunnan-Guizhou Plateau plus the Hengduan Mountains, all of which the ancient people simply could not go over. This is why some Chinese in ancient and medieval times travelled to India for the Buddhas scriptures did not go directly to the south, but they had to go northwest, take the Hexi Corridor to today's Afghanistan area, before starting to turn south to India; and the east of China is the vast Pacific Ocean, impenetrable for the ancient people.

Note that this fully enclosed landscape, the only place in which food can be produced, is the Central Plains. Put yourself in the place of what would have been the situation if ancient China had not suppressed commerce and industry? Business is far more profitable than agriculture, but in ancient China, business could not get grain back. Not only you could not get food back, you had to trade grain for non-essential luxuries as a cost, with attractive profit. It was exactly opposite of ancient Greece, where commerce was precisely the process of exchanging the most basic means of livelihood, grain, through the Mediterranean Rim; whereas commerce in China, on the contrary, was the process of losing grain. That is why

China had to adopt a state policy of suppressing commerce and industry, which was not only profitable but also caused the loss of strong labor from the land. If such an issue left unchecked, eventually no one would like to devote himself in farming. This was also the reason why China has a saying *more sons more blessing* since ancient times.

Under such a survival condition, if the industrial and commercial practices that interfere with agricultural civilization had not been suppressed, I am afraid the Chinese nation would starve to extinction thousands of years ago! Please understand what I am talking about, even a political state policy as a local cultural phenomenon can be limited by geographical and physical conditions. This is the reason why Guan Zhong, when he was the prime minister of Qi, proposed that profit comes from one channel, meaning that industry and commerce should be suppressed and only agriculture should be encouraged, thus the profit comes from only one channel. Later generations made various explanations, saying that only the rulers could effectively control its dictatorship should they stuck the channel of profit and the resources for people's survival, and so on. Such sayings lack of understanding the deeper aspects of China's existence and cultural origins.

When we Chinese say individualism, we turn to immediately understand it as selfishness. This is actually wrong. Individualism is not selfishness, it is just a social view, and its opposite is called socialist social view. It was discussed first by the ancient Greek wise men 2600 years ago, called liberalists and republicans.

The so-called individualist view of society means that in order to build the best social structure, the rights and freedom of each individual must be guaranteed first, so that the best social structure can be built, which is called the individualist view of society; the so-called socialist view of society means that in order to build the best social structure, each individual must be willing to give up some of his or her rights and freedom, so that the social structure built can guarantee the peaceful existence of each individual. This is called the socialist view of society.

The basic cultural form of any commercial and industrial civilization must be *an individualistic view of society*, while the basic cultural form of any agricultural civilization must be a socialistic view of society. And the more purely agrarian civilization is, the more emphasis must be placed on collective cooperation and social coordination, and the more visible hands must be needed to control it. In other words, the socialism we practice today has very little to do with the introduction of Marxism into China, and we were easily gravitating towards it, because we have a natural affinity with it, because we were already some kinds of naturally primitive socialist society formed 3,000 to 5,000 years ago.

I am talking about the original meaning of the words *socialism* and *individualism* in their literal sense, and I am not denying any new interpretations or propositions of modern sociology. The point is that all cultural phenomena and civilizational structures are actually the successive products of natural processes, that is, the synthesis of natural and personal spontaneous factors, which is called the structure of existence. The difference lies in the fact that the natural factors change more slowly, while the spontaneous factors change more quickly. What I mean is that the personal spontaneous factors, which are generally called man-made factors, are in fact one of the natural factors, but the later the derivation, the more unstable the existence or survival body is, the faster the decay rate, which can be said that the survival situation is deteriorating. Therefore, from a macroscopic point of view, it is still not separated from the general concept of survival structure that I have repeatedly used earlier.

For the above reasons, the more primitive human civilization is, the greater the influence of natural factors on human survival and human society formation, the weaker the subjective factors of human beings themselves; conversely, the more recent human civilization is, the less the influence of natural factors on human survival and human society development, the more prominent the subjective variables of human beings themselves. As a result, the progress of human civilization has become a process of man-made disasters instead of natural disasters, and the process of increasing human productivity has become the same process of increasing human social unrest. This is why we feel today that the influence of natural factors on human social movements has been weakened and diluted to a negligible degree, and this is also the reason why it is difficult for us to understand the origin of ancient cultures and civilizations today.

We also need to know that today's Western civilization has become so powerful and universal that we are assimilated by it today, but Western civilization is actually the reproduction and promotion of ancient Greek civilization.

What does this phrase mean? Let me give you an example. Today's Western democracy is called a bicameral democracy, with the upper house called the Senate and the lower house called the House of Representatives. In fact, 2,600 years ago, ancient Greece was a bicameral democracy. The upper house was called the House of Peers, also called the Senate, and the lower house was called the Citizens' Assembly. The free market economic system that is practiced in the West today was so widespread in Ancient Greece 2600 years ago that 60% to 80% of the population of Ancient Greece gradually moved to the entire Mediterranean Rim due to their activity of commerce, which means that the clan structure was completely dispersed.

Even today's Western judicial system was largely formed in ancient Greek times. The ancient Greeks did not trust judges, and thought that judges were also human beings, so why should he decide the life and death of the accused like God. So the ancient Greeks had to find a group of ordinary people who did not know the law to form a jury. Note that the judge had no power to convict. Both the prosecutor and the lawyer faced the jury to argue, and the common folk on the jury, using not their knowledge of the law but their common sense of life, decided whether the defendant was guilty or not. If the jury determines that the defendant is guilty, only then can the judge exercise his or her sole sentencing power and determine that the defendant is sentenced to a number of years in prison or deported to exile, depending on the written or unwritten law of the day. We can see the Chinese translation of jury (a group of people accompanying the judging process) is a complete mistake, for they are the group of people with the power to pass judgment, while judge is actually the person accompanying the judging process. Even such a judicial system was largely established in ancient Greece 2600 years ago. That's why I say that today's Western civilization has nothing significant to offer, but is merely a reproduction of ancient Greek civilization. The ancient Greek civilization was not designed by anyone, but was a spontaneous process, a structure of human existence made possible by the geography and natural physical conditions of the landscape.

Once any structure is formed, its inherent regulations force it to operate in a given direction. This is another expressing the phrase *path dependence* that I use today.

Let me give you an example. There is a type of deer in biology called antlered deer, whose male antlers grow extremely wide, actually larger than the body length of the deer. The fact is that the deer's antlers growing too big is very unfavorable for their survival, more difficult for it to run through the dense forest to escape predators. But why would the antlers grow bigger and bigger? It is because when the species was first formed, the female antler only chose the male with larger antlers to mate, which means that sexual selection was involved in natural selection, forcing the antler to grow bigger and bigger until it became extinct.

Let us see another example, all the birds' tail, or tail feathers, in the world are very short in length. It serves only one purpose, to keep the balance of the body position when the bird is flying at high speed. But there is a bird called the peacock, which male one grows its tail extremely long. In fact that if the tail feathers are too long it won't be good for the bird, as it will seriously limit the bird's flight height and flight speed, not helpful to it to escape from natural enemies. But why do peacocks grow their tail feathers bigger and bigger? It is because when the peacock species was first formed, female peacocks only looked for the male with larger and most gorgeous tail feathers before they were willing to mate with them, in other words, sexual selection was involved in natural selection, thus forcing peacocks to grow their tails bigger and bigger until they were endangered.

Once a structure is formed, its inherent prescriptiveness forces it to run in a certain established direction. When Eastern and Western civilizations took place back then, they were not really that far apart. The so-called Eastern civilization was a purely agricultural civilization; the so-called Western civilization, the spark of which, the ancient Greek civilization, was actually a semi-agricultural and semi-commercial civilization, and the difference between the two was extremely small. However, there is an ancient Chinese idiom called "the slightest difference between a hair's breadth will produce a thousand miles huge difference later", which is like shooting two arrows at a point of origin with a small angle, but when the two arrows are shot to their far ends, the distance between them will be greatly increased. From such a small difference between the East and the West, the culture eventually extends into two completely different and polarized, so much so that the compatibility is extremely poor, and the forms are always opposite civilization divergent pattern.

What am I talking about? I'm talking about the first basic element of civilization occurrence, the structure of subsistence.

Next, we discuss the second major differentiating factor in the divergence of human civilizations or the divergent evolution of Eastern and Western civilizations, the way of thinking.

Origin of Writing and Social Constructs in Shang Dynasty China

We talked about the origins of human civilization, which is a product of the natural structure of subsistence.

We talked about a primitive agricultural civilization, whose very quality of existence was unindividual, group, and harmonious, and which finally evolved into a cultural and social configuration of collectivism and statism with the creation of groups and states.

Industrial and commercial civilization, with its individualistic social and conceptual configurations, is also a product of the natural structure of subsistence. This is why Marxism, which in modern times took place in the heart of Europe, in Germany and England, did not develop in the industrial and commercial countries of the West, but ran into the great agricultural countries of the East. Because we were already a socialist society in the literal sense of the word three thousand years ago.

It expresses the inertial strength inherent in the structure of human civilization, and it also makes present the reasons why the matching relationship between productive forces and relations of production, between economic base and superstructure, does not really correspond to each other in the actual history of human civilization.

We understand these things first, then we can understand the epiphenomenal principles and epiphenomenal causes of the origin and motivation of civilization. I say epiphenomenal causes because there are actually some deeper determinants, a topic we will expand on later, even on the last day of the course.

Now we will focus on the differences in the ways of thinking between Eastern and Western cultures. Before we turn to this topic, we will first talk about the state of the social and civilizational configuration of China in the ancient times. (It helps to deepen the understanding of some elements of the later lectures.)

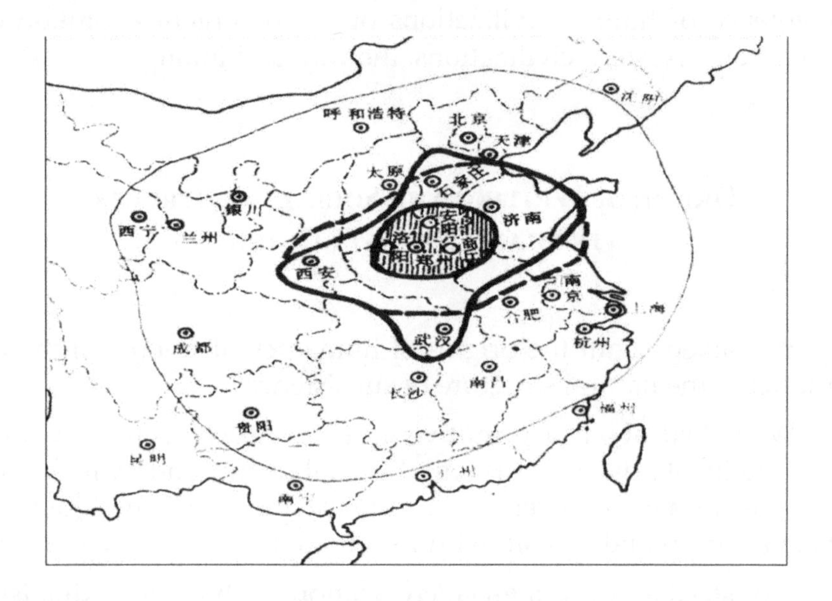

Look at this map. Eastern civilization, or Chinese civilization —in the early years, it was called Central Plains Civilization, which was limited to a small area centered on Henan, including Shanxi, the south of Hebei, the west of Shandong, the north of Anhui, etc., which is circled in black in the middle of this map. This small area, which is called the Central Plains Civilization, is also the origin of the original word China. The so-called China initially referred not to the great power system, but to the relationship between the civilization of the Central Plains and the surrounding uncivilized regions. In ancient China, the uncivilized people around the Central Plains were collectively called Yi Di, and roughly speaking, they could be called Northern Di, Western Rong, Southern Man and Eastern Yi, respectively, all of them means uncivilized regions, and the small area of civilization in the middle surrounded by them was called China.

The civilization of the Central Plains, with the continuous development of the farming range and its social culture, gradually expanded into the Chinese civilization, the so-called Chinese civilization, which is the solid line and the dotted line outlined with a thick pen on the map above.

What is the meaning of Hua Xia? Hua refers to the spread of civilization from the Central Plains to the Guanzhong region in Shaanxi. There is a mountain in Guanzhong region in Shaanxi called Mount Hua, and the words Hua for the mount and Hua for flower are generic, which means that the mountain has five peaks that open like a flower, so it was also called Mount Hua in ancient times and later called Mount Hua. Xia refers to the lower reaches of the Yellow River, that is, the civilization of the Central Plains expanded eastward to the lower reaches of the Yellow River. Xia (for summer) and Xia (lower place) are homophonic with similar connotations, in ancient are generic, approximately related to the warm climate of the coastal region. This extension of the Central Plains civilization to the east and west is called the Huaxia civilization. Further later, look at the big circle outlined by the thin line outside, which is the so-called Chinese civilization, which is close to the middle antient times. Here we can see the origin of the expression "the Yellow River is the mother river of Chinese civilization".

We will next talk about the social structure of the Shang Dynasty in a rough way.

In ancient China, there were many legends about the three emperors Yao, Shun and Yu. But in fact, the creation of oracle bone characters by the East Asians occurred only 3,300 years ago in the middle of the Shang Dynasty, and thus our previous history was all legendary, and it was the appearance of oracle bone characters that created the age of credible history. It is easy to give us the illusion, without knowing such things, that the Chinese system of great power was already in place. It is important to know that human civilization developed gradually from primitive clan societies, and the emergence of states was quite around Xia Dynasty. Regarding Yao, Shun and Yu, we can't actually say who they really were, although Confucius gives great credit to these legendary saint-kings.

During the Republican era, a famous historian named Gu Jiegang once said that Yu was nothing but a worm. What does this statement mean? Let's take a look at the form of the three ancient characters Yao, Shun and Yu. This character (甲骨文 金文 小篆 楷体) is the origin of the Chinese character "土" (Tu) in mold inscriptions, and the addition of a person below the two soils (甲骨文 小篆 楷体)characters is the initial form of the character "尧" (Yao), which is the origin of the traditional character "堯" (Yao); then look at the character "舜" (Shun), which has a hand and claw on the top, a through symbol on the bottom, and then two footprints on the bottom in a semi-abstract picture. What does it mean? Yao expresses a person buried in the earth, while "舜" (Shun) expresses a person buried under the earth and being pulled out of the pit by other people with their hands, with his two feet stomping continuously to break free from that state of live burial. Finally, in the character "禹" (Yu), a long worm (snake) is drawn and () then a symbol is placed where it pokes its head out of the earth, and this character is "禹" (Yu). As you know, in ancient China, humans were also called worms, and all animals were called worms, tigers were called big worms, snakes were called long worms, and humans were called human worms. So the whole process of drawing a man from being buried in the earth, to pulling his hands and feet out of the earth, and finally emerging from the earth is the origin of the three characters Yao, Shun, Yu.

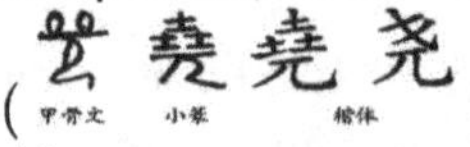

What do I want to say by this? It is that we do have very suspicious legends in ancient history, as we find from the written symbols that such legends are very different from the usual understanding of the three saint emperors and the five holy emperors and so on.

The oldest and clearest historical record that the scholarly community can pursue in the credible history is the Shang Dynasty, and the history before the Shang belongs to the non-credible legends. The Shang Dynasty was not a state structure, it was a confederation of tribal chiefdoms ruled in turn by a coalition of ten tribes. Therefore, we must understand that in ancient times there was no common ruler and no state system. As recorded in the Yao Dian (Records of Yao's regime), Yao "harmonized all the nations" and Shun "Ban Rui (bring peace) in all the groups", and even Xunzi in the Warring States period, in his Enriching the State, he said that "in ancient times there were numerous nations". Therefore, the

Shang Dynasty was a social form of clan and tribe confederation. To clarify this point is a basis for understanding the development of the East Asian social structure later.

The Kings of Shang Dynasty were all marked with the ten characters of Tian Gan (heavenly stems), which are Jia, Yi, Bing, Ding, Wu, Ji, Geng, Xin, Ren, Gui. In 1899, Wang Yirong first discovered the oracle bone scripts, and later Wang Guowei discovered that the oracle bone scripts were marked with ten characters of the Heavenly Stems, which corresponded to the titles used in the Records of the Grand Historian. This made the oracle bone scripts an important source for historical research.

Why did these ten tribes use Tian Gan (heavenly stems) as their symbols? It is because in the early civilization, these ten tribes were able to make unique tools to exchange or trade with each other, so they took pride in this, and then used it as their tribal totems or emblems, which finally formed their unique symbols of each tribe.

For example, the character "甲" (Jia) in the early oracle bone script is a cross. What does it mean? At the beginning of human civilization, when clans began to clash with each other occasionally, they fought with a wooden stick as weapon in one hand and held a cross made of two branches tied together as a shield in the other hand. (甲文 金文 小篆 楷体) It indicates that the Jia tribe was particularly good at making shields.

The emblem of the Yi tribe looks like this, (甲文 金文 小篆 楷体) and the character is "乙" (Yi). What does it actually depict? It is a drawing of a rope. You may think there was nothing to be proud of in making a rope. But you do not know, the difficult for ancient people to knead a rope was too high. Because at that time there was no chemical fiber, and plant fiber were very short, early plant fiber can only be extracted from the wild hemp, such as flax, etc. First of all, they had to soak the flax in water, to compost the fleshy part of it, and then peel off the short cellulose from it, and then gathered into a bundle, twisting the strands into a long rope, allowing no knot in the middle. The difficulty of twisting a rope was equivalent to the high technology of today's making a rocket, so the tribe that could make ropes used it as their totem, which is the origin of the Yi tribe and the word "Yi".

Look at the character "丙"(Bing), (甲文 金文 小篆 楷体) what is it

actually? It is a tool for drilling wood for fire. As I said earlier, the ability to use fire is unique to human beings and could be considered the clearest indicator of the initial development of human beings. The earliest identified ancestors of the ancient Chinese was not Nuwa or Fuxi, but the Suiren. What is "Sui Ren"? It is the legendary person who first used flint to make fire. You know that it was very difficult for ancient people to get fire. In a natural state, fire was only available when thunder and lightning started a fire in the forest. At that time, people brought the fire back to the cave, the community must arrange men to take care of the fire in turn, every moment someone designated had to constantly add wood to the fire to keep it burning; if it once extinguished, the whole tribe would immediately fall into the cold and starvation, cooking and heating all became a problem. Therefore, in the far antient times it was a difficult thing to manually get fire anywhere, anytime. Think about it, hitting the stone could only get the sparks, as there was no gasoline at that time, only by hitting the sparks to ignite the dry leaves or branches, I could not figure out how this could be achieved. In fact, mankind began to keep a standing fire since wood-drilling fire. First find a grooved hardwood as the chassis, and then find a soft wood stick, press it on the grooved hardwood and keep hands rotating it, so that the wood friction could start heat, smoke, then a fire, and then use the ignited off wood chips to ignite the prepared hay, so as to obtain a man-made fire. The Bing tribe may be proud of inventing such an important tool, so they use the character Bing as their totem symbol. Therefore, Bing always has the meaning of fire, such as later man adding a character of fire side to make it the transcribed character Bing, which means to be lit up in history.

The character "丁" (Ding) depicts a cross-section of a copper ingot, ( 甲文 金文 小篆 楷体) which was gradually transformed into the character "丁" later.

It is actually the tribe's earliest mining, smelting, and making of copper, which led to the formation of the Ding tribe emblem.

The character "戊" is a drawing of an ancient weapon. First, a Ge is drawn, and (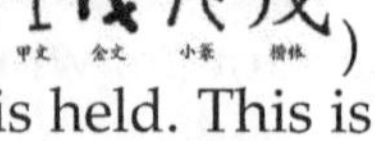 甲文 金文 小篆 楷体) an indicator symbol is drawn in the place where it is held. This is the origin of the character Ge, which signifies that this Ge tribe is particularly good at making weapons.

The character "已" (Yi) indicates that the tribe is particularly good at tying things with ropes. (甲文 金文 小篆 楷体) Tying things with ropes in knots is a complex and difficult action. For example, sailors to fix the sail position, dock mooring, etc., if the knot is not firmly tied, it will be a very dangerous thing, knotted rope in many ways, different occasions need different methods of winding knots. The Yi tribe is good at this skill, so they use it as their own tribe emblem.

Let's look at the character "庚" (Geng) actually draws a drilling tool. ( ) As you know, jade culture has existed in China thousands of years before the creation of writing. Jade is a very hard stone, so if we want to cut or polish something today, we have to find a harder material to polish it with. The hardness of jade was already close to the highest level of natural rock, so what did the ancients use to pierce or shape jade? At that time there was no diamond sand, people could only use ordinary sand much softer than jade to do continuous grinding, such as using a wooden stick to press the gravel constantly rotating, the sand quickly turned into powder, and then change the sand to continue the polish. According to the record, making a hole in the jade in far ancient times may take years or even decades, for this reason some slaves could be detained under the dry well, forcing them to constantly polish it every day, and it may even need several generations to figure out a jade. Later, when a tribe invented a special drilling tool, which is the origin of the word Geng.

Look at the character "辛" (Xing). ( ) It is actually a drawing of a wooden chisel, a woodworking tool used in the antient times for mankind to make wooden articles, including building houses out of wood. The tribe invented this tool Xing as a symbol of their skill.

The character "壬" (Ren) actually depicts a bone needle or a javelin. (甲文 金文 小篆 楷体) In ancient times, even if a human being only wears a skirt of animal skin, he had to have the tools to cut and sew. Sharpening a bone needle is very difficult, so this tribe used Ren as the emblem.

It is obvious that the character "癸" (Gui) is a pictographic depiction of an ancient human spinning brick the spindle used in the antient times to weave hemp thread and linen, and its spinning state is drawn. (甲文 金文 小篆 癸 楷体) And this tribe was good at waving linen, so Gui became their symbol.

These ten tribes intermarried with each other, thus forming five major tribes ruling in turn, or at first just taking turns to preside over the rituals of the entire confederation, and then gradually transformed into a power structure, which is the basic social structure of the Shang Dynasty.

Since Cheng Tang, the five tribes have been ruling together; since Pan Geng moved to Yin, the Shang dynasty gradually stabilized, but the kingdoms of the chiefdoms were mainly composed of the Geng Xin clan, the Jia Yi tribe, and the Bing Ding tribe as the core alliance body, forming a King's reign in turn among the Geng Xin - Ding and Jia Yi tribes, with Wu Ding reign as the prime period. Therefore, the oracle bone divination texts contained several places the name Wu Ding (wife's mother, Fu Hao), Di Xin (King Zhou of Yin), and Di Yi (so-called father of King Zhou). In addition, because of the "mother is respected by her son's supreme position" system of sacrificing the mother as her son being the King, it is possible that Fu Hao was not the wife of Wu Ding, but the mother of Wu Yi, or the general name given to woman who was revered as the King's mother; nor Di Yi was the father of King Zhou, but the previous King of Jia Yi tribe, King Zhou and Pen Gen were of the same tribe.

According to the record, the destruction of the Shang Dynasty was caused by the internal conflicts, and later was destroyed by Qi Zhou coalition joined by traitors of Shang Dynasty. Downfall of evil virtue was falsely labeled mostly by the victors. That is, the Geng Xin tribes split with the Bing, Ding two major tribes, after the Kang Ding, Wu B, Wen Ding, Di Yi two groups of Yi Ding reign in turn, Geng Xin tribe elected King Zhou into power, and then moved the center of Kingship to their own tribal station (Chaoge, that is, today's Qi County), Weizi, Bi Gan, Qizi of Yi and Ding tribes had rebellions separately, till King Wu started invading King Zhou, the eve of the battle of Muye, the Shang state of chiefdom alliance had long fallen apart.

The above quotation shows that Shang society was a tribal confederation social structure after the era of tribal alliances. (See Tang Han's research work on ancient history with the help of mold inscriptions)

It is possible that this state of rotating King reign continued until the early Zhou Dynasty, and likewise collapsed at the time of King You of Zhou, leading to the eastern migration of King Ping of Zhou and the unstoppable chaos of the Spring and Autumn Period.

There is a very absurd story in history that King Wen of Zhou once went on a trip and saw an old man named Jiang fishing with a straight hook in the Wei River. After a moment of talking with him, King Wen of Zhou invited him to be his state counsellor and military advisor. If you were the king, would you so casually find a crazy old man to be your military advisor?

The actual situation is not at all like that. According to the *Book of Verses*, the Zhou tribe probably first migrated gradually from the western Tianshui area to the vicinity of Bin County in northern Shaanxi before migrating and settling in the land of Qi Zhou. The original text reads, "Ancient Duke Danfu, who came from the west riding horse, led his tribe to the water side of Qixia, and his tribe had marriage with local Jiang tribe, so they build settlements and lived there." Antient Danfu was the grandfather of King Wen of Zhou, and he led the Zhou tribe to Qishan Zhouyuan on the side of Wei Shui (River Wei), and had a marriage with the local indigenous Jiang tribe, so that there was a place to build their houses.

The so-called two surnames of Zhou and Jiang, Jiang Shang and Ji of the Zhou dynasty, they were actually a two tribe-combined tribal relationship. It is likely that Jiang Ziya was the head of the Jiang tribe, and the two formed a joint power structure, and even formed some kind of relationship of ruling in-turn. This is why in the early years of the Western Zhou dynasty, we find that the Ji and Jiang surnames occupied the best areas of the Central Plains, while other tribes not related to the Ji and Jiang surnames, except for a few original service states, were mostly subdivided into barren areas on the periphery of the Central Plains.

And until the early years of Zhou Dynasty, we find that a strange system of Zhaomu was formed. The so-called Zhaomu refers to the names of King Wen of Zhou, King Wu of Zhou, King Cheng of Zhou, King Kang of Zhou, King Zhao of Zhou and King Mu of Zhou, the fifth and sixth generations of the two kings were Zhao and Mu. When we mention Zhaomu system today, the first thing that comes to mind is the funeral system of the ancient emperors. That is, the first king (including later emperors) buried in the middle, his son buried on the left, his grandson buried on the right, and so on, it is always the same, forming two lines of intergenerational burial of the cemetery form (until the Ming and Qing dynasties as well). How did this system come about? In the past, it was unclear, only when you understand the relationship behind the transition of power, you can understand that it is actually the historical remanence from the Shang and Zhou tribes ruling in turn, after the death of the king, he must be buried back to the original tribe's graves. It is easy to see that it is named Zhaomu system, probably expressing the early years of the form of power alternation relationship perverted between the Western Zhou's Ji and Jiang surnames tribes.

This conclusion has not yet been clearly proved by the historical research circle. And as a reasonable corollary, it implies that the gradual institutional transition of mankind from tribal alliances to state forms or feudal societies system was probably a process of continuous gradual change.

Hieroglyphs and East Asian Mold Inscriptions

We move on to another topic, the influence of thinking styles on the differentiation of civilizations.

To talk about ways of thinking, we must talk about paleography. Why? Because writing or written symbols has a major impact on form of human thought.

That is why in the early years of the Western Han Dynasty, as recorded in the ancient book *Huainanzi*, the original words were expressed in this way: "Cangjie made scripts, the sky rains grains, the ghosts cry at night." What does this passage mean? It says that since Cang Jie created writing, rain fell from the sky was grain, and ghosts cried in groups at night. Why does it use such an amazing tone to depict the creation of written symbols by humans? It is because the occurrence of written symbols played a somewhat foundational role in the subsequent way of thinking and thought of mankind.

Before the emergence of written symbols, human thought and consciousness were in a stream flowing state, or what we call the stream of consciousness in psychology; after the emergence of writing, the schematic system of external written symbols became the basic framework for the presentation and derivation of human thought, thus creating the structure of human explicit thought.

This is, of course, only one of the main factors that allow ways of thinking to be formed. In the following part of my speech, I am not saying that the formation of human ways of thinking is only due to the influence of written symbols, but written symbols are obviously an important influencing factor. By talking about this major influence, it will be easier for us to understand how the shaping and differentiation of ways of thinking is a spontaneous process.

Let's start with the ancient Chinese characters. As you know, the scripts we use is called hieroglyphics. Today, of the 221 countries and organizations in the world, the only one that uses pictographs is China. All other nations and countries use phonetic scripts. It is easy to have a major misunderstanding that phonetic script is the main source of writing. Make no mistake, remember that the original tribes of mankind either did not have writing, but all those who first invented writing symbols were all pictographs. Phonetic scripts was a fairly recent, secondary type of writing symbol. For example, ancient Egyptian hieroglyphics; for example, ancient Babylonian cuneiform, which is actually a variant of hieroglyphics; ancient Chinese writing is also hieroglyphics.

Since 1899, when Wang Yirong discovered the oracle bone inscriptions, the number of oracle bone fragments with oracle bone inscriptions unearthed by the archaeological community in Henan Yinxu and other places in China has reached 100,000. After studying them, it was found that there were about 4,500 characters in the ancient oracle bone scripts, and the Chinese characters we use today are over 10,000, which are the result of the gradual evolution from 1,500 oracle bone scripts in later years. Why were the other 3000 scripts obsolete? It is because originally, writing and language were two systems.

Linguists of the past, including Aristotle, said that language is the sign of thought, and words are the sign of language, and therefore words are the sign of signs. That is, it is widely believed that written symbols are a direct product of language, something that is probably mistaken. In fact, humans have been talking for about 100,000 years, but humans have writing for only the last 3,000 to 5,000 years, and writing initially had nothing to do with language. Language is transmitted from the mouth to the ear, writing is transmitted from the hand to the eye. The written symbols, or hieroglyphs, were initially nothing more than a picture in a living scene, so they were not fully connected to language at first. As writing developed, it had to be combined with language in order to be used effectively, so those symbols that could be ideographic in monosyllables, that is, with a single vocalization to express the mind, were able to be preserved. The symbols that were overly complex in the early days and had to be understood in a long series of words to make them clear were discarded. This is the reason why only 1500 of the 4500 scripts eventually evolved into the Chinese character writing system.

The ancient Chinese script is called oracle bone scripts. The so-called oracle refers to the turtle shells, and bone pieces refers to the shoulder blade of a cow, which is the earliest writing material for engraving scripts. Then followed by hundreds of years into the Bronze Age, the bronze casting or molding of the text, known as Jinwen (mold scripts), also called inscriptions. So we call the ancient Chinese pictographs oracle bone scripts as a whole, which occurred about 3300 years ago.

It is important to note that the so-called hieroglyphs are a picture of a living scene. There is a clear difference between Chinese hieroglyphs and ancient Egyptian hieroglyphs; Chinese hieroglyphs are semi-abstract, while ancient Egyptian hieroglyphs are drawn in a very figurative way.

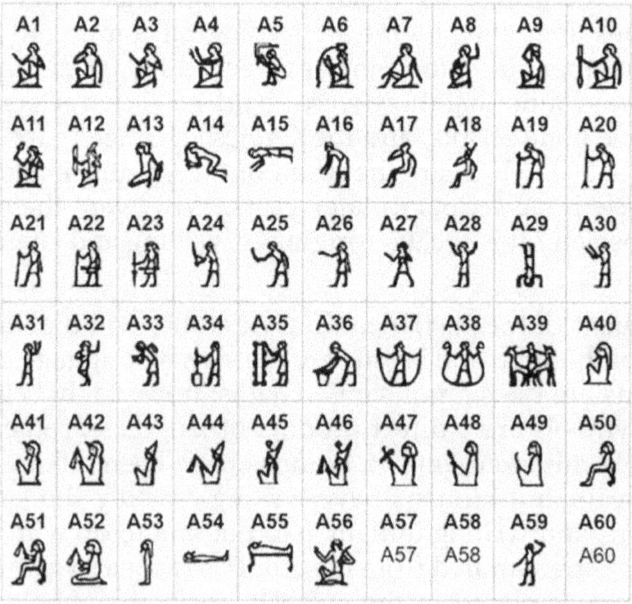

A1	A2	A3	A4	A5	A6	A7	A8	A9	A10
A11	A12	A13	A14	A15	A16	A17	A18	A19	A20
A21	A22	A23	A24	A25	A26	A27	A28	A29	A30
A31	A32	A33	A34	A35	A36	A37	A38	A39	A40
A41	A42	A43	A44	A45	A46	A47	A48	A49	A50
A51	A52	A53	A54	A55	A56	A57	A58	A59	A60
						A57	A58		A60

Table of ancient Egyptian hieroglyphic characters for 'Man'

Let me give you an example. For example, in ancient Egypt, if one wants to draw the character man, he draws a very realistic human being with a head, torso, arms, legs and feet (draw a picture of man on the board). However, in the oracle bone script, we see a human being ( ) as a symbol, which actually draws the sideway of a person walking. In the ancient Egyptian script, a bull is also drawn in a very figurative way (draw a bull on the board), which is the bull in the ancient Egyptian hieroglyphic script, where a bull is drawn in its entirety and in its complete configuration. However, the Chinese oracle bone script for bull only shows its horns, (甲骨文 金文 小篆 楷体 牛) which is the origin of the Chinese character " 牛". In ancient times, it was pronounced "moo", imitating the sound of a bull, which is an onomatopoeic character. When drawing a sheep, it draws a goat horns, and this is a sheep (甲骨文 金文 小篆 楷体 羊).

ANCIENT EGYPTIAN HIEROGLYPHIC "BULL" SYMBOLS

So why was the hieroglyphic writing in ancient Egypt very figurative? It is because ancient Egypt produced a grass called papyrus, and the ancient people peeled this grass to form a writing material similar to paper. Then they plucked reed sticks at the Nile River, split them and dipped them into the black ink of wood ash, so they could draw smoothly on the papyrus, so their pictographs were very realistic. China in the aera of East Asia where was no such grass, and paper was invented only after the Han Dynasty, so the ancient Chinese writing materials, could only be on hard turtle shell or cow bone, and then use a stone knife or bronze knife to carve on it, which is the reason why the ancient called pen as knife pen. Due to the limitation of writing materials, the ancient Chinese pictographs had to be abbreviated or semi-abstracted. This is the reason for the morphological difference between antient Chinese hieroglyphs and ancient Egyptian hieroglyphs.

We will discuss one more issue below.

The ancient Chinese scripts, each character has one meaning and each character has one syllable, which is called monosyllabic script, and also is completely different from the pinyin script, which is a multi-syllable script. The human larynx and tongue can only pronounce about 400 monosyllables differently, so by definition, there should only be 400 Chinese characters. In fact, the number of Chinese characters is so large that under this physiological vocalization limitation, a large number of homophones are bound to appear.

So how the homophones were created in ancient times? It has a basic principle that words pronounced with the same sound generally contain some degree of the same meaning.

Let me give you an example. For example, this is an oracle bone script (甲文 金文 小篆 楷体). What kind of character is it? It's the word for "but". Today the word "but" is already a function word and a preposition. But you must understand that ancient Chinese writing does not have function words and prepositions, because they were not needed. Because the ancient text does not have a grammatical and logical structure, it is a system of pictograms. Therefore, early writing, each word is a notion word, there is no function word, and each word has its own meaning, compound words do not hold.

For example, "池塘" (Chi-Tang), Chi means a square pond, and Tang means a round pond. Has anyone ever seen a pond that is both square and round? So the word Chi-Tang is not valid. Another example is "朋友" (Peng-You). Peng is a picture of two strings of ( ) shells (money), and You is a piture of two hands, which are half-held (甲骨文 金文 小篆 楷体). What is the meaning of Peng? People who earn money together and work together are called Peng; what is the meaning of You? People who share money together are called friends; each character has a meaning. As we know, humans are such a species that they can share the pain together, but not the gain, so the word Peng-You is not valid. Another example is “荣华富贵” (Rong Hua Fu Gui), there was one of the earliest encyclopedic dictionary in the pre-Qin era, called *Erya*, it says “grass is called Rong, the tree is called Hua”, that is, the grass grows very lush called Rong, the tree grows luxuriantly called Hua; ancient Chinese merchants are rich, but not noble; we can see that glorious, gorgeous, rich, noble, each word is a meaning. The proliferation of compound words came about after Buddhism was introduced to China in the middle of the Eastern Han Dynasty.

So looking back at the word “而” (Er), what does it mean? Look at my beard, there is a glimpse of beard at the top and a stroke of beard at the bottom, because there are two strokes of beard, so it is pronounced Er. What other word is pronounced Er? Why does the word ear sound like Er? Because you have an ear on your left and an ear on your right. There is another character pronounced Er, this character is “日” (Ri), in the area of Henan and Shaanxi where oracle bone inscription was discovered, “日” is not pronounced Ri, read Er, the sun called “日头” (er tou), why? Because in the morning there is a red sun rising from the east, and at dusk there is a red sun setting in the west. So any word pronounced Er must have the meaning of two pieces. Therefore, in ancient times, homophones, or characters with a similar basic configuration, were considered to be generic characters and often used interchangeably. Therefore, if you read ancient books, really ancient books, you will find that the ancients wrote a lot of miswritten characters, which are not called miswritten characters but called generic characters. So, you do not miswrite characters today, in fact, you do not have much culture.

Let’s see the three principles of making pictograph.

In the early days of mankind, the tribes either did not have writing or those who had writing but only pictographs. The first element in the construction of pictographs is the principle of ideogram, which is a picture of a living scene. In I-Ching, there is an eight-word expression for the creation of symbols in the early years of mankind: “taking things near body, taking things from afar”. This is the main source of pictograms, which find symbols as near as in the body and as far as symbols in objects. (There are various interpretations of ancient scripts, all of which are speculative and inconclusive, so this lesson is for reference only.)

Let me give you an example, for example, we have seen this character in the oracle bones, what is it? (甲文 金文 小篆 楷体 凡)

It's the character for "凡" (Fan). What does it depict? It's a bit indecent, the anus that you see when an ancient man bent down without pants. Ordinary persons have dirty anus, so this character is Fan, means the ordinary, which is pronounced very close to the word "粪" (Fen) for feces. Then if add a bar in the middle, notice this symbol, which we see a lot on the rim of ancient bronzes, (甲骨文 金文 小篆 楷体) it is the character "用" (Yong), the word for use. Why is its use? The ancients did not have toilet paper, but they could not run around with shit in the anus, so they picked up a wooden stick from the ground and wipe clean the anus, and the stick is very useful, so it is the character "用". This is called "taking things near body".

I will draw another symbol, () what is this character? It's a "齐" (Qi). What does it say? All the ears of the wheat in summer looked neat in the field. This is the oracle bone script [the upper part of the traditional Chinese character " 齊 " comes from this configuration (甲骨文 金文 小篆 繁体 简体)]. This is called "taking things from afar".

Let's look at one more character (), what is it? "帝" (Di), the word emperor used in the Yellow Emperor and the Yan Emperor, etc. In order to understand this character, you must first understand this painting. It has an inverted triangle drawn at the top, a through-symbol drawn to the bottom, and another through-symbol drawn horizontally. What does it mean? First of all, you should know that whenever you see an inverted triangle in ancient Chinese characters, it refers to the female. The female sex organ grows inside the abdomen, unlike the male sex organ that hangs out between the legs. Then the most important sign of female sexual organs is the inverted triangle distribution of pubic mound and pubic hair, so draw an inverted triangle to represent women, and draw a positive triangle to represent men.

These two symbols are used all over the world, not only by the Chinese. For example, the ancient Jewish and modern Israeli emblems are called "Star of David". This is still the design on the flag of the State of Israel today (). It is a positive triangle superimposed on an inverted triangle. See if this is the Jewish six-pointed star? It is the symbol for the intercourse between man and woman, the intercourse symbol between yin and yang, drawn by antient man in the age of fertility worship.

So let's go back to the word "帝" (Di), what does it mean? The following through-symbol represents the children and grandchildren, and the horizontal through-symbol represents the relative cousins of the aunts and uncles, its original meaning refers to the most ancient woman who could be traced back in the clan group, and she was called emperor. We must know that in ancient times, the early clan society was matrilineal, and a clan society was a blood group. Its internal marriages were prohibited, no sexual relations allowed, otherwise incest could lead to serious deformation diseases among the kids of the community or even lead to tribe demise. Therefore, in the early years of mankind, its group marriage system is mostly practiced as the combination of two clans, of course, there were also interactions between multiple clans from time to time; otherwise, in long period of time, incest still cannot be avoided. That is, men of this clan went to that clan, and men of that clan came to this clan, all at night, and returned their homes at dawn. All the children stayed in the female clan for birth and raise up. Because of the inter-clan marriages, people never knew who the father of a child was, a child's father could be any man from another clan. Therefore, people could only find their own female ancestors, so they called the most ancient female ancestor who could be traced in each clan at that time "帝".

By the end of the Shang Dynasty and the beginning of the Zhou Dynasty, society was generally patriarchal and people of that time no longer knew the original meaning of the word, so the male ancestors or kings were revered as emperor, such as the Yellow Emperor, Yan Emperor, the First Emperor of Qin, etc. This is obviously the wrong use of the ancient script "帝".

So which word was used to address male ancestors in ancient times? It was the character "且" (Qiě), what is this picture? () It directly draws a male reproductive organ. This character was not pronounced Qiě back then, nor was it a function word, it was pronounced Zǔ. How did it become "祖" for ancestor? It is because human beings gradually transitioned from the era of fertility worship to the era of sacrificial civilization, so when faced with the scene of sacrificing to heaven and earth and ancestors, a T-shaped ()

sacrificial platform was first drawn next to the sacrificial platform, and then sacrifices were placed on the platform, (甲文 金文 小篆 楷体) and the so-called sacrifices were cow, pig, sheep and other animals slaughtered in sacrifice to heaven and earth and ancestors, and these sacrifices were dripping blood(甲文中形体各异的"示"字).

See, is this character "祖" (Zu) the source for the word ancestors today? (甲文 金文 小篆 楷体) It expresses the step-by-step process and evolution of pictographs with the change of human social and cultural structure, and the corresponding change of the character shape, which we call the principle of ideogram, the first principle of establishing ancient pictographs.

The second is called Principle of common experience.

Please hear that my purpose of talking about the oracle bone scripts or mold inscriptions is not to give you a lesson in literacy, but to discuss a major issue, even a philosophically fundamental issue, the issue of way of thinking. Of course, it is true that we are no longer literate today to a large extent, so there is also a need of giving a remedial literacy lesson.

The second way that humans construct pictographs is called the "principle of common experience". In other words, at least the upper level of the community must have a common experience of the symbol, and generally know the meaning of the symbol, in order for it to be accepted.

Let me give you an example, for example, there is a character called "闯" (Chuang). (小篆 楷体)Why not draw a cow or a sheep inside the word gate? You know that the ancient people were exactly as smart as we are today. As I said earlier, it is impossible for human intelligence to change significantly in just 40,000 years, not to mention the fact that it took only 3,000 to 5,000 years to create the characters. So at that time, people's intelligence was exactly equal to today's, except that their concern was the basic issues of survival - grassroots issues such as clothing, food, housing and transportation, in which the amount of information was extremely small. They handled such a low amount of information with great wisdom, so think how much the ancients could have pondered these issues. This is where the value of ancient culture lies.

The ancients kept animals observed extremely fine, they found that all animals out of the pen door was very slow, because the animals were crowded before they ran out of the pen, if they run too fast, ramming each other, it was easy to injure each other. Any animal, including wild animals, once injured will certainly die. Therefore, all animals go out of the pen door would slow down, horses were the only exception. The ancients observed extremely detailed and found that the horse ran out of the stable jumping, so painting a horse inside a gate to represent the character "闯" (Chuang) break out.

I'll draw another picture (甲文 金文 小篆 楷体 白) , and the character is "白" (Bai) meaning white. What is this drawing? It has drawn a nail cap, which shows the semilunar membrane underneath the skin. Why did he draw a fingernail to represent the word white? It is because the ancient people were doing rough work, hands were always black, the only thing that could retain the white color of the hands was the nail, so they draw a nail to represent the meaning white. All these things are symbols created by the ancients in their common life scenes, so the meaning of those symbols will be obvious to everyone.

I will draw another symbol (甲骨文 金文 小篆 楷体 止), which I drew earlier. What is this character? It is a semi-abstract picture of the footprints left by the ancient people who did not wear shoes and socks and simply stepped barefoot on the soil. However, we should pay attention to the meaning of this character, which in ancient times did not mean stop, but "止" (Zhi) of the toe. If you draw two footprints (甲骨文 金文 小篆 楷体 步) in front and back, what is this character? Step, the "步" (Bu) of walking. It is a character that developed from the oracle bone script, then curved into a figure in the small and big seal script, then changed to the regular script, and then changed from a curved pen to a straight one.

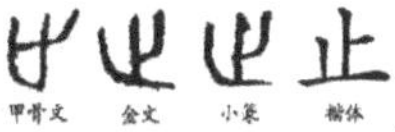

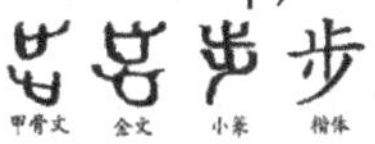

What can we learn from this character? We can find that the so-called civilizational progress is the process of trying more and more to solve things but only making things worse and worse.

The ancients did not have wagons and horses, barefoot walking in their dozen square kilometers of clan territory and it was enough to solve all their basic survival needs. What do you want today when you drive a car or fly a long way? You're still just trying to fill your stomach. Have you solved the issue of walking? Not really, you just solved more and more things, but make things worse as you solve them. Take the car for example, you want to build a car, you must first dig a mine, right? After mining, you have to smelting metal ore to get steel, then you have to manufacture thousands of parts to assemble a car. And you need rubber to make the tires, and a lot more; then you still cannot run it! You have to pave the road, set up traffic lights ...... and then the police has to be there constantly directing the traffic, even so many drivers may hit their cars on the poles cripple themselves. Was there any one ancient people walking to let himself hit in the trees, then nose collapsed?

We should understand that the progress of human civilization has not solved any problems, it has only solved it into more and more problems; and the more it solves, the worse it gets. Let's take the automobile as an example. According to the United Nations, the world has an average of 3 million vehicle casualties a year, killing about 250,000 to 300,000 people a year just because of automobile traffic accidents, which is equivalent to fighting a large-scale local war every year. That's not all of the story, as we haven't even counted the large amount of petroleum resource waste, ocean pollution, air pollution and all other big troubles it causes.

From these ancient scripts, we can see that the ancient people had a deep understanding of their conservatism, that is, they did not recognize the civilizational development of human society, but were skeptical of it, as they had their profound understanding of it. That is why we say that primitive thought contained in the ancient scripts and antient cultures have profound meanings.

The third principle of character creation is called humanistic principle, which means that the human being is the center, or the human conceptual form and dependency needs are the basis for drawing all the image symbols.

For example, in your vision, mountains appear as rolling peaks, so you draw this picture, ( ) which is the origin of the character "山" (Shan). Water, a semi-abstract picture of a river is "水"(Shui) ( ). Look at this picture, ( ) what is this character? "女" (Nü) woman. What does it depict? In ancient times, there were no tables or chairs, not even sitting on the floor, so people took a kneeling position, sitting on their heels. A woman sitting on her heels, put both hands in front of her belly, showing a quiet sitting posture. This image of a woman sitting in a static position is the origin of the character "女" (Nü) woman. So, as you can see, all the characters are created with people in mind, expressing the symbolic perception of people. These are the three basic principles of pictographs.

I repeat, I speak about ancient scripts, quoting mainly from the research of Tang Han, supplemented by the views of other oracle bone scholars, to give the content of this part of the lecture. If any of you are more interested, you can read more of the related books.

How the Meaning of Oracle Scripts were Formed

We discuss a little bit below how the meaning of pictographs was formed.

Let's look at the character "人" (Ren), ( ) which is a drawing of the side of a person walking. However, in the early days of the oracle bone scripts, we also see this character, which ( ) we pronounce today as "大" (Da) big, which is not correct. In the early oracle bone scripts, this character actually means a drawing of the frontal position of a person standing.

How do we know? There are a large number of characters that are built on this symbol. For example, if we draw a horizon line underneath, it is the (甲骨文 金文 小篆 楷体) character for standing is "立" (Li). For example, if we draw a person, and then draw a walking stick in his hand, and( )later add a mouth to represent the sound of the walking stick hitting the ground, this character is "奇" (Qi). What does it mean? It means a person with a crippled leg, so the original meaning of the character "畸" (Ji) is deformity, and because the crippled person looks strange, the character "奇" is slowly derived later from the character "畸" for deformity.

Look at another character, still drawing a person standing in front, and draw(甲骨文 金文 小篆 楷体)two hands underneath (by the way, in traditional Chinese characters, whenever you see "又" (You) a hand is drawn, while in simplified Chinese characters it does not count, because the symbol "又" is abused in simplified Chinese characters), with( ) a stream of water drawn between the two hands? What is the meaning of the word "泰" (Tai)? First, the meaning of tall, second, the meaning of comfortable. So we have the words like comfortable, at ease, released, etc.

Why does it have this double meaning? You have to see the painting first. What exactly is the painting? A man is peeing with two hands holding his little one. Why does the painting of a man peeing have the meaning of tallness? Because the difference in height between men and women is very small, and men look particularly tall when they are peeing. The ancients did not wear pants, only around a skirt of animal skin, while women could not stand to pee, or she would pee scatted on her legs and feet, very indecent. Therefore, women since ancient times, were squatting to pee, while men were standing to pee. At the moment of peeing, the man looked especially tall, so the character "泰" had the meaning of tall, and so the civilized people of the Central Plains at that time called the highest mountain around the Central Plains as Mount Tai. Then why does this character "泰" have the meaning of comfortable? Because it's hard for you to hold your urine, it is called internal urgency. You must hurry to find a place to pee off before you will feel again at peace. So the meaning of released, comfortable, and at ease emerged.

What am I talking about? I am talking about the origin of the meaning of any pictograph, especially the semi-figurative and semi- abstract oracle bone script symbols, which were not derived from logical deduction, but were given in figurative analogy.

Please note the difference between logical deduction and figurative analogy. Let me draw another character, (甲骨文 金文 小篆 楷体) the horns of a ram, this is the character "羊" (Yang), a sheep. If I draw the character "大" (Da) big, underneath, what is this character? "美" (Mei), the character for beautiful. What is the meaning of this character? In the past, many scholars of oracle bone scripts interpreted it as "the sheep is beautiful because it is big", which is a very problematic interpretation. Why do you say that a sheep is beautiful when it is big? The lamb is beautiful! The interpretation is wrong. The actual meaning of the character is that a man who is as strong or fit as a ram is called beautiful. Please note that when the ancients said beautiful, they used it to describe a man. If we point at a man today and say he is beautiful, he must have goose bumps all over. Today the meaning of beautiful has long been used for women. So was it the ancients' mistake, or is it today people's mistake?

Let's look at the history of biology. All animals are male beauty, you will not see female beauty in the animal kingdom. For example, all male pheasants have fancy big tails and handsome physical appearance, while all the females are gray. Then look at the lion, the male lion mane is broad, a majestic attitude, while the female lion is all a shrinking face. So why the animals are all male beauty? It is because the female social status is very high, it does not need to be beautiful. As you know, all animals only in a situation of infighting, that is, in the rut for female reproductive resources. What is a scene at this time? All the female animals crouched next to each other, watching the male animals in front of them to show beauty, show strong or competitive fighting.

Why do females have such a high social status that they do not use beauty? It is because female reproductive resources are very scarce. What does this statement mean? You know that all animals' rut is only once or twice a year, even if we humans may have it every day, a man's sperm content in an ejaculation is about 200 - 400 million, while a woman produces only 13 - 14 eggs a year, indicating that female reproductive resources are very scarce. Therefore, in the entire animal kingdom, the social status of females is very high. Nowadays, women dressing themselves up to seduce men, only mark that their social status has fallen greatly.

It is important to know that in all animals and even in the early days of human civilization, their marital relationships were group marriages. The pair marriage system is the result of the civilization of mankind, the gradual masculinization of society, and the ensuing privatization, at which time, if the male wants his private property to be inherited, he must know which child is his offspring. It is due to this factor that dyadic marriages took place, and it was the male dominated society that transformed women into reproductive subordinates of men.

It is evident what the civilization process is. It has perverted we humanity! Such a process is called civilizational progress. The meaning of the ancient script contains many thoughts of early human civilization and the deep understanding of social and even natural problems that humans originally had. Moreover, we find that there is a huge difference in the evolution of the characters between the ancient script and the regular block characters.

Let me give you three words as examples. First, look at the character "盗" (Dao), which today means robbery, violently taking other (甲骨文 金文 小篆) people's belongings. But in the oracle bone script, what does it depict? It depicts a person stealing meat from someone's pot, with his saliva dripping from the corners of his mouth, which is called "贼" (Zei) theft, which is typical of what we call a thief today. Look at how the character for "贼" is written in mold and small seal script. (金文 小篆 楷体) It starts with a shell, which we all know that the East Asians used shells as currency in the pre-Qin era, called shell money. Then a person is drawn on the left or in the middle, and an ancient weapon is drawn on the right side - a Ge (dagger-axe), and an indication symbol is drawn at the place where the hand holds. This character is the origin of our character "贼" (thief) today. Please look at this picture, what is it? A person holding a weapon in his hand and forcibly robbing other people's property is called a "贼", that is exactly the meaning of the character "盗" (robbery) today. Only the antient script or character "寇" (Kou) remains the (甲骨文 小篆 楷体)same in form and meaning, with a house drawn on top, a man with his head covered below, and a hand holding a weapon next to it. This is the character "寇" (Kou), meaning to rob in doors.

What can we tell from these three characters? The ancient scripts have long undergone changes and even flip-flops in the meaning of characters in the course of historical evolution.

I say this to show that when you look through classical literature, you are bound to have serious misinterpretations when you use today's Chinese characters to understand them, and this is the reason why we often see many scholars today speaking about ancient cultures and ancient classics with a large number of errors. Only with a certain understanding of paleography can we decipher ancient literature. And Chinese writing has been passed down from one lineage to later generations, and this writing system has never been interrupted; therefore, only the ancient Chinese culture can systematically retain the thoughts of primitive primary civilization intact.

All ancient scripts are so figurative that to understand them you must have the ability to go back to the original life state of the scene, which of course is quite difficult. For example, look at this character "安" (An) safe and peace, (甲文 金文 小篆 楷体) it starts with a house and then a woman sitting in a beneath it. What does this character mean? It doesn't mean what it means today. If you have visited to the Yangshao site, Half Slope site, you got to know it refers to the primitive human clan society in the era of group marriage, most of the other people in the clan lived together to sleep in a bunk, they only provided young women in peak of fertility a separate house, to let them live in there at night, for what? To receive men from other clans. This unique scene of group marriage was the reason for the formation of the character "安" (An), the word now means safe.

I'll draw another character "家" (Jia), (甲骨文 金文 小篆 楷体) or a house with a pig inside. Please note that this pig must be a male pig, so it has to draw the reproductive organs of the male pig. That's why in the ancient books, when you see the character "家", there is a dot on the left side of the three strokes, which is the male pig's genitals. What does it mean by "家"? You know, the ancient people raised pigs, but they did not raise boars. Because raising pigs required a lot of time, and also required a considerable amount of grass, mixed partially with grain. Therefore, the ancients only raised sows, because sows of fertile could expand the breeding stock. But only sows couldn't give birth to piglets? The ancients built low-walled pens for sows that had been bred to be mature and did not have the wild capability to jump and run. Every night, the male wild boar would jump into the sow pen to breed with the sow, and the boar ran away at dawn. This situation of boar sneaking into the sow pen was depicted as the character "家", which is now the meaning of home for human beings, it is a bit of interesting like boar into the nest of sow.

Let me give you another example. (金文 小篆 楷体) It draws a man with a mouth next to it, what is the character "信" (Xin)? Do you know what is the meaning of "信"? It is not only the meaning of trust and honesty, it originally meant that the ancient asked another one to send a message to his friends or relatives in distant places, and the person who sent the message, conveyed the message in its original form, not adding or missing anything, this is the character called "信" (true to the original).

Let's look at the character "恒" (Heng), which means constantly, and eternal. (甲文 金文 小篆 楷体)This character is the origin of the character "亘", which was later transferred to the character "恆", which means constant. It refers to the continuous existence of the moon from the evening until dawn next day. This is the origin of the word "恒" or "亘".

How was the character "夜" (Ye) night, depicted? The antient first draws a man facing front, then add a crescent at his side, the moonlight casts his figure to the other side, so a sketch is added to the opposite side, and this is the origin of the character "夜" night (金文 小篆 隶书 楷体). So, we can see it is all figurative descriptions. And this is the character "瓜" (Gua) for melon, when I was in elementary school, I could not understand why this character means melon, because melons are round things, how could melon be drawn in such an ugly shape? However, if we draw it in mold inscription, you will immediately know why it is a melon. In mold inscription, (金文 小篆 楷体)a melon stand is drawn first, and then a melon is hung below it. Isn't a character so vividly depicting a picture of melon "瓜"?

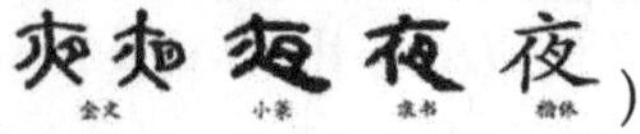

Since Chinese characters are figurative symbols, how do they express abstract meanings?

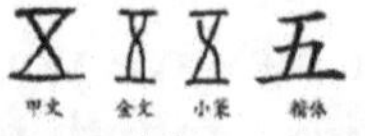

For example, the number characters "一, 二, 三, 四" (Yi, Er, San, Si) one, two, three, four, man can extend his fingers horizontally to express that, the ancient four was also drawn with four bars at first. (甲文 金文 小篆 楷体)Only later did it become straight out face of a fist gesture, which is the source of four. What about five? Because there are five fingers on the palm of the hand, so five was drawn in this shape in the early days, (甲文 金文 小篆 楷体)and it was only later the character "五" (Wu) was created by zigzagging and gradual changes. For number six, the character "六" (Liu), the index, middle and ring fingers are retracted into the palm of the hand, and the thumb and little finger are placed upside down, (甲文 金文 小篆 楷体)which is the origin of the character "六". For numbers seven and eight, the characters show separately up for (甲文 金文 小篆 楷体)"七" (Qi) and down for(甲文 金文 小篆 楷体)"八" (Ba), that is, with the thumb and index finger to open up and turn the gesture up and down, so there the saying goes "seven up and eight down".

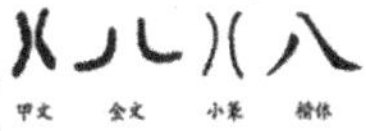

In ancient times, a hand was drawn with only the index finger bent out, (甲文 金文 小篆 楷体)which is the origin of the character "九" (Jiu). (甲文 金文 小篆 楷体)How about character "十" (Shi)? The whole arm is stretched out to represent "十", so in the oracle bone scripts, a point is placed in the middle of the vertical bar, and this is the character "十" for ten.

How to express the abstract meaning of hundred, thousand, and ten thousand? It is not possible to draw a hundred or a thousand things, right? This question is not difficult for the ancients. Look at the character "百" (Bai) drawn by the ancients, the character is hundred. (甲文 金文 小篆 楷体)Add one cross to it and it is one hundred, add two crosses and it is two hundred, add three crosses and it is three hundred. We have seen such symbols in the oracle bone scripts indicating three hundred. Then what is the meaning of the two circles or the curved line inside the circle of the character "百"? The inner circle or the inner line represents the lips, and the outer circle represents the beard, using the number of men's beards to represent "百", that is, hundred.

Look at the character"千" (Qian) (甲文 金文 小篆 楷体) thousand, this is a number used to describe a man with a lot of shin hair on his lower legs.

Lastly, the character "萬" (Wan) for number ten thousand, which is a very concrete drawing of a scorpion, (甲文 金文 小篆 楷体) with the large pincers on its head and the poisonous needles on its tail clearly drawn, and an indicator symbol in oracle bone script, where the poisonous needles can sting. This is the character "萬"

in traditional Chinese. Why is a scorpion drawn to represent "萬", ten thousand? It is because scorpion stings is very painful, and few of us today have ever been stung by a scorpion, so you don't know that if accidentally you are stung by a scorpion, it will hurt so much that you want to roll around on the ground. The ancient way of building a house was to dig a nest downwards, and in the process of digging a house sometimes uncover a stone piece, you would occasionally see a nest of scorpions, that is, a female scorpion surrounded by hundreds of thousands of small scorpions. A female scorpion lays 400 to 1,000 eggs or more at a time, and if it hatches all these eggs, you see hundreds or thousands of scorpions wriggling around. Since the scorpion stings were so painful, it gave the ancients a strong visual impact, so the ancients drew one scorpion to represent ten thousand, that is the character "萬".

What can we learn from this? In a nutshell, the so-called progress of civilization is the process of replacing natural disasters with man-made ones.

Let me give you an example. The ancients lived in houses that were initially ground nests, and earthquakes at that time did not form a disaster at all. Therefore, we hardly see descriptions of earthquakes in the records of ancient times, but instead we constantly see descriptions of solar and lunar eclipses, because the ancients considered solar and lunar eclipses to be an ominous celestial event. Why is it that earthquakes, something we consider a serious natural disaster today, did not pose a threat to the ancients? It was because the house was dug downwards into the ground to form a nest, on top of a thatched hut. Even if the earthquake was shaking, it only could only shake that straw shack down, at most causing a little superficial injury, never seriously to the bones. Until after the middle antient times, the ancient books began to gradually see records of the earthquakes. Why? Because humans began to build houses upwards, and even build additional floors to a house, so the house's center of gravity lifted higher, when the earth shakes a little, the house immediately collapsed. We can see that the earthquake disasters are *man-made disasters rather than natural disasters*.

The human civilization progress is such a process of accumulating and superimposing all kinds of disasters, which has always been the case since ancient times, but now it has become more intense.

The foregoing is a cursory explanation of ancient Chinese phonetics and pictographs, and we can see it as a refresher class in literacy. Today, we are quite unfamiliar with the origins of ancient Chinese characters and the formation of their original meanings, and people have long confused pictographs for purely abstract symbols. However, the main purpose of this lesson is not so, but to illustrate the influence of pictographs and different writing symbols on ways of thinking. Therefore, what I will say later is the part that you should pay special attention to.

DIFFERENCES AND CAUSES OF EASTERN AND WESTERN MINDSETS

We move on to the second thematic part of the divergence of primitive human civilizations - the differences and causes of the Eastern and Western ways of thinking.

As I mentioned earlier, the reason why the book Huainanzi in the early Han Dynasty used such amazing words as "the sky rains grains and ghosts cry at night" to describe the creation of written symbols by human beings is that although the ancients could not argue in detail about its relationship with the human way of thinking, they could deeply feel the great impact of the occurrence of written symbols on human civilization. Not only did it give us an additional tool to record and accumulate and pass on human culture and ideas, but more importantly, it had a significant impact on the way of thinking. We will now look at the inner logic of the written symbol and its interactive response to the logic of human thinking.

I have divided it into three groups for the discussion.

First, the word form is logically deduced.

In fact, I have already covered this meaning when I talked about oracle bone scripts earlier. Let me give you another example. Look, I draw a picture: first a mouth, add a straight-out symbol on it, and a flesh moon next to it, (肉)What is this character? "胡" (Hu). ()What is the meaning of the character "胡" (Hu)? The ancients described the uncivilized people outside of the

Chinese civilization and called them the Hu people. If you were to explain the difference between uncivilized people and civilized people today, you could talk a lot of nonsense and might still be unable to explain the difference between them. And it was enough for the ancients to draw just this figure and symbol to show the difference, then what did he draw? He drew the visual characteristics of the uncivilized people: those who eat bloody raw meat and have a fishy-mutton smell coming out of their mouths are called Hu people.

Therefore, the character "胡" (Hu) is all related to smell. For example, after the antient script was transformed to the regular script, people added a rice character next to "胡", which is the character for food burnt smell "糊", and how you can detect when something is burnt, the first thing is to smell it. Another example is to add a three-dotted water next to it - "湖", called lake water. What is the meaning of the so-called "湖" lake? Water flowing to the lowlands, accumulated into a flat pool, water no longer flowing; not flowing water will be stale, you walk around such lake will smell the water stale. You can see, the transitive characters of "hu" are all related to smell. All other meanings derived from this character are all analogically related to figurative thinking.

The character "胡" (Hu) is very important in China, for example, when we talk about carrot today, we mean that the radish came from the Hu people; when we talk about Huqin today, we mean the zither that came from the Hu people; when we talk about Erhu today, we mean the two-stringed zither that came from the Hu people. We also often scold others as "胡说" (nonsense). What does it mean by "胡说"? Because the Hu people speak like birds and civilized people don't understand them. The meaning of so many characters made words is a figurative extension of this one character "胡", which has nothing to do with pure logic. Therefore, we call it figurative symbols or figurative thinking, and its counterparts are abstract symbols and abstract thinking. Remember, figurative symbols lead to figurative thinking training in the way of thinking, which is called glyphic logical deduction.

Second, word order logic deduction.

I'm still going to give you an example. We said earlier that this is ( ) a person, so if we draw two people in a row, ( ) his character is "從" (Cong). What does "從" mean? A person follows another person is called following. If we draw two people in opposite directions, this character suddenly becomes "比" (Bi). () Why does drawing two people in opposite directions mean a race? The ancient people went out to work in the morning and walked lazily, but at the end of the day, they returned from work, each one walked faster than the other, so the meaning of race was hidden in it, which is the origin of the character "比".

I drew a similar character with two people back-to-back, () this character actually points to one direction, "北" (Bei) the north. Why does this character indicate north? It is because we are in the northern hemisphere in East Asia, the sun always runs in the south, at noon, when you face the sun, a person's shadow must spill behind you, forming a back-to-back pattern with you, and it must point to the north, so the meaning of this character suddenly transforms to direction, north. Notice that this character also has another meaning, "败北" (failure), called defeat. Why does it have the meaning of defeat? It is because if you win the battle, you have only one direction, charge forward; if you lose the battle, you would turn back and run away, you got two faces, so it has the meaning of defeat. The ancients recorded anything by drawing a comic strip, so the text is concise. Thus, we once saw in ancient literature describing a situation of a big war, actually with only four characters, "King's army went war, defeated." (The ancient text has no punctuation.) It means the king led us into battle and defeated.

If I draw a person forward and then draw a person backward. What is this character? ()The character "化" (Hua), change. Today, if a philosopher were to explain what change means, he might need to write a thick book on it, but the ancients just drew this character and that was enough. What does it mean? A person from standing to lying down, from living to dead, is the character "化", meaning change.

The four characters listed above form a sequence of characters, all of which are graphical symbols constructed from a human character, yet there is no logical connection between them. They each express completely different and independent word meanings, and there are only figurative analogies of derived meanings between them in different scenarios. This long-term training of acquiring word meanings in visual figurative images eventually leads to a special solidified pattern of figurative thinking. It is important to understand that figurative symbols contain a large amount of information. Let me give you an example. The 1 megabyte of storage in our computer today can hold 1 million bytes, which means it can hold 1 million Latin letters, equivalent to about 65,000 Chinese characters. But it actually can not store a picture or a photo, what does this mean? It means that there is a much larger amount of information in pictures and characters. Because of the intuitive and rich information contained in them, we can build analogical and metaphorical concept extensions in figurative symbols, and the way of thinking becomes very simple and effective, without the need for complex deduction in the logical system, and this is where the impact of figurative symbols on the way of thinking is strong.

I'll draw another set of characters in sequence. First draw a sun and a horizon line under it. What is the meaning of the character ( ) "旦" (Dan)? It is the earliest time of the day, when summer the sun rises above the horizon at four or five o'clock in the morning. Let me draw another character, ( )first a tree, please note that this character is the origin of the character "木" (Mu) wood. Let's draw a sun in the middle of it and a crescent next to it. What time does it mean? The sun is already halfway up in the morning around six o'clock, and the crescent in the west has not yet set. This is the character "朝" (Zhao), morning, the second section of morning.

If I draw a sun and a straight-out symbol underneath, this character is "早" (Zao) morning. ( ) It is equivalent to our present 8 o'clock in the morning, when the sun has already risen a pole high, which is also equivalent to what we call "上午" (Shangwu) before noon. If I draw only one sun, ( ) this character is "日" (Ri), which means "中午" (Zhongwu) noon, that is, the sun is at middle of day. If I draw one sun and four grasses next to it, ( )please note that each of the grasses( )is a character "生" (Sheng) life. What is this combined character? "暮" (Mu) twilight, meaning evening or dusk, the sun goes down to the grass nest. As I said before, the Central Plains is a plain and there are no mountains, so we generally say that the sun has set, but the civilized people of the Central Plains say that the sun has gone down into the grass nest. Please see, I have drawn five suns, and it surprisingly draws out all the cosmology of the ancient Chinese.

The early Chinese cosmology is the *sky vault* legend, that is, the earth is a flat plate, the sky is like a vault buckled in the earth, also known as the theory of sky round and earth square. Today we still call a place as "地方" (Difang) ground square, which is related to this cosmology. When I mention this theory, you will immediately think of the geocentric model developed by the famous ancient Greek scientist Ptolemy. His work was early translated by the Arabs as *Astronomy in a Nutshell,* and the original Greek name, the real name, the full name of this book is *The Mathematical Compendium in Thirteen Books,* which is actually a huge system of motion derived from complex mathematical logic. The geocentric theory established by Ptolemy was a logical model, and at the same time, during the Han Dynasty, one of the greatest astronomers in history, Zhang Heng, emerged in China, which means that Zhang Heng was exactly contemporary with Ptolemy, to what extent? The age difference between the two men was only 12 years. Zhang Heng built a geocentric model for the Chinese, but it was a water-driven armillary sphere, a physical model. What does this show? It shows that scholars in the East and the West do research in very different ways. Westerners make logical models of ideas, while Chinese scholars make figurative models of objects. The logical model is meticulous and malleable. What does it mean? The more complex the structure, the more flaws it has. When later generation finds flaws in the logic, he can change the doctrine and create a new model of thought. The figurative model, on the other hand, is so strong and stable that you will never be able to change it. So the Chinese have been using the sky vault legend and geocentric doctrines till the Opium War (1840s). So what is the problem presented here? The difference of ways of thinking between scholars of the East and West. One is a logical abstract model, or abstract logical thinking mode, while the other is a physical figurative model, or figurative comparative thinking mode, thus deriving a completely different way of thinking. In turn, the way of thinking becomes the weaver and bearer of the whole cultural connotation, which causes a fundamental divergence between Eastern and Western cultures in their basic configuration and quality of thought.

Third, word group logical deduction.

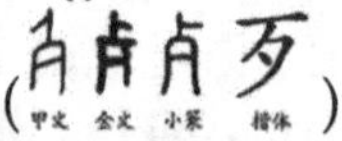

Here is a piece of oracle bone. It draws 5 characters () but speaks of a very complex event, saying a child with a long tongue whose mother was stung by poisonous scorpion or spider and died, but due to her unusual death she was not allowed to be buried in the clan public cemetery. Only these 5 characters tells so complex a story? The first character draws a child. The second character draws a mouth and then a long tongue on the outside, which is the earliest image of the character "舌" (She) tongue. The first two characters mean a child who always stretches his tongue out. When the ancients named a child, they would often use one of the physical characteristics of the child as his nickname, so this child is called "子舌" (Zishe). The third character below is a bit more complicated, the one on the right is a mother. "Then a poisonous insect or a poisonous spider is drawn in the middle; a corpse is drawn on the left side, and the legs are completely stiff, and a sign is marked in the stiffed legs, (歹 甲文 金文 小篆 楷体)this character is "歹" (Dai), not good. Look at the whole character, a mother woman stung to death by a poisonous spider, the death is not auspicious. Such a complex picture its meaning is not possible to express in a single syllable, so this character was eliminated in the later development. The fourth character is "不" (Bu), ()which starts with an inverted triangle and three drops of water at the bottom. What does it mean? The inverted triangle represents the female yin, and the water drops underneath represents a woman's menstruation or period, at which time she will refuse to have sex with man, and this refusal symbol is the origin of the character "不" no. Finally, a tomb is drawn with a person lying inside. What do these 5 characters express? A child with a long tongue, whose mother was stung by a poisonous insect or spider and died in an inauspicious way, and therefore she must not be buried in a clan cemetery. It is amazing that such a complex narrative, a story with so many meanings, is expressed in only 5 characters.

Look at how similar it is to a literary text, which is composed in this way. In fact, its ideographic process is equivalent to a comic strip. This is the figurative coherent relationship between ancient Chinese words and texts, so this is what I meant when I said earlier that the text structure in ancient China had no grammatical-logical relationship.

Since it is such a figurative pictorial system, and since the information contained in the pictorial symbol system is larger, it does not need to resort to abstract and complex logical thinking to take forward the conceptual composition of its ideas, then its way of thinking tends to be figurative, tends to be analogical, and does not tend to be linear in its derivation of relations. The long training of this way of thinking has led to the formation of a cultural state unique to the Chinese, which I call the skill culture system. That is to say, Chinese culture favors the production of technology and art, or its main culture is most conducive to the production of technology and art.

Let me give you an example. In the Song Dynasty, Ma Zhiyuan wrote a poem called *Autumn Thought*, which reads, "Withered vines, old trees, and dark crows, small bridge flowing water and house, thin horse old road west wind, sunset, heart-broken man in desolate land." This poem is very famous. Note that there is no punctuation in ancient poetry. Please look at his entire verbal structure, in which there are no function words, prepositions or adverbs, that is, no grammatical-logical connections. Withered vines, old trees and dark crows, he did not need to talk about how the old trees were wrapped by the withered vines, and as a result, he wrote the best words. Another poet Wang Wei wrote a poem with two lines of 10 words, the most desolate line I've seen depicting a grand western landscape, and he phrased it like this, "The desert with straight lonely smoke, the long river with round setting sun." The desert and the lonely smoke use only one adjective, straight; the long river and the setting sun use only one adjective, round. He did not need to describe about a scarcely living peasant hut in the desert and cooking smoke curling up at night, but it turns out to be the best poem. What does it show? It shows the unique way of figurative thinking and the coherent sequence that figurative symbols must have. Figurative symbols are the extensions of petroglyphs carved in caves by humans 20,000 years ago, and they are very simple symbols. Placing these figurative symbols directly in order, they form a very beautiful picture, a dynamic serial ideographic system. In other words, Chinese pictographs are naturally colored, unlike the Western spelling words which are all grayish conceptual norms. For example, we describe man and woman dating as flowers under the moon, we speak of man of unrestrained as a horse galloping in the sky, and we mention coitus as rainy cloud...... all these kinds of descriptions reveal a subtle and elegant style. Therefore, it is particularly conducive to the production of art and culture.

As we all know, people of art need figurative thinking, rather than abstract rational thinking. So, the Chinese tendency of figurative thinking is particularly suitable for creating a unique art culture. Therefore, among the great literary figures in ancient China, except for the development of scriptures by some individuals among the hundred schools of scholars in the pre-Qin era, and the scriptures in the state of scattered logic, most literary figures in the past generations were artists, such as Qu Yuan, such as Li Bai and Du Fu; such as the poems in Tang Dynasty and the iambic verses in Song Dynasty. Even the Eight Great Men of Tang and Song, their articles are mostly prose, not complex and esoteric in thought, the beauty of words and the beauty of the context is what made them great. In a word, they were all aestheticians. Thus, ancient Chinese culture was extremely capable of creating art.

Let me give you an example. After the Sui and Tang dynasties, semi-abstract paintings emerged in China, which is known as Chinese painting. Chinese semi-abstract painting in the last thousand years has reached a very high level. Western abstract painting, on the other hand, did not occur until one or two hundred years ago in modern times, and its greatest characteristic, I can only use one word to describe, ugly of no comparison. Needless to say, compared to ancient Chinese paintings, compared to Chinese semi-abstract paintings, Western modern abstract painting is too far away. But because Western culture has become the mainstream culture today, its most ugly paintings can still be sold at high prices. I believe that if China gradually rises, Chinese ancient paintings will be the paintings with higher value. I suggest if you have money, buy more Chinese ancient paintings, which will have a very high value preservation.

Chinese culture, first is particularly conducive to the creation of art and, secondly, conductive to the creation of technology. Here I have to correct a concept that we confuse today with science and technology. Please note that science and technology are two different things when analyzed from a primitive state. Technology is to practice in advance, and then sum up the experience thoroughly in a theory, this is called technology. The so-called science is the opposite way of thinking, it is logical modeling in advance, and then build a laboratory to test it with practical experience, this is called science. Chinese culture produces a technical system, but never produces a philosophical system, that is, never a philosophical and scientific system. What is philosophy? I have to make a clarification, but only the simplest summary here: By philosophy, I mean a pure logic game played by a group of adult children in ancient Greece. The product of the extension of this purely logical game is called science. (We'll talk more on this in Western Philosophy later)

Let me give you an example. Copernicus established heliocentrism back in his days without any evidence, he simply found serious flaws in Ptolemy's geocentric model of thought. He envisioned, or rather he merely conjectured, that Ptolemy's logical model would be simpler and more rigorous if the sun was placed in the middle and the earth and other stars were made to orbit around it, for which he had no evidence at the time. This is why 50 years after the death of Copernicus, Bruno was burned in the Sun Square by the Inquisition for advocating Copernicus' doctrine, and the people cheered; until 70 or 80 years after the death of Copernicus, Galileo supported Copernicus' heliocentric theory in his later years, and was also sentenced to house arrest by the Western Inquisition, and there was no protest from the academic community; the reason was that Copernicus' doctrine did not have any evidence. It was not until nearly 100 years after the death of Copernicus that the three major evidence gradually appeared, which is the Venus surplus and deficit, light line difference and stellar parallax.

What am I talking about? I'm talking about how science and technology are two completely opposite thought processes. Technology is a practical experience in the first place, and afterwards find a theory to put it together; philosophy and science is a logical model in the first place, only afterwards to find evidence, or to use empirical observation to empirically prove, we call this way of thinking philosophical way of thinking. Let me give you an example: mankind has never known how genes are formed. In recent times, it has been unclear whether genetic factors are granular or liquid. For example, if both parents are tall, the offspring will be taller; if the parents one is tall and one is short, the offspring will have an unequal distribution of height, and the average height will be medium; from this point of view, the genes are in a liquid mixture. But reversely it was found that a certain genetic or biological trait would be expressed as a separate, prominent likeness, which again appears that the genes are granularly present. Thus, even after Darwin and up to Mendel, the basic histology of genetic factors was not found. By 1953, Watson and Crick constructed the genome shape in a purely logical way, based on the representation of biological genetic phenomena, which is the famous double helix gene model. At that time, the molecular structure of genes was still invisible to humans, not under the light microscope. More than a decade later, the tunneling microscope was invented and the X-ray diffraction fractal technique emerged, only to find that their base chain conformations were actually indistinguishable from the theoretical model.

What does it show? The logical modeling comes first, and the practical test follows second, and this thing is called science. That is why in the history of Western philosophy, in the mainstream of philosophy, you do not hear the phrase "true knowledge comes from practice". We Chinese say this phrase the loudest, because our entire cultural system is a technical system, is a concrete practical system, is a system of experience. But we should note that the knowledge we have today has little to do with practice. Think about this: when we say matter today, what is matter? We say it is molecule, we say it is atom, we say it is elementary particle, can you see it with your eyes? When we say life today, we say it is made up of cells, we say it is made up of genes, can you know it with your eyes, with your experience? So we should understand, our modern knowledge system is all the product of logical deduction.

China used to be one of the four ancient civilizations in the world before the Middle Ages, and even reached the highest level in the world during the Tang and Song dynasties. During the age of technology, that is, before the age of science, Chinese civilization actually created more than 60%-70% of the world's technological system, but when it came to the age of science, Chinese culture suddenly declined, because the technological system is a hard-state trial and error method, it repeatedly tries and errs in actual operation, so its scope is narrow, and it takes a long time and multiplies the difficulty. In contrast, the scientific system is constructed on a logical model, and once it is proved to be established, it then sweeps all related fields, resulting in the great efficiency of the soft trial-and-error method. This is the reason and reflection for the sudden decline of Chinese culture in the scientific era and in the way of thinking.

The next question involves the question, why did the West produce a philosophical cultural system? When I talk about this, you must think that I am slandering Chinese culture again, because I say that Chinese culture does not produce science. I repeat, I lecture only about the facts, not about the good and the bad. If you want to understand the major differences between the connotations of Eastern and Western cultures, you have to understand the reasons why such connotations occur, and this is called the facts. Only by understanding this, can you understand the fundamental fulcrum of the inner qualities of different cultures.

Phonetic Words and Philosophical Culture

Why did Western culture produce the philosophical system? How did the philosophical system derive its way of thinking? We will discuss this topic below.

For this reason, it is necessary to briefly explore the origin of the phonetic words.

Phonetic word occurred in the circum-Mediterranean region, and it probably first occurred on the eastern side of the Mediterranean. In ancient times there was a small race called Phoenicia, the so-called Phoenicia, it means purple-red. That is, the Phoenicians smashed a kind of mussel from the sea to make a purple-red dye, and the clothes they dyed were bright and did not fade, so the people around them called them purple-red people. This is the origin of the name Phoenicia.

Because it was close to the eastern side of the Mediterranean Sea, the Phoenicians traded extensively in the Mediterranean Rim as early as 3,000 years ago, surprisingly accounting for more than 50% of the oceanic trade at that time. Around 1000 B.C., this part of Phoenicia and its surroundings gradually produced linear scripts, the precursors of phonetic words, and evolved 22 approximate symbols of the 26 Roman letters. So under what circumstances did phonetic writing occur? I have already given a hint above: it must be in the relatively convenient communication conditions, so that in a state of semi-isolation between the original tribes could continue to travel, frequent trade, multi-lingual collision, only in such a special open landscape conditions, could the phonetic words be formed.

For example, in the Mediterranean region, due to the open landscape, various ethnic groups and tribes came and went, either in business or in war, and cultural exchange activities continued under ethnic disturbances. When a man came to another tribe, he could neither read the hieroglyphic symbols of the other tribe nor understand what the other tribe was saying, what could he do? He had only one solution left, which was to mark down the pronunciation of the other language with phonetic symbols. You made a phonetic symbol, I made another phonetic symbol, and people would eventually use only this phonetic system in mutual communication, and throw away the different pictograms that each originally used, and this was the origin of phonetic words.

Please understand what I mean by this paragraph. It is that phonetic writing is a symbol system that developed late in the hieroglyphic script, and it must have occurred in a semi-isolated, semi-open geographical environment. It is another cultural secondary condition after the survival structure. Therefore, phonetic writing could never have arisen in China because it did not have this specific state of geographically separated communication conditions.

Once the phonetic writing occurs, it immediately leads to a serious problem - the loss of the concept of written symbols. For example, if I write an English word sun here, the word is this symbol in our Chinese characters, (⊙) and Chinese people know what it is when they look at this symbol, "日" (Ri) sun. But who sees the word sun and knows intuitively that it is the sun? If I say I am standing on sun, you may think sun is the earth; if I say I am sitting on sun, you may think sun is a chair. The concept of the word sun comes from the meaning following the predicate, for example, the ancient people said "sun is the abode of the sun god", and we modern people say "sun is the celestial body of hydrogen fusion". Note the letters of the word sun, which has no concept! All its concept comes from the predicate part after the word is, and the predicate part gives the meaning or definition to it, so that the phonetic symbol sun has a concept.

Our human mind consists of three main parts, concept is the most basic element which can be seen as bricks and mortar. Then comes the proposition. Note that a proposition is never a title of an article. A proposition means that the predicate part behind the predicate gives a meaning or definition to the subject in front of it. We call this kind of grammatical structure proposition. This is the second part of the component of ideas. The third part of the component of ideas is the compounding and derivation of propositions.

Please be advised that we call the sum of these three components as thought, and its most basic component is the concept. But once the phonetic words appeared, the concept actually disappeared in the symbols, and it had to be established in the abstract logical derivation of propositions for each lexical item. This led to the fact that every word they said, every thing they did, and even every concept and problem they thought about, had to run their thinking under the rules of strong logic, resulting in a grotesque condition of thinking, which I call logical compulsion.

For thousands of years, people have not been able to present concepts directly in characters and symbols, but must run their thoughts and ideas under the compulsion of grammatical and logical sequences, thus forming a logical structure of abstract thinking and a system of ideas, and this system of ideas and its way of thinking has created the pure logic game. As soon as I say this, you should understand what pure logical games are, i.e., philosophy in particular. That is why philosophy is called love wisdom and not practice. It is the evolution of pure wisdom, and the logical model of this pure wisdom is called philosophy, and the post-derivative differentiated form of this thing is called science. Therefore, we say that "philosophy is the mother of science", so we call the unique cultural connotation created by the abstract way of thinking *philosophical cultural system*. It is completely different from the Chinese *skill cultural system*, thus creating a sharp division and separation between the Western way of thinking and the Eastern way of thinking.

Let me give you an example. Western philosophers discuss all problems by reducing them to *being*, so-called *inquiry into being*, because *being* is the most fundamental property of everything. But how is the word *being* written in the Western language? It is actually written with a *Be* and then followed by *-ing*. "*Be*" is the non-tense central word for is, which is the neutral word for is, was, are, and so on. "*Be*" becomes the progressive tense *Being*, and this word is existence. This is why the Chinese found it very difficult to translate the concept of being in Western philosophy, and even today we still do not translate it accurately as existence. The academic community sometimes calls existentialism *be-ism*, sometimes *existentialism*, sometimes *ontology*, and in any case, it is not clear how to interpret it properly.

Why is it sufficient to take out the predicate tense to represent the existence of all things? It is because everything is after is. Such an abstract way of expression is indeed difficult for us Chinese to understand, and it expresses the great difference between the Eastern and Western ways of thinking and language structure. In this forced system, all concepts, all thinking, and the existence of everything must run on a logical abstract chain of derivation in order to be established. This structure of thought, in which logical forms are extracted to form a commentary on everything, is called the "philosophical model of thinking". It is very important to understand this point, since this is how the cultural divide between East and West occurs and gradually separates.

Let me give you another example on how the Chinese express the concept of existence. In the oracle bone scripts, an inverted triangle is drawn first to represent a woman, (甲文 金文 小篆 楷体)then a vertical line is drawn in the middle to represent a woman's menstrual period and the birth canal of a child. "才" (Cai), this is the character for talent, why is it talent? Because the ancients believe that only women who can give birth to children are the most talented, this statement is very reasonable. Man is very capable, he could at most build a bullock cart, but could he try to build a person? Next to the character "才", draw a child in it, (金文大篆 小篆 隶书)this character is "存" (Cun), there is. The ancients knew that women alone cannot give birth to children, there must be men to sow the seeds, so they drew a "阳" (Yang) male next to the character "才", (金文 小篆 在 楷体) and this character is the word existence.

As I speak of this, some of you may think that I am highly praising the Western culture. Don't be mistaken, my lectures are all neutral language, no good or bad. In fact, I don't want to praise anyone, nor do I want to criticize anyone, I just want to explain the reason why different civilization systems could occur, and this is what you should pay special attention to.

When we say that Chinese culture does not produce science, in a way, you can also see it as my praise of Chinese culture, if you must evaluate it emotionally. Because it is science that has brought great disasters to mankind. Our environmental pollution, ecological destruction, climate anomalies, and weapons of mass destruction today have pushed mankind to the brink of extinction, all of which are the products of science, the creation of evil.

Chinese culture does not produce science, and if you want to praise it really, you can say that Chinese culture is not involved in evil creations, but what is the point of saying that? Would you gain any new understanding of Eastern and Western cultures? It won't. So, please note that I am not in any way trying to praise or belittle any party in my lectures, I am just trying to give you a truthful account of how cultures and types of civilizations diverged, and this is the part that you have to pay special attention to understand. So unlike other scholars who generally praise Chinese studies, I do not praise traditional Chinese culture, and I do not admit that Chinese culture can save the world or save humanity. Because Chinese culture has long been in decline, because the so-called Chinese culture is a typical agricultural civilization, and the so-called Western culture is a non-mainstream industrial and commercial civilization that happened in the distant past. So instead of calling them East or West civilization, Eastern or Western culture, we should call them agricultural civilization and industrial and commercial civilization to be more accurate. I don't admit that traditional Chinese culture can save the world, because we have no way back, because we can't go backwards to agricultural civilization. So the persistent touting of Chinese culture shows its lack of fundamental understanding of the meaning of Chinese culture and the characteristics of Chinese culture.

Nor do I admit that Western culture represents the future, even though it is the dominant culture of the entire human world today. For any culture must be a system that has the effect of preserving the survival of its carrier, and we regard this effect of preserving the survival of its carrier as culture's main characteristic. So, a culture that has been undermining its carrier is a sign that it is in decline.

Please think about why the traditional Chinese culture has declined.

Because it is an overly refined and rigid agricultural culture system, which has severely hindered the transformation of the Chinese nation from an agricultural civilization to an industrial and commercial civilization in modern times, so it has brought great damage to the Chinese nation, so it has bankrupted, so it has declined. Then Western culture today is bringing even greater harm to the entire mankind, so it marks the decline of Western culture. Therefore, I neither admit that Chinese culture can save the world, nor do I admit that Western culture represents the future.

So what are the values that each of the Eastern and Western cultures has? Chinese traditional culture, because it preserves the fundamental level of human civilization, and the more primitive and lower level it is, the more fundamental, decisive and stable it must be, therefore, it constitutes an important reference system for the future re-creation of human culture and civilization. Western culture is the spiritual embodiment and materialized foundation of industrial and commercial civilization, therefore, when the next civilization of mankind is carried forward by industrial and commercial civilization, it is the direct port and channel of transmission and spreading itself. This is the value of Eastern and Western cultures in the re-creation of culture and civilization for future mankind, and the most essential commentary and method for understanding culture (soft intellectual properties), civilization (hard social structure), and the connotation of thinking or thought form (the core of human intelligence).

In the mid-20th century, a new philosophical school called postmodern philosophy emerged in the West. But what is postmodern philosophy? Nowadays, a large number of texts have been translated by the academic community, and you can read these books and get dizzy and confused about what it is trying to say; when we have come to the point of my lecture, the meaning of postmodern philosophy is already highlighted. What is the central concept of postmodern philosophy? Deconstruction, what does it want to deconstruct? the structure of Western philosophical culture. It believes that it is the Western philosophical cultural thought system that has caused the systemic crisis of all humanity today. Western philosophers know very well that the roots of their philosophical cultural system were deeply rooted in the phonetic words. They therefore raised two objections: first, reduce the phonetic-centrism, that is, oppose the phonetic words; and second, reduce the logocentrism.

Look at *Logos,* which is the Latin word, meaning *words and order*. This ancient Greek concept is the predecessor of the common word *Logic* today, and *Logic* means "逻辑". Notice what the postmodern philosophers are against? They are against *phono-centrism* and *logocentrism*. In other words, they know that the Western philosophical culture system is derived from phonetic word and logical abstract thinking, so they raise these two objections. We can thus see that the most intelligent people in the West have realized today that Western culture does not represent the future. Only if you understand the origins of the respective civilizations that occurred, only if you understand the basic qualities of culture, and you understand the lineage of its development, can you understand the essence of culture and civilization and its prescribed trends. Obviously, mankind is about to face the construction of a third crop of cultures and civilizations. Only when you understand such a sequence of civilizational occurrences, can you truly see the major historical events that are coming upon you, and you can truly build the ideological and cultural projects that correspond to them.

Let's summarize this lesson below.

If you have listened to my entire class today, you should understand that I have only talked about one thing, what is *culture*. As I have said repeatedly before, culture is nothing more than the sum total of the livelihood behaviors and systems of consciousness expressed by such an intellectual creature as human beings, that is, it is no difference from our existence itself. All of our human survival activities can be considered as cultural survival activities. Therefore, if you want to understand what a human being is, if you want to understand what the humanity is, if you want to understand what human civilization is, you must deeply understand the underpinnings of culture.

Culture is something that has three basic characteristics: first, the structure of survival. This is the natural or spontaneous relationship between your living environment, living conditions, and your own survival needs. These are the first underpinning that makes culture occur, which I call structure of survival. Second, the way of thinking. Because of the difference in written symbols, derived from the difference between figurative thinking and abstract thinking, which led to a huge split between the cultural connotations of the East and the West, resulting in the formation of the basic characteristics of the East and of the West, which is called way of thinking. Third, the enveloping effect. What does it mean? People generally think that "culture is naturally expansive", but this is a very problematic statement. In fact, no human culture, no model of human thought has anything to do with truth. What does this statement mean? We will discuss it in our philosophy class later. Since no culture and no model of human thought is the truth, why does it serve as a system of guarantees for the effective maintenance of human existence? It is because it constitutes a self-consistent closed structural system under which we are enveloped and at peace. Therefore, culture is not naturally expansive, but rather obscuring. It is only in the process of collision and exchange that the expansion of culture takes place, and this is something you must deeply understand.

Let me give you an example. The ancients, the ancient people of the West, they believed in theology since ancient times. Until modern times, the West, through the Renaissance and the Enlightenment, kept trying to break out of the shell of theology. If you ever read the *Decameron* written by Boccaccio in the Renaissance era, all the vicious attacks on Christianity and its clergy. The Enlightenment era, when scholars such as Diderot and Voltaire and a number of others were constantly attacking the repressive structure of Western theology, it was the midwifing process of the coming scientific age. But even so, the vast majority of people in the West today still believe in God, and the number believe in science is no more than 20% believe. What does this tell us? It shows the enveloping effect of culture.

Let me give you another example: Chinese people are no difference from Westerners in terms of intelligence, but the core of traditional Chinese culture was only "ruler rules, subject subjects, father fathers, son sons", and it was only a social structure of human relationships within a blood system, where all of its culture was concentrated, and it completely ignored natural science, so much so that in the Ming and Qing dynasties, if you read the Ming and Qing histories, an emperor, whose mother was not the empress, that is to say, he was not born by the first wife, but the child born to the emperor's other concubines, and after he became emperor, from filial piety, he had to elevate his biological mother to the position of Empress or Empress Dowager. For example, Ming Xiaozong came from a humble little palace maid from Guangxi, and his father Ming Xianzong accidentally gave birth to him when he happened to visit this palace maid and slept with her. Since his father's proper empress was a very jealous woman, she went to great lengths to deliberately mutilate all the children born to other concubines, even the child's mother, so as to ensure that she would be able to inherit the throne if she had a biological royal son in the future. This led to Xiaozong being raised in secret since childhood. After he ascended to the throne, he wanted to make his mother, the former palace maid, the rightful Empress Dowager, which became the top priority of the entire court for a while.

Chinese bureaucrats, the top elite of the Chinese literati, were actually grouped together in caring about what way and what name to use for the emperor's biological mother, which was surprisingly a matter of national importance, which was surprisingly a core connotation of mainstream culture. Another example, when the Empress Dowager Cixi of the Qing Dynasty, wanted to retire in her later years (1894), why did the Guangxu Emperor use millions of taels of silver to build the Summer Palace in order to please her? And that was when the Sino-Japanese naval war was imminent! We look at it today and say that Empress Dowager Cixi was ridiculous, Empress Dowager Cixi impeded the country! But you have to go back to that era, you have to know that this was one of the most normal moves of Emperor Guangxu to consolidate the orthodox ideology of the country and the thousand-year patriarchal system, and what he expressed was the patriarchal basis of the culture of kinship and filial piety. So at the time, he didn't seem absurd at all, he was absolutely normal. For thousands of years, the Chinese culture has closed itself in such a primitive blood culture, in fact, their level of intelligence is no difference from the Westerners, but they have touched nothing of the huge naturalistic system, living in a strong state of cultural obscurity. What does it express? It expresses the most profound obscuring effect of Chinese culture. Therefore, please understand that culture is not naturally expansive, but has an enveloping effect in the first place.

These three qualities of culture make us understand that, from a large country or a nation to establish its own national culture and ethnic culture, to a small enterprise, a group, or even an individual, it has to establish its own group culture and personal culture, so that you have to conform to the above three principles.

In other words, firstly, you must find the elements related to the structure of your survival at that time, which become the basic premise for the derivation of your own culture; secondly, you must find the way of thinking and behavior that is compatible with this structure of survival; thirdly, you must realize that any culture has a maintenance effect in the early stage but it will have undermining effect in the late stage, so you have to open a gap in the cultural system composed of the above two elements, so that the heterogeneous culture or other cultures can collide and communicate with you, thus producing the dissolution effect to the obscurity, that is, the expansion of the future path of survival. I repeat, if any country, nation, or even humanity as a whole wants to seek the next phase of culture, create the next phase of civilization, and find its future path of survival, it must construct new ideas and new cultures for the future based on these three principles.

As I speak here, I'd like to mention one more topic: what is effective learning? If your listening, your reading, and your learning are only operating in the normal channel, under your original thinking model, I call it ineffective learning, because it means you are still in a state of obscurity. In today's era of rapid changes in human existence, you can call it effective learning only if you are open to different voices. Our lecture today, including the series of lectures that follow, is based on the cross-reference between Eastern and Western culture and Eastern and Western civilization as the background of the whole lecture, which shows the different voices of Eastern thinking when the mainstream Western civilization has already covered the world; which also, at the same time, tells you from a profound level the origin and characteristics of the Western culture, so that we could find a breakthrough while we live in a state of obscurity formed by Eastern way of thinking. So if you are listening to my class today and you think that my presentation seems a bit perverse and out of the ordinary, then you have heard it, because that is effective learning.

Well, that concludes our class for today.

Q & A After Class

Okay, we're going to answer questions. Each of you may have one question at a time, so as to leave time for more questions from others.

Questioner: After listening to your lecture today, I have a deep impression that agricultural civilization and industrial civilization were not designed by anyone or any philosopher, but they were formed naturally under the circumstances and conditions of the time. So if this is the reasoning, does it mean that this new culture or civilization in the future, in fact, any thinking ahead of time is not helpful? Or maybe it will not be formed until it reaches that condition; when it reaches that condition, it will be formed naturally. If that is the case, then is it true that our study here today, even if we know the reason for it, does not actually change anything or the course of history?

Mr. Dongyue: This is a very good question, and I will answer it. I said earlier that the original civilization and civilization process of human beings are not the result of human choice, nor are they the result of human planning and design in advance. But please note that I am not denying another phenomenon, only that I did not expand on that topic, that is, the higher the level of human civilization, the more information is available as civilization develops, the more human beings have to construct their future behavior patterns and social constructs through models of thought, making them as a precursor. Please note that the two are not contradictory. Starting from Plato's *Ideal State*, from Laozi's *Daodejing* to the issues Confucius discussed in the *Analects*, mankind has actually set out to design his own future social model. But be noted, what was the premise or the bottom of his design model being defined by? For example, Plato's model of the ideal state and Confucius' model must be different, and why were their models different? It was because they could not choose the ground which had been prescribed! Then although the process of human civilization is the process of information increment, which makes the future development of human beings has to be revealed through rational logical design, this design is not the main cause of the original creation, but the driving force of the civilization process, or I call it the personalized expression of the natural will, which is its accurate connotation. So I think you are right, that if mankind still wants to seek a way out of the future, in this highly civilized and highly information-augmented age, he has to resort to the establishment of a new model of thought and logic as its precursor, and the emergence of this logical model itself is the product of some involuntary natural force, only it is manifested as a precursor element. If the creation of new ideas and new models is a necessary node in the natural process, then it marks the point at which our future existence may have to unfold in order to be realized. That is why the majority of human theories constitute only a disaster for the development of human society, that is, instead of being realized, it causes problems for humanity, because it does not really convey the intrinsic requirements of the natural will itself. A few doctrines, on the other hand, become the cornerstone of the construction of human civilization, because the authors unconsciously act as the personalized mouthpiece of the natural will, and that is the difference.

Questioner: Teacher, I would like to ask, because you talk about the Eastern culture and Western culture cannot represent the future, then if they both integrate, we often say 1 + 1 is greater than 2, which one will be more dominant to absorb the other side? My next question is that in ancient times, the story of King Chu was fond of thin-waist women, and just now you talked about the personalized mouthpiece of the natural will, so as a politician or entrepreneur, is it possible for him to change and reverse such a trend because he understands the principle of weakening compensation or the source of this culture?

Mr. Dongyue: Of course, it is possible, but it doesn't have to be a reversal, but rather an adaptation and expansion. Please remember that any personal power of human beings comes from new ideas. What is the greatness of the so-called great politician, the so-called great social activist, the so-called great military man? Not great in himself, but great in being the bearer of a certain new idea. Let me give you an example, for example, George Washington, where did his strength come from? His strength came from the democratic and republican system of thought established by a group of European scholars in the modern era. Let me give you another example, in the Second World War why Germany actually defeated the whole of Europe at the beginning and achieved or nearly achieved the one of the two brief unification in European history, one was done by Napoleon and the other was done by Hitler. You know that Germany was a defeated country of the World War One, it was a very weak country, the First World War ended in November 1918, but just 21 years later, in September 1939 it started the Second World War, the Germans used only a few months to defeat the entire European allied forces, what made it possible? It was because when the First World War was about to end, there were some strange weapons that military men could not understand at that time, such as tanks and airplanes. At that time, the tank was as bulky as a big water tank, and the speed was only 5km per hour; the early aircraft were all wooden planes, propeller planes, and it could not set the machine gun in front, so one machine gun from ground could hit its propeller broken, and the pilots had to shoot at the enemy planes with pistols. It was such a bad weapon that military men at that time could not understand what it meant, so all of them regarded it as an auxiliary weapon for infantry or cavalry. After the World War One ended, a scholar in Britain explored the prospect of these weapons a little bit, but did not go deeper; while the German military academia paid more attention to it, including the famous German war general Guderian who later participated in World War Two. They studied the new changes brought about by these weapons and then established a new idea in military science, that is, they realized that such mechanized and armored weapons would form the main battle force, the main assaulting power, which was the ideological basis for the later three-dimensional blitzkrieg method to unfold. Because the German military community had the most systematic organization and development of this new idea, it made Germany, the weakest of the European powers at that time, the most powerful force at the beginning of the Second World War. What do I want to express? The strength of new ideas! Please remember that the prerequisite for anyone to produce a powerful behavioral effect is that you have an understanding of contemporary new ideas and integrate them into your own spiritual and behavioral system. Of course, this is too much and too difficult for an ordinary to achieve. If you can do it, you will be a great man.

Questioner: You mentioned that civilization is a disaster against human nature, that human problems will be solved more and more, and that human beings will lead themselves to an irreversible path of disaster, which may lead to their own destruction. On this premise, my question is: After you've seen all the truths, do you still love the world? If so, what is your faith? If not, how do you live with the world? How do you find your goal in life and support yourself in living it?

Mr. Dongyue: This question is a bit advancing. We have just started this lecture series, and what we are going to talk about later, you have to follow the 12-day course of nearly 80 hours, gradually deepen the understanding, layer by layer, before you can see its real full picture, and even that is not enough, you need to read the book. My concern is not to discuss that there is life and death, not to discuss the inevitable end of human civilization, I am only discussing why the higher the level of human civilization, the deeper the crisis. The discussion of this issue is a matter of basic theory. Because the public generally think that the higher the level of civilization development, the more survival advantage we will have, which may be a major misjudgment. Only when we have a clear understanding of this issue can we find a way out for the future survival of humanity. Therefore, I emphasize that my doctrine is not about death and destruction, but about what development and progress really are and how we will deal with this issue in the next period. If I discuss the issue in this way with pessimistic overtones, it does not have any effect on my life. Please think about what your ultimate goal is after you are born, there is only one goal, the grave; but does it affect your optimism in life? Not at all, you still muddle through life, happy, and eventually go to the grave. So even if I say that our future existence is at great risk, even if I say that our future existence is threatened with death, people today can still be rampantly arrogant, they can be optimistic and self-congratulatory, they can still have endless z-turns. It is because we lack a vision of the ultimate problem, or even if we have a vision, we act in a muddled way, so we are in more and more trouble in the future. If we know today that the future is a terrible path, and we can restrain ourselves from being so optimistic in the present, then we might have a future. So including myself, even though we know there is trouble ahead, we still need to have a sense of joy and happiness in our life. But you must understand and be careful that this sense of joy and happiness, may be exactly the ecstasy or narcotic that leads you to remote disaster.

Questioner: In 1935, there was a professor named Hu Huanyong at the National University of the Republic of China, who drew a line from the Heihe River in the northeast to the southwest to Tengchong in Yunnan, which is now called the Hu Huanyong Line. In the northwest of the *Hu Huanyong* Line, 64% of the country has only 4% of the population, while in the southeast of the Hu Huanyong Line, 36% of the country has 96% of the population. Chinese culture and civilization were initiated from the middle part of the Hu Huanyong Line, a line that had a huge limitation on the development of China's economy and population, including culture. One of the questions I would like to ask is: What is the role of the Hu Huanyong Line in the development of Chinese culture? I would like to hear your insights. Another question is: I wonder if it is possible to break this trap in the future.

Mr. Dongyue: I have paid attention to this study, and it is not difficult to understand it at all. I mentioned in class that Toynbee discussed a problem called the moderate challenge doctrine, that is, places with too good or too bad natural conditions cannot be the birthplace of civilization. It is easy to understand that the place west of this line is too poor in natural conditions, so it can neither become the birthplace of civilization nor the main base for civilization survival and development. In the future, this place may become a blessed place because today human beings are tossing and turning, with climate anomalies, greenhouse effect, and rising sea level. 80% of human beings live in coastal areas today, and in the near future these areas will be submerged. So I suggest that you do not buy houses in the coastal cities of Shanghai, Guangzhou, Shenzhen, buying a house there will be a waste. On the contrary, those today's desert land, the future may be an important survival area for human beings. However, when it comes to that day, you flee to that place, it may not produce good result, because there will be a bigger disaster following you, even if you climb to the top of the Himalayas, you can not get rid of the disaster. So it is better for us not to wait for that waste land to become a blessed land, but to let both our state of thought and our state of existence remain or the present state be delayed as long as possible.

Questioner: Sir, just now you said that any structure, once it is formed, it will run in a given direction, which is equivalent to path dependence, right? You said that *path dependence* is determined by its intrinsic properties, but what determines this intrinsic property? Or who determines it?

Mr. Dongyue: Once a civilizational structure is formed, it must have a momentum of inertial movement. When we talk about inertial motion, we immediately think of Newton's classical mechanics, but in fact human civilization also has this quality. Marx called it "the dead catching the living", that is, the traditional human culture has a strong hold on the subsequent human civilization. The reason for this lies in what I said earlier: the more primitive and low-level things are, the more fundamental, decisive and stable they are. This statement sounds very simple, and to really understand its meaning, you have to read and understand my book A Unified Theory of Evolution, which has a hypnotic effect. What I am trying to explain here is why all the ancient civilizations of mankind have basically declined, ancient Egypt, ancient Babylon, today's Syria, Iraq, ancient India, of which the best antient culture preserved is in China. Why did China, among all the ancient civilizations that declined, also did not escape the tragedy of cultural and civilizational decline, and had a humiliating recent civilizational history in the last hundred years of the 19th and 20th centuries, but developed better in the recent past? It is because we had a very thorough cleaning of traditional culture! That is why I have a high respect for the New Culture Movement, the group of Republican-era philosophers who advocated the overthrow of Confucianism and caused great damage to traditional culture and national education back then. Please listen to what I am saying, Chinese traditional culture does not represent the future, it has long been in decline, it cannot even save the current society, we have to save ourselves with the help of a cultural system that matches our survival situation, this is one of the reasons why China's contemporary transformation is intense and rapid. On the one hand, we have to deny traditional culture and clean it up to some extent, but on the other hand, as I said earlier, modern and contemporary culture must have the effect of undermining and maiming, while we have to rely on traditional and ancient culture in order to recreate a new culture that matches our future survival. This contradiction and dilemma are the major issues that scholars today must be concerned with, that is, to find the focal point and convergence point of these two civilizations and cultures, which are extremely incompatible, and to find the ideological guidance and cultural direction for the future survival of mankind, which is the frontier issue facing Chinese and even global culture. This is a cutting-edge issue for Chinese and even global cultures. Its depth is evident from its cultural paradox or cultural role paradox.

Questioner: Survival is the instinct of any living creature, so I would like to ask: Our culture (and civilization) has developed to such a point that it has resulted in an undermining effect, because we have over-reached to the extent that we have sacrificed the survival of the environment and other living creatures, so from this perspective, what is the appropriate scale of survival? What kind of survival attitude should we adopt from the perspective of individuals or groups, or from the perspective of human beings, in order to make our future better?

Mr. Dongyue: You raise a good question, but there is one issue I have to clarify. I talk about the degree of existence as the independent variable and the degree of compensation as the dependent variable. It is not our greed that causes our degree of existence to decrease, but it is the decrease in our degree of existence that causes our greed to get worse. The depth of this relationship is in the determining element, the way it is determined, and you have to read and understand my book *A Unified Theory of Evolution*. But the issue you discuss is indeed a major one, that is, if mankind is still to seek its future existence, its way of expanding and mobilizing human greed in the present, with the high speed of development and the pursuit of progress is by no means the way out. It therefore calls for a new cultural cognition of mankind in general, a cultural cognition that itself calls for the suppression of the incremental compensation of mankind. We won't go into this topic here, but if you're interested, you can read my book *The Decline of Humankind*, but the book is not available in bookstore now.

Questioner: Mr. Dongyue, since you talked about the construction of the third crop of human civilization, I was thinking, isn't the first crop the construction of human civilization in the pivot age? Then what is the second crop? Or are you saying that the East is a crop and the West is another crop and the third crop is the integration of the East and the West? Just this question, thank you.

Mr. Dongyue: First of all, let's understand what is the pivot age, a concept proposed by Western scholars. It means that around 600 B.C., a group of heavyweight thinkers emerged from all over the world and all ethnic groups at the same time. For example, Laozi and Confucius in China; Siddhartha Gautama in India; Thales to Socrates and Plato in ancient Greece; the Jews emerged as the original creators of the *Old Testament*, some say Isaiah; and so on. In short, we will find that around the 6th century B.C., a group of great thinkers emerged all over the world at the same time, which is called the pivot age by Western scholars. What it actually expresses is that the evolution of human species and the occurrence of human civilization is a natural process, and at the same point of this natural process, because human beings are the same species, they reach a certain unified level of intelligence development. When I say that mankind has only had two civilizations, I mean that the first one is called agricultural civilization and the second one is called industrial and commercial civilization, and we have actually experienced only these two civilizations so far.

Today there are many claims, such as information civilization, life science civilization, space civilization and so on, but in fact, at least today I can't tell it is not the end of the commercial and industrial civilization to show the form. Therefore, in a broad sense, we can still consider it as the late stage of industrial and commercial civilization, in the sense that mankind has experienced only two civilizations in the past. (However) this second crop of civilization, the industrial and commercial civilization, has so far gone over the cliff to the end of the road. Therefore, when I say that a third crop of new cultures and civilizations is coming, this is what I mean by that. So what is the extent of its approach? What is the critical pattern we are facing? You won't know how imminent it is until you hear the whole 12-day course.

Questioner: Teacher, you mentioned today that there is a huge cultural gap between China and the West, and that there seems to be no way to integrate them, so I was wondering if there is any culture that can guide our Chinese companies or products when they fight in the international battlefield in the future. Or how do you think Chinese companies or cultures have a chance to make an impact in the international arena? Thank you, sir.

Mr. Dongyue: It seems that you did not attend the opening ceremony yesterday. I said yesterday afternoon that what I discussed was useless, because the deeper discussion of philosophy or the system of thought is all about the fundamental issues, that is, the question of *Dao* that I talked about at the beginning of today's class. The so-called *Dao* is not what you can dominate, but what dominates you, which is the basic state of my course. If I'm bold to give you an answer, isn't it to teach fish to swim, because I study the ultimate issues, and you are the expert in business management, isn't it ridiculous if I tell you how to manage the business? But I would like to make a short explanation based on your question. I said that there is a poor cultural compatibility between East and West, which is a historical phenomenological description. I compared the process of compatibility between the two different cultures before and after the introduction of Indian Buddhism into China and the past 170 years since the Opium War, and the differences are too great. It shows the difficulty of the cultural transformation that occurred in the modern era for the Chinese, and I have to say that today this integration of Eastern and Western cultures is still extremely poorly done. It is difficult because you have to have both a deep understanding of traditional Chinese culture and a deep understanding of the Western cultural underpinnings. However, in recent times, a deviation has occurred in the Chinese study of the West, that is, we are eager to seek our liberation through the promotion of the Western academic application level, that is, the science and technology level. This is why we have smashed our national education on the one hand, and learned only the superficial things of Western culture on the other, that is, what can be applied, which is why I said in the previous lesson that the cultural structure of Chinese people today is a situation where "our national culture lost mostly its value while Western culture learned only superficially". This is the basic cultural structure of the Chinese people today, which is of course a very bad situation. Then it is obviously a deep and arduous task for the Chinese to find the compatibility between Eastern and Western cultures. We have to find not only the deep reference part of Eastern culture, but also the possible extension channel of Western culture in the future, and then to build a new cultural system, or new civilization survival system, on the convergence of these two or even more other national cultures, which is of course an extremely difficult task. Because of the recent emptying of national studies and the superficial things of Western studies, the real underlying cultural integration in a broad and deep direction has just begun in China. We can only hope that more will be built in these areas in the future.

Let us take one last question to end this afternoon.

Questioner: Hello, Mr. Dongyue. I have a specific question about the morning lecture. When you talked about the social organization system, you said that the human nature of Chinese civilization is good because it continues the cultural heritage from the clan era. I would like to clarify with you that the reason why Western culture advocates human nature (originally) evil is because their civilization was interrupted, so that the structure of survival changed later? For example, when the Greek civilization was formed, such a traditional concept of human nature (originally) evil emerged. Thank you.

Mr. Dongyue: That's not my explanation. My explanation is: the process of civilization development is the process of continuous corruption and degradation of human nature. Therefore, the more primitive human beings were, the better human nature must be; the more civilization develops, the worse human nature must be. Since Chinese culture is rooted in the lowest level of human primitive civilization, it explored the issue of human goodness. Conversely, because of the excessive exchange in the Mediterranean Rim, they developed progressivism, so they develop at a higher rate, and so they abandon and lose their primitive culture at the grassroots level.

Therefore, by the time they were able to discuss the issue rationally, their local civilization had already entered the stage of human evil. Therefore, my answer to the question of "human nature is good and evil" is not a question without an answer, it is not a question like "whether there is a chicken or an egg first", but a very definite answer: the more primitive human beings are, the better human nature is; the more civilized they are, the more evil human nature is. The more civilized we are, the worse human nature becomes. What is the meaning of this topic? We will continue to discuss it in later lectures.

That concludes our session for today.

2

Recollection of Laozi's Ideology

Preamble

Today we will talk about Laozi, and the title of the lecture is Recollection of Laozi's ideology. I will start with a basic description on this course.

Laozi is the patriarch of Chinese thought and culture. What is the meaning of this statement? The hundred schools of thought of the pre-Qin era in China actually included not only literati, scholars, and thinkers, but also politicians, military men, diplomats (also called eloquent persuaders at that time), and so on.

In terms of chronological order, the first Man of the Hundred Schools of Thought is most likely Guan Zhong, the chancellor of Duke Huan of state Qi, the first of the Five Hegemons of the Spring and Autumn Period. The reason why we say Laozi is the patriarch of Chinese thought and culture is that, as a literati thinker, Laozi is indeed the first Man of the hundred schools of thought of pre-Qin era in China.

The Book of Laozi is one of the most profound and difficult books to read in the ancient Chinese classics. Let me explain this statement: Laozi's ideology is so profound that, compared to all subsequent Chinese literary scholars, he has reached a height that none of later generations has ever reached.

As I said repeatedly in my earlier lectures, that Eastern and Western cultures are always opposite. They are often opposite not only in content and form, but even the ways they develop and operate are quite different. Western culture goes from simple to complex, from low to high, through theological stages, philosophical stages, and scientific stages. Chinese culture, however, runs in the opposite way: it comes down from the high to the low.

Let me give you an example. The entire foundations of Chinese national thought all occurred in the pre-Qin era, that is, before the first Emperor Yingzheng of Qin Dynasty unified China. Since that time there has been almost no more significant development of Chinese thought and culture, except for one thing, that is, the introduction of Buddhism from India into China in the middle of the Eastern Han Dynasty. Even if we go back to the pre-Qin era, the highest point of thought is still expressed in the first patriarch of pre-Qin thought, Laozi. So, even China's cultural development is the opposite of the West's, not from the lower to the higher level, but from the higher to the lower level.

Laozi's book, *Daodejing*, is not the original book named *Lao Zi*. In the early times before Qin Dynasty, the books of each reverend thinkers were labeled with their surname followed by the character Zi (which means a reverend thinker). For example, Meng Ke's book was titled *Meng Zi*, Zhuang Zhou's book was titled *Zhuang Zi*, and Han Feizi's book was titled *Han Zi*. It was due to one of the eight great writers of the Tang and Song dynasties, Han Yu, who was called Han Zi, so the name of Han Feizi's book was changed from *Han Zi* to *Han Feizi* after the Tang and Song dynasties. Then, the original title of Laozi's book is *Lao Zi*. In the *Records of the Grand Historian* there is the word, "Book of *Lao Zi* in two parts: the upper and the lower".

The title of the book *Daodejing* is said to be labeled to the book by a famous scholar of Laozi, called He Shang Gong, in the early years of the Western Han Dynasty. And we should note that Laozi's book *Daodejing* is never about human morality in the general sense, because his word *Dao-De* has deeper meanings.

Laozi is the only philosopher in the history of Chinese thought, and there are some deep characteristics of narrow philosophy latent in Laozi's thought. Moreover, from a certain aspect or angle, the height of Laozi's thought is no less than that of any great philosophers in the history of Western philosophy. Therefore, we say: Laozi's vision is unique and far-reaching.

Since ancient times, there have been many commentaries on the doctrine of Laozi, accumulating over 2,000 years, the amount could be numerous. However, there are many divergent interpretations and misunderstandings on Laozi's thought. By the time of the two Han dynasties, Laozi's doctrine, as a superb imaginary ideology, had sunk to the practical ideas of Huang-Lao's study. Let me explain what is meant by the study of Huang-Lao: the so-called Huang refers to the Emperor, Lao refers to Laozi; the study of Huang-Lao is to deflect Laozi's imaginary ideology of philosophy. This is of course a serious devaluation of Laozi's lofty thinking.

And, as what is the meaning of *Dao* in the book *Lao Zi,* late generation is not at all clear. Tea has the way of preparing tea, wine has the way of preparing wine, literature has the way of sublimating literature, martial art has the way of training martial art, even dinner has its way of enjoying taste of dishes. But what is the meaning of *Dao* that Laozi said? rarely people can speak clearly.

Let me make it clear what are we talking about today? Today we are going to talk about the original intention and the main line of Laozi's ideology. The so-called original intention is the original intention of fundamentalism, that is, what Laozi wanted to do back then; the so-called main line is the 5,000 words of Laozi's book, what its basic thought lineage and thought orientation is. If you can understand this lesson, then at least you will be able to know what Laozi is talking about when you read Laozi's book in the future; if you can't understand this lesson, then you will have some kind of gain and feeling every time you read Laozi's book, but you won't understand what Laozi really wants to say after all.

There was a famous scholar and friend of Lin Zexu in the late Qing Dynasty, named Wei Yuan. He once had a comment on the book of *Lao Zi,* he said, "Laozi *Dao,* the Way of the Ages; the book *Lao Zi,* the Book of the Ages." Note that the word Ages, in the Chinese cultural tradition, refers only to the time when Pan Gu separated the heaven and the earth; in Western paleogeology, it specifically refers to the period when the primitive earth and primitive paleontology were born, called *Tai Gu Zhou*. As we know, Laodan, or Laozi, as he is commonly known, lived in the late years of the Spring and Autumn Period, and he was the teacher of Confucius. Confucius born in 551 B.C. And according to Hu Shi, Laozi would have been about 20 years older than Confucius. In other words, Laozi should be born roughly in 570 B.C. How could Wei Yuan have used such a word *Tai Gu* (Ages)? This is obviously a question.

During the years of the Republic of China, there is a famous scholar Lü Simian, he said in his famous book *Pre-Qin Scholarship*: "The book *Lao Zi* contains very ancient meaning, and the whole book talks about women's power superior to men's power, these are sufficient to sign its early era." What does this passage of Lü Si Mian mean? He said that if you look back at Laozi's text today, you will find that the book of *Lao Zi* is "very ancient in its diction and meaning", that is, the text he used is much older than the Spring and Autumn period, and the whole book means that women's power is superior to men's power. It is obvious that he indicates the book belongs to the era of primitive matriarchal society. Therefore, Lü Simian says that these two points are sufficient to show that the book *Lao Zi* was written at an earlier time.

Let's look at the book of *Lao Zi* below. In order to better explain this, I must first mention something else.

In 1973, Chinese archaeology in the Mawangdui Han tomb, Changsha, Hunan, unearthed two sets of silk books of *Lao Zi*. The so-called silk books was written on nice textile silk, and the book *Lao Zi*, was divided into book A and book B. The unearthing of the silk books *Lao Zi* (hereinafter referred to as silk books) made the academic circle realized that *Daodejing* we now have is not the original book of *Lao Zi*.

It has long been known to scholars that the book *Lao Zi* is actually a composite combined with commentaries of four later literati. These are the commentaries of Heshang Gong in the early Western Han Dynasty, Yan Zun in the early Eastern Han Dynasty, Wang Bi, a famous scholar in the Cao Wei region in the era of Three Kingdoms, and a historian named Fu Yi in the early Tang Dynasty. The so-called *Daodejing* is a composite of these four major commentaries, so scholars call it the popular version. In other words, it is clear to the scholarly community that it is not the original text written by Laozi.

After the unearthing of Laozi's silk books, people studied and found that there are many textual details of differences between the silk books and *Daodejing*, and the silk books were written in an era far earlier than *Daodejing*. For example, in the silk book B, the first sentence of *Daodejing*, "*Dao* can be *Dao*, not ordinary *Dao*; name can be name, not ordinary name", was expressed as "*Dao* can be *Dao*, not constant *Dao;* name can be name, not constant name". The fact that the word Heng (constant) can be used means that this book appeared in the early years of the Western Han Dynasty before Emperor Xiaowen Liu Heng. Because the ancient Chinese custom keeps the name of the emperor sacred, the word used in the emperor's name could not be used again by the people of the time. In the same way, in silk book A the word Bang was constantly replaced by the word Guo (state) in *Daodejing,* it is clear that the silk book does not avoid the word Bang, which was used by Liu Bang, the first Emperor of Han Dynasty, indicating that the silk book A should have appeared the time of pre-Qin era.

Although we now can not prove that the silk books is the original *Lao Zi,* but at least we can say that the silk books of Laozi is a textual version closer to the Laozi era than *Daodejing.* In comparison, we find that the *Lao Zi* text used words and phrases extremely ancient, and the meaning is more profound.

We will do a brief comparison of the texts below.

In the popular version of *Daodejing, Chapter 62,* there is a passage: "Establish the King, son of Heaven and set up the court three councilors." Pay attention to the meaning of this sentence. In primitive clan societies, or before civilization, there were no privileges, no political institutions, no violent control, and no government among human blood social groups. Then, with the development of human civilization, social tensions increased, so people had to establish privileged, powerful control institutions, such as the establishment of a king, the king manages the society with the help of the three councilors and nine ministers, this is called "establish the King, son of Heaven, and set up the court three councilors".

However, in Laozi's silk books, this passage is expressed as "Establish the King, son of Heaven, and set up three villagers". Let's look at the character Xiang in the oracle bone scripts. This is the origin of traditional Chinese character "鄉". What is the meaning of the word *Xiang*? First of all, look at this picture, ( )in the middle of which is an ancient food vessel, with food piled up on it, and two people sitting on either side. The meaning of this word is: people who are related by blood can sit together to eat, called Xiang. As I said earlier, the original human clan society was a blood kin society, when the members of the society were structured by clans and blood relatives, and those who could sit together to eat must be blood relatives. For example, in the real rural regions of China, each village is a blood group, and people from the same village are not allowed to intermarry, and when a person goes out of town and meets his fellow villagers, he is called *Xiang Dang* (folks of same village), the word *Xiang* is used in this sense.

However, this character is also the origin of another Chinese character "卿". (甲骨文 金文 小篆 楷体)What is the meaning of *Qing*? It means guest and visitor. Why did this character change from "鄉" (villager) to "卿" (guest/visitor)? It is because human society developed from a blood clan society to clan alliance of tribal forms, and the tribes were superimposed on top of each other as tribal alliance, and the tribal alliances were further superimposed to be the prototype of a state. For example, I talked previously about the clan-tribe confederation of the Shang Dynasty, and only after that was the prototype of the feudal state in the Zhou Dynasty. In other words, the development of society transcends blood gradually. So in the era of clan alliances or tribal alliances, the person who comes to you and sits with you for dinner is probably not related to you by blood, but as a guest from afar. Therefore, the second character "卿" is derived from this character, which expresses the corresponding changes in the form and meaning of the character as human society develops.

It is worth noting that Laozi did not even use the phrase "establish the king, son of Heaven, and set up the three *Qing* (ministers)" in this place, and *Daodejing* has been changed to "set up the three *Gong* (councilors)", while the silk books actually still use the most original "set up the three villagers". Bear in mind that Laozi was the head officer of history library in Zhou Dynasty, that is, the advisory of all knowledge to the royal family, the highest representative of national culture, he could not have not known the word *Qing*. Therefore, we have reason to suspect that the word *Qing* might not even have appeared at the time when the book *Lao Zi* was written.

Let's look further down. In the sixth chapter of *Daodejing*, Laozi says, "The door of the mysterious mare is called the root of heaven." First of all, what do we understand by "the root of heaven"? Laozi called *Dao* as "the root of heaven", because Laozi believed that it was *Dao* that gives birth to all things including the heaven and earth. But what did he use to describe his most cherished *Dao*? He used the word *Xuan Pin*.

Let's take a look at the oracle bone scripts of the character *Xuan Pin*. In the oracle bone scripts, the character "玄" *(Xuan)* is a drawing of an umbilical cord. (甲骨文 金文 小篆 隶书 楷体)*Xuan* has two meanings in Chinese: first, it means black, darkness, such as wearing black clothes in ancient times, it is called wearing *Xuan*-colored clothes; second, it means far, far away. So, why drawing an umbilical cord is to represent these two meanings? It is because a pregnant woman has just given birth to her child, and the placenta connected to the umbilical cord is still in the womb, and the place where the umbilical cord connects is a dark and distant place, so the word *Xuan* has a corresponding meaning.

Next, look at the character "牝". (甲骨文 小篆 楷体)The character "牝" is a pair of horns, representing a cow, and the draw a cow tail, and draw a mark on it, this is the word *Pin*, means a mare. "牝" is a common Chinese character, and its counterpart is *Du*, (甲骨文 金文 小篆 楷体) which also draws a pair of horns, but with a male genitalia on the right. The word *Du* refers only to a bull in far ancient times, and later on it refers to all male animals; then the word *Pin* (mare) refers to a cow in ancient times only, and later on it refers to all female animals. What is the meaning of *Pin* (mare)? If you open the tail of the cow, you can see the female genitalia, the black and red genitalia, so it is called *Xuan Pin*. "The door of the mysterious mare" is a metaphor to describe *Dao* as "the root of heaven", it gives birth to all things including the heaven and earth, just like the reproductive organ of a cow continuously gives birth to calves.

This expression of Laozi obviously could not have occurred at the end of the Spring and Autumn Period, when Confucius had already proposed the great caution between men and women, which was later expressed by Mencius as "men and women are not to be close to each other". It could only have occurred in the era of primitive fertility worship. By the end of the Spring and Autumn Period, such a straightforward and rough word was obviously no longer acceptable in the grand scheme of things. We can thus see how far antient Laozi's text could be.

In chapter 28 of *Daodejing*, Laozi says, "Know the male and stay with the female", which means that one should know the character of the male and keep the character of the female. He also says in chapter 52, "The world has a beginning, that is the mother of the world". Here beginning refers *Dao*, what he uses to describe *Dao*? Once again, he uses the word Mother, yes, he uses the word Mother to describe the beginning.

From these two passages, we can see that Laozi gives a very high commendation to women, reflecting the idea of the higher social status of women in the primitive matriarchal communities. This shows that the text of *Lao Zi* is very ancient, it probably did not come from the late Spring and Autumn period.

Let me make a note that our lecture today is still based primarily on the text of *Daodejing*. Although there are many detailed differences between the silk books and *Daodejing*, the good thing is that *Daodejing* did not completely drown out the main idea of Laozi's thought. In order not to over-academicize this class, we use *Daodejing*, which you can read every day, as the text for the lecture, and it does not prevent us from understanding the original intention and main line of Laozi's thought.

Laozi says in his book, "Those who understand me are few, those who follow my code are rare, and that is why the sage wears coarse linen and holds his jade next to his skin." Laozi clearly knew that it was very difficult for his book to be read and understood by the world, and that those who could read and understand his book were very scares; those who could act according to his principles were rare and noble. It was clear that Laozi understood at that time that it was not easy to read his thoughts.

Laozi, the Man

In the following, we will talk a little about Laozi, the man.

Who is Laozi? There are scarcely a few words about Laozi in various ancient books like *Chronicle of Zuo, Protocol of Rite, Book of Han, Wen Zi, Zhuang Zi, Biography of Lü, Confucius Family Talks*, etc.

In these ancient books, there are usually only a few sentences or a few words about Laozi. For example, where did Laozi die and how did he die, only 11 words were found in *Zhuang Zi.*

The most important and detailed account of Laozi's situation is found in Sima Qian's *Records of the Grand Historian · Biographies of Lao Zhuang Shen Han*, even which is only about 700 words found. In contrast, Sima Qian's biography of Confucius even reached more than 10,000 words. This leads to who Laozi really is, has been entangled by historians, and can not be settled clearly.

Till the Republican era, the most famous Chinese scholars of that time, like Liang Qichao, Qian Mu, Feng Youlan, etc., all of them believed that Laozi was a man of the mid-Warring States era, which was much later than Confucius, for the reason that Sima Qian himself did not even figure out who Laozi was.

Sima Qian said in *The Records of the Grand Historian* that Laozi was a native of Lixiang Qurenli in the County of Chuku, with the surname Li, the name Ear, and the style word Dan. He was the historian of the Zhou royal family.

But Sima Qian couldn't tell who Laozi was, so he actually used word like "or said", "or said", to give examples. He said that Laozi could be the Dān, that is why we call Laozi as Laodān today. But he also said that Laozi could also be another person, also named Dān, who also was a historian of the Zhou royal family, but in the middle of the Warring States period. Then he also said that Laozi's seventh grandson "served the Emperor Xiaowen of the Han Dynasty", that is, Laozi's seventh grandson worked as an official for the Emperor Liu Heng of the Han Dynasty. Ancient people married very early, generally people of one generation do not exceed 20 years to the next generation, even we assume one generation 30 years, 7 generations backward can only be about 200 years. If we push backward 200 years from Emperor Wendi, Liu Heng, of Han Dynasty, then Laozi is indeed a man of mid-Warring States era, a hundred years or more later than Confucius.

Moreover, in *Daodejing*, the popular version of Laozi's book, we see a large number of words from the Warring States and even after the two Han dynasties. As I mentioned earlier, Chinese words do change with the times, and the meanings and forms of characters also undergo certain changes. The scholars who study *Daodejing* find a lot of traces of words that are much later than the Spring and Autumn period, for example, words such as "benevolence against righteousness" and other words from the mid-Warring States era, were the subject of debate between Confucianism and *Daoism*, but all appeared in *Daodejing*. This is certainly one of the reasons that later people doubt what era Laozi was from. In fact, it is obviously because that *Daodejing* is a composite of all commentaries by later generations.

The ancients did not have the printing facility, and when a book was written, it had no way to circulate. It was transmitted by each person copying it by hand, and in the process of transcribing it one by one, it was inevitable that mistakes in writing and errors occurred, and not to mention that some people added their own interpretations to it. Therefore, the presence of later words in the text of Laozi's book does not prove that the book was not written in the distant past.

However, it will lead to a lot of trouble and misunderstanding, and even lead to Sima Qian being confused about what is going on. Therefore, Sima Qian had to say, "Laozi is a hermit." A hermit is one who lives in seclusion. In other words, since Laozi was a hermit, so Sima Qian could not figure out who Laozi was.

Now let us sort out about the status of Laozi. We will talk about it in four parts: first, about his place of origin; second, about his honorific name; third, about his historical deeds; and fourth, about his disciples.

We talk about Laozi's life, on the one hand, is to let you have an understanding of Laozi, the man, so as to facilitate a better understanding of Laozi's thought; on the other hand, is to give you a demonstration of the traditional Chinese culture, the way of how to study the evidence.

Let's first look at Laozi's place of origin.

Sima Qian said that Laozi was a native of county Ku in the state of Chu, which is a very doubtful, because Ban Gu says in his *Book of Han ·Geography*, county Ku did not belong to the state of Chu. In the Spring and Autumn period, before the State of Chen was annexed by the State of Chu, that is, in the time of Laozi, it (county Ku) should belong to the State of Chen. Gu Zuyu, a famous scholar in the Qing Dynasty, recorded in his book *Notes of Chronicle and Territory* that county Ku was not a county in the Spring and Autumn Period, and till the Han Dynasty that the place Ku was set up as a county. At that time, it was not called Ku but Xiang. In *Book of Han II*, it was recorded: "... Ku of state Chen, was called Xiang in the Spring and Autumn Period". This clearly shows that Laozi was not from the state of Chu.

Moreover, Chu was a state of southern barbarians. As I said in my previous lecture, a place with too good natural geography cannot be the birthplace of agricultural civilization, so the agricultural civilization of Chu and its overall cultural development was relatively late, until the middle of the Warring States era, it was regarded as a southern barbarian by the civilized countries of the Central Plains, and named it the state of thorns. The sixth ruler of Chu, Xiong Qu, was recorded in *Records of the Grand Historian ·Rulers of Chu*: "Xiong Qu said: 'I am a barbarian, won't be posthumous titled of central states.'" The king of Chu himself admitted that he was a barbarian in the south and would not get the posthumous name of the civilized people of the central states. The word posthumous refers to the honorific title added to an ancient king or nobleman after his death. Here it shows that the king of Chu admitted that he was a southern barbarian and did not accept or admire the civilization of the central plain states.

As late as the middle of the Warring States period, Mencius still said in his book *Teng Wen Gong*, "Nowadays, the southern barbarians of bird-speaking people are not the way of the previous kings of central plains." In the opinion of Mencius in the middle of the Warring States period, state of Chu was still a land of southern barbarians. The so-called "bird-speaking people" means the people there were uncivilized and speak like birds, which civilized people in the central plain states could understand. However, Laozi was the highest representative of Chinese culture at that time, as per the common sense, he could not have grown up in a culturally barbaric land, because the educational resources at that time were by no means as widespread as they are today. Therefore, it is suspicious to say that Laozi was a native of Chu.

It is said in the *Book of Han II* that the place of Ku was part of Chen, which makes us think that Laozi could have been from the state of Chen. What kind of country, or what kind of feudal state was Chen? Chen was the feudal state of Shun, the descendant of Yao, Shun and Yu, and therefore, Chen had a profound literary style. It is said that King Wu, Jifa, of Zhou Dynasty, married his eldest daughter Daji, to Guiman, the Duke of Chen, and Daji was fond of literature, witchcraft, history, since she was young, and her arrival further contributed to Chen becoming a major town of Zhou culture.

In this sense, there seems to be a basis for saying that Laozi might be from the state of Chen. But the book of *Zhuang Zi* repeatedly says that Laozi lived in the place of Pei, and Pei does not belong to Chu or Chen. Yao Nai, a famous scholar in the Qing dynasty, said in his book *Overview of Laozi*: "*Zhuang Zi* contains the saying that Confucius, Yang Zi Zhu went to south of Pei to visit Laozi, and the surname of Lao is from state of Song, and the place Pei is the land of Song." What does it mean? It says that Laozi often lived in Pei, and it also says that the surname Lao comes from Song, and the place Pei belongs to the state of Song.

In this way, Laozi looks like a native of Song. It is important to know that Song was a feudal state of the noble people of Yin Shang, and *Book of Zhou* records that "only the Yin ancestors, they have books of various kinds", which means that in East Asia at that time, only in the Central Plains of Yin Shang (Dynasties), there were writing and books, while all other tribes and races did not have writing yet. Therefore, it makes sense to say that Laozi was born in Song.

There is another incident worth mentioning. After the destruction of the Shang Dynasty by King Wu, Jifa, of Zhou Dynasty, he moved a significant portion of the remnants of the Yin Shang nobility to Guanzhong, the area around the Western Zhou capital of Fenghao, so that these cultured Yin Shang nobles could serve the newly established Zhou royal family. We can see a record of this in the archaeological excavation of the bronze Wall Plate. (Its inscription recounts the submission of the Weishi family of Shiqiang to the Zhou during King Wu's conquest of the Shang, and the family's service in the Zhou Dynasty for six generations.) Therefore, it is reasonable to infer that Laozi's ancestors or Laozi's family may also have been Yin Shang immigrants and were moved to Guanzhong, that is, to the Qin area in Shaanxi. This is because we have seen a description of Laozi's funeral in *Zhuang Zi ·Inner Chapter·Master of Health and Life*, where the original quote says: "When Laozi died,

Qinyi went to condole and came out after three crying-howls". He said that when Laozi died, a man from Qin named Yi went to the funeral to condole and came out after only three dry howls. This was the only record of Laozi's death, and it shows that Laozi died in the land of Qin.

This leads us to further suspect that Laozi was likely to be a relic of the Yin Shang Dynasty, because that place is the most cultural, and only that place could have shaped such a cultural personality as Laozi. Besides, Laozi's family moved to Guanzhong in Shaanxi Province in the early Western Zhou Dynasty and served the Zhou royal family ever since, but they could not help but deeply miss the inherent culture of the Yin Shang of the old dynasty. At that time, official positions were hereditary, so Laozi's family worked as historians for generations, and later moved to Luoyi with the Eastern movement of the Western Zhou. Eventually, because of the ancient Chinese custom of returning to one's roots, Laozi left Hangu Pass in his later years and returned westward to Qin, where he died, which is a possible proof of his origin.

Let's look at Laozi's honorific name below.

Laozi's surname is Li, his name is Ear, his style character *Dan*, and there is another legend character, called *Chong-Er*. Please note that Laozi's surname, first name and style character, all are pretty special.

First, we may ask is, why was Laozi not called Lizi? Because in the pre-Qin era, normally the *Zi* was labeled together with his surname. Why was he called Laozi? As per common practice, he should be called Lizi. Even though there are too many people with the surname Li, he was the first ancestor of culture, so if he was called Lizi, the descendants would not repeat it after him. But he was called Laozi, where did his name come from?

The first argument is that Lao is the surname or clan of Laozi. For example, Hu Shih said that Laozi's surname was "Lao and his clan was Li", while most scholars believe that Laozi's surname was "Li and his clan was Lao". Let me explain the surname, we use the surname to include family name and clan name together today, but in ancient times the family name and clan name are two concepts. The word surname means maiden, that is, from a matrilineal lineage, all the offspring in the original blood group has a common emblem called surname. I said earlier, human society from blood society gradually developed to a transcend blood society, so the people of clan society eventually inevitably will disperse. After people scattered, each retain the original surname, but in addition to their surname, they add a differentiation label, called *Shi*, family name, so the family name *Shi* was less than the surname, and later *Shi* was included in the concept of surname. So, Laozi was probably *Shi Li*, clan name Lao. This is the first explanation to the source of the name Laozi.

Secondly, Laozi is a title of respect. Because the Chinese have a custom, call others a little older to show respect for others. For example, if someone is not too old, you call him Lao Wang, and if one is just old, you call him Wang Lao. So, Laozi could probably the respect name for him from later generations. This is the second source of the name Laozi.

Third, nicknames. How should I say it? A sentence quoted from *Taiping Guangji* (*Miscellaneous Records of Peaceful Society*)·*Legends of the Immortals* of Song Dynasty era, saying that Laozi "was born with a white head, so he was called Laozi". It says that when he was born, his head was full of white hair, so he was called Laozi. In the Eastern Jin Dynasty, there was a book called *Book of Mysteries*, which said, "The mother of Li was pregnant for 81 years and under a plum tree she cut her body left side under armpit and gave birth to her child." It says that Laozi's mother was pregnant 81 years with Laozi in her womb, and Laozi was 82 years old when he was born, so he had a full head of white hair, and because the pregnancy was too long to labor from the birth canal, so she had to cut open her left side under armpit and pull him out. This claim is of course absurd. But Lu Deming, a famous scholar of the Ming Dynasty, also contains in his *Classic Interpretation* that Laozi was "born with a white head", saying that he was born with a full head of white hair. It seems that this was a very obvious characteristic of Laozi.

Then look at the name of Laozi. Laozi's name is *Er* (ear), and his style character is *Dan*. The ancients named their children in many different ways, one of which is to look at the physical characteristics of this child. Then Laozi's name and style character are both related to his ear. Laozi's character is *Dan*, what does this *Dan* mean? Xu Shen, the first ancient Chinese character scholar in the Eastern Han Dynasty, said in his book *Shuowen Jiezi* (*Explanation on

Meaning of Characters): "*Dan* is big pinna." What does that mean? It means that his pinnae are very wide. Also, in the early Ming Dynasty, Song Lian said in his book *Features of Famous Scholars*, "*Dan* is pinna without helix", which means that the ears are large but have no helix. You can imagine that if this character *Dan* describes Laozi's ears, then his ears must be oversized, weak and drooping, which proves that Laozi was born with some abnormalities.

By the time of Tang Dynasty, since the Emperor of Li-Tang Dynasty was not entirely Han blood, but more than three-quarters of Emperor Li Shimin's lineage was ethnic Xianbei, so he named Laozi Li Er as his ancestor, in order to prove that he was also a Han nationality. Therefore, the Tang Dynasty honored *Daoism* as its state religion. At that time, there was a Buddhist monk named Fa Lin, who was dissatisfied with Li-Tang Dynasty's respecting *Daoism*, so he spoke against Laozi, saying that his father was "born without ears and one eye blinded" He said that Laozi's father was born without ears and one of his eyes was blind.

In the *Siku Quanshu (General Catalogue of the Four Categories) ·Overheard History*, it is recorded that "the royal historian of Zhou was born with no ears and one eye blind". This royal historian of Zhou refers to Laozi, who is said to have been "born with no ears and one eye blind".

Then based on these records, combined with modern medical knowledge, I can reasonably infer that Laozi suffered from congenital albinism when he was a child. Because it is impossible for us to imagine that Laozi's mother carried him for 81 years and gave birth to him with a head full of white hair. Knowledge of modern medicine tells us that the longest pregnancy cannot be more than 14 months, otherwise is stillbirth, and the normal pregnancy is only 9 months. Then Laozi was "born with a white head", which means he probably had a congenital disease called albinism.

When we walk in the street, we sometimes may see someone with pale skin, all body hair white or white hairs, and even light pigmentation on the iris of the black eye. Patients of such, due to insufficient pigmentation of the iris, the sun ultraviolet rays invade the fundus of the eye in large quantities, damaging the retina, and they are prone to become one eye blind during their teenage years. Therefore, based on these records, it is reasonable to speculate that

Laozi was an albino back then, suffering from congenital albinism and blindness at one eye. Because of his abnormal birth appearance, he might be often ridiculed by other children when he was a child. This made him afraid to meet people as a child, and thus caused a secondary psychological disorder called juvenile claustrophobia, which is the reason why he still behaved as a hermit in his later years, even though he became the first patriarch of Chinese culture.

If this inference holds true, then Laozi's congenital anomaly could also be a series of syndromes. It is important to know that congenital genetic disorders usually do not inherit just one disease, but carry a group of genetic defects in parallel down the line, resulting in some kind of multiple heterozygous syndromes. Therefore, it is difficult for us to imagine Laozi lived a long life. *Records of the Grand Historian* record that "Laozi lived 160 years old, or he is said to have lived about 200 years old, because he cultivated his life by monasticism." That is to say, he lived for 160 or around 200 years, and I think this statement is also very doubtful. Because if Laozi suffered from so many congenital abnormal diseases, it would be very difficult for him to live a long life. What I mean is that the records in the history books are not clear, and we need to do some other examination about Laozi's life.

Let's Look at the Historical Facts about Laozi.

Since Laozi's family had inherited the Zhou dynasty as historians for generations, they later moved with the dynasty, from Haojing in Guanzhong to Luoyi in the Eastern Zhou, and from then on they moved around in the heart of the Central Plains. At the end of the Spring and Autumn Period, as recorded in *Chronicle of Zuo*, in the 22nd year of Duke Zhaogong of state Lu (520 B.C.), when King Jing of the Zhou Dynasty died, the succession to the throne led to internal strife in the royal family and a civil war that lasted for more than a decade, which was known as Wang Zichao Rebellion. It is said that Wang Zichao fled to state of Chu with so large number of classical books that the library and archives under Laozi's control were virtually useless, so Laozi resigned or was dismissed from his post. He became jobless and homeless, and wandered about at the age of 50 (according to Gao Heng's study, Laozi was about 57 years old at that time).

After that, Laozi wandered or shortly lived in states of Chen, Pei, Lu, or even Chu and Song, and in his later years, he went westward through the pass, returning to his roots, and died in the land of Qin, which is the brief history of Laozi.

We will slightly talk about Laozi's disciples.

Laozi had many disciples. People generally know that only Confucius had three thousand disciples and seventy-two sages. In fact, Laozi's disciples are more famous, such as Confucius, Yang Zhu (known as Yangzi), and Wenzi. Who is Wenzi? According to *Records of the Grand Historian,* Fan Li's teacher was called Ji Ran, and this Ji Ran was Wenzi. In other words, Fan Li was the disciple of Laozi's disciple. And then there are Yinxi, Kang Cangzi, Juanzi, Baiju, etc. So there are many disciples of Laozi.

But since Laozi was a hermit, the way he led his disciples is completely different from that Confucius did. He did not allow his disciples to follow him, and they came to him for questions, and they left after they got their answers. There is a historical record saying that Yang Zhu, the most important disciple of Laozi, once insisted to follow him around, but was reprimanded and driven away by Laozi. It can be seen that Laozi, as a hermit, was so completely hidden that even the way he took his disciples was different from the ordinary people.

This is a brief introduction to the life of Laozi.

Laozi's Writings and His Relationship with Confucius

Let's talk about the writings of Laozi.

There are also many doubts about Laozi's writings. In the *Records of the Grand Historians ·Laozi Hanfei Biography,* it was written: "Laozi cultivated *Dao De,* the priority of his learning is to self-imposed anonymity, he lived in Zhou for a long time, and he saw the decline of Zhou Dynasty, so he left ......" and then it said: "when he came to the Pass, the officer in charge Yinxi said ......", that is, after Laozi resigned from his official position, he traveled west to Hangu

Pass, and the chief of Hangu Pass, Yinxi said, "Your reverend will be hidden away, may I ask you to write a book for me." He held Laozi in the Hangu Pass and forced him to write a book. "So Laozi wrote a book of two parts, talking about *Dao* and *De* in about 5,000 words, and then left, no one knew where he ended up." Legend says that Yinxi then took off his official clothes and went away, becoming Laozi's only disciple following him in his later years hidden in the Zhongnan Mountain.

I am also skeptical of this account from the *Records of the Grand Historian*.

First, from the record of Laozi's thought, he already has a relatively systematic view of the universe, society and life, which cannot be a sudden and impromptu random work.

Secondly, the writing materials before the Qin and Han dynasties were mainly *Jan* and *Du, Jan* is the documents written on bamboo strips, while *Du* is the documents written on wooden strips. At that time, there was no paper, and the preparation of writing materials was very troublesome. For example, bamboo *Jan,* man has to cut down the bamboo, then shaved into bamboo strips. Bamboo is wet and curved, easy to deform, so man has to bake it. After that, the bamboo piece is not considered done, but also need to take heavy stone pressure on it, gradually air dry, and then cut it into bamboo strips with grooves at two ends, so as ready for writing on it. Then take the cowhide rope to tie up all the written strips, rolled into a roll, two rolls, three rolls, stacked up. In Laozi's time, Hangu Pass was a barbaric place, the western frontier of the Central Plains civilization, and it seems impossible and unnecessary to have a large number of writing material of *Jan Du* at this frontier.

Third, looking throughout the world more than 2,500 years ago, we hardly see any thoughtful masterpieces, except for certain narrative texts, except for Laozi, because his family line was historians, and their job was to record history, using pen to record, and that's why Laozi became the only sage we see in ancient times who could record his thoughts in writing.

You know, ancient literati did not write books, they passed on their ideas by teaching disciples. Confucius, for example, had no writings himself, and after his death, his disciples collected his words together, which is the *Analects*. Another example, the Buddha, Shakyamuni, preached for 45 years while he was alive, but he never wrote until after his death, when the bhikkhus who had heard sermons he preached were gathered and assembled many times to form the Sutras. In the history of ancient Greek philosophy, we know that none of the philosophers before Socrates had a clear text. Socrates himself did not write anything, thanks to his good disciple Plato. Plato wrote a great deal, and most of his books are dialogues with Socrates, and this was how Socrates' ideas were passed down to us, so much that when we read Plato's texts today, we can hardly tell whether the ideas expressed in them were those of his teacher Socrates or his own.

This shows that in those ancient times, it was very rare to leave a thoughtful masterpiece by writing. 5000 words or so is a small piece of writing today, but as a thoughtful work, it was enough to be considered a masterpiece back then. It is inconceivable to say that such a valuable thing was made on the spur of the moment in a short period of time by being held in Hangu Pass. In my opinion, it takes effort of a person's whole life, and may even include the continuous effort accumulation of several generations of the whole Laozi family lineage in a span of hundreds or even centuries to form such a highly difficult text. Therefore, regarding the formation process of the book *Lao Zi*, the description in *Records of the Grand Historian* can also be doubted.

The following is a summary of the testimony of Laozi's life and his texts.

First, Laozi may not be Laodan alone, but a general term for Laodan's family line. As I mentioned earlier, ancient officials were hereditary by blood, and Laozi was probably the ideological representative or virtual bearer of more than one person in his historian family line. Since Laodan had taken in or taught several famous disciples, such as Confucius and Yang Zhu, these famous disciples eventually lit him up in history, causing people to mistakenly regard Laodan as Laozi.

Secondly, Laozi's family originated from the relics of the Yin Shang Dynasty, and was moved to the central part of the Western Zhou Dynasty in Qin after the destruction of the Shang Dynasty, and then moved to the eastern capital with the Zhou royal family. In his later years, Laodan resigned from his official position, wandered through many countries, and went westward to Qin and died there, returning to his roots.

Third, the surname and name of the Laozi family line was not clear. The surname Li may be a remnant of his ancestor's work as a ritual official of the previous dynasty. Li Er and Lao Dan were both nicknames or forbidden names of Confucius' teacher, who may, in the early years, have suffered congenital albinism and secondary claustrophobia, so he became a hermit.

Fourthly, the book of *Lao Zi* should be a record of the thoughts of Laozi's historian family, which may not be the handiwork of Laodan alone. Moreover, we cannot exclude the falsification and alteration by many people from the Warring States and even after the Han and Wei dynasties, including Zhou Taishi Dan, but the book's original meaning and ancient meaning were not lost.

Fifth, the extant texts of *Lao Zi,* whether they are authentic texts or unearthed ancient copies, cannot be identified as the original family text or the initial handwritten text of Laodan, but can only be regarded as different transcriptions or annotated texts in various stages of transmission.

This is the rough testimony that we can give about Laozi's person and Laozi's text. It is important to state that the above opinion is based only on unreliable historical documents and occasional unearthed archaeological data, and it is largely indicative of the traditional Chinese academic style of conformity, so it is not conclusive and still needs to be proved or disproved by more conclusive research and excavation in the future.

We will talk slightly about the differences between Confucius and Laozi.

It is conclusively proven that Confucius was a disciple of Laozi. Although many scholars doubt this, it is recorded in many ancient books, including Sima Qian's *Records of the Grand Historian,* Li Daoyuan's *Water Classic Commentary,* and Bian Shao's *Laozi Inscription* of the Eastern Han Dynasty, that Confucius in his life visited Laozi at least three times.

The first time, when Confucius was about 17 years old, he met Laozi and asked him about rituals; the second time, as recorded in *Records of Grand Historians,* when Confucius was 34 years old, he was sent by Duke Zhao of Lu to Luoyi, the first capital of the Eastern Zhou Dynasty, to ask Laozi about *Dao* about rituals; the third time, as recorded in the *Zhuang Zi*, when Confucius was about 50 to 51 years old, he went to the place Pei of state Song to meet Laozi, and asked him about learning. Therefore, it should be confirmed that Confucius was a disciple of Laozi.

However, the cultural character of the two men, Confucius and Laozi, was diametrically opposed. Confucius' cultural character was extremely positive, and the most representative of Confucius' cultural tone was the phrase in the *Analects*, "Knowing that it is impossible and doing it." This is the original phrase of what we usually call "knowing that it cannot be done, but doing it", which means that I will try to do it even though I know it cannot be done. It expresses a cultural attitude of active participation in social transformation. Therefore, later scholars summed up Confucius' doctrine with two words: "entering the world".

Laozi, however, was the opposite, with an extremely negative cultural character. What best represents Laozi's cultural character are the six words that keep appearing in *Daodejing*: "Do nothing but nothing left undone." It means, I do nothing but nothing is left undone. In other words, in layman's terms, it means I did nothing but everything is done. It sounds absurd to us today, but what Laozi means is that *Dao* has given birth to all things including heaven and earth, but no one has ever seen any superfluous action of *Dao*, which is called "doing nothing but nothing left undone". We can see from this sentence that Laozi's cultural character was extremely negative, so negative that he did nothing.

So, later people made a summary of Laozi's cultural tone, which is the opposite of Confucius' "entering the world", called "out of the world", meaning out of the human world, stay marginal from society. This is why Sima Qian added a sentence in *Records of the Grand Historian ·Biography of Laozi and Han Fei*", saying "the way of life in the world is different, so no interaction from each other", referring to the obvious difference in the "way of life in the world" between Confucius and Laozi, even though they were teacher and disciple.

I speak about this point in order to give you a deep understanding of the negative mood of Laozi's text. If you all read *Da-*

odejing and do not experience this rhythm, you will not be able to understand what the point of Laozi's advice to mankind really is.

In the year when Confucius was 34 years old, he made a special trip to Luo Yi to pay homage to Laozi as his teacher. There is an account in the *Records of Grand Historian* that records in detail the conversation between Laozi and Confucius. Of course, how this dialogue was known to Sima Qian is a very troublesome issue. Sima Qian's history books, all of which are in the style of biography with vivid dialogues in them, which can almost be regarded as literary models, so its authenticity of details is obviously very doubtful. But Sima Qian's *Records of the Grand Historian* have been verified by later generations and are often accurate. Therefore, although we dare not say that the words recorded by Sima Qian must be original true, we can at least view it in this way, that is, the meaning of the words in Sima Qian's *Records of the Grand Historian* and that spiritual orientation behind the language will not be too different in general.

Let's look at the dialogue that Sima Qian recorded when Confucius met Laozi at the age of 34. Laozi said, "The man you speak of, has died and even his bones are decayed." Let's make it clear here that what Laozi said to Confucius were all words of reprimand and criticism, with cold air coming out of his nose. The meaning of his words is that the man you Confucius always talk about, is dead so long that his bones have rotted away, so why do you mention him? The person here referred to is Duke of Zhou, Jidan of Zhou Dynasty. We all hear a lot that Confucius said he dreamed of the Duke of Zhou, Jidan quite several times. Who was the Duke of Zhou? He was the brother of King Wu, Jifa of Zhou and the first prime minister of the Western Zhou Dynasty. Since King Wu died soon after he conquered Shang, his son succeeded to the throne, which is the famous King Cheng, Jiyong of Zhou Dynasty. As King Cheng was young, his first minister, Duke of Zhou, Jidan, presided over the state, and established the entire ritual rule, the political system of the Zhou Dynasty.

Duke of Zhou, Jidan laid down the ritual rule of the Zhou Dynasty, which is known as "making ritual and music". What is ritual? You should not understand ritual as etiquette, courtesy. The meaning of the word ritual in the Zhou dynasty refers to the sum of national political laws and regulations to civil manners and rituals. To make rituals, that is, to establish the political authority of feudal patriarchy of the Zhou Dynasty. Making music, you should not understand music as general music. By music, Confucius and Duke of Zhou meant the playing of music and music at large rituals. The so-called large-scale rituals are actually the declaration of the state's ideology. Just like today's music accompaniment for the two sessions (NPC and CPPCC), you cannot just listen to the music, you have to listen to what the theme of report at the two sessions talking about, this is called "making rituals and music". Because Confucius had great respect for the feudal Zhou ritual created by Duke of Zhou Jidan in his early years, so he often "dreamed of Duke Zhou, Jidan".

The whole doctrine of Confucius is in fact a theorization of the political operation of Duke of Zhou Jidan's "making rites and music", which is the essence of Confucius' doctrine. Therefore, Confucius kept referring to Duke of Zhou, Jidan. So, Laozi criticized him, saying that this man was dead so long that his bones were rotten, why you keep mentioning him all the time? Then Laozi reprimanded Confucius," I heard that a good merchant hides his money deeply as if he is empty, and a gentleman flourish in virtue and looks like a fool." Laozi said that a good merchant hides his wealth as if he is poor, and he never shows he is rich; a gentleman, even if he has great virtue, must show humble, or even foolish, in appearance. So, what did Laozi mean by this passage? He is obviously criticizing Confucius for being overly ostentatious and preaching around, and expressing himself overly and harshly. Then Laozi goes on to say, "remove the pride and much desire on yourself, the state of lust and the lustful ambition, are all unhelpful to you." That is to say, get rid of the pride and lust in you, and rub off your arrogance and grand ambition as well, as these won't do anything good to you. As you can see, Laozi's words to Confucius were all straightforward and critical.

Let's look at what Confucius said about Laozi below.

According to *Records of the Grand Historian*, "Confucius said to his disciples when he left Luo Yi ......", that is to say, Confucius left Luo Yi and returned to Lu and said to his disciples, "Birds, I know they can fly; fish, I know they can swim; beasts, I know that they can run". These three sentences no need to explain. He went on to say, "Those who run can be lured into trap." The meaning of the character *Wang* (trapping net) is to deceive. That is to say, for animals, man can dig a trap and over it with straw mat, then surface it with soil and dry leaves, thus animals can be lured into the trap. He also said, "for swimming fish can be caught with bait of fishing line", that is, for fish swimming in the water, you put down a fishing line with a hook bait underneath, and you can catch the fish up; he said next, "the flyer can be shot with lined-arrow", the lined-arrow is an ancient arrows specifically used to shoot birds, because if you shoot birds with ordinary arrows, the injured bird may fluttered desperately into the river reeds, then you can not find the prey, so the ancients designed a special lined-arrow, tied a long string behind this arrow, so when the injured bird fall on the ground you can pull the string to get the bird, this is lined-arrow. He then said, "As for the dragon, I don't know how it rides the wind and clouds and goes up to the sky". The meaning of this passage is, I never see a dragon, and I do not know what a dragon looks like. He finally says, "I see Laozi today, and he is like a dragon!" this is the famous saying of "like the Dragon". He said he saw Laozi that day, and he finally knew what a dragon looks like, which shows how highly Confucius thought of Laozi.

I cite this paragraph to illustrate two points. Firstly, Laozi did not give Confucius, his disciple, any good comments, but only criticism. But Confucius, as a student, respected Laozi as his teacher highly and regarded him as a dragon. Confucius said a famous sentence: "Morning hearing *Dao*, evening death is acceptable." This statement implies a different meaning, that is, Confucius may not in his life have understood what Laozi's *Dao* actually is talking about. We can thus see the profundity of Laozi's ideology.

We have talked about Laozi's life, Laozi's text, and the different cultural character between Laozi and Confucius, all of which are just a background to clarify later the main idea of Laozi's ideology.

Laozi's Doctrine of *Dao*

We enter the Laozi text below.

The book of *Lao Zi,* contains the upper and lower chapters. In the handed-down version of *Daodejing*, the upper part is the *chapter of Dao*, and the lower part is the *chapter of De*. So, what exactly is the *chapter of Dao* about?

Let me begin with a synopsis: *Dao* focuses on the cosmic and natural view, and *De* focuses on the social and life view. What is the meaning of this statement? First of all, we should know that all the Chinese scholars of the pre-Qin dynasty were concerned with the sociological aspects of human nature, and scarcely any of them were concerned with the natural aspects. This is in sharp contrast to the ancient Greek philosophy, where all the philosophers, except Socrates, were concerned with the concept of nature and cosmology. Thales, the first philosopher of ancient Greece, left a famous allusion of "falling into a well while watching the sky", which was summarized by later generations as "looking up at the stars". But strangely enough, all the famous Chinese pre-Qin scholars were concerned with the sociology of human nature, so much so that the natural and cosmological views were almost obsolete.

What is the reason? Agricultural civilization led to a population boom, which led to extra tension in human relations and resource relations, which caused all Chinese scholars to be concerned with the sociological issues of human ethics. But there is a loophole here, when they discussed the social issues of human ethics, that is, the humane issues, they lacked a deep foundation or premise of grounds. For example, Confucius preached "the way of a gentleman", preaching that one should be this way or that way, but he never mentioned where these *shoulds* were derived from. Laozi's thought is profound, he wants to ask the ultimate cause of this world. Therefore, when reading Laozi's book, you should pay special attention to two sets of words, one is called the *way of heaven*, and the other is called the *way of man*. The word human way that we talk about today in humanitarianism comes from Laozi's *way of man*. The so-called *way of heaven* is the view of the universe, the view of nature, the general rules and laws of the operation of heaven and earth. Therefore, the way of man is the way of human civilization, the way of human society, and the way of human behavior. According to Laozi, if you only talk about the way of man, then where is the basis and foundation of the way of man? Obviously, you must first investigate the laws of operation of the way of Heaven, which has given birth to all things including heaven and earth and even human beings themselves, before you are qualified to discuss how the way of man should operate. We regard this line of thought as the inquiry for the ultimate, and the inquiry for the ultimate is one of the three major features of ancient Greek philosophy in the narrow sense. This is why I said earlier that "Laozi is the only philosopher in the history of Chinese thought".

In order to understand Laozi's *Daoism*, we must first understand the character *Dao* in the oracle bone scripts.(甲骨文 金文 小篆 道 楷体) The character *Dao* in the oracle bone script starts with a crossroad, and this character is "行" *Xing* (walk). (甲文 金文 小篆 行 楷体)In the middle of the character "行", there is either a footprint painted on it, or there is a head and face painted on it. Regarding the image of the latter, there are many debates in the academic circle, and some of the opinions are more concentrated, they think that this character actually paints the image of a child in the process of delivery, with the head already coming out of the birth canal. This statement is also valid if applied to the interpretation of the "gate of the *Xuan Pin*" in Laozi's book. Let's look at the mold inscription, which describes this character more clearly. It first draws a big road with a fork in it (at first both sides are drawn, but later one side is omitted), then a strand of hair, then a big nose under the hair, and this middle character part is the character *Shou* (head) that we often use today, (甲骨文 金文 小篆 首 楷体) and then a footprint is drawn underneath, and this character is the origin of *Dao*. What does it mean? When you walk on a straight avenue, you can see the face of the person coming from far away, which is called *Dao*.

You must find it strange for the way I say it and wonder: on what road would I walk and not see the face of the person coming from the opposite direction? You know, each ancient Chinese character is a meaning. *Dao* (road), refers to the artificially built straight avenue; Jing (road) refers to the curved path that naturally stepped out, for example, if you're hiking, from afar you can hear the voice of the opposite people talking, but you cannot see the opposite people, this is called road.

These is another word to describe road, it is the character "径" (Jing), which means a short-cut, or off the track. Let me draw a sketch, look at this character, it looks like the character "井" (Jing) well. You read ancient books and may see a term *井-shaped field system*, that is, the field is divided into nine pieces. What does *井-shaped field system* mean? It has two meanings, its most primitive meaning arose in the clan era, at that time the clan is a commune, is the original communism, there is no private ownership. As the clan commune later developed into a clan alliance or even a tribal alliance, privatization at this time gradually occurred, but the entire tribal alliance still keeps a lot as the original part of the clan's communal land, this is the earliest form of the *井-shaped field*. At the beginning of the Zhou Dynasty, the *井-shaped field system* changed, and the eight pieces of land around the clan lot were individuals' or tribal rented fields or private fields, and the middle piece of land became the king's field, that is, became the public field, and everyone had to finish their work in the public field before they cultivate their own private fields. Therefore, the *井-shaped field system* was very complicated. Don't underestimate such a *井-shaped field*, the total area in fact is quite large, usually thousands or even tens of thousands of *mu*, we can almost use the term of square kilometer to say it. Suppose a person wants to walk from a certain point on the edge of the king's field to another point of the diagonal, he should follow the ridge of the field so as not to trample the crops, but no one wants to walk this way, because he has to take two edges of a triangle; so everyone would rather trample the crops in the king's field to step out a middle way in it, which is a short-cut. This is called off the track, that is to say, he is not taking the right path, but the short-cut, called crooked path "径".

Laozi said in *Daodejing*, "The big road is very smooth, but people are prone to paths." It means that people prefer to take the crooked path even the big road is clear and smooth. Obviously, Laozi saying this in the beginning of *Dao chapter* is to accuse humanity of doing thing against the way of heaven.

Then, what is the origin of the word *Dao*? It is important to understand that Laozi was discussing metaphysical issues, and the early symbols were constructed by the general public in their physical daily lives. Therefore, it was very difficult to find metaphysical concepts to name back then. Therefore, Laozi borrowed *Dao* (Broadway) to express the laws of the operation of the heaven and earth. What is the origin of the word *Dao*? It is the first avenue in Chinese history that was built in the early years of the Western Zhou Dynasty, which was called *Zhou Dao*. How do we know? There is a line in the *Book of Verses* that says, "Zhou Dao is flat and smooth like polished, and straight like a shot arrow". It means that the broad road is as flat as polished and as straight as a shot arrow.

As you know, before King Wu destroyed the Shang Dynasty, the capital of the Zhou tribal alliance and its political center had been moved to the area of Fenghao in Guanzhong, Shaanxi; but after that, the vast territory of Yin Shang that it conquered and needed to govern and manage was in the Central Plains, so the royal family of the Western Zhou had to place a significant part of its administrative and military forces in Henan in the early years, and for this purpose, it established the first accompanying capital, Luoyi. In order to facilitate the mobilization of administrative and military forces, Duke Jidan of Zhou built the first straight road in Chinese history between Haojing and Luoyi, which is the Zhou Dao. Then Laozi used this Zhou Dao as a metaphor for the way of cycling of the heaven and earth. Therefore, please note that Laozi's *Dao* and *De* are separate concepts.

Each Chinese word means one thing, so don't combine the words *Dao* and *De* together. As I said earlier, the meaning of *Dao* and *De* in *Daodejing* is never the meaning of morality in the sense of human morality. Therefore, you must first understand *Dao*, which is somewhat similar to what ancient Greek philosophy called Logos. The meaning of the word Logos, if I didn't make it clear yesterday, I will repeat it today, is a general term for speech and order in ancient Greek. The word order refers to objective laws, and speech refers to subjective statements, that is, the search for the ontological connection between them and the law of existence in the state of indistinguishability between subject and object. In that case, Laozi's *Dao* is somewhat similar to the ancient Greek concept of Logos. What he wants to express and inquire is the law of the cycling of the heaven and earth, which is the first thing we should understand.

Let's look at the first sentence of the opening chapter of *Daodejing*: "*Ways* may be spoken of *Dao*, but they are not the eternal *Dao*; Names may be cited as names, but they are not the eternal name." Nowadays, scholars from all walks of life have very complicated interpretations of this sentence, and some people even move the punctuation marks around, which makes people confused and unsure of what to say. So, what did Laozi want to say when he started with this quote?

To clarify this point, let me start with some digressions. In the modern period of classical Western philosophy, a philosopher named Leibniz appeared in Germany, and he once discussed the problem that philosophy needs its own special written symbols. As I said earlier, our normal language and written symbols are constructed by ordinary people in their physical daily life, while philosophy expresses metaphysical issues, and everyday language is not enough to express philosophy. Therefore, Leibniz's argument that philosophical expressions should have its own special symbols is quite valid. For example, in mathematics, you cannot use everyday language to express mathematics, neither in English nor in Chinese, mathematics has its own special symbols; for example, in music, the pentameter is its special symbol; and in computer programming, you cannot use everyday language to program a computer, it must use special logical symbols, i.e., computer language, to make it work. It is logical, then, that the scope of philosophical expression is not at all on the intuitive level of everyday life, so it is all the more important that it should have its own proprietary symbol system. Unfortunately, it does not, because the problem it wants to discuss is the collection of the physical and the annotation of the physical, and therefore it cannot completely get rid of the physical pointing and the physical appeal, which makes philosophical formulation very troublesome.

Let's look at Hegel, who said in his famous book *The Phenomenology of Mind*, that his philosophy loses much of its original meaning once it is expressed in words or language. What does he mean by this? It is still that everyday language is not enough to express philosophy.

Let me give you another example, Siddhartha Gautama. You know, Buddhism is the most flamboyant, philosophically deepest, and logical system among all the religions in the world, and we'll talk about that in a future Buddhism class. It is written in the scriptures, "The World Honored One flicked a flower, and Kasyapa smiled." It says that the Buddha preached without saying a word, but twirling a flower in his hand, and the bhikkhus listening below were bewildered, only a disciple named Kasyapa smiled slightly, and the Buddha understood that he was a sober person. The Buddha also said, "The Dharma I know is like the leaves on a tree, and the Dharma I preach is like a leaf on my palm." Meaning, the Dharma I know is living leaves on a tree; but once I preach it, it is already a dead leaf plucked from the tree and placed in my hand. This classic passage is still speaking, expressing profound philosophies through language and words, is really difficult to be exhaustive.

Okay, so let's look at the opening passage of *Daodejing*. Laozi said, "*Ways* may be spoken of *Dao*," what I call *the Way of Heaven* can be expressed as *Dao*; but "not the eternal *Dao*", that is, you cannot express in normal language, you have to use extraordinary language to express. He goes on to say, "Names may be cited as names, but they are not the eternal name." By names, he means the properties of things that we can perceive and the name that we can give to each of the perceptible objects. He said that you can name the properties of objects, but you can't name them in normal language, you have to use extraordinary language to name them. Look at this, Laozi's statement is the same as Leibniz, Hegel and Siddhartha Gautama. Words like these can only be experienced and expressed by someone who has thought deeply and long about philosophy and stated it in written symbols. This is the reason why most scholars are prone to get it wrong.

In addition, there is another layer of meaning in this statement, that any expression of deep thinking is extremely awkward and difficult. It is very difficult to read philosophy books, including the original works of any philosopher in the history of philosophy, because his thinking is not at all on the same level as the ordinary thinking of a normal person, and therefore his context cannot be made to fit in with the normal context. He even had to create words or define the concepts of the existent words. This makes you open his book, you know every word, but once it is arranged in a sentence, you do not know what it is about. This is how people feel when they read my book *A Unified Theory of Evolution*. It is not that I consciously want to make it very difficult to write, but the first obstacle to the expression of any profound thought, philosophical thought, is the problem of "not the eternal *Dao*" and "not the eternal name". This is the reason why Laozi knew that his thoughts and texts were difficult to be understood by the world, and that is why he had the prophecy of "Those who understand me are few".

Let's look further down, Laozi said, "Profound and still more profound is the gateway of all mysteries." That is to say that the way of heaven he is pursuing is somewhere extremely deep and dark, and that inaccessible place is the gateway to all the mysteries, the root of the birth of all things. Obviously, the issue he discusses is not within the scope of our normal thinking and normal perception. He goes on to say, "The clear feeling of the valley spirit is called *Xuan Pin,* and the gateway of *Xuan Pin* is called the root of heaven and earth." I have already talked about this before. I will explain what "the clear feeling of the valley spirit is called *Xuan Pin*" means. This phrase has caused many misunderstandings. Please note that the word *valley* "谷"(Gu)is most likely a generic word for the word *desire* "欲"(Yu)in this place. If you understand it as "the clear feeling of the spirit of desire is called *Xuan Pin,*" the sentence will immediately flow smoothly. As we all know, any life, any organism, is around the central axis of sexual proliferation, all living organisms in the end is only a temporary means of transport for genetic production and dissemination of more genes, this is a biological argument. Therefore, Freud explored the spiritual aspect of human beings and found that their mental disturbances were actually related to sexual repression in one's early childhood, which shows his deep understanding of the substratum of life and spirituality. This is the reason why Freud's professional theory, as a psychologist, is close to a philosophical doctrine, which is widely spread and has far-reaching effects. Freud called this sexual impulse or force the ego, using the word libido, which is somewhat similar to what Laozi called *spirit of* (*valley*) desire. Therefore, the desire mentioned here refers to the most powerful sexual desire of life, which he said is "the gateway of the profound (female) earth", and this desire will never be destroyed. Of course, Laozi only used sexual desire to describe the origin of the inner workings of heaven and earth, and he said, "The clear feeling of valley spirit is called *Xuan Pin*", thus revealing the *Dao* that can give birth to all things including the heaven and earth, to indicate that *Dao* is the original cause of the creation of heaven and earth and the inexhaustible cause for the continuation of all things.

Laozi goes on to say, "*Dao* gives birth to one, one begets two, two begets three, and three begets all things." This statement has been interpreted by many scholars to mean that Laozi had already conjectured about modern cosmology 2600 years ago. This statement superficially exalts Laozi, but it shows a serious deviation in his understanding of Laozi's book. The reason is that the primitive human culture is a model of thought formed in a state of relatively low information, while the modern cosmology is a highly developed science, until the early 20th century, after the advent of Einstein's theory of relativity, to establish a new model of cosmology that is sufficient to contain a great amount of information. Therefore, it is obviously inappropriate to compare Laozi's *Dao* with modern cosmology, as the two are not comparable at all.

It is important to note that in Laozi's time, the amount of information was extremely low. So what Laozi said, although it was metaphysical, he expressed it in a figurative way as much as possible. By "*Dao* gives birth to one", he refers to a certain original one or *Tai Ji* state before *Dao* gave birth to the two things: heaven and earth. The so-called "one begets two" refers to this primordial chaotic state of *Tai-Ji* (meta-one) that subsequently gave rise to the two things, heaven and earth; the so-called "two begets three" refers that these two things, heaven and earth, then gave birth to animals, plants and human beings; the so-called "three begets all things" is that animals, plants and human beings, and finally gave birth to all things under the sun. When I say the word *all things*, I mainly mean the billions of living things, including of course the endless human-made things. Therefore, what Laozi expresses in this passage is a certain degree of figurative metaphor to trace and look at the *Daoism*.

The phrase of Laozi is too common for you to read today. But you should know that when this sentence was uttered 2600 years ago, if you understand it, then you will be very shocked. Because there is an implicit meaning in this statement: everything including heaven and earth are evolved gradually. Please note that we have learned a lot of evolutionary knowledge today, you think this is a common sense, but you should know that the ancients saw all things between heaven and earth are arranged on a flat surface. 2000 years ago, *the Bible ·Old Testament*, in chapter 1 Genesis, it said that God created everything in the world in 6 days. Think about it, when you were young, when you first understood the world, could you think that the world is actually evolved instead of being presented in its entirety? There is no way you could think of that. You know, the concept of evolution did not spread in human academia until with difficulty the 19th century. And it was indeed extraordinary that Laozi actually held such a profound concept that all things came from evolution 2600 years ago.

Looking back at the ancient Greek philosophers, Thales, the first Greek sage, left only one sentence to posterity, which made him to be regarded as the founding father of ancient Greek philosophy in the narrow sense, that is, "water is the origin of all things". This phrase is all wrong when we look at it today, but why does this phrase mark Thales' position as the ancestor of Western philosophy? It is because this phrase also implies a very advanced and broad vision that "everything in the world evolves and develops gradually from some primitive state", thus starting the beginning of ancient Greek philosophy. Therefore, we must not take this statement lightly, it marks Laozi's far-sightedness and the high level of philosophical thinking that Laozi's doctrine has reached.

In *Daodejing ·chapter 21*, Laozi says, "The initial state of *Dao* is nothing but trance", saying that *Dao* begins in a trance-like state. What does *trance* mean? It means that the visual, auditory, sensory and experiential state cannot be captured clearly and cannot form a clear idea. That is to say, Laozi still expressed abstract deep thoughts in a figurative way as much as possible back then. We can see from these words the difficulty of Laozi's writing. He goes on to say that "there is something mixed up, born before heaven and earth", and he says that there is some state of existence that has been chaotically presented before heaven and earth appeared, which is of course a very powerful conjecture.

Be Good as Water

Let's see what Laozi said about "*Yi, Xi* and *Wei*". In *Daodejing · chapter 14*, it says, "To see but not seeing it is called *Yi*, to listen to but not hearing it is called *Xi*, to grasp but not catching it called *Wei* (tiny)." What is the meaning of this passage? First of all, we should know that the only channel for us human beings to obtain external information and external knowledge is the five senses, that is, vision, hearing, smell, taste, touch, other than that, we have no other source to obtain external information.

But Laozi said, you cannot have any capture and perception of the *Dao* by virtue of this channel, which is called "to see but not seeing it, to listen to but not hearing it, to grasp but not catching it", so we can see that Laozi wants to talk about *Dao*, but how difficult it is! He actually had to go beyond the normal human perception channel to capture the root of everything including heaven and earth. This mysterious expression, which lacks a proof link in the middle, i.e., is incompatible in the broad sense of logic, later became an important origin of ideology for the mystical Chinese *Daoism*.

In my Laozi class today, I will only talk about the most important and core part, sorting out the main thrust of Laozi's doctrine and main line of thought back then. Laozi said, "Applying the *Dao* of the antient times to harness things of the present." What does he mean by "to harness things of the present"? It means that if you want to master the way of operation of human civilization and civilized society today, you must "applying the *Dao* of the ancient times", that is, grasp the *way of heaven*, only then you are qualified, have the possibility, and have the basis to discuss the *way of man*. Look, is this what I said earlier, that the core of *Daoism* is the cosmology? Only when you grasp the cosmic view can you grasp the human world view, humanistic view, social view, and life view. In this sense, Laozi has reached the ultimate philosophical height.

In chapter 16 of *Daodejing*, Laozi says, "Heaven is *Dao*, and *Dao* is the eternality, and till the end of life won't peril." Please note this sentence, he said that Heaven is *Dao*, or Heaven is the closest to *Dao*. Then what is its main characteristic? *Dao* is eternality, what he emphasized is its constancy, stability, foundation and inseparability. He says that only when you grasp this thing can you keep yourself intact lifetime, that is, you can persist and control for a long time. The deeper meaning behind this statement is that Laozi wants to investigate the origin behind the world's immediate flux. If you are familiar with the history of Western philosophy, once you hear me talking about this, you will immediately think of the first period of ancient Greek philosophy called the ontological age. In the early years of ancient Greek philosophy, existence and ontology were pursued. What the antient Greek philosophers called existence was never the presentation of all things in front of them, but they considered these things to be illusions, because these things were constantly changing and erratic. They believe that all real existence must be eternal existence, unchanging existence, and indivisible existence, which can be called existence. Therefore, this statement of Laozi is very similar to the object of the ancient Greek philosophy, and expresses the equal level of thinking of the East and the West in the pivotal era.

And we should also note that this sentence has another layer of meaning, or say even more important key point, that is, since Laozi used "*Dao* gives birth to one, one begets two, two begets three, three begets all things" to express the sequence of evolution of all things, then, his sentence "Heaven is *Dao*, *Dao* is the eternality" expressed the difference of permanence and stability in this evolutionary sequence, isn't it? Otherwise, why would he talk about "*Dao* is the eternality"? He is obviously saying that things that are not the *Dao*, things that are superficial, are not sustainable, and there is no stability to speak of. Therefore, I say that Laozi has an observation and conjecture about the stability state of the evolutionary process, or the state of loss of stability.

Then Laozi said, "Heaven and earth are not benevolent, they treat all things as straw-tied dogs; the sages are not benevolent, they treat the people as straw-tied dogs." Thus, many people say that Laozi was a cold and thin-hearted person. But what exactly did Laozi want to say in this statement? First of all, let's look at the character "刍" (Chu)(甲文 金文 小篆 隶书 楷体). There are many debates in academic circles about what *Chu* really means. In the ancient script, the character *Chu* is drawn with a hand holding two bundles of grass, which means straws.

Therefore, some oracle scripts scholars believe that the character "刍" (Chu) means a puppy dog that fell into a nest of grass, a puppy without a mother to take care of it. However, most scholars believe that *Chu-Gou* means straw-tied dogs. We all know the ancient worship heaven and earth and ancestors need to put sacrifice on the altar, the sacrifice is divided into extravagant and simple ones, the so-called extravagant one includes large animals like cattle, pigs, sheep, and the simple one refers to small animals like chickens, ducks. For the ordinary people, even the cost of simple sacrifice is also high for them, so they use grass-tied animals, paper animals, to replace the real sacrifice as their offerings, which is called straw-tied dogs, referring to something very cheap and low. I used to doubt the validity of this statement, because we can rarely see such things as straw-tied dogs. Once I went to Tibet and saw a straw-tied sacrificial offering in a Tibetan museum, which is called *Rong-Guo* in Tibetan; then I believe this straw-tied dogs sacrifice holds good.

So what does this phrase actually mean? Laozi first talked about the way of heaven and earth, saying that there are not many complicated things between heaven and earth as there are in human civilized society, and that before all the creations of the way of man glowed, the way of heaven was silent and inactive, and it regarded all things as straw-tied dogs, that is, it regarded all things as very low, and never gave any false care, as a result of which all things developed in accordance with the trend, and constantly and steadily survived. He said that since the natural way of heaven acts and operates in this way, the way of man should also follow it. So next sentence followed "the sages are not benevolent, they treat the people as straw-tied dogs", he said that those who truly manage the world should therefore do nothing and should not use the excessive tricks derived from civilization, for they only disturb and destroy the human condition. In this statement, it is still marked that Laozi, when discussing the way of man, how mankind should operate, man should first look at how heaven and earth operate. And there is an implication in this statement, that is, Laozi is against all those fancy operations of human civilized society. He believed that too many ideas, too much preaching, too many means of human civilization are actually harming the survival of human beings, which is against the way of heaven. Therefore, we must understand that Laozi's doctrine of *Wu-Wei*, that is, let things change its own way without interventions, comes from the summary of the *Way of Heaven*.

Here I would like to emphasize what Laozi meant by sage. The ancient Chinese scholars all cited the term sage, such as Laozi, Confucius, Han Feizi, and so on. By sage, Confucius referred to a person who is virtuous and has a high position of authority, so Confucius classified people into three classes: sage, benevolent and gentleman; by sage, Han Feizi referred to a king of a state, who has the power of dictatorship and is proficient in magic; it can be seen that different scholars of pre-Qin era used the concept of sage with completely different connotations. But sage used by Laozi is the original meaning of the word sage. Let's look at the way the character sage written in oracle bone script. (甲骨文 金文 小篆 楷体) It starts with a very figurative ear, a mouth next to it, and a person underneath it, which is the origin of the traditional Chinese character "聖"(Sheng). What does it mean? In a clan-based society, there was no government, no violence, no privileges, no rule of law. The elder of the clan, the old grandmother in matrilineal society or the old grandfather in patrilineal society, listens to the opinions of all the clan members, and then he or she mediates disputes, negotiates and manages the clan community gently.

So please note, what is the doctrine of Laozi? Confucius said, "I follow the Zhou", which means he follows and obeys the feudal ritual system of the Zhou Dynasty. Then we may say Laozi is "I follow the Shang", that is, he follows and obeys the clan and tribal way of life of the Shang Dynasty. We can see that Laozi highly appreciated the primitive society of human beings, i.e., the early civilization and even the uncivilized state. Therefore, Laozi's sage is completely different from the concept used by Confucius, Han Feizi and later generations, because Laozi believes that before the civilization of human beings, there was very little human intended interference in society, and this natural and gentle way of dealing with the world is in line with the way of inaction of heaven and earth, which is the meaning of this passage of Laozi.

Laozi goes on to say, "The superior is as good as water." This phrase is familiar to us. The original meaning of the phrase is, *the superior* means the best state, and *as water* means like water. The meaning of the whole sentence is that the best state is like water. So what does Laozi mean by *as water*? He is using water as a figurative thing to describe, or to compare the natural way and natural state of the operation of Heaven. This is surely not easy for you to understand, because there is a deep meaning behind this statement of Laozi. So, he continues with the following sentence: "Water is good for all things but it does not compete." That is, water nourishes all things but does not compete with all things. Please note this sentence, why did he say such a plain word statement? It is because he wants to criticize human civilized society as a competitive structure. As we all know, when human beings were in the primitive clan society, its social form was truly communal, and the only time communism in human history was called clan commune, where there was no private ownership, and there was no competition among human beings. Then after the civilization of human beings, private ownership occurred, and social relations between human beings became tense, forming a pattern of intense competition, which brought about the disorder of the world and the unrest of the people. Therefore, Laozi said, "Water is good for all things but does not compete", the meaning of this sentence is to criticize human civilized society to run against the heavenly way.

He then went on to say, "It flows to places which most people detest, therefore it is closer to *Dao*." The meaning of this statement is that water always flows downward and accumulates at the lowest point to form a flat pool. Because it behaves in a downward manner and stays in the lowest position, which most people detest. The most people he refers to here is the civilized people, and his statement is still a criticism of civilized people, because civilized people always strive for upstream, for higher position, for better condition. But Laozi thought that there was no such competitive pattern in the operation of heaven and earth, no such impulse to move upward. Therefore, he says, "Therefore, it is closer to *Dao*," saying that the state of water is the closest, and almost equal to the presentation of *Dao*. In other words, the basic intent and point of the phrase "superior is as good as water" is to criticize human civilization for running contrary to *Dao*, the Way of Heaven, which is the core meaning of this phrase.

WEAKNESS IS THE EFFECTUATION OF DAO

The central part of Laozi's *Daoism* is Chapter 40 of *Daodejing*.

It is generally believed that *Daodejing*, sections 1 to 37, is the *chapter of Dao*, and sections 38 to 81 are the *chapter of De*. But you may have noticed that the core section of Laozi's *Daoism* are in the *chapter of De*, what does it mean? the irrationality of the division of sections into chapters. It is impossible to know who made the sections and even the chapters of Laozi's book. But the academic community is basically sure that division of the 81 sections is the falsification made by later generations. Therefore, when we read Laozi's book, we will find that its sections are disordered and its logical relationships are incoherent, which, of course, is probably a direct reflection of the state of the original book of *Lao Zi*. This is because, as I said earlier, it is possible that the book of *Lao Zi* did not originate from Laozi alone, but was a superimposed record text of the assembled concept developed by Laozi's family line as historians for generations. If this was the case, it is naturally difficult to smooth out its logical relationship. This is one of the reasons why we infer that the name Laozi may not refer to Laodan alone.

Let's look at the full text of section 40 below. Section 40 of *Daodejing* has only 21 words, so I'll read it for you: "Reversion is the motion of *Dao*, weakness is the effectuation of *Dao*, and everything under heaven is born of being, and being is born of nonbeing." This is the full text of section 40. Most scholars believe that the most important phrase of Laozi's *Daoism* is "reversion is the motion of *Dao*". What is the meaning of the phrase "reversion is the motion of *Dao*"? It means "things will go opposite when they reach their extreme", which expresses a typical dialectical logic. Regarding dialectics, many people think that it is the core of Laozi's book, and that reading Laozi's book is to read dialectics.

But I would say, if you read Laozi's book and only find dialectics, then I can be sure that you simply did not understand Laozi's book, you simply can not figure out what Laozi wants. First of all, we must understand that dialectics and dialectical logic is by no means the high end of human rational logic, it is instead the most elementary stage of human rational logic. After the founding of the country, because we introduced Marxist philosophy into China as the main body of philosophy, and one of the main components of Marx's philosophy is Hegel's dialectic, so the domestic ideological domain has elevated dialectic to a frightening height. Logically, in fact, dialectical logic is only the most primitive level of the logic of human rational thought. In terms of the history of civilization, the way of thinking used by human beings at the earliest and lowest stage is the dialectical view.

For example, *I-Ching* is a non-written symbol system which is a thousand years earlier than the oracle bone scripts, and it initially has only two lines, Yang lines represent male, Yin lines represent female, which is the simplest expression of the original dialectical view. All of the ancient thinkers used the method of thought is dialectical, such as Laozi, such as Confucius speak of the middle course. The early philosophers of ancient Greece all were basically users of dialectical logic, such as Parmenides who proposed existence and non-existence, such as Heraclitus who proposed a clear dialectic, and then Plato who used dialectical concepts all the time. One reads Plato's *Ideal State* and discusses all issues in dialectical view. It was not until Aristotle, the last philosopher who gathered the best of ancient Greek philosophy and established the first human logic, that he considered dialectical logic to express the chaos of thinking. Then Aristotle examined each of these 48 combinations of premises and found that 34 of them were invalid combinations and only 14 were valid combinations; then he continued to strip and argue little by little, and finally formed the first logic in human history, which is *formal logic*.

As I spoke about this, those who are familiar with the domestic philosophical community will immediately claim that formal logic is, in Hegel's view, precisely the reaction of dialectical logic. We can see that Aristotle's rectification of logic is precisely a correction of dialectical logic against the original chaotic and vague formulation, a clarification and sorting out of that state of disorganized thinking. So if you read Laozi's book and only read dialectic, you are indeed of too low a standard. There is a more serious problem here, dialectic is just a tool of thought used by Laozi. Pay attention that anyone who use a tool or method of thinking at a certain period of time is not up to your choice, so I think it is very problematic to call the spontaneous operation of thinking programs as methodology. Because the way your thinking unfolds is not the result of your choice, but the result of information increment of different times and of dealing with problems of different complexity, which naturally influence or even stipulate your logical thinking and mobilization state, and make it impossible for you to choose. In the ancient times of mankind when the amount of information was low, the thinkers of that era were using dialectical logic consciously and unconsciously, because they had no choice. Then Laozi's use of dialectic would have been nothing more than a temporary tool of thought.

Think about it, what does tool mean? If you build a bridge on a river, it proves that the river is not your destination, otherwise what is the use you build a bridge on the river? Then Laozi's use of dialectics is just a transitional means, or just a temporary boat or bridge for him to reach the destination of his thought, then it is certainly not the ultimate goal of Laozi's thought. Therefore, if you read Laozi's book, and you only find dialectics in it, I should say that you've lost your way. Dialectics implies that "things goes opposite when they come to the extreme", or in today's terms, "A and B can be transformed in between", which implies that we humans have a way back, we can go back to the old times. Thus, the earliest expression of dialectical logic, "reversion is the movement of *Dao*", leads to a very famous and common Chinese term, reaction. The word reaction is derived from the phrase "reversion is the movement of *Dao*", and it expresses the inevitable point that dialectical logic brings out that things go the opposite when they come to the extreme. Since Laozi uses dialectical logic, his doctrinal intent eventually turns out to be reactionary.

In my opinion, the most important part of the central part of Laozi's *Daoism* is the second sentence: "Weakness is the effectuation of *Dao*." It is really worthwhile to explore in depth what this statement means. The majority of scholars, and it can even be said that almost all scholars since the two Han dynasties, have interpreted or commented on this phrase as "weakness is better than strength", and "softness overcomes strength", which are of course the original words of Laozi, but in fact this phrase has another meaning. Generally, people only stay in the literal sense to interpret it, it seems that the saying "softness overcomes strength" is also quite justified.

Because there is an allusion in the ancient literature that Laozi once studied with Chang Cong as his teacher when he was young. When Chang Cong was dying of old age, Laozi went to visit his mentor, Chang Cong opened his mouth for Laozi to see and asked "Do you see if my teeth are still there?" Laozi said "No"; Chang Cong asked "Do you see if my tongue is still there?" Laozi said, "Yes"; Chang Cong finally asked, "What does it mean?" Laozi replied, "The strong will perish, but the weak will survive." This is the origin of the allusion to "softness overcome strength". Most people interpret it in this way, but I don't think it's good enough to understand Laozi's thought system. As I said earlier, Laozi has a deep vision of evolution. If he has this insight, then Laozi's "weakness is the effectuation of *Dao*" should be a dynamic expression given in this evolutionary channel, and cannot be a static depiction. If he expressed "weakness is the effectuation of *Dao*" on a dynamic axis, and if he had the confirmation that "Heaven is *Dao* and *Dao* is the eternality", that is, he was aware of the constancy and stability of the original existence and the variability of the evolutionary process, then what he said "weakness is the effectuation of *Dao*" cannot exclude the implication that the phenomenon of weakness is the way to realize *Dao*. I repeat: the phenomenon of weakness is the way of realization of the *Dao*! Thus, regarding the central meaning of Laozi's *Daoism* and the understanding of the phrase "weakness is effectuation of *Dao*", two schools of thought have emerged, with the vast majority of people expressing it as: weakness is the form of the action of *Dao*; while I interpret it as: weakness is the evolution vector of *Dao*.

So let's see, what are the expressions Laozi used while he explores the issue of weakness on the vertical axis of evolution? Laozi talked about "the longevity of heaven and earth", and *Daoism* later interpreted as "long life and long vision". In the original text of Laozi's book, there is a sentence that says, "When things in their prime will become old, which is no longer close to *Dao*, and being not *Dao* will soon demise". Laozi said that if a thing develops quickly, it will age quickly. He said this is not *Dao*, this is no longer *Dao*, and if anything no longer fit in with the way *Dao* works, it will soon demise. Obviously, Laozi in *Daoism* contains a vision of pursuing stability but not obtained. He also asked, "Heaven and earth cannot last long, how can man do?" In other words, the most primitive things, heaven and earth, cannot last forever, so the weakening of human beings is naturally predetermined and has become a self-evident trend and result. Here Laozi compares the strengths and weaknesses of the existence of heaven and earth with that of man, which obviously contains a vision of weakening development. He even directly asserts: "The softest thing of the world, gallops over the hardest thing of world." What he called *the softest* is *the weakest*, and who is this *weakest*? It is human. He says that man is able to ride on the strongest of the world, that is, everything that is much stronger than man is mastered by man. Obviously, this thought contains the unique consideration of questioning and comparing the occurrence of the phenomenon of weakness.

He found that weak survivors with a declining existential stability, such as human beings, have the ability to harness matter with very high existential stability. The fact that he makes such a strange comparison and discussion indicates that he had an inquiry into the direction of the evolution of matter in terms of the difference in the degree of strength and weakness, which is well expressed between his words. It is only that all scholars who have interpreted Laozi's text since the two Han dynasties have never seen the problem in this way, because there was not enough information back then, while we stand in today's era and look back at this statement of Laozi, we will find that Laozi was the only thinker who had the earliest conjecture about such issues.

The central meaning of Laozi's *Daoism* ultimately boils down to two words - softness and weakness. Softness and weakness is the general outline of Laozi's *Daoism*. Please note that he summarizes nothing but the two words softness and weakness, which is a very strange phenomenon. Most people interpret it to behave in a soft and weak way. But Laozi is talking about the *Way of Heaven*, and the topic of "behaving in a soft and weak way" has nothing to do with the operation of the *Way of Heaven*, and it has nothing to do with Laozi's saying " Heaven is *Dao*, *Dao* is the eternality", "not *Dao* will soon demise," and so on, is also quite incompatible. The two words *softness* and *weakness* appear 11 times in the 5,000-word text of *Daodejing*, so it is a basic summary of *Dao* by Laozi. It has many other expressions, such as "Nothing in the world is softer and weaker than water, in attacking the strong and hard nothing can surpass water". Laozi used various expressions, including the use of water and people, to constantly argue the issue of softness and weakness. Including "Nothing in the world is softer and weaker than water, yet in attacking the strong and hard nothing can surpass water." This example is to describe the relationship between man and things, and the relationship between the weak and the strong. So we need to remember that the core of the *Daoism* comes down to the two words *softness* and *weakness*.

About Laozi's *Daoism*, its more refined proofs, its more complex meanings, we will discuss them later in the topic. We have only touched the surface of the textual aspects for now.

Laozi's Doctrine of *De*

The main theme of *Dao chapter* is about cosmology and world-view, or rather about cosmology and nature-view. Its central idea is section 40 of *Daodejing*, and its most important phrase is "weakness is the effectuation of *Dao*", which means that the phenomenon of weakening is the way to realize *Dao*. It boils down to two words: *softness* and *weakness*.

Let's move on to Laozi's *De chapter*. The central idea of *Deism* is to talk about social and life views, from the *Way of Heaven* to the *Way of Man*. In fact, strictly speaking, Laozi was more concerned with the social problems of human nature, which was common to all Chinese thinkers in the pre-Qin era. Therefore, *De chapter* is the main focus of Laozi's book, and therefore in the silk books, *De* comes first and *Dao* comes second.

So what exactly does *De* mean? We have to look at its oracle bone script.

In the oracle bone script, the character (甲文 金文 小篆 楷体) "德" *De* starts with a big road and a fork in it, and then a big, figurative eye is drawn next to it, and then a straight-out symbol is drawn on top of it. When it came to the mold inscription, a heart was added to the bottom, and this is the origin of the character "德" *De*.

What does it mean? First, we need to understand this character: walking on a thoroughfare with a fork in the road, keeping your eyes straight ahead and walking wholeheartedly, this is called *De*. In other words, walking along the road is called *De*. What kind of road do you follow? Follow the road in accordance with the Way of Heaven is *De*. Therefore, we must pay attention to the fact that the *Dao De* that Laozi refers to is not what we call human morality in our daily life, but refers to the Way the Heaven operates, and to act in accordance with it, that is, to act in accordance with the *Heavenly Way* is called *Dao De*.

Then, the Chinese later called the ethics as morality, which is indeed a high level of wisdom. Because the ethics of human beings, in fact, changes and transforms with the operation of human existence in accord with *Dao*. But you must first understand the deep meaning of Laozi.

Moreover, one should also note that this character is not pronounced *dé* but *děi* in the region where the oracle bone scripts was formed, such as the whole area across Henan and Shaanxi. For example, in the Guanzhong region, to say that a person lacks virtue, one would say that he lacks *děi*. What is this single sound *dei*? A farmer driving a bullock cart or wagon gives the bullock or horse oral urge to go straight.

Farmers drive bullock carts or wagons and give four single sounds as oral commands to the oxen or horses. First, *jia*, let the oxen or horses start moving; second, *de* (pronounced dèi), let the oxen or horses go straight; third, *wó*, let the oxen or horses turn; fourth, *yù*, let the oxen or horses stop.

Take the first word and the fourth word out from the four commands, and form a word called *Jia Yu* (harness/yoke). The second sound command *de*, is used to urge the oxen and horses go straight along the road. This is the original meaning of the word in the oracle bone script. Therefore, we must remember that the word *De* means to walk along the road, and to live in accordance with the way of heaven is called *De*.

When we mention *De*, people would think that it must refers to virtuous people. Wrong! By *De*, Laozi meant material virtue. The original words of Laozi in the silk books are "Everything respects *Dao* and values *De*"; in *Daodejing*, these words are expressed as "all things respect *Dao* and value *De*". Both phrases are exactly the same meaning that all things have *De* (virtue).

We are familiar with a phrase that was once used as the motto of Tsinghua University, called *Hou De Zai Wu* (thick virtue bears much things), which was actually derived from here. But many people interpret it wrongly, interpreting *things* as humans, and *virtue* as ethics. What Laozi said is *things' virtue*, the so-called "thick virtue bears much things," originally means that the heavenly way is practiced by all things, so that all things have *De* (virtue) and are nurtured.

So, what did Laozi mean by this statement? He is saying that all things have *De*, except for man who does not have *De*. So this statement implies Laozi's criticism of civilized mankind. That is why he said, "Man follows the way of Earth, Earth follows the way of Heaven, Heaven follows the way of *Dao*, and *Dao* follows its own way, *Nature*." The word *follow* here means to do as what the example shows, saying that man should follow the example of Earth, Earth should follow the example of Heaven, Heaven should follow the example of *Dao*, and *Dao* follow its own way, that is, *Nature*.

Please note the so-called *Nature* here. The concept of *nature* here does not mean the natural world, which was introduced to China from the West in recent times. The word *Nature* here means *naturally*, which refers to the spontaneous evolution and state of evolution of *Dao*, which is called *naturally*. Therefore, Laozi added another meaning to *De* by saying, "complementing the naturally of all things and not daring to do anything further", which means to follow the way all things operate and never dare to make any superfluous action, and this is called *De* (virtue). What does he mean by this phrase? He is further criticizing human civilization, which has too much sophisticated projects and too much further movements, violating the way of heaven and losing the virtue of things.

Therefore, he says the following: "do not glorify the talented, so that people will not contend", because the difference between virtuous and talented, between virtuous or not, is all something made up by civilized people, but in fact, it contains the contention for fame and profit; "do not value rare goods, so the common people will not steal", the rare goods reflect the value of high and low, and the value is only a measure of greed. We understand that everything in the world is originally no difference in value, in nature. Can we say that gold is more valuable than granite? No, there is not any difference of noble or low between them; "do not display objects of desire, so the common people's minds will not be confused." that is, do not make opportunity to flaunt human desires, without the passions and greed fully mobilized by civilization, people's hearts will be quiet, the society will be safe and peaceful; "doing nothing, there is nothing ungovernable", this to say, don't do anything superfluous, don't do anything civilized, thus the human world could be truly ruled without chaos.

If you think that I am misinterpreting, then look at Laozi's further elaboration. He says, "When *Dao* is lost, *De* (virtue) appears; when *De* is lost, benevolence appears; when benevolence is lost, righteousness appears; when righteousness is lost, propriety appears." What is this passage about?

The first thing we must understand is that if people emphasize something, that means they must be missing or lack of. For example, today we shout the slogan of "eight honors and eight shames", it is because we have long lost these things. Lu Xun once gave a testimony on Confucius, he said Confucius traveled around the warring states for 13 years, during which he must frequently encountered with various difficulties. Why he demanded "food is never cooked fine enough, meat is never sliced thin enough"? It was because he was always hungry, and when he had a chance to eat a big meal, his stomach was filled round up, and then he had to drive far away; since there were no tarmac roads and no rubber tires at that time, his wagon with wooden wheels went up and down, which made his stomach drooping. In other words, Lu Xun concluded that Confucius suffered from a serious stomach problem based on only one thing: he must have been lacking something before he shouted something.

Whether or not Lu Xun's testimony about Confucius is valid, we need not to care much, but at least we need to understand that once you see people emphasize something, it must be what they are missing. Please note this passage from Laozi, he said when *Dao* is lost, *De* appears;" when people start shouting *Dao* and *De,* it must be because they have lost *Dao*; "when *De* is lost, benevolence appears", when people have lost even virtue, then they begin shouting benevolence; "when benevolence is lost, righteousness appears", when you can't even keep your benevolent heart anymore, you talk about righteousness; "when righteousness is lost, propriety appears", after you have lost *Dao, De* (virtue), benevolence and righteousness, you have to talk about propriety.

As I said earlier, the so-called propriety refers to the sum of the state's political legal system (patriarchal moral system) and its civil rituals and ceremonies. It is when we lose all these things, morality, virtue, benevolence and righteousness that the civilized human society begins to control the violence with severe law punishment. Obviously, Laozi's meaning is very clear, he believes that civilized people must be out of morality and lack of virtue.

Laozi went on to say, "Superior *De* is not about virtue; it therefore has virtue; Inferior *De* does not want to lose virtue; it therefore has no virtue." What does *superior De* mean? It is the state of true virtue, the virtue that all things have. What does it look like? No virtue! That is, you cannot see that it has virtue. In fact, this is the true virtue. He said, "Inferior *De* does not lose virtue." This *inferior De* mentioned here is the virtue that people shout with their mouths and hold in their arms. He said, on the surface, he does not lose virtue; but in fact, he does not have virtue.

If you still find my explanation not really convincing, then let's look at Laozi's direct expression of *De* (virtue). He even used the eight words "The feature of great virtue is to follow only *Dao*".

First of all, let's look at the meaning of the character "孔" (Kong) hole. When we say this character today, we are talking about it in some compound word, such as *Kong Dong* (hole), where both holes are linked together. As I said before, in ancient times, each word had one meaning, and the word of compound characters was not valid. What is a *Dong* (hole)? A cave or a tree hole that has a cavity inside and a big hole directly seen from outside, which is called "洞" (Dong) hole.

What is "孔" (Kong)? Let's look at the mold inscription. First, (金文 小篆 孔 楷体)we draw a child, and this character is *Zi*, but the child's mouth is consciously drawn more pointed, and then we draw a very figurative breast next to it, and this character is *Kong* (hole). What is the meaning of *Kong*? There is a cavity inside, but you can't see it from outside. When a mother breastfeeding her child, there has never been a big hole in her breast that flows out milk to feed child. This state of having a cavity inside but not seen from outside, i.e., nothing is revealed but has a substantial content, is called *Kong* (hole).

The fact that Laozi purposely used the character *Kong* to describe the "feature, or appearance of *De*" shows that virtue itself does not have its own independent form. Therefore, he added four words "to follow only *Dao*", which are meant to highlight what is the connotation of *De*? It is simply to follow along the road. Then he said, "*Dao* gives birth to all things, and *De* raised them," which means that *Dao* gives birth to all things in the world, and all things are in consistence with *Dao*, they are raised by *De*, which is called *De*.

Therefore, he also said, "Growing, rearing, mellowing, maturing, nurturing, and covering." The word *Ting* here means to change and mellow; the word *Du* here means to supervise and manage;

and the word *Fu* here means to cover and receive. Then, "Giving birth to but not possessing, having things done be but not taking advantage, leading but not controlling, which is called profound *De*", he said that by following *Dao* (the way), all things can naturally germinate, grow and mellow, and develop. This a state of hidden but actually powerful in reproducing and controlling all beings, is called *Xuan De,* profound virtue, that is, virtuous in the dark. As I said, *Xuan* has the meaning of darkness. The word *Xuan De* should be familiar to everyone. During the Three Kingdoms period, Liu Bei, a famous politician, gave himself a style name, *Xuan De,* the word is derived from this.

He went on to say, "Stop all channels, close all doors, blunt the sharpness, resolve the difference, harmonize the light, blend in with dust, which is called *Xuan Tong* (profound commonality)." Let me explain this passage. What does *Dui* mean? It is the five senses. As I said earlier, the only way for us humans to obtain external information and knowledge is through the five senses: sight, hearing, smell, taste and touch. Laozi said, "stop all channels", that is, block your five senses, do not receive too much information from the outside; "close all doors", where the door refers to the spiritual world, close the door of your spirit. He said, "blunt the sharpness;" here the word sharpness refers to the ambition of civilized people, and he said, to blunt the sharp ambition of civilized people; (only in this way) can the disputes in civilized society be resolved, which is called "resolving the differences;" the following is the famous idiom of "harmony with the light and dust", which means that civilized people should reduce themselves to, or restore themselves to, the light of nature and the dust of nature, which is called *Xuan Tong* (profound commonality). Only in this way can you secretly be in harmony with the heavenly way, blend yourself in the heavenly way. Therefore, *Xuan Tong* is another expression of *Xuan De,* which is a clearer example to criticize human beings not reaching the state of *Xuan De* and *Xuan Tong.*

In short, we can see that Laozi, as usual, in the *chapter of De,* has been criticizing civilized human beings for losing the material virtue. And in the *chapter of Dao,* he has been criticizing civilized human beings for deviating from the *Way of Heaven*. If I say this and some of you still find it suspicious and still think it is not enough to prove that Laozi meant this, let's look at another original passage of Laozi.

He said, "The one who is endowed with *De*, may be likened to *red infant* (a newborn infant)." These are the original words in the silk books. *Daodejing* says, "Those who are endowed with *De* are likened to newborn infants." There is no difference in meaning between the two. Laozi makes it clearer here: only a newborn infant "is endowed with *De*", only an infant has a thick virtue. In other words, once humans grow up, they become virtueless.

First of all, I would like to explain what a *red infant* is. A *red infant* is a baby born within one week, that is, only a newborn baby can be called a red infant. Because the newborn's skin is very thin, the capillaries under the skin can be seen in general, the baby appears red, so it is called red infant. Why does it refer to only newborns within one week? It is because jaundice occurs in all babies after 4 to 7 days of their birth and is clinically known as physiological jaundice. Therefore, babies born after one week are no longer called red, but yellow.

Why is this so? Because the fetus is nurtured in the mother's body, and after 6 months, the fetus becomes bigger and its oxygen demand increases, but the only way to supply oxygen to the fetus is through the mother's two lobes of lungs, which used to supply oxygen to one person, but now have to supply oxygen to two people at the same time. What particularly troublesome is that there is only one artery - the umbilical artery - to supply oxygen to the fetus, and there is no other way, so the fetus will be seriously deprived of oxygen. So, what does any animal do if it is persistently hypoxic? There is only one thing it can do, and that is to increase the number of red blood cells.

As you know, red blood cells contain a large protein molecule called hemoglobin, which is a solid component of the blood that specifically complexes oxygen molecules, i.e., transports oxygen. Ask yourself why would you have a plateau reaction when you go to Tibet? It's because Tibet is a plateau more than 3500 meters above sea level, the oxygen content of that place is about 40% lower than the oxygen content of the plains at lower altitudes, so when you travel there, you will have an acute hypoxic reaction, which is called plateau reaction. Then what about Tibetans? He settles in that place for a long time, in a state of chronic hypoxia, and he has only one way left, which is to increase his red blood cell count. If the Tibetan is given blood test, his red blood cell count shows 40%

to 60% more than the red blood cells of the plain people.

Then as the fetus is hypoxic, and in the last month or two of gestation there is persistent hypoxia for the fetus, so its red blood cells proliferate. With the delivery, the baby opens his mouth and cries, his own two lobe lungs suddenly open, oxygen supply suddenly becomes sufficient, so a large number of red blood cells appear redundant, so within a week period, some red blood cells lyse, which is clinically called hemolysis. Hemolysis is medically a very dangerous issue, because the molecular amount of hemoglobin is too large to pass smoothly through the renal units - glomeruli and tubules - and thus be excreted by the kidneys. Instead, it has a serious damaging effect on the nerves and nuclei of the brain, and must be rapidly degraded by the liver into small molecules of bile pigments and bilirubin, which are then excreted through the feces and urine. This is why people who have hepatitis have an increased jaundice index due to impaired liver function.

Newborns have an excessive supply of hemoglobin on the one hand, but on the other hand, its liver function is underdeveloped, so all newborns will experience a jaundice process around 4 to 7 days of life, clinically known as physiological jaundice. I would like to make a note here that most children do not need treatment and will pass naturally; however, if it is too severe, it does need to be treated promptly in the hospital, otherwise it can cause serious neurological damage and kidney damage.

Generally speaking, during the jaundice period, 60% of newborns show yellowing of the skin and sclera, and 40% you can't see. However, if you take a blood test for jaundice, the jaundice index is all increased, so after one week of birth, the child is no longer called red baby, but yellow.

This paragraph is to tell you that the term red baby refers only to a newborn child. And you must know that the intelligence of a newborn baby is not even as good as that of an ordinary adult animal. In other words, the intelligence of a newborn is not as good as that of an adult dog or cat that you have at home. Why? Because the brain capacity of a human newborn is actually only 27% to 30% of his adult brain capacity, which means that it is surprisingly not up to one-third of his adult brain capacity.

It is important to know that the brain capacity of all animal cubs is at least half of its adult brain capacity. Cows and horses, for example, have about 70% of their adult brain capacity, which is why cows and horses can waddle around their mothers within half an hour of birth. Even apes, such as chimpanzees, gorillas, their newborn brain capacity is more than 50% of adulthood, so the newborn chimpanzee, do not need the mother always hold it, it will cling to the mother's mane, the mother moved around to jump between branches, the child will never be thrown off. Only human infants due to low brain capacity, his nervous system failed to fully develop, so that even the muscles to maintain their own posture can not be effectively controlled, so all rely on the mother's carrying in the arms, actually six months it cannot move, simply like a paralyzed patient.

Why is that? It's because man, the monkey, suddenly became upright. People should know that uprightness is a terrible thing because it causes a large increase in brain volume. In fact, all postnatal animals as well as reptiles, its brain capacity in the process of genetic mutation, will be randomly changed, that is, the brain capacity tends to randomly increase. However, once the brain capacity of all animals increases, they are inevitably eliminated by natural selection. Why? Because it will lose its motor balance.

What does this mean? Let me give you an example. For example, give you a bamboo pole, you pick up the pole roughly horizontally in the middle, I hang a little weight in the front end, this bamboo pole immediately tilted down; however, if I hold this bamboo pole upright, you can even set up a bucket of water on it. That is, when the animal keeps crawling movement, the body length is distributed laterally, so if the head weight changes slightly, its motor balance will have to be coordinated again, otherwise, it is difficult to hold body balance. But once humans are upright, the top brain volume changes, the center of gravity does not shift significantly, that is, it does not affect the balance of movement.

Thus, it was only after erection that apes developed brain capacity on a large scale, without being eliminated by natural selection. Just 3 to 5 million years ago, the average brain capacity of reptilian apes, including hominids, was only about 400 ml, while by Homo sapiens, it plummeted to more than 1350 ml in just a few million years. As you know, the increase in brain volume will bring out a serious consequence, that is, difficult birth. The baby's head is so big that it can suffocate the mother, because the mother's birth canal is still the same as that of a reptile. That is, the human female birth canal still remains under a rigid skeletal support that is called the pubic symphysis in anatomy science. Therefore, a fetus with too large a brain can get stuck in this part of the mother's pelvis, causing difficult labor; that is why, among all animals, the disease of obstructed labor is seen only in humans. In ancient times, a woman's first birth was called a primiparous birth, and there would be one mother death out of every 10 primiparous births due to obstructed labor. Also because of this reason, all humans are born prematurely, that is, you must be born early when conception has not yet matured, when the brain has not yet grown large enough, when the head is not yet suffocated in the birth canal. Therefore, the entire human brain capacity at the time of after birth, is only less than a third of the adult.

Let me give you an example. When you were in elementary school, your teacher gives you a four-operations question that put you fail to solve it, and when you grow up, you look back and see that it was so simple that it was not even worth mentioning. Why is that? It is because your brain did not grow mature. Human brain won't complete its development to a mature state until the age of 17 to 20. What am I trying to say by this? It is that the newborns have low intelligence and barely reach the intelligence of adult animals, but Laozi said that only at this time can a person be considered endowed with *De*. We can see that Laozi has made it very clear that civilized people are mobilizing their intelligence, forming a social structure to achieve greed, forming a competitive situation, forming a highly intelligent group, which is actually a bad process of deviating from the heavenly way and losing material virtue.

Attempts Nothing and Nothing is Left Undone

The central idea of Laozi's *Deism* is in section 37 of *Daodejing*.

As I mentioned earlier, sections 1 to 37 are the *chapter of Dao*, but the central section of the *chapter of De* runs back to the *chapter of Dao*. One of the most important phrases is this: "*Dao* in its eternity does nothing, yet nothing is not undone." He did not say what *De* is like, but said what *Dao* is like, which explains what state *De* (virtue) is. As I said earlier, Laozi's description of *De* (virtue) is "the appearance of *Kong De*", "superior *De* is not virtue". In other words, Laozi always believed that *De* (virtue) does not have its own independent form, but its only connotation is "to follow *Dao*, nothing but be with *Dao*".

Therefore, when Laozi elaborates on what *De* (virtue) is in the central section of the *Deism*, the expression he uses is "*Dao* in its eternity does nothing, yet nothing is undone." To sum up, there are only two words: *Wu-Wei* (*doing nothing intently*); like in the *Daoism*, only two words to sum up: *Rou-Ruo* (*softness and weakness*).

The key here is, what exactly is the meaning of *Wu-Wei*? Most of the scholars explain *Wu-Wei* as something to do, something not to do, saying that this is *Wu-Wei*. Is that right? Obviously not. When you listen to this lecture, you should understand that Laozi is against the use of intelligence by human beings, and Laozi is against the radical process of mobilizing intelligence in civilized society. And something to do, something not to do is an intelligent choice of on what to do. Therefore, *Wu-Wei* cannot mean something to do, something not to do.

In the Song Dynasty, there was a famous scribe, a great scholar, and also a theoretician named Zhu Xi, who had a commentary on Laozi's *Wu-Wei*, which he summed up in four words, namely, doing nothing at all, meaning that doing nothing is called *Wu-Wei*. This interpretation is somewhat close to Laozi's original meaning. But this statement still has problems, because even a wolf, it has to find sheep to eat; even a sheep, it has to find grass to eat, how can people do nothing and still survive? Therefore, Zhu Xi's interpretation is still not valid.

So what exactly is the meaning of *Wu-Wei*? I have not seen a truly thorough and logical interpretation in all the ancient and even modern commentaries on Laozi's *Daodejing*. Therefore, I will give a unique definition and commentary here for your reference.

What is *Wu-Wei*? Laozi is against all civilized actions, and this is called *Wu- Wei*. Let me emphasize once again that Laozi opposes all civilized actions. The word *Wu-Wei* appears 10 times in the 5,000 words of Laozi's *Daodejing*. He says, "*Wei Wu Wei, Shi Wu Shi, Wei Wu Wei* (no intent in doing things, no worry in mind, no desire for tasteful food)". He said, what do you need to do? Nothing; he said, what do you need to deal with? Nothing; because all the things that civilized people do, all their actions are superfluous in Laozi's view, and all of them are against the way of *Dao-De*; he said, eat meals of not tasteful, even your meals should not be tasteful. Think about it, before the civilization of human beings, there was no oil, no soy and vinegar in food, so food was tasteless, still expresses the complete pre-civilized state of existence.

As I speak, you should be able to understand that Laozi's social view is extremely reactionary.

Laozi's social view, his summary and view of the human way, is commended in section 80 of *Daodejing*. The last section, the 81st section, focuses on "truthful words are not beautiful, beautiful words are not truthful", that is, trustworthy words do not sound pleasant, sound pleasant words are not trustworthy. Laozi said, my words do not sound beautiful, but you should be careful, only these are the most trustworthy. Obviously, section 81 is the final sum of his whole book, that is, the final confirmation of his previous arguments. And the penultimate section, that is, section 80, is Laozi's definition of the highest ideal expressed in the *Way of Man*, that is, the return to the humane state in line with the *Way of Heaven*.

What does Laozi say? Let me paraphrase his original text below. He said, "Let the states be small and population be sparse; let them have no use of mass-scale tools" What does "small state and sparse people" mean here? It is the primitive clan society. It was the state of community organization before the civilization of human beings, which is no different from animal kinship society.

As you know, in the primitive clan society, the average population of each settlement was about 30 to 80 people, which is called "small state and sparse people". When we say *state*, we immediately think of a big state system, but you should know that when the word state was formed in the oracle bone scripts, that is, during the period when the oracle bone scripts occurred, and even during the period when the oracle and mold inscriptions appeared, the word *state* had never existed in the world, because the Shang Dynasty could only be considered a clan and tribal confederation (the jurisdictions of the subsequent dynasties were still considered its countryside), not at all a *state* in the modern sense. Further, the clan era, tribal era, moreover, there is no such semantic sense of the state. Therefore, the small state and sparse people" that Laozi said, the *state* is never the concept of state in the later sense.

Let's take a look at the oracle bone script for the word *Guo* (state). ( ) It starts with a small mouth, and then draws an ancient weapon, *Ge* (dagger-axe), next to it, with an indicator symbol where it is held in the hand. It means that the mouth (mouth) represents the survival system, and the *Ge* (weapon) represents the defense system. A primitive clan is a survival unit and has its own means of protection, which is the state of the clan. In mold inscription or *Xiaozhuan* script, a border was added, which is the origin of the traditional Chinese character "國"*Guo*. What is this border? It is the walls and trenches of the "國" (Guo) state.

As you know, in the rural hinterland of China, each village is a blood group, and there is no intermarriage between people of the same surname. Certain larger villages have their own border walls and even their own border rivers. Please recall those villages in the center battlefield of the Huaihai campaign, where the walls and rivers around those villages were piled with corpses. It shows that many villages in the past had this border-shaped defense structure, and the blood structure of this survival defense system is called state. Therefore, what Laozi's called "small state and sparse people" only refers to the primitive clan society. And primitive clan society, I stress again, is no different to any animal kinship social organization form.

What does it mean by "什佰" (Shi Bai) tool? It refers a civilized apparatus invented by civilized people that can replace dozens or even hundreds of people. For example, the ancients built a bullock cart, one cart can carry several tons of things, these things are dozens of strong young men cannot carry, this is called "什佰" *Shi Bai* tools. Laozi said, "let them have no use of the large-scale tools", that is, let them abandon these efficient apparatuses of civilization.

He went on to say, "let the common people fear death and have no desire to migrate far." As I said earlier, the ancient people lived within their own clan territory of a dozen square kilometers and never traveled far to make a living, which is called "no desire to migrate far". What does it mean by *fear death*? You know, all animals, including humans, their nature must be afraid of death. Because all animals and human neural constructs and their mental reactions are based on the principle of avoiding harms. Therefore, in the seven emotions, there is an important thing as the basis, that is fear. This emotion originates from the amygdala nucleus of the limbic system of the brain and is an important action regulator of the human mental system.

It is a protective mechanism. Because ancient men lived in the jungle, in crisis, if they did not have a feeling of fear and an escape response, they could not have safety and security. It's like pain is seen as a protective mechanism in medicine, clinically, because if you don't have a sense of pain, you lack a defensive protective stress response in your perceptual system. Let me give you an example, for example, of a clinical condition called peripheral neuritis. The patient loses the sensory peripheral nerves in the distal extremities and loses the sense of pain and even the sense of temperature. This disease of the patient is very scary. He may hold a sharp object in his hand and gets damaged, but he doesn't know it; he gets warmth from a close fire in winter and talks to the person next to him, when he turns back and find that his hand is burnt, but he doesn't know to retract his hand. So, you can see what pain is? It is a protective mechanism.

What is fear? It is a protective mechanism. Thus, all creatures, all animals, including humans, their nature must be afraid of death. Only civilized people will create a bunch of nice words, like brave, sacrifice and so on, and then just send you to the battlefield as cannon fodder. That's why Laozi said "let them fear death and have no desire to migrate far".

He went on to say, "though there are boats and carriages, let there be no occasion to ride on them". "Although there are shields, armor and weapons, let there be no place to store them"; he concluded, "Let the people restore the skill of knotting and put it to use." This sentence is very straightforward, that is, to make people go back to the time when there was no writing and rudimentary cognition, but live on by knotting and using.

Laozi goes on to say, "What is the best state of social management for human society"? He used four phrases: "relish their food, appreciate their clothing, feel secure their dwelling, and happy with their customs." It means that if you eat raw meat and drink blood, you feel sweet; if you wear a skirt of animal skin, you feel beautiful; if you dig a dwelling, you feel secured in; if you shout rough sounds and twist your body in ugly dance, you feel very happy.

Then he said, "neighboring lands in sight, sound of their fowls and dogs can be heard, but the people never visit each other." What is the meaning of this passage? You know that human primitive clan society, as I said earlier, is no different from all animal kinship society. Then, all animals, in estrus must form a blood relative social unit, and then occupy a piece of territory, to start the process of breeding offspring survival succession. The same kind of animals are never encroaching on the territory of other families, animals will do some scent markings around their respective territories. It's like when you walk your dog outside, you always see the dog keep lifting its hind legs to pee. What is it doing? It doesn't have a bladder infection, but it is the remnant habit of its instinct to scent mark its territory as a wild dog. That is to say, all the animals never have mutilation of the same species between them. Although wolves eat sheep, wolves never eat wolves, and even if their groups are next to each other in a separated state, they generally will not violate each other.

The primitive human clan society that Laozi speak of, is like this state. Before civilization, human survival mode, social state, is no different to all animal kinship society. Therefore, at that time, human beings never had conflicts and disputes, not to mention wars between clans or tribes. This is called "neighboring lands in sight, sound of fowls and dogs can be heard, but the people never visit each other", which is Laozi's highest social ideal. What is it? Regression to an animal-like, uncultivated, uncivilized state of existence!

Laozi's Reactionism and Conservatism

Laozi not only expresses his reactionary view of society in section 80, but he also emphasizes it throughout the book. He says, "Return to its roots", "Return to the infant", "Return to *Wuji* (prior to *Dao*)", "Return to simplicity". All of them are telling you to go backwards. This is the meaning of the word reversion.

He went on to say, "I have three treasures which I hold dear.

One is compassion, the other is frugality, and the third is refraining from being ahead of the world." Today's people are so bold that they change the phrase to "dare to be the first in the world". Laozi said, I have three treasures, I always hold dear and never relax, this is called "I have three treasures which I hold dear". Which three treasures? "One is compassion", what is the meaning of compassion? We generally understand it in the compound word "慈悲" *Ci-Bei* (kindness and compassion), this understanding is not good. The original meaning of the word kindness is a person looking at another person who actually is living a very good life, a very normal life, you still feel that his life is not good enough, still feel sorry for him, this sentiment is called kindness. It only refers to those who are mothers now, who look at their babies and children, who are actually living a normal, good life, but you still feel that they are not living well enough, and you still want to help them, and you still feel sorry for them, and this is called kindness.

In primitive clan societies, the sentiment of kindness was the dominant sentiment of the society at that time. What is the meaning by this sentence? You know, primitive clan society, children are raised by the whole society, because at that time it was a group marriage custom, the child could not find a father, the father is a man of another clan, the child was born to live in its mother's own clan. All the members of the clan were the child's blood relatives, including the women, who were either the child's sister, aunt or possibly grandmother; and the men, who were either the child's brother, uncle, or possibly uncle's uncle. In short, in the whole clan society, everyone is related by blood, and the community raises children together. Therefore, the sentiment of kindness is the mainstream of the clan society, which is the opposite of today's civilized society. What is civilized society about? It is about success and excellence. What is success? You are very capable, see other people are living like pigs, you are very proud of yourself, this is called success. What is excellence? You stand out from the crowd, see others are a bunch of stupid asses, so you feel complacent, this is called excellence. So, we can see, the mainstream sentiment of civilized society, and the mainstream sentiment of primitive clan society is the opposite.

"Second is frugality". When we say frugal today, we immediately think of hard work and simplicity, that is, the meaning of frugality. Not true! The ancient meaning of the word frugality refers to the sense of not wanting anything more than enough to eat and wear. You know, after all animals are fed and clothed, they don't want any more. Who has ever seen a monkey wearing a gold necklace around its neck? All animals wear warm things is a natural solution, it grows fur. Whenever late autumn comes, it will grow a layer of fine fleece under the fur, which is called *Qiu Hao* (fluff), in order to keep warm in winter (*Ming Cha Qiu Hao*, the idiom of seeing the tiniest hair, is derived from this); the next spring, before the summer comes, it loses its fluff in order to facilitate the summer evacuation of body temperature. So people who have dogs or cats know that in the early summer, the fluffy hair flying all over the house, why? It is losing fluff. Therefore, all animals, it is a natural solution to the problem of wearing warmth.

All animals, it won't have more needs other than eating. Let me give you an example, such as bears, why do bears hibernate? Hibernation is a biological term that refers only to cold-blooded animals, that is, animals whose body temperature is not constant, their body temperature fluctuates with the fluctuation of the external temperature, such as fish, such as snakes, this is called cold-blooded animals. When they come to winter, the outside temperature is too low, the body temperature drops, so they can not move, this is called hibernation. Bears are warm-blooded animals, that is, thermostatic animals, the same as us humans, it does not have the quality of hibernation, why would it hibernate? In fact, it is not called hibernation, it is called dormancy. It is because there is nothing to eat in winter, so it eats a lot in autumn, when everything and fruit is ripe. In autumn an adult bear can eat more than 40 kilo food a day, it gains weight quickly and accumulates thick subcutaneous fact. In winter, when there is no food left, the bear has to hide in a cave and stay still, reducing its basal metabolic rate to the lowest level. When the next spring comes, it is thin to the bones, and then comes out again to look for food.

What does this mean? It means that animals want nothing other than foods, and just to the amount they need. The only exception is rodents, mice, voles, and squirrels. Rodents in the fall will bring food into their holes to store, such as pine seeds and so on. But even if it does so, it only collects food enough to eat in winter, not a little more. Because if it hides too much food in the hole, after the winter passes, the next spring warm climate brings abundant rainfall, air humidity increases, the left food in the hole will mold, it has to move the moldy food out, it is not so stupid. Therefore, before winter comes it hides food in the hole just to the limit it needs. Only we humans are the exceptions, greedy, grab endlessly!

Think about it. What is human civilization? The so-called human civilization is the process of constantly mobilizing and realizing human greed. Yuval Harari said in *A Brief History of Mankind* that everything in human hands, i.e., all the tools and means of living used now, can be regarded as luxury goods. This is true. Think about what you had in your hands when you were a monkey. Nothing! All the things you use today are not necessities, but luxuries. Man's greed is immense and civilization is highly developed. In other words, the mobilization of human greed has contributed to the rise of civilization, or rather, the enhancement of civilization and greed mobilization, the two stimulate each other, forming a positive feedback relationship, so the wheel of human history rolls forward.

Let me give you an example. In economics, there is a term called *Engel coefficient*. What is the *Engel coefficient*? The lower the percentage of your total income that you spend on food, the lower the Engel coefficient, the more civilized you are. So what is civilization? It is nothing more than the process of mobilizing and achieving greed.

Therefore, Laozi said "the third is refraining from be ahead of the world", that is, do not dare to innovate, do not dare to promote the development of civilization. Because if you continue to innovate, continue to promote the civilization process, then you will move towards that bad, erratic civilization society of less and less compassion, less and less frugality.

We can see from here that Laozi's view of society has a tendency to be "anti-civilization, anti-culture, and anti-progress". If you use these words today, you will immediately associate them with *anti-humanity*. Make no mistake! Laozi was never *anti-humanity*, but rather he wanted to preserve humanity. He believed that the constant promotion of civilization, the constant increase of culture, and the constant pursuit of progress were in fact maiming the existence of humanity. That's why he wanted to promote the opposite way.

Laozi has many other expressions in this regard, which I have condensed into two sets of words adopted by Laozi himself: the first is "forsake intelligence and abandon knowledge", and the second is "wear plain clothes and embrace simple life".

The so-called forsake intelligence is to abandon all the wisdom that civilized people can mobilize; the so-called abandon knowledge is to reject all the knowledge that civilized people create. What does it mean to "wear plain clothes and embrace simple life"? The word plain clothes refer to unbleached clothes; simple life refers to easy and the least demand life; the so-called "wear plain clothes and embrace simple life" means to let mankind regress to a pre-civilized, simple, primitive clan society.

Therefore, Laozi said, "The rule of sage is to keep their minds empty, their bellies full, their wills weak, and their bones strong." What does it mean to "keep their minds empty"? It does not mean to study with a humble mind, but rather the opposite of next phrase, "keep their bellies full," so, it means to throw away all the wisdom and knowledge in their minds, and just to fill up their bellies. And "keep their wills weak", is to wear down and weaken the ambition of civilized people. Think of the monkeys in the jungle, who had the ambition to transform the world? Then he says "keep their bones strong", which means to keep only one's body fit and bones strong. It is very much in line with what we call today "well-developed limbs but simple-minded", which is the state Laozi appreciated most.

Therefore, Laozi also said, "Always keep the people ignorant and desireless, so that the wise do not dare to act." This means that the best state of existence is to keep all people away from knowledge and desire, and never enter the civilized sequence, which is the "rule of sage".

He went on to say, "Five colors dazzle one's eyes, five sounds deafen one's ears, and five tastes spoil one's palate." Too bright colors will hurt your eyesight; too loud sound will hurt your hearing, you wear a headset in your ears all day long, your hearing will be harmed; stimulating food and drink will hurt your mouth and tongue. The following sentence is: "galloping and hunting, lead one's mind mad." Think about it, what is the state of civilization today? Isn't it "galloping and hunting"? In ancient times, civilized people rode horses and ran at high speed, and nowadays we drive cars and race at highways, which makes us feel excited and unrestrained. Then he said "rare goods, turn one's conduct awry", all people are pursuing luxury goods, LV bags and so on, resulting in their behavior completely deviated from the normal way of living.

That's why he said, "to pursue knowledge, you increase day by day; to follow *Dao* you decrease day by day". He said that when people pursue knowledge, they want to learn the more the better. However, if you want to follow *Dao*, to practice *Dao* you will lose more and more until you have nothing, that is, "to follow *Dao* you will decrease daily, till you have nothing to keep in mind," it means you should continue to remove the burden of civilization until you completely abandon it. We can see that Laozi is unapologetic and clear about his anti-culture, anti- civilization, anti-progress and other conservative views.

So, why did Laozi have such a reactionary *Deism* view of society?

You know, in those days, East Asian civilization was limited to the Central Plains, and its periphery was full of uncivilized people. Laozi saw it with his eyes, he did not need logical reasoning, he intuitively was able to find: in the Central Plains civilization caused social tensions, treacherous minds, deceitful behaviors, battle fields, bloodshed everywhere. The Shang Dynasty destroyed the Xia, the Zhou Dynasty destroyed the Shang, and in the Spring and Autumn Period, more than 180 vassal states fought one another. While the surrounding primitive clan society, that is, the uncivilized society of uncivilized people, was in a quiet and peaceful state.

Thus, in visual contrast, Laozi was able to comprehend that civilization was a disaster! Civilization is trending badly! The text of *Lao Zi* expresses his reactionary view of society very clearly. Not to mention scholars, anyone who reads Laozi's books carefully, his reactionary nature is immediately apparent.

But why do we seldom hear scholars lecture like this, and why do we seldom hear scholars have such a commentary on Laozi like this? It is because most people simply cannot understand what reactionary means. You know, in the history of human thought, all great thinkers tend to be reactionary. On the contrary, normal human beings will never be reactionary, as they cannot be reactionary even if they want to, because the world evolves in one direction.

Let me give you an example. For example, our modern history always says that Yuan Shikai is reactionary, this argument is actually not valid, or at least it is incomplete, we should remember that Yuan Shikai was one of the most advanced figures among the bureaucrats of the late Qing Dynasty. He strongly supported learning from the West during the foreign affairs movement, and in his later years, when he became governor of Hebei, Tianjin and Beijing big region and minister of the premier's office, he created eight firsts in China: he built China's first modern army; he established China's first modern police system in Tianjin during his tenure as governor of Hebei, Tianjin and Beijing big region; he also established the first telegraph and telephone bureau in China's history in Tianjin; under his promotion, he established the first telegraph and telephone bureau in China's history in Tianjin; he promoted the construction of the first officially recognized modern railroad in China's history, the famous Bei Jing-Zhang Jiakou Railway with Zhan Tianyou as the engineer; not only that, he also established the first modern school and modern girls' school in China and back then The girls' school could not recruit students because of the old-fashioned concept that women were not allowed to show their faces, which was called "never go out of the first door, seldom walk across the second door". The girl's school could not recruit students, then what did Yuan Shikai do? He actually sent all his eight concubines to the girls' school to study as girl students; he was really an advanced man.

Yuan Shikai in his late years claimed to resume the empire system and he was the emperor, which was indeed a reactionary action. But you need to know that after he claimed the restoration of the empire for less than 83 days, he died of disease suddenly, result of which left China 11 consecutive years of chaotic rule of the Northern Warlords. What does it mean? It shows that ordinary people can't be reactionary even if they want. But we can find that all great thinkers are inclined to be reactionary. This shows that reaction must contain some kind of profound meaning that is not understood by ordinary people.

Let's look at the facts below. In the history of human thought and culture, if you look closely, you will find a very strange phenomenon, which I call "the thinkers who react" and "the doers who misinterpret". That is, the thinker always tends to be reactionary, and the person who implements the thinker's ideas in practical operations, because he fails to be reactionary, so he has to misinterpret the thinker's ideas in order to implement in social practice. This is a very common phenomenon in the history of human civilization.

I give examples. Laozi was reactionary, as we already mentioned. But after the two Han dynasties, Laozi's doctrine actually became the doctrine of a Huang-Lao school, which became a strategy of governance. As we all know, in the early years of the Western Han Dynasty, the doctrine of Laozi prevailed, and the rule of Emperor Wenjing was achieved by applying Laozi's principle of "rule by doing nothing". It embraced the saying of Laozi "ruling a big country is like cooking a small fish", which is indeed the original words of Laozi, meaning that ruling a big country is like frying a small fish in pot, you must not toss it around too often, otherwise, you will turn it into fish scraps.

But why did Laozi speak this phrase? If you read the book of *Lao Zi*, if you listen to this lesson, you should understand that Laozi's basic proposition could be clarified by four sets of phrases – let the country be smaller, people be more foolish, things be thriftier, and tools be simpler. This is Laozi's true ideal. The phrase "ruling a big country is like cooking a small fish" appeared in *Daodejing*, is actually just a side metaphor to prove the importance of doing nothing, which is not the theme of Laozi's thought.

I repeat, the basic idea of Laozi's thought is to let the country be smaller, people be more foolish, things be thriftier, tools be simpler. Many people interpret Laozi's doctrine as conspiracy and trickery, and even think that the way of warriors was originated from Laozi. This is totally a misinterpretation of Laozi. But the doctrine of Laozi has been misinterpreted for 2000 years.

Let's look at Confucius again. What was Confucius' highest ideal? *Restrain oneself and restore propriety*. What is the meaning by "restraining oneself and restoring propriety"? To do one's best to resume the past social propriety of the Zhou dynasty, standing at the end of the Spring and Autumn Period, but trying to regress to the time when Duke Zhou Jidan made rites and music in the early years of the Western Zhou dynasty, this is called *restrain oneself and restore propriety*. Therefore, during the Cultural Revolution, Confucius was criticized as a reactionary Confucius, which was not a mistake at all.

So, we can see Confucian doctrine advocates reaction, advocating a return to the intact feudal system of the early Western Zhou Dynasty, but how much terribly it was eventually misinterpreted? From the time of Emperor Wu, Liuche, of the Han Dynasty, uniquely embracing Confucianism, the anti-feudal system of the great monarchy dictatorship became the symbol of the times in which the banner of Confucian doctrine was flown. This is obviously a serious distortion of the original intent of Confucian doctrine.

Let's look at Plato again. Plato wrote a book, *The Ideal State,* which I think many students here may have read. In this book, Plato makes a series of reactionary claims. For example, he advocates communal ownership and he opposes any privatization and private property. When was mankind communal? Only in the era of the primitive clan commune. So remember, the faster you run forward, the farther you will be away from communism.

Plato also argued that dyadic marriages and families should not be formed; he was against dyadic marriage. Imagine when mankind was not in a dyadic marriage? It was in primitive clan societies, before civilization, humans were married in groups. Plato even opposed the private raising of children by families, he advocated that children should be raised by society. Think about it, when did we have children raised by society? Again, it was in primitive clan society. It is clear that Plato's basic concept was also very reactionary. But Plato's doctrine eventually led to the development of Western philosophical thinking, and he became the ideological founder and theoretical promoter of modern Western classical philosophy and its radical scientific trend.

Let me give you another example - Rousseau. What was Rousseau? He was the thinker for the bourgeois revolution, as Marx did for the proletarian revolution. In other words, Rousseau was the theoretical banner of the bourgeois revolution. Rousseau wrote a famous book, *The Social Contract.* Please note that as early as 2600 years ago in ancient Greece, their basic social structure and social thought was contract society.

What is the Social Contract about? Rousseau suggests that civilized human society is a state in which public will is gradually formed. We can understand the word public today as public will or public power, and he asks how public will and public power are formed. It is because human beings have gradually moved from the state of nature to the contract society, that is, they have gradually reached some kind of unwritten or written consensus and contract, and each person has ceded part of his private rights, thus constituting public will and public power. Therefore, it should strive to protect the basic private rights or natural human rights of all people, and may impose necessary sanctions on those who violate the public will. But if the public will and public power end up depriving and harming human rights, it is a violation of the contract, and the individual has the right to seek redress or even to recover his private rights. His doctrine eventually formed the theoretical basis of modern Western democracy.

If you listen to my expression in this paragraph, you will think that Rousseau's thought was very advanced. Don't be mistaken! In fact, Rousseau deeply believed that contract society is a very bad social state, which makes people of born free, to always live in chains. He said that the general public did not know how mankind had somehow fallen into this age, and he intended to clarify this question. He deduced that the best golden age for mankind was the one, he specifically used the term natural state, that is, he believed that the best state for mankind was when mankind was living like monkeys in the jungle.

If I say this, and you think that I have misread Rousseau. Then let's take a look at Voltaire's reply to Rousseau in 1755, when he sent his famous anthology *On the Origin of Human Inequality* to Voltaire, then the great French Enlightenment philosopher, who read it and wrote back to Rousseau. In his reply, Voltaire said: "Having seen your new anti-human work, I thank you for it. It is unprecedented to use such cleverness in an attempt to make us all stupid. Reading your book, one cannot help but long for crawling on four limbs." It is clear that Voltaire read Rousseau and knew that this guy was particularly reactionary.

There are many more examples I could give, but due to time constraints, I won't go into them any further.

We will find that the most important thinkers in the history of human thought have tended to be reactionary. It shows that reaction must contain some kind of connotation that cannot be understood by ordinary people.

We analyze and interpret this phenomenon below with the help of a large informative cognitive model.

Law of Weakening Compensation

The history of human civilization is a spontaneous process with an increasing amount of information. Any pre-cited problem can be stretched out and clearly presented only as the amount of information increases. Then let us pull out the general map of natural science in the 20th century to form a new cosmology with a large amount of information, so that we see how the whole cosmic evolution is in a process.

The development of the natural sciences in the 20th century has led to the breaking down of the boundaries between the various disciplines. For example, what is meant by life? The definition of life has never been clear to humans. Huxley, the self-proclaimed dog of Darwin, who was also a famous biologist, was once asked what life was. He couldn't answer it, so he flirted with the idea that life is the escape from death.

It was not until the middle of the 20th century that mankind suddenly came to understand that life was in fact nothing more than a molecular code. This led to the creation of a new discipline, molecular biology. The emergence of this discipline broke down the boundary between biology and molecular chemistry. At the same time, or even before that, a new discipline called physical chemistry was created. Because what we usually call chemical bond is nothing but really a redistribution of energy in the electron cloud of the physical shell of an atom. In order to know what the structure of a molecule is, you must first know what the structure of an atom is, and thus physical chemistry emerged. It in turn erased the boundary between chemistry and physics, and so, everything unfolded as a pattern of a series evolution in one system.

In 1859, Darwin published his famous monograph on biology, *On the Origin of Species*, and the doctrine of evolution was born. In Darwin's work, you can see an evolutionary history of 3.8 billion years of living things, from primitive single-celled organisms to human beings, from simple to complex, from low to high, in a specific stage of evolutionary trend. However, it was then discovered that this evolutionary phenomenon is not only limited to the biological world, that is, biological evolution was preceded by molecular evolution, which is the evolution of organic macromolecules from small inorganic molecules, and then the evolution of biopolymers, including biocoded molecules. This did not end here, and it was then discovered that molecular evolution was preceded by atomic evolution, a table of chemical elements that evolved from hydrogen, the first element, to 92 natural elements. This is not the end. It was discovered that there was also particle evolution before atomic evolution, from the energy singularity 13.7 billion years ago, suddenly burst out the first three elementary particles, which are quarks, leptons and bosons, which evolved a large number of other particles and 92 natural elements.

A complete panorama of the evolution of all things is thus fully unfolded, constituting a general situation of the unity of all things and the homogeneity of all things. In this huge spectrum, we will find a very strange phenomenon, that is, the more primitive and lower the material existence form or species, the higher its degree of existence; the more evolved and developed the material existence form or species, the lower its degree of existence. What do I mean by degree of existence? To make it simple, there are three indicators to match it: first, the greater the mass distribution in the universe, second, the longer the duration of its existence in the universe, and third, the more stable its state of existence.

I'll give examples below. Elementary particles have been occurring in the universe for 13.7 billion years, and it is still by far the most massive form of matter existing in the universe. The previous physics considered the total amount of matter in the universe to be the stellar system, but it was soon found to be incorrect, because according to the mass of the stellar system, it simply cannot sustain the gravitational structure of the existing cosmic galaxies. It is calculated that to maintain such a gravitational structure, the total mass of matter needs to increase at least by a factor of 5 times, thus the concept of dark matter was introduced; furthermore, since recent astrophysics has found that the galaxies in the universe are rapidly moving away from each other, which is the so-called redshift phenomenon, then, according to the previously projected burst energy in the universe, the energy level to support this rapid escape is not enough, so the concept of dark energy is derived. Although physics cannot say what dark matter and dark energy are, most physicists believe that dark matter and dark energy must be some kind of odd mass or energy hidden in elementary particles or quantum states that are still unobserved. And according to calculations, dark matter and dark energy account for about 95% of the total mass of the universe, and stellar systems account for only about 5%. The elementary particles and quanta are the earliest primitive forms of matter, but they have the largest mass distribution, the longest evolution time and the most stable state of existence in the universe, and have been so for 13.7 billion years.

Let's look at atoms. The so-called star is the atomic state of existence, hydrogen nucleus constantly fusion, fusing into helium nucleus to release energy, which is solar energy. A periodic table of chemical elements is the gradual evolution of 92 natural elements from the number one element hydrogen. And you will find that the more primitive and more anterior the element, the greater its total mass in the universe and the more stable its state; the more posterior the element, the smaller its total mass in the universe and the more unstable its state. For example, the last natural element, uranium, was used by mankind to make the atomic bomb because of its instability. Thus, in stars, the mass distribution between hydrogen and helium varies greatly, with hydrogen alone occupying about 79% of the mass of the average star, another 19% or so being helium nuclei, and the rest of the posterior natural elements accounting for less than 1% to 3% of the mass in most main sequence stars. We find that the more primitive and lower the element, the greater the overall mass.

The above scenario is even more remarkable if we continue to look at the other matter distribution relations of the stellar system. In the solar system, for example, the Sun accounts for 99.86% of the total mass of the solar system; if we consider the eight planets as molecular matter in their main bodies, then the eight planets plus interstellar matter account for only 0.14% of the total mass of the solar system. Moreover, we will find that the planets, although occurring later than the Sun, will definitely perish before the Sun. Contemporary astronomical research suggests that in 4 to 5 billion years, the Sun will become a red giant, which will expand in size, swallowing up the perihelion planets such as Mercury, Venus, and Earth, and causing their molecular matter to dissociate back into atoms under high temperature and pressure. In other words, we will find that the star occurs before the planets but dies later than the planets. It takes more than a hundred billion years for a red giant to become a white dwarf and then a black dwarf before it dies, but planets in the molecular configuration do not last long and are doomed to die earlier. Once again, it shows us the higher and more complex the matter, the lower the mass of existence, the shorter the duration of existence, and the degree of existence tends to fall.

This phenomenon becomes more obvious when we reach the development of the biological stage.

The living matter only covers the surface of the earth, spreading into a thin layer of biosphere, it is not even a billionth of the total mass of the earth, the mass further decreases significantly. And we will find that the more primitive and lower species, the stronger the existence, the greater the amount of their existence.

Let me give you an example. The most primitive organisms on earth are single-celled organisms that occurred 3.8 billion years ago, and single-celled organisms are so vigorous that they almost never grow old, get sick, and die. Think about it, what is the single-celled fungus that exists today? It is a continuation of the bacteria that split in two 3.8 billion years ago. Unless the resources are limited, so the number of divisions is limited, it continues to divide and proliferate, and there is no such thing as old age and death, so the state of survival is balanced, or the process of life and death has nothing to do with aging; on the contrary, the more advanced the species, the more urgent the cycle of life and death.

Single-celled organisms have existed for 3.8 billion years and have never gone extinct. Not only has it never gone extinct, it is still the most massive and strongest species on earth. It is called single-celled algae in the ocean, if its total mass is not greater than the sum of the mass of all marine organisms a number of times more, then the basic food chain of marine life would have collapsed, marine life would have systematically disappeared. It is called single-celled bacteria on the surface, and is likewise the species with the greatest mass, even the formation of soil involves the participation of bacteria. How vigorous is its life force? -- It is able to survive unharmed in the liquid of volcanic craters at temperatures above 90 degrees Celsius, it is able to survive under the high pressure of 10,000 meters under the deep sea. As for human diving, if you dive below 30 meters, you will have a fatal disease of high pressure. It survives as usual in the strong acid and alkali liquid in the waste mine pit. The single-celled organism that pollutes *Taihu* Lake and *Dianchi* Lake today is called blue-green algae, also called cyanobacteria, which is one of the most primitive single-celled organisms 3.8 billion years ago. So we see the strength of life of primitive single-celled organisms.

Instead of doing itemized examples below, such as sponge creatures, mollusks, squamates, arthropods, etc., let's look directly at the medium level vertebrate reptile dinosaurs. Dinosaurs survived on Earth for only about 160 million years, but they suddenly became extinct 65 million years ago. When we talk about the extinction of dinosaurs today, we say that it was caused by the accidental impact of an asteroid on the Earth, which is the famous catastrophe theory; but there is a problem with this statement. This is because biologists have found that the extinction of dinosaurs went through a process of at least millions or even more than millions of years, that is, long before the asteroid hit the Earth, the phytophagous dinosaurs became extinct because their food - ferns tended to be replaced by angiosperms, causing the phytophagous dinosaurs to become extinct first, which is also known as the flowers wiped out the dinosaurs, and then the carnivorous dinosaurs, whose food chain was based on phytophagous dinosaurs, became extinct one after another. Thus, the extinction of dinosaurs began to occur gradually millions of years before the asteroid impact. Moreover, even if the asteroid hit the Earth 65 million years ago and eventually led to the sudden extinction of all dinosaurs, one question cannot be answered: why did a large number of other species lower than dinosaurs not become extinct?

Lastly, we look at the higher organisms, the mammals, and bear in mind that we humans belong to one genus of the mammals.

Mammals have occurred on this planet for a total of only 70 to 90 million years, yet the vast majority have been extinct long before humans came into being. Its existence is extremely low and its population size is extremely small. Let's look further down the list, the most advanced class of mammals is called primates, and the most advanced group of primates is Homo erectus. Homo erectus existed on earth for 3 to 5 million years, as I mentioned in my lecture earlier, but suddenly all of them became extinct 70,000 to 25,000 years ago. The modern Homo sapiens, the human race of today, has existed on the earth for less than 200,000 years, and I think it is not far from extinction.

In short, when we look things at a larger scale, we will find a situation: the lower and more primitive the material existence form or species, the higher its potence of existence or degree of existence; the more evolved and more advanced the material existence form or species, the lower its potence of existence or degree of existence. We also find an even stranger phenomenon: the lower the degree of existence of a substance or species, the higher its properties and abilities. Why do I call ability as property? It is because the so-called biological ability, such as human perception, is actually a gainful substitute for the original physical sensing property.

I'll give examples below. The highest degree of existence of elementary particles, have the lowest properties or capabilities, they only have strong and weak forces; when it came to atoms, electromagnetic induction appears; when it came to molecules, Brownian motion appears; when it came to single cells, receptors appear on cell membranes, which can actually distinguish the vast majority of atoms and ions in the universe; when it came to flat animals, vision and nerve nets appear; when it came to vertebrates, five senses and lower nerve centers appear; when it came to primates, higher nerve centers and cerebral cortex emerge; when it came to humans, the frontal neocortex and the ability to reason emerge.

That is, we will find that the higher the degree of existence of a material form or species, the lower its properties and capabilities; the lower the degree of existence of a material form or species, the stronger and greater its properties and capabilities. Please note that it is exact opposite to our general perception or intuitive appearance. People usually think that the stronger the capability, the more advantageous the state of existence is. Wrong! On a larger scale, the stronger the ability, actually the lower the existence, and the two become a strictly inverse functional relationship, so strict that it can even be calculated almost precisely.

We need to understand that we can see the state of all things clearly only after we pull up the scale. Let me give you an example, man's ancient vision was extremely small, and he saw the earth as a flat plate, so he formed the theory of the sky vault, that is, the sky is round, and thought that the earth was a flat plate resting on the back of a turtle, and the sky was like a vault buckled on the ground.

The ancient Greek philosophers from Pythagoras, Plato, Aristotle up to Ptolemy, they observed that the moon's gain and loss and lunar eclipse movement is actually a change in the relative position of the earth and moon and the earth's arc shadow projected on the moon, they stood on a large scale far above the earth's position, and established the earth theory and later the geocentric theory. Since then, the scale was further stretched, and so far this scale has been as large as the spacetime scale of 13.7 billion light years, that is, light travels 13.7 billion years at a speed of 300,000 kilometers per second. Such a large spatial scale is the sight and perception margin of our present-day humans, and that is how we developed the modern view of the universe.

And we should also note that the phenomenon and the essence are always the opposite. If you rely on your eyes, the sun clearly rises from the east and sets from the west, and it is clear that the sun revolves around the earth, but in fact it is the earth that revolves around the sun. So when we pull up the scale, you will find that it is completely different from the general idea and material form that we have established in our common sense.

We will find that in the process of evolution of matter, the degree of matter existence is decreasing, while the abundance of matter properties and the ability of compensation is increasing in inverse proportion, I call this phenomenon law of weakening compensation, or, I call the logical rectification model of this phenomenon the principle of weakening compensation. This law or principle continues to be implemented in the history of human civilization, for example, the pre-human civilization of the Paleolithic Age lasted for more than a million years, the agricultural civilization lasted for about 10,000 years, and the industrial and commercial civilization is only 300 years, and today it has been covered by the information civilization. I can predict that the information civilization will never last more than 100 years before it will be overwhelmed by the next worse wave of civilization. We will find that the more advanced the structure, the more unstable it must be. It continues to be expressed throughout the history of human civilization without interruption, i.e., the higher the properties and capabilities, the lower their potence of existence, and probably this is the general law of the evolution of the universe.

Nowadays, we human beings are desperately trying to improve our abilities, thinking that we will gain an advantage in survival and even immortality by doing so, putting forward radical slogans of higher, faster, stronger. What do you want to do? There is only one goal ahead of you, and that is, to run quickly to death and destruction, which is the evolutionary process of things and the prospect of the human world on a larger scale. This doctrine effectively explains the serious reality of why the higher the level of human civilization, the deeper the crisis. As we all know, it was not until after the 1960s that people discovered that the high level of civilization we have today is bringing a series of major disasters to all mankind.

Let me give you an example. Let's look at environmental pollution first. We humans today have polluted almost all of the three most abundant substances on earth: air, fresh water, and soil. Due to air pollution, once the rain falls, the pollutants in the air will spill into the soil with the rain, plus because we have polluted 97.85% of the earth's freshwater resources since long, that is, all rivers, and lakes are polluted, perhaps now only limited streams of the deep forests are left unpolluted, farmers can only irrigate the land with polluted water, resulting in full soil pollution. As early as nearly a decade ago, the global soil scientists did general research, and they found that the earth's existing agricultural soil pollution rate of is up to 60% or more. What kind of damage does pollution actually do to us? We can't say now, but you should know that every meal you have today, every bottle of water you drink, and even every breath of air you breathe, you are damaged by pollution.

In the 1950s, the Dutch medical profession found that the sperm count of Dutch men had dropped significantly. The news reached the United Kingdom, and the British medical profession began a survey, pulling out the year 1950 sperm test reports of men in major hospitals in the United Kingdom and comparing them with the year 2000 sperm test reports of men in major hospitals, and found that the normal sperm count of men in the United Kingdom dropped by 45% in 50 years. When this information reached China, the Chinese Academy of Medical Sciences carried out a research, pulling out the year 1975 men's sperm test report and year 2010 men's sperm test report to do a comparison study, and they found that the normal sperm count of Chinese men fell by 30% in 35 years. You know, all mammals before their extinction the first sign is the decline in male sperm count.

Let's look at the ecological damage. According to the United Nations Wildlife Fund research, now every hour there are 3~6 species extinction, at least 75 species extinction every day, 30,000 ∽ 60,000 species extinction every year, the biological community called it the sixth biological extinction on Earth. And the extinction rate is extremely high, much faster than the previous five times. You know the species that are now extinct are much lower than us humans, that is, the species of much higher degree of existence, even they are rapidly extinct, how far we humans are from extinction?

Let's look at climate anomalies. In year 2009 climate conference was held in Copenhagen, Denmark, with the world's heads of states in attendance, why? The level of climate anomalies on the planet today has become a serious threat to the survival of all mankind. What was the topic of discussion at the conference? The issue of two degrees Celsius. What does that mean? In less than 250 years from the first industrial revolution in 1788 to today, we humans have raised the average temperature of the earth by almost 1 degree Celsius. We know that the Earth's temperature is supposed to fluctuate, but its natural fluctuation cycle is extremely long, hundreds of thousands or even millions of years before a fluctuation cycle occurs, and the general direction of fluctuation is cooling, forming ice ages. But humans in the post-industrial period so far, in just a few hundred years actually quickly raised the average temperature of the Earth 0.8 ∽ 0.9 degrees, its rate is thousand times more than the natural Earth climate fluctuations.

Why is the conference set to discuss the issue of two degrees Celsius? It is because if mankind raises the average temperature of the earth by more than two degrees Celsius, then a substance called solid methane, which is commonly known as combustible ice, hidden under the permafrost of Siberia and the shallow sea of the Arctic, will be released from the solid state to the gaseous state and enter the atmosphere, and the greenhouse effect of methane is more than 20∽25 times that of carbon dioxide. In other words, if human beings raise the average temperature of the earth by more than two degrees Celsius, then the time bomb of solid methane will explode and there will be no possibility for human beings to solve the problem of climate anomalies from now on.

However, some scholars calculate that according to the current rate of human industrialization, we should know that the industrialization of Africa, South America and Arab countries has just started, and if we continue to develop at this rate, it will only take 30 years, around 2050 or even before 2050, the average temperature of the earth will rise by more than two degrees Celsius. Some scholars also calculate that to interrupt this process, at least 70% of all human factories and their industrial products, including cars and airplanes, need to be shut down now. Is this possible? At the Copenhagen climate conference only to reach an agreement on reducing emissions, it ended in failure; recently, another Paris agreement was made, but the countries argued and compromised to the minimum, and the United States withdrew. Therefore, we can basically conclude that mankind has lost the future of solving the climate anomaly.

Let's look at weapons of mass destruction. Back at the end of the last century, the United Nations counted the world's nuclear weapons stockpile at the time, and the results was an equivalent of 2.5 tons of TNT nuclear equivalent sitting under the seat of each of the world's billions of people, enough to blow up all of humanity dozens of times. This is not including the more vicious genetic weapons, biochemical weapons, weather weapons, etc.

Please note that while we are highly civilized today, but mankind on Earth is on the side of an abyss of total crisis. Man survived very hard in ancient times, but as a species he was generally safe. The result of our high-level development and progress today is that we are at risk of extinction. So I say, fundamentally, today mankind remains ignorant of the situation of his own existence, and there may be major problems with our cosmology and worldview. Almost no one in today's academic and intellectual circles, whether in the East or the West, has ever really studied this issue in depth. All scholars in the East and West are advocating faster development and are pushing for faster progress. But no one is clear where do we really want to go? We are desperately chasing each other forward, but no one can say what our goal is. Where are we running to? What is our future? In an age of so much information, all of humanity and its intellectual community are in a state of total blindness and obscurity.

On the contrary, Laozi had already sounded the alarm on this issue 2600 years ago. What is Laozi's *Daoism*? I said earlier that "weakness is the effectuation of *Dao*", and I said that its deeper understanding is that the phenomenon of weakness is the way to realize *Dao*. The core point and anchor point of this theory is *Rou-Ruo* (softness and weakness); What is the core point and anchor point of Laozi's *Deism*? It is *Wu-Wei* (let things move on with no interventions), that is, do not enhance your ability. In other words, Laozi's *Daoism* and *Deism* are precisely focused on the two points of weakening compensation. He is the only thinker in the history of human thought who first speculated on this natural phenomenon, so I say that Laozi's vision is far-reaching and unique. Laozi said in his book, "the sky will be torn apart when it is not clear", it seems symbolizing the atmospheric pollution; he said that "the earth will be deserted when it is not clean", making a vague prediction that the earth's soil and rivers will be polluted; he said, "grains will be exhausted when cereals are not yielding" making a prediction about the depletion of rivers and the shortage of water resources, which will lead to the problem of grain production; he said, "every being will be extinct when life is no way to survive," making a prediction about the sixth extinction of living things; we can see that at far antient time, Laozi was as discerning as a torch.

Many scholars disagree with me when I talk about Laozi in this way. Our ancient Chinese culture of commenting on the scriptures can be summed up as: "One who annotates the six scriptures, is inspired by the six scriptures". I follow the original text of the scriptures closely and made comments on them without adding any of my own opinions or views. I followed the original meaning of Laozi's text strictly, even if this original meaning is totally incompatible with our current mainstream ideology, even if it is expressed as a most reactionary image, I am still faithful to the original text. That is why I started this lecture by saying that the original purpose and main line of our lecture on Laozi is to strictly follow the text of Laozi and I will not to make any later distortions or interpretations, which is called "One who annotates the six scriptures," but below is the part that "one is inspired by the six scriptures".

It is not *Dao* without others' Laughter

Many scholars think that Laozi's *Daoism* and *Deism* have nothing to do with my principle of weakening compensation, which is just my nonsense derivation.

Before I wrote *A Unified Theory of Evolution*, I had read *Daodejing* and thought I understood it, of course I was young at that time. When I wrote my book to the halfway of volume one, I suddenly realized that I might not have understood *Daodejing* at all, so I opened it again and read it from the beginning, and only then did I understand the deep meaning of Laozi.

"Being inspired by the six scriptures" is actually a necessary step to interpret the texts of antient literatures. If you do not have any new vision or insight when you read the texts of your predecessors, what are you reading? How can you call it reading? Only when you can get the inspiration caused by the texts of antient literatures, that is, the increased current background information has a greater strength of interpretation on antient literatures, can you interpret the more profound insight out of it. This is called reading; this is called learning. Therefore, it is quite normal when one "is inspired by the six scriptures".

Let me give you an example. When Darwin wrote the introduction for his book, *The Origin of Species*, he goes so far as to specifically thank Malthus. Malthus, as you may be familiar with, was not a biologist, he was a demographer and a sociologist. His main doctrine is the population theory, which holds that population grows geometrically, while human means of subsistence or production capacity grows arithmetically, so that the momentum of human population growth and its prospects for survival and development inevitably lead to famine, pestilence and war, through which reach the relative balance between population and resources. Regardless of the correctness of this doctrine, it did cause a major enlightenment to Darwin, making him realize that the reproductive potential of organisms is far greater than the realistic survival of organisms, that is, the reproductive capacity of any organism appears too large, while the realistic resource conditions allow the survival of species is set at a very low natural threshold. Malthusian population theory was a major source of enlightenment for Darwin, giving him a deep understanding of how intraspecific competition played a role in evolution. This study, which had nothing to do with Darwin's biology, was acknowledged by Darwin in the introduction of *The Origin of Species*. This is called "being inspired by the six scriptures", and this is the true way to study.

The value of an ancient idea, the doctrine of its predecessors, lies in the fact that it contains an explanatory power that can be widely developed. I borrow a phrase from Hegel to the effect that the entire inner prescriptiveness of a blooming flower is contained in that tiny seed. Therefore, if you cannot uncover and reveal the explanatory power implied in the concise narratives of your predecessors, it proves that you do not have research skills, and that you do not have the ability to control and consolidate the amount of new information. Therefore, a really good reading must first achieve "one who annotates the six scriptures", that is, faithful to the original; at the same time, it must also achieve "being inspired by the six scriptures", that is, to achieve a new comprehension based on a deeper interpretation of the large amount of information; this is the standard way to do research and academic work.

Laozi was unable to make a systematic proof of this stuff back then, and he expressed it confusingly because of the lack of information. I say he got four and a half out of five wrong. He said that *Dao* is "soft and weak", but he could not say what this softness and weakness is, and he could not prove it systematically. He praises softness and weakness at one time and criticizes it at another. For example, he says, "When things in their prime will become old, which is no longer close to *Dao*, and being not *Dao* will soon demise", which is obviously a criticism of softness and weakness. He said, "Heaven is *Dao*, *Dao* is eternality, then no danger till the end of life", which is obviously the opposite praise of softness and weakness. However, he also said, "Nothing in the world is softer and weaker than water, but in attacking the strong and hard nothing can surpass water" and "The world's softest thing gallops through the world's hardest thing", you can see his appreciation of softness and weakness in these two sentences. His expression is confusing, why? There was not enough information to make a systematic proof. This has led to many deviations and superficial statements in the interpretation of Laozi by later generations. That is why Laozi himself said, "Whichever heaven disapproves, who knows why? Even the sages will find it difficult." (See *Daodejing*, section 73.) He says that who can tell what Heaven and Earth dislike? Even a sage would be puzzled! Actually, that's because there wasn't enough information back then. The above quotation also shows that Laozi was well aware that he could not elaborate and prove thoroughly the issues he discussed. But we should not forget that Laozi's *Daoism* points to *weakening*, which is called "weakness is the effectuation of *Dao*"; Laozi's *Deism* points to *compensation*, which is called *Wu-Wei*, that is, do not enhance your ability; such a precise correspondence between the two points shows that Laozi had a deep thought and speculation that he could not prove for the time being.

All major changes in human thought began with some kind of conjecture. The physics of today is a continuation of the atomic theory conjecture proposed by Democritus and his teacher Reuben in ancient Greece 2500 years ago. Therefore, even if Laozi's views are not clear and seem to be confused, the high academic value of his ideas is unparalleled, and for this reason we certainly have to give Laozi a very high evaluation.

We have mentioned several mistakes in Laozi's doctrine, which are manifested in various aspects. The so-called half right is the conjecture of softness in *Daoism*. However, Laozi speaks of *Wu-Wei*, saying that human beings become contrary to *Dao* of Heaven in their more and more actions in doing things, advocating *Wu-Wei* (no intervention in things moving on) of pursuing *Dao* through daily decrement" is in line with *Dao* (Way of Heaven), Laozi is obviously wrong. Because we find that the more advanced the biological species, the more powerful their capabilities must be; the more develops human civilization, the more increased human capabilities. In other words, the increase of material properties and capabilities, including the increasing technological capabilities in the history of our civilization, is precisely a product of the evolution of the Heavenly Way, not at all an act against the Heavenly Way. It can be seen that Laozi was wrong on this major issue. Laozi excluded the phenomenon of humanities, that is, the phenomenon of human civilization, from the Heavenly Way and Material Virtue. The phenomenon of civilization is only the personalized expression and social embodiment of the final stage of the evolution of the universe, and that's all.

Because Laozi held the concept of dialectics, which connotes the circuit of things that go the opposite whenever reach its extreme, Laozi advocated reaction and returning to the primitive, pre-enlightened animal-like social group of blood relatives. And we know today that the dialectic does not hold, that the world is evolving in one direction, and that we have no way back. So the situation we face today is far more treacherous than Laozi predicted back then, because our backward direction is a dead end, and our forward direction is a dangerous one. Laozi at least thought there was a way out by going backwards, but this way out does not exist, and we are in a dilemma today. Only stupid human beings still think that going forward and advancing at high speed will give us a survival advantage, we are happy because of this, we are crazy because of this, and then we confusedly continue to be arrogant until we go to death. Only Laozi sounded the alarm for the bad trend of human civilization 2600 years ago, so I can never overly give Laozi high rating, even though he seemed out of place at that time.

I can anticipate that you may have many questions at my lecture, many of you will debate with me, saying that we are so capable today that we can go beyond the principle of weakening compensation. Make no mistake! A rule of material evolution under large scale that drives and governs us is *Dao*. And we generally look at the level of specific things and only discuss what we can drive and dictate. The more important is that we should first understand what we are governed by, and this is the fundamental concern, and this is what the cosmology is about, and in short, we need to find humanity's place in nature. Philosophy is nothing more than life in the universe! It deals with the ultimate question, with the unchangeable rules of your situation. It is the value of the study of useless learning that leads to and looks at the future of humanity from this basic theory, traces the future path of existence from a higher standpoint, and provides logical signposts for it. It is important to know that in every little bit we can prove this principle of weakening compensation and the trend of its weakening or criticality, which is the law of nature that Laozi called "weakness is the effectuation of *Dao*".

Let me give you an example. Some scholars once argued with me that nowadays it is civilized, at least people no longer defecate in the open, which is a good thing, right? But don't forget, in ancient times the population was small, and open defecation did not pollute the environment at all, only fertilized woodland and farmland. Today all residents use flush toilets, feces and urine go into the septic tank only softened without further treatment, then directly flow into the rivers. Seven billion people's feces and urine directly polluted all the rivers, we think about how terrible is this situation. Only domestic sewage pollution, not counting industrial pollution, chemical pollution, all the rivers and lakes are badly polluted. Once I went to the southern countryside and saw the big rivers floating full of feces. This is the consequence of human progress from antient defecating in the open into using flushing toilets today. Look at the garbage siege, a small and medium-sized cities produce hundreds of tons of garbage every day, not to mention huge cities everywhere, but how can we humans manage to treat that tremendous amount of garbage each day? You know that the ancients produced no garbage at all, the ashes of the burning fire is grass ash, peeled onion and garlic and other vegetable leaves, animal bones all were composted to organic fertilizer, good for crops, so no garbage. Today we use a lot of artificial materials, from plastic to various heavy metals and electronic products, these things all become pollutants that we simply cannot deal with. How do you treat it? If you buried them deeply, once it rains, the rain water ooze down and percolate the soil, dissolve them, mix with them, then carry them to pollute the groundwater, which in turn is communicated with fresh surface water; if you burn garbage, it immediately produces more than 40 kinds of air pollutants, including serious carcinogens such as dioxins, so European countries in recent years turned to a negative attitude for the burning of waste disposal. We can see that every little progress humans make, in fact, we cannot avoid causing reversed harm in long terms.

Some people say that we are changing from fuel to electric cars today, and it should be a benign measure of progress, right? You're wrong again! You should know that a piece of wasted No. A battery, which you discard casually, it pollutes a square kilometer of groundwater after corrosion and breakage, which is why the sorting of waste batteries needs to be particularly strict. Then think about a battery car, it carries the battery amount at least equivalent to nearly a thousand No. A batteries, how will you deal with it later? From production to recycling disposal, what will you do with them? You gather a large number of harmful substances originally scattered in the surface rock layer, cohesively purified them and bring into the environment of human survival, how do you return them to their original place? What kind of pollution it will cause in the long run? You can never predict it today. People need decades or even hundreds of years to understand a thing, the short-term arguments you make today are not enough to avoid the problem in the future. Those seem to improve the environment, pollution-control measures, in the long run may be a greater disaster, a new source of pollution.

Some leaders say that we build nuclear power plants today as a solution to environmental pollution because they do not produce greenhouse gas emissions. But do you know what the state of nuclear power plants is in terms of reprocessing? Leave aside the fact that nuclear power plants cannot solve the problem of nuclear leakage caused by natural disasters or man-made accidents, we assume that nuclear power plants are 100 percent absolutely safe, and that nuclear waste alone cannot be disposed of by humans. You know that even with the most modern high technology, nuclear fuel rods can never be 100% depleted of their radioactive energy and material, and a large percentage of it becomes nuclear waste. Where to put it? Wrapped up in lead barrels and buried in the ground, but any lead barrels are not strong enough to last three or four hundred years, hundreds of years later the lead barrels will still break down. And the heat it emits, the unit heat of nuclear waste, is so high that it is more than 1.5 times the heat of the same volume of solar matter, so it is enough to melt the surrounding rock layers and contaminate the entire groundwater in a radioactive way. As I said the groundwater communicates with the surface water in a circular way, thus causing radioactive contamination of the entire surface. If put it to the bottom of the sea, all marine life is bound to get radioactive contamination, we know that the Fukushima nuclear power plant in Japan leaked out of the cooling water, nuclear contamination of the cooling water is getting bigger and bigger, an amount nowhere to store, so there is only one way, that is to discharge the contaminated water into the sea, and contaminant is still so much so that it is discharged in the western side of the Pacific Ocean, the Americans took seawater measurements on the east coast of the Pacific Ocean and found that the amount of radioactive substances in it is greatly increased. So, you have to be careful, you eat sea fish today is an implicitly dangerous thing. What we can do with it? There's one way left, ship nuclear waste to the moon, but it's so expensive to do it that you simply can't support the tolerable cost of supplying large amounts of electricity. Clearly it is not a safe way to produce, it is not a sustainable way to supply energy, and it is a pathway much more terrible by simply delaying the self-deceptive pollution. In short, we will find that every human progress, that even a tiny innovation, put in the long term it will have the harm effect.

We humans are short-sighted, and our general wisdom in the world is simply not enough to foresee the distant future. Our basic way of survival is that what problem we face, we find the opportunity to solve that problem, as for what consequence the solution of this problem in the future will produce in the long-term, people simply cannot foresee it. Therefore, if we look at the whole history of human civilization, it shows such a bizarre phenomenon: in order to survive in the present, we have to release a small devil; when the small devil is in chaos, we release a middle devil to subdue the small devil; eventually the middle devil is in chaos again, then we release a big devil to subdue the middle devil; in the end, the shadow of the devil envelops the whole human race. This is the true picture of the vicious civilization process, and this is the reason that the more development and progress we face from ancient times to the present, the more precarious the situation of our survival is. And its basic motive and its basic theory, comes from this law of evolution of the universe - the principle of weakening compensation, no matter we understand it or not, it will determine the future fate of mankind.

I will briefly talk this much about the grand doctrine of Laozi. Let's see another topic, about Laozi, the lazy ant's sigh.

In his *Daodejing*, section 20, Laozi has an expression that is a typical lazy ant grumble. I will first explain what is meant by lazy ants. Biologists have found that ant colonies, whether foraging or relocating, are generally in legion, but there are always a few lazy ants, which do not participate in the collective activities of the ant colonies, but wander outside the ant groups, wandering alone in different directions. In fact, these lazy ants are the most dangerous and hardest workers, because they lose the shelter of the group, and lose the clear direction of food resources. Then why do they wander alone elsewhere? Biologists found that the more pronounced the phenomenon of lazy ants is in any ant colony, the more secure this colony's overall security and long-term survival prospects are. Because ant colonies act in unison, they quickly exhaust the resources they find in front of them, and are then left in limbo and immediately in a survival crisis. Only those colonies with individual lazy ants, as they are often scattered around searching, actually seeking new survival resources for the ant community, finding the direction for the next large-scale group action of collecting food sources, so those ant colonies are safer, though their lazy ants are the most dangerous and lonely individuals. So, let's return to Laozi, the thinker of the human community, I would say, is the lazy ant of mankind. He was doing useless things, often saying strange things that no one understood, he was a typical alien, even rejected by the mainstream ideology of his time, and suppressed by the mainstream society of his time. However, he represented the future of mankind's overall survival and development, and became a pioneer or prophet in the search for the future of mankind.

So in Laozi's book we find this charming lament, he said, "people are bustling, like enjoying a great feast, like climbing a terrace in spring", that is, the ordinary people are lively, happily enjoying life, enjoying the spring sunlight, while "I stay alone quietly, showing no sign of action", I stay alone myself, lonely and quietly; he then said, " It all has to do with my fool's heart! and common people think everything is crystal clear, while I am alone dull and dumb," and "all ordinary people see everything sharp and shrewd, but I am alone simple and slow". In fact, anyone who can see far away won't be able to see near, so he always falls into the hole in front of him. He goes on to say, "All people have something useful to do, but I am alone incorrigibly stupid." All people have abilities, but I am stubborn and have nothing to offer; "I am alone different from others, and choose to be nurtured by mother *Dao*". As I mentioned earlier, Laozi used the word woman or mother to describe *Dao*. We can thus see that Laozi's thoughts not only guided the foundation of the entire Han Empire hundreds of years later, but also enlightened us 2000 years later.

Let's talk a little bit the detailed features of Laozi's doctrine. As a heavyweight thinker, anything he says, you dare not take lightly. For example, he appreciated hysteresis, he said that we should keep the low primitive state and not advance to the high civilized state. Think about what I just said about the principle of weakening compensation, that is, the law of weakening evolution, which is actually an expression I have mentioned before: the more primitive and lower things are, the more fundamental, decisive and stable they are; on the contrary, the more progressive and advanced something is, the more lightly soaring, turbulent and destabilizing it is.

Let me give you an example. You can live without a computer today, you can live without a car, don't you dare live without food? Food is the most primitive and lowly of human creations, but it is the most important resource for human life and death. Let me give you another example. I said earlier that dialectic is the lowest stage of human rational logic, but why is it that in our daily life and work, more than 90% of the time and occasions, more than 90% of the problems we face, people involuntarily adopt mostly dialectical concepts? It is because the lower the level, the more useful it is.

In my class yesterday, I said that progressivism is an import from the West, and that it is due to the fact that the Mediterranean region is an open landscape that has been overly communicative and rapidly progressing since ancient times, so it has lost the most original cultural ideas, and therefore the basic idea and the basic cultural tone it produces is progressivism. But again, I say, has anyone really examined, on what basis do you say that progressive is good. Today, when we examine progressivism through the doctrines of Laozi, we find that the idea of conservatism in the original Chinese culture is indeed profound and of great value. Therefore, in my opinion, the Chinese people's obsession with the Western concept of progress today may be deeply poisoned.

The more primitive and low-level things are, the more you have to maintain. Think about the financial crisis and sovereign debt crisis in Europe some years ago, who was the most secure? Germany, Switzerland. Why? Germany retained its traditional manufacturing industry, Switzerland retained its traditional handicraft industry, and as a result they were not affected by the turmoil of this civilizational storm. Look at what the United States is doing? From Obama to today's Trump, the United States has focused on recalling the traditional manufacturing industry of the United States, and the United States has been highly subsidized the most primitive primary industry - agriculture, so far, the United States is still the world's largest exporter of agricultural products, thus laying the foundation of its strongest and most stable country in the world. What is it doing? Seeking an effect of lagging stabilization.

So we must pay attention to the fact that many of our concepts today are problematic, such as innovation. What does innovation mean? We always think that innovation means the future. Make no mistake! We humans are not the only ones in the world who innovate. Without 3.8 billion years of biological variation - which we can consider as biological innovation - where on earth would human beings come from? But if you look closely at the survival rate of mutations in biological history, what has mutation brought? Basically, all of them are deformities, aberrations, and elimination. Therefore, what is the most important manifestation of sexual proliferation? It is inheritance, the original copy of the parent's genes. Although biological variation has created complex biological chains and higher organisms, it is important to know that, as observed in the history of biology, the probability of biological variation being retained by natural selection is less than 1%, that is, there is a 99% probability that any mutated organism is eliminated by natural selection. What is innovation? Innovation is first of all a risk, only secondly it represents the future. And the future opened up by innovation is a weaker, more destabilized, more volatile, less existential future, a future in which species die out faster and faster. That's why Laozi said, "dare not to be ahead of the world". Therefore, I hope that you will deeply understand Laozi's doctrine, because it is about the survival of humanity, because it is about a fundamental theory and logical goal of the next phase of the cultural and civilizational rebuilding of humanity.

Okay, let's summarize this lesson.

What does the so-called thinker's reaction actually mean? It is equivalent to putting a pair of rear-viewing eyes on the back of human head. You know, our human field of vision is only 180 degrees in the forward direction, which is biologically called the rear-view blind spot. The lower animals, even medium animals, their eyes are on both sides, such as fish, such as horses. Each of their eyes has a 180-degree field of view, and the two eyes form a full 360-degree field of view. So the fish does not have to turn around, it can see behind if the shark is in pursuit of it; you'd be better not mess around behind a horse, the horse does not have to turn around, a lift of rear hoof will kick you in the vitals. So why have humans lost their rearward 180-degree vision? It's because the primate apes evolved gradually tens of millions of years ago, and they evolve into Homo erectus three to five million years ago, a process that was increasingly treacherous for their survival. Think about it, an upright monkey suddenly fell from the tree, it was initially loopy legs, it can not reach the fruit of the tree, chasing animals but ran not as fast as animals, so it immediately faced a survival crisis, how did it do? It has only one way, through natural selection to gradually adjust its sides eyes to the front. Why adjusting the eyes from two sides to the front is the first step to wisdom and survival? It is because with two eyes looking equally at an object in front of you, you are able to produce a sense of accurate distance measurement of forward-facing objects. So if you temporarily have an eye disease and the doctor snaps a dressing on the eye, I suggest you not to drive at this time, because you will probably rear-end the front car, due to your losing the sense of distance measurement for front objects.

So what does the thinker's reaction actually mean? Maintaining or restoring the full 360-degree vision of the lower beings. Since human beings have lost their backward vision, ordinary people have also lost their backward thinking. Thinker maintains the full field of vision of the thinking state, and is then perceived by us ordinary people as reactionary, so much that we dare not call him reactionary and then misinterpret him. This thing is called reactionary thinking. So don't just accuse people who tend to be reactionary and conservative in their vision and thinking, accusing them only means you have a narrow vision.

In ancient China, Confucius and Laozi were described with two famous quotes: "Without Confucius there would be no heroes of progress; without Laozi there would be no heroes of conservative." Today, human civilization is highly developed, with remarkable achievements, and a considerable percentage of you here are considered successful people. But you should remember that if you are a successful person, then the most important thing you should do is not to be aggressive but to maintain your achievement. Marx wrote a famous line in the *Communist Manifesto*, saying that the reason why the proletariat should be active in revolution is that he has nothing, and what he has gained is the whole world, and what he has lost is only a chain. But for the successful, the man of property, you'd better not be cautious, otherwise, what you lose could be your good life, and what you gain is probably just a chain. In fact, today's human beings are equivalent of overconfident, overhyped successful people, for human beings, there should be also a restraint of their own not to be overly positive, overly arrogant; otherwise, not knowing the negative conservative, not knowing timely retreat, that would lead to self-inflicted disaster. This is a major issue for future generations to understand the profound connotation of Laozi's negative philosophical thinking. There is a famous saying in Laozi's book: "Without laughter it is not *Dao*." It means that if his doctrine is not laughed at by ordinary people, it proves that he is still far from *Dao*! What I am talking about today is quite different from the current public opinion and mainstream cultural concepts, but that may prove what I am talking about is very close to *Dao*.

Okay, that concludes our Laozi lesson for today.

Q & A after class

Questioner: Hello, teacher! Yellow people have an inexplicable inferiority complex in front of white people, which I believe is an unconscious inferiority complex. I feel that Westerners are not only better than us in logic (thinking ability), but also in design, architecture, and music, which seem to surpass the East in all aspects. I wonder how you perceive this?

Mr. Dongyue: I will answer briefly. First of all, you feel that the logical thinking ability of our people is bad today. I have long said that human beings are one species, there is no difference in intelligence, but the general trend, the general composition of the national culture is biased towards the state of skill culture. We have already westernized today, our elementary school, secondary school and university are all learning Western culture, so today you mobilize the ability of mathematics, physics, chemistry, these are not the products of Chinese culture. As for the West, its sensual and artistic aspects have been greatly expanded after the Renaissance, in fact, it was quite advanced in the ancient Greek era, which is related to its extremely high intelligence mobilization. In contrast to its abstract logical thinking, the philosophical cultural system it created constitutes the entire material and technological structure of human existence today, and the gap between the two is much larger in comparison to this level, and we are discussing this topic in this sense.

But I would like to talk a little bit about what you call the inferiority complex that we Chinese still have today in facing the West. Today, China's economy is growing at a very high rate, but we do have an inferiority complex. Why? We have basically made no significant intellectual or cultural contributions to humanity in the last 1000 years of our history. Let me give you an example. According to some statistics, among the 4,000 and 6,000 laws or theorems in science, the Jews account for less than 1% of the world's total population, but contribute about 15%, and the Chinese have accounted for about 20% of the world's population, but we contribute less than 1%. In recent centuries and even in recent millennia, we Chinese have contributed little to the world's spiritual and cultural aspects, and this is the reason for our inferiority complex. We must pay attention to the fact that we are only rich, which are called parvenu. You know that in the Emperor Kang-Qian era during Qing Dynasty, China's GDP (Gross National Product) was one-third of the world. And when the United States was at its strongest, its GNP was only 22% of the world. But it was exactly during the Emperor Kang-Qian era that the West developed rapidly, from Newton to Montesquieu, who proposed *the separation of powers*, as well as Locke, who wrote his *Treatise on Government*, Adam Smith, who wrote his *Wealth of Nations*, Mueller, who proposed *representative government*, and Rousseau, who completed his *Social Contract*, the rapid development of the West, leaving China of huge economy far behind. So the fact that you are economically developed today in no way signifies that you are powerful, much less that you will be respected. For a nation to be respected does not lie in how much money you have, but in your cultural contribution, your spiritual contribution to humanity, because spirituality and culture are the cornerstones of human existence.

Let me give you another example. Russia abolished serfdom only in 1861, and although Russia began to learn from the West after Peter the Great, and by the 19th century it was called policeman of Europe by Marx, and was considered a powerful country, Russia was actually despised by the West at first. However, in the 19th century, a number of important cultural figures emerged in Russia: Mendeleev, the founder of the periodic law of chemical elements and the first originator of chemistry as a science; Lev Tolstoy, Turgenev and other world-class literary figures; Tchaikovsky, a world-class musician; and Lebin, a world-class painter...... It immediately attracted the attention of the West, where it was predicted that Russia would become a powerful country. Sure enough, Russia became a superpower in the 20th century. However, after becoming a superpower, its culture was suppressed and it declined again. So it's not enough for a country to be economically developed, you have to make a spiritual and cultural contribution to humanity, and only then will the West really respect you. Okay, any more questions?

Questioner: I'd like to discuss two small issues. First one, how do you know what is more important; the second one is that often what you don't know is more important than what you do know.

Mr. Dongyue: You ask me how I know which thing is more important? Let me quote from Laozi: "Whichever heaven disapproves, who knows the reason, even the sages find it difficult." You've got me down with this question, because I'm not even a sage. But I want to tell you that we will find that in the history of human civilization, exploring the basic theories of useless science has had a more significant impact on humanity. Newton merely talked about the state of the operation of celestial mechanics, which you can't even use in your daily life, but it started the whole industrial age, and we call the industrial age the Newtonian age. Einstein discussed the bending of space-time, can you use it? You can't use it at all, but we call it the Einstein era today. Therefore, it is the most important topic to explore the study of emptiness, the study of uselessness, the study of *Daoism*, and the study of fundamental theories. Even though I can also say it conversely, that it was these great figures who became the beacons that led our humanity to peril.

Okay, any other questions do you all have?

Questioner: Hello, sir! In your class, you used the method of enlarging the scale to give this gradient pattern diagram of sustaining, but the method of illustration is still the example and induction method. I believe it is for our easy understanding. Is there any other way to prove the gradient of sustaining? Thanks!

Mr. Dongyue: My lecture needs to please the audience, so there is no rigor to speak of. The better it sounds to you, the less valuable it is. When I write my book, I will never accommodate the reader. It is not my business whether you can read it or not, I only pursue the rigor of logical proof. Therefore, please note that if you want to understand my ideas, listening to my lectures does not help much, you need to read the book. My whole book *A Unified Theory of Evolution* is 300 to 400 pages thick, but it only does one thing, that is, the proof of the principle of weakening compensation. Remember, learning is proving! What you call my induction is actually one of the methods of proof after hypothesis. The book is divided into three volumes: Volume 1, on natural philosophy; Volume 2, on mental philosophy; Volume 3, on social philosophy; the last two volumes are all deductive proofs. The sum of all things in the universe is no more than these three fields, which are used to complete the systematic proof of the principle of weakening compensation. Therefore, you have to read, not just listen to the lectures as a gateway to understand my doctrine, but this course only serves as an introduction, a guide, and a prelude.

Questioner: After listening to this class today, I feel very heavy-hearted. I would like to ask, at present, the most technologically advanced United States, I feel that people like Elon Musk and others, making rockets and electric cars, are pushing mankind to a point of no return, and I wonder if there are people like Mr. Dongyue in the United States who can point out the truth of the problem. And then my question is: Is humanity still savable? How can it be saved? If there is no salvation, how many years are left?

Mr. Dongyue: I can't answer your second question because I am not a fortune teller, I can only talk about trends. In fact, I am not that pessimistic, I think there is still a long time frame for human survival, it depends on whether human beings can properly recreate their next civilization, please read my book *The Decline of Humanity* for answer to this question. As for your claim that the US is the most advanced and therefore most likely to drive humanity to disaster. I don't think that is necessarily the case! China is developing today at a much higher rate than the US, so don't leave China out of the game, China is the most radical developer today, holding up the most radical view of development.

So, just yesterday at the beginning of the class I talked about how Chinese traditional and even modern history has allowed the Chinese to have a broader perspective. We studied the West in the modern era with an open mind, and then experienced the typical agrarian civilization and the violent clash between it and the industrial and commercial civilization, and then unfolded our horizons. We even went one step further than the West and tried out the communist movement in advance, and we are today running more rapidly than the capitalist countries, so we are well qualified to be more forward-looking than the Americans and Europeans. Because our forward direction unfolds as they do, and our backward resources - primitive cultural resources - are deeper and more solid than theirs. When my doctrine was first created, after the book was written in 1998, I thought how could such a simple thing be discovered by me? I thought I might be merely repeating what others had done. In the last 20 years since the book was written, I have not seen a similar formulation of the doctrine in the West. I do not want to say that this doctrine is the most forward-looking, I just want to say that this doctrine is the result of drawing on the core of the Eastern conservative theory of the unity of heaven and man and combining it with the logic of Western philosophical thinking, so it still has some uniqueness, at least to this day. Although I am ashamed to say that I do not know whether my book is the last word for mankind or a gospel for its future.

Okay, any other questions do you have?

Questioner: Hello, Mr. Wang! *Daodejing* says, "The Way of Heaven is to take from the wealthy to supply the needy" and "The Way of Man is different, it take from the needy to enrich the wealthy". So I would like to ask Mr. Wang, what is the relationship between the Way of Heaven and the Way of Man?

Mr. Dongyue: Actually, I have already made it very clear in my lecture. The so-called *Way of Heaven* and *Way of Man* of Laozi is actually the Principle of Weakening Compensation, or rather, the Principle of Weakening Compensation is a modern proof of Laozi's *Daoism*. The passage you mentioned is only equivalent to the Matthew effect mentioned in the Bible, which does not involve the root of the problem. *Daodejing* has many messy words because he did not have enough information and the proof was not clear, so he said many words in contradictory. Let me give you an example. For example, in the paragraph "To pursue knowledge you increase daily, to practice *Dao* you decrease daily, decreasing more and more, till the point of nothing in mind", he means that if you engage in knowledge, you will get more and more; but if you follow *Dao*, you have to reduce more and more. What should be the result of decreasing more and more according to the principle of weakening compensation? It should be to the point of great capability, not to the point of nothingness. Because the more you lose your degree of existence, the more your degree of compensation must expand inversely, so this expression of Laozi is wrong. It can be seen that a large number of expressions in Laozi's *Daodejing* are confusing, and a large number of expressions are figurative analogies, not logically derived rigorous conclusions, such as "the superior is as good as water". Therefore, the premise of reading Laozi's book is that you have to understand the logic of his thoughts, which is the key to read and understand him. That is why I said at the beginning that we will only talk about the original purpose and main line of Laozi's doctrine today, that is, you should focus on searching his basic ideas when reading Laozi's book.

Questioner: Hello, sir! I would like to ask a question about "food and sex are human nature". It is very difficult for all of us to break through this temptation, and we are always bound by this kind of human nature, and this kind of nature is always binding us behind. But for our society as a whole, including what you said yesterday, our human society has gone through an agrarian civilization, which is a result of natural selection. Then we have reached today, our social development, including the resulting pollution, and climate anomalies and other problems, from another point of view, is it also the result of natural selection? Because our human nature determines that we will definitely go after more things.

Mr. Dongyue: I didn't use *natural selection*, I used *natural process*. If you read my *A Unified Theory of Evolution*, there is a sentence in it that is quoted everywhere: "Humanity is the expression of all beings; human being is the miniature of the universe." It is that all our human impulses and operations today are actually some kinds of natural driven state that we cannot help ourselves, so we cannot escape from the law of weakening compensation, and this is where the biggest problem lies. How to deal with this problem is the primary issue that human beings need to focus on in the future.

Questioner: Mr. Dongyue, I have come across your theory, and I think the human race is definitely hopeless. The reason why you are still discussing the possible continuation of the human race is that I think you have a slight illusion from the standpoint that you are a human being and a part of the human community. My question is, at this stage of the human race, the existence of things like the state and nationalism, if we want to slow down or change a little, they may be the biggest obstacle. I would like to have your opinion on the future trend of states.

Mr. Dongyue: Read my *The Decline of Humanity*, which discusses these specific issues. I will now answer the question about my seemingly pessimistic and fanciful doctrine. First of all, I am not the most pessimistic, there is a group of scholars in the West who are much more pessimistic than I am. For example, Stephen Hawking, although he does not know the principle of weakening compensation, says that the survival period of human beings on Earth is only one or two hundred years, and he suggests that we should hurry to emigrate to other planets. My doctrine is not that pessimistic at all. Read my books, especially *The Decline of Humanity*, and I say that if mankind handles it well there is a long late survival. Humanity today is equivalent of middle-aged 40 or 50 years old, man of this age group is still tossing and Z-turning, working desperately or fighting fiercely with others, will have an ugly death for sure. However, if a middle-aged person with the spontaneous rhythm of physiological aging and the transformation tends to comprehensive negative, that is, psychologically gradually will become depressed, physical strength tends to exercise less, more maintenance, no more tossing and Z-turning, and to maintain a good condition, more self-care, it is not impossible to eventually live through 80 or 90 years of age. If you calculate it this way, before Homo sapiens has about 200,000 years of survival as young adults, after that there should probably be several thousands of years of life!

Naturally, I can't provide specific numbers because the principle of weakening compensation can't have the parameters so far, there is not enough information. If the amount of information continues to expand in the future so that it can be substituted into the parameters, this problem should be able to be calculated precisely, but it can't be done now, so I never discuss the exact timing and details. But I'm not as pessimistic as you suggest. As to whether I am under illusions, I just want to make the point that I in no way think that humans can violate the law of weakening compensation and exist indefinitely, so I have no illusions. But a foundational theory never happens out of thin air, and a foundational theory emerges, and if it is correct - and since nothing is truth, I say if it is correct, or if it is appropriate - then it must have some sort of pro-survival impact on human culture in later generations. That's my hope, and that's the potential value of this theoretical system.

Questioner: Hello, sir! Ever since I heard about your doctrine six years ago, I have taken this doctrine as the cornerstone of my values. My question is, if Laozi's *Daodejing* presupposes your theory of weakening compensation, and Laozi is backward-looking, reactionary and good-oriented, and various other doctrines are forward-looking, positive and evil-oriented, and if civilization development is evil-oriented and civilization regression is good-oriented, then how will I grasp the degree of good and evil, development and conservatism in the future?

Mr. Dongyue: I can't really say anything about such a specific life issue. However, you should pay special attention to the fact that you cannot regard my doctrine as advocating reaction, because my saying that Laozi's doctrine is reactionary is precisely one of the major flaws of Laozi's discourse. Read my book, you will find that I say the world is a one-way evolution, you want to be reactionary or go backward, but you can never do that, so my doctrine never advocate reactionary. It's not that reaction is bad, it's that you can't be reactionary. Some people read my book and say that my views are nihilistic and that there is no point in living after reading it. My book is telling you exactly why you can't be nihilistic even if you want to be, why you must be more and more tossing and Z-turning, why you must be more and more arrogant. It is because the amount of compensation is always increasing, the property of being-for-itself is always expanding, and the will to survive and the tendency of dynamic freedom are increasingly soaring. Therefore, to interpret my book, one must deeply and systematically comprehend it. As for what to do at the application level, I really can't say any, and if you discuss problems with me at the application level, I have no words to say.

Questioner: Hello, teacher! Due to the misinterpretation of Laozi by later generations, the theory of Huang-Lao was created as a result. In the future, I believe there will be also misinterpretations of your doctrine according to the decreasing degree of existence and increasing degree of compensations, what is your opinion and attitude towards this kind of thing? And on this basis, which misinterpretations do you like, and which ones do you dislike? Thank you!

Mr. Dongyue: I have no way to answer what has not yet happened in the future. As for if my doctrine is correct and valid, it will be misinterpreted by future generations, I think that must be the case and is inevitable. Human species is so strange in that the best things that come to their hands can eventually be completely trashed and deformed. Just look at how beautiful an ideal communism was, but it turned out that Stalin and Pol Pot made a mess of it. Someone in the West once said, "Freedom! Freedom! How many evils have committed in thy name!" Such is the way of man, that the best things are distorted or defiled by man into the mud pits. Therefore, I do fear greatly that future generations will take my doctrine to justify or excuse sin. Not to mention posterity, contemporary people have already performed this way. For example, in my book *The Decline of Humanity*, I speak of controlling population size, i.e., reducing the quality of human biological reproduction, as an important part of maintaining one's continued existence. I also specifically emphasized which sensible and reasonable flexible ways to do it, and never to force it by means of mass killing living beings. Subsequently, someone voiced on the Internet that Wang Dongyue advocated the mass extermination of human beings. See, not to mention the future, there is already bad trend today. So I said in *The Decline of Humanity* to the effect that if my doctrine is applied in a way that is contrary to heaven and heavenly conscience, then I would rather face destruction.

Questioner: I would like to ask if it is possible to verify that the theory of *A Unified Theory of Evolution* actually be revised and even evolve through the occurrence and revelation of some future events, instead of becoming a definite conclusion now that everything will definitely end and everything will definitely be moving in a negative direction.

Mr. Dongyue: The main theme and direction of my doctrine is not to say that mankind is hopeless, not to discuss that there is life and there is death; this issue does not need to be discussed. I am only asking: Why is it that the higher the development of human civilization, the deeper the crisis? In other words, I am trying to warn mankind how to seek the next stage of survival. I do not have any confidence in this, nor do I think that the solution proposed in the book *The Decline of Humanity* is necessarily feasible.

The only thing I have confidence in is the principle of weakening compensation, although it is not the truth, and most likely only a temporary correct logical model. If my doctrine is not the truth, it is too likely to be falsified by future generations, but even if my doctrine is proved wrong one day, it will only be a different way of explanation, and the weakening compensation will be transformed from a principle to a phenomenon, but it will never completely dissolve and fail, just like Newton's theory of gravity was falsified and replaced by Einstein's new explanation of the bending of space-time, but the Earth still rotates around the Sun in a way that is consistent with the gravitational relationship. Furthermore, I would like to make one more point, if you look at the history of human thought, the position of human beings in the natural world has fallen all the way down: initially second only to God, so much so that they inhabited the center of the universe; then they became heliocentric and fell down to the ordinary planets; then they became the disciples of monkeys. In short, when examined in terms of thought forms, the situation of human beings is more and more degenerate and worse and worse. Based on this, I can predict that if my doctrine is one day falsified by future generations, it must be replaced by a doctrine that is even worse than mine, which is very likely. So you'd better not to expect the appearance of that doctrine, especially not to expect that it will turn everything for the direction of good.

Questioner: Hello, sir! I would like to ask a question, that is, you mentioned that Confucius was to enter the society, a state of positive life-view, but he actually also said that he would go back to the Zhou dynasty; that Laozi was to exit from the society, and he mentioned that he would go back to the Shang dynasty. My question is, you mentioned earlier that in the last 1000 years in China, after Laozi and Confucius, there were basically no significant contributions to human thought in the world, is it because whether they were entering the world or leaving the world, enterprising or conservatizing, the original motive behind them was to go back to the past? Because they all want to go back to the past, from the one direction point of view, there is no such a state or appeal to evolve or move forward. Is this a core reason why no new ideas have been produced in China in the past 1000 years?

Mr. Dongyue: I said that relative to the pre-Qin era, after the unification of China by the first Emperor, Yingzheng, of Qin Dynasty in 221 B.C., China had no more intellectual contributions in the field of thought that exceeded the pre-Qin era. In the second 1000 years after A.D., we had no significant contributions in almost all major cultural fields. The reason for this is complex, and certainly related to the conservative tone of traditional Chinese culture, but it is not the root cause; it is the result of many constraints. On this topic, in the next Western philosophy class, I will give an in-depth explanation of the phrase "philosophy (love of intelligence) is the mobilization of intelligent reserves", and if you listen to that class, these questions will be answered.

But I want to affirm that one element contained in your question holds true, that the conservatism of Chinese culture has somehow restrained China's rapid development, if it is not a causal relationship, at least a parallel one. Then it signifies that the cultural shift of mankind to passivity and conservatism may still be valid, may still seek some means of stable survival, and may have a chance of being realized to some extent or to a very small extent. Thus the value of the conservative ideology - the keynote of this cultural thought in the East - is enormous.

Of course, my explanation does not refer to any specific event. For example, some people say that I am politically conservative because I "advocate dictatorship and regression"; some people think that I am old and therefore I like old-fashioned things. This actually has nothing to do with specific issues, nor does it have anything to do with my political, social or life views. My theory does not involve the discussion of any specific issue, but only extrapolates in pure logic.

Overview of the Western Philosophy (I)

Preamble

We are talking about Western philosophy today. I will start with a basic description on this course.

I'll start with a description of the course. The Western Philosophy course is the only course in our 12-day program that focuses on the core of Western culture. This course takes up two days. Though not a lot of time, it's a very important course. And this course is particularly brain-challenging, and the reason for brain-challenging is our extreme lack of knowledge of this way of thinking.

What are we talking about today? We are not going to talk about Western philosophy as a whole; as this course requires at least 200+ credit hours, but we only have two days for it. So we are only going to talk today about the basic overview of Western philosophy, that is, only the most basic level of Western philosophy. What we want you to understand here is how is the thinking of Western philosophy derived? What is the basis of its thinking? How are the channels of its thinking expanded? What is the effect of its thinking? Or I can summarize it in one simple sentence: you have to find the *philosophical sense,* or *philosophical interest.*

That is, after listening to this class you have a basic sense of Western philosophy, you have a basic understanding of the model of how Western philosophy unfolds its thinking, then this class will have served its purpose. With this foundation, you will at least be able to understand what philosophers discuss when you open a philosophy book in the future, and understand his starting point, his way of thinking, and the way he derives his conclusions. Therefore, I emphasize again that what we are talking about today is only an "overview of the foundations of Western philosophy".

I say that Chinese culture has long been in decline, so what value does it still have? It is an important underlying reference system for mankind to recreate the next culture and the next civilization in the future. For example, last time I talked about Laozi's *Daoism, Deism*, and *Conservatism*, which is a basis for human beings to construct new ideas in the future, or A reference.

Then, again, I said that Western culture in no way represents the future, because it is already undermining humanity today, and therefore, humanity faces a major cultural transformation of next phase. But the next cultural transformation of mankind must take place on the basis of the mainstream culture of today, that is, the philosophical thinking (philosophical and scientific thinking) of the industrial and commercial civilization. Therefore, although Western culture does not represent the future, it is the port of the next culture and the direct continuation of the next civilization. Therefore, a deep understanding of the process of the formation of Western culture and its current state is the basis for the extension of the subsequent series of ideas, which is the purpose and the original intention of this course today.

Let me start by saying what philosophy is. The word philosophy is familiar to everyone. What we usually call philosophy, I call it philosophy in the broad sense. The so-called broad philosophy, to use the ancient Chinese saying, there is a passage in *I-Ching* that says, "Those above the physical form (incorporeal) are called *Dao*, those in the physical form are called material articles." That is to say, as long as one reaches the metaphysical thinking, it is a broad philosophy. The so-called material form is what you see physically; the so-called metaphysical is the thinking that goes beyond intuition. The way I am talking about philosophy is in no way the Western philosophy. Because once any of us unfolds our senses, the consciousness behind our senses will immediately and unconsciously elevate what we sensed to a level of summary, and this level must be metaphysical. Let me give you an example. Have you ever seen a horse in the world? You will never see one. What you see must be a yellow horse, a black horse, a stallion, a mare, a big horse, a small horse. Horse is just an abstraction, you never see a horse in the world, all you see are specific, figurative horses, not the sum of abstraction of horses. But once you use your vision, you immediately arrive at the idea of horse, which is the most elementary abstraction of metaphysical. If you consider metaphysical as philosophy, then it is only the unconscious sublimation of human surface consciousness, which does not constitute the philosophical pursuit in real sense.

Therefore, I would like to emphasize that the philosophy we are going to talk about today is called *philosophy in the narrow sense.* The word philosophy that we all use in our daily lives is usually used in the broad sense. One does not have to study anything, one does not have to do any deep thinking, so long as one speaks, or discusses issues that go beyond the intuitive level, it can be included in the broad sense of philosophy. Therefore, it is very far from the real narrow philosophy.

Well, the so-called narrow philosophy is only found in ancient Greece. What is the meaning of this statement? According to the famous British historian Toynbee, there were at least 600 civilizations in the world in the ancient times. Among these 600 or even thousands of civilizations, the only one that produced a narrow philosophy was Ancient Greece, while all other civilizational regions and cultural types did not produce a truly narrow philosophical system.

So, the philosophy we are talking about today is by no means the general impression of philosophy that you have in your daily life. Philosophy is pure virtual probing, or called labor in prospective concern. Therefore, people's past understanding of philosophy is close to zero.

A famous Chinese scholar, Qian Zhongshu, once said in his novel *The Siege* in a flirtatious tone that there are only scholars of philosophers in China, but there have never been any philosophers. What does he mean by scholar of philosopher? It is a scholar who studies certain philosophers. For example, Nietzsche experts, Heidegger experts, Kant experts, etc., this is called scholars of philosophers. A true philosopher is one who studies philosophy itself in the narrow sense, the ultimate questions that are beyond the reach of the ordinary human mind. It is necessary to make it clear that the study which discusses at a deep point is called philosophy.

I say that Chinese culture traditionally does not produce

philosophy in the narrow sense, nor does it have the basic philosophical-scientific thinking. Note the meaning of the phrase philosophical-scientific thinking, which means "philosophy is the mother of science", that is, scientific thinking is entirely an extension of philosophical thinking.

I say Chinese culture, its basic state is the culture of technology art, that is, the culture of technology and art. And philosophical-scientific thinking is a unique line of thinking. Therefore, when we talk about philosophy, we only talk about the history of Western philosophy. This is the reason why we call traditional Chinese culture the history of Eastern thought, not the history of philosophy.

Why, then, do we have such a lack of understanding of philosophy? It is because we have had a problem with the focus of introducing Western culture in modern times. Since the Opium War in 1840, the earliest movement in China to learn Western culture was the Foreign Affairs Movement. The so-called foreign affairs movement was to learn the technology of the barbarians in order to overwhelm the barbarians, that is, to focus on learning the superior technology of the West or the practical aspects of science only, hoping that this would quickly overwhelm the West. We started to learn Western culture from this starting point, but science is only the subsequent extension of Western philosophical thinking, which is almost the surface of application. This has led us to study the West, from the very beginning, but only at the level of the application of Western science and technology, which makes us lack a systematic training process for a deeper exploration of Western philosophy.

By the beginning of the last century, during the New Culture Movement in 1916, Hu Shih introduced Western philosophy to China. Hu Shih received his doctorate in philosophy in the United States, but his mentor was John Dewey - the great master of pragmatist philosophy. Therefore, the Western philosophy introduced by Hu Shih was the philosophy of pragmatism. As you know, this line of thought is very close to the ancient Chinese idea of learning to apply, but it is still quite far from the true depth of Western philosophy. Therefore, to a large extent, it has seriously misled the Chinese to look deeper into Western philosophy.

After the founding of the country, we then proceeded to study Marxist philosophy as if it were Western philosophy. Here, it is necessary for me to explain the relationship between Marxism and Western philosophy. First, it is important to note that the core of Marx's own scholarship was not in philosophy. Despite what Marx said, his scholarship consisted of three parts, one of which was Western philosophy. The center of Marx's research was called political economy, which means that it was not pure economics, but a study of the political structure of society from the perspective of economics. In his words, it is called political arithmetic. Marx had studied the writings of the first progenitor of political economy, Wilhelm Giedi, who, he said, had pioneered political arithmetic. This is a central part of Marxism. I admit that Marx reached extraordinary heights in this area. And the first volume of Marx's *Capital*, especially the part that discusses money and value, is amazing in its way of thinking, in its expansiveness of writing, in its clever use of philosophical ideas. But Marx was not a philosopher after all. You know, Marx's whole life, except for his doctoral thesis on the ancient Greek philosopher Epicurus, he hardly saw any special philosophical thesis, nor did he have any philosophical monograph. Marx was only an applier of philosophy, but not a philosopher.

Real philosophers, even real scientists - please understand the distinction between scientists and engineers - people who really study the basic science, they are only concerned with the problem of knowing the world, but never the problem of transforming the world. Because human intelligence, for any person, even if he mobilizes all his intellect, never let any trace of his energy distracted, wholeheartedly focus only on the study of how the world works, he won't thoroughly understand it after all his life. This is why those who really study philosophy and science, that is, those who study profound learning, are never concerned with practical issues. So, please remember that a true philosopher is only concerned with knowing the world and never with the problem of transforming it, which he believes is someone else's business.

And Marx famously said that previous philosophy was concerned only with knowing the world, while his philosophy wanted to change the world. What does this mean? It shows that Marx was a philosophical applier, an engineer of the philosophical world, not a philosopher. So if you study Marxist philosophy as if it were Western philosophy, I am basically sure that you are a philosophical amateur.

And one should also note that Marxist philosophy has not followed the mainstream of Western philosophy, nor has it deepened the basic problems of Western philosophy in recent times. What does that mean? Marxist philosophy is called dialectical materialism. You know that since Descartes, except for Locke, there is basically no real materialism. Because at this time, most materialists have actually fallen into the philosophical amateur, they no longer know what problem philosophers studied at this stage.

And when I briefly mentioned dialectics, dialectical logic, dialectical thinking in the previous Laozi class, I said it is the lower stage of rational human thinking. Even if you don't study Marxist philosophy and you simply go through the classical Chinese pre-Qin literature, what is the philosophical outlook will you have? It must be dialectical materialism. Traditional Chinese thinking has always been materialistic - "seeing is believing, learning is applying", it is the inherent basis of our thinking in Chinese culture. Even if we do not study Western philosophy, even if we do not study Marxist philosophy, what is the basic method we use to develop our thinking? It must be dialectics. Because the basic structure of Chinese logic, starting from *I-Ching*, is dialectical thinking.

In other words, Marxist philosophy is not an importation of new philosophical ideas into China, but a reinforcement of China's inherent philosophical lineage, nothing more. In my last lecture, I said that China was already a socialist society thousands of years ago, and I said that agricultural civilization must have constructed impersonalism, that is, a social configuration based on social groups.

That is to say, then, we now look back on Marxist doctrine, both in terms of socialist concepts and dialectical materialistic ways of thinking, as in fact a reinforcement of traditional Chinese social configurations and traditional ways of thinking. As such, it has allowed us to break through the limitations of our original thought in no real sense, but rather, to a greater extent, has solidified and obscured our understanding of other heterogeneous scholarship.

Therefore, you have to empty your head of the so-called philosophical preconceptions, and we start from the beginning to understand Western philosophy in the narrow sense, that is, from the seeds of the lineage of thinking that began in ancient Greece. Only then can we really build up the most basic sense or knowledge of philosophy.

Since philosophy is the mother of science, the slogan of *New Youth*, the magazine that led the New Culture Movement back then, was two things: *Democracy* and *Science*. In other words, from the Foreign Affairs Movement "to learn the technology of the barbarians" to the New Cultural Movement "to raise the banner of science", we Chinese today have become fully scientific in the field of culture and education, so much so that our national policy today is called, *outlook of scientific development*.

What we don't know is that science is based on philosophy, which is a large and informative extended model of philosophical thinking subspecialized. If you do not know what philosophy is, you will not be able to understand what science is at all. That is why I say that today the whole country is in a situation of Scientology, that is, we have turned science into a new religion. It is not too much to call it *Scientology*.

Please think about it, our Chinese attitude toward science today can be described by the word faith, that is, science is the same as God. As long as the something is said to be scientific, we will have not the least doubt about it, as we believe science is the objective law, is the truth.

But what does it mean by objective laws? What does truth mean? What does perception mean? What does knowledge mean? All these most basic questions have never been explored. Because of the underpinnings of science, its thinking does not actually flow at the level of the application of science, which leads to the fact that if you do not have a deep study of Western philosophical thought, you do not know what science is, and you may even have a major misunderstanding of science. This is why, since the founding of our country, we have studied all along scientific lines from elementary school, secondary school, and university, and the secondary school students we send to compete in the World Olympics in subjects such as mathematics, physics, and chemistry often come out on top, yet we have contributed very little to scientific innovation and invention, because we have always lacked understanding of the thought underpinnings at the grassroots level of science.

Therefore, our lesson today is, to a large extent, a remedial lesson on the basic thinking of industrial and commercial civilization. In my last lecture, I said that the basic culture and way of thinking corresponding to industrial and commercial civilization is called philosophical-scientific thinking, which is the reason for our scientificization today. If you lack understanding of its deep structure, then you cannot really understand the basic thinking of industrial and commercial civilization, its form, its effect and its development prospect.

It is actually very difficult to make the subject of Western Philosophy clear. If you stand at the foot of a mountain and look up at it, you will never be able to see it all clearly. To understand and grasp a discipline, you must stand higher than it at a certain point to look down on it, then it is possible to see the whole picture of the thing. Look up at high mountains, being trapped in Mount Lushan, both idioms in fact express the embarrassment that you cannot fully view and understand something. Therefore, we have to stand on a different high point today, overlooking the source and thinking of Western philosophy, so that this topic can be truly in-depth, even if my lecture is limited to the basic overview of Western philosophy.

What is *Philosophy*?

Let's get to the point.

First of all, what is philosophy? Let us look at the comments made by some Western philosophers. Schopenhauer says: "A man would not be a philosophical man if he did not see all men and all things as mere visions or phantoms at all times." What is the meaning of this statement? If you look at external things and you see them as real, and you think that seeing is believing, then you are very far from philosophy. The starting point of Western philosophy is to say that the world as we see it is all illusion, all falsehood, and this is one of the most basic starting points for exploring philosophy.

Please note, what is the spirit of our traditional Chinese culture? It is called Seeing is believing. This basic concept alone closes the door of philosophy completely. Please think about what is meant by seeing is believing, and know that our human eyes have developed from billions of years of biological evolution. In other words, if you look at the world with the attitude that seeing is believing, then you are no different from animals.

If you think that what you see with your eyes is real, then all your insight, all your knowledge, is only in the state of animal-like recognition and reaction, that is, you are only in the intuitive identification of different objects A, B, C and D, but not in the state of higher intellectual thinking. So remember, if you see everything, if it is not an illusion or a phantom, then you are far from philosophy.

Let's look again at what Russell said: "Is there such a thing as wisdom, or does what seems to be as if it were wisdom, merely the very refinement of folly?" What does that mean? All of us think we are wise, and we use wisdom every moment, every minute. But what is wisdom? Has anyone ever explored this question? Why does wisdom happen? What is the use of wisdom? What is the result of the use of wisdom? Why does the use of wisdom often lead to folly? We have never thought about these questions, but philosophers do not believe in the eyes at first, and then in wisdom, and they want to ponder wisdom itself, which is the entry-level question of philosophy.

Aristotle said, "People in the ancient (past) and modern times should begin their philosophical explorations with a sense of wonder at all things in nature." I would like to ask you, do any of you today sees ordinary things that exist in the world and you feel a sense of wonder and excitement? We usually judge a person's maturity in this way, that is, when he is still in the childish stage, such as a child, he feels amazement and wonder at everything he sees, he keeps asking questions and keeps asking why, which is the expression of a child's childish state; but when a child grows up to be an adult, one of his important signs is that he takes everything for granted, and he no longer has doubts, which is the expression of maturity. But Aristotle said that the starting point of philosophy is to be always amazed and inquisitive about everything and anything in nature. In other words, the development of adults, no more sense of wonder, no more questions, this is called closed thinking. Reaching this point is equivalent to losing your philosophical mind completely, but it is the regular state of all our normal people.

Let's look again at Kant's statement, "The philosopher's business is in pursuing what is called self-evident." That is, what is the philosopher doing? He is pursuing questions that are self-evident without asking them, that is, questions that do not constitute questions are what the philosopher is pursuing.

Let me give you an example, for example, what does *thing* mean? What does *existence* mean? What does *knowledge* mean? I think everyone agrees that this is a no-brainer. But if you think deep about it, can you explain what matter means? Can you explain what existence means? Leibniz, Schelling, and Heidegger all asked the question, "Why does Being exist but nothing does not?" What is *being* and what is *nothing*? Furthermore, we use knowledge all day long, but what does *knowledge* mean? Hume once made a proof that all knowledge is not valid, which led Kant to explore knowledge itself, and later he wrote a thick book about it, to explain what knowledge means. Please think what does proof mean? Can this be a problem when none of us would have thought of it? Actually, it is a big problem.

We generally believe that seeing is believing, the eye sees, that is the proof. When I say there is a cup here, and I see it with my eyes, then the question of whether the cup is here or not, is proven. But this is not proof. All learning is just a system of proof. If you see with your eyes and then you have finished proving, would there be any learning in the world? This is what I said earlier, the animal has completed all the proofs of seeing with the eyes, but that is only the non-intelligent state of existence of the animal.

Remember, all proofs are called logical proofs. So what is a logical proof? How to develop logic in order to achieve proof? Anything that is not proven is a falsehood. Then what is "proof"? These questions, which everyone thinks are not problems, are precisely the questions that philosophers want to investigate deeply.

Huxley said that "agnosticism is the only reliable philosophy". Of course, this statement is not entirely true, but he illustrates the point that in Western philosophers and scientists, the basic concept they hold is agnosticism, which is the opposite of our Chinese concept of knowledge. We believe that knowledge is the thought or fact that leads to a definite conclusion and no longer wavers. That is, we believe that all knowledge must be something that has a definite answer before it can be called knowledge! But this is the opposite of Western philosophical thinking.

The dominant thinking in Western intellectual circles is agnostic. That is, they create a whole system of science and then they say that the world is unknowable. What is this *science* they are talking about? There is a popular saying in the West: "When man thinks, God laughs." It means that as soon as we expand our perception, as soon as we think we know, we fall into folly and laughter, seeing that knowledge itself is a profound doubt that needs to be pursued endlessly.

And what does it mean to insist on an agnostic view of the world? It expresses a permanent skepticism of all certain knowledge and conclusions. If your previous knowledge is certain, if you have never built up the idea that there is a correct answer, a standard answer, from elementary school, high school, and university, then you are very far from true philosophy and science.

Michelet speaks: "Metaphysics is the art of methodically channeling oneself into the clouds." What does that mean? It means that once you have a definite view, you are out of the quest for knowledge, and once you keep pursuing your doubts, you will lead yourself into the clouds, and you will not reach a definite conclusion. But the state in which you are led into the clouds is the philosophical or intellectual state.

If you attend this two-day class, and after listening to it, you are led into the clouds, you have understood a little bit of this class. If after listening to this lesson, you arrive at a new truth, and you give a definite answer, then you have suffered this lesson for nothing.

There is a quote from Heraclitus, who said, "I have heard many people talk, and among these, not one of them realized that all were far from wisdom." What does that mean? We should know that in our daily lives, and even in the course of our unusual intellectual inquisitive conversations, we are not actually mobilizing the depths of intelligence; we are actually all far from what philosophers call wisdom. Philosophy is an extremely specific mobilization of an intelligent movement, and that is the basic state of philosophy in the narrow sense.

Let's talk about the concept of philosophy, which is an etymological synthesis of the Greek words phileo and sophia. phileo means love and sophia means wisdom, which is the meaning of philosophy as love of wisdom. This is what philosophy means: love of wisdom. The first person what used this term was probably Pythagoras, the first Greek philosopher of theory.

In modern Japan, the Meiji Restoration was a comprehensive study of the West, and they first translated the word philosophy into Chinese. As you know, before the Meiji Restoration, the main body of Japanese scholars used Chinese characters, and the katakana that is popular now was used by peddlers and common people back then, and was disdained by literary scholars. Japanese scholars used to translate the Western word Philosophy into "哲学" (Zhe Xue) in Chinese, and it should be said that the translation was very good, because the character "哲", in the ancient Chinese means "明智" (Ming Zhi) wise; Therefore, "哲学" means the study of wisdom.

But if I only talk this much, you still don't know what philosophy is. The key question is, what does it mean by "爱智" (Ai Zhi) love wisdom? First of all, I would like to say here that all the important scientists of the modern West, and I don't mean engineers at the applied level, must have been people who had a deep understanding of Western philosophy. Let me give you an example, Newton's classical mechanics, whose original book was called *Mathematical Principles of Natural Philosophy*, Newton did not think he was doing science in the least, he thought he was studying natural philosophy. Let me give you another example. Someone once asked Albert Einstein what was his theory of relativity? Einstein replied that the universe is like a clock with an unopenable case, you never know how the universe works, and all of us who do science are just standing outside this clock with an unopenable case, constantly guessing and simulating the way this cosmic clock works. What does this statement mean? It means that science is by no means objective truth, and you can't open the case of the universe, you curiously look at it working in an orderly way, but you can only make a logical model of an analogous nature, in order to explain the possible ways of its unfolding movement.

I still take clocks as example. As you know, clocks work in various ways, mechanical watches are driven by gears, electronic watches are driven by electronic oscillation, and atomic clocks are driven by atomic cesium. Cesium oscillates more than 9 billion times per second, and then the vibration frequency of Cesium is used as the base for time calibration, and the clock is called an atomic clock, so it is extremely accurate. In other words, the watch that we make today have various types, but you never know how this clock of the universe works, and since you can only stand outside, your speculation about it is always a simulated conjecture, which is the expression of Einstein.

Einstein said in a pamphlet, *The Truth of Relativity*, that all science, like psychology, is merely a matter of bringing one's empirical elements into harmony (to that effect) with the logical system. He did not say that my logical system is in complete agreement with the objective truth, he says that it is simply a matter of letting my empirical system, that is, what I perceive, come to some state of self-consistency with my own subjective logical system, and he says that this is called the truth of relativity.

Origin of Philosophy

In the West, people who really understand science must have a basic philosophical thinking, which is completely different from our view of science. But it is precisely this radically different view of science, which actually comes from a radically different philosophical view, that has led to the development of their science in a deeper and deeper way.

If I say it this way, you may not understand what is loving wisdom. Let me put it in another way. Since the civilization of mankind, there are basically three ways of using wisdom: the first is called *faith in the Lord*; the second is called *emphasis on virtue*; and the third is called *love of wisdom*.

Let us first look at *faith in the Lord*, that is, organizing culture under religious faith. From ancient times to the present, the main part of mankind, the basic way of using wisdom, is to believe in God - that is, to believe that the world was created by God, or by Lord, and if I am convinced of this, all problems are solved. Therefore, I don't need to think about it anymore, because God has already arranged everything in order, and this is called faith in the Lord. When you hear this, you should understand that the first intellectual effect of faith in God is obscuring and repressing.

Of course, I need to make a supplement here. In the history

of Western thought, theology, philosophy and science are in one linage. That is to say, theology pursued the idea that the ultimate of the world is God, and then philosophy pursued the idea of how God, the ultimate power, manipulates the world, and thus constitutes the subject of philosophical inquiry. Thus, philosophy in its early years was merely the handmaiden of theology, and science was merely an extension of the philosophical line of thought. In other words, in the history of Western thought, theology, philosophy, and science are successive in one linage. This philosophical inquiry into theological questions is found only in ancient Greece and continued in the West after ancient Greece through the modern Renaissance. Everywhere else in the world, theology itself has remained largely in a state of inquisitive finality. That is, the idea that God has answered all the questions. As long as I believe in God, all the questions are not a problem. This is the basic state of theology outside of Greece, outside of the modern West.

Let me give you an example, as you know, in the 7th century AD, Islam was formed in the Arab region. When Islam was first formed, Muhammad, a clerical organization - a political organization and a military organization at the same time - quickly unified the Arab region and formed the Arab Empire. The Chinese Tang Dynasty called it the Great Empire of Eclipse. The Great Empire of Eclipse expanded rapidly, occupying the entire Middle East region, and then raiding its territory up to North Africa, threatening Europe from the east and west like two pincers, one in the direction of Turkey on the eastern edge of Europe, and the other in the direction of Spain in the southwestern corner of Europe, posing the threat of swallowing up Europe. In the 8th century AD, after the occupation of Egypt, the Great Empire of Eclipse selectively translated the ancient Greek documents left in ancient Egypt, that is, the documents left in the library of the ancient city of Alexandria, into Arabic before they were burned. As a result, Europe lost all of its ancient Greek ideas after Rome.

As you know, the modern development of Europe began with the Renaissance. Don't be misled by the term Renaissance, which refers to Da Vinci, Raphael and Michelangelo. The Renaissance was actually the recovery of ancient Greek literature and the rational spirit of ancient Greece, which led to the Renaissance. In the 11-12th century, the Christian legions in Europe restored Spain, and then began a famous Latin translation movement, which was to use Latin to translate the ancient Greek literature preserved in Arabic, and this process initiated the Renaissance. And then literary figures, such as painters and sculptors like Da Vinci, Raphael, Michelangelo, plus a group of other cultural scholars, such as Dante, Petrarch, and Boccaccio, re-promoted the ancient Greek humanistic and rational spirit through their literature and art, which startled most people and formed a new perception of popular society, and as literature and art is something that can easily influence the public, it makes the submerged ancient Greek literature and the inheritance of ancient Greek thought neglected. In fact, the primary merit of the Renaissance was to retrieve the ancient Greek literature and the ancient Greek rational thought line back to Europe, and this thing constituted the epoch-making force of the Renaissance.

The Arabs had translated ancient Greek texts, and a few of these Islamic scholars studied these sources in depth. This led to the emergence of a few extremely rational scholars in Arab societies who reached high levels of philosophical attainment when medieval Europe was plunged into a dark and repressive Christian atmosphere. In mathematics, for example, and in optics, most of the earliest breakthroughs or achievements in the Medieval Ages were related to the Arabs. However, because Islam is the highest purpose of faith, it suppressed the expansion and evolution of the overall culture of Islam, resulting in the Arab culture region, the region covered by Islam, in a state of faith suppression, it is impossible to develop the entire modern scientific system of thought, and eventually made the Arabs become the bearer of ancient Greek culture, that is, the role of passing the torch, while their own culture is gradually declining, losing the potential for significant development. The Arabs became the bearers of the ancient Greek culture, that is, the torch bearers, while their own culture declined and lost the future that could have been achieved.

Please note that *faith in the Lord* is a state of intellectual repression, both in Arabia and in Europe. In the late Roman period, Christianity became the state religion of the Roman Empire after Constantine the Great established the formerly oppressed Christianity as the state religion, that is, after the famous Edict of Milan. Since then, the West gradually fell into the Dark Middle Ages. The term Dark Middle Ages is not really appropriate, but from the point of view of the promotion of ideas, it was indeed a dark and oppressive era. What does it mean? It means that the culture of faith in God was not a precursor to the development of wisdom in the mainstream, but a force for obscuring information and suppressing wisdom. The ancient Greeks also used to believe in gods, and they believed in various gods. The ancient Greek gods all seemed very naughty, very mischievous, jealous, aggressive, wanton, and lustful, even to the point of incest, all the weaknesses of human nature they had. From a certain point of view, they are just another manifestation of the mortal personality on the heavenly stage, or the unreal mobilization of the mediocre human nature in the realm of transcendence. Since ancient Greek theology was such a loose and tumultuous chic state, instead of constituting a repression of thought, the theology of ancient Greece back then became a launching point for the mobilization of ancient Greek wisdom. Socrates once said, to the effect that when man mobilized his intellect to the extreme, when he pursued it to the height of the gods and still refused to rest, that is, when he was determined to find out what the gods were capable of, that was the beginning and the end of philosophical inquiry. This was the peculiar relationship between ancient Greek philosophy and theology.

Let me take another example and look at Pythagoras. The Pythagoreans were both a learned order, an ecclesiastical order, and a political order, which ruled the ancient Greek region of Croton for twenty years. They were first and foremost an ecclesiastical organization with a theological faith called Orphism. So what was their philosophy studying? The study of how the gods manipulate the world, and from this point of view the investigation of the functioning of the gods themselves, which constitutes the whole system of Pythagorean number theory philosophy.

I made two points: first, that theology, philosophy, and science are one and the same, and that the early days of philosophy were about pursuing the ultimate in theology; and second, that this line of thinking about pursuing the ultimate in theology is found only in ancient Greece and in modern Europe during the budding era of philosophical science. In any other part of the world, theology instead constitutes a repressive and obscuring force of thought. We call this form of subjective culture, which constitutes a repression of thought, the culture of *faith in God*. This is an important aspect of the use of wisdom in the early years of mankind.

The wisdom direction of the *virtue-oriented* lineage is most clearly expressed in the traditional culture of ancient China. East Asia is the most typical region of agricultural civilization, and an agricultural civilization can cause the population to skyrocket a hundredfold. It is because the crop we produce on each acre of land, converted into energy that can be used by the human body, is roughly equivalent to 260 times the amount of energy you get from letting the acre of land grow grass, then the animals eat the grass, and then you go hunting animals. This led to the population grew a hundredfold once agricultural civilization develops. While the population grew, land resources were limited, bringing about excessive tensions in human and resource relations. As a result, the scholars of the pre-Qin era in China devoted all their energy to dealing with human and social problems, which led to the main lineage of pre-Qin culture and traditional Chinese culture, all concerned with the topic of human and social problems, which is expressed as the restraint and rectification of interpersonal relationships, and we call this lineage of learning virtue-oriented culture. So from ancient times to the present, moral discussion, ethical discussion, and social concern have been the whole basis, even the whole outline, of Chinese culture. This lineage of culture then makes all the avenues of your mobilizing your intellect in other areas blocked.

Therefore, from the pre-Qin era to the modern opium war, China has rarely had a naturalistic inquiry as a whole. Even the literati, a class of scholars whose job it was to pass on their culture, were hardly concerned with naturalistic issues, not to mention the natural sciences, and so the naturalistic line of thought was basically blank throughout. The emphasis on virtue culture obviously obscured the possibility of Chinese thinking to create a new branch. That is why Confucius left behind the famous saying, "Attacking the heretical, to avoid the harm of it." What does that mean? He said that thoughts outside of the culture of *virtue-oriented* were called heretical, and that the only way for people to get rid of the harm it might bring was to keep attacking heretical thoughts. This shows how deeply Chinese culture repressed different thought in the virtue-oriented era. All ideas outside the system of virtue-oriented were commonly called heretical culture. Therefore, Confucius's conduct as a teacher was summarized in the *Analects* by his disciples as "Confucius never speaks of weird force or diversified deities". It means that Confucius never talked about things that were not related to the culture of *virtue-oriented*. This is the second way of using human wisdom.

Since the human civilization, there are basically three ways for mankind to use wisdom, the first is called *faith in God*; the second is called *virtue-oriented*; and the third is called *love of wisdom*. Philosophy, the whole core of it is the love of wisdom. The so-called love of wisdom means that all the trivial matters of daily life are not discussed, but only the problems brought about by wisdom itself.

For ordinary people, what problems do we use our wisdom to solve? It is only the problems that arise in daily life and work. That is, the problems to be solved at the practical level are the main direction we use our wisdom, so we beautify name as learning to apply. But the ancient Greek philosophers believed that what can be applied is the finished state of learning, and it no longer constitutes a subject that scholars should continue to pursue. Therefore, anything that can be used is the stuff of the craftsman. It is the study of what cannot be used that is called scholarship. This kind of study that has nothing to do with practical use, and that is purely useless, is called philosophy. It is the just opposite of the Chinese idea of *learning to apply* and *knowledge to practice*.

We Chinese believe that a culture or a doctrine that is understood and recognized by the majority of people is a sign that it is closer to the truth. However, in the Western philosophical circle, in the culture of love of wisdom, it is quite the opposite, which believes that the majority of people cannot actually enter this level. It believes that if you study a problem that the majority of people can appreciate, then it proves that you are still far from wisdom. Let me give you an example. When Newton's book *Mathematical Principles of Natural Philosophy*, which deals with classical mechanics of gravity, was first published, most of the physics professors in Western universities could not understand it, because the mathematical equations and calculus in it were just invented by Newton. But it was Newton's book, which could not be understood by ordinary people, that created the industrial age. Today, we call the industrial age the Newtonian age. The calculations used by technicians and workers to make each gear are all branch equations derived from Newton's classical mechanics.

Let me give another example, Einstein's theory of relativity, special relativity was completed in 1905, and general relativity in 1916, and produced almost no social response. It wasn't until 1919 that Eddington, the chief scientist of the Royal Academy of Sciences, led a group of scientists who split up to observe total solar eclipses in Africa and South America. Because the theory of relativity says that a massive object bends space. That means then that a star behind the Sun, after the total eclipse obscured the light of the Sun, should be seen next to the Sun according to Einstein's calculation. Eddington sent two groups to observe the total eclipse, and indeed saw that a star that should be behind the Sun in astronomical calculations, appeared on the side of the Sun, indicating that space was curved and the light went not in a straight line but in a curve, and the calculations all agreed exactly with Einstein's prediction of the curvature. So, Einstein became famous in 1919, and the news was published on the front page of all newspapers around the world. But at this time Eddington declared that there were only two and a half people in the world who could read Einstein's paper, and he belonged to that half only. It was this study of relativity, which only two and a half people could read and understand, that became the basis of the entire human cosmology today. Today we are entering the nuclear age, the electronic age, which can also be called the Einstein age. What do I want to express? I want to express that popular culture is very far from the realm of truly profound thought. The more a doctrine, an idea, a book, is appreciated by the public, the further it is from the truth. Don't take popular culture as the high end of academic study.

Philosophy, or love of wisdom, is an extreme, excessive and overwhelming mobilization of intelligence. What does this phrase mean? Let me explain one more layer. It is worthy to know that all of us, all of your body organs have functional reserves. For example, the heart, our heart in the resting state per minute output, that is, about 5 liters of blood per minute heart beat, this is enough to maintain your life in a normal state. However, when you run long distances or exercise vigorously, your heart's output per minute increases six times to more than 30 liters, and the difference from 5 to 30 liters is the cardiac reserve. You should know, all of our organs, there is a functional reserve. For example, breathing, normally you only have one side lungs working is enough. A patient with severe lung disease may need to remove all the lungs on one side of the chest cavity, but it does not affect his normal breathing. Two kidneys, if you remove one to transplant it to another person, you will never occur uremic syndrome, all of this is called functional reserve. It is important to know that human intelligence also has a functional reserve. All of us are not able to mobilize this functional reserve under normal conditions. What can be called love of wisdom? It is the extraordinary mobilization of the functional reserve of the wisdom.

Please note I say two things: first, intelligent reserve mobilization is incredibly difficult; second, any functional reserve mobilization is harmful. For example, if you over mobilize your heart functional reserve to run a marathon and run too much fatigue, you may die suddenly. Then, human beings mobilizing their intellectual functional reserve can also cause great damage. I am not referring damage to the individual; I am referring damage to humanity as a whole. I just want to emphasize here that only the mobilization of the intellectual functional reserve is what can be called philosophy, or love of wisdom.

You know, our intelligence was developed when we were apes in the jungle. Think about it, you were in the jungle relying on hunting and gathering, i.e., gathering plants, hunting animals, you lived in such an environment, how much intelligence did you need to mobilize back then? You were in almost the same state as all animals mobilizing intelligence, there is no difference, that is the norm of our intelligence endowment. Most of us, in fact, use our wisdom in this normal state. But the narrow philosophy of love of wisdom does not stop at this point; it considers all such normal animal-like activities of intellectual discernment and perception to be outside the question I want to explore. I want to mobilize and bring into play the substratum of wisdom that is completely different from this type of conventional intellectual activity, and this is called philosophy, or love of wisdom.

In other words, the love of wisdom activity in the narrow sense of philosophy is the over-mobilization of the potential of intellectual reserves. Let me give you an example. A leopard hunts an antelope, how does it run? It must be lurking there, waiting for the antelope to come up to it before it starts to run. The antelope never runs in a straight line to avoid the leopard, it zigzags and turns all the way around to avoid the faster pursuer who is running straight. Before the leopard lurks, it observes the terrain, for example, it sees that there is a scrub forest on this side and the animal cannot run past it. Then when it chases the antelope, the antelope first runs in the direction of the bush, the leopard does not follow close behind, but will run in a straight line, it knows that the antelope must turn, so it moves along a straight line, taking one side of the triangle. In other words, the leopard is actually able to calculate, but it will never create the Pythagorean law that $a^2 + b^2 = c^2$. It does not have to calculate so precisely, it deals with the problem in an intuitive sense, which is called normal use of intelligence.

But what does the philosopher do? He would not need to calculate, if he were chasing an animal, he would do exactly the same, that is, he won't run the two sides of the triangle. But instead of chasing the animal, he sat indoors and tried to calculate the relationship between the two sides of the triangle and one side, using a precise mathematical model. This way of using intelligence, which is not directly related to daily activities, is called intelligent reserve mobilization. Do you think you need to calculate the Pythagorean Law if you are hunting an animal? Of course not, if you calculate the Pythagorean law, the animal would have run away. This means that for your survival it is better that you do not over-mobilize your intelligence.

The deep mobilization of intelligence, which on the surface does not appear to be related to your everyday practical survival activities, is the point of using intelligence in the narrow sense of philosophy. Please note the Pythagorean law I just mentioned, which was first discovered by Pythagoras, the ancient Greek philosopher.

Let me give you another example. Computers today can calculate hundreds of millions of times per second, but if you let them to recognize human faces, to recognize dog faces, cat faces, it is very difficult. But we humans, and even all animals, have no difficulty in recognizing facial differences between individuals of our own kind. What does this mean? It shows that recognizing faces is a very complex calculation. But why is it an extremely parsimonious act in our ordinary use of intelligence? It is because during our billions of years of biological evolution, our way of using intelligence has been compressed into a series of simple response modules, that is, we have turned a complex algorithmic problem into a neural docking relationship of simple responses. This has made our way of using intelligence very simple and fast. But please note that although it is very efficient, this efficient and shortcutting process discards all the sophisticated computational aspects in between.

So, what is philosophy doing? Mobilizing the sophisticated links in between and figuring them out. Who needs to do such a futile task in their daily life and work? This kind of futile and impractical study, in which the intellectual potential has to be fully mobilized and fine-tuned, is called love of wisdom. Therefore, please remember that philosophy is concerned with issues that have absolutely nothing to do with the application of everyday life, it is the refinement of pure wisdom, it is the mobilization of the reserves of pure wisdom, it is the over-exertion of the potential wisdom. We call this thing love of wisdom or philosophy in the narrow sense.

So, Aristotle summarized philosophy by calling it *metaphysica.* What does that mean? After physics. What Aristotle called physics is the material entity that you can visualize with your eyes and think about with your brain, and philosophy is the deeper inquiry that comes after it. It is almost identical to the Chinese term "形而上学" metaphysics, but with different connotations. Chinese metaphysics does not involve the extreme mobilization of intellectual reserves, but is expressed only as the primary organization of intuition by consciousness. The ancient Greek philosophy in the narrower sense of after physics refers to the sophisticated refinement of the intellectual form that follows intuitive physical phenomena.

Thus, in the modern era of classical philosophy, there is a figure of Germany named Leibniz. He once expressed it in this way, saying that philosophy needs its own dedicated system of symbols. He proposed a term ordinary symbols. What is meant by ordinary symbols? The language and symbols that we use in general are constructed in the material everyday life, whereas the problems that philosophy discusses are the system of figuring out the depths of metaphysical thought or wisdom itself, so the everyday language that we build in the material intuitive world is not sufficient to express philosophical problems. According to Leibniz, we must create a universal symbol. Note the original meaning of the word universal, not in the sense of commonplace, but in the sense of universal. That is, it has to be used both material common life and metaphysically, and only when such a sequence of symbols is found can it be used for philosophical expression. What does it mean? It means that the philosophical context of thought is not in the everyday context of thought at all, so that the philosophical expressions are not in the everyday context at all. We have to extract and study this wisdom that is not mobilized in everyday thinking and everyday contexts, and after studying it clearly, we have to disperse it and implement it at the unrealistic level or refer to it at the realistic level, so that the system of learning thus created can be called a philosophical system.

This is why neither ancient philosophy nor today's science is in our daily operation of thought, neither is within the scope of our intuitive insight. The learning it mobilizes and creates is invisible to the eye. This knowledge system thus created is called the product of a logical game reached in the philosophical realm of thought. It is the product of this purely logical game that constitutes the entire body of knowledge we have today. It is from this starting point that philosophy gave birth to the entire modern system of human knowledge and thought. That's why you don't see the mainstream Western academics, except for a very few empiricists, speak the phrase "practice produces true knowledge" in Western philosophy from ancient Greece to modern times. They do not speak this phrase, and only we Chinese repeatedly speak this phrase. Because practice does not constitute a system of knowledge; the real system of knowledge is constructed in the process of intelligent reserve mobilization and the refinement of purely logical games. That is why a philosopher once made this statement about Western philosophy in a narrow sense: "What is called philosophy is a purely logical game played by a group of large-sized children in ancient Greece." I would like to invite you to finely speculate on the actual meaning of this seemingly joking statement.

More about Ancient Greece

I have talked so much before, but I have only talked about what it means by love of wisdom. We start from this starting point because we want you to understand that in your daily life, your daily study, and your daily thinking is very far from philosophy. In order to enter the intellectual reserve function of philosophy, you have to stay away from the cultural atmosphere of chicken soup. Then, as I said earlier, "Philosophy in the narrow sense is found only in ancient Greece." Please recall my first class, which I said was the foundation of all the courses. In that class, I talked about the so-called Western civilization called the circum-Mediterranean civilization, that is, the region along the circum-Mediterranean formed the only fully open landscape in the conception of ancient human civilization. The circum-Mediterranean region includes North Africa, the Near East and Southern Europe, so why did the narrow philosophical lineage occur only in ancient Greece? This is a question that needs to be explored.

First of all, I would like to emphasize once again that the ancient Greek culture is a collection of cultures around the Mediterranean. We have seen many books that say that ancient Greek culture originated from ancient Egypt and ancient Babylon, the sources of Eastern culture, but this is very problematic. Because from the West European outlook in modern times, the Middle East, the Near East and West Asia all are called the East. Therefore, many scholars now regard ancient Egyptian civilization, ancient Babylonian civilization, the Near and Middle East civilization, and the Two Rivers civilization as all oriental civilizations, which is incorrect and misleading by the concept of the East as the Western Europeans call it in recent times. Ancient Egypt, Mesopotamia, Crete and the Aegean islands and their coasts, including even Asia Minor, were completely integrated in the formation of ancient Greek culture, so they are collectively called the circum-Mediterranean region, which is the cradle of typical Western culture. Therefore, ancient Egypt and ancient Babylon should not be called the East, it is actually the overall hotbed of Western culture.

The question is, why did the ultimate focus of all cultures in the entire circum-Mediterranean take place in ancient Greece? Well, we have to look at ancient Greece as a place below. Notice this map, which shows the whole area of ancient Greece. Ancient Greece was a place where agricultural civilization was difficult because of its rocky terrain and poor soil. The rainy season was not until winter, and the dry season was stuck in the summer when the climate was warm and sunny and everything was growing, so its vegetation growth conditions were misaligned, creating huge obstacles to crop cultivation. It faces the Mediterranean Sea and is sandwiched between Europe, Asia and Africa in the middle of this inland waterway, which makes it extremely convenient for trade and cultural exchange, creating a semi-agricultural, semi-commercial civilization in the primitive era of mankind. The industrial and commercial civilization required a state of extreme intelligent mobilization in order to make its development possible.

Why, then, did narrow philosophy ultimately fail to occur throughout the circum-Mediterranean, in ancient Egypt, for example, or in ancient Babylon, for example? To put it in perspective, the earliest place where mathematics and geometry took place was not on the Greek peninsula, but was first demonstrated in ancient Egypt and the Near East. But because ancient Egypt was a Nile civilization, and ancient Babylon was a Two-River civilization, and all large-river civilizations were agricultural civilizations, and agricultural civilizations did not need to mobilize intellectual reserves, nor to mobilize sophisticated logic.

To understand this, we have to look at this map. Note that ancient Greece was never the Greek peninsula of today. The Greece of today is very different from ancient Greece in terms of geographical scope. Ancient Greece included Asia Minor and the Near East, the Greek peninsula, the Apennine peninsula, the southern tip of the Italian peninsula, and the islands of Crete and Sicily, a large area known as Ancient Greece.

First look at the right side of the map. There is a place called

Lydia in the east of ancient Greece, and there is a row of words called Ionia underneath. You should know that the earliest natural philosophy of ancient Greece took place in the Ionic region, and Thales, the first saintly philosopher of ancient Greece, was born here in a place called Miletus, and founded the Miletus school. As you look further up, there is a place in Asia Minor called Thrace, which is also not part of Greece today. Thrace produced two important figures, the creator of atomism, Leucippus and his disciple Democritus. Then look at the Greek peninsula. At the lower southern end of the peninsula is the famous Athens, which produced the main body of ancient Greek philosophy, and where the three great figures of ancient Greece - Socrates, Plato, and Aristotle - were active. Looking further to the left of the map, this is the Italian peninsula, the southern part of the Apennines, a place that was also part of Greater Greece in those days. To the northwest of it, there is a city-state called Elea, which gave rise to the famous Eleatic School, represented by Parmenides and Zeno. And slightly south of it, there was a city called Croton, where the Pythagorean school took place.

In addition, in the Near East on the eastern side of the Mediterranean Sea, which I talked about in my first class, there was a small state called Phoenicia. The Phoenicians were responsible for 50% of the ocean shipping and trade in the Mediterranean Sea during the ancient Greek era, and because of their extensive trading activities, they created the phonetic script, or rather the main body of the alphabet of the phonetic script, i.e., it had already created 22 of the 26 Latin alphabets 3,000 years ago. The Phoenicians then spread throughout the circum-Mediterranean region, and later developed Carthage, a powerful rival of the ancient Roman Empire, all these historical events are related to the Phoenicians. The actual situation may be that the phonetic script, which gradually spread from around the circum-Mediterranean to Crete and eventually to ancient Greece, was the prerequisite for creating the structure of grammatical and logical thinking.

This part of ancient Greece is a geographical structure divided into fragments. It included the Near East, Asia Minor, the Greek peninsula and the southern Apennines, as well as many islands in the Aegean Sea and Crete. This fragmented geographical structure made it a unique structure of existence that could not accomplish political unity. Thus, ancient Greek civilization was a typical city-state civilization. Each city-state constituted a living colony and a cultural fractal. This fragmented geopolitical relationship, as well as the special open landscape and unfavorable agricultural environment that I mentioned earlier, resulted in a semi-commercial civilization, which, together with the non-unitary and pluralistic political and cultural pattern, created the conditions for free and open exchange of ideas in ancient Greece. In other words, the occurrence of ancient Greek philosophy was not deliberately designed by a few people, but it was a system of thinking shaken by a special geographical landscape and living structure.

As we all know, a unified political entity can easily form an overly rigid mainstream culture under the strong repression of a regime structure, which makes the development of other ideas always appear as incompatible heterodox forms. The fragmented political structure of the city-states and the specific geographic pattern of ancient Greece made it possible for different thoughts to occur among different jurisdictions and regions, and then it had sufficient conditions for communication, which in turn led to the constant collision and fusion of different ideas. The long process of agitation, variation, differentiation and reorganization played a spontaneous role in promoting the mobilization of intellectual potential, and this is the reason why the ancient Greek philosophical culture was created.

Overview of Ancient Greek Philosophy

We turn next to three kernels of thought in ancient Greek philosophy.

First, the concept of knowledge. What is the concept of knowledge? It is your basic attitude and basic view of knowledge.

Let me start with a quote from a young contemporary Israeli historian, Yuval Harari: The mobilization of human civilization's thinking began with *conscious ignorance*. He also called it the *revolution of ignorance*. What does this mean? It means that in a non-intellectual culture, our basic idea of knowledge is called all-knowing, that is, we believe that we know everything about our concerns, that we are in a state of omniscience.

But the cognitive revolution of human beings actually started from a state of ignorance. Think about an animal, such as a monkey or a wolf, when it sees a fruit or a sheep in the surrounding jungle, what is its reaction? I know very well that I see a sheep, I know very well that I see an apple, and I will never doubt or think about the sheep or the apple itself. This is called all-knowing.

The vast majority of our early human states of mind, and even today's, have always been in the complacent state of knowing it all. That is, in everyday life and work, if you aim to deal with practical problems, then your thinking process is always in a state of clear knowledge. But ancient Greek philosophy started with the opposite, with ignorance, with the idea that we do not know anything, or that what we think we know is in fact nothing more than an illusion. This is the first premise for the mobilization of intelligent reserves.

So the word being discussed in ancient Greek philosophy, which I mentioned earlier, is simply the predicate Being. What does it express? It expresses not knowing anything, with the implication of continuing to ask. It is the predication that follows the predicate that gives the subject its concept. So we see that the meaning of Being in antient Greek philosophy is very unusual. It does not admit that what we see with our eyes is something in existence. It says that what we see with our eyes is an illusion, and that it has to investigate a certain determining element behind this thing, which is called Being. Therefore, it does not admit what I see is what I know from the beginning.

Socrates has a famous saying, "I know that I know nothing." -- which actually is an important starting point for ancient Greek philosophy. Socrates always invited people to discuss problems, saying I am ignorant, so I sincerely ask you for answers, at which point the other person usually acted as if he knew everything, and answered Socrates' questions one by one. Socrates kept asking questions, changing the angle, until the other person's answer contradicted his previous answer, and finally had to bow his head and admit his ignorance. This street game of Socrates was called the midwifery of knowledge by later generations.

As we can imagine, this kind of constant questioning of others initially appears to be asking for advice, but later degrades others from *a state of knowledge* to *a state of ignorance,* and makes them fall from a state of feeling very lofty and perfect to a very childish and absurd situation. This, of course, makes the interlocutor very annoyed. That is why Socrates was finally sentenced to death by the ancient Greeks through voting. What was the purpose of this act of Socrates? To remind you that everything starts from ignorance! To warn you how absurd it is when you think you know! Think about it, most human beings in general are in a culture of faith in God or virtue-oriented, what is this state? This is the state of certainty, so you will stop asking questions. If your knowledge is certain, you don't have questions, and if you don't have questions, you don't think further, and your mind is thus closed.

Aristotle once said that all philosophical inquiries begin with amazement. What does amazement mean? I am amazed only when I am ignorant of what I see. If I take what I see for granted, then the inquiry stops. The so-called amazement must be prerequisite at ignorance. This is what is called the ignorance revolution.

Let me give you another example. Back in China's first book, the *Book of Shang,* one of the texts called the Yugong, in which it had all the geography of China spelled out, called the Little Jiu Zhou. At that time, it was called Jiu Zhou, instead of Little Jiu Zhou, though its depiction was actually different. In the Warring States period, a man named Zou Yan, the one who invented the doctrine of the five elements, used the five elements to deduce the Great Jiu Zhou, that is, it has completed the whole world geography. We can imagine what you could do to illustrate the world in that non-navigational era, which was completely based on conjecture. But this conjecture actually became definite knowledge, so we no longer had any doubt about what the world was, and we entered the state of omniscience. All the parts that are ignorant are things that do not need to be known. It was not until the Kang-Qian period of the Qing Dynasty, when a map of China hung in the imperial court, that it gave an overview of the geography of China and then concluded that all places outside of China were barbaric places not worth caring about.

As I said in the first lesson, East Asia is a typical closed landscape, with the Siberian tundra to the north, the Pamir Plateau to the west, the Hengduan Mountains to the south, and the vast Pacific Ocean to the east. This predetermined the Chinese view of the world, which was only the central country, called *land under heaven* (the world). From the small Jiu Zhou to the Great Jiu Zhou, the Chinese already considered themselves to have a complete and systematic understanding of the world in the pre-Qin era, and this view did not change until the 17th and 18th centuries. We can see how solid and confirmed the state of our knowledge.

Let me give you another example. At the beginning of the Great Age of Navigation, that is, the fourteenth and fifteenth centuries, the Portuguese, at that time, first began to follow the west coast of Africa, seeking to reach the East by sea. At that time, they had a map of Europe with the surrounding area, which was limited to a very one-sided part, and the part along the west coast of Africa was all blank, and the whole Africa was drawn with only a clue of the west coast. It left a large number of questions, making people want to explore when they saw this map, and they were eager to understand the unknown places. Because it hung a question mark of ignorance, a lure of ignorance, the age of great voyages was able to take place. Ignorance is the prerequisite for inquiry, inquiry is the development of ideas, and it is ideas that create knowledge. Therefore, it is important to determine whether one's conception of knowledge is in a state of confirmation or in a state of ignorance. It is the starting point for all thoughts to unfold, and this is the first one, called the concept of knowledge or the concept of ignorance. The first of these three kernels, which I am laying out, is the underlying reason for you to understand why the ancient Greeks had that kind of whimsy.

The second core of ancient Greek philosophy is called *ontological truth*.

When it comes to ancient Greece, many people talk about it from Thales to Aristotle, but in fact, you can't understand why there is such a whimsy line of philosophy in ancient Greece. The ancient Greeks did not admit that the world we see is existence, and his deduction is like this: the world we see is always changing, mountains will collapse, the earth will crack, rivers will dry up and change their course, people will age and die, and everything is in flux. The ancient Greeks thought that these things were illusions and never the real existence. He believed that a real existence must be eternal, unchanging, and indivisible, and only that something can be called existence. He therefore asked about the hidden core behind the world seen by the eye, which dominates the world of flux, and which is constant in itself, and which he thought was called *Being* (existence).

The first phase of Western philosophy is called ontology. What is ontology? The true existence behind the phenomena, behind the intuition, is called ontology. His thinking is very strange, for he does not admit that seeing is believing, and its premise is called *seeing is not real*. Why does he have such a strange idea? This is exactly the opposite of our simple Chinese view that seeing is believing. I used to say that Eastern and Western cultures are always the opposite. This opposite point in its way of thinking is very peculiar, why is it so?

As I said before, *Being* in English is just a predicative link verb, because the phonetic script itself has lost its concept, which is the most basic building block of human thought. When a phonetic script hangs there, it does not have a figurative symbol, so you do not know what it is, you have to give it a meaning in its grammatical-logical structure, and in the middle of all propositional sentences there must be a link verb, and the link verb brings out the predicate that is the source of the concept of the subject, so the link verb is called Being. What does it mean? It means that Being is a question! "Being" caused major difficulties in translating Western philosophy in modern China, because what we call existence is what we actually see, while what westerners call "Being" is an invisible inquiry. This is why there was a debate when it was translated: should it be translated as existence? Or should it be translated as is? That is why the term existentialism is sometimes called is-ism until now. What is the meaning of is-ism? Is "is" a question? What does "is" ask? What is "is"? That is, the word "is" must be followed by a question of what, and this is the potential compulsion that the lexical item "Being" necessarily creates. When it is presented as being, it is not fixed as a system of reality, but becomes an interrogative state.

What the Chinese call *existence* is about the reproduction by men and women, their offspring, children and grandchildren, and the continuity of generations. It describes a confirmed state; *Being*, on the other hand, is a non-confirming and inquiring state, and this is the difference between the being and the existence we are talking about. Therefore, in the West, there is a concept missing in our traditional Chinese culture, called phenomenon, that is, it does not recognize what you see as reality.

Please note that *reality* and *phenomenon* are two concepts, what we see is only phenomenon, which is an illusion of manifestation. This is called phenomenon, and the master behind the phenomenon is called reality, which is the meaning of the ancient Greek theory of being, also called ontology. It believes that the thing behind the phenomenon that you cannot see is the real existence, and this concept leads to the modern essence. The terms phenomenon and essence that we keep using today actually originated from the ancient Greek inquiry of *being*.

What will be the final dynamic of this inquiry? Let me cite the example of Harari, who said that "the origin of human civilization began in fabrication". What does that mean? It means that I do not recognize what I see as real, but I have to trace origin and fabricate the illusion of what I see, thus civilization is created. He said, the monkeys, for example, are knowledgeable, they have knowledge, they even have language. When one of the monkeys saw an eagle, it will make a unique cry, saying "the eagle is here," because the eagle will snatch away the baby monkeys, so all the monkeys rush to take the baby monkeys to hide. These monkeys also make another strange call to warn the whole group that a black bear is coming, as the bear poses a threat to them.

So how do humans behave? Man was exactly the same as the monkeys, first confirming the sensory facts, identifying eagles and bears. But when man suddenly started to make up stories one day, he said "the bear is our protector", thus civilization began. The Yellow Emperor of China, his tribe was called the Bear Clan, what does this mean? The bear is the guardian god of their tribe. So the founder of Chinese civilization was the Yellow Emperor. What does that mean? When he was able to virtualize reality as existence, when he did not admit reality as existence, when he fabricated a purely ideological reality, it started the breaking away of the human being's thinking from animals, and thus launched the civilization process. This ability to recreate or reshape reality with the help of thought is what we call hypothesis in philosophy and science.

As you know, the basic way of unfolding Western culture is hypothesis and proof. What does it mean by hypothesis? I do not admit that what I see is real, it is only an illusion or a phenomenon. Since all I see are illusions, what is the reality and true existence? I can only trace through hypothesis, which is called fabrication in common parlance and hypothesis in academic terms. It is only when there is a *hypothesis* that you ask questions, and when there is a hypothesis that you need to *prove*. If you don't make assumptions, why do you need to prove them? Since it is a hypothesis, the proof that seeing is believing is of course invalid, because what is seen is false, so what is seen is not enough as a proof. So the proof that is added to the hypothesis is not the sum of the regular state of seeing or consciousness, but the product of some kind of sophisticated logical program, which is called *proof*.

Traditional Chinese scholarship has lacked the premise of "hypothesis or assumptions" since ancient times. Chinese culture is summed up in four parts: "scriptures of Confucianism, records of history, works of scholars of pre-Qin era, and collections of literatures". Among the four, the records of history is the most important component. There is a classic statement in historiography that we have repeatedly emphasized - "History does not allow hypothesis". That is, Chinese scholarship as a whole does not accept hypotheses. But human civilization began precisely with hypothesis. In fact, Chinese people (including other civilizations) have been fabricating since ancient times, but they refuse to admit it, so they do not actively assuming anything and seek proofs about it, so their thinking will come to a standstill, and the subsequent process of proof will not be able to start. This is the reason why narrow philosophy occurred only in ancient Greece, where assumptions were constantly made and proofs were constantly sought.

And it is a question of what is meant by proof. We are going to keep talking about this issue later. I now remind you that you will understand what proof means when I talk about the concept of logic in broad sense later. I may not repeat this question at that time. I will make a rough statement about proof here. When you were in high school, your teacher gave you a problem of quadratic equation with two unknowns, and told you to calculate and solve this problem. You could do it in a few lines to arrive at the result. But if the teacher to you to prove this problem, if you were not a mathematician, you could not complete the proof of this quadratic equation with several dozen pages of derivation, this sophisticated process is called proof. There is a saying in the West: Learning is proof. Learning is never to declare the truth directly, it never means that you immediately come up with a definite answer and say you have finished it; rather you must first make a hypothesis, and then logically step by step to prove it in depth, this is called learning, this is called proof. If you read Newton's work *Mathematical Principles of Natural Philosophy*, the whole book is just a proof of what gravity is, and even what force is. If you read my book *A Unified Theory of Evolution*, the whole book only proves one principle - the principle of weakening compensation, and hundreds of thousands of words in the whole book are only a systematic proof of it, so it is particularly hard to read. Because the proof is a purely logical inference, one ring is fixed into another in chain, and no missing ring is allowed, and this process is called proof. And all real, all learning is actually the result of assumptions and proofs, which is called ontological truth, which is the ontology of ancient Greek philosophy.

I will explain a bit more here to help guide you in listening to the lessons that follow. The ancient Greeks thought of our sensory organs as nearly an orifice of vacuum, that is, the ancient Greek philosophers of that time did not yet realize that our perceptions themselves were prescriptive. Therefore, they imposed perception directly on objects without inquiring into perception itself. This stage in ancient Greek philosophy is called the ontological stage, also called natural philosophy.

Subsequently, that is, since Plato, they have actually discovered that our perception itself is not a vacuum. If our perception is prescriptive, then you are not qualified to ask about existence if you do not first figure out what perception is, isn't that so? Because your perception itself is prescriptive to "being" and "existence" with distortion. Thus, since the modern era, Western philosophy has moved from the ontological stage to the epistemological stage, which is another topic we will talk about later.

We will begin with the general state of mind of ancient Greek philosophy, and our entire focus today is on ancient Greece. Why? Because it is the only thing that can lead you to understand the origins of Western philosophical culture. So remember, when ontology took place, when natural philosophy emerged in ancient Greece, it was premised on not recognizing what is seen as real. It had to inquire what follows behind, and the inquiring itself could only be done through hypothesis. If neither our senses nor the unfolding of our consciousness are sufficient to prove that hypothesis, but instead provide false result, then the proof has to be accomplished through purely logical deduction, that is, by having a purely logical hypothesis followed by a purely logical proof, which constitutes the beginning of philosophical and scientific inquiry.

Now we move to the third kernel, *precise logic*.

What is *precise logic*? Since the evidence provided by the sensory organs is not recognized, and the logical thinking behind assumptions and hypotheses has to be used for proof, then how does logic prove it? This requires that the logic itself be able to operate in a particularly refined and rigorous manner, so that it is not random or arbitrary, but necessarily derived and unmovable, and this kind of thinking and reasoning procedure is called precise logical proof. So please note that when I talk about thought, logic, and reasoning, I am not talking about general reasoning, but about precise logical reasoning.

Among the existing human learning, there are roughly only three things that require the mobilization of precise logic: first, mathematics, geometry; second, physics; and third, philosophy. If you study mathematics, you will find that it's one ring buckled to another, there is nothing behind the number. For example, if I say 3, what is 3? It can be 3 cups, 3 computers, 3 tables or 3 people, etc. Anything can be, but nothing is it. When I arrange such purely abstract logical symbols and then perform a chain of derivative proofs or algorithmic solutions, this process constitutes the whole of mathematics, of geometry. The reason why geometry was particularly important in ancient Greece is that the early years of human mathematics unfolded on geometry. What does this statement mean? You know that in primitive times mankind did not have a number sequence, so the mathematical calculations of early mankind had to be done on geometric figures. In ancient Egypt, in China, and in the West, geometry and mathematics were the same thing in the early years. That is why there is a sentence written on the outer wall of Plato's school: "No entry who does not know geometry", which is equivalent to "No one who does not know mathematics is allowed inside". Everyone who has studied mathematics should be well aware of the complexity and detail of mathematics, which shows the precision of precise logic.

Let me give you another example. Thales, the first philosopher of ancient Greece, was born in the 7th century B.C. and unfolded his ideas in the 6th century B.C. Thales left only one sentence: "Water is the origin of all things." Why he became the first philosopher of the West and the first pioneer of philosophy is a topic we will discuss later. According to the history of ancient Greek philosophy, Thales traveled through ancient Egypt, and as a young man he was particularly keen on geometric calculations. He stood on a cliff by the coast and looked at a distant ship, and through the triangle formed by the diagonal line of his viewpoint and the straight line of the sea level, he was able to accurately calculate the distance between the ship and his position. What was he doing? He was training himself in geometric mathematical thinking. Many of the philosophers in ancient Greece had the experience of traveling around the Mediterranean Sea. Standing under the pyramids in ancient Egypt, they could determine or roughly determine the height of the pyramids by visual calculation, which is typical of geometric mathematical training and geometric mathematical application. Few types of civilizations, and few early literati, in those primitive times were able to use and mobilize precise logic as universally and persistently as the ancient Greek philosophers did.

Let us take a brief look at the state of human intellect. We humans and all creatures can be divided into five levels of consciousness, I would say simply. I spoke earlier about Harari, and the stories I quoted are from his book, *A Brief History of Humankind*. He has recently published another book, which I think many of you have read, called *A Brief History of the Future*. In *A Brief History of the Future*, he discusses a problem in which he says that human consciousness is the algorithm, or the arithmetic of precise logic. He says that he understands this today because of the advent of the computer age. He even says that the residual consciousness that lies outside of precise logic, that is, the primary consciousness outside of algorithms, is actually completely ineffective and even harmful. A computer or robot, for example, does not feel pain; pain is something in consciousness, not related to algorithms. You take a needle and prick a human fingertip, he feels the pain, but you take a needle and prick a robot, it is not painful. But robots run algorithms that are much more sophisticated and efficient than yours. Therefore, human low-end consciousness is a redundant and even harmful thing. He also gave a very interesting example, he said that just like the aircraft flight, it is not unavoidable to make a roaring noise, consciousness is this noise, noise has no use, it cannot push the aircraft forward at all.

Is Harari right in this statement? It's very awfully wrong. Where does human consciousness come from? You have to sort this out first. The consciousness of all our creatures as well as human beings can be divided into five levels, namely: the unconscious level, the subconscious level, the lower conscious level, the upper conscious level, and the sophisticated logic level, also called the consciousness level of thought. What is the foundation on which your whole perceptual system of any living creature, including human beings, is laid? It is laid on the transmembrane potential of the cell membrane and the bioelectrical conduction of the nervous system. This part, which we cannot mobilize in the upper conscious level or manifest consciousness, is called the unconscious. Please note that I choose a term coined by the psychologist Jung, but what I mean by it is much deeper than that.

The second level is called the subconscious. What is the subconscious? Please note that the concept I adopted was established by Freud, but the meaning of my choice of words, although more similar to Freud's original meaning, may have a broader scope. How can I put it? It is the sum of the functions of the neural structure of the organism and its internal perceptual maintenance system, also known as the sympathetic nervous system or the vegetative nervous system, constructed on the basis of the physical movement of the cellular transmembrane potential, i.e., micro-physiological electromagnetic induction. It is important to understand that once life occurs and evolves into a multi-cellular, multi-organ organism, its internal coordination becomes very complex, so our human nervous system has a low-end remnant that specializes in regulating the internal functioning of physiological structures. For example, your heartbeat, breathing rate, gastrointestinal motility, reproductive mechanism, etc., you do not have to take the manifest consciousness to govern it. Who manages these things? They are all regulated by the vegetative nervous system in an orderly manner.

Since all living organisms act around the central axis of sexual proliferation, Freud speaks of sexual repression in early childhood, which can bring about severe psychopathy, and he calls this thing the *subconscious*. I give it a broader expression, expanding it to the neuroregulatory system of the inner structure of the whole organism. This thing lurks beneath the manifest consciousness and cannot be controlled by you on your own. For example, you cannot use your explicit consciousness to control the beating of your heart, nor can you use your explicit consciousness to regulate your gastrointestinal movements, which is the second foundation layer of biological consciousness.

The third layer is called the *lower conscious*, which is our lower nerve centers, such as the spinal cord in the spinal canal in the back. When we ride a bicycle, if you know how to ride a bicycle, and you can control it skillfully, then your two legs can do circular movements without special attention, you can ride a bicycle and think about complex problems at the same time, and you won't fall down or hit on a tree. It is your spinal lower conscious system, the lower sub-central nervous system that presides over it. For example, if you prick your finger with a needle, you will immediately have a painful sensation and a retracted hand response, which is a strain protection mechanism triggered by the peripheral sensory nerves feeding back to the lower central reflex arc. Random, instinctive combined internal and external perceptual responses like these constitute the lower conscious.

Then there is the *upper consciousness*, which is already the fourth level, also called explicit consciousness or motivated consciousness. It is at this level that you start to use intelligence, or what you usually call wisdom, intelligence, intellect, IQ, etc. This is the upper consciousness part, which is also called *manifest consciousness* in psychology. The average person floats on this level and thinks he is so smart that he brags about it everywhere, not knowing that he is actually only an inch further than the beasts and apes who use their intelligence.

Finally, there is a fifth level above this one, which is the unique potential of Homo sapiens or the superiority of philosophers' mobilization, which is what Harari called algorithmic consciousness (or algorithm), or may call *thought consciousness*. Please note that I am using the concept of ideology, which is in no way related to what we usually call in domestic politics someone "with a bad thought consciousness" or "with a good thought consciousness". What I mean by *thought consciousness* is *precise logical consciousness*, because that is the only part that can really be called thought. Our daily intellectual activity is based on a modular response to the general external environment that was formed over billions of years, so we have already used our intelligence to a state of satisfaction at the level of manifest consciousness, which is the fourth level.

The precise logical consciousness requires special mobilization, that is, you have to be constantly trained over time. It is originally only a *latent ability*, a *weak wisdom*, and does not directly manifest itself as a ready intelligence. It's not like you see an obstacle and choose a side of a triangle like an animal, and think you've done something important, but rather you have to do the Pythagorean Theorem or Proposition. You have to reach penetration in such a complicated logical path, so as to achieve the precise operation of the details of thinking, which is called precise logic, which is the highest level of the sequence of human thinking.

As I said earlier, computers are still not perfect in recognizing human faces, dog faces and cat faces, though they run hundreds of millions of high-speed calculations per second. But why do we humans find it easy? It is because we have long compressed it into a neural network linked to the *response module*. But on the other hand, it becomes very difficult for humans to perform sophisticated logic use. To what extent is it difficult? We study mathematics from elementary school to university for more than a decade, and probably less than one in ten thousand of us can become mathematicians, i.e., people who can readily translate all problems into *equations* and *algorithms*. What does it tell us? We have to mobilize that uppermost level of algorithmic consciousness, and it is actually a super potential to mobilize. That is, algorithmic consciousness is only in our potential, not in the normal realization of universal intelligence. We have to mobilize it with the help of painstaking and continuous training, which I call *intelligence reserve mobilization*, in order to enter the high level of thoughtful consciousness, that is, precise logic consciousness or precise logic for short. So we see that the ancient Greek culture started its training at this level in its philosophical beginnings, and it was from this level that the intellectual foundation of ancient Greek philosophy in the narrow sense was solidified.

I repeat, the basic core of ancient Greek philosophy includes as follows: first, the revolution of ignorance, i.e., its conception of knowledge is always in a state of emptiness and inquiry; second, the true existence of ontology, i.e., it does not admit that the cognition acquired in superficial intuition is true knowledge; and third, precise logic, the only way to achieve a high level of mobilization of human intellectual reserves is through the training of such thinking. The synthesis and condensation of these basic qualities is the true starting point of philosophy in the narrow sense.

Initial Inquiry of Ontology

We move on to discuss the topics explored by ancient Greek philosophy. Again, I repeat that we won't talk about the history of Western philosophy in this class, but only talk about an overview of the foundations of Western philosophy. Therefore, with regard to ancient Greek philosophy, I will only give you a basic framework.

I will talk about it in flashbacks, starting directly from Aristotle. As you know, Aristotle was the last famous philosopher of ancient Greece, and became the master of ancient Greek philosophy. Why do I talk about ancient Greek philosophy, starting from him? He said that when you look at all things, you have to ask about *existence* or the *essence of existence* (please note that once I say *inquiry into existence*, I am not talking about phenomena at the *level of intuition*), you will definitely ask about the four causes. Aristotle's so-called four causes, I will now make a brief discussion, the first is called material cause, the second is called formal cause, the third is called dynamic cause, the fourth is called purpose cause.

I will explain each of them. What is material cause? Ancient Greek philosophy asks why everything is different, and this question immediately leads to the simplest answer, that is, everything is different because it contains different materials. A porcelain cup, for example, contains clay; a steel cup, contains metal; a wooden utensil, contains plant fibers; a human being, contains countless cells; and so we believe that the different categories of external objects are due to the different materials they contain.

But let's note that in the 20th century, a famous American physicist named Gell-Mann emerged as the discoverer of quarks, for which he won the Nobel Prize in Physics. He wrote a popular science book *Quarks and Jaguars,* in which he raised a question: Everything is made up of quarks and electrons, so why is there a difference between everything? This question asks why, if the proposition is true, there are differences in the composition of everything, given that the constituents of everything are the same. It is important to understand that this question has remained unanswered to date. When the ancient Greeks asked that the reason why everything is classified differently is because of the difference in the underlying material, his intention was not to reach any definite conclusion, but to form a follow-up question. This is called the material cause, not the material effect.

Thales, the first saintly philosopher of ancient Greece, left only one sentence: "Water is the origin of all things" - and because of this he surprisingly became the first philosophical founder of ancient Greece. We listen to this sentence today, he was all wrong, because water is not the essence of everything. Water is hydrogen-dioxygen, two hydrogen atoms with one oxygen atom, obviously water is not the source of everything, because the atom is not yet the beginning of everything. Where do atoms come from, please? You have to go back to the elementary particles, and where do the particles come from? You have to go back to the singularity energy. At a glance, Thales did not go back to the origin. But why did he become the first progenitor of Western philosophy? It is because his statement contains the question that everything itself is not ready-made and does not emerge simultaneously, but has a source that derives it in a gradual manner. It contains two meanings: first, there is a primary cause behind all things; second, all things evolve.

Please think back to my talk about Laozi, whose *Dao* is also the same inquiry. That is why I say that Laozi is the first and even the only philosopher in the history of ancient Chinese thought. But Laozi's *Dao* ends here, while Thales' questioning is much naiver than Laozi's, so there is still room for further questioning. But you don't know what Laozi's *Dao* is, and you can imagine infinitely, and there is no way to find out. You can consider the question to be satisfactorily answered, while Thales' answer constitutes a new question, so it is not the ultimate conclusion. When he said "water is the origin of all things", he immediately got into a big trouble, then what is the precursor or the origin of water, please?

There is a reason why Thales said this. Intuitively, where there is water, all things will flourish. Where there is water, vegetation sprouts; where there is irrigation, grain grows; where there is moisture, maggots grow; where there is water, fish and shrimp are produced; and even babies are born from amniotic fluid. Observing that the presence of water inexplicably leads to the occurrence of things that were not there before, Thales made the assertion that water is the origin of all things, which seems too crude today. On the one hand it expresses that there is an original cause behind everything that needs to be pursued, and on the other hand he tries to give a tentative answer to this pursuit, and the naiver and concrete this answer is, the more likely a breakthrough to it is sure to occur.

Then his disciple Anaximander criticized his teacher, saying that water was not right because there was a source of water itself that needed to be pursued. Anaximander said that there is something more fundamental behind water, and I don't know what to call it, so Anaximander gave it the strange name of amorphous. However, Anaximander's disciple, Anaximenes, said that amorphous was too nebulous, so he gave it another root and identified it as "Qi". The Chinese have been talking about "Qi" since ancient times, and their figurative thinking is slightly similar to that of the Miletus school. But the Greeks did not stop here, and then a series of philosophers continued to inquire, such as Heraclitus, who said that it was fire, because fire can deform anything, fire can recreate new states of matter, and the sun is a fire that never goes out, and everything grows by the sun. So his statement is valid, or at least another question in relation to the previous one. But what is the origin of fire?

So Anaxagoras went on to propose the seed theory, which suggests that the origin of all things must have had a seed-like point of origin, somewhat like the return of Anaximander's amorphous form. He said that the composition of all things can be proved to be a combination of four things, namely *water, fire, earth,* and *air,* which he said constituted the basic material elements of all things. This view is somewhat similar to the Five elements theory of the Warring States period in China, which can be regarded as the Four elements theory. When I talk about this point, you should realize that there was a similar inquiry in the pre-Qin period in China.

However, it should be noted that the material cause was only one of the four causes in ancient Greece, and it eventually bore an amazing fruit: the *atomic theory* proposed by Leucippus and his disciple Democritus. They argued that anything concrete as the original of the material is not valid, because what you can see is an illusion, and there must be something behind it that you cannot see, but it must really exist, and it must be the material essence of things. They said that this thing should be given a special name, atom, i.e., the most primitive and essential being, the meson, and thus the *atomic theory* was born. That is, at the time of Leucippus and Democritus, they had already deduced from pure logic that everything, no matter how diverse, is actually composed of one or a few combinations of elementary particles, and this idea is at the forefront of today's physics, or more precisely, is the precursor of modern physics. This is the overview of the pursuit of material causes.

Let's look at the second cause summarized by Aristotle, which is called the *form cause*. When we talk about form today, we mean content and form, and we say that something always has content and always has form. The so-called content includes the material, and the so-called form is its external form. It is often easy to draw the inference that content determines *form*, which sounds very reasonable. But you notice that Aristotle said the opposite, he said form determines content. It is difficult for us Chinese to understand this statement. The key here is what is meant by *form*? The ancient Greek philosophers never discussed form in the intuitive realm, but by form they meant logical form! Let me change the term to what we can easily understand today, which is *perceptual form*. The first founder of this concept was Pythagoras, and Pythagoras' whole philosophy was actually about the *number-theoretic formal system.*

It is important to understand that the Pythagorean system of number theory is not arithmetic or mathematics, as we generally refer to it at the application level. The core of Pythagorean thought is expressed in a phrase called "everything is number". What does that mean? Pythagoras found that everything can be reduced to a logical relationship of numbers. He said that everything is an illusion, and if everything is abstracted into a number-theoretic system, a mathematical logical system, and if everything conforms to this system, then this "number-theoretic logical formal system" is the origin behind all phenomena, because it has more universality and unity, which is called "Everything is number". Please recall that I said earlier that "the essence really exists" and that existence does not appear in intuition. Then, to go beyond intuition, there are several ways to ask questions, one is to ask about the inherent material, which results in atomism; the other is to ask about the universally applicable form, which is actually the perceptual form or logical form. I think people who have learned mathematics know that what is mathematics? It is nothing but "the formal system of numbers".

Pythagoras said that "everything is number", which means that everything is nothing but a mathematical logical form. Since everything is this thing as the essence, or rather, everything takes this form as the basis of its own existence, so by extension, it can certainly be said that "form determines content", that is, your perception of the logical form determines or prescribes the appearance of all things. This is why Pythagoras is regarded as the progenitor of the "theory of rationalism" in ancient Greek philosophy. Please note that what I call "theory of rationalism" here, is called idealism in China. I suggest that you do not criticize idealism indiscriminately before you find out where the idea of idealism comes from. Remember that Pythagoras did not consider the logical form of number theory as something subjective, but as the original determinant behind the objective world, even though this determinant turned out to be a logical sequence, or logical program form. This is the ontological pursuit of the Pythagorean order.

This thing was brought to Athens through his disciples. After his death, his disciples scattered to Athens and then passed their ideas to Plato, who then realized what his teacher Socrates meant when he said, "The intuitive knows nothing, but the true being is the *idea.*" In fact, Socrates himself did not know what *idea* was at that time, and he expressed it as the *shell of God* or the *memorial of God*. It was not until Plato accepted the influence of Pythagoras' doctrine and confirmed that *idea* is a mathematical and logical form that Plato's *idea* theory had a substantial core.

What is meant by *idea* theory? The *idea* is the *logical form of the mind* behind everything, which is the essence of everything that happens or the source of knowledge. That's why Plato said, "Everything is just a part of an *idea*". For example, any table will perish, but why does it survive in the world? It is because the carpenter has the idea of the table in his mind, so the table lives forever. The table is nothing but a part of the *idea* of table. It might sound absurd you or hard for you to understand, but please take it easy and listen to my further lecturing. It makes so much sense because what you call each and every thing is actually a product of some kind of cognitive idea that you are not aware of.

To summarize, what is this *idea*? It is the way of perception or the form of logic. Then there was Euclid, who we know today as a geometrician, but make no mistake, Euclid was a philosopher. He did not do geometry at all for application, and I repeat, the ancient Greeks did not care about application, at least the ancient Greek philosophers did not care about application. They think that anything that can be used, are the things of the craftsman, simply not worth their efforts to study again. Euclid's book was called Theory of *Forms*, just like Pythagoras' mathematics was called Theory of *Numbers*. Please note that there is a big difference between theory of *numbers* and arithmetic, which has been used in China since ancient times. Pythagoras' mathematics is a system of number theory, and a system of number theory refers to a system of logical forms, so please distinguish these two. One is arithmetic for calculation, a practical technique; the other is the original of all things, a precise system of logical forms. One was created for application; the other was created to inquire about the ultimate of the world. In fact, Euclid wrote his book to prove the validity of Plato's conceptualism, so he named it Theory of *Forms*, or *Formal* Theory. The Chinese later translated it as "几何" (Ji He) *Geometry*, because the Chinese word "几何" (Ji He) means how much, and a phrase in Cao Cao's poem, "Be happy to sing with wine, life left how much mine," sighing life is short, not much left. Therefore, the Chinese borrowed the ancient word "几何" and turned his book into a tasteless translation.

Euclid composed all the rules of *shape* in a purely logical way. In reality, a triangular mountain can collapse, a rectangular ground can be deformed, a linear river can be diverted, in short, all the *shapes* in the intuitive vision are in flux. But in the theory of *forms*, that is, in geometry, the concepts of triangle, rectangle, circle, and line are clearly defined, eternal and unchanging, with some kind of established logical relations or a priori regulations between them.

Therefore, Euclid used geometry, that is, *formal* theory, to prove that the origin behind the world is *idea*, and then came Aristotle's *formal* logic - the first logic in human history. The name of this logic, created by Aristotle, is *formal logic*. Note that it does not refer to the shape of an object, it refers to your thought *form*, or it refers to your perceptual *form*. In your thought form, 2+2 always equals 4, 3×3 always equals 9, it does not change. This given logical form determines the floating illusion, determines the presentation of things, and is actually prescribed by the *idea* in order to ultimately explain how everything exists, which is called formal logic. He then says that you derive the knowledge of everything in the logical form.

What is *logic*? Aristotle gives a definition: "a necessary derivation." That is, when you are given a certain material, a certain premise, you logically deduce the conclusion is given, this predestined conclusion is constrained by the logical form, so this logical form is the true core of things. We will talk more about this topic later.

I have talked about material cause and formal cause, which are two ways of pursuing the question in the early days of ancient Greece. The inquiry of material cause led to atomic theory, and so far the whole of human physics, from atomic physics to particle physics, has not yet finished exploring this problem; the inquiry of formal cause eventually led to the number theory form, geometric form and even logical form, and the logic of mankind, i.e., the structure of precise logic, has not been exhausted so far. These two lines of inquiry have been pursued from ancient Greece to the present day, and are still being pursued.

Aristotle goes on to conclude by saying that after these two lines of inquiry, one question remains unaddressed: What is the motive force for the operation or survival of all things? So he proposes the *motive* cause. Then he asked: What is the final destination of the operation of all things? Where is its goal? This is called the purpose cause. As we all know, there are certain laws for the evolution of all things, which naturally imply the two major questions of the power source and destination, that is, the beginning of movement and the trend of movement, to which Aristotle did not give a clear answer. The ancient Greek philosophers also had a lot of speculation, but under the conditions of the time, they could not reach a decent conclusion, so three things were raised as the subject of discussion: the first is God, which is of course a kind of escape, but Socrates said that behind God is an endless line of inquiry and clues, which is probably also the reason why Aristotle's theory of purpose contains some kind of subjective intention; the second is the *good*, that is, the best thing that human beings have been pursuing, which constitutes another way to explore the motivating; and the third is *wisdom*, that is, knowledge, as in ancient China, *knowledge* and *wisdom* are equally indistinguishable, meaning that these questions can be answered unless you pursue them endlessly in knowledge and wisdom.

Obviously, even when Aristotle proposed the theory of the four causes, he finally failed to exhaust his questions, and as a result, let these four causes remain expressed as a continued pursuing state, which is the general presentation of ancient Greek philosophy. It thus formed an important system of thinking methods, namely, deep inquiry and precise logic. Please note these two points I made: incessant inquiry, how? By conjecture and hypothesis. And for the hypothesis given to be established, or at least recognized at the time, they had to be verified through precise logic.

There! Let's look back at China. I would say that Laozi's *Dao* is largely consistent with Thales' inquiry. Moreover, Laozi's *Daoism* even includes the question of the *formal* cause except for the question of *material* cause. There is a saying of Laozi, which many people may not pay attention to, which says: "I know the world without going out of the house, and I see the way of heaven without peeping through the window." This sentence means that I know the world without going out of my house; I know how the way of heaven works without even looking through the window. He goes on to say, "Those who go far away from home, will know very little." He said that the more you go out to practice, the more your activity is, the less knowledge you will gain.

This passage of Laozi is a typical ancient Greek style pure wisdom inquiry, he does not recognize that "practice makes true knowledge". This is why we say today "read ten thousand books, travel ten thousand miles", is really a waste of time as did Confucius. Confucius traveled among the states one another for 13 years, and indeed traveled ten thousand miles, but he ultimately accomplished nothing. In China, only Laozi, who was determined to inquire about *Dao* - the essence behind the illusion of things, and he categorically denied that the general way of perception could gain knowledge, so Laozi is really the only Chinese philosopher in the pre-Qin era that can be compared with ancient Greece.

However, why did Laozi's philosophy become one of the three mysteries during the Wei and Jin dynasties? Why did the ancient Chinese philosophy later evolve into metaphysics and did not extend into a philosophical thinking system? What was missing? It was missing the deep inquiry and precise logical proof. Please understand what I am talking about. The Chinese pre-Qin era started with the philosophy of *Daoism* but ended in metaphysics, while the ancient Greece started with the same philosophy and ended with science. The difference lies in whether or not deep inquiry was carried out, that is, later people kept asking questions, questioning, refuting, and using precise logic to organize to make up for or innovate the flaws revealed by this hypothesis-proof system. It is a series of explorations that took thousands of years to forge philosophical thinking and subsequent scientific thinking.

And we should note that when Aristotle spoke of *form determining content* and when the ancient Greek philosophers spoke of the *idea* as the origin of all things, although at that time the problem of *idealism*, that is, the problem of epistemology, that is, the problem of the prescriptive nature of the spirit itself, had not yet been explored, it had already laid the groundwork for subsequent development. So if you read Aristotle's book, he discusses categories, and by *categories* he does not mean categories of the objective world, but modules of your logic and thinking that have some fixed connections, something he calls *categories*. I'm not being precise on this, I'm just trying to make it clear, and if you want to know the details and the meaning of it, you have to read his original work. This thing deeply influenced Kant, so Kant later organized the famous four groups of *twelve categories* to discuss the problem of *a priori rationality*.

This lineage of material inquiry, formal inquiry, logical inquiry, and ideological inquiry constitutes the long-term extension of Western philosophical thinking, which is the beginning laid by ancient Greek philosophy. Its beginning was never the conclusion that "water is the origin of all things", or "fire is the origin of all things", or "number is the origin of all things", but the extension and development of these conclusions due to the implementation of deep inquiry and precise logical proof, i.e., the constant mobilization and training of the hypothesis and proof system. Its starting point is the fact that the cognitions we obtain at the level of general perception are unverifiable illusions, which is the beginning of narrow philosophy. This beginning was refined over centuries in ancient Greece to form a lineage of precise logical systems. Just read Apollonius' proofs of conic curves, pure mathematical proofs, read Euclid's original 13 volumes of *Geometry*, and then read Aristotle's reasoning on formal logic, and you will know how far-reaching the ancient Greek philosophers went back then to mobilize the height of their intellectual potential.

Germination of Science

We spoke earlier about ancient Greek philosophy, which was the beginning of Western philosophy, its underpinnings in terms of intelligent mobilization and ways of thinking and its overview.

Thinking back, is the development of this philosophical underpinning and thinking inevitably leading to science? Consider the combination of the inquiry of material cause line and the inquiry of logical-formal line, is this the basic way of thinking and inquiry of scientific activity today? Even in the ancient Greek era, science was expressed as natural science before Aristotle, that is, before the formation of a division of the bureau, all kinds of knowledge together, but this is the natural philosophy itself, that is, the ancient Greek natural philosophy and natural science is exactly the same thing, and natural science as the precursor or germ of science, its basic style as early as in the ancient Greek "natural philosophy period" in ancient Greece.

Let's see below, how does scientific thinking derive from philosophical thinking? How is the basis of philosophical-scientific thinking formed?

From Thales' inquiry into the origin of all things, to the Miletus school's successive inquiries, to Pythagoras' proposal that the formal system of number theory is the core of the world, to the completion of the Platonic transformation and its theory of ideas, a line of precise logical thinking has been forged.

I need to explain a little bit about the Platonic transformation here, and I mention this repeatedly because Plato, as a disciple of Socrates, had an important change of thinking. In addition to being more concerned with the pursuit of thought, Socrates implemented a significant part of his energy into social issues, and the main discussion of Plato's most famous work, *The Ideal State,* is biased toward this aspect.

As I mentioned earlier, the Pythagorean school once ruled Croton, but Pythagoras himself died in a political struggle, and his school was scattered, with some of its students going to Athens. At this time, Plato encountered the ideas of the Pythagorean school and was shocked to learn that in the south of the Italian peninsula, to the west of ancient Greece, there had been a line of pure mathematical and logical thought that explored the origin of the world. As a result, Plato underwent a major shift in his thinking, taking up the sophisticated mathematical logic of the Pythagorean school and injecting the essence into the *Theory of Idea.* The elevation of the *theory of idea* became an important guide for later generations in scientific thinking and in the search for the deeper essence. The modern West has a famous philosopher Whitehead, who once made a comment to the effect that the whole process of development of Western philosophy and science is actually a footnote to Plato's thought. Think of Euclidean geometry, which is nothing more than a testimony to Plato's theory of idea, which is purely a philosophical inquiry. We look at mathematics and geometry today and think of it as a tool of science; make no mistake, it is a forge of philosophy.

Plato's student, Aristotle, went one step further. Aristotle changed the original statement that "the essence of things is behind the illusion" and proposed the *entity theory*. The so-called *entity theory* means that the world of illusion itself is the physical expression of the true existence of *ideas*. You cannot look at it completely, but you have to investigate it in order to find the essence. This correction by Aristotle led the whole philosophy and subsequent sciences to turn toward the study of *object reality,* and Aristotle himself was the founder of the science of subdisciplines. The so-called *science* is the subdiscipline of natural science or natural philosophy, and we call this *subdiscipline* as *science* for short. If Aristotle had not explored the science of subdisciplines from the perspective of *entity theory* (substantialism), it is likely that the budding science, especially the modern empirical science, would have lost its footing. He had already studied physics, metaphysics, logic, biology, political science, ethics, and so on, in as many as 19 categories, and this was the beginning of the division of science, the beginning of the expression of science.

Aristotle also had many failures, including a major regression in his neglect of pursuing mathematical and logical methods from Pythagoras to Plato, though he made up for it somewhat with formal logic. So, if you read Aristotle's essay on the science of subdisciplines and you will find it full of errors. But these errors do not matter at all, because it is this idea that is most enlightening.

As you know, Galileo proposed the free fall experiment and derived law from it; in fact, this experiment was related to a wrong discussion of Aristotle's, that is, Aristotle as early as 2000 years ago he discussed the issue of free fall, and he thought that light things must fall slowly, while heavy things must fall fast. Although this was in line with common sense, it was later proven wrong. But I would like to ask, except in ancient Greece, where else in the world have ever discussed such questions? Would the Chinese in ancient times have bothered to discuss questions about free fall? Therefore, the question is not whether the discussion was right or wrong, but whether you had the perspective and the idea, and whether it became a problematic focus, which is the key issue, from which, there is possibly the extension further later.

Going back to Euclid, he made precise logic to such an extreme that he used abstract points, lines and surfaces that do not exist in the world, I mean there are not abstract points, lines and surfaces in the world, in reality you can find a chalk point, a fly point, but can you find an abstract point? You can find a silk line, the edge of the table line, can you find an abstract line? You can find a table top, floor, bed surface, can you find an abstract surface? Euclid actually used these purely abstract things to propose in his work of *Geometry* with 5 axioms, 5 postulations and 23 definitions.

I'll start with the definition. What does he mean by *point*? It is called a point if it has only a position but not a size; and what does he call a *line*? It is called a line that has only length but not width. He gave this definition, and so on and so forth 23 items, and then he proposed 5 axioms and 5 postulations from them. Today we call axioms and postulations, all as axioms, or axiomatic systems. This is the way any rigorous logical project today must use, called the *axiomatic method*, which began with Euclid.

I will give two examples of these axioms: the first axiom that a line can be made between two points; the second axiom that any line can be extended infinitely. He started from the simplest logical origin, which is self-evident, and deduced 48 theorems step by step, and then combined 5 axioms, 5 postulations and 48 theorems, and then deduced 476 propositions, which completed the whole 13 volumes of plane geometry, and later people could hardly add any theorem from then on, such a precise logical conclusion made people amazing, and its influence is so much that from Descartes to Spinoza, to Newton, to Einstein, to Russell, all of these people's philosophical enlightenment, actually due to their reading Euclid's *Geometry* in their teenage years, greatly impacted and open-minded. Therefore, Euclid's *Geometry* laid the foundation of the entire sophisticated derivation of thinking models.

In the ancient Greek era, science unfolded simultaneously with each other. Archimedes, for example, deduced in precise logic the calculation of the area and volume of a geometric body surface and derived the buoyancy theorem and the principle of leverage. The problems he explored have been fully aligned with those discussed in modern science.

Then to Ptolemy, as you know, Ptolemy's geocentric theory is regarded as a laughing stock by us today, but it was really a huge precise logical project back then. The Arabs translated Ptolemy's work as *Astronomy in a Nutshell*, which is not the right name, the original Greek is called *Mathematical Compendium in Thirteen Books*. That is, Ptolemy back then divided the entire celestial movement into multi-layered celestial orbits for precise mathematical calculations, establishing a sophisticated geocentric astronomical system that influenced Western agricultural civilization for 1400 years, and its precision almost in most cases can predict lunar and solar eclipses, which is the definitive launch of Western astronomy and even natural science.

In fact, before the time of Ptolemy, heliocentrism was already proposed in ancient Greece, and this is the famous Aristarchus (we will talk about him later). At the same time there appeared a man named Eratosthenes, who actually took the circumference of the

Earth back then, and made it almost precisely determined. You know, at that time, the rest of the world, basically did not realize that the Earth is a sphere, basically still in the stage of thinking that the earth is a flat plate, "round heaven and square earth theory", while Eratosthenes has the circumference of the Earth, that is, the equatorial circumference, done a fairly accurate determination and calculation.

When we look further, we find a series of scientific acts and figures very similar to modern scientific activities have emerged during the ancient Greek era. Hiero, for example, had already discovered in ancient Greek times that air could be compressed and tried to use compressed air as mechanical power. A man named Acheta, as early as the 4th century B.C., invented steam-powered devices, and was said to have used them to make elaborate flying machines wooden pigeons. In the 2nd century B.C., Heron also used steam power to make pneumatic balls and a variety of mechanical toys. We know that steam used as power was the beginning of the first industrial revolution of mankind in the 18th century, and the exploration of these issues came to prominence in the form of scientific precursors as early as the era of ancient Greek natural philosophy.

Why do I prefer to talk about philosophical-scientific thinking as a system? It is because the so-called science is a sub-disciplinary large information volume processing of philosophical thinking models, and we call this philosophical thinking model that has to be sub-disciplinary in the process of information increment by another name, *science*. Therefore, wherever philosophy in the narrow sense does not arise, there is no culture of scientific systems in the true sense.

As I said earlier, ancient Greek philosophy was a purely logical game played by a group of big size children in ancient Greece. They were called big size children because they were not concerned with practical matters, but only focused on logical games, just like children who play games without utilitarian motives and without distractions. This childish state is precisely the prerequisite for their achievement of precise logical deduction and the mobilization of their thinking potential. The so-called pure logic game is that it must be free from the constraints of practical operation, and once a learning comes from practical operation, its deep-thinking inquiry will be replaced by shallow trial-and-error observation.

If you take a pragmatic approach, where all learning comes from a pragmatic purpose, then it is limited to a goal-oriented condition, and once the learning is implemented, it is then interrupted. If the question is raised and the thought is drawn only from the pragmatic point of view, then the purely logical game in the linage of narrow philosophy has no place to occur. Moreover, the pragmatist must regard the object as true, which naturally and immediately closes off the prospects for deeper inquiry.

I have always said that the concept of *ignorance* and speculation of phenomenon as illusions were the starting point of ancient Greek philosophy. This state of mind was inherited in the classical period of Western philosophy, which brought forth Francis Bacon, the first philosopher who initiated the modern scientific thinking. Bacon said that mankind-built knowledge is never beyond the limits of the four illusions.

First, the *racial illusion*. If racial illusion is not easy to understand, I will call it *species illusion* instead. That is, the picture of the world that each person perceives must be a model of your perception, not an objective reflection of the object. To take the simplest example: a bat does not have eyes, and it gets its representation of the world by emitting and receiving ultrasonic echoes, while we humans get our representation of the world by visual perception. If we are in a cave with a bat, the bat is always in such a dark place that its visual and light-sensitive organs are ineffective, so its main receptor is an ultrasonic echo radar receiving system, which must form a very different cognitive representation from that of a human. This suggests that what you call the world is always a model of your subjective perception, which is called the *racial illusion* or *species illusion*.

Second, the *cave illusion*. Plato once suggested that people in general cannot help but be cognitively trapped in the cave dilemma, as if people locked in a cave could only see the figures projected on the cave wall. Here I would like to explain it in another way, which is more familiar to the Chinese - the well bottom frog. That is, each of us has an extremely limited field of vision or knowledge, just like a frog in a deep well, the sky it sees is always only as big as the mouth of the well, so it thinks the sky is only as big as the mouth of the well. No one can have no limitations, so the world that each person talks about must be his or her own limited world, which is the second reason why the illusion can happen.

Third, Francis Bacon expressed it as *market illusion*. It's like a marketplace of merchants, each selling his product in a different way, portraying his product in a different way, and advertising his product in a different way. You are influenced and disturbed by these different information, and then you can only make a choice and judgment in this chaos of confusingly contradictory information.

Fourth, the *theater illusion*. That is, what each of us calls the world must be the product of our own inherent ideas or preconceptions. It is just like when you go to see a play or a movie, the plot is developed according to a specific logic. If you just follow the plot, you will think that the plot is the result of natural evolution, but it has actually been framed by the playwright before it is staged, which is called theater illusion. Each of us actually has a pre-formed conceptual script in our mind, and you open your eyes to the world on the basis of this conceptual script, so the world will also appear as the logical form of your conceptual script. For example, if you are a materialist, then you see everything as material, and you can cite countless supporting evidence, and it will always be true; on the contrary, if you are an idealist, carrying an idealist script, or you hold a materialist idea, then you see everything in the world as a derivative of the senses. But the problem is that whether you are materialistic or idealistic, the various evidence you bring out is the very issue itself that needs to be pursued, and therefore the evidence is never valid, which is called the theater illusion.

Let me give you another example, if you are a Marxist, then all human social movements, in your opinion, evolve according to the class struggle and historical materialist way, and you consider it to be the truth. But if you hold another theoretical system, then again you will present all kinds of evidence that human society evolves according to the logical path of that theoretical system. In other words, any view you have, including your whole worldview, the way it unfolds, is actually regulated and shaped by some preformed basic idea.

Thus Francis Bacon argues that the knowledge of men in general, if unexamined, is nothing but a heap of falsehoods. He expounds on these aspects in a way that sounds quite vivid, enough for us to understand the reason why the Greeks saw everything as false.

Three Main Characteristics of Narrow Philosophy

Let's further discuss the three basic characteristics of narrow philosophy.

The first characteristic is to *pursue the ultimate*. We generally look at things or deal with problems, is a specific object at hand for multi-factor analysis. For example, if you look at a ceramic mug is good or not, there are many factors affecting it: the quality of the initial porcelain clay, the fineness of grinding porcelain clay, the clay form, the mould color, the kiln temperature, and so on, so many factors, are combined to affect a porcelain mug quality.

Let me give you another example, if you have a cold, it can be caused by multiple factors. The flu is not only the result of a viral infection. When a flu virus comes, some people get it and some people don't, some people get it lightly and some people get it badly, why? Because there are differences in people's innate immune quality. It is also important to know whether you were already having a cold or not, because having cold can lead to a temporary decrease in immune resistance, and the virus that used to reside normally can suddenly become a disease-causing virus. In addition, your physical condition, psychological stress, fatigue, diet changes, and other factors all may have an impact on whether you have a cold or not.

However, such multi-factor analysis may lead to a series of problems. Why do we need a laboratory for scientific research? It is to be able to block out all the multiple factors, only one factor in a time, under the same conditions of comparison to study the amount of each factor on the matter, the study of this one factor, and then dump it, and then get another factor in for isolated study. But even if you do a single study of all the factors separately in the laboratory, the question remains unanswered. Because the number of permutations among the factors is an infinite number, you can never reach a truly definitive insight or conclusion for any problem in the context of multi-factor analysis.

So, when philosophy first started to run its thinking, it did not recognize the multi-factor approach to discussing problems as viable. Its purely logical rules of play require that the first or only cause, the ultimate cause, must be pursued. The first cause precludes causalism, because since there is only a first cause, there is no first effect that can be transformed into the next cause. We know that the chain of thinking in causalism is that from the cause turns out the effect, the effect becomes the cause, and so on, ad infinitum. As I will say it later, discussing issues in the chain of cause and effect is going to be a serious deviation. The discussion of the first cause is to inquire into the ultimate cause that has the only unifying power, which is called pursuing the ultimate.

There are two ways to pursue the ultimate.

First, the first cause is sought in what is called ontology. That is, to search for the first cause in the external world, which is typical of ontology.

Second, find the logical pole, that is, find that starting point of pure logic in the logical derivation.

For example, when I was talking about Euclid, he started from axioms, postulations and definitions. Why did he start from the simplest point, which is self-evident, and end up discussing very complex problems? It is because he must first find the logical pole as the only point of origin to start thinking, so as not to fall into the confusion of many heads. Therefore, pursuing the ultimate includes both the ultimate of the thinking and the ultimate of the object. For example, theology has determined that the source of creation belongs to the heavenly court, and it has enabled the later philosophy to inherit the theological idea of pursuing the first cause, which is why I have repeatedly said that theology, philosophy and science are one line of thought.

Theology is the beginning of the most primitive and crude simple model of human thinking in the pursuit of the ultimate. In his book *History of Western Philosophy*, Russell explained the relationship between theology, philosophy and science, saying that both theology and philosophy explore ultimate causes, which is the consistency between theology and philosophy; and philosophy and science have one thing in common, they both use reason as a tool; but science explores specific problems, so science is different from philosophy and theology in this place, and Theology differs in that the tool it uses is faith.

Although Russell's way of making this distinction seems too simplistic, he roughly illustrates the first characteristic of philosophical thinking. It is that it inherits the line of thought that theology pursues the ultimate, which is the key point that makes philosophy different from general learning and general science. And we should note that if we speak of the logical pole as a key part of the pursuit of the ultimate, then we should note that this logical pole is drifting, and human beings are always pursuing it, which includes the re-examination and forward movement of this logical pole.

Let me give you an example. When Euclid was doing geometry, he was setting up that all geometric phenomena occur on the plane. In Euclid's time, no one ever thought that space could be a surface. It was not until the 19th century that a famous figure named Riemann appeared in Western mathematics. Riemann realized that the world was constructed on a surface. Then if this world was somehow displaced at the beginning of space-time, that is, at the logical starting point of Euclid's derivation - from a plane to a surface - the whole geometric construction would be completely turned upside down. So in Riemannian geometry, you can't make a straight line between two points, and the first axiom doesn't hold, because space is a surface. Moreover, the sum of the interior angles of a triangle is equal to 180 degrees in plane geometry and greater than 180 degrees in surface geometry. Therefore, the entire geometric construction will have to be completely reworked, which is called logical pole shifting. Riemannian geometry later formed the basis of the mathematical formulation of Einstein's theory of relativity and his theory of space-time bending.

It is clear that the idea of pursuing the ultimate, including the drift of the logical pole, constitutes an indicator of the depth of philosophical thinking. Since science is the inheritance and development of philosophy, science, at least the basic science, also has the same deeper meaning of pursuing the ultimate in its nature.

What we are generally familiar with is actually applied science, and true philosophical science is not practical. Let me give you an example, when Newton was studying classical mechanics, the doctrine of gravity, he was pursuing the ultimate, he was pursuing the way God manipulates the world. After Newton finished his work *Mathematical Principles of Natural Philosophy*, he actually spent almost 10 years or so of the second half of his life studying alchemy, which became a laughing stock in history. Why did he study this problem? After he thought he had figured out the way God manipulates the world, his next problem was to figure out the materials God used to create the universe. So he did alchemical research for years, which ended in failure. Finally, Britain took care of him by making him head of the Mint to make a small fortune and live a good retirement.

We can see from this matter that the great scientist is also pursuing the ultimate, almost exactly the same way as theology and philosophy. The scientific training we have received in general is mostly engineering or applied science training, that is, training at the level of engineers, which takes us out of the realm of philosophical thinking that originally pursues the ultimate. Because we learn science more from the perspective of application, our science education is far from the real sense of deep philosophical thinking. The second characteristic of philosophy is *logical reflection* in the broad sense, or *reflection* for short. (At present, this concept is misused everywhere as the word introspection, which is wrong!) What is meant by *reflection*? The meaning of this word is that using the thought to think about thought, that is, using the thought to turn around and examine what the perception itself is, or rather, using the thought to interrogate the thought, to interrogate the perception, this is called *reflection*. This is the beginning of a typical idealist philosophy.

When we read the writings of ancient Greek natural philosophy, many say that those were the simple materialism, but this is not correct. Because in those days there was no direct investigation of mind and perception, that is, *mind* was not yet a problem, so there was no such thing as materialism, because *materialism* must be relative to *idealism* in order to exist.

In retrospect, the early years of mankind were like simple materialism or intuitionism. Because at that time, it did not occur to people that our perception itself was something that needed to be worked out. So in the ancient Greek natural philosophy period, it directly pursued the ontology, directly pursued the object, and this direct pursuit of the object is the practice of imposing *thinking* on external objects, which is called *direct thinking*.

When ancient Greek philosophy developed to the point where

Pythagoras used numbers to explain everything, there was already a germ, what we call everything is really nothing more than a logical form. When it came to Plato, he had explicitly summarized it as an *idea,* saying that the essence of the world is nothing but an idea for us, in other words, nothing but a model of our perception. In fact, Plato did not realize that there was another layer of difference in this issue, that is, he did not distinguish whether the idea was subjective or objective, but by this time, the *mind,* that is, the subjective idea, had already emerged secretly.

By Aristotle, he already made formal logic, but the epistemological problem, that is, the idealist interrogation of the *mind,* still did not come to the fore. Why? Because at that time, the ancient Greeks were not yet clearly aware of the prescriptive nature of our perception.

Let me give you an example so that you can understand it the other way around. The ancient Greek philosopher Empedocles, who proposed the *four roots theory,* had a classic statement about what *knowing* is and what *perception* is. What did he say? He said that our perceptions are all orifices in a vacuum, and that external objects emit something that he named *streams,* which you can now understand as information. He said that external objects emit streams that enter our consciousness through the sensory orifices of the vacuum. He said that this vacuum orifice has a characteristic called "the same attraction and different repulsion", what does it mean? What does it mean? It means that it absorbs things that are the same and rejects things that are different. For example, he said that there are two orifices in our eyes, water and fire, and through the orifice of fire, we see light; through the orifice of water, we see darkness. Since our perception is the orifice of the vacuum, then of course we are objectively perceiving the world.

Empedocles goes on to say that external objects emit streams that eventually enter the bloodstream and are then mixed through the heart to form our knowledge. This is exactly the same as what we Chinese have been saying "thinking in our hearts" since ancient times, only we do not formulate it as a philosophical inquiry, as Empedocles did.

So what exactly is our perception? Is it prescriptive? Or is it a vacuum of orifices? How does this vacuum orifice perform? Or how does it receive information? We Chinese have not discussed it in depth, but in a hazy way, our view is in full agreement with Empedocles. This is the earliest materialistic reflection theory in human history.

We will talk below about why materialistic reflectionism does not hold. Think about that time in ancient Greece when the mind, ideas, and logic were already unfolding, and it became a precursor to later inquiries into perception and the study of what perception is. It must then lead to the question: if our perception is not a vacuum of orifices, if our perception itself is prescriptive, that is, if the process of perception requires separate processing of information, then how do you know that the *knowledge* you obtain is not the product of subjective processing, but the reflection of the objective object as it is? In other words, if we don't know what perception is, if we haven't investigated the inherent prescriptiveness of perception, we are not qualified to ask about the object, because you can't tell whether the object you are talking about is an objective object or your subjective object, isn't that so?

Thus, when ancient Greece inquired into the external essence and launched *direct thought*, what followed inevitably was *reflection*. In other words, the epistemological question of idealism is a necessary sequel to the object question of materialism. In other words, the epistemological question and the idealist question are the higher questions or the deeper questions that materialism necessarily leads to.

I am in no way praising idealism here. We will talk more on what idealism and materialism actually mean, and what evaluation we should give them later. I just want to remind you that when philosophy begins to ask what perception itself is, when philosophy begins to ask whether perception itself has its own identity, when philosophy begins to interrogate thought with thought, philosophy enters the second deep stage, which we call the *reflection* stage, or the epistemological stage.

Let me give you some examples. We humans can only receive external information by virtue of our five senses: sight, hearing, smell, taste, and touch, except which we do not have any other channels to reach external objects. So let's look at these five senses, are they orifices in a vacuum or not? No! They are all clearly defined in their own way.

Our vision, for example, accounts for about 80% of the external information collected by humans, but what is vision? It is just a light-sensitive organ. Any object that does not emit light, reflect light, or refract light, it does not exist in vision.

What is it that vision obtains through light sensitivity? It is brightness. It is important to know that light is energy, called light quanta, and light is not bright. Light hits any object and that object does not produce brightness. Light stimulates the retina, the retina converts it into bioelectricity, which enters the optic center through the afferent nerve, and the optic center illuminates this light energy as brightness, which then gives the object we are facing an outline in terms of light perception. Brightness itself is a misinterpretation of photon energy.

And, more importantly, our vision only sees one hundred thousandth of the cosmic spectrum, that is, our vision can only see 400 ∽ 760 nanometers wavelength of light waves, light waves outside of this narrow band, we can see no more. Below 400 nanometers is the ultraviolet, X-rays, gamma rays, and the long light waves above 760 nanometers are infrared, there are tens of thousands of times beyond the two ends of the spectrum band, all Not within the range of our human vision.

And the world has no color, what we call color is actually just an illusion of the wavelength of light waves, in the 360 nanometers of light waves we can see, we can distinguish it into at least 150 colors. That is to say, the world is no color, color is only different light wave wavelength through the optical center of the illusion. It can be seen that as soon as we have opened our eyes, we immediately distorted the world. We distort light quanta as brightness, and we mistake light wavelengths for colors.

And the world is also no sound, what we call sound is actually the energy of the external vibration wave through the air shock to the outer ear eardrum, and then the outer ear membrane shock and then conduct to the inner ear into bioelectricity, through the afferent nerve into the auditory center, the auditory center mistakes this shock energy illusion for the booming sound.

If our eyes were a spectrometer, if our ears were a vibrometer, what would this soundless, colorless world look like, can you imagine? That thing might be the real world, and just might be.

In other words, as soon as we come into contact with external information, we immediately distort and process it. The moment we receive external information, the so-called external information has become subjective information.

In a word, what we perceive is always the shape of our subjective world, not the objective world itself. Please understand deeply that our perception is not set for truth, but set for survival.

Why do we have to distinguish 360 nm light waves into 150 color illusions? It is because if we were to deal directly with the spectrum of light waves, it would become a very complex problem. Light waves are continuous, stepless variable, from 400 nm to 760 nm, there is no separation, and we have to distinguish it into completely different color differences. If we can't do that, it will be a terribly dangerous thing. For example, when you were a monkey in the forest in yellow leaves in autumn, to find and pick a slightly red peach, you must be able to see from a distance that the slightly red peach hidden deep in yellow leaves, in fact the wavelength of yellow and red is only a few nanometers or tens of nanometers in difference. If you can't distinguish it distinctly as a different color difference, the monkey will surely starve to death, isn't that so?

For example, if you see a five-colored snake, and you start to calculate its wavelength combination, then your brain, even if it is as big as a classroom, may not be able to process it in time. If you can instantly misperceive it as a different color object, and you will be able to form a clear discriminatory relationship right away, which we call *recognition survival model* or *simple recognition mechanism.*

Therefore, we can only maintain our survival most economically, quickly and effectively by misperceiving the world, and therefore I preach that our perception is *not set for truth-seeking*, but *set for survival.*

Some may say that our sense of smell and taste should always be true knowledge! Then you are wrong again. Why do we taste fruit as sweet? It's not that the fruit is objectively sweet, but because you have to taste the energy it contains as a comforting sensation like sweetness before you will eat it. We all know that fruit is full of glucose, but in fact it is not in the form of glucose monosaccharide, which is very low in the biological world, in the natural plant world.

We humans get our energy from three sources, glucose, also known as carbohydrates, then fat, and protein. Glucose mostly exists as a disaccharide, which means that two glucose molecules make up one fructose molecule. Since the sweeteners in fruits and plants - carbohydrates - that the body can use for this energy mostly exist in the disaccharide structure, that is why we have evolved to experience disaccharides as explicitly sweet.

Later, we cultivated grain. Humans could not find starch in far antient times because it exists in grass seeds, and starch contains much more glucose than disaccharides, but why do we eat starch today without any taste? The rice and flours you eat are not sweet, because you have been eating it for just a few thousand years, and you have not had time to make energy-distinguishing taste sensory adaptations to it in the too-short evolutionary process.

Why do we feel that meat smells better than fruit? It's because lean meat contains 18% fat, and fat has more than twice the energy of carbohydrates. One gram of carbohydrate contains 4 calories of energy, while one gram of fat contains 9 calories of energy, so you feel very good when you eat meat because it contains higher energy.

Why do you smell stool bad? It's not that stool naturally has odorants in it, but you have to evolve to smell it as a very unpleasant odor. Because the stool is the residue of the energy you consumed, and if you do not smell it as an uncomfortable odor at this moment, you may swallow the stool back to body, which is a useless waste, so you smell the stool must be smelly. But why do flies always keep crawling on the stool? It is because there is still energy in the stool that the flies can use, so the flies must smell the stool as fragrant, otherwise why do they crawl on the stool whenever available? We can see that sweet, fragrant, and smelly these sensations, not because the substance naturally has a certain taste element, but from the point of view of survival, if you can get energy out of it, in the process of billions of years of evolution, you must set it as a comfortable or uncomfortable sensory classification.

Similarly, anything that is bitter must be something that is harmful to the body. It is not that it objectively contains bitter elements, but because in the process of adaptive evolution you are eliminated by natural selection if you do not taste as bitter the toxins that cause damage to the organism. You can only qualify for survival if you experience what causes damage to the organism as an unpleasant repulsive sensory response in the setting of the senses. So bitterness is not objective, but subjective, and whatever causes damage to you, you must set it as bitter. Therefore, anything that is bitter must be something toxic, and so, it is better for you to eat bitter melon with care, at least not in large quantities.

Further, all drugs are poisonous, whether they are bitter or not. Today human beings have created a large number of chemicals, most of them are strong poisonous agents, but they are colorless, odorless and tasteless, why? It is because they do not exist in nature, so we have not differentiated them in the evolution of our senses, so they are causing more harm to us today.

In short, your senses are inherently prescriptive, set according to energy-seeking resources or organismic protection mechanisms rather than truth-seeking. For this reason, at the moment you receive any information, you must process it in a way that illuminates it as the most concise and bioenergetically efficient response. It is clear that the world we speak of is always our subjective world, and cannot be the objective world itself, which we cannot arrive at directly.

One might say that my feelings, my sensibility, are faulty, but my reason, my logic, has the potential to correct this bias. If you think so, then you are wrong again!

Three Characteristics of Narrow Philosophy (continued)

There are really only three major ways in which we humans use logic, that is, use thought, basically.

First, pure logical thinking. For example, mathematics, geometry, etc. The problem with purely logical thinking is that you don't know exactly what it is in relation to the object. For example, in mathematics, each number can contain anything or nothing behind it, it is nothing more than a purely logical algorithmic number sequence system. Then the purely logical algorithm itself only follows its own logical pattern, but what is its relationship with the world you can never figure out. Thus, mathematics has developed to the point where there are a large number of mathematical models that are mathematically valid, but we cannot find its correspondence with natural external objects. So mathematics and geometry are typically purely logical expressions of the inner workings of the human brain.

The second way of using wisdom is called *induction*. Let me give you an example, for example, you see that the swans in Asia are white, you go to Europe and see that the swans in Europe are still white, you go to Africa, you go to America, the swans are all white, so you inductively come to a conclusion, saying "all swans are white". But there is a problem here, you have not exhausted the list of swans in the world. If by chance you come to Australia one day and suddenly find a black swan, the original inductive conclusion of "all swans are white" will immediately collapse. Obviously, the inductive method has a natural flaw, it can only falsify, not prove. That is, it can only prove that your previous conclusion is wrong, but never prove that your current conclusion must be right.

For example, you can conclude today that "all swans are either white or black", which seems right on the surface. But you have only finished summarizing the swans on Earth, how do you know that there is another swan on an alien planet that is not green or red? You can never observe all the swans in the universe exhaustively. Therefore, the inductive method can never give a conclusion that can really get a valid proof.

The third way is called *deduction*, which is a subsequent application of induction. For example, you already know that "all swans are white", and then you deduce that if there are swans in Australia, they must be white too. "All swans are white" is called the major premise, "There are swans in Australia" is called the minor premise, and "The swans in Australia must be white" is the conclusion, which is what Aristotle called the typical triad deductive method. But the deductive method has a problem, that is, its premises are inductive. And since its premises are qualified by induction, it can only prove, not disprove, the opposite of induction. I repeat: the inductive method can only falsify, never prove, while the deductive method can only prove, but never falsify.

Note that we humans use logic in only these three ways: pure logic, induction and deduction. But they are all flawed, and are prescribed by the laws of our innate thinking. They are another model of distorted thinking based on the non-true material of the senses, which is re-processed by an innate law of thought. Therefore, the result of its processing must be a further distortion on top of the original sensory distortion before you can reach a thoughtful conclusion. This is why, all our perceptions cannot be true knowledge.

What am I talking about here? I am talking about *reflection*, that is, the use of thought to question thought in turn. The reason I call it logical reflection in broad sense is that logic in broad sense includes all stages from sensuality, perception to rationality. Then we take the narrow logic, that is, we take our thinking to examine our senses, we take our thinking to examine the three patterns of thinking in turn, this is called using thought to interrogate thought. We can take thought in the broad logic and turn it around and examine the sequence of perception and the sequence of thought, which is called reflection. This is how epistemology unfolds. I say this in the simplest scientific formulation to show you that there is a reason for *idealism*, and it is the longitudinal problem that is necessarily derived from thinking materially and straightforwardly about the world and its objects. Only by examining this question clearly will you know what your *knowledge* itself is, and what the limits of knowledge are, and then what your knowledge is, and so on and so forth. Spiritual questions can be discussed in real depth.

The third feature of philosophy in the narrower sense is called *scientific foresight*. Philosophy inevitably leads to science, because the so-called science is the state of philosophical thought model of the large amount of information sub-disciplinary processing. For example, when we talk about mathematics and geometry today, these things were created by a group of philosophers like Pythagoras and Euclid. They were not trying to create tools for scientific applications, they were trying to find the ultimate cause of the existence of the world, so they were purely philosophical products, though they are the most fundamental way of thinking about the whole range of scientific tools we have today. The *atomic theory*, for example, was the ultimate conclusion of the ancient Greek philosophers' search for material cause, and it was a product of purely logical deduction. It was not until the 19th century that Rutherford made it into a model of a stellar system, with a nucleus in the middle and electrons orbiting around it in the void.

All the questions we explore in atomic and particle physics today are in fact the questions posed by the atomists Leucippus and Democritus 2500 years ago. So far the frontiers of physics have not been explored. The questions we are exploring today in particle physics are still the same questions that atomism dabbled with in advance, which is called scientific foresight. This is a major feature of philosophy, which is why I have repeatedly said that philosophy and science are the same thing.

In his later years, Russell wrote a pamphlet called *The Problem of Philosophy*. He had devoted it to the question of what the difference between philosophy and science is, since they are products of exactly the same way. Russell expressed it as, what is called philosophy is a forward-looking non-deterministic discussion of scientific questions. Please recall that the atomic theory, that is, more than 2,000 years before mankind was really close to studying the atomic problem precisely, philosophers had deduced in pure logic that everything in the world was composed of one or several basic elements. At that time it was impossible to have a very rigorous model of the atom and to treat it deterministically and mathematically. The result of such a study, which discussed the problem in advance but could not reach a precise quantitative analysis, is the philosophical state of scientific foresight.

A philosophical question is an advance exploration of a scientific question, an advance pursuit or preparation of a topic in case of insufficient information. As such, it carries the role of a precursor and leader of scientific questions, and constitutes a precursor to the subsequent unfolding of science. Science still cannot explain what the spirit is, because it cannot get the spirit into the laboratory, and nor can it explain what society is, because it cannot get the society into the laboratory either. Therefore, as usual, these questions can be explored today only at the philosophical level, in the form of models of philosophical thought.

Why is it that most of those who engage in philosophy in China are scholars of philosophers? One of the important reasons is that philosophy is not separated from science, philosophy and science are the same thing. Since the current system of higher education in China, literature, history and philosophy and mathematics, science and chemistry are distinctly separate, science and arts two separate ways, no intersection, which makes the majority of people engaged in philosophical research unfamiliar with the natural sciences.

You know, all the philosophers of the ancient Greek era were basically natural scientists back then. For example, Aristotle, then Pythagoras was a mathematician, Euclid was a geometrician. In modern classical philosophy, all the important philosophers were natural scientists of their time. Descartes, for example, was a mathematician, physiologist, and mechanist, and Kant, for example, was the originator of the Kantian-Laplace nebula, and taught about 40 or more courses in the natural sciences for nearly 20 years before he pursued his philosophical studies in his middle and late years. Hegel, for example, was very familiar with chemistry. Russell, for example, was so interested in mathematics that he tried to commit suicide at the age of 15, but was moved to terminate it one day when he saw the blood-like sun in the sky at dusk, and according to him, he survived because mathematics was so beautiful. I am telling you that the real philosophers of the West must be the natural scientists of the time, who were usually very familiar with the natural sciences, or at least proficient in one of them. This is one of the reasons why the separation of arts and sciences in domestic education has caused the study of philosophy stagnated in China.

We will discuss one more issue below. Because of the poor philosophical literacy in the country, we often hear inappropriate interpretations against philosophical science. On the surface, these interpreters draw on certain recent scientific advances, for example, we have recently seen a large number of new philosophical explorations of quantum mechanics circulating on the Internet, including certain scientists who are talking nonsense there. For example, in view of the emergence of quantum entanglement, some people say that Buddhism is therefore scientifically valid, and even make the philosophical assumption that there are a bunch of quanta in our brains and that our so-called external world is nothing but the product of the super-distance entanglement of these quanta, meaning that the external world does not exist, etc. Why are these claims so problematic? It is because they lack understanding of how the internal interplay of philosophical thinking can be reached.

I suggest you read this article by Schrödinger, one of the founders of quantum mechanics, called *Nature and the Greeks*. He says that the problem of quantum entanglement is first expressed as a series of doubts that philosophical thinking still needs to be deepened. For example, quantum entanglement, that is, the discovery that two or more quanta of the same quantum are always moving super-spaced at the same time. This hyper-range force, according to Schrödinger, has two questions that have yet to be pursued. First, the question of whether space is continuous. We generally feel that space is continuous, but it is possible that space is discontinuous, and the so-called hyper-range quantum entanglement may be a specific manifestation of spatial discontinuity. Second, what is meant by wholeness and individuality? When you look at two or more quanta and they are entangled at super-range, you think of them as two or more individuals, which is conceptually debatable. They are probably as a wholeness, not independent individuals. Human beings' conception of wholeness and individuality is necessarily rectified and researched. (I think there is another possibility: the phenomenon of quantum entanglement expresses a state in which multidimensional space-time has not yet unfolded at the quantum stage or quantum level of physical evolution.)

It is very prudent to note Schrödinger's way of expression: he does not immediately overturn the philosophical system on the basis of a small scientific progress, but discusses the deeper points of scientific research on this issue. For example, in the 17th and 18th centuries, some Western philosophers, on the basis of their research on animal or human physiology, rashly made the theory that the social structure was merely an internal and external match of the human physiological structure, which was later proved to be completely nonsense. So I would like to make a point that it may be feasible to make immediate philosophical subversive assumptions about the latest advances in quantum mechanics, but you must remember that the assumptions need to be followed by precise logical proofs. If the proof cannot be unfolded, you must explore whether the basis of your claim itself still needs deeper investigation.

Let me give you an example, quantum mechanics talks about energy. The so-called quantum is the smallest packet of energy, that is, the smallest unit of energy. But so far physics, including quantum mechanics, can not say what energy is. You know that mankind in the past can not say what matter is, after Einstein special relativity solved the relationship between space-time, his successive logical deduction, the conclusion that energy and matter is the same thing. This is the famous mass-energy equation $E=mc^2$, where energy is equal to mass times the square of the speed of light. It established for the first time that matter is a specific transformed form of energy, and for the first time mankind knew the ultimate scientific formulation of matter. But the question remains: what is meant by *energy*? This question, even in relativity, even in quantum mechanics, still has not been finally answered. So before a scientific system has a final argument, you eagerly take it for philosophical argument, obviously your proof system can not reach. So, although philosophy and science is a system, and there is a foresight correspondence between the two, still you have to make a precise logical proof, rather than just give a conclusion.

Why must those who do philosophical research be scientifically qualified? It is because science provides the most effective new information. Please listen to this statement of mine. We are in the information age today, and a great deal of information is coming to us. But information is never knowledge. Information must be rectified by precise logic before it constitutes knowledge. Information is objective, knowledge is subjective. Information is transformed into knowledge only through the precise rectification of subjective broad logic. Since science is the outgrowth of the precise logic of philosophy, so it provides the most effective increment of new information and thus becomes the basis on which all new philosophical ideas can take place, and this is the relationship between philosophy and science.

Let me reiterate that philosophy is the foresight of science, and science is the precise provisional expression of philosophical problems. We will discuss one more issue below. We have seen certain scholars in China who consider themselves to be very well versed in the sciences, who have disparaged philosophy, saying that it is dead, that it discusses pseudo-problems, and even that it is pure nonsense, such statement is a sign of complete ignorance of the intrinsic relationship between philosophy and science. It is important to remember that science is guided by philosophy and occurs, that science itself connotes the soul of philosophy, and that philosophy is a forward-looking discussion of scientific issues in the absence of sufficient information, so philosophy and science are originally one family. Moreover, philosophy must outlive science; philosophy derives science and philosophy leads science. Although science is a precise formulation of the forward-looking problems of philosophy, it is not the ultimate truth, and it will be falsified and subverted by a new round of philosophical forward-looking inquiry and questioning. And science must be the most short-lived thing, because the more progressive and advanced something is, the more wavering it must be, while the lower and more primitive things must have the quality of foundational, decisive and stable. Therefore, we can foresee that when the day of the demise of science comes, philosophy will continue to exist, just as theology still envelops more than 80% of mankind when philosophy is already in a shaky and turbulent state today. The point here is that no scholarship is the truth, it is merely a destabilizing progression of ideas, a natural evolutionary or spontaneous decay process of an incremental model of information rectification.

I have repeatedly emphasized that science is never the truth, something that is very clear to all scientists in the West. Let me give you another example here, the same Schrödinger, one of the creators of quantum mechanics, who in an article entitled *Science and Humanism* explored the issue by saying that science must be biased, and this bias was not discovered until the study of quantum mechanics. It is why scientists usually place themselves outside the world system, becoming an external and solitary observer. In fact, man is a component of the world object system, and man observing things must cause object interference. Moreover, you observe everything as a coupled product of borrowing your own prescriptive perceptual properties and applying them to external objects. You simply cannot transcend the external object system, and you simply cannot observe the object alone. But science in general always sets itself in an external, isolated state or position, and therefore the results it gives are bound to be biased.

In the past, since science only studied macroscopic problems, this bias may not be visible or may be negligible. In quantum mechanics, Heisenberg proposed the *principle of inaccuracy*, that is, the observer himself must have perturbed the object of observation. From a philosophical, reflective point of view, your perception itself is prescriptive, and it will cause distortion to the object system; from a physical, straight thinking point of view, you yourself are part of the external object, and it will cause disturbance to the dependence relationship; this is an unavoidable scenario, how can you examine the object objectively, alone and externally? Remember, therefore, that all scholarship, including all science, is only a subjective cognitive model of the object, not a true description of the objective world.

I have made three exegetical points about the basic state of philosophy. The first, to pursue the ultimate. Instead of exploring the problem at the superficial multi-factor level, we keep investigating the ultimate cause and approaching the logical pole in the chain of thought unfolding to form an axiomatic system of argumentation. Secondly, logical reflection in the broad sense. This is where philosophy is far superior to science in terms of its depth of vision. Third, scientific foresight. It is the scientific elements and scientific questions in the case of insufficient information in advance of the inquiry, so it has a pioneering role in leading the birth of science and guide the development of science. We refer to this system of thought in general as the philosophical-scientific mode of thinking.

Additional: Positivism of Model of Dependency

We discussed earlier the basic characteristics of philosophical thinking, and we can make some more comments about it below.

First of all, uselessness is like a foundation. Because it is a purely logical game, because it does not focus on practical application, that is, it is not limited by the practical application, so it is able to unfold in depth. It is just like when you build a building, first you have to build the foundation, which takes up the most important part of a building. But the foundation is not inhabitable, and this unusable part of the foundation in our thought building in philosophy, and philosophy is to lay this part.

Let me give you an example. Legend has it that Thales looked up at the stars every night, and one day he accidentally fell into a dry well. His handmaiden, his maid, fished him out of the dry well and asked him, "You can't even see the mouth of the well in front of your nose, why do you look up at the stars all day? Thales smiled awkwardly and said, "I can't see the dry well under my nose, so I am Thales. " We know that the word *stargazing* comes from this story of Thales. Later people used to look up at the stars to express the profound and useless state of philosophical thinking. What does it mean? It means that to look far into the sky, to think deeply, not to seek practicality, to concentrate the mind, to explore the deep logical potential of thought, is the basic way of thinking and intelligent mobilization of philosophy.

Second, it is *bizarre and esoteric*. It is the philosophy that explores mostly very strange and very remote questions, even questions that are out of the question. The Pythagorean school, for example, was all about how the gods of the Orphic sects operated in the world. They built the whole logical system of number theory in a purely mathematical way. It is important to know that Pythagoras, back then, had already calculated all the twelve laws of sound in a mathematical way, and no later generations could add any more theorems to it. His school would go into such an abstract pure mathematical problem, which is unimaginable in the traditional Chinese culture. Consider the hundred schools of thought of the pre-Qin Chinese scholars, and the problems they discussed, how did they ever have purely mathematical, purely logical problems.

Pythagoras had a student by the name of Hippasus. He once discovered a very strange phenomenon, that is, the proportional relationship between the length of the sides of a square and the diagonal is actually *an infinite acyclic decimal*. That is, there is never an end after the decimal point. Such infinite acyclic decimals can be found in many ways, such as pi, the ratio of the circumference of a circle to its diameter, which is also *an infinite acyclic decimal*, and the square of 2, which is an infinite acyclic decimal, which is what we call *irrational numbers* today. The discovery of infinite acyclic decimals (irrational numbers) by Hippasus caused a great shock to the Pythagorean school because he violated the basic principles of the Orphicists and the Pythagorean school that had always interpreted the world in the canonical way of rational numbers.

People need to know what an infinite acyclic decimal means. Why is it called an irrational number? It is because the numbers can be arranged continuously on the number axis. If a number point is suddenly found on a logical probe has no exact location, and the decimal point is followed by an infinite noncyclic extension of the number, it means that the number point has no place on the number axis. Geometry describes space, and mathematics to some extent describes time. As far as our general sense is concerned, space and time are continuous, and therefore in mathematics, in general number theory, the straightforward sense of the number axis is a continuous system. But with the discovery of irrational numbers by Hippasus, a major trouble arises that the number axis is actually broken, and it is possible that time and space are discontinuous. That is, there is a series of loci in a number axis that are actually wobbly and indeterminate, which gives a serious shock to the religious beliefs of the Pythagorean school.

How far did the impact go? Hippasus was so violently attacked by the other members of the school that he had to flee to avoid trouble, and he was found brutally killed while crossing a river, and his body was thrown into the river. It's really amazing how serious the ancient Greeks were, as to the point of killing someone in order to keep their purely logical games!

The Pythagorean Order actually had many extremely absurd rules back then, such as not being allowed to eat beans, not being allowed to sit on the bottom of an overturned barrel, not being allowed to bend down to pick up things on the ground, hearing a white rooster crowing as ominous, and so on. As a sect, it shows an extremely absurd aspect. But it explores the origin of the world from a religious perspective, and the degree of logical precision actually leads to the discovery of irrational numbers and the endless pursuit of irrational numbers. Eventually it was not until the second half of the 19th century, more than two thousand years later, that the mathematical meaning of irrational numbers was really clarified. We can thus see the extent of its grotesqueness and profundity.

Let me give another corresponding example. As you know, Western missionaries entered China at the end of the Ming Dynasty, and the most famous early one was Matteo Ricci. After Ricci came to China, he took in a Christian follower and student, the famous Xu Guangqi in Chinese cultural history. Later, Xu Guangqi and Matteo Ricci collaborated in the translation of Euclid's *Geometry*. Xu Guangqi made a statement about this, saying that the book *Geometry*, though seemingly useless, is a basic tool for anyone who wants to train in precise logical thinking. This shows that Xu Guangqi had a deep understanding of Euclid's geometry in those days.

Xu Guangqi translated the original *Geometry*, which was at the end of Ming Dynasty, more than 1000 years later than the ancient

Greek era. But when the translation reached the sixth volume, Xu's father died suddenly. Although Xu Guangqi himself had joined Christianity at this time, the Chinese culture of virtue still exerted a heavy pressure on him. According to the Chinese culture of filial piety, he had to go home to mourn the death of his father, so he was forced to interrupt his translation work and return home to mourn for his father for three years. When he returned to his hometown three years later, Matteo Ricci had already passed away, and their joint translation of the original *Geometry* was interrupted and became a remnant. It was not until after the mid-Qing Dynasty, more than 200 years later, that the original *Geometry* was translated in China.

What does this example show? It shows how great the difference is between the culture of virtue and the culture of love of wisdom. Even Xu Guangqi, who had already understood the essence of the love of wisdom culture and had been immersed in it for a long time, was greatly hampered by the social atmosphere of the virtue-oriented culture, so much so that his translation was interrupted. This situation of being held back by a virtue-oriented society and that of being encouraged by the love of wisdom culture, where every move is suppressed and bound by strong interpersonal relations and the other is fighting for a mathematical problem of rigorous calculation, reflect two completely different cultural states of life or cultural situations.

Third, pure logic engineering. That is, it explores problems without any realistic meaning. Let me also give you an example of a problem that Plato explored in his essays after his intellectual transformation due to his contact with the Pythagorean school, namely the problem of the positive polygon. For example, a positive pentagon, a positive octagon, a positive hexagon, a positive 32-sided shape, you can zoom in infinitely, make more and more sides of this, draw a circle, stick to the circumference, and keep making inner tangent equivalent polygons, which is called a positive polygon. Why did Plato explore such a useless and strange problem? Please try to imagine how the circumference of a circle can be measured. It is important to know that curves cannot be measured precisely, and so the length of the circumference of a circle cannot be calculated precisely. There is only one way to do this, and that is to make more and more positive polygons to the point of making an infinite number of polygons, and then measure the straight-line distance of each side, so as to arrive at the closest calculation to the circumference of the circle.

We speak of calculus as having been invented by Newton and Leibniz at the same time, and this was already in the 17th and 18th centuries. But as early as Plato in ancient Greece, the purely logical investigation of the relationship between the square polygon and the circle as a mathematical calculus had already begun, which shows how far such pure logic has been used. Please compare this with our Chinese culture, which is quite different from this kind of thinking. Our culture has a very different style, in the words of Confucius, "to describe but not to fabricate", which means that I only describe what has been done before, and never innovate or fabricate. It is completely opposite to the style of pursuing the ultimate, constant inquiry, and continuous depth. Philosophical thinking is about hypothesis and proof, and the process of proof requires that there should be no logical break in the loop, and that the process should be advanced step by step in pure logic. The Chinese culture speaks of "imparting deep meaning in a few words", that is, using the least amount of brain power and language to reach the most significant value judgments and conclusions, which is the opposite of precise logical proof.

Another feature of philosophy - scientific foresight - discuss in advance the outlook of the problem induced by pure logic. And the basic culture of Chinese society I call it human social concern, or to use an ancient Chinese term, "社稷" (She Ji) social care. *She* is the Chinese sacrifice to the deity of land, and *Ji* is the sacrifice to the deity of grain. The Chinese "社稷" is the foundation of Chinese agricultural civilization and its corresponding social structure. The contrast between Chinese culture's social concern and Western philosophical culture's expression of purely logical proof, constitutes a major division between Eastern and Western ways of thinking.

Therefore, we can summarize Western philosophy in two sentences. In the first sentence, it is the game of wisdom and the logical channel. It begins with games, ends with channel, and is intermediate to science. The so-called channel opens up the path of precise logic and expands the future of rational thinking. In the second sentence, it is the logical foundation of rational movement. The so-called rational movement means pure logical reasoning, which is the training process and operational basis for the whole rational thinking to unfold. This pure logical game is equivalent to the basic operating system in the computer that you cannot see or adjust, with this basic operating system, the application software can continue to work and develop on it. Please imagine, if your computer does not have this basic operating system, what your computer will become, to what extent your application software will be shallow, this is the basis of rational movement. In our national way of thinking and cultural configuration, these things are precisely the most lacking.

Even if we study the philosophy-derived sciences from the West today, we have not departed from the traditional pragmatic way of thinking that operates at such a shallow level. Chinese scholarship has always spoken of "learning to apply" and "combine knowledge to action", which is the exact opposite of the ancient Greek philosophies of the West that specialize in useless learning. In his book, Xunzi said, "Learning stops when it works", that is, if a study can be practically applied, it has reached the most thorough depth. The same view of Confucius is expressed in a passage in *The Mean*, which says, "Learn, ask, think, discern, and practice. The whole purpose of thinking and discernment, or the whole high point of thought, ultimately comes down to the point of *practice*, that is, once it can be applied, that is the end of learning. Zhu Xi, an important founder of the Song and Ming philosophies, said, "Much learned is not that good as knowing what is the important, knowing what is the important is not that good as really practicing it". He said that the breadth of learning lies in being able to sort out the main points of knowledge, and he said that the main point of knowledge lies in being able to implement it into practice, which is the measure of Chinese scholarship. It expresses the basic form of Chinese culture or other cultures outside the philosophy in the narrow sense. This led to a limitation of the mobilization of the intellectual potential of other civilizations, which led to ancient Greek philosophy finally becoming the most subsequently extended channel of thought.

As far as I lectured here, I think you should understand that all our human knowledge is not a direct reflection of the objective world, but a subjective perceptual model or a subjective logical model. The so-called cosmology and worldview, you must understand that it is in no way a true reflection of the universe and the world, it is essentially nothing more than a logical view, or more precisely, any cosmology and worldview is in fact nothing more than a system of subjective logical models, which is the ultimate intellectual effect of philosophical inquiry. That is why I have repeatedly said that all knowledge is only a subjective model of thinking, not a true reflection of the objective world. Understanding this point, you can understand the essence of human culture and thought. Human civilization is not built in the objective world, but is paved in the passage of ideas of thinkers. It must be understood that all animals live in the objective world, so why do they not create civilization? Human civilization is the product of the mobilization of human intellectual potential, the virtual, hypothetical and rigorous proof of pure thought, and then the logical system of knowledge, which is continuously updated and extended in turn.

These are all basic concepts that we all have to establish, and it is very different from our original concepts. But you can only truly understand the basis of human culture, human civilization and even the composition of human knowledge if you understand these things.

Since our knowledge is only a subjective logical model, how can this logical model guide our actual existence? This is, of course, a serious question. That is, our perception operates in a closed channel, and we do not have another channel besides the perception to reach external objects. Therefore, I describe it in my book as a metaphysical confinement. The so-called *metaphysical confinement* can be understood in a simpler way, as perceptual channel confinement. Because what we call the world is always the world in our subjective perception, and we do not have another channel to reach the outside world other than the subjective perception channel. That is why, even in China today, some people propose *omniscience,* which means that the world we speak of is always the sum of our subjective perceptions.

In fact, this idea has long been given proof in the history of Western philosophy, but it is not enough to stop at this point. For here there is a question: what is our perception? Since our perception is only a closed subjective channel, why is it valid for interfacing with our actual life, i.e. the external world? Moreover, why is our logical model of perception constantly changing? These questions cannot be answered by *omniscience* alone. So omniscience only says that our world is always our model of perception, which is philosophically equivalent to an introductory overview, i.e., to the simplest statement of fact. But why is this presentation or statement valuable? It is because it corrects a very common cognitive error, namely, the assumption that our perceptions are a true reflection of the objective world. In fact, all our perceptions, all our thoughts, all our knowledge, all our doctrines are not a true reflection of the objective world, but merely a model of thought.

But a question occurs here, why is this model of thinking valid? Why is it expressed in our daily life as fully interfacing with the world? This is a question that we will discuss step by step later. I hope that when I discuss these questions below, you can hear the rhythm of it even if it is not directly or specially addressed to this issue, it is difficult to make it understood.

Let's all look at Stephen Hawking's formulation of the problem. I cite it because Hawking had a greater influence and because he was a famous contemporary scientist occupying the faculty position of Newton's chief professor of physics at Trinity College, Cambridge that year. As I said earlier, the truly great scientists of the West are very familiar with Western philosophy, because philosophical scientific thinking is a system. Even if Western scientists do not read the original works of ancient Greece or even the history of Western philosophy, their way of thinking is deeply influenced by these things, just as the vast majority of Chinese people do not read Confucius, Laozi, or Han Feizi, but the traditional Chinese culture has a very deep influence in our spiritual bottom. Stephen Hawking once expressed the relationship between our knowledge and the world in his philosophical book called *The Grand Design*. He used a phrase called *model-dependent positivism*. Please note, as I said at the beginning, that the world we see is not considered by the ancient Greek philosophers to be the *reality* and *true* of the world, but only an illusion. The *reality* is the *real existence* behind the *illusion*. What is *reality*? The model of thought is the *real*. Therefore, Hawking says that human knowledge is nothing but a *model-dependent positivism*, and the model on which it depends is the model of thought, that is, the model of perception.

He gave an example, he said it was like a fish being kept in a circular fish tank. Since the wall of the fishbowl is a curved surface, the fish in the fishbowl sees the external world as always imaged in a curved mirror, so it must think the world is like the world we see in the curved mirror, a distorted image but all of us are unaware of itself. He says that our human perception is equivalent to that curved projection of a fishbowl, and that our perception is not a vacuum, not a direct reflection of the external world. Therefore, we have to use our perceptual prescriptiveness to shape a rendered model of the external world, and then use this model to interface with the external world, which is called "model-dependent positivism". I think anyone who understands natural science should be able to understand the meaning of this statement. For example, in our human perception system, we live in a four-dimensional world, that is, three dimensions of space and one dimension of time. Einstein combined space and time together, and this is the four-dimensional world we live in. However, in physical logic, ten and eleven dimensional models of the world have been derived today. Which model is true? We can't say it clearly, because our perception is limited.

Hawking gave another example, he said that everything in science is just a logical derivation of the product. For example, he said that scientists have never seen an electron, although all of our scientific and technological applications today are based on the electron, but no one has ever seen an electron. Because the electron is only a phenomenon discovered by Thomson in 1897 through cathode rays. The electron stream from the cathode ray tube, if you put a constant magnet underneath, the current itself will be deflected, which is the basis for the logical derivation of the electron as a negative charge system, please tell me who has seen the electron?

Then there is the quark, which no one has ever seen. A quark is a logical component of a hadron structure, for example, the proton is part of a hadron structure. In today's physics experiments, quarks are never hit, that is, physics in theory are considered to have no free quarks. So what is this thing called a quark? It is a product of a logical derivation of physics particle phenomena. No one in the world has ever seen a quark, and no one has ever been able to prove that a free quark exists, and that is science. What is science? A model of precise logical derivation, so please understand that it is on this system that we have built our worldview, cosmology and knowledge system today.

So you read my book, 20 years ago I said in my book that our human perceptual representation can be presented in at least three levels. Perceptually, I call it *intuitive representation*; intellectually, I call it *cognitive representation*; and rationally, I call it *model representation*. Coincidentally, it is exactly the same as the expression model-dependent positivism. Consider that the world we are dealing with today is constructed on a mathematical coordinate system. Is there a coordinate system in this world? Coordinates are just an ideal model, just a logical model. But you can only understand the world on this system. So again, I emphasize that all our knowledge is nothing but a subjective model of thought, something that Western scientists are very aware of.

Hawking goes on to explain further, saying that there are four criteria for distinguishing a good or bad model, or for building a model: first, it is elegant; second, it cannot be adjusted arbitrarily, i.e., it is very accurate; third, it can be tested by predictions, etc.; and fourth, it can be falsified, i.e., it can be proven wrong in the end. Please pay attention to these four criteria: What do you mean it is elegant? How do you determine whether it is elegant or inelegant; how do you determine that it is accurate? If it is ultimately falsified, it is not precise enough, or at least not certain; it can be predicted, which means it can be confirmed with the senses, which is called empirical evidence in science. If you look carefully at these four articles, none of them are non-subjective.

And Hawking cannot answer three questions: First, why does logical model change? We all know that the human cosmology, worldview and knowledge system are in flux, and are constantly being falsified before creating new logical models and new theories and doctrines. Why is the logical model always unstable? Second, he said that a good logical model must be convenient, that is, the case of the universe cannot be opened, you can stand outside and guess how the clock works, so you have multiple models of operation, which model will you take? Hawking thinks that whichever one is convenient will be adopted. But is correct just convenient? In fact, human logical models or doctrinal systems have been getting more and more complex and inconvenient, so much so that the vast majority of people today are reduced to scientific amateurs, which is in fact increasingly inconvenient. Third, what do the concepts of model, correctness, and convenience mean? We have no answer in Hawking's work. There is clearly room for deeper questions and inquiry in the exploration of philosophical issues. Once you understand the questions raised by ancient Greek philosophy and the eventual development of scientific results, the boundaries of human thought are still endlessly expanding. Human knowledge, human understanding of the world, has so far remained a marginal exploration, and this is the deep state of the underpinnings of human knowledge as revealed by philosophy.

That is all I have to say about the foundations of philosophy. You should understand one thing by this point, that is, the philosophy of idealism, the philosophy of epistemology, which is actually an inquiry into the human spirit, a product of the continuous depth of human thought. It is not a problem that you can simply deal with in a critical and negative way. In the history of philosophy, the deeper the realm of human thought goes, the more it derives from a field of study that is constantly differentiated and refined scientifically, and this is something you should be especially careful about.

Dialectics: the Initial Form of Rational Logic

If you understand the previous part, you may have a fundamental shake in your original worldview of materialistic reflection. In fact, we are only looking at the "survival maintenance effect of cognitive processes" from a different perspective, or rather, we are re-examining the *universe-life* interrelationship, which does not exclude the objective existence of material systems and their fundamental role.

The dialectic is discussed below. Because the basic intellectual structure of the nation is dialectical materialism, then it is very important that we discuss *dialectical logic* a little bit. I don't want to subvert your original views at all, I just want to tell you that if you want to understand Western philosophy, if you want to understand the roots of science, you have to know the way human thought is stretched and applied.

Let's look briefly at the dialectical order of thought. As I already said in my Laozi class, that dialectic or dialectical logic is the primary stage of rational human thinking, so please remember my statement. Since one of the important components of Marxism is Hegel's dialectic, the dialectic is elevated to the frightening level in this country, and dialectical logic is considered to be the highest end of the logic of human thinking. This is a major misunderstanding, so I will address this issue with the simplest possible clarification. I will not phrase it in a purely philosophical way, but try to phrase it in a way that people can understand, although I may get into a slightly more complicated issue when I discuss formal and ideal logic below. I don't know if I'll be able to make it clear to everyone, so let's try.

What does it mean that dialectical logic is the lower stage of human rational development? First of all, we should know that from the history of human thought, dialectical logic is the earliest form of human rational logic. China as early as 3300 years ago, oracle bone inscriptions have not yet formed, *I-Ching* as the representative of the two lines of Yin and Yang culture was already popular, so the initial foundation of the original Chinese thinking is realized in the dialectical method. This topic we will expand later when we talk about *I-Ching*. As you know, the earliest thinkers in the history of Chinese thought, such as Laozi (he says "reversion is the movement of *Dao*") and Confucius (he says "the middle"), established the concept of dialectics. In the West, the earliest philosophers in ancient Greece, such as Heraclitus, including Parmenides, including Plato, all used dialectical thinking.

Dialectical thinking is expressed as the earliest model of thinking in the history of human thought. Why? It is because early human beings were very low in information and used dialectical logic to deal with rational problems, showing the most parsimonious state. The most typical expression of the simplicity of dialectics can be seen in this way: the two points of AB can be transformed into each other, which is called contradiction theory in our Chinese description. Let's see how simple the dialectical model of thinking is. It says that beyond A is generally called B, which is equivalent to what we say in the theory of contradiction, that beyond the spear is generally the shield. As you know, there are thousands of things beyond the spear, not all of them are shields. But how does dialectical logic deal with it? It treats all things other than A as B, that is, all things other than spears as shields. But there are so many things other than spears, such as cups, microphones, computers, and tables, which are not shields. But in dialectical logic, it is a shield, or something other than A is a B. This is obviously an extremely crude logical model.

What problem does it deal with? It deals with the law of identity of the *formal logic of knowledge, A=A*. What does this mean? We will talk about it later. I just want to tell you that dialectical logic is the simplest model of human thought to deal with the problem of the law of identity, that is, the problem of *A=A*. In other words, dialectical logic is a typical relativistic model of subjective constructs. What does that mean? How do we use it in dialectics, in everyday concepts? For example, what do you mean by front and back, up and down, left and right? If you take a few steps backward, the original back becomes the front, that is, front and back, high and low, left and right, all these concepts are relativistic concepts. Why do we deal with concepts in this way? Why do we not have a definite front, a definite back, a definite top, a definite bottom, a definite left, a definite right? It is because our human existence is in a state of temporal dislocation. I can only say that it is a kind of oscillating way of survival in which human beings are forced to search for positioning and fixation due to the state of dislocated existence or the tendency of dislocated evolution. I can only ask you to read the book after class and figure it out for yourself.

Dialectical logic, is a collation of shaky states in the way humans establish cognition and discrimination. As I said, human perception must break down the stepless variables of external objects into clear boundary variables, such as when you take a continuous wavelength of 360 nanometers of light waves and have to split it into more than 150 distinct color perceptions. It expresses the need to establish a discriminative response, which is very complex. Dialectical logic is a model of subjective rectification that overcomes this shakiness in the most concise way.

You may not fully understand what I have talked about, so we will talk more about it later when we talk about formal logic.

When human beings understand the world in their early years, just like when we are in childhood, we see the world as complete, constant, or stable and unchanging at that time. It is only when we reach a certain level of age, a certain level of intellectual development, and a certain level of increased information that we discover and understand that the world is actually fluid. At this stage, dialectical logic has to deal with a question, or human intellectual logic has to deal with a question, that is why do things change? And how does it change? Dialectical logic is the simplest way to deal with this fundamental question, and this is the source of the explanatory model that "A and B can be transformed into each other".

Dialectical logic belongs to the logic of understanding, which is Hegel's own formulation. Hegel believed that after the logic of understanding, there is a higher logical form than dialectical logic, which he called logic of speculation. It is clear that Hegel himself did not consider dialectical logic to be the highest logical stage. The reason why dialectical logic shows the greatest use in our daily life, and even more than 95% of the cases we use it, is because the more primitive and lower the level, the more foundational, decisive and stable it is. The simpler the model, the more effective it is, the easier and more stable it is to use. Therefore, we use logic models in everyday situations by choosing the simplest and most primitive underlying models.

The human lower center is called the subconscious and is determined by the spinal cord. As I said earlier, for example, if you ride a bicycle, after you become really good at it, you are giving it to the spinal cord to manage, instead, when you are learning for the first time, you have to mobilize the high end of the mind, mobilize the cerebral cortex, try to control yourself, and even so you could not avoid falling down. What does it show? It shows that the way we humans use our intelligence is to leave the task of regulation to the lower centers or the lower end of logic to run as much as possible. So once you get good at something, you no longer have to use the cerebral cortex to control your bike, but leave it to the spinal cord. It shows that the lower the end, the more effective and stable it is, and that's the way humans use their intellect. So dialectical logic expresses its validity only by its low end and stability, which are the basic characteristics of dialectical logic. So never think of dialectical logic as the high end of human logic.

High-end logic presents itself when you are faced with many complex conditions and an increasing number of objects presented that you can no longer handle with simple logical models. So it is not valid to call philosophy or logic a method of thought. The word method of thought can easily give us the illusion that you can choose a certain method of thought at will, but in fact the way we use our intellect is not our choice. When you are in the primitive low information stage, or dealing with simple problems with low information, you will unconsciously use low end logic. When you are faced with a high-end complex problem, you unconsciously have to use high-end logic to deal with it; there is no choice here.

Hegel famously said something to the effect that the fact that a person does not know the physiology of how the esophagus peristalsis moves does not at all prevent his esophagus from continuing to move properly. The meaning of this quote clearly tells us that the method of thought you use does not lie in whether you can actively choose to deploy it in your manifest consciousness, but in the amount or complexity of information you face when dealing with a problem, and at this moment you will naturally mobilize the corresponding method of thought, even if you are not conscious of it, which is the manifest state of our different logical levels.

Hegel deliberately made it extremely complicated when he addressed the issue of dialectics, but in fact his method was very outdated. For more than 2000 years ago, ancient Greek philosophers and the Chinese *I-Ching*, all the way to Laozi's *Daodejing*, were discussing dialectical thinking in depth. So why did Hegel have to use dialectical logic? It was because he wanted to respond to the dilemma of paradox left by Kant's exploration of the ultimate problem of reason and the relationship between object of being-in-itself and the mental subject. So to understand Hegel, you must read Kant, and then you must read what Hegel's *absolute spirit* means. Hegel says that the alienation of the *absolute spirit* is the system of objects, and the process of perception is the same process of bringing it back to the idea, which is called the *positive and negative operation* of dialectics. Hegel's *absolute idea* is indeed justified, and it is nothing but the inheritance of Plato's *idea theory*. The background of the idea is that after the recent classical philosophy clearly realized that our perception is a subjective closed channel, the other investigation he made on what we human beings say is the object, which he could not find the proper way to explore, so he borrowed the most primitive and concise dialectical logic model of human beings to wrangle. Therefore, the key to understand Hegel's philosophy is to understand that the *absolute idea* means the insurmountable of the closed system of perception itself, which is the reasonable element in Hegel's philosophy.

Since Hegel made an inappropriate and excessive elevation of dialectic in his *Logic* and *Phenomenology of Spirit*, Russell, one of the important founders of modern logic, once made this comment about Hegel's philosophy in his book *History of Western Philosophy*, and I quote him, "Hegel's doctrine is almost entirely false. " I declare that I do not think Russell's evaluation is absolutely correct, but Russell's evaluation of Hegel's philosophy in terms of logic is justified. The criticism he gives from the standpoint of high-end logic against the primitive low-end dialectical logic itself being over-elevated is insightful, and it is something that one should pay special attention to.

We will briefly talk about the relationship between dialectical logic and high-end logic below. To clarify this issue, let's first look at the formal logic proposed by Aristotle. In China, those of you who have studied Marxist philosophy from secondary school to university have often seen Marxist philosophy use two terms created by Hegel: one is called *dialectic* and the other is called *metaphysics*, and you are familiar with these two sets of terms. Metaphysics, in Marxism or in Hegel, means a philosophical way of looking at things in a static way; dialectics means a philosophical way of looking at things in motion. But what does metaphysics actually mean? As I said earlier, it is equivalent to what Aristotle called "metaphysica after physics," so the word *metaphysics* stands at the base and depth of ancient Greek philosophy in a narrow sense, which is a valid Aristotelian expression of the word *philosophy*, or a proper translation. In fact, the logic established by Aristotle is called *formal logic*. The so-called *formal logic* is to remove the specific elements of the object and see how the logical form works, which was summarized by Aristotle as three laws, called "the law of identity, the law of exclude middle, and the law of contradiction", and then the fourth law added by the modern German classical philosophers Wolfe and Leibniz, is called "the law of sufficient reason". Hegel precisely designated it as the typical form of logic of understanding.

Let's look at the state of the three or four laws of formal logic. The first law of formal logic is the *law of identity*, the simplest expression is called *A=A*. It sounds like a repetition of the same word without any difference between the subject and the predicate, but why is it the most important core law of formal logic? It is important to understand that the human perceptual system is designed to reach a discriminative response. If we are faced with a single object, there is no need to recognize the object, that is, there is no need to identify the object, is that right?

Let's assume that when the universe first occurred, there were only two things in the world: quarks and leptons. For an electron, a lepton, or a quark, each of them has a single object: the electron faces only the quark, and vice versa, the quark faces only the electron, and nothing else, which is called *A=A*. That is, when the object is divided from *one* to *many*, if it still faces a single object of knowledge, then there is no selective obstacle for it to establish dependence with the object. But imagine that the evolution of the universe is a process of differentiation, the universe is initially a singularity, which is expressed by Parmenides as "existence is one"; think about Laozi's saying "*Dao* gives birth to one, one to two, two to three, three to everything". Here both express the process of differentiation. Then the universe initially differentiated from the singularity of energy, quarks, leptons and bosons, and then differentiated into *many*, and these most basic particles then evolved, or rather, conformally differentiated into more basic particles and 92 natural elements, and these 92 natural elements continue to differentiate into nearly 10 million kinds of molecular substances, and these molecular substances, in the process of conformation and differentiation, then differentiate into hundreds of millions of species of organisms. We will find that the evolution of matter in the universe is a process of differentiation.

When you are confronted with many objects, you can only depend on one object per unit of time. It is important to understand that the process of differentiation is the deteriorating of the original *one*, so all differentiated objects have an inherent tendency to seek unity, and we call this process *dependence*, or *structure*. The means by which we achieve dependence and structure are called *affective attributes of sense-responses* or, by extension, *perceptual attributes*. So when objects are multiple, all objects are your dependencies, your conditions of existence, or your conditions of survival, and you can only depend on one object per unit of time, what do you do at this time? Of course, you have to identify and capture the primary object of dependence among many objects, and not to confuse and shake among many objects, which is called *A=A*.

Vision began to appear 500 million years ago in the most primitive lower aquatic animals, the flat worms. At the time of single-celled organisms there were no sensory organs, and cells performed external substance recognition and external energy metabolism through receptors on the cell membrane, which could only discriminate between some of the atoms and ions in the universe. As natural differentiation became more complex, by the stage of flatworms, vision appeared, the first of the five sensory organs to occur. According to biologists, the most primitive vision does not see multiple objects, but only the dependent conditions associated with its survival, which is called *A=A*.

It is very difficult for us to teach a philosophy class because if I use the words *A=A*, everyone will fall asleep, so we have to use scientific language and intuitive experiments to give a lecture. This kind of lecture is far from the philosophical thinking that you can really understand the pure logical derivation, so you should not consider this class as a complete philosophy class in the real sense, it is only a basic overview and enlightenment of philosophy.

Let me tell an experiment. Biologists make a disk, put a toad on it, and fasten a glass cover on this disk, and detain the toad in it. Then hang an insect-like bar on the outside, but stand it up longitudinally and rotate it outside, but there is not reaction from the toad, indicating that it is invisible to the toad. When the external bar is lowered and the appropriate vibration is applied, the toad will follow the bar in a circle once the disk is rotated again. It indicates that this time the toad began to have a visual response. This experiment shows that the toad's vision can only be effective if it sees a bar moving in parallel, which is to imitate the image of a wriggling flesh worm. At the time of development of a highly evolved oviparous animal like the toad, its vision was actually still limited to a single object, and it could only see the striped crawler on which it depended, and it automatically excludes other irrelevant multiple objects from its perceptual perception, which is called *A=A*.

Let me give you another example. A bird is trying to find a worm in a tree, and bird as a vertebrate flying animal its perceptual objects are already highly multiple, it can see the trunk of the tree, the branches, the leaves, the flowers, and the stripes on the bark. Then it must distinguish the insect that is very similar to the bark cracks among these multiple objects, and it cannot just hit the tree trunk or keep flying around the leaves, which will excessively consume its biological energy and is completely ineffective. So it must choose to catch the insect among the infinite number of objects such as A, B, C, D, etc., which is called *A=A*. That is, in the multiple objects, the first time to find the primary dependency of the recognition reaction, called *A=A*.

The second law of formal logic is called the *law of exclude the middle*. Its philosophical expression is *A is B or not B*, what does it mean? It means that when multiple objects have been presented, *A, B, C, D* ......are all differentiated, and while I want to depend on *A*, *B* is interfering with me, and I have to keep distinguishing between A and B. In the complex process of distinguishing between *A* and *B*, I first have to determine which object I want to depend on. In the process of complex discrimination, first of all, we have to determine the object *A* that we want to rely on, and secondly, it must also be clearly identified as *B* other than *A* different objects, that is, there is no wandering situation, which is called the *law of exclude the middle*. It can be seen what is the law of the row, *A=A* cannot be maintained, *A=A* by more than one object interference, and for this reason, and quickly eliminate such perceptual interference, called the *law of exclude the middle.*

The third term of formal logic is called the *law of contradiction*, or the *law of non-contradiction*. Its philosophical expression is *A* is not *non-A*. What does it mean? It means that *A* has been shaken in the law of the row again, because there are more and more differentiated objects, *A* has been submerged in too many objects, and it is difficult to determine what is *A*. I have to search for many objects again and again, and after the initial recognition, I have to confirm it again to make sure that I have not made a mistake in recognition, or have not disturbed the recognition, which is called *A* is not *non-A*. This is called *A* is not non-*A*. It is the state of overcoming the wavering of the *A* itself by sifting through the *A=A* law (the *law of identity*) after the recognition of the law of *A* is *B* or not *B*, so it is called the logic of understanding.

Please note that I am expressing what *understanding* means here. *Understanding* is the act of judgment that has to arise when the object of plurality is shaken, and when the shaking of the object of confirmation occurs, it is called *understanding*. Note that the word *judgment* means *discernment*, and only when the object is multiplicative does it need to be discerned. If you have only one object, for example, an electron facing only one proton, then it does not need to be discerned. When the object is multiple, you have to discriminate among the objects, and only when the discriminating is done and you can make a decision, and only then can a discriminative dependence reaction occur, which is called *judgment*. Therefore, in philosophy, *judgment* is a very important concept, and *discernment for determination* is called *understanding*.

If the object is single, it is called sensuality, so the most primitive sensuality does not need to be judged. For example, the electron does not need to be judged in the face of a proton, or the toad does not need to be judged in the face of a vertical bar, which is not within the scope of its senses. It is not until multiple objects lead to understanding that the act of judgment becomes necessary, and therefore *formal logic* is classified by Hegel as *logic of understanding*.

What does *rational logic* mean? When the objects are divided into infinite numbers, we can no longer recognize the infinite number of objects in the entity pattern, i.e., we can not intuitively realize the discriminative confirmation of *A=A*, so we must categorize the objects into concepts, and then deal with the conceptual, not the real objects, thinking model deduction, and then finally return to the physical response, which is called rational movement. In essence, rational movement is the abstraction and categorization of objects into concepts, and then doing imaginary reasoning reactions. Its purpose is still to judge the overloaded multiple objects, except that this time the hard-state physical judgment is no longer available, but must run on the soft-state logical concept of the sandbox of thought, which is called rationality.

The logic of understanding, as expressed by Aristotle, proposes the law of identity, the law of excluded the middle, and the law of contradiction, an elaboration that is itself rational, abstract, and conceptualized, but the question it answers and explains is the question of understanding judgment. I think you should be able to hear the meaning of my passage, that is, formal logic deals with the problem of understanding judgment, but not with physical objects like a bird, but with the rational model of the state of understanding physical discriminations at the level of rational logic, by way of conceptual derivation. Or rather, the effect reached is a rationalized model account of the logical response form of understanding, which is called the formal logic of understanding. It was later added by Wolf and Leibniz as a *law of sufficient reason*, that is, when you make judgments of A, B, C, D, etc., your judgments have to be based on continuity and have a deducible order. progress to the transitional level of *rational logic*, which is the reason why the fourth law is not in Aristotelian *formal logic*, that is, the *law of sufficient reason* has been expressed as the subsequent intermediary state of *rational logic*.

Brief Description of *Ideal Logic*

We will briefly discuss the state of the further development of understanding formal logic into rational logic. This part will still be difficult for you to hear. This course will not go into detail about logic, because logic is so complex that it has to be derived even from non-literal symbols, and if some of you are interested, you can read the monographs on logic by Russell and others. So I just want to make a summary of the high state of rational logic that is formed by the derivation and development of formal logic upwards.

When mankind entered the state of philosophical thinking, that is, after Plato, Aristotle, and even in the modern scientific era, it was by no means possible for the true thinkers to apply dialectical logic to the problems when studying more complex problems of systems. The amount of additional information and the complexity of the object at this time already had to be handled with the help of high-end rational logic. The scope of rational logic is very wide, from the most basic dialectical logic gradually developed to ideal logic.

It is necessary to clarify that when I talk about logic here, I am referring to logic in a narrow sense, and we will expand and interpret logic itself and the meaning of logic in a broad sense tomorrow.

I will first explain the meaning of the term *ideal logic*. I call the highest level of rational logic *ideal logic*. Please pay special attention to the word *ideal*. When we say ideal today, we mean a utopian wish, and we call this thing ideal. But we should pay attention to the original Chinese concept of the word "理想" (Li Xiang), its literally translation means *pure reasoning*. When the objects tend to be infinitely multiple, and then judged on the physical system, the process is completely impossible, so we have to categorize thousands of intuitive objects into a concise, abbreviated conceptual system, and then make a reasoning judgment. This is called rational or rational logic, which enters the soft thinking of discriminating and seeking to determine.

When rational logic unfolds, the perceptual element, that is, the physical object element, is withdrawn from the concept, that is, there is no longer a physical object in the concept, and this is called the thought of pure reasoning. For example, in mathematics, 3 refers to anything and nothing, it is always suspended in the physical object. 3 is nothing but a pure conceptual symbol, there is no physical element behind it, and then the deduction on it is called the thought of pure reasoning. For example, if we say "cup", you cannot find a cup in this world, you can only find a ceramic cup, a plastic cup, or a stainless-steel cup, you can never find a pure cup, the cup is an abstraction. But when you say cup, the physical object is still behind it, that is, the concept does not exclude the perceptual material. Although when you say cup, it has been abstracted, it has been conceptualized, it does not exclude the sensual material, so it is not a purely reasoning thought, it is a thought mixed with sensual elements.

When you raise the level of abstraction, you have to extrapolate at a more virtual level because the object is so complex, that is, you have to do layers of virtual logic. For example, who has ever seen a *creature*? You have first seen a certain horse, a certain wolf, a certain sheep, a certain tree, and then you categorize them separately and say this is called an animal, that is called a plant, which is already abstract. But it is not enough, you further abstract it by saying that animals and plants are alive and can be summed up as *living things*, which is another layer of abstraction on plants and animals. At the time you keep abstracting, the sensual elements are gradually filtered out of the concept, and when you have abstracted all the concepts to the highest degree, the sensual elements are completely shed, and only pure reasoning is done, we call it *ideal*. Please understand this point: logical reasoning at the level of *pure reasoning* is called *ideal logic*. Let me give you another example. When Einstein proposed the theory of relativity, he did an ideal logic experiment. He said that when you travel at the speed of light, what will be the state of things? What would be the state of time and space? Can you run at the speed of light? That is simply not possible. His whole model of scientific theory is based on a purely logical and ideal deduction, which is called *ideal experiment*. We regard such a model of thinking as the high state of rational logic, and I call it *ideal logic*.

Let us see below the purely reasoning thought filtered out of the perceptual element, how it is expressed in mode corresponding to the way formal logic.

The first one is called *law of simplicity*. It corresponds to the *law of identity* of perceptual logic. Remember that we humans, and indeed all animals, perceive only for the purpose of reaching a cognitive-dependent response; keep in mind that our perception is not set up for truth-seeking, but for survival. Survival is achieved in a series of multiple object differentiation and mutilation, so you have to develop your perceptual process as a discursive sequence, that is, a discursive state facing multiple objects. When the amount of object differentiation is small, you can directly correspond perceptually and intellectually; when the amount of object differentiation is too large, you must transform it from a hard physical state to a soft conceptual state for virtual derivation, a process called rationalization. Then, since all our perceptions are only survival systems of discursive responses, when there are many objects, the discursive dependence of the *law of identity* (*A*=*A*) is transformed into the simplicity of a higher degree of abstraction. By *law of simplicity*, we mean that *A*=*A* is transformed into "*A*-system equals *A*". The "*A*-system" is the whole series of *A*, *B*, *C*, *D*, *E*, *F*, *G* ......, which is a series of differentiation related to *A*. Let's rectify it into a logical lineage, called *law of simplicity*. Please pay some attention to this paragraph to understand the meaning of the object in the concept of the tendency to multiplex, and then in the concept of multiplex to organize it into an *A*, called *law of simplicity*.

Let me give you an example. For example, we humans use *force* in all kinds of situations. Today in the industrial age, you make a gear, you make a crankshaft, you make a connecting rod, you have to use mechanics. But what is *force*? if you can not rectify it into a point, an abbreviated *A*-system, you will never know what the *force* is. Humans have been using *force* for tens of thousands of years. Humans have been hunting animals with guns and javelins for tens of thousands of years, and they have been using arm strength, foot power, and physical strength, but they never knew what *force* was until Newton finally put it into an equation: the equation of gravitation. We are all familiar with the gravitational equation, gravity is equal to the product of the mass of two objects as the numerator, the square of the distance between the objects as the denominator, and then multiplied by the gravitational constant. In other words, the entire real force, the infinite figurative force, is turned into such an extremely abstract equation. At this point, we get the ultimate answer to what force is, at least in Newton's case, the simplified answer, so the state of thousands of forces is expressed simply as gravitational force.

Let me give you another example about the momentum of the force. Newton divided gravitational force into three laws. The second law, the law of momentum, is expressed as follows: $F=ma$, that is, force equals mass times acceleration. It expresses the momentum, the state of a thousand forces as a simplest equation. This is called the *A*-system, that is, the state of thousands of forces is expressed as *A*, which is called the *law of simplicity*. It is like a bird focusing on a single worm in a forest of thousands of objects, focusing on a single point in the concept of thousands of objects, and taking this single point to unify the overall relationship of thousands of objects. This is the upgraded state of *A*=*A*, which is called the *law of simplicity* and expressed as *A*-system = *A*, in which rational logic crosses over perceptual logic to deal with greater information.

Let's look at the second one, which is called the *law of arranging order*. Please remember that it corresponds to the *law of excluded the middle* in logic of understanding. The *law of excluded middle* is expressed in the formal logic of understanding as *A is B or not B*. In other words, the judgmental response to one object per unit of time is shaken, so it is necessary to choose and confirm between *A* and *B*, between multiple objects, which is called the law of excluded the middle. Then at the high end of rational logic, the state of ideal logic, it is transformed into the combination of "*A* is *B* and *C*, and *D* ......". That is, it no longer does the excluding, but the sorting of order. That is to say, it clarifies the relationship between *A* and all *non-A*, so that the relationship between *A* and *non-A* is coherent, called the *law of arranging order*.

I will give an example below. I need to repeat it again that when I present examples of problems in a non-logical and intuitive way, they may not be appropriate or precise, and they are only meant to assist in understanding the philosophical abstractions. For example, before Darwin established his theory of biological evolution, biology was very much complex. As you know that *everything* refers mainly to living things, because there are only a few million inorganic species, but in the biological world there are tens of billions of species, including extinct ones. Therefore, the most knowledgeable with the most sophisticated learning among human beings were the taxonomists, such as Carl Linnaeus and Georges Cuvier. They simplified the classification of hundreds of millions of species of organisms, and subdivided them into kingdoms, phyla, orders, families, genera, and species. There are tens of billions of species, and then categorized upward; above the genus, the genus will be reduced; the more genera and then subsumed into families, the family will be even less; in this order of recurrence, and later categorized to the phylum, such as Protozoa, Chordata, etc.; each phylum and then categorized upward called the kingdom, such as the animal kingdom, plant kingdom, fungal kingdom, the more subsumed is more streamlined. But even so, with these seven levels of categorization, the total number of objects is still countless. And what did Darwin do with it? He used the principle of "natural selection" to sort all organisms into an evolutionary hierarchy, so that everything is presented in one system, that is, a clear chain on a sorting series. I just want to tell you what kind of model state it is to ascend from the *law excluded the middle* to the purely rational *law of arranging order*, which is called the *law of arranging order*.

The third is called the *law of eliminating contradictions*, which corresponds to the *law of contradiction*. The *law of contradiction* in formal logic is *A* is not *non-A*, which means that the shaken *A*=*A* must be confirmed again, and it must be clear that *non-A* must not be confused with it, which is called the *law of contradiction*. This is called the law of elimination of contradiction. In high-end ideal logic, it is expressed as the *law of eliminating contradictions*, it is achieved not by excluding all the things other than *A*, but by dissolving the boundaries and contradictions between them. This is called the *law of eliminating contradictions*. I mentioned Darwin earlier, who said that living things derive from one point to another, or can be reduced to a certain point, rather than breaking up into an infinite number of points. For example, all organisms evolved from single-celled organisms, for example, vertebrate reptiles can be categorized as aquatic chordates when they look backward, and then as amphibian reptiles when they trace back to the original direction, and finally as terrestrial reptiles. This state of *A* = *A* comes from *non-A* or derived from *non-A* by eliminating the gap or contradictions between *A and non-A*. This is the high end of ideal logic of *law of eliminating contradictions.*

The fourth is called the *law of tracing back to the origin,* which corresponds to the *law of sufficient reason*. The so-called *law of sufficient reasons,* in fact, cannot help but import the state of multi-factor analysis, which will bring confusion in thinking. Therefore, in the high-end ideal logic, it is necessary to trace the origin to an ultimate point, so the *law of sufficient reason* is ultimately expressed as the ultimate trace of the *law of tracing back to the origin*. Where will it trace back to? The return to the *law of simplicity*. That is, the law of tracing back to the origin is the conceptual reversion to the first law, the most important law of dependent realization, the *law of simplicity,* in the final collation of multi-element objects. It is equivalent to the confirmed non-moving state of the logic of understanding *A=A*. Only one is judged on the physical confirmation, and the other is organized on the conceptualized large amount of information. Human high-end rational logic is the same way extension of animal logic of understanding, not the reverse transition of dialectical logic. Dialectical logic is expressed as the transformation of *A* and *non-A* into each other, while in fact the logical progress of human beings is a deep and same way development of the lineage of understanding logic, rational logic, and ideal logic. Its connotation is essentially dealing with the difference in the amount of information, or with the increment of information, which is the state of ideal logic.

In Hegel's and Marx's formulations, it is said that formal logic sees problems statically and that dialectical logic sees it dynamically, this formulation is clearly incorrect. For even formal logic, or rational logic by extension of formal logic, although it has to determine *A=A*, it in no way says that *A* is always the same, it deals precisely with *A=A* in the extension of rational logic, with the logical relations of the variables of this *A*. It's like if we say cells, you want to study cells, you have to let the cells express as a static model, you can study them. But it in no way excludes the fact that cells can change, change from prokaryotic to eukaryotic, from unicellular to multicellular. If you don't work it out statically, you're talking about dynamics as a chaotic model. You figure it out statically before its dynamics, momentum and the amount of movement can enter into precise analysis, so the strict pursuit of the concept of static thinking and static formal logic in no way indicates that it denies the dynamic contemplation of objects. The expression of formal logic and dialectical logic as one being static and the other dynamic, may be valid in the state of animal logic of understanding, but not in the ideal logical form of the rationalization of formal logic and the development of the continuity of formal logic in human beings, knowing that the static study of problems is the basis for the derivation of dynamic variables. I hope that you will hear my remarks and thus understand that the narrow criticism of formal logic of the dialectical past is inappropriate.

I'll bring the lesson here. You can at least get a sense of the foundational operating state of philosophical thinking, the way it is pursued, and the limits of dialectical materialism. We have to understand that Western philosophy starts from such a most basic state of thinking, from a logical game that gradually derives a refined decomposition of the model of human thinking. Then this model of thought is continuously sculpted, and within this abstracted model of pure thought - which has no connection with reality and experience or even pragmatism - a greater amount of information is fed in constantly, leading to a sophisticated logical rectification, a process that constitutes the human capacity for thought. This mobilization of potential is expressed in the study of philosophical thinking and logic on the one hand, and in the pursuit of objects and what lies behind them and in the construction of sophisticated logical models on the other hand, which eventually leads to the sub-disciplinary presentation of philosophical thinking in the scientific era, thus forming a philosophical thinking system.

That's all for today's class of Western Philosophy, which will be continued tomorrow. The following time is set aside for interaction and discussion.

Q & A After Class

Questioner: Mr. Dongyue, my question is this: Philosophy is the precursor of science, and philosophy is the pursuit of theological inquiries, so may I ask what is the relationship between philosophy and theology?

Mr. Dongyue: I said that philosophy is the mother of science, so let me say another sentence that theology is the mother of philosophy. Because theology is the ultimate inquiry of man at the most primitive stage and with the least amount of information. What was the most concise, least informative, and most intuitive response of man in a very primitive age, thousands of years ago, when he had to ask the questions of what is going on in all things and why does the world exist? To create one or more personalized Gods. So this is how Russell phrased it, he says that both theology and philosophy are ultimate inquiries, and that both philosophy and science employ the tools of reason. Theology is the ultimate inquiry, the ultimate inquiry about the universe, except that it belongs to a model of inquiry with a very small amount of information. When the amount of information increases, it expresses itself in human intellectual presentation as doubt, or as amazement, and then questions the simple model of theology, and asks about the inadequacy of theology to rectify the universe simply by God, and how God rectified the universe, like Pythagoras, like Newton. This led to the next step of discursive processing with a large amount of information called philosophy, so early philosophy and theology have been linked together. Whether in Pythagoras, or in Socrates, all the way to Newton, theology and philosophy were always entwined. To a large extent, philosophy has been in the service of theology, which is a basic lineage in the history of human thought. I draw your attention to the fact that the history of human thought, if summed up in the simplest terms, is the process of dealing with ever-expanding increments of information, which is the most fundamental connotation of the history of human culture and thought. At the same time, according to my principle of weakening compensation, the more primitive and lower something is, the more foundational, decisive and stable it is. Therefore, the stability of theology does not lie in its truthfulness, but in its primitiveness, because the more primitive something is, the more stable it is. So when I say that something is stable, remember that it is the same as if I were saying that something is primitive and backward.

Yes! Any more questions from everyone?

Questioner: When you summarized at the end, I didn't understand much of what you were saying, and I didn't write it down when you summarized at the end. Can you repeat the summarized part again, though I don't think I can understand it even if you say it again.

Mr. Dongyue: It was a little difficult for me to reorganize the summary of the later part of the lecture while I was out of my mind. So when you listen to my class, you need to concentrate and try to catch every sentence of it. If you didn't understand this lesson, or didn't understand it completely, it's okay, after September all my lectures will be online, please review them online.

Questioner: Hello, teacher! The four theorems of ideal logic you mentioned, from the law of simplicity to the law of arranging order to the law of eliminating contradictions to the law of tracing back to the origin, feel like an evolutionary cycle. After returning to the law of simplicity, does it mean that a logical change is made and another channel of thought is opened?

Mr. Dongyue: The question is well posed, but the topic is very deep. I have repeatedly said earlier that the core of the logic of understanding is the law of identity *A=A*. Keep this statement in mind. What is the so-called *A=A* that I repeat again? *A=A* is a kind of rectification of multiple choices, as only one object could be depended upon per unit time, which cannot be disturbed by other multiple objects, and this is called *A=A*. The law of arranging order, the law of eliminating contradictions etc. are all rectification to effectively maintain *A=A*. So *A=A*, the law of identity, is the core of the logic of understanding. Then rational logic deals with the problem, no different from perceptual logic, and still solves the problem of dependence. Our perception is not set up for truth-seeking, but for survival. Therefore, all human beings' knowledge and intelligence are only for survival, and there is no difference in this respect; the only difference is the change in the amount of information. Since the world is differentiated and evolved, information is in the incremental process during the development of the universe. As the amount of information increases, to the rational logic stage, it is a non-intuitive model of greater information, that is, a soft conceptual reasoning model. What does it have to accomplish? It still has to accomplish the same effect on which perceptual logic depends, so that the simplicity of ideal logic is exactly the same as the law of identity in the perceptual logic, which is its central dimensional subject. All the laws that follow it are *auxiliary laws,* which are only a soft sequence of treatment to facilitate the implementation of simplicity, or to keep the law of identity from faltering. Therefore, they are the same thing, but the difference is only in the amount of information. Rational logic changes in the mode of intellectual processing, but its subject matter does not change at all. When I come to this, I will say one more topic, and that is the topic of logical change. If I talk about these two logical models and you think that we have covered all of the world, you've misunderstood it. Because information is constantly incremental, what we have summarized is only the logical processing model in the low information and high information stages. But even though the logical processing model is relatively fixed, the connotations and patterns of the logical model are constantly changing. As an example, Russell, who was a very good mathematician, once co-authored a book with Whitehead. I suggest that students with solid mathematical skills should read his book, which is called *Logics of Mathematics*. The book uses mathematics to rectify the sloppy state of logic and language used by humans on a daily basis. He believed that only by rectifying the model of human thinking in mathematical precision logic could he show what a state of human thought and perception is. So after Russell finished this work, he used to be proud that he had finished dealing with all the problems of the foundations of human knowledge. For if the logical foundation is dealt with, and all human knowledge runs on this logical model, then there will be no intellectual doubts for human beings in the future.

But then a figure emerged that fundamentally overturned this conclusion of Russell, and this was Einstein's good friend, the famous mathematician Gödel. Gödel argued in pure mathematics that in any isolated system of number-theoretic forms, if that system is logically self-contained, it must be imperfect, or incomplete, which is called Gödel's first theorem. He went on to derive Gödel's second theorem: conversely, in any isolated system of number-theoretic forms, if a logical system is complete or perfect, it must not be self-consistent. These two theorems of Gödel overturned Russell's conclusion that the problem of knowledge is necessarily complete when logic is studied to completion on a logical basis. What he means is that the human logical system is inherently flawed, and that when logic reaches intrinsic self-consistency, there must be an insurmountable hole beneath this self-consistent system; if this hole is to be filled, the self-consistent system cannot be realized. The former expression is Gödel's first theorem, and the latter expression is Gödel's second theorem. This is a bit complicated to say, and you have to go study the relevant logic. But it illustrates the point that any logically self-consistent theoretical system has an incomplete logical hole underneath it, leaving it in a perpetual state of imminent subversion. What pops up to subvert it? Incremental information! So the fact that the logical model is complete, in no way means that the model of human thought has not changed since then; this is a very complex issue, and I can only express it to that extent.

Questioner: Hello, Mr. Dongyue! Regarding the last paragraph, can I understand it in this simple way: if I want to know the world, I need to make a classification of it, and this classification, no matter what I study, is actually a model of thinking. So does this model make sense? Or is it reasonable to study this thing? In fact, it depends on whether it conforms to the last few laws of logic model. For example, if it conforms to the law of simplicity, the law of arranging order, or the law of eliminating contradiction, then the results of the study may be more reasonable. I don't know if I can simply understand what you discussed in the last paragraph. Thank you!

Mr. Dongyue: That's a good point generally, but that's not enough. Because this is only a purely abstract formulation of a model of logic, or a model of logic. And actually, any model of thought that you build, or any theory that you build, or an explanatory system, it requires a proof. That is, you have to prove it out step by step logically, and I mean proof in the broad sense of logic. What does broad logic mean? I'll talk about it tomorrow, except that the proof process must conform to the ideal logical four laws I mentioned. If you only correspond to the four laws in general, but you do not complete the proof of precise logic in information processing, it is still suspicious as a theory. What does it mean to be correct if our perceptions are not for truth, and do not contain truth judgments, i.e., if any of our knowledge has no relation to truth? We will devote tomorrow to this topic. I hope that when I discuss this topic tomorrow, you can concentrate on it, so that your question today can be answered.

QUESTIONER: Sir, recently I was chewing on your book *A Unified Theory of Evolution*, and I have a question here. Since the degree of existence is the independent variable and the degree of compensation is the dependent variable, and the degree of existence is not affected by the degree of compensation, but it goes all the way down, that is, this degree of existence keeps weakening as the first cause, and at the same time this degree of compensation is limited by the degree of existence and the threshold of existence. Then, for a certain species, there should be a maximum at a certain stage, which is one of the reasons you mentioned, like saying that Laozi could not formulate the theory of relativity in his time. According to this theory, no matter how people pursue development and progress today, that is, no matter how they increase the degree of compensation, it should not affect the degree of existence of human beings, because it has an upper limit. Then why do you propose that we need to control development now and not to look at our future completely with a developmental perspective?

MR. DONGYUE: I didn't say the degree of existence is not influenced by the degree of compensation. I said that the degree of existence is the independent variable and the degree of compensation is the dependent variable. I will not say the basis, but first of all, I said this is a limited statement. What does it mean? As you will read and find it later in the book, I say that the degree of compensation and the degree of existence are the same thing, that is, the gain of the degree of compensation is the way the decay of the degree of existence is realized, and I specifically emphasize this statement in the later paragraphs. As I said in my lecture earlier, I said that our human model of recognition, that is, our perception, is that we must decompose the continuous state of external objects into fragmentary states, which is a subjective setting necessary for our human perception, because we must establish a recognition-dependent response. Therefore, when humans discuss any problem, they formulate a problem into several concepts for deduction. This is something that cannot be helped, it is prescribed by the limits of human logic, so I hope you understand.

When I set the degree of existence as the independent variable and the degree of compensation as the dependent variable, this is necessary for a refined analysis within the limits of human logic. Therefore, I express later: the gain of the degree of compensation is the way the decay of the degree of existence is realized. Why do I say that the decay of the degree of existence determines the increment of the degree of compensation? It is because the degree of existence reaches the highest value of satisfaction when everything is without any property of compensation. Only those who have read my book know the meaning of this statement. That is, in the singularity state of the highest degree of existence, there are no attributes, and if the attribute gain is the first nature, then we should see the attribute existence first, and then the degree of existence. Thus at the logical pole, attributes cannot be used as fundamental variables.

However, since the gain of the degree of compensation is the only manifest form of existential decay, the expression of attributes or attributes gain, when we speak about the posteriority problem concerning human beings, keeps appearing in the foreground, while the existential degree occurs in the background. This is the reason why our discussion of the problem is increasingly focused on the issue of compensation. Thus, when I speak of the increasing human attributes capacity, which marks a serious weakening of human existence, I speak of the fact that humans cannot just increase their amount of compensation, which seems to say that the reduction of compensation can enhance existence, as if the reasoning is reversed. In fact, I am trying to tell you that constantly increasing your capacity is a sign that your existence state tends to become critical. As for whether humans can scale down their variables of compensation, you should be highly skeptical of it if you really read my book.

QUESTIONER: Just to follow up the gentleman's question, I've actually been confused about the *finite range of sustaining*. There is a theory that the existence of living planets in the universe is a very probable event, maybe hundreds of millions, maybe more, I don't know how many. In this case, there are so many planets with life, why did you make human beings the last stop in the range of sustaining? Actually, I was thinking that you could make it one of the stops, but not have to be the last stop. Because I remember you said in one of your videos that if aliens came, this philosophical theory of yours would collapse, but if you left an opening for yourself, this philosophy would not necessarily collapse. What makes you so confident that humanity is in the last stop of sustaining? That's what I'm trying to understand.

Mr. Dongyue: We will expand on this issue on the last day, the 12th day of class, and I will only make one point now. To do scholarship is not to play with machinations, that is, when I argue for a law or a theorem, I must follow strict logical regulations. If I leave an opening, superficially my doctrine can never collapse, but it must lose its precision and rigor. As for what I mean when I say that everything in this universe is sustaining within a finite range, that humans are one of the species with the weakest degree of existence in the universe, and that the future of human beings will hardly have too much room for development, we will discuss these words on the last day of this series class. I only emphasize one point here, a doctrine, a principle, for it to be able to hold, it must never hold on Earth, it must hold in the whole universe.

Theoretically there could be an infinite number of aliens or extraterrestrial beings of higher intelligence, but why are they never encountered? What would happen if there were highly intelligent beings on planets in the universe that are billions of years ahead of our planet? Think about it, our human civilization so far is only tens of thousands of years, the civilization with writing is only 5,000 years, we are not far from the end of the game today, then, on the planet that happened billions of years earlier than us, if it has intelligent life, if its development has no boundaries, it should have been able to cross the entire universe today, but why did not come to Earth? The academic community calls it the Great Filter, meaning that there is an unknown Great Filter blocking interstellar travel. What is the Great Filter? It is the principle of weakening compensation. That is to say, any living creature, including higher intelligent creatures, its intelligence substitution reaches a certain height, marking its existence degree tends to zero, which is the reason why alien highly intelligent creatures, although they may be extremely numerous, finally cannot come to Earth.

Questioner: In today's lecture, you said that many people nowadays are superstitious about science and even become followers of the Scientology. Then all of us here today are probably followers of the principle of weakening compensation. In the spirit of the ancient Greek inquiry, we reflect along the way. Can you imagine, by purely logical reasoning, where is the possible breakdown of the principle of weakening compensation? Where exactly will it go wrong? My own judgment is that there are two possibilities: one is that it does not have a detailed mathematical reasoning yet, and a new science may be developed in the future; the other is that we have too little information now, so we cannot stand in a higher dimension and look at this problem from a top view. My real question is whether you, Mr. Wang, are great enough to cross this cultural obscurity and subvert your own theory, that is, to cross the second S-curve, as Professor Li Shanyou said. Thank you!

Mr. Dongyue: If you read my book carefully, you will find that I repeatedly emphasize in my book that my doctrine is in no way the truth. If I want to reach self-consistency in logic, I will never admit that my doctrine is the truth; it is only a temporarily correct logical model. All science is only a temporarily correct logical model, and this is true of all doctrines and theories, and my doctrine is no exception. But there are conditions for overturning a doctrine, and not just you want overturn it. Newton's doctrine was correct for 200 years, before the emergence of Einstein's doctrine, and even Maxwell's field equations came out, Newton's doctrine still could not be subverted. In other words, any doctrine is falsified, it is necessary for the amount of information to develop conditions, so my doctrine is by no means the truth. But if you want to falsify it today, it's hard! And I myself have a limited life span, if I could live 800 years, then I would go and falsify it. Unfortunately, the amount of information to falsify it may not appear before I die. So let me emphasize again, my doctrine is not the truth, but it is a correct model that matches the amount of information available today, and it has nothing to do with greatness, but only with whether the model itself can meet the logical tri-consistency. As for the question of logical tri-consistency, we will discuss it tomorrow.

Questioner: Sir, please tell me, what is understanding? What is rationality? What is sensuality? What is logic? What is theorem, object, phenomenon, form, and validity? After listening to these two lectures, I am a little bit confused about what is what and what is truth. How many important philosophical concepts are different from the ones we are used to? Can you tell us more? Thank you!

Mr. Dongyue: I think you got the flavor of the class. If you feel that all your past concepts, which are called self-explanatory things actually become problems, it marks your entry into the realm of philosophical thinking. But I really can't give you all the answers to your questions in this class, in this Q & A. For even if you read my *A Unified Theory of Evolution* intensively, you will only get answers to some of the questions unless you use it to make profound and larger deductions. Here I will only explain a little bit about one question: What is meant by object? What is meant by objective body? Once we say object, we generally think that object is objective body, that there is no difference between the two, but in fact, we are very wrong. The objective body is the thing that existed before our subjective perceptions covered it, that is, the thing that is not within the scope of our perceptions is called the objective body. An object that is covered by our perception, or distorted by our perception, is called an object. I explain this one example just to show you that any foundational concept, any self-evident concept that you think is unproblematic, is actually in need of proof. If you read my *A Unified Theory of Evolution,* I will also discuss in detail in it what the difference between object and objective body is, in three separate discussions. Of course, the prerequisite is that you are interested in reading the relevant chapters of the second volume, *The Philosophy of Mind,* of the book *A Unified Theory of Evolution*. But I think it is very good for you to ask questions like this, because it is a sign that you are willing to explore what you used to consider unproblematic, and only when you enter this state will your mind be stretched and you will start to mobilize your intellectual activity again, although it is the misfortune of human beings to mobilize their intellectual activity on a large scale. Good! Do you have any more questions?

Questioner: Sir, a question has been puzzling me for weeks, and my confusion is about reductionism and holism. I come from a chemistry background myself, so reductionism always made sense to me, until I started researching and thinking about it systematically about a month ago, and found holism. Reductionism is a layer-by-layer deconstruction, and holism goes back to looking at the connections between each element, which also seems to make sense, and then I was exposed to the first cause. In particular, I would like to ask you, sir, is there any relationship between first cause, reductionism and holism? Or do they have nothing to do with each other?

MR. DONGYUE: You have raised a very troublesome question. After Einstein's theory of relativity was published, he once had a major argument with Bohr, one of the founders of quantum mechanics, who proposed probabilism, while Einstein proposed reductionism or determinism. From the point of view of quantum mechanics, things are probabilistic; from the point of view of Einstein and previous scientific and philosophical thinking, everything is deterministic and reductionist. This issue has been debated so far without end between Einstein and Bohr, between relativity and quantum mechanics. As far as the history of human thought is concerned, causality, reductionism and determinism, to a large extent, express the state of completion and the state of formation of a theory and an idea. I am not saying that it is the truth, but emergentism, holism, occurrenism, etc., are usually expressed in theory as a study that is not yet complete, or a theory that is not yet finished. So in a way, looking at quantum mechanics today seems to overwhelm relativity for the time being, but in fact even Schrödinger admits that quantum mechanics is not yet complete. So this is the only way I can answer the question you asked.

But I would like to add that no matter what the theoretical doctrine is, what is expressed in the general outline of its model of thought is a human perceptual defect, not a human reaching the discovery of truth. The key issue here is that if your perceived defect is inevitable, then you are not trying to overcome this defect, but to achieve a cultural maintenance effect in this defective model, or to achieve the correctness of the theoretical model, not in achieving its truthfulness and lack of defect. Let me give you an example, when I talk about everything being decaying, when I talk about the degree of existence being a decaying quantity, yet I cannot answer why everything is decaying to begin with. Although I can take the law of entropy in physics to express my correspondence with it in my *A Unified Theory of Evolution*, no one has been able to answer the question of why entropy is increasing so far. Then as the amount of information increases, the logical pole of this problem will move forward and the problem may be solved, but even if the problem is solved, the next limit boundary of the logical model will still be formed. The critical point at which any logical pole drifts is yet another blind spot, and this is the hollowness flaw that Gödel's law is intended to express. But even if a theory is falsified, if it was originally correct on a large scale, then the entire phenomenal world it reveals does not disappear, even though it changes in the way it is explained. This is the reason why any theory that has ever been correct is of great academic value.

Questioner: Sir, I just had a question that I didn't understand. The formal logic, dialectical logic and ideal logic we are discussing are all precise logical systems, is the ideal logic model your creation? If so, what are the other models of logic in the world today? What is the place of this ideal logic model in your system of thought?

Mr. Dongyue: About logic is a very complicated topic, and we try to avoid logic discussion in these two days of class. I had to discuss a little bit of logic of understanding and ideal logic this afternoon, and it was really a topic that I had to talk about if I wanted to make the dialectic and basic logic issues clear, and I will avoid such too complicated topics tomorrow. Logic is a very complex discipline that uses thought to investigate the state of thought itself. Aristotle originally created what he recognized as logic only as deductive logic, called the *necessary derivation*. Later on, the logical community gradually discovered that human logical forms go far beyond deductive logic, so inductive logic, dialectical logic, mathematical logic, semantic logic, and other logics arose. In my doctrine, I have only given a framework summary of the high-end logic of human reason in the second volume of *Philosophy of Mind*, in *A Unified Theory of Evolution*. I have not seen the same formulation by other scholars, but I have just made a little bit more of a cogent summary of the high form of logic than others, and that's all. But if you understand it, you will at least understand human logic in the broad sense, or the way it is called human perceptual property gain. What do these words mean? You do have to read *A Unified Theory of Evolution*. We are lecturing today on philosophical topics that are relatively new to us, and I am lecturing these lessons from my philosophical off angle, or from a high point of philosophical discussion, and I just want to give you the most basic account of what Western narrow philosophy really is. It certainly leaves too many questions for everyone, but if you listen to these two days of class, you can get a little taste of philosophy when you read those books from now on, then this class has a lot of value for you, a lot of gains. Because reading philosophy books is very difficult, it is purely logical deduction, and it uses and runs concepts in a way that is not in the realm of our daily life and work, so philosophy seems very obscure and deep. So why does Western philosophy discuss these strange questions? I am giving you an account of this most fundamental thing, so that you can find a sense of philosophy, and know what problems the unfolding of the philosophical state of mind actually confronts, or what problems human beings face when they mobilize the state of uncovering their wisdom to the utmost. Therefore, we should not seek the truth in this class, but the negation of the truth in this class, which is the real value of this class.

Good! That concludes our lesson for today.

Overview of the Western Philosophy (II)

A Historical Proposition: How *Cognition* is Related to *Being*

We spent a day yesterday focusing on the basic state of mind and the underlying philosophical thinking of the origins of ancient Greek philosophy. From yesterday's lecture, you should be able to understand that philosophical thinking is a unique system of thought.

We focus today on the difficult questions that have been discussed in recent classical Western philosophy.

I am by no means mistaken when I say that philosophical thinking is the underlying logic of scientific thinking. Please imagine how far-reaching avenue of thought has been opened for mankind by the philosophical logical extension of Euclid's *Geometry*. If we had studied geometry in secondary school, and instead of the current test-taking approach, where students just bury their heads in a bunch of arithmetic problems, we had followed the logic of Euclid's axiomatic system and taught them, what a sophisticated system we would have been taught and built up in the way of thinking and its models. Newton, Einstein, Leibniz, Spinoza, Russell, and others were all impressed by Euclid's *Geometry* when they read it as adolescents, and thus began their philosophical scholarship.

I make this point to show that philosophy may seem useless on the surface, but it is the underlying groundwork for thought. One's behavior, one's thinking, is governed by one's own underlying logical model. This thing determines the picture of the world that is presented in your cognitive representation. Your world picture, your world model, is a product of your thinking model, and the way you behave operates on your thinking model, your world model, or worldview model.

Please think about how important this training of the bottom of the mind is. Missing this thing, how much regret and lack will be brought about by only talking about science and technology at the application level.

Okay, I'll address one more issue. In addition to the Arab civilization, which played a role in transmitting the ideas of ancient Greece, there was also a direct line of succession, which I would like to briefly explain here.

Why does the West trace its cultural roots in historiography to the ancient Greek-Roman cultural system? It is because the former has had a profound and long-lasting influence on the culture of the latter.

Ancient Rome went through three eras. The early period was called the Age of Kings. The most simple way to understand the kingly era is that it is equivalent to the era of the clan or tribal confederacy. The second period of Ancient Rome was called the Roman Republican Age; it was only after B.C., marked by Julius Caesar, that Ancient Rome entered the Roman Imperial Age. During the early and middle periods of the Roman government, that is, during the Roman Republican era, the basic culture of ancient Rome was inherited from the ancient Greek culture. Therefore, the basic ideological atmosphere and even the basic political and social forms of the Roman Republican era were all Greek structures, including its bicameral democracy, noble senate, citizen's assembly, and the election system of consuls and tribunes, and so on.

The reason for the imperial era was the gradual expansion of the Roman Republic into the northern part of the Apennines, the Italian peninsula, which was under natural climatic conditions suitable for agricultural development. As soon as it entered into an agricultural structure, the republican system fell apart and the imperial era began.

Due to this reason, the Roman Empire split in the 4th and 5th centuries AD. Later, when the Western Roman Empire fell, the Eastern Roman Empire moved to the area around present-day Turkey to establish its own capital. The famous ancient city of Istanbul in present-day Turkey, which was called Constantinople, became the center of the Byzantine Empire. It was here that some of the ideas and documents of ancient Greece were preserved, and this became a second channel and source for the later Renaissance, when ancient Greek ideas and documents were revived. This topic is intended to add to the institutional qualities of agricultural civilization, the rupture of ancient Greek culture, and the multi-source relationship of the Renaissance.

Today, we will focus on the fundamental question of the relationship between *knowing* and *being*, which was explored in modern Western classical philosophy. Classical philosophy began in the early 17th century with Descartes, continued through the 18th and 19th centuries, and finally came to an end with Hegel. This period refined the basic logical and methodological system of scientific thinking, and more importantly, it explored issues far beyond the scope of ancient Greek thought, and far beyond the limits of the general scientific horizon, thus building a basic system of intellectual weapons for the foundation of the future post-scientific culture of mankind, including the critique of science.

Therefore, understanding today's lesson will not only help you to understand the basic spirit of the scientific era, but will also serve as some kind of inspiration for the underlying deconstruction of scientific systems and the construction of the foundations of the future post-scientific era.

The ancient Greek era was devoted to the pursuit of ontology, but they were never able to remove the background of mental projection in the process of pursuing ontology. From Pythagoras' system of number theory, to Plato's theory of ideas, to Euclid's theory of forms, the pursuit of ontology and the pursuit of the mind were actually presented as one system. It was not until the expression of Aristotelian formal logic that the question of the mind became an important topic of inquiry. At this stage, the question of the mind has come to the fore, but not to the foreground. But it already implies a strange set of problems, namely, the confusion between *knowing* and *being*. For when you say *being*, you are talking about the *being* in perception or *being* projected in the mind, and when you summarize the *being* and the *reality*, you find that any of your allegations and conclusions are nothing more than a conceptual model.

Then the question of *knowing* and *being,* in this state of confusion, without distinguishing between them, has led to the emergence of some fundamental problem. Thus, from the ontology of direct thinking about objects to the epistemology of mental reflection, that is, to the investigation of the prescriptive nature of the mind itself, is the basic characteristic of classical philosophy.

It involves such basic questions, almost common-sense questions, but they are extremely difficult. For example, what is *knowing*? Where does *being* lie? How can you prove *being*? Because all your proofs are logical proofs, how do you know that your logical proofs point to the *reality*? What is the content of *knowing*? What is the momentum of *knowing*? How do you express the extension of *knowing*? These and other fundamental questions constitute the major issues and questions of modern classical philosophy.

So, let's start again with ancient Greece. As you know, the first person who introduced the concept of *being* in ancient Greece was Parmenides. Parmenides, of the Elea school, proposed *being* and *non-being*.

What is the *non-being* he refers to? Philosophical opinion is divided. The *being* is an extension of the *being* that is sought after behind a certain illusion. The what does *non-being* refer to, which constitutes a serious question. Therefore, the *non-being* of Parmenides can be interpreted from different perspectives, one of which is that it is an intuitive representation of the mental world, for the ancient Greeks were inquiring about the *reality* behind this false appearance and considered that thing as *being*. Zeno, a disciple of Parmenides, made four famous paradoxical deductions about what is *being,* including what is *one,* what is *many,* what is *motion* and *stillness,* in other words, what is *space* and what is *time,* he made a series of bizarre deductive arguments.

I need to mention here a really amazing person by the name of Gorgias. He actually came up with the famous three propositions in ancient Greek times. He said first, nothing exists. No matter exists, because what you call *being* is an idea behind an appearance or an illusion. He then goes on to make a corollary, he says that even if something exists, there is no cognition. For what your perception has reached is only the false image or phenomenon. He goes on to make a third expression, he says that even if there is cognition, which is beyond words, that is, unable to express with words.

These three words of his predicted the three major processes of Western philosophy. First, ontology. What exactly is *being*? Is there a *being*? Secondly, epistemology. Even if there is a *being*, how do you identify it? This is precisely the central difficulty of epistemology in the second stage of classical Western philosophy. Third, there is the semantic turn in contemporary or modern philosophy. That is, since the way we perceive the world is a logical system of subjective perception, and the realization of this logical system is expressed in a system of linguistic structures, which has its own intrinsic regulations, this leads to the operation of language beyond the ties of logic, and to its own independent operation, which leads to the disturbance of the logical system. This is the problem discussed in the contemporary philosophical semantic turn. Looking back at Gorgias third word, even if there is cognition, the cognition is beyond words, is inexpressible.

It is indeed very surprising that Gorgias, in the ancient Greek era, should have predicted the direction of the entire history of Western philosophy and the formulation of fundamental questions. Without seeing the whole process of Gorgia's argument, we can see from Gorgia's statement that the germ of ancient Greek philosophy contains all the genes and seeds of the subsequent evolution of Western philosophy, and that the subsequent philosophical developments are merely extensions and iterations of ancient Greek philosophical thought.

Moreover, we will find that as early as the time of Gorgias, philosophy had already expressed the tendency to drift away from *ultimate origin*, that is, from the inquiry of the origin of the world to the inquiry of perception, and from the inquiry of perception to the inquiry of language. This process formed the general trend of Western philosophy towards frivolity and superficiality. This is why in the 20th century, the famous philosopher Heidegger proposed to return to ancient Greece to inquire *being* again.

We are going to talk about Descartes, the first modern Western classical philosopher. Descartes, a 17th century French philosopher, was also a famous mathematician, physicist, physiologist, and mechanist. The coordinate system we use today, the plane right angle coordinate system and the oblique angle coordinate system, is the invention of Descartes, so it is called Descartes coordinate system. It is Descartes who invented analytic geometry.

We can thus see Descartes' fundamental intellectual strength in natural science and philosophy. As I have said repeatedly, philosophy and science are inseparable, and once they are separated, once they are divorced from the natural sciences, there is no way to explore philosophy, no way to develop philosophical ideas, and it becomes very difficult to understand philosophy in the true sense of the word.

Descartes was a Frenchman, and France was still in an autocratic era, more than 100 years before the French Revolution. Descartes' real academic career therefore began after his exile to the Netherlands. The Netherlands was the first place in the West to complete the bourgeois revolution and establish a capitalist system. It broke away from the era of Spanish rule and completed the Netherlandish Revolution in 1609 after almost 50 years or so of war, which was much earlier than the bourgeois revolution in England in 1640.Thus the Netherlands, in the early or first half of the 17th century, had a relatively relaxed political and cultural climate. This is one of the reasons why Descartes, a Frenchman, finally managed to make a difference after his exile in the Netherlands.

The most general statement of Descartes' philosophy is called *dualism*. The term *dualism* means that Descartes believed that the world needs to be explored in two directions. He says that the world has a *material entity* and a *mental entity*. He said that the property of the material entity is extension, which means time and space. He says that the property of the mental entity is thought.

Descartes then discusses the question, whether the world as we know is the birth of mental entities or the reflection of material entities? He goes so far as to start from such a fundamental point that he says that when he finds himself dreaming, his dreams are so real that he cannot perceive in the least that his dream is an illusion, and when he wakes up, he finds that the dream is just a dream. So he made a follow-up question, he said how do I know that I am not in another dream state when I wake up? So the corroboration of our perception itself is a question.

When I talk about this, you should immediately recall an account by Zhuangzi in the pre-Qin era, which is the famous story *Zhuang Zhou Dreams of a Butterfly*. In his book, Zhuangzi said that he dreamed at night that he was a butterfly, "so vivid as a butterfly", and when he woke up, he found that he had become Zhuang Zhou, "so real as Zhou". In other words, when he dreamed, he felt that he was a realistic butterfly, and when he woke up, he found that he was a realistic Zhuang Zhou. So, he asked, "Did the butterfly become Zhuang Zhou, or did Zhuang Zhou become the butterfly? He was already confused about who he was.

The allusion of "Zhuang Zhou dreaming of a butterfly" is almost identical to the beginning of Descartes' discussion on *knowing* and *being*. The difference lies in the fact that, while Zhuang Zhou dreamed of the butterfly as an amusing joke or witty argument, it ends abruptly and does not go on to probe; Descartes, on the other hand, starts to ask questions and queries, to probe into the underpinnings of *beings* in perception. This is the difference between a system of metaphysics that is based on layers of inquiry, deep investigation, and precise logical proof, and one that merely swirls around the surface of the problem.

Descartes' doubts about his own perception inevitably led to a big problem, as he says, it becomes very difficult for me to prove the existence of anything, because since what I call *being* is *being* that happens in the perceptual system, and my perceptual system itself is erratic and difficult to prove. How do I know that my inquiry into *being* is valid and reliable, given that my perceptual system itself is indeterminate and difficult to verify? So he made the famous assertion: *I think, therefore I am*. In other words, Descartes believed that I am at a loss for other external inquiries, and the only *being* I can confirm is *my thinking*. That is, my thought is there, my skepticism is there, and the only *being* that I can confirm is this thing. This can be said to be the only non-logical and valid direct proof of what *being* is.

Notice that this is a very complicated statement. He says "I think, therefore I am", which many people interpret as Descartes saying "I think, therefore I am, my flesh is". Make no mistake! Descartes' "I think, therefore I am" is focused on "I think", so it can only prove that my mind is *being*. Many people interpret this as "I am", including my physical body as a material entity, but this is not correct. Because if you read Descartes' original text, what he discusses is how I can prove that my mind is *being* and later I can also implicate that my body is *being*.

He specifically discussed a brain tissue called the pineal gland, located near the thalamus. He says that this area produces "mind-body sympathy", which then leads to the presence of my bodily substance. Therefore, we must pay attention to Descartes' "I think, therefore I am", the "I am" (*being*) only means "thinking" is *being*, whichistheonlyvalidproofof*being*Thisistheonlyvalidproofof*being*.

We should also note that Descartes' expression is called "I think therefore I am", and the English translation brings out the *therefore*. The meaning of therefore is "because of, so", so this translation is problematic, or perhaps Descartes' expression is problematic. Because "I think" is not the cause of "I am", the word *therefore* is a faulty translation. His expression should be "I think I am" or "I think that I am".

Descartes confirmed the existence of thought through the valid proof of "I think I am", but he could not deny the existence of the external world, or he could not exclude the existence of the external world in his intuition, so he had to go through a series of logical derivations to gradually prove the existence of external objects.

Lostness of Both *Cognition* and *Being*

Descartes makes the observation that the central part of our knowledge is *innate ideas*. He then goes on to say that we have two channels of access to knowledge, one called *ideas of the senses* and one called *ideas made by the mind*.

Descartes' *innate ideas* was severely criticized because, in the view of materialistic reflectionism, it was complete nonsense. Later, Kant's effective "a priori" proof proved the validity of Descartes' unfolded *innate ideas*.

Kant's *a priori intuitive form* and *a priori logical form* are in fact the proof versions of Descartes' unexplored *innate ideas*, which shows that Descartes had actually touched on some fundamental depths of the problem when he explored the epistemological issue, or *mind* or *knowing* as a separate issue, but the system of argumentation had not yet been developed.

Descartes' dualism, then, necessarily brings up a problem. Please think about this problem in purely logical terms and do not discuss it intuitively. I have repeatedly emphasized that we human beings use thought, especially today or at the end of civilization, you have to get rid of the senses as much as possible and develop a purely logical way of thinking.

Why? Please think about what our sensory system is for. It is the basic way of cognition and survival maintenance when we lived in the jungle back then. For example, if you go to the African savannah, lions, hyenas, wolves and leopards surround you, what makes you survive at this time? You rely on your ears and eyesight. Your eyes have to be very bright, as we all know, the animals' vision is much sharper than ours, when you have not seen the animal, the animal has long seen you, when you see the animal, the animal is ready to pounce on you; your ears should be able to hear the small sounds in the forest, the animal's latent behavior may pose a threat to you; your sense of smell has to be able to detect the scent of other animals in the downwind or even upwind direction, or even the odor of an individual of the same kind, otherwise the act of courtship or even the motivation to find food cannot be implemented. So what do you use to survive in the jungle? With the senses, with sensual acuity.

But when you gradually get out of the jungle hunting era, then the survival situation changed greatly. The so-called age of civilization, that is, nature no longer provides humans with any means of survival, all the means of human life have to be prepared by humans themselves. By the time we enter this era, the ability of human beings has risen to the top of the entire biological food chain, and human beings no longer have to devote their main energy to dealing with the threats in the jungle, but have to project their main energy on understanding and transforming the world. What will be the process? --the process of sensory degradation! Thus widening the margin of lushness of thought. This is why the human beings today have a tendency to blur their vision, a general degradation of hearing, and a basic disappearance of the sense of smell.

So, when you enter the realm of survival where you have to deal with a huge amount of information, you have to get rid of the senses. You have to operate your perceptual and mental systems on a different level than your sensual intuition, in order to reach the more complex conditions of existence, which is why human beings resort to philosophical thinking in order to mobilize the potential of their intellectual reserves.

So on this basis, when we speak of esoteric philosophical thoughts, please always take care to get rid of the bondage of intuition and enter the realm of purely logical and rational thought.

Then the dualism opened by Descartes will logically present a problem: since you can only prove that your *knowing* is there, and since all your *being* is in *knowing*, you do not have another channel to reach the external object than perception, what makes you say that there is an external object? That is, Descartes' dualism, although for the first time from the beginning of classical philosophy, mind as an object, called the entity of the mind, was presented as a positive subject to be pursued and explored, it immediately generated a serious problem, that is, if what we call *being* is only *being* in perception, and perception is a closed channel, and we do not have another channel outside of perception to reach the external object, then on what basis do you say that the external object exists? How do you know that what you call *being* is not a purely mental derivation? This, of course, constitutes a serious doubt in terms of pure logic. In other words, Descartes' proof of *being* is a *dogmatic judgement.*

When I say the word *dogmatic judgement*, you should think of Hume. I am developing a problem-oriented lecture on the basic ideas of classical philosophy, because only in this way can you understand how their thinking unfolds.

Thus, in Descartes' dualistic state of "half materialism and half idealism", the next clear answer must be brought out, which is Beckley's *subjective idealism*. If you do not study philosophy deeply, you will think that Berkeley is a complete madman. When Berkeley put forward his doctrine, he was widely recognized as a psychopath even in Western Europe, which is rich in philosophical ideas. Berkeley proposed this discussion by saying that I cannot prove the existence of external objects. Based on Descartes' question and his understanding of Newtonian optics, Berkeley directly proposed that "things are a collection of ideas". Since Descartes' dualism can only prove the element of *knowing*, there is no way to prove the element of material entities. If I say that what you call *being* is *being* in perception, please note that it is not for Descartes individually, but for all of us, what you call *being* is *being* in your perception. Remember what I said. So, how do you know that what you call external object is not a collection of your perceptions?

Thus Berkeley makes the famous triple assertion that *things are collections of ideas*; that *to exist is to be perceived*; and that *objects and sensations are originally the same thing*. Berkeley's expression is so extreme that he completely denies the existence of an external world, but it holds logically.

Thus Beckley's proof that *knowing* cancels out *being* became a philosophically valid proposition, thus constituting a serious shock to the English empiricist Hume. It was only when Hume came across Beckley's doctrine that he suddenly realized that what we call *knowledge* was a serious void. We have no idea what *knowledge* is or what *knowing* is. Because we generally think that our knowledge is knowledge of external objects. But Beckley effectively proves that what you call *knowledge* has nothing to do with external objects, or at least you can't prove that it has anything to do with external objects.

In the era of classical philosophy, there were two schools of thought: the empiricist school, represented by England, and the rationalist school, represented by Germany. The so-called *empiricism* is the idea that perception is the experience of external objects. The so-called rationalist school, which is expressed in the German series as the philosophical problem or the problem of *knowing* and *being*, is supposed to be a purely logical process of proof.

Hume was thoroughly empiricist, very thoroughly. Empirically speaking, it is materialism on the surface, that is, all our knowledge comes from the experience of external objects, or the perception of external objects, which is typical materialism. But please note that it is precisely the typical materialism that must deduce typical idealism, and that the two are the same thing, or are somehow necessarily related in their logical deduction.

Since then Hume has posed a series of questions. Hume says that since our knowledge is nothing but the product of experience, how can there be so many non-empirical elements widely gathered in knowledge? As we all know, Locke once proposed the *blank tablet theory*, that is, our mind is like a blank tablet, and the projection and writing of external objects on the blank table constitute the content of our mind and our system of knowledge, which is a typical materialist formulation. In Locke's formulation, it is obvious that he brings out a serious problem, that is, he thinks that our perception is a vacuum of orifices, and that perception is not prescriptive, which is the essence of the *blank tablet theory*, which is obviously an extremely superficial view, and an obviously wrong view.

When I spoke yesterday of reflection, of the prescriptive nature of the senses, of sight, of hearing, and of the metrical nature of induction, deduction, logic, etc., you know that perception is not a blank empty, not a blank tablet, not a vacuum of access. Then even if one insists that there is some truth in materialism and blank tablet theory, even if one traces it from Hume's empirical perspective, if all our knowledge is an empirical reflection of objective things, we still need to ask where the non-empirical elements of knowledge come from? Hume, for example, discusses the puzzling problem that holonomic judgments cannot be derived from idiosyncratic judgments.

Strictly speaking, judgment is divided into single judgment, special judgment, and general judgment. I will only make the most abbreviated elaboration here. What does it mean? What we see in our experience is figurative. You can only see a big horse, a small horse, a yellow horse, a red horse, a male horse, a female horse in your experience, but have you ever seen a *horse* that does not have these empirical properties? *Horse* is a conceptual abstraction, *horse* is an all-inclusive judgment, but there is no such *horse* in experience.

So where did you get your *horse* from? Where did you get your all-inclusive judgment? Because all of our human knowledge must be based on a series of allometric judgments. That is, we have to find the universality of everything in order to construct knowledge. Please imagine which of the knowledge contained in every sentence you speak is a single judgment and a special judgment? When you say that a horse is an animal, from the concept of *horse* to the concept of *animal*, they are all nominal judgments, things that are not found in experience. You can only find a specific monkey, a specific horse, a specific crocodile, a specific elephant, but you can never find an animal. The word *animal* is an all-embracing judgment.

But it is such a statement, which hardly constitutes knowledge: "A horse is an animal", that does not hold in experience. Thus

Hume argues that all our knowledge has nothing to do with experience, and that what we acquire empirically are only figurative elements, while our knowledge is universal elements, a collection of all-embracing judgments.

So, how are those things outside of experience in what we usually call knowledge derived and constructed?

Hume goes on to explore one more issue in pure logic when he says that all our human knowledge is based on the chain of thought of the law of cause and effect. Think about it, isn't it true that a tree grows because it has seeds? The seed is the cause of the tree. A man is born because he has a mother, and the mother was the reason he was able to be born. Then again, genes are the cause of all biological traits or biological phenotypes. In short, everything you know is constructed on a sequence of thinking about the law of cause and effect. But notice that there is no law of cause and effect in your experience, there is only you in your experience, there is only your mother, there is only the tree in your experience, there is only the seed. But the whole process of "the seed is the predecessor of the tree" does not exist in your experience, and the causal relation you are talking about does not exist in experience, especially in the experience of individual judgment.

The fact that all human knowledge is constructed on a causal sequence makes Hume deny the basis of all human knowledge construction from a purely materialistic and purely empirical point of view. His denial and questioning, which is called *skeptical philosophy*, is based on precise facts.

Hume goes on to ask what we mean by *cause and effect*. Empirically, it is simply the repeated presentation of a thing in temporal and spatial order. That is, one thing always comes before another thing in time and space, and then another thing occurs, so you set up the relationship between these events, non-empirically and subjectively, as causality. But this setting is not valid, because there is a problem here: you have not yet figured out what *time* and *space* mean.

Please note that these things that we take for granted, the so-called *self-evident things*, are the very things that philosophers seek to investigate. Hume suggests that if what we call causal connections do not themselves present themselves directly in experience, but are merely expressed as recurrent presentations arranged backwards and forwards in space and time, then we must ask what time and space are. If we do not explore this question, not only will the law of cause and effect not hold, but the entire knowledge structure will collapse. And are time and space real? What exactly is it? Is it a mental phenomenon? Or is it an objective being? Hume raises a series of doubts, a very thoroughgoing skepticism, but one that is built into an extremely solid logical inquiry.

You should know that in our daily life, the statement of cause and effect is mostly confusing, and the cause-effect relationship is credulous and shallowly compared in experience. For example, in terms of temporal relationship, you can express it this way, and even the ancients did express it this way, saying that the rooster crowing is the cause of the sun rising. The rooster crows at 4 or 5 o'clock every dawn, and the sun rises after the rooster crows. In terms of time sequence, the rooster always comes first, does this cause-and-effect relationship hold? Logically you would think it is ridiculous, but in the empirical sequence it holds.

Russell made an even more interesting analogy when he said that a man kept a flock of turkeys and came to feed them every day on time, and it seemed to the turkeys that the owner was the reason for the food, but they didn't think that one day the owner would come with a shotgun or a knife. ......That's why Wittgenstein asked the question, Hume asked the same question. "The sun rises in the east" is only a hypothesis, because you say that "the sun rises in the east" is an empirical product, and an empirical product of induction, but induction can never be exhausted, so "the sun rises in the east" is only a hypothesis, an unsupportable hypothesis. We know today that this statement is true because the sun will become a red giant in 4 billion years and it will never rise from the east again, as it will fall straight off until it melts the earth. Isn't that the case? So the skepticism discussed by Hume proposes that at the empirical level we can never gain knowledge, and clearly proves that the inductive method is invalid.

And it is obvious that all of our human knowledge was established on the basis of induction, so that the whole edifice of human knowledge collapsed, because Hume's proof was valid, and this was the beginning of agnosticism. Thus, Hume suggests that the previous investigations into the law of cause and effect, into the construction of universal knowledge, and even into what *real-*

ity itself is, are all merely subjective judgments. This argument of Hume's shook Kant to his core.

Peak of Classical Philosophy and Its Legacy

We turn briefly to Kant below.

Immanuel Kant, the pinnacle of modern Western classical philosophy. Kant never studied philosophy too seriously until he was 40 years old. He taught in universities, teaching mostly natural science classes. He taught for more than 20 years, never realizing that knowledge itself was actually a problem. He happened to read Hume's work and was greatly shaken. He found that after 20 years of teaching all kinds of knowledge, what he called *knowledge* was itself a loophole, a doubt, a fundamental confusion. This prompted Kant to think deeply about what knowledge is and how our human cognition is constructed, and other philosophical questions.

He had to start, of course, with the basic doubt raised by Hume, which is what is space? What is time? For Hume had argued that the empirical perception of space and time could not be clarified, that it was merely a background representation of the successive occurrence of things. Kant therefore asks what is meant by time and space, what is meant by causal connection, what is meant by all-embracing judgments, where they come from, and how they form the cognitive structure ......, After repeated reflection and rigorous reasoning, he finally achieves his system of *a priori philosophy*.

To speak of Kant, we must first speak of three sets of words, or three sets of concepts.

First, experience. Please note that the term *experience* in philosophy is slightly different from the term *experience* in our daily life. By *experience* in our daily life, we mean the accumulation of knowledge in general practical activities. The original meaning of *experience* is not the same, it means that we use our senses to know the object or use our senses to acquire the elements of the object. For example, the senses of sight, hearing, smell, taste, touch, and so on.

Second, *a priori*. What is meant by *a priori*? Something that is prescribed before experience is called *a priori*. That is to say, the thing that has already prescribed your mode of experience and system of experience before your experience has occurred is called *a priori*.

Third, *transcendence*. It refers to those pursuits that are "beyond the boundaries of experience", that is, non-phenomenal knowledge that can only be achieved through reason, which does not have a specific empirical object like knowledge, and thus necessarily forms *idea*, which is called *transcendental*.

Let me make these three concepts clear. Hume demonstrates that *experience* cannot lead to a derivation from causal to holistic judgments. There is no direct element of causal connection in experience, and the inductive method does not hold. Then, of course, Kant must discuss what our *experience* is. Where does the force behind our connection to *experience* come from? Where is our all-embracing judgment, our causal judgment, all these things, that is, what is the foundation of knowledge, outside of *experience*? He proposes *a priori*! Before your experience you are prescribed by subjective endowments. We perceive light energy as light, which is an *a priori* prescription; we perceive wavelengths as colors, which is a model of vision that is prescribed before we open our eyes.

Kant, who did not have this amount of information, actually deduced that our perception is *a priori prescriptive*. That is, a "prescriptive metric of experience" or a "prescriptive platform of ways of experiencing" is shaped long before your *experience* occurs. He then suggests that time and space are merely *a priori intuitive forms*. Please note the word *form*, once I use this word, we will immediately go back to the concept of the ancient Greek use of this word. In other words, there is no way to discuss whether time and space exist objectively or not.

Kant said, I only know that if my experience is to happen, it must have a platform. This is my language, not exactly Kant's original words, because they are too complicated to say it clearly, so I change it to modern language for your understanding now. Then my *perception* and *experience* itself must have a carrier, a platform, if it is to happen, and this platform is time and space, which are our *a priori intuitive forms*. Time and space are our *a priori intuitive forms*. He said that the so-called causal connection and the so-called all-embracing judgment come from the *a priori category stipulation*.

The word *category* seems to be no different from *scope* in our everyday language, but in philosophy it is a special term. The first person to introduce the concept of *category* was Aristotle, and Kant explored it further. Kant said that our holistic judgments and causal connections are constructed on *a priori categories*. He divided the categories into 4 groups of 12, so I will not expand on each of them, I will just give an example. For example, if I say, "Bush Jr. must be the president of the United States," you will find it very problematic. But if I say "2+2 necessarily equals 4", you will have no problem on hearing it. There is no such thing as 2 in the world, 2 is a purely abstract symbol; there is no such thing as addition and multiplication in nature, but why do you have no doubt when I say 2+2=4, 2×2=4?

This comes from the derivation of the purely logical *categories*, that is, the *a priori categories* of "necessary, contingent, and probable", which are constructed in the innate logical model of *prior experience*, bringing you such a lineage of thinking results. So when you hear "Bush Jr. must be the president of the United States", you think there is a problem. It is not acceptable in your *a priori category*. 2+2=4 is not in the world, but it holds in your a priori category. Kant goes on to deduce that where do your logical forms and logical procedures come from? It still comes from *a priori prescription*, which he calls *a priori logical forms*, a separate set of concepts above the empirical level of logical prescriptions.

I just talked about time, space, and experience, which are called *a priori intuitive forms*. Everything that you can logically organize, including causal connections, is *a priori logical form*. In other words, this is the perceptual prescriptiveness given *before experience*. He says that *experience* only provides information about phenomena, but does not directly provide the connecting elements behind the phenomenal information. Therefore, the world we perceive is always the phenomenal world. What we call existence is always a system of phenomena in perception. Where is the *objective object itself*, he says? On the other side! He gave a self-coined term, *the object itself*, also called *the object in-itself*. He said that the objective world itself, which is beyond the reach of our perception, is not within the scope of our direct perception, but is transcendent, which is the famous *transcendent realm*.

The *phenomenal world* and the *thing-in-itself* are thus divided, and the proof of *agnosticism* is thus reached. As I said earlier, the dominant idea in Western culture is *agnosticism*. Please consider isn't it that Kant's doctrine is the most effective proof of human knowledge? Your knowledge is not a reflection of the external world. The external world only provides you with some fragmented information, but how to organize this information is determined by your subjective prescriptive nature itself before you receive the information. This is what I was talking about earlier, that perception is not set for truth, but set for survival. What is your *a priori property* given by? It is given by the adaptive requirements of biological evolution to maintain your survival.

Isn't it so? This seems to be a very simple common sense today, but in the time of classical philosophy, it needed to be proved layer by layer by precise logical deduction.

And Kant goes on to raise an even more problematic issue, saying that we humans always have a tendency to mobilize our intelligence or reason to the extreme. But once you mobilize your intelligence or reason to the extreme, you will inevitably seek to reach an absolute, indivisible, infinite and eternal transcendental as a result of your thinking.

When you think about it, Kant is spot on with this statement. We in general must think that the existence of the world is absolute. The ancient Greeks believed that behind the illusion of the world, there must be a stable, indivisible, eternal and continuous *true being*. For example, in Newton's time, people unconsciously thought that the law of gravity was absolute, infinite, and all-encompassing. Today, in the age of relativity, we think that Einstein's doctrine and his cosmology are absolute and all-inclusive. People always seek to reach a consummate, absolute, and infinite idea when they mobilize their reason and intelligence to the utmost.

But Kant says that our *experience* is always limited. Your *experience* does not unfold in the infinite at all, the infinite has nothing to do with *experience*. Think about it, you can see concrete objects, but can you see the infinite universe? You see a concrete person, a concrete table, a concrete star, a concrete sun. All you see are finite existents; experience unfolds only in a limited scope, and knowing operates only in a limited process. It is the infinite and the absolute that mobilizes reason to reach the ultimate pursuit. All *experience* and *perception* operate only in a relative system, but always pursue the infinite in the mobilization of the highest idea and the highest reason, which constitutes a major drawback of the use of reason.

Thus, Kant says, once humans enter this highly mobilized state of reason, they immediately become dichotomous. The so-called *dichotomy* or *antinomy* means that incompatible and contradictory conclusions are all valid, which eventually leads to the confusion of fundamental knowledge. It is evident that Kant was already aware of the drawbacks or limitations of human perception, experience, and its narrow logic at that time. And the higher human beings mobilized their reason, the more obvious this drawback and limitation became.

By reflecting on Hume's question, Kant was able to establish a system of *a priori* knowledge, so that for the first time mankind would know exactly what we call knowledge. What you call *knowledge* is never a mere reflection of external objects, but a combined system of external information and your subjective inherent perceptual prescriptiveness, or the *a priori prescriptive pattern*. Is this the case? It was not until Kant's *a priori theory* was proved that mankind knew for the first time what human knowledge was and what the structure of knowledge was. If you have not been mobilized and trained by the system of perception, the system of thought and the system of logic, what you receive is not called knowledge, but only information. If you take a flawed a priori perceptual system or a priori logical system to organize information, you can imagine what situation will arise. Humankind high end perceptive part is not in the surface of human manifest perception, it is only a potential that needs to be mobilized and trained for a long time, and the information processing system thus constituted is called *a priori organizing model*, which is called *knowledge*.

Therefore, it is important to separate *information* from *knowledge* here. By the way, let me correct a common misconception. People say that knowledge is endless, and what we know is just a drop in the ocean of knowledge. Zhuangzi has an expression, he said, "My life is finite, but knowledge is endless, devoting the finite life to endless knowledge, impossible." What he means is that my life is finite and knowledge is infinite, and to pursue infinite knowledge with a finite life is an impossible goal. This sounds like a statement that is acceptable to everyone... Wrong! Remember that knowledge is finite, and it is constructed with your a priori perceptual ability. And perceptual ability is a gradual thing that happens gradually, and knowledge is only enhanced to the extent that perceptual structure and perceptual ability are developed. Please do not confuse the endless information with the endless knowledge. And whether information is endless and infinite or not is something that needs to be traced and re-investigated.

What do we mean by information? Information is the sum of existence, a marginal dependence effect based on the process of differentiation of everything. In other words, if everything is not differentiated, there is no information. The weakening evolution of the universe is the process of differentiation, and the process of differentiation is the process of generating information. If the evolution of the universe is realized within a finite range of sustaining, then the total amount of information must also be finite. In this finite ocean of information, any person or species dealing with this information cannot and does not have to deal with the whole of this finite amount of information; the amount of knowledge he deals with must be given by his perceptual ability or a priori logic. Therefore, not only is knowledge finite, but information is also finite. It is therefore incorrect to say that the ocean of knowledge is infinite and that our knowledge is only a drop in the ocean of the unknown.

In short, understanding what knowledge is, understanding the relationship between knowledge and information, understanding the separation between the phenomenal world and the object itself, and understanding the conceptual distinction between object and objective body are the fundamental issues for us to establish *the knowledge about knowledge* in philosophical logic.

Let me briefly mention two more topics. When Kant proposes that the objective body is on the other side, and the object in-itself is on the other side, our perception only floats in the phenomenal world, and the original being of the world is unknowable, this makes an insurmountable gulf between *knowing* and *being*. It is important to realize that the recognition of this gap should be considered a significant progress. For in Berkeley and Hume, the existence of matter has been abstracted, the possibility of knowledge is in doubt, and even what *knowing* is a total void. So by Kant's development, it can be said that a series of significant achievements have been made. Then Kant says that what we have achieved by mobilizing intelligence and reason to the extreme is a dichotomy, an irreconcilable contradiction and paradox.

In order to deal with this problem, Hegel established his system of *mental phenomenology*. From recent classical philosophy and even ancient Greek philosophy, Hegel has clearly realized that what we human beings call *objective objects* or *systems of existence* are in fact only *mental existence* closed in the channel of perception. Therefore, we are not qualified to discuss whether there is existence beyond perception. This question is logically a pseudo-question, and there is no need to discuss it at all. Therefore, he proposes to return to the ancient Greek Plato's thesis that the origin of the world is an *absolute mind* that replaces or dissolves the unreachable external *absolute being*. The so-called *absolute mind* is also called *absolute idea*, which, to put it in a simple way, means that what you call the world is always the existence in your mental realm. This is something you cannot transcend, nor can you break its marginal limits. If we want to understand something and figure out what state it is in, we have to find its boundaries and then compare the conditions at both ends of the boundary to be able to distinguish its differing states. But the perceptual channel is completely closed, and you can't open the boundary of this perceptual channel, and the comparison of conditions at both ends of the boundary is destined to be impossible. Therefore, what you say about the world is always your mental world, which is absolutely right.

Accordingly, Hegel proposed that the *absolute mind* is the origin of the world, or reasonably speaking, at least what we humans call the world is always just an unopenable *absolute mind*. On this point, the core of Hegel's doctrine is established. Then what is the world? What is the object? What is what Descartes called a *material entity*? What is what we call *external being* in our intuition? How to bridge the gap drawn by Kant? Hegel thus presents the most primitive dialectic, saying that the *external object* is merely an *alienated presentation* of the *absolute mind*. You see this external transformation or alienated form of the *absolute mind* as an object, but in fact it is only a derivative reflection of the *entity of the mental idea* that governs everything. When you get to know it, it returns to the *absolute mind*, which is Hegel's usual explanation of *dialectic of positive, negative, and unity*.

What is the rational element of Hegel's philosophy? It is in the confirmation of the closure of perception, which is its rational element, that is, the core formulation of his idealism or idealism is valid, but it is precisely his dialectical formulation of "the alienation of the absolute idea into the existence of the external world" that is pure nonsense. That is why I say that if you really read Hegel, you will find that the rational elements of his philosophy are precisely the targets of our criticism. To understand Hegel, you must read Kant; to understand Kant, you must read Hume; to understand Hume, you must read Beckley; to understand Beckley, you must read the previous doctrine of dualism and Descartes; this is the basic line of thought of modern Western classical philosophy. This is the basic line of thought of the modern Western classical philosophy. In this way, to Kant and Hegel, the problem of *knowing* and *being* in classical philosophy seems to have been finished.

If you confirm that Kant is the high point, the problem of *knowing* and *being* is dealt with as a definite model of agnosticism. If you accept Hegel's statement, the dichotomy between *knowing* and *being* is completely dissolved by means of the *Absolute Mind.* This is the end of the discussion of the fundamental problem of *knowing* and *being.*

I am sure you are not satisfied with what I have said here, because obviously more questions follow. Where does our *knowledge* come from? What does it mean to be mental? Where is the origin of mind? What is meant by a priori stipulation? Why is it necessary to have a priori regulations? What are the a priori rules shaped by? If our *knowledge* is only a subjective setting within the closed channel of the mind, then why do we need this superfluous and unnecessary *knowledge*? And one more thing: Why does our knowledge work in practice? Questions such as these obviously become more serious problems. Unless you close your eyes to these questions, you can say that the questions of classical philosophy have been fully answered. This is why, at the end of the 19th century, a series of modern philosophies emerged in the West, represented by Kierkegaard. They no longer pursued the originality and spirituality of the world, they no longer asked these fundamental questions, which they believed had either been explored or were not explored at all. So they returned to the inquiry of the self, which is the typical of existentialist philosophy, which I would say originates from a fog and goes deeper into a loss.

As we all know, Heidegger's *Dasein* actually expresses the problematic turn of the *selfness of knowledge* and the *knowing of my-*

self. He does not investigate where the "*I* " comes from, nor does he investigate where the *knowledge* comes from. He sets up the starting point of all things in the beginning point of *determinate being* and the definite point of *determinate knowing*.

The word *Dasein*, which was called *determinate being* in classical German philosophy, was originally a questionable concept. Nowadays, it has become the starting point of the ultimate inquiry in modern Western philosophy, which is obviously a great regression, though it shows some kind of rationality in the logical argumentation of avoiding difficult points or blind spots.

Looking back at classical philosophy, *mental inquiry* and *epistemological inquiry* become a necessary *natural inquiry* and *ontological inquiry*. In other words, the "materialistic confrontation with objects" inevitably leads to the subsequent result of the "idealistic reflection on the mind". This process of inquiry establishes the basis of our *theory of knowledge*, the foundation on which the scientific system is built, and also the ideological weapon for the future post-scientific system, or scientific criticism. Although it is an unfinished inquiry, it is an important port of thought for tracing the basic line of thought of the present scientific age of mankind and for the future beyond the scientific age, and it is crucial to understand this.

Limitations of *Materialism, Idealism, and Agnosticism*

We talked earlier about the basic ideas of recent classical Western philosophy and its epistemological framework.

I am presenting this lesson in an extremely brief and not sufficiently precise rough comparison. But I hope that you are able to listen to the way these philosophers developed their ideas of proof, and that only by following this thread will you be able to understand the general approach and the ideological content of the discussion of problems in Western philosophy in recent times.

For example, Leibniz proposed the *windowless monad theory*, which is very difficult to understand. What is a *windowless monad*? Leibniz said that inorganic matter and plants also have knowledge, called micro-knowledge. Mimosa, for example, is a plant whose leaves can sense your touch, and when you touch it, the leaves will immediately contract, so Leibniz's statement is good. Not only plants are sentient, but inorganic matter is also sentient. Please think about what is meant by a molecule? Isn't it an electromagnetic induction relationship between an atom and another atom through the energy of the electron cloud of the outer shell, or electromagnetic recognition relationship or electromagnetic acquaintance relationship? Isn't this a kind of micro-sensing?

Leibniz also said that animals have a *sensual soul*, which is a very accurate statement. If we humans go back to the jungle, what do you do to survive? With sensuality, with a keen sense of sight, hearing, smell and so on. So he says that animals have a sensual soul, and this statement is valid. He says that the human self-consciousness is called *rational soul*, and this is also very accurate. When you get out of the jungle and enter the civilized age of thought construction, you have to shed your sensuality gradually and then build a purely rational logical mind, and he calls this thing the rational soul. Even then, he says, you still can't reach the origin of things, so he sets a higher mental summation at the top, called *the wisdom of God*. Please note that once I talk about God, please go back to the idea that Socrates saw God as the abode and channel of ultimate inquiry.

So, what is Leibniz talking about when he talks about *windowless monads*? The ancient Greeks deduced that everything is made up of one or several basic elements, without any practical basis. Today's physics proves that it is valid, and our whole world structure today is built on atomic physics, particle physics. But at the epistemological stage, what we call the world is the closed mental world in our perceptual channel, and the atomistic problem of course needs to be reinterpreted, so Leibniz proposed the *monadic theory*, which you can understand as follows: physical atoms become *mental atoms*, or material monads become *mental monads*. It is very difficult to interpret his ideas, and you can only understand that what he calls *monads* is actually *mental atomism*, which is the basic element of mind, if you build on the epistemological problems of classical Western philosophy. If what we call the world is only the mental world, then what are the basic elements of the mental world? This is, of course, a question that needs to be explored, and this is called *windowless monads*. By *windowless*, it means that the monads do not communicate with each other. That is, the micro-knowledge of plants, the sensual soul of animals, and the rational soul of human beings cannot communicate with each other. But they are internally harmonious and consistent, that is, they are progressively consistent in the final appearance, which is called *predetermined harmony*. You cannot read Leibniz's book if you do not understand the difference between existence as discussed in classical philosophy and existence as discussed in ancient Greece.

Let me give another example, Schopenhauer. When you read Schopenhauer's book, you must find it very obscure. He himself summarized two sentences: "The world is my will"; "The world is my appearance". What do they mean? Why is Schopenhauer's philosophy called *voluntarist* philosophy? It is because Schopenhauer discovered that all people, all living things, and even all inorganic things have a will that is driven, or more precisely, are driven by some kind of internal will that is uniformly enhanced and cannot be controlled by itself. Our system of perception, that is, our appearance of the world, is a secondary product driven by that willful desire that cannot be restrained.

So he says that philosophy in general is limited to the study of the level of perception and appearance, and does not look into the deeper grassroots force that drives the movement of appearance and perception, which is actually the will to survive. The will is something that you cannot control, but it is the driving force behind all your subjective abilities. He says that everything has a will, but that this will is constantly evolving and increasing. Then he says that the object-in-itself that Kant throws on the other side is actually the will, and he uses the existence of the will on the other side to drive the existence of perceptual appearances on the other side in order to bridge the gap between the Kantian phenomenal world and the object-itself, and therefore he thinks that he has made a major discovery, and therefore he especially despises the poor sermons of Hegel in dealing with the Kantian problem. Obviously, only if you understand Kant, can you understand Schopenhauer, and Schopenhauer's entanglement with Hegel. Schopenhauer's voluntarism unfolds a different paradigm of discussion. He gives our later aesthetic inquiry, including the revelation of the nature of beauty, a logical precursor for making inferences. For more on this topic, please read the chapters after chapter 104 of my *A Unified Theory of Evolution*.

What do I want to illustrate? the knowledge and intellectual expansion of human beings, from the ancient Greek inquiry into ontology to the mental exploration and epistemological analysis of modern classical philosophy, which has spread and broadened the whole picture of the human mental world.

When I talk about this, it is easy to create a serious misunderstanding that you will think I am an idealist. Make no mistake! I have repeatedly made it clear that idealism does not deal with one fundamental question - what is the mind? What is spirit? What is perception? Where do mind and perception come from? How does it really work? What is the momentum of its development? How does it shape its operational prescriptions? These are obviously questions that idealism cannot answer.

But you cannot criticize idealism in one way or another, because idealism clearly answers the major question that the human mental constitution and perceptual channels are not vacuums, but prescriptive. That is why I say that since Descartes, all materialists, i.e., materialists who criticize idealism, have long been philosophical amateurs - they no longer know what the philosophers of the age are actually exploring.

But I am by no means an idealist. Please pay attention to what materialism is, it evidenced that it had no sense of what *mind* is, and it does not even know that perception itself is prescriptive, and that perception itself is an object and subject of inquiry. This expresses the extreme naivete of materialism and the elementary stage of human wisdom. Please think about this: when a wolf sees a sheep, will it doubt whether this sheep is mental or material? A person who does not start thinking, who stays in the state of direct feeling like an animal, must be materialistic. If you ask an ordinary person or a peddler whether the world is material or spiritual, he will laugh at you for being mentally ill. So, materialism expresses itself as ignorance of mental and perception, as blindness to the fact that mind has its own regulations, which is the primary stage of materialism. But there is another stage of materialism, which is that you can only clarify what is the origin of the *mind* if you go deeper into the process of material evolution. What is the *mental phenomenon* all about? Why is it only a *property* of things and not an entity?

On this subject, please read my *A Unified Theory of Evolution.* What am I saying? I am telling you that I am not an idealist, although I have a high opinion of idealism, but I am not a materialist either, because all things contain perception and mind, mind is the property of things, and perception is the compensated property of all things. I will briefly discuss this topic later in the course.

Therefore, remember that the debate between materialism and idealism is meaningless. Because the early materialists, such as the ancient Greek natural philosophy, were not aware of the existence of *mind* at all, that is, they had no enemies, so nothing of the kind form argument. In the age of idealism, you are not qualified to identify the object if you have no understanding of mental prescriptions, so it is not necessary to argue, there is no premise for argument, and they were not even bothered to argue.

If we want to discuss the *mind-matter problem*, that is, *inductive (sense-response) properties* between *things and properties of things*, then they are exactly the same thing. Therefore, the debate between materialism and idealism is purely a pointless argument, and is a manifestation of the lack of understanding of the deeper connotation of each side.

Let's look at agnosticism. Agnosticism has an antecedent question that it does not answer, and that is, what is *knowledge*? The so-called *unknowability* is a tacit assumption that we should be able to acquire true knowledge. Since our knowledge is ultimately found to be unattainable, our knowledge floats on the phenomenal plane and our *truth* is always a distorted product of our *a priori forms of perception*. Therefore, it is considered *unknowable*. But if you listen to my lectures, I have repeatedly said that *knowledge* is not set for truth-seeking, but for survival. It is not for seeking *the truth of subject-object conformity*, it is for seeking existence and reality, that is, to seek for the reality of natural dependence, which has nothing to do with seeking truth. Seeking truth is a delusion, a meaningless fiction. If so, the problem of agnosticism is solved. For since *knowing* is not seeking truth, but seeking survival, and *knowing* does achieve the compensated effect of seeking survival, how can it be said to be *unknowable*?

So, I repeat, the flaw of agnosticism is that it tacitly assumes that *knowing* is a delusion of truth, and this is the fault of agnosticism. I also reiterate here that I am neither an idealist nor a typical materialist. While I hold idealism in high esteem, I also believe that idealism does not address the root of the problem by inquiring into "the origin of mind, perception, and spirit in general"; this origin can only be *matter*, although it is precisely this *matter* or the *decay of matter* that leads to the *properties of mind* or *perceptual obscuration*. There is a false default of truth-seeking under agnosticism, and so this so called *unknowability* is not grounded if this default is removed.

This is the actual situation of the three major philosophical schools. If you look at them from another high point, the differences between them will be dissolved, and they will even appear to be an evolutionary correlation of the same system.

Implication of Dynamic Genesis of *Cognition*

I will briefly explain the topic of what is *knowing*.

The discussion here is based on *A Unified Theory of Evolution*, but I have tried to keep it as brief as possible and still focus on the relationship between *knowing* and *being*. Descartes says that the world is dualistic: the property of the material entity is extension, and the property of the mental entity is thought. He sets the perception, the mental entity, and the object, the material entity, in a dichotomous relationship on parallel horizontal axes, and he does so on the basis of "I think, therefore I am". However, if I make the opposite proposition, "I think therefore he is" or "I think he is", this proposition is also valid. Please think about why there is "I think". If there is no object, if you are not a relative being, if you are an absolute being, do you need to *think*? Do you need to *perceive*?

Assuming that the world is *one* and *being* is *one*, such as the state of singularity, the universe is in the most primitive state of existence before differentiation, at this time everything is *one*, the only *one*, there is no other There is no other being. What is the result? This singularity state of energy has no properties, so physics calls it a singularity.

What does *singularity* mean? It means that it does not have any perceptible properties, or it does not have any properties. Because our perception is only the perception of the properties of the object. If a thing has no properties, it has no way to be perceived. In this case, you can't get any observable or verbal elements from it by any means, including physical, mathematical, and other scientific instrument interventions, i.e., it has no properties to present.

The singularity is the state with the highest degree of being, the point at which no compensation is required and properties do not occur at all. The evolution of things is a process of weakening and decay, and when things decay, weakening is differentiation, or in my book: weakening = differentiation = deterioration. Being is *one*, and gradual differentiation into existence is *many*, which is called *all things*. Any *many* is a part of *one*, or a remnant of being is *one*. Any mutilated part always has an inner urge to return to unity, which leads to the induction (*sense-response*) property, that is, it can only achieve the recognition and return of its own lost mutilated part through the induction property, which is called *dependence* or *dependent structure*.

There are many kinds of attributes, and the most basic attribute is the extended attribute. By *extended attribute*, we mean the properties of time and space. As you know, according to modern cosmology, the singularity state has no time and space. The next is the *induction (sense-response) property*, such as the initial differentiation of the proton and electron, then the electron to return to unity with the proton, with what way to do? It must be coupled with the proton's positive charge property by means of its own negative charge property, which is called electromagnetic induction in physics. It is actually the precursor of the later *perceptual property*. This is due to the fact that the higher the degree of being of matter, the lower the amount of property occurrence; the lower the degree of being of matter, the higher the amount of property compensation.

We can see from such a relationship that the initial singularity is, on the contrary, the most stable state of being. It therefore specifies a basic threshold of being, called the "universal constant of threshold of being". Without this threshold as a constant, the decay of the existence of matter would not be necessary to reach a compensation relation for the occurrence of properties. (For details, see the relevant section of *A Unified Theory of Evolution*)

The process of development and gain of perceptual attributes culminates in the compensation of perceptual attributes, which is the origin of the mind or mental source of human beings.

It is clear that mind is not an independent entity of being, and Descartes' formulation is wrong. For if "I think, therefore I am" is a proof, there is an unanswered question: Why is there "I think"? "I think" must be because there is a problem with "I am", it must be because "he is", and "I" is compatible with "he is". *I* and *he* are inseparable, *I* and *he* are a necessary dependency, and only then "I think" can happen, can occur. So, the converse is also true - "I think, therefore he is". In Leibniz's words, the lineage of "micro-knowledge, sensual soul, rational soul" is enhanced to reach a route of mental development: the evolutionary process of everything is the process of gaining inductive (*sense-response*) properties.

The decay of degree of being is an independent variable and the gain of degree of compensation is a dependent variable, which are inversely related. The so-called compensation is the attribute compensation or attribute gain. There are many kinds of attributes, such as extended attributes, which are spatial-temporal attributes; inductive attributes, which are later developed into perceptual attributes; dynamic attributes, which are later developed into freedom attribute; the structural properties, for example, later developed into social structures. The early structure of matter was extremely simple. The primordial singularity had no structure, and it was differentiation that led to the need for dependence and the achievement of structure. So the higher the form of existence, the more complex the structural state. They are all products of the compensatory gain that occurs accordingly with the process of decay of the degree of being.

If we focus only on the affective attribute of sense-response, this is the basic look that allows the philosophy of mind to unfold. From here it becomes clear that perception is prescribed by upper and lower limits, that is, perception is not arbitrary. For example, an electron senses a proton, its perceptive ability is called induction in physics, expressed as an extremely low, extremely weak state, and it can only sense a positive charge. And the perception limitation, that is, the limitation of not being able to really feel, is already shown in the moment when the induction property first occurs. For example, the electron sensing proton, as you know, orbits an electron around a proton, which is the number one element on the periodic table of chemical elements - hydrogen. The electron sensing proton, it will never know the other elements of the proton, such as it will not know the mass of the proton, the shape of the proton, the color of the proton, it can only use its subjective sensing property, that is, a negative charge to sense the corresponding sensible attribute of the proton, that is, that positive charge. Moreover, it cannot even really sense the positive charge, because the moment it senses it, the negative charge couples with the positive charge and achieves the electric neutrality.

If I put it this way, and you don't get it, I'll discuss it again when we get to the molecular stage.

Let's first discuss a key concept, what does it mean to be a *subjective body*? What does it mean to be an *objective body*? What is a subject? The subject is the mirror image of the objective body. In the primordial stage, you can set any party that is mutilated as the subject, and then its other party is the objective body; but conversely, when you set its other party as the subject, it is the objective body itself. What is the subject? The subject in its original state is the transposable state of the objective system, which is the origin of the subject.

So, fundamentally, we humans are nothing but an object molecule that cannot be extracted from the objective world. Therefore, science, by leaving itself alone, by assuming that it has nothing to do with the object, by externalizing itself and acting as an observer, is itself doomed to trouble.

Okay, back to the molecular phase of the discussion. Let's say an acid and a base. If an acid molecule is set by you as the subject, correspondingly set the base molecule as the object, or of course you can set it the other way around. Then the acid molecule uses its acid root as the sensing property, and it does not sense the molecular structure of the whole base molecule, but only the base part of the base molecule. And the result of its perception is never a base, but a salt reached at the moment of collision and coupling between an acid and a base, and the product of the acid-base neutralization reaction is a salt. So if you can ask *acid*: "What is *base*? The answer must not be *base*, but *salt*. That is, at the moment of perception, your subjective perceptual property must be a coupled distortion of the perceptible counterpart of the object, so that the dependence between the sensing parties can be reached, isn't that so? And the limit of your perception is that you do not seek omniscience, just as an electron does not need to know the mass, shape, color, and other elements of the proton. It only needs to know the positive charge of the object, or even distort the positive charge of the object to be electrically neutral, and its perception is already satisfied.

What is satisfied? Satisfy the stable dependence between electrons and protons. Is that right? This is called knowledge, and this is called the original induction requirement of knowledge. Remember what is the most basic structure of the whole mental system and nervous system of our body? It is electromagnetic induction! That is, the transmembrane potential of the cell membrane, the bioelectric impulses, that is, the electrical impulses coming into the nerves, and then the rectification of this electromagnetic induction system in the brain centers such as the visual center and the auditory center. Isn't that so? It is the lowest level of all our mental activity, which I expressed earlier as the unconscious base. We are simply superimposing the compensative structure on top of this base layer, step by step.

About 500 million years ago, vision appeared in platyhelminths, later the neural net, and later the ganglion, which is the precursor of the nerve centers. Then came the hypocenter, followed by the epicenter, and finally the higher cerebral cortex. Such an evolutionary superposition process constitutes the *sense* of atomic molecules, to the *sensibility* of flat animals, to the *knowledge* of vertebrates, to the rationality of human prefrontal cortex.

In other words, the process of gaining sensory properties in the structure of natural object evolution is realized layer by layer in the neuro-organizational architecture or mental perception system of our human body, without missing a single step. It predestines you at the most basic point that your perception itself is not seeking truth, but seeking dependent response, or seeking to reach dependent structure. So even after developing to the post-derivative perception stage of human beings, you are still subject to this rule.

In Kant's doctrine, *mind* still fails to find its source, and the source of *knowing or knowledge* has never been found in the entire Western philosophical epistemology, even before Descartes considered the mind entity to be a system of being that corresponds equivalently to the material entity. Today, we can see very clearly in this model that there is only one system in the world, and that *mind* is merely a property of the gaining product of the material-evolutionary system. Moreover, Kant cannot explain why our perception can only stay in the phenomenal world.

What does it mean by *phenomenon*? It's just a coupling of inductive properties! That is, your perception does not happen for nothing, your perception comes from the extension of the subjective sensory properties of the object evolution series - from the negative charge property of the electron to the acid molecule's acid property to the human perceptual property - you are using your subjective sensory property to couple the corresponding sensory properties of the object, and the coupling process is the distortion process. Because the result of the distortion process is a dependency realization, it satisfies the perceptual survival effect, which is the source of the *phenomenon*. Since perception is only a coupling of properties, the derivative vehicles outside of properties are never within the scope of perception to be pursued, which is called *thing-in-itself*. This is the reason why the insurmountable transcendent realm of Kant's philosophy is possible to occur. Is this a clear answer to these questions?

And we find that there are upper and lower limits to perception. That is, when your potency of being is high, your sensing attribute or perception capability must be very low; when your potency of being is low, your sensing attribute, which develops into a perception attribute at this time, must already have a corresponding gain in its degree, that is, your perception capability manifests as very powerful. You know, this process is definitely prescribed. You will never see a fish that can do the basic calculations, nor you will see a monkey that can do calculus. Why? Because this perceptual increment or inductive (sense-response) attribute increment does not match its state (degree) of being.

Let me give you a simple example. Mosquitoes need to suck the blood of animals or humans during their breeding in the fall, when it will launch a group attack regardless of death casualties, in order to achieve the effect of survival continuity. Because the female mosquitoes need to have the blood plasma of animals for its enough nutrition and energy to reproduce. Because the mosquito's potency of being is high, capable of laying eggs in large numbers, so its perceptual properties remain at a lower state. That is, when it attacks to suck your blood, it is defiant. If you are in a state of defense, 10 mosquitoes attack you, there may be only one or two mosquitoes success in sucking blood, while the other eight or nine are to be killed by your slaps. From the human point of view, the mosquitos are blind and stupid, as they are completely unable to calculate the loss and gain ratio of their breeding behavior. Buy if we see it from the mosquitos' side, even each time only one mosquito succeeds in sucking the blood it will assure the continuation of the species reproduction.

In contrast, as human beings, we need to calculate carefully in any economic activity, because if the amount of loss is always greater than the amount of gain, and you won't stop the ongoing business, you will soon go perish. It is because your degree of being is too low, your perception of capability to calculate must be very high, so that you can sustain your own feeble survival. The mosquito's degree of being is on the high side, the reproduction volume is extremely large, it each oviposits hundreds of eggs, and its breeding period is very short. If it has the same perceptive capability as humans, knowing that their probability of success is less than 50% and retreat, the mosquito would have long been extinct. It is precisely because of its individual stupidity that ensures the effective continuation of the species. Therefore, we can see that low perception is a kind of protection effect, high perception is a kind of critical survival effect.

Origin of Mind: *Gain of Affective Attribute*

Let's go back to recall the part where I was speaking at the very beginning of this class, I spoke about a quote from Russell, What is wisdom? How do you know that wisdom is not a refined folly?

If you understand my previous lecture, you will understand that wisdom is really a kind of refined stupidity, which signifies that you are in a bad critical state of existence with very low degree of being. In this system of thinking, we can clearly explain the upper and lower limits of *knowing*. Its lower limit is determined by your degree of being, and its upper limit is determined by your degree of compensation, that is, by your threshold of survival satisfaction constants, which is our perceptual momentum. In other words, our knowledge is not an arbitrary aggressive amount, but a naturally prescribed amount. We find in this theoretical model both the source and the momentum of the mind, as well as the basic provisions for the operation of the mind.

It's like the study of biology, you want to probe the basic state of life, and it's very difficult for you to take the human body as a specimen. Where do you have to go? You have to go back to the level of cytology. It's like today when humans do genetic engineering, in the laboratory, it's all about using the most primitive single-cell organisms, like E. coli, to do research. Because on the simplest model, the most complex latent forms and prescribed elements of all the properties are expressed.

Similarly, if we want to dissect the spirit and go back to its original point, it will appear as a very simple yet very clear state. All the contradictions between existentialism and epistemology, all the answers to the deep questions of philosophy, are thus profoundly revealed.

I have only made the simplest theoretical model statement of *affective attribute of inductive (sense-response) gain* here. What am I trying to say? The degree of *knowing* is limited by the degree of *being*! Your *capable to know* is an attribute expression of your *capable to be* state. Then your *state of knowing* and *prescriptive nature of knowing* determine your *form of knowing* and *content of knowing*. This is the fundamental cause of mental phenomena, or the model of mental being in today's large amount of information. Therefore, when I talk about *perception*, I express it systematically in the progressive steps of *sense-response, sensibility, knowledge,* and *rationality*.

So one should note that in the mental level or mental layer of human beings, what we call sensuality, knowingness, etc. are no longer pure. Because what we call such things is the general state under the envelope of reason. In terms of genesis, there was no sensibility when there was only induction of sense-response in the beginning. For example, electrons and protons, for example, acid roots and bases, they have no sensual organs, there is no such thing as sensibility, they are pure induction. The first sensibility occurs, for example, when a flat animal has only vision, and its vision can only see its dependents, but nothing else, and this is called pure sensibility. At this time, it does not have knowledge because its object is single, or its visual object is single, so it does not have the need to discriminate between multiple objects, which is called pure sensibility.

Then in chordates and vertebrates, as all things continue to differentiate, the objects become multiple, and then the intellectual judgment reaction, or the judgment-seeking reaction, is presented, which is pure knowledge, without reason. At this time, reason had not yet emerged. Then comes to the human reason, after the human reason iterative occurrence, when humans talk about knowledge, sensibility and even induction, in fact, it has long been unable to pure. What they said about sensuality has actually been mixed into perception, and what he said about perception has actually been mixed into reason, that is, in the full sequence of induction, sensuality, perception, and reason, you can no longer make it purely stripped. So, when humans refer to perception, you won't be able to have pure induction, sensibility, knowing, and rationality, because you can't strip them out separately anymore. They are an infinitesimal variable, or a continuous increment without compartmentalization. Kant unconsciously used a book title like *Critique of Pure Reason* in order to explore this question, seeking to explore as much as possible what pure knowing, pure reason is all about, and ended up in a lot of trouble.

When humanity is in a very low degree of being, the differentiation of the dependent object is so large that it is impossible to discriminate and determine the physical state, and has to carry out large amount and large quantity of virtual reasoning in the logical concept, this time marks that you have entered the rational state. The higher end the rationality is, the more it is expressed in the state of abandoning or discarding perceptual material, which I call ideal logic, that is, striving to reach pure rationality. But since the higher end the vehicle is, the greater the increment of compensation is, it must be in a state of greater drift. Because it is a gain of attributive compensation of reduced degree of being. The lower the degree of being, the more destabilized the state is, and therefore the higher the degree of compensation, the more destabilized the state must be. This is the reason why I have repeatedly said in my lectures that "the more primitive and lower things are, the more fundamental, decisive and stable they are".

We will also see this very clearly on the level of perception. The primordial state of affective attributes of sense-response is under the subconscious or unconscious mind that we cannot mobilize. When we look at sensibility, it must be much more stable than knowingness. We see that plants are always green, but in fact the green color is an illusion, just an illusion of light wavelength. But we see that the plant is always green, it will never change in the perceptual sense. Even before the monkeys, animal vision already saw plants as green, and this has never changed. Even if we realize today that green is just an illusion of a certain wavelength of light, the leaves still appear green, and reason does not change perception at all.

But when we enter into knowing, that is, when we make a judgment about any green thing and examine its relationship to our dependence, for example, when you were looking at a green apple between green leaves, it becomes a state of nonplus when you have to make a judgment, find and determine whether it is edible or not. A green apple may or may not be ripe, and an unripe green apple tastes bitter. As I said earlier, it is not that it is objectively bitter, but that it needs to protect the unripe seeds inside when it is not ripe. The reason it grows into a round and sweet form later is so that animals can devour it, and then the animals cannot digest the internal apple core, thus helping the fruit tree sow its seeds by excreting feces. So when it does not grow ripe, it must express itself as an unpleasant taste that is toxic to animals, and that is why we feel very bitter when we eat green apples that do not grow ripe. And you might be harmed by eating it, because its metabolic intermediates contain many undesirable active substances including nitrites.

So, when you are in the midst of a green vegetation, choosing which object is the necessary dependency of the moment, this process of knowing judgment is a state of unstable, a state that cannot be determined, or is difficult to determine. It is completely different from the stability that we see in the purely perceptual green. And when we get to the rational stage, when we talk about why plants happen, why they grow, why they evolve, it has become a product of rational logical deduction, and so it has no stability to speak of from then on. In ancient times we said it was the creation of God; in the Middle Ages the West said it was because there was some mysterious and inexplicable activator, vital element in it; later on, it was rigidly classified by botanists; later on, it was said by Darwin to be the product of gradual evolution; later on, it was said by Mendel to be the stipulation of genetic factors ......; and the list goes on and on, rapidly transforming. That is, on the rational model, it is a constantly variable and unstable state.

In short, we find that at the level of our perceptual attribute of compensation, it still expresses the dynamic state, the lower level, the more stable; the higher level, the more unstable, which is caused by the law of constraint. That is why, where a brilliant philosopher, such as Kant, who did not have this amount of information and this theoretical model, actually deduced centuries ago that the high development of pure reason would bring out the inappropriate idea of dichotomy. Look at Hume's famous saying, "Reason is nothing but the servant of the passions". That is, we find in our daily life that our lower perceptions, such as emotion, are in fact an expression of our knowingness, and that they dominate our reason, not our reason dominates our knowing.

Highly intelligent philosophers have been questioning the high use of intelligence by humans for centuries, so we hear all sorts of voices from Hume, Kant to Russell flirting with high intellectual rationality. So if you want to know what is mind? What is perception? What is the prescriptive nature of mind? What is even the object? What is the objective body? What is the subject? you have to re-explore them all in the context of much more informative model construction. But these model constructions are premised on the logical paths and logical steps that have been explored by thousands of years of human philosophers, without which all our subsequent explorations would not have occurred. So I have to make it clear that even at the stage of Western classical philosophy and even modern philosophy, human exploration of philosophical problems is far from exhausted. To say that "philosophy is over" is to be ignorant of the fact that philosophical problems must continue to present themselves as information increases.

And I would also like to state here that much of what I am teaching now you will not see in my writings. For I have no need to repeat what has already been discussed by my predecessors, but I only inquire deeply into what has been left over from previous philosophers. Therefore, my doctrine is nothing but a proof of a completely new basic principle, and this proof system runs through the three fields of *natural existence, mental existence* and *social existence*, which is something that no one has been able to do before, that is, to use a single principle to link through the three systems. It is important to understand that the total system of existence in the universe, as we call it, never goes beyond these three fields, and that science in general focuses only on natural existence.

Then if my model is to be built, it must be based on the problems discussed by previous philosophers step by step. Therefore, when I do the proof of the system, I do not discuss again the problems that have been dealt with by my predecessors, but I only bury my head in the proof of the new principle, and in the process of this one lineage proof, I only comment on the origin of the problems and their solutions wherever they were involved. In this way, I have proved the whole system, deconstructed the history of philosophy, and given a point-by-point commentary on the occasion, and this is the structure of the exposition of my book *A Unified Theory of Evolution*. The reason it is difficult to read is that you have to understand the state of the problems discussed by the philosophers and the flaws that remain. And I will not rehash these issues. Moreover, it is followed by the extraction of additional information from the whole of contemporary natural science, which makes it a difficult read. But if one reads it, it is really an extremely simple basic principle. I am here through this round of lectures, to illustrate the heights reached by recent classical Western philosophy, to present the problems it discusses, and to sketch the shape of new model solutions to these problems.

Definition of *Logic* and Its Path of Formation

So far, we have generally sorted out the levels of epistemological inquiry undertaken by modern Western classical philosophy in succession to ancient Greek philosophical thought. Now, Let us discuss some other related issues, which are not systematic enough but belong to thematic exposition, so that we can clarify some common conceptual confusions and may serve to correct our misconceptions about a lot of major issues.

We will first discuss logic. The concept of *logic* was not clear in ancient Greece, and was expressed as logos, which means "the sum of words and order". When we listen to the meaning of this word, it actually means some kind of "law of subject and object without distinction". When people then realized that the relationship between the object of perception and perception itself, though possibly the same thing, still needed to be separately investigated, the concept of *logos* was gradually differentiated and derived, and the word *logic* was born.

The first person to use the concept of logic was Aristotle, but he did not use this symbol. This word was later transformed from the Latin word logos. Aristotle gave a definition of logic as *necessarily derived.* That is, Aristotle recognized logic back then as only deductive logic, that is, if the major premise is given, and then the minor premise is given, the conclusion is certain and unique. He regarded this thing as logic.

Based on our exploration of the entire epistemological hierarchy and the subsequent extensional development of logic, we know today that logic contains two meanings: the *necessary derivation* of thought reasoning, and the *a priori specification* of the perceptual sequence. By logic we usually mean only logic of thinking or logic of rational thinking. In other words, our past concept of logic is expressed only in the stage of thinking "rational reasoning".

Then there is a question: What is the coherent relationship between rational logic and perception, sensibility and even the underlying induction (sense-response)? This question has never been explored in the past, nor can it be explored. Moreover, all philosophers, including Kant, Hegel, and those of contemporary logicians, believe that logic, reason, and even the sum of sense, knowledge, and rationality are possessed only by human beings, and they call this thing reason, wisdom, and regard it as the exclusive possession of human beings.

But by the 20th century, with the development of natural science, it became very clear to us today that the human perceptual system was gradually created in the long process of biological evolution. And we find that rational logic is based on perceptual logic, and formal logic is the rational expression of animal perceptual logic, as I mentioned earlier.

What is the basis of logic of understanding? It is logic of sensibility! Once we used to say senses, feelings, sensuality, we would never let it be associated with logic. But we know today that it is just a metrical mechanism or programmed sequence of recognition hidden behind our subconscious or subliminal consciousness, which of course should be called *logic* because it also meets the definition of "necessarily derived". Let me give you an example. Today we just input a large number of 0s and 1s to the computer, but the computer presents us with a very realistic and dynamic image. For example, you can play a video game, you can play soccer on this virtual soccer field, you can drive a car, the scene is vivid and real. But what do you input to it? What you input to it is a series of numerical information elements of 0s and 1s.

So think about it, what is our sensibility? What the outside world feeds us is just light quanta, and that is for vision; for hearing, it feeds us just vibrational waves; for smell and taste, it feeds us just certain molecules, molecules that are good or bad for our body. But why do we manage to rectify it into a series of concrete and realistic representations? Obviously, in the visual center, the auditory center, and the whole perceptual center, there must be a logical organizing system underneath that we cannot mobilize, just like a computer is equipped with a basic operating system that cannot be mobilized by ordinary people, that is, a system that organizes this information according to a certain program or rhythm, and the result of this organizing is our perceptual representations.

Therefore, even if we cannot mobilize it today and cannot find its specific metrical expression, we can be sure that there is an "a priori rectified metrical" or "innate programmatic provision" behind it, so we can consider it as much as possible as "perceptual logic" as well as "logic of understanding". I believe that as the amount of human knowledge and information increases further, these things will eventually be sorted out. If so, a complete and coherent logical channel will be revealed.

Strictly speaking, there is another layer below the sensibility, which is the *electromagnetic induction logic*. For example, if an electron recognizes the positive charge of a proton with its negative charge, it reacts in a certain way according to a fixed pattern, which we can also call *inductive logic*. For such a simple to complex, surface-to-internal logic, I named it logic in the broad sense. Accordingly, I renamed the so-called logic of thinking or logic of reason as *logic in the narrow sense.*

Until now, people have only focused on narrow logic and have not yet realized that there is a broad logic that needs to be explored. However, ignoring or neglecting the broad logic will certainly raise a series of questions, such as what is the origin of logic? How does the evolutionary process of perception or logic unfold? If perception is not true, how can it be valid? Since rational logic often denies perceptual experience, what is the basis for the respective validity of perceptual empirical life and rational narrow logic? Finally, why and how can an a priori perceptual channel or sequence of broad logics arrive at a model-dependent positive dependence? Questions such as these are by no means easy to answer by studying narrow logic and its models of rationality alone.

In the passage of this generalized logic, the more primitive and lower level of logic, the simpler must be its logical structure and logical metric; the higher the degree of compensation of the higher logical form, the more complex must be its logical structure and logical metric. This is completely consistent with the evolutionary process of the structure of material entities. That is, in the sequence of matter evolution, we find that the structure of matter evolution is a process of continuous superposition and succession. The particle structure is superimposed on the atomic structure; the atoms continue to differentiate and combine, which is the molecular structure; the molecular structure continues to be composed, which is the genetic structure or cellular structure; the cells continue to mutilate and integrate to form a multicellular organism, which is called the organismic structure; the structure formed by the continued mutilation and combination of the organismic structure at its extracorporeal level, which is the social structure.

We will find that the structure of material entities is a superimposed and cumulative process from simple to complex. Then, at the same time, the gain of affective attributes of sense-response is also matched, i.e., from simple to complex, from lower to higher levels, and the corresponding structural and attribute compensation of the same extension occurs, so as to reach the effective dependence of the level-by-level recognition. This is the origin of the entire affective sense-response hierarchy, perceptual channel or broad logic.

Why is it necessary to derive the concept of *broad logic*? We will discuss this separately later, and I will start here with a cursory reference to some of the empirical evidence that is available in terms of biological research today. As I said, I will present this lesson in as intuitive or scientific a way as possible to make it easier to understand. Let's look at contemporary biology devoted to the genesis of bio-sensory responses or bio-logical sequences. I have previously talked about electromagnetic induction, molecular Brownian motion, and receptor responses on cell membranes, and I will not say more about these. We turn next to the inductive surrogate incremental states of neural response systems, including sub-neural response systems, as visualized in biological experiments. We discuss this issue in order to show how narrowly philosophers in the past considered *perception* and *logic* as unique to humans, which also led to serious biases in their perception of these issues.

It is important to know that the most primitive organism, a single-celled organism, already has some kind of perceptual ability, which is expressed in biological experiments as kinetic tendency response. Let me give an example, of an anaerobic single cell, that is, it does not need oxygen to survive, and biologists do experiments on such single cells. These single cells are aquatic organisms, and the biologist drops a bubble of oxygen into the water, all the single cells will keep drifting and eventually all move away from this bubble of oxygen, which is called *kinetic response*. That is, at the single-cell stage, it does not have sensory organs, not to mention nerves, but it has receptor responses on the cell membrane, and it can already produce the most rudimentary directional movements in terms of dependency recognition.

Then there is the so-called *tropism*. Let me still give you an example, the phototropism of cells. As you know, all cells, including single-celled organisms and all living things, its energy source is ultimately solar energy. Then all the food collected by heterotrophic organisms, including us humans, is nothing but the accumulation of solar energy. Solar energy is concentrated in autotrophic plants, animals eat plants, and humans eat animals, and in the end, all that they eat is solar energy. Since the energy on the earth's surface comes mainly from solar energy, all primitive single cells have some kind of phototropic reaction, that is, the spontaneous reaction of chasing light sources and surviving, this reaction is called *biological phototropism*. This reaction is called *biotropism*. It is even expressed as the phenomenon of "moths fly to flame" in insects. It also forms the evolutionary basis of the *eye*, that is, the *eye* is such a complex organ, in fact, the original single-cell phototropism in the long hundreds of millions of years gradually developed out of a multi-cellular photoreceptor structure.

This phototropism, which has been developed from the primitive single cell 3.8 billion years ago to today, is very persistent. For example, a newborn baby just opened his eyes, if you hang a light bulb at home, he lay in the cradle, you will find that his eyes are always fixed on the light bulb, this is the expression of primitive biological phototropism in humans. Therefore, you should pay special attention to the brightness of the lamps used in the home when you are raising babies, it must be on the low side, otherwise too much light will cause visual damage to babies.

There are many types of tropism responses, such as negative tropism expressed by plants, which means that they always grow against gravity, hence the name "negative geotropism". If you bring down a tree and keep it in parallel to the ground, as long as it is still alive, the branches from the tree trunk will grow back vertically to the ground, which is called negative tropism. Plant roots always grow downward, which belongs to "geotropism". These primitive tropisms are expressed very firmly in the whole biological system, such as phototropism, geotropism, negative geotropism, etc., which are all expressions of the tropism response.

Next level sense-response in organisms is called *reflex*, which is a more advanced response state after the emergence of the neural arc. The so-called *reflex* is to start with the receptors, for example, we get information from the senses, forming bioelectricity, through the afferent nerve to the center, the center after processing and then through the efferent nerve, in the form of electrical impulses to the effector, such as the arm, such as the leg, so that they can have actions. Such a process from the receptors to the nerve center, after the information is organized, and then output into a behavioral effect, called the *reflex arc*, which has formed a neural network system of intellectual response state.

And then next is called *instinct*. As you know, animals have a variety of instincts. The so-called *instinct* refers to certain innate subconscious behavioral capabilities. Darwin in his book *Origin of Species*, specifically described the animal instincts, which mentioned some instincts are very complex. For example, in the subsection *Special Instincts* of the chapter *Instincts*, Darwin discussed the honeybee building a nest, that hexagonal nest is the largest proportion of space and the smallest consumption of materials a building structure. If you use mathematics, it is a very complex series of equations needed to derive the results. But the bee does not need to do the math, it relies on instinct alone to build its own hive into the most material-efficient, volume-efficient, and particularly stable housing structure. This modular, a priori behavioral response is called *instinct*. In most of our human cases, the basic somatic-intellectual response is still driven by instinct. At this stage of development, a knowing nature beyond sensuality has emerged.

The next term is *motivation*. Motivated behavior marks the gradual emergence of a sense of autonomy, that is, you have a goal-setting behavior plan. This is followed by the development of *freedom of consciousness* or *freedom of will*. We will find that over the 3.8 billion years of evolution of living things, the increase in perceptual capacity has been a gradual and consistent process.

And we also need to know that the old belief that *intelligence* is something that only humans have, and *learning ability* is something that only humans have, is completely wrong again. Contemporary biological research has found that *learning* behavior actually occurred as early as 500 million years ago in mollusks. For example, the octopus, biologists prepared two cards, yellow and white, and then constantly let the octopus in the two cards to choose, once the yellow card to give electric shocks, once the white card appears to put food. After at least 24 electric shocks, the octopus evaded and retreated when it saw the yellow card and went to feed when it saw the white card. This suggests that learning has already occurred in this lower aquatic stage of mollusks.

Another example is to let a primitive gastropod species like the snail walk a maze. Initially, the snail cannot get out of the maze, but after repeated training, the snail can eventually get out of the maze at once, which shows that the snail has the ability to learn.

Darwin took the Beagle ship around the world that year and went to the famous Galapagos Islands in the south-central region of the Pacific Ocean. In this archipelago he found that the same ground finches appeared to have different calls. He observed many other anomalies, including slight differences in the shape of the bird's beak, which led to his discovery of *interspecies*, thus disproving the misconception that "species are given by God at creation". Darwin realized that between the different islands of the archipelago, despite their proximity, the same birds made different calls, thus confirming that the calls of these birds were acquired. As another example, biologists conducted an experiment in which a bird called moraine rook was born and then separated from its parents and raised in captivity, and its natural call was very difficult to hear. However, if the bird is allowed to grow up with its parents, its call as an adult will be pleasant. This shows that the call of this bird is learned. It can only lure the opposite sex with a melodious call, which is part of the courtship learning process.

These examples show that the ability to *learn* is by no means unique to humans, but was already present in very primitive lower animals. Biologists have gradually studied the growth of the learning phenomenon in biological evolution and have summarized it as follows: the most primitive and simple learning is called habituation learning. The so-called habituation learning is to learn not to respond to repeated irrelevant stimuli, in order to save physical energy. The most typical example is the experiment with tuning forks for spiders. A spider crawling on a spider web, you use a tuning fork to make a noise, the spider is initially very alarmed, but if you let the tuning fork noise constantly presented, the spider eventually no longer does any unnecessary reaction to the noise. This shows that the spider has adapted to this environment through learning, which is called habituation learning, a very low-level, primitive initial learning.

The next step is *learning by imprinting*. It refers to the gradual increase in memory capacity that guides later behavior. Let me give you an example of a duckling that has just been born and the biologist detaches it from its mother. As soon as the duckling opens its eyes, it is assumed that the first object it sees is a green paper-box, which the biologist keeps tugging, and the duckling will always follow the movement of the green box. Then, wait until this duck grows up, it always does not recognize the mother, even until the courtship, its object of the opposite sex must be held in the green box, otherwise it is not interested, this is called learning by imprinting. As you know, this thing also has a very profound impact on us humans, such as first impression. We humans are usually the most stubborn about the first impression we make of something, and even if the impression is false or wrong, it becomes very difficult to correct it later. This is actually the precipitation of primitive learning by imprinting in human intelligence.

It continues to develop into *associative learning*, that is, the formation of a preparatory response procedure evoked by several interrelated stimuli. The typical manifestation of this is the conditioned reflex. When I say conditioned reflex, you should recall the famous experiment conducted by the Soviet biologist Pavlov. When you feed a dog, you ring the bell before each feeding, and keep doing so repeatedly, and eventually you just ring the bell, even if you don't give food afterwards, on hearing rings the dog's saliva and gastrointestinal digestive juices start to secrete, which is called conditioned reflex, a kind of associative learning.

This is followed by *trial and error learning*, which means that through the experience of behavioral effects, one can repeatedly adjust one's behavior. For example, various types of maze walking experiments.

This is followed by *insight learning*, that is, the ability and method to deal with the current unfamiliar situation based on past experience. For example, a transparent glass plate is placed in front of the animal, and food is placed behind the glass plate, so generally the lower animals will keep ramming the glass plate, but a little more advanced animals only need to ram a few times, the hominid chimpanzee just by touches it with their hands, it will at once understand, and go around the glass plate to get food, this is called insight learning.

Finally, we move on to *reasoning*, that is, the use of concepts and general principles to deal with specific situations and problems with complex implications. It is here that reason comes to the fore. In other words, we find that both the progression of perceptual abilities and the expansion of learning behavior are the product of a gradual process of biological evolution.

It can be seen that human perception, or human wisdom endowment, is by no means unique to human beings, nor is it suddenly born on earth, but is the result of the gain of the inductive attributes of the entire sequence of physical biological evolution.

CAUSES OF RE-FORM OF LOGIC

Let's talk about what exactly does broad logic deal with.

As we mentioned earlier, our perception is only a subjective cognition we reach about things, and in the end, it is only a model of thought, or a logical model, not a true reflection of things. So, why does it work? That is, why can our perception achieve certain behavioral effects? And the greater the amount of information, the stronger the perceptual compensatory function seems to be, why? It is because our cognitive model is a complete channel of communication with the outside world in the broad sense of logic. Therefore, according to this *model,* that is, depending on this *model,* we can form an effective interface with the external reality.

Only by clarifying the relationship between the consonance of broad logic and external things in a "model-dependent theory of knowledge" can we understand why our "perception is not true but valid". And we have another problem to explain, and that is logical change.

That is, our perceptual process eventually arrives at a logical model, we can abstract the general logical model into a narrow logical model, which generally can be called a theoretical model or doctrinal system. In any case, it is not a true reflection of the objective world, but merely a subjective construction that deals with external information a priori. So why do we have these logical models, which are always renovating and changing?

As you know, our *cognitive world* is not fixed, our understanding of things is constantly changing, and we improve our civilization process by constantly changing our cognitive model. For example, our view of the universe has undergone at least five major changes. The earliest one was the *heaven vault* theory, that is, the sky is round and the earth is a flat plate, and the sky is like a dome covering the earth. Think about the primitive tribal people, standing at the door of their own tribe to see the earth, see the universe, in the sense of intuition of course he established the heaven vault theory of the universe. What does this cosmology match with? It matches with the way of hunting and gathering, with the small-scale territorial survival. Then it came to the *geocentric* theory, when the geocentric theory appeared, it requires a larger amount of information. It effectively sustained Western agricultural civilization for 1,400 years under Ptolemy's theoretical model. Then came Copernicus' *heliocentrism*, which opened the door to the scientific era. Then came Newton's *absolute space-time theory*, which pried the opportunity of the first industrial revolution; and finally, Einstein's *theory of relativity* and the *modern cosmology* based on the theory of relativity, have created the Einstein era, on which the nuclear age, the electronic age, and even the so-called information age are now based.

We find that our logical models, including the cosmological model, are constantly changing. What does the change in the logical model indicate? It shows that our cosmology is never a true reflection of the objective world, but only a subjective logical model. This truth should be clear. In the case of the solar system alone, it will take at least 9 to 10 billion years for any significant change to occur in the solar system, which has existed for 5 billion years today. It will be about 4 to 5 billion years before today's Sun is close to exhausting its intrinsic hydrogen fusion energy and enters a red giant or even white dwarf state, and the entire pattern of the solar system will change significantly. But our theoretical model of the universe has changed at least five times in just 3000 years. It means that our cosmology is not a reflection of the objective world. If our cosmology were a true reflection of the objective world, it would have remained stable for 5 or 10 billion years without any change.

Since the logical change of our cosmology has led to the continuous expansion of human civilization, what is the state of logical change? What is the motivation? This is the first question we need to explore, which in turn involves the logic in the broad sense.

Note that there are two states of logic in broad sense: the first is coherence of general logic, or the self-consistency of general logic; the second is the failure of general logic.

The so-called consistency of general logic or self-consistency of general logic is a state in which there is no conflict and disagreement in the internal structure of logic at the rational, intellectual and perceptual levels, and this is a state in which the problem is solved and confirmed; on the contrary, when the amount of information increases further, the previous general logic cannot maintain the coherent state, there appears an internal contradiction and fracture, we call this *general logic failure,* which inevitably brings a new round of logical change.

Let me give you an example. About Ptolemy's doctrine of geocentrism, we know today that it is wrong, but in those days, Ptolemy's doctrine represented the highest level of all human astronomy, and it was a very complex logical project. On the original Greek text, it was titled *Mathematical Compendium in Thirteen Books,* and the book made a very complex exposition of the motion of the heavenly bodies. You know, it is very difficult to investigate the celestial motion with the geocentric theory, because the planets and the Earth originally orbit around the Sun. Now you have to make the Earth the center, and the Sun and all the stars, including stars and planets, move around the Earth, and you have to rectify it into a complete and self-consistent model.

So what did Ptolemy do? He went so far as to divide the celestial wheel into two layers: the principal wheel and the mean wheel. Think about how complex a motion the planets are, as they orbit the sun (which was thought to be around the earth at the time), each orbiting together in different orbits and on different circumferences at different speeds. So you can observe with the naked eye, the five planets - Venus, Jupiter, Mercury, Mars, and Earth, which could be seen directly back then, the orbits of these planets, standing on the Earth, were actually irregular, they were back and forth, left and right. With the Earth as the center, it is really difficult to summarize them in such a dynamic form in a regular state.

But why was Ptolemy's geocentrism so well established for thousands of years? It is because it matches our underlying logic, our low-end logic, our sensible logic! Because we watch the sun rise from the east and set from the west, in our senses, it is obvious that the sun revolves around the earth, so Ptolemy's geocentrism, extending from the model of sensible logic to rational logic, he had to find the matching relationship between the two, and this doctrine could not be recognized until the matching between the two was opened, which is called the self-consistency of general logic.

If I haven't convinced you by saying this, or if you haven't quite got it, I'll give you another example. You know, hundreds of years before Ptolemy, there was a famous scholar in ancient Greece in the 3rd century B.C. named Aristarchus. He actually proposed heliocentrism at that time, but it was submerged in history. Why? Because if it is heliocentric, then the Earth must be in motion, that is, the earth must be moving around. If the Earth is in moving state and in a large scale moving around the sun, then at that time, immediately the inconsistency of the general logical sequence or the failure to match the various levels of general logic will occur.

Think about it, we look at any object, if that object is stationary, and the observer is in motion, then the relative position of the object must not be fixed. You let three points into a line, if you set two static reference points, and you are a wandering moving point, then the relationship between these three points will constantly shake, is not it so? But when you stand on the Earth and look at the star, it is actually never moving. Back then this problem could not be explained, because if the earth moves, the position of the star in the sky dome can not be conserved. It was not until after the modern Galileo, theoretical problems like light travel difference and stellar parallax were all solved, only to put this doubt dissolved.

Let's think it again, there is one difficult problem to face. Let's not talk about the trouble caused by the earth being a sphere and rotating motion, let's leave this issue aside for the time. In the year without the theory of gravity, if the Earth is rotating, then will people fall off the Earth? Let's not discuss this issue yet, and just imagine the confusion necessarily caused by the rotational motion of the earth. According to the heliocentric theory of the year, you can do a rough orbital calculation, the Earth's motion speed should also be very high, about 40,000 kilometers a day. Such a high speed of motion, you throw up a ball, how can you stand in the same place and receive this ball? As a result of such a motion of the earth, the ball must have fallen far away, but we are indeed on the earth, and are able to catch the ball thrown vertically high and back to the hands. This problem could not be solved until Newton used the concept of *inertial force* to explain it. In other words, the heliocentric theory proposed by Aristarchus back then, even though it was a theoretical model in the narrow sense of logic, it did not match and was not self-consistent in the broad sense of logic, that is, in the perceptual verification, so Aristarchus' doctrine was buried in history.

What am I talking about? The self-consistency of general logic is the basic condition for a theory, a doctrine, or a model of thought, to reach a then balanced, correct, and acceptable state. We can thus see the importance of the state of general logic itself. However, as the amount of information increases, the general logic, which originally appeared to be coherent and self-consistent, becomes inherently contradictory. At this point, the original theoretical model breaks down, and this is called "logical change leading to the development of human civilization". So, what exactly is the force that causes logical change to occur? It is simply the increment of information.

I have said repeatedly earlier that the process of development of all things in the universe is the process of information increment, and this natural process continues to be expressed in the history of human civilization. Therefore, the lower the level of human civilization, the lower the amount of information processed, and the higher the level of civilization, the higher the amount of information processed.

The so-called *logical change* is a product of the increment of natural information compensation. When the amount of information increases to a certain level, the previous model of low information rectification cannot accommodate the new amount of information, and the original model of logical thought will then break down.

For the simplest example, let's look at Newton. Newton's doctrine has been repeatedly proven to be the truth, and it is surprisingly effective in predicting the orbits of the planets. When Newton's doctrine first appeared, most physics professors could not read it because the mathematical equation calculus was his own unique invention. Newton's doctrine was gradually accepted and exclaimed to be "like a god who discovered the laws of nature", and its predictions were so accurate that they predicted the existence of Uranus. At first, with the development of telescopes, a new planet, Uranus, was found, which was the first planet invisible to the naked eye besides Venus, Jupiter, Mercury, Mars, and Earth, but the orbit of Uranus did not conform to the calculation of Newtonian mechanics. At this time, people did not say that Newtonian mechanics was wrong, they say that Uranus orbits were wrong. According to the calculations of Newtonian mechanics, some scholars believed that there was some unobserved planet in another orbit in the periphery interfering the orbit of Uranus, so people calculated beforehand the orbit and mass of that star that should exist according to Newton's mechanics theory. As the development of telescopes continued, the star was accurately found decades later, and it is the famous Neptune.

Newton's doctrine is thus repeatedly proven to be the truth, but Newton's doctrine can only deal with macroscopic events, macroscopic object motion can be explained by gravity. When microscopic phenomena are revealed, that is, when there appeared an additional amount of information about the microscopic world, such as Faraday's discovery of electromagnetic induction and Maxwell's electromagnetic field equations, the motion of the microscopic world cannot be explained by gravity in any way. Because the gravitational force is related to the mass, a very large object will show gravitational force, in the four major forces of physics it is the weakest force. Think about it, the gravitational force of a large earth can not resist the electromagnetic force of a small magnet, of course, this statement is not accurate. You drop a set of keys on the ground, you can take the magnet to lift the set of keys above the ground, the gravitational force is so weak. How can such a weak force explain the motion of particles in the microscopic world? As such, Newton's doctrine could not match at all with this new amount of information, and Newton's doctrine then collapsed, and Einstein's theory of relativity came into being. The theory of relativity emerged because it can effectively solve the unified principle of action of macrocosmic world motion and microcosmic world motion by readjusting the space-time relationship, which is called logical change, which is called the original logical model breaks down and changes with the increment of information.

Therefore, we can understand the meaning of human knowledge progress and knowledge renovation only in the continuous operation of self-consistent and dis-consistent systems of general logic and in the process of logical change with the spontaneous increase of the amount of perceived information.

Well, by now you should have even a vague sense of the overall state of human knowledge and the overall cognitive landscape in general. Next, we discuss some marginal issues.

We will discuss what *truth* is first. The term *truth* is widely used, and the idea it contains is very attractive. The pursuit of truth has traditionally been a human dream or considered to be the dynamic energy of the human mind. However, if you understand my previous lesson, you should understand that *truth-seeking* is something that is very difficult to achieve at a deep epistemological level. What is it that we usually call *truth* and what is it that we usually think of as *truth*? We can roughly divide it into the following five items.

What we usually mean by *truth* in the most meaningful sense is the conformist view of truth. By *conformism,* we mean that your subjective perception matches the objective object exactly, which is what we usually mean by truth, and which is the most common view of truth. This is the first concept of *truth* that deserves deeper investigation.

The following four items are not really important, so I will only list them a little and not say more.

The second is the *self-consistency theory,* which means that if a theory is self-consistent, then it is the truth. This obviously does not work, because anyone can arrive at a self-consistent doctrine or a self- consistent system of explanation for anything if he or she wants to say, but that is not precise logic, so the self-consistency theory is obviously not valid.

The third item is *pragmatism*. The so-called pragmatism is typically expressed in practical philosophy, that is, people belief that any doctrines have practical effects are the truth. But this does not hold true, why? We will discuss it later.

The fourth is the *convention theory,* which means that any opinion, as long as it is recognized by the vast majority of people, is considered the truth. But in fact, this is the philosophy of the ignorant, because the truth has always been in the hands of a few people, and so the *convention theory* is easy to refute.

The fifth last item is called *intuitionism,* which is the theory that seeing is believing.

We don't need to talk about any of this anymore, we are only talking about truth in the sense of *conformism*. As I have said repeatedly before, our perception is not *truth-seeking*, and we must distort external information in our senses the moment we receive it. Perceiving light quanta as brightness, light wavelengths as color, vibrational wave energy as or mistaken for loud sound, and so on, our perception itself in no way provides us with the truth. And the logic of thought that we structure on top of our direct senses, narrow logic, does not correct this parochialism. It is precisely a further rectification of the a priori subjective thought pattern on top of the distorted material construction provided by the senses, and therefore it must be a further parsimonious distortion on top of the distortion.

Therefore, in terms of the perception model, it is impossible for us to obtain the truth. We should note that the words *truth* in Chinese translation is made of two characters "真理" (Zhen Li) *truth* and *reason*, which cannot be put together in themselves. The so-called *truth* must be your feeling, your logic, that is, your reason, the original truth that is not imposed on it. The so-called *reason* is your perceptual attributes overlaid on it, distorting the truth to obtain information and form a logical line of reasoning. Therefore, if there is *truth*, there is no *reason*, and if there is *reason*, there is no *truth*. The Chinese word "真理" is not valid! This is like the Chinese word "客观" (Ke Guan) *objective view*, which is not valid, if you want to *view* it, it must not be an *objective*. Once it is *objective*, it must not be *viewed* by you, so the Chinese term itself is not valid. Therefore, we should pay attention to the fact that our so-called "真理" concept should be removed from our knowledge system or cognitive system.

So let's move on to deal with a question that is the criterion of truth.

We are all familiar with a famous saying in China: "Practice is the only criterion for testing the truth." This is the inevitable conclusion derived from the philosophy of pragmatism or the philosophy of practice. But whether practice can test the truth or not is a question that needs to be pondered. For we find that we do not see such a formulation in true Western philosophy. Spinoza and Hegel had a statement about the measure of truth when they said, "The measure of truth is truth itself." This statement is equivalent to saying "Truth is truth"! This is a reduplicative statement, a tautology, and the predicate gives nothing more than what the subject asks, so this should be an invalid answer.

But why do they, as philosophers, give such a tautological and repetitive expression? It is because practice cannot test the truth!

I am only exploring purely philosophical issues here, and we are not involved in political issues. China proposed back then that practice is the criterion for testing truth, because Deng Xiaoping's reforms encountered obstacles and had to use such a philosophical approach to seek a breakthrough and change in the previous theoretical framework and political landscape. This has nothing to do with the issue I am going to discuss today, and I am not discussing it in relation to that political controversy; we are only inquiring a little bit about the purely academic and philosophical aspects.

Think about this: Can truth be tested by practice? Why did Spinoza and Hegel say that the measure of truth is truth itself? I still take the bat as an example. As a species with a completely different mode of perception than we humans, the bat captures external objects and targets in a radar response with ultrasonic echoes. Whereas we human subjects get 80% of our information from vision, that is, we build world representations in a photoreceptive way. If we and bats are in the same cave, the representations that this cave provides to bats and us humans must be different simply because our respective modes of perception are different. Can practice then test who is right and who is wrong? It is important to know that the bat's perceptual model and its perceptual representations are very effective in practice. It can fly at high speed in a mosquito state, itself also high-speed movement, and then through the radar-type ultrasonic echo, accurately capture this small insect, its accuracy is no less than we humans shoot a missile, shoot down a plane. If the test of practice is valid then it is the truth, then the bat has the truth, but the bat's truth is completely different from our human's picture of the world, and our human's appearance built up with vision, and the behavior is equally valid, so which is the truth? It is evident that practice cannot test truth! Or rather, practice cannot test perception!

Because all practices and activities are given and shaped on a perceptual platform, it is called "unconscious *taking as true* on the perceptual platform". That is, you do not consciously recognize it as *true* at all, and you do not even realize that it is necessary to distinguish truth from falsehood before and after perception or from perception itself, which is a completely blinded normal state. In other words, you are not consciously aware that your perception is *distorted*. Without reflection, you will not realize that your senses and thoughts are actually distorted with respect to the object. In the end, everything we do, everything we practice, is done on a "*non-true* perception platform" that we do not consciously recognize as *true*, so there must be a natural match between your practice and your way of perception. I think this logical relationship should be very clear, in a nutshell: practice tests the truth invalid!

However, it is obvious that when a doctrine is logically self-consistent in the broad sense, has practical guidance, and has repeatedly proved its validity, it is precisely a sign that the truth is about to collapse. In other words, instead of testing the truth, practice can only test the collapse of the truth! Let me cite the example of the geocentric theory again, thousands of years of Western agricultural civilization, are built on the geocentric theory, and even the Chinese heaven vault theory, have effectively guided the Chinese agricultural civilization. Visually, the sun clearly revolves around the earth, and on a practical and empirical level, you can test it any way you want, it is right, it is correct, and it is ironclad. But when you repeatedly test it without problems, it means that it is about to break down.

Let me give another example. Aristotle explored the problem of *free fall* in the ancient Greek era. He followed common sense, according to the practical way to prove that a heavy object and a light object falling at the same time, the heavier object must hit the ground first. This view is never wrong if you want to actually try it. You take a stone, take a piece of paper, while throwing down, the stone must fall to the ground first, in practice repeatedly test will never be wrong. How did this conception collapse? Galileo actually used a purely ideal logic experiment, and overturned it. We know that Galileo's logic experiment, called the "reductio ad absurdum". He deduced in pure logic, if the heavy things fall fast, and the light things fall slowly, then the light and heavy two things tied together, what will happen? Logically speaking, the light and heavy two things tied together, the weight is greater, should fall faster; but from the other side, the light thing falls slowly, if the light and heavy two things tied together, the light thing will drag the heavy thing, so that it slows down. Therefore, logically, the two contradict each other and cannot be self-consistent. Thus only in the pure logic of the concept Galileo has determined, that the light and heavy things must be the same speed of fall! Then to deal with the problem he only did some slope experiments and settled it. He did not have to run to the Leaning Tower of Pisa and throw down two iron balls, large and small, this thing did not exist in the history of science, it is only a complete fabrication, a legend. What does the example show? A truth that has been repeatedly tested empirically and in practice without problems, in fact, implies a foretaste of its collapse. So, instead of testing the truth, practice can only test the collapse of the truth! This is the only conclusion we can draw from a purely philosophical discussion of this issue.

Momentum of *Truth*

The trend of truth is discussed below. We always say in general that mankind is gradually approaching from relative truth to absolute truth in the long run of knowledge. That is, our perceptions are becoming more and more realistic. This is almost a common sense in everyday experience, or in the general history of ideas telling. The more advanced the theory we find, the more accurate it seems to be, and the more it is able to correct previous failures. Therefore, it is generally accepted that the trend of human cognition, whether in common sense, intuition, or scholarship, is increasingly toward truth.

However, if what I have said is confirmed, it means that our perception is not a vacuum orifice, and that our perception is a distorted appearance or distorted knowledge of the object by coupling it with our own subjective perceptual attributes to capture the corresponding perceptible properties of the object. If this statement holds true, the situation will not improve regardless of the stage of perception or sensing. Even at that stage of physical sensing, the electron senses the proton by its negative charge property, not by nothing; even at the stage of the acid-base molecule, the acid senses the base of the molecule not by the vacuum, but by its acid root. Therefore, you cannot use your own nothingness to perceive things outside. Your perceptual process is to borrow your own subjective attributes ("subjectivity"), or call it subjective sensing capability, or compensatory gain perceptual property, to capture the corresponding sensible property of the object. For example, your eyes are only light-sensitive organs, that is, they have only subjective light-sensing attributes, so you can only perceive the corresponding luminous or reflective properties of external objects. This can be clearly verified in physics and in sensory physiology. So, if our perception is to capture and process information through our own subjective perceptual attributes, called a priori perceptual forms or a priori perceptual regulations, how can we truly have *objective cognition* or *objective truth*?

Moreover, we find that in the process of material evolution, or even biological evolution, our incremental knowledge is reached by the gain of our perceptual attributes. For example, the sensing property of electron is extremely thin, only negative charge, so the amount of information it collects is extremely low, only positive charge or electrically neutral; the sensing property of molecule is also very weak, so it can only take the acid root to sense the base, and as a result, it senses into salt; to flat animal, it only has vision; to vertebrate, it produces five senses and low level center, that is, we will find that in the course of the evolution of things, the inductive property and its gain into the perceptual attribute are constantly expanding, and the reason why you can process more and more information is predicated on the fact that your subjective perceptual attributes is increasing. If this holds true, then logically speaking, the greater your perception, the greater the amount of information you process, and the more advanced your knowledge form, then it must be due to the more subjective elements attached to your perception, the more perverted the perceptual coupling, that is, the greater the perceptual distortion.

Isn't it the case? Logically we can only conclude that this is the case. Accordingly, the process of induction or perception development must be a process of diminishing cognitive realism in the *conformist* sense, or, as I put it in the second volume of *A Unified Theory of Evolution, Philosophy of Mind*, the amount of information increases and the amount of truth decreases. Because the more information you have, the more subjective perceptual attributes you have, and the more coupling and distortion of objects you have.

Therefore, our perception must not be getting closer to the truth, but must instead be getting farther and farther from the truth. This is logically self-consistent, backward and forward. What a phenomenon does it match with? It matches the increasing invalidity of our human knowledge, that is, the increasing speed of falsification of knowledge.

We all know that the more our knowledge evolves, the faster it is proven wrong. In today's information age, it is said that knowledge is renovated every 10 years. What does that mean? It means that the more advanced the knowledge model, the thought model, the theoretical model, the lower the truth content, and therefore the higher the degree of faltering. This is completely consistent with my earlier statement that the more primitive the sensory level is, the more stable it is, and the more advanced the perceptual level is, the more volatile it is.

Therefore, if we were to deduce the way and trend of truth development from a purely philosophical and rational point of view, we would find that our perceptual process is becoming more and more bewildered, or the rate of perceptual distortion is tending to increase. This is another expression of the trend of crisis in the process of human civilization from a mental and epistemological point of view.

Let's discuss another question, what does it mean to be *correct*? Since our knowledge has nothing to do with truth, that is, no doctrine of knowledge, including scientific systems, contains a judgment of truth, how can we test a model of thought, a doctrine, or a theory to see if it is *appropriate* or *correct*? I don't know which word is more precise, because the word we use every day is *correct*, maybe it is better to use the words *appropriate* and *suitable*. It has nothing to do with whether or not it is the truth, but whether or not your degree of existence matches your degree of compensation, or to put it more philosophically: whether or not your amount of compensation is sufficient to meet the existential threshold of the amount of existential loss. We call this thing "knowledge of effective compensation" or "effective perceptual state of compensation". In short, it is still the same: all knowledge and all perception are not set for truth, but set for reality or existence only. If existence is not stable, knowledge is also volatile; if knowledge is volatile, existence is also unstable; the two are mutually expressive.

So what do we use to judge what is *appropriate* or *correct*? I have set three philosophical indicators, called the *logical three consistencies*. Please note that when I talk about this part, you should recall what I meant when I said at the beginning of the course that "proof, only refers to logical proof".

The first indicator of the appropriateness and correctness of a doctrine or a model of thought is *self-consistency*. It is divided into two levels: first, the narrow sense of logical self-consistency. That is, in your rational logic, your theory and doctrine in the process of logical proof does not contradict itself. For example, Galileo's reductio ad absurdum, which I mentioned earlier, pointed out that Aristotle's common sense of free fall was not self-consistent in the narrow sense of logic, and therefore it collapsed. Second, the broad sense of logical self-consistency. That is, not only at the theoretical level, the rational level without contradiction, but also matching with the whole perceptual channel, i.e., perceptual logic and sensible logic. As I mentioned earlier, Aristarchus' heliocentric theory was not recognized because in the general logic it was not self-consistent, and it was not compatible with the geocentric theory at the level of perception and basic logic. Although it was actually correct, it did not express as correct, so it was not accepted. This is what called logical self-consistency meant.

The second indicator, *other-consistency*. By *other-consistency*, I mean that we cannot contradict other doctrines that have not yet been disproved, unless there is sufficient evidence to disprove them. Let me give you an example. I said earlier that materialism is not valid. For if materialistic reflectionism holds, then today's physics, optics, the relationship between wavelength and color perception, and sensory physiology must all be overturned. Maybe these things are wrong in the future, but if you can't prove it at the moment, then your doctrine must match it, and this is called other-consistency of general logic.

Let me give another example, Einstein's doctrine came out and could not completely disprove the appropriateness and correctness of Newton's doctrine in the macroscopic field, so after Einstein established the special theory of relativity, he had to then work on the general theory of relativity, that is, he had to deal with the matching relationship between the theory of gravity and space-time bending. He solved this problem well before the theory of relativity was established. Another example is about Newton's doctrine. As I said earlier, Newtonian mechanics is very accurate when applied to Uranus and Neptune, but using this theoretical system to calculate Mercury's incoming phenomenon, no matter how you calculate it, you can't get it right. Mercury is the closest planet to the Sun, due to the rotation of Mercury, the resulting rotational momentum will bring about a certain deflection of Mercury's orbit, which is called Mercury deflection, which is an angular momentum of Mercury's deflection of 1 degree, 33 minutes, and 20 seconds in a 100-year cycle. However, using Newton's theory of gravity and classical mechanics to calculate, there is always a difference of 43.11 seconds, and the exact corresponding value is never found. So, some scholars, in the same way as they did to Uranus and Neptune, said that there must be some undiscovered asteroid in the vicinity of Mercury that interferes with its motion, but no matter what, they could not find it. This was the problem until Einstein's theory of relativity appeared, and using Einstein's theory of relativity to calculate Mercury's deflection was very accurate and precise. What does it mean? It means that Newtonian classical mechanics is only an approximation of Einstein's relativity, that is, Einstein's relativity is a complete realization of the coverage and other-consistency of Newtonian mechanics, so Einstein's relativity is established. This is called *other-consistency of general logic*.

The third indicator, *future-consistency*. The term *future-consistency* refers specifically to the state of accepting and accommodating the new amount of information. That is to say, it is able to accommodate the new information better than the original logical model. It is important to note here that the model of theoretical ideas in philosophy and science is very strict and precise to the extent that it does not allow arbitrary adjustment. And it must be universal, that is, it must not have any counter examples to the relevant problem to which it corresponds. If any counter-example appears, your doctrine collapses, and you cannot deal with the problem of inconsistency by adjusting your own doctrine. It would be absurd to fine-tune our theoretical model and say that it is universally applicable. So, the philosophical model of thought is very rigorous, and even more so at the stage of scientific precision, and this is the lovely part about science. It has to undergo rigorous testing and withstand constant criticism and impact. Then when the amount of information increases, the original model must continue to maintain the precise pattern, and be able to accommodate this amount of information, the model will be expressed as "continue to be appropriate" or "continue to be correct", otherwise it immediately collapses, this is called *future-consistency*.

For example, I talked about Newton's doctrine earlier, it was so effective in explaining all problems by gravity in the macroscopic realm, but it could not handle the microscopic world movements that emerged after the 19th century. It is completely unable to deal with this additional information and new phenomena, so Newton's doctrine then degenerated into a background reference. We should know that there are many problems with Newton's doctrine, and I will give an example here: Newton said that gravity is the source of all forces, but gravity, such as the sun's attraction to the planets, to the earth, what is the transmission of this force? What is the medium through which this force is transmitted? How is this super distance effect achieved? Newton could not answer this question. Therefore, Newton assumed that the so-called vacuum of the universe was filled with a substance called *Ether*, which he said acted as the medium of gravity transmission. But the Ether could not be found, so Newton once left a paragraph saying that his own doctrine might be very absurd. Obviously, Newton was aware of this problem, and if the Ether could not be found, the doctrine of gravitation would have serious flaws. We know today that vacuum does not exist, because the so-called vacuum also contains a lot of energy waves, the so-called *vacuum* is actually an ocean full of energy fluctuations, but it is not the Ether. The physics and science community has not been able to find the Ether, so there is a major hole in the bottom of Newton's doctrine that cannot be filled, so much so that Newton himself is anxious.

Until Einstein's doctrine appeared, proving that gravity is actually just a presentation of the curvature of space, as long as the spacetime relationship is adjusted, there is no need for the Ether as such, the Ether is a completely redundant concept, and from then on the physics community does not have to explore whether the Ether exists. We can thus see that it is a very difficult situation when the original model cannot accommodate, cannot be renewed with the occurrence of new information, new phenomena. This is another important indicator of correctness.

I'll give you another example, look at Darwin's doctrine, he said the more advanced the species the more adaptable it is, the more survival advantage, which is called the "survival of the fittest". This is Darwin's original words. But Darwin himself did not notice a phenomenon, that is, the more advanced species, the more adaptable species, and the faster the extinction rate, which does not match Darwin's "survival of the fittest" research conclusions. Moreover, we used to believe that the more human beings progressed and developed, the more survival advantages they must have. Since the 1960s, people suddenly found that the more we developed and the more we progressed, the deeper the crisis became, that is, the human race faces an increasingly serious overall survival crisis. The emergence of these new information and phenomena has led to a failure of consistency between the original biological evolutionary model and the humanistic progressive model, and thus it led to the advent of my "principle of weakening compensation", which can explain what is the "evolutionary adaptation phenomenon" all about, the increasing adaptation is the expression of compensation gain; and it can also effectively explain the inner reason why the more species evolve, the faster they die, and the new phenomenon that the more human civilization develops, the higher the degree of their crisis, so my theory is in line with the tri-consistency of general logic, that is, self-consistency, other-consistency and future-consistency.

I just want to clarify one point here: what does it mean to be *correct* in a theory? What does it mean to be *appropriate* for a *non-true* logical model? It must be logically in three-consistency! Note that *properness* or *correctness* is just to answer the topic of *perceived untruth*, which has been many times vividly expressed in various ways in the history of human civilization. Let me give you another example. As early as the 3rd century B.C., a philosopher named Eratosthenes appeared in ancient Greece, and he had already calculated the circumference of the Earth, that is, the maximum circumference of the Earth, quite accurately more than 2200 years ago. As you know there are two numbers for the circumference of the Earth, one is the equatorial circumference 40,076 km and the other is the meridional circumference, or radial circumference 40,004 km, which is the exact measurement today. In the 3rd century B.C., Eratosthenes erected a pole to measure the sun's shadow at the vernal equinox at a place called Aswan in the upper part of the Nile, which is in southern Egypt. As you know, the Spring equinox and Autumn equinox are the two seasonal points when the direct point of the sun falls at the equator. Eratosthenes erected a pole in Aswan at the Spring equinox, and sent his colleagues to set up a pole in Alexandria, a city in northern Egypt on the lower Nile, to measure the length of the sun's shadow at the same time. Since Aswan is close to the equator and Alexandria is far from the equator, the lengths of sun shadows measured at noon in the two places are different. By measuring this difference in the length of the sun's shadow and performing precise mathematical calculations, Eratosthenes was able to actually calculate the circumference of the Earth with great accuracy at that time, which was nearly 40,000 kilometers, a very small difference from today's values.

You know, Ptolemy also gave the circumference of the Earth in his geocentric model, but it was a value with a huge error, which was calculated to be 18,000 Greek miles. One Greek mile is equivalent to 0.1517 kilometers, please multiply it, 0.1517 times 18000 is how much? The circumference of the earth is actually only a few thousand kilometers, which is a serious error. However, Ptolemy's geocentric theory in general is logically coherent in broad sense.

In 1492, Columbus made an absurd decision. According to Ptolemy's geocentric theory, he got to know that the earth is a sphere. Then since the Earth is a sphere, from Europe to the East India will not need to go east, he thought he could go completely west, complete opposite direction can also lead me to reach India. And, if he goes east, from Western Europe to reach India he has to follow the west coast of Africa south, and then around the Cape of Good Hope, and then into the Indian Ocean, to take a very winding long distance to reach India, a long way, the sea conditions are very complex. Columbus envisioned that he goes west, just cross the Atlantic Ocean, and he should be able to reach India, and the distance is much shorter, because the Ptolemaic measurement of the Earth is very small. Columbus calculated accordingly, obviously much closer than the distance previous people had experienced around the Cape of Good Hope. If Columbus knew the correct calculation Eratosthenes did, he would surely be terrified, definitely he did not dare such a long voyage. We know that he only had three wooden boats of small tonnage, accompanied by 87 members, actually traveled 70 days. He originally expected that they should be able to arrive around ten days plus, but they just could not see the land, the whole ship personnel became so pessimistic, due to the lack of fresh water, food and other essential supplies, they were almost in a desperate situation. Columbus finally asked to hold on for a few more moments and finally found the coast of the Costa Rican Islands. This extreme adventure led to the discovery of the New World. Columbus had no idea that he had reached the New World, and until his death, he thought he had reached India, so he called the natives *Indians*, which is the origin of the name *Indian*.

What am I trying to say here? I want to further clarify what is *correct*. It is the error of the time that is considered *correct*! Had Eratosthenes' calculations been known to Columbus at the time, or had Columbus known that Ptolemy's calculations were wrong, this major event that launched Western Blue Civilization would have been delayed or even disappeared. It shows that *correct* not a search for truth, but rather an expression of a fallacy at the right time, *correct* is only a mutual match with the survival situation, or rather a state of compensatory satisfaction to sustain existence, and this thing is called *correct*. This is the derivative relationship or survival maintenance effect of all perceptions.

The Nature of *Science*

We will discuss the last issue below - what is science? This topic will be the closing part of this lesson.

Today is the age of science, and everyone thinks they know very well what science is. But in fact, as I have said repeatedly, philosophy is the mother of science, and if you do not have a true understanding of the roots of philosophy, that is, the underpinnings of science, you actually do not know what science is. What we usually mean by science is that which can be empirically proven. A theory is reached from experience, from objectivity, and then verified by experience and practice, so science is also called empirical science, or in philosophy, positivism.

But even in the West, where philosophy and science were born, the definition of what science is has not been found. It was not until the last century that a philosopher specializing in science appeared in the West, named Karl Popper, and this philosophy was called philosophy of science. Karl Popper gave a definition of science for the first time, which is called *falsificationism* for short, and it was really astounding. What does *falsificationism* mean? It is opposite the meaning of *proof*, so it is called *falsificationism*, that is, any learning that can be proven wrong is called science.

Let me repeat, Popper said that science is a term for *learning* that can be *falsified*. This is the opposite of what we usually understand by science as truth, or at least relative truth, and undoubtedly objective law. Please understand my previous lesson, all our human knowledge is just an a priori closed perception model, and what we call laws are always subjective laws, how can they be objective laws? Popper made an argument, he said that science is never called science if it is empirically valid. He says you look first at non-science, such as theology or philosophy, and it is very difficult to falsify it. Who, may I ask, can prove the existence of God or disprove the existence of God? You can neither prove God exists, nor can you falsify it, saying that God does not exist, and since it cannot be falsified, it is a non-science. What gives you a sense of "theological proof" is that a person who believes in God uses all kinds of illusionary evidence to prove the existence of God, for example, that he can even see miracles and experience the apocalypse, which is solid evidence, but you just cannot disprove it, so it is not science.

Then look at philosophy, which is also generally very difficult to falsify. Can you prove materialism wrong, for example? Or can you prove idealism wrong? You can't disprove it! Because the evidence you present is itself the very thing you are supposed to prove. If you hold a materialist idea, then any piece of evidence you produce is valid; conversely, if you hold a idealist idea, any piece of evidence you produce is equally valid, such as proof that any object is a derivative of an idea. In short, the evidence you provide is exactly what you need to prove, and therefore invalid. You can neither prove it with certainty, nor can you falsify it at all, so it is still not science.

But throughout the history of science, all scientific theories are ultimately proven wrong. Karl Popper cited the history of science specifically for this purpose, and I will use his way to make a paraphrase, of course, not entirely accurate. Ptolemy can be considered the first rigorous scientist in human history, he established the geocentric model is accurate and effective, guide the Western agricultural civilization for more than 1400 years, it has been repeatedly proved correct and effective, the result today is completely reduced to the history of science laughing stock.

Looking at Copernicus' heliocentric theory, it is important to understand that it started out as a purely conjectural model. Copernicus was in the 16th century, when the Renaissance had been launched and ancient Greek texts had been translated. Copernicus, as a cleric, had traveled and studied in Italy as a young man. Italy was not yet unified and was divided into various city-state republics, such as the Republic of Venice, the Republic of Florence, the Republic of Milan, etc. That fragmented political structure constituted the social cradle of the Renaissance at that time. Copernicus came across Ptolemy's system of geocentric doctrine and its mathematical model in Italy, and after careful study, found that Ptolemy's doctrine had many flaws and was overly complicated in its calculations and cumbersome in its overlapping celestial wheel design. He envisioned, and he only assumed or conjectured, because he had no evidence, that if the sun was placed in the middle and the earth and all the stars were made to orbit around the sun, then Ptolemy's entire astronomical-mathematical system could be significantly simplified and the many flaws in the original system of logical models that were not well thought out could easily be remedied, and so the heliocentric theory was established.

You should know that Copernicus established heliocentrism back then without any evidence, almost similar to the embarrassing situation that Aristarchus faced in establishing heliocentrism in ancient Greek times that I mentioned earlier. This is why Copernicus, a Polish man, could not publish his works until his death. He finally commissioned a friend to go to Germany, which was divided into hundreds of small states (at that time Germany was still only a geographical term and could not be considered a unified national polity at all), and found an opportunity to publish it secretly in that place. It is said that Copernicus saw the sample of his work before death and he was glad to see it and died in peace. Fifty years after the death of Copernicus, Bruno supported his doctrine and was burned in the Sun Square by the Inquisition, to the cheers of the crowded people. Seventy or eighty years after the death of

Copernicus, Galileo late in life published vaguely supportive of Copernicus' heliocentric views, was sentenced to house arrest by the Inquisition, while the academic world was quiet, almost without protest. Why? Because there was no strong evidence for Copernicus' doctrine. It was not until nearly a hundred years after Copernicus' death that Copernicus' doctrine was confirmed, thanks to the development of the telescope, from Galileo's first discovery of Venus's surplus and deficit, followed by the theoretical construction of the optical parallax and stellar parallax.

I tell this allusion in order to make you understand what science is, which is a conjectural structure that first builds a model of an idea, rather than a practice that produces true knowledge. After Copernicus' doctrine was introduced, after only two or three hundred years the main body of his doctrine was proven wrong. Copernicus thought that the sun was the center of the universe, but today we know that the sun is not even the center of the galaxy; Copernicus thought that the orbits of all planets around the sun are positive circles, but today we know that there are no positive circular orbits, all planetary orbits are elliptical. Copernicus' doctrine showed a major error hundreds of years later, and was wrong in general and only partially valid within the solar system.

Let's look at Newton. As I mentioned earlier, Newton's classical mechanics emerged as a way to accurately predict planets that had not yet been observed, but this theoretical *correctness* only lasted for more than 200 years before it was pushed to the back of the line by Einstein's theory of relativity. As a result, Einstein declared that his doctrine was only a "short-lived transition". It is important to know that Einstein's doctrine has a prerequisite and assumption that the speed of light is absolute, that is, the speed of anything in the universe can not exceed the speed of light. Many issues such as these have faced major challenges so far, which is the reason why the scientific community is currently making efforts to go beyond Einstein's doctrine.

So now we see that the science is even all wrong, and it is getting wrong faster and faster, that is, it is being falsified faster and faster. This means that scientific theories are becoming less and less true! This is what we call *science*: a system of scholarship that is getting less and less true, that is being falsified more and more quickly, and that is repeatedly proven wrong. This is completely different from our common perception of science as objective truth and objective law.

Popper goes on to say that it is generally believed that the model of human knowledge is based on a process of "from observation to theory". But in fact, science is the opposite: it is "from theory to observation", it is "speculation and refutation". That is, it first builds a theoretical model and then seeks to prove it one by one in the laboratory or in actual observation. Therefore, the scientific act is a continuation of the typical purely logical line of thought in philosophy. Popper expressed it as "problem (P1) - test theory (TT) - eliminate error (EE) - new problem (P2) ", that is, initiating with the formulation of a problem; followed by tentative theory construction or thought model construction; then focusing on the elimination of errors; and finally being subverted by the emergence of a new problem. He calls the cognitive outcome reached by this sequence of thought science, and it is one of the best, or relatively best, definitions of science we have seen so far.

I make this point in order to break the superstition of science. We Chinese are in a state of Scientology today because of our lack of understanding of the relationship between science itself and philosophy and the underlying structure of human perception. The question here is whether (objective) facts lead to logic or (a priori) logic leads to facts? Some people say that this is a pointless tangle of *the chicken or the egg,* but I do not think this is necessarily the case.

Popper divided the world into three layers, what he called *world one,* which is what we call the objective material world; *world two* refers to our mental level and perception state; *world three* is the content of our mind and knowledge system. The key issue here is the part of *world two,* that is, your perceptual regulations, states of consciousness, and thought models, which you have to figure out, otherwise you will never understand the relationship between *world one* and *world three.*

This definition of science by Popper is certainly not complete. Let's put this topic aside for now and return to it at the end of this lesson.

Let's now look briefly at the division between science and technology. As I emphasized in my first day of lectures, Chinese culture is called *skill culture* - technology and artistic cultural forms; Western culture is called *philosophical thinking* - philosophy and scientific way of thinking; these two are completely different. It is important to understand that technology and science are two different things, and it is only after the modern scientific era, when basic and applied sciences were finally combined or developed into a huge reverberant system, that we can discuss *science* and *technology* together. Before the Middle Ages, science and technology are completely two thought channels, technology is the practice in front, and then find a theory to put it together; philosophy and science, on the contrary, is the idea of modeling in front, and then open a laboratory with practical experience to test, so science and technology are very different ways of thinking, please be sure to distinguish clearly.

Compare the difference between science and technology: technology is a hard-state operational trial-and-error approach, and science is a soft-state logical trial-and-error approach. Because technology is faced with an object or problem, repeatedly and continuously at the level of operational behavior trial and error, and thus achieve technical results. For example, the four major inventions of China, the compass is not theoretical modeling in the front, the Chinese at that time, do not know the impact of the Earth's magnetic poles on the constant magnet, they just found it by chance to levitate the constant magnet, it always points to the north and south, which is entirely a product of experience; gunpowder, is the alchemists in order to refine the elixir of immortality, and they blindly try to add a variety of things to the furnace, and then an accidental explosion, which came out the product of explosion as gunpowder; paper making and movable type printing, is the invention of artisans in daily production activities, they are not at all with the establishment of theoretical logical model of a sequence of behavior, which is called technology. So in ancient times, when mankind had not yet entered the scientific era, based on the large population and the complexity of social needs, China became a technological power, ahead of its time in the field of technology, but in the scientific era it could not avoid rapid decline, why? Because science is a soft state logic trial and error method, it first reached a result in the model of ideas, that is, scientific logic, with deductive methods to sweep all aspects of the trial and error effect. Thus science accelerates technology, the former (scientific logic) expands technology, the latter (soft state trial and error) accelerates technology, because soft state logic experimentation is of course much more convenient than hard state object trial and error; at the same time, science refines technology, because the modeling of ideas is the embodiment of sophisticated logic, and therefore can achieve sophisticated deduction of technological development; science also systematizes technology, that is, from connotation to extension, it shows a wide range of connections. This has led to the rapid rise of a barbaric West, which has just emerged from the darkness of the Middle Ages, since the dawn of the scientific age.

So we must understand that science and technology are two different things, and the scientific era is based on the foundation of thousands of years of philosophical refinement. In the history of science there has been a phenomenon that can be called "logic is more true than fact". When I say this, some people would say that this is an arrogant idealistic cry, and I have seen this criticism of me on the Internet. Please note the philosophical and scientific implications of this phrase. As I have said repeatedly before, all our perceptions are merely the product of a priori forms of perception. Our perceptions are prescriptive, and our knowledge derives from the subjective operation of processing we apply to external objects. This is why Wittgenstein opens his *Treatise on the Philosophy of Logic* with the statement, "The world is the sum of facts, not the sum of things." What does that mean? It means that what we humans call the world is the sum of logical facts, not the sum of objective things. Because whatever we call a *thing* is actually just a reproduction of a *fact* in our model of perception.

Hegel famously said, "Everything that is real is rational, and everything that is rational is real." Let's note that this quote was once not phrased in its entirety in this way. What we usually talk about, or hear in class, is the statement, "Whatever is existing is rational, and whatever is reasonable is existing." This is easy to misunderstand, because what we mean by *reasonable* is a very broad concept. Note Hegel's words, "Whatever is real is rational, and whatever is rational is real." What does that mean? What we call *reality* is "reality on a logical model", or "reality rectified by reason", which is called "whatever is What is *real* is *rational*. "

In the 16th century, there was a famous astronomer in Denmark named Tycho Brahe. He was the best and most outstanding astronomer before telescope was invented, and he observed the sky with the naked eye for more than 20 years. Because of his great contribution, the Danish royal family set up the largest astronomical observatory in the world for him at that time in a place called Boon Island. He observed the heavens closely every night and made detailed records of the thousands of stars he could observe with the naked eye, including the slightest changes in the orbits of the planets, and he was actually able to observe the difference of 8 minutes in the orbits of the planets. Note that a circle (circumference angle) is 360 degrees, 1 degree then divided into 60 minutes, 1 minute then divided into 60 seconds, he was able to observe 0.13 degrees of 8 minutes difference, accurately mapping the planets orbit of such a subtle difference. However, since Tycho Brahe embraced the idea of geocentrism, he did want to correct it, so he actually created a hybrid model of heliocentrism and geocentrism: all the planets revolve around the sun, and then the sun carries the planets around the earth. He made such a hybrid model, but it boils down to geocentrism - the Earth does not move to avoid the dilemma of the heliocentric theory. Because he had the basic idea of Ptolemaic geocentrism in his heart, he observed the stars for 20 years, cherishing that he would make a great achievement in astronomy, and until his death he lamented "how he wished to make a great discovery", but he finally failed to do so.

In his later years, Tycho Brahe accepted a disciple called Kepler. Kepler was very young, in his early 20s, and had been Tycho Brahe's protégé for just over a year before Tycho Brahe's death. Kepler had been exposed to Copernicus' heliocentric idea, please note that it was only a heliocentric idea, and then when he opened the astrological records of Tycho Brahe, he clearly found that Tycho Brahe's observations could effectively prove that Copernicus' heliocentric idea was valid, but only the problem of the 8 minutes difference of the planets could not be explained. At this point Kepler realized that the 8 minutes difference could mean that the planets' orbits were not circular and that Copernicus had made a mistake! But he didn't have any ready-made mathematical model to use. By chance, he found in the library the *Theory of the Conic Curve* by Apollonius more than 200 BC.

I will briefly talk about Apollonius below. Apollonius was a famous philosopher, naturalist or scientist in ancient Greece. Apollonius finished all the mathematical models of different sections of a cone back then. As we all know, a cone, make a parallel section is a square circle, make a dip section is an ellipse. Apollonius finished all the mathematical equations of various models of conic curves back then, and he had no idea what the use of this thing is. Kepler stumbled upon this paper, and he threw the elliptical mathematical model of Apollonius' conic curve directly in the sky, which actually happened to be the orbits of the planets. Bear in mind that the orbit of the planets in the elliptical model is very complicated, because from the center of the ellipse, the planets elliptical orbit must have a perihelion and an aphelion, the planet orbit to the perihelion its speed accelerates, orbit to the aphelion is slowed down, it scans the elliptical sector area per unit time is always equal. Apollonius finished proving this strange mathematical model in that year, but he did not know what use it had, and the result was that Kepler threw this mathematical model directly into the sky, which happened to be the orbit of the planet, and it was not bad at all. This incident made the contemporary philosopher Whitehead exclaimed: "Matter has not yet appeared, the mind has long been first", Einstein also once commented on this, saying that "logic and discernment guide the facts."

Well, after I finish this allusion, please recall my earlier quote from Hegel: "Everything that is real is rational, and everything that is rational is real", that is, "logic is more real than fact". What does that mean? What we call the world is the body of our logical model. When I say this, you should also think back to one thing - the *idea theory*. Are ideas true, or are facts true? We would normally think that facts come first and ideas come second. Wrong! It should be that the idea comes first and the facts come second. If you hold the idea of geocentrism, it is the astronomical fact of Tycho Brahe, and if you hold the idea of heliocentrism of Copernicus, it is the astronomical fact of Kepler. Kepler was therefore called the *celestial legislator* in recognition of his ability to calculate the precise position of any planet's orbit. What does this mean? Logic is more real than facts! It expresses the correspondence between the model of human cognition and the model of the world we are referring to. Even if a logical model is created without knowing where it will be implemented as a fact, it will eventually be realized as a fact. I draw your attention to the understanding that this system is called *science, system of knowledge, worldview* and *cosmological model.*

Then I have to discuss the following question, why all scientific theories ultimately but to take the empirical test, called experimental observation. That is, the highest end of sophisticated logical models, but ultimately to be tested with the lowest end of the eye, despite the eye is not true, but to be tested with it, thus science is also called empirical science. As I said earlier, empirical evidence and proof are two different things. Proof refers to broad logical proof and narrow logical precision modeling, and empirical evidence refers only to underlying perceptual logical verification, so they are two concepts. But the question is, if logic is more true than fact, why do we need to test it with low-end perceptual logic? Please pay attention to understand the two points I repeatedly mentioned earlier: First, human perception communicates with the external world through the channel of self-consistency of general logic, so if your theory is reached at the high-end narrow logic, but fails to be verified at the bottom of the general logic, it indicates that the whole general logical channel has not yet been opened. Secondly, the more primitive and bottom-level things are, the more groundbreaking, decisive and stable they are. It is this principle of weakening compensation that makes any high-end logical precision model must ultimately be verified by the most rudimentary underlying perceptual experimental observation, which is the reason why *science* presents a paradoxical form on the surface.

So, we can say "logic is more true than facts", but you can't say "logic is more reliable than facts". The logic here refers to narrow logic, that is, you cannot say that reason is more reliable than sense, because the lower end of things has more stability. To understand this passage, you have to go through my whole lecture.

Logical Path of Knowledge Innovation

So let's discuss the following question: Is Popper's definition of science as *falsificationism* correct? At a cursory glance, it seems to be valid, but it is not. Why not? Because if we expand the boundaries of cognitive phenomena beyond the scientific horizon, that is, if we review the history of cognition on a larger scale, the situation immediately changes. We will find a phenomenon: the more primitive the cognition, the more difficult it is to be falsified; the more advanced the cognition, the faster it is falsified. This has nothing to do with science; it is true for the whole series, from theology and philosophy to science.

You can't say that theology is unfalsifiable, it's just difficult to falsify and it is extremely stable. Nor can you say that previous philosophy cannot be falsified; again, it is just difficult to falsify. For example, read my *A Unified Theory of Evolution*. I say that God is falsifiable because God's compensation is too great, and his attributes and powers are too high, and he is called "omniscient, omnipotent, and omnibenevolent," so he cannot be there earlier than us, much less possible at the beginning of the creation of the universe, but only be there after us. This is why the original title of Harari's book *A Brief History of the Future* was *From Homo Sapiens to Homo Deus*, which is an excellent formulation. Likewise, it is not impossible to falsify the definitive theories of the philosophical past, such as materialism, idealism, agnosticism, etc. If you understand my previous lesson, you will know that they can be falsified, and that they cannot be logically consistent in the broad sense, nor can they be logically other-consistent. It is just that the falsification of philosophy is more difficult than the falsification of science and requires more information than the general science, that's all.

And we can stretch the scale even further. As I said earlier, induction is more stable than perception, and perception is more stable than knowingness, and knowingness is more stable than reason, even in the inorganic and animal stages. If we take the whole history of cognition, that is, the whole evolution of the inductive attributes gain, and do not limit it to the history of human cognition, we will find that the lower and more primitive cognition must be more stable. The electromagnetic induction between electrons and protons, for example, must be the most stable, more stable than that wavelength of light that appears as green in all plants or leaves when viewed perceptually. Thus, falsificationism manifests itself on a large scale as a natural general tendency for all cognitive outcomes of higher end and more volatile.

If so, falsificationism would be defined not just for the scientific stage, but for the entire history of cognition. So falsificationism as a definition of science is not valid, is it not? Because *definition* means that the concept you are discussing is framed in terms of *clear boundaries* of its connotation and extension. So Popper's falsificationism cannot be used only as a definition of science, but as an expression of the *destabilizing tendency* of all cognitive history. Since Popper's search for fundamental philosophical questions was not deep enough, he already found that the rate of scientific correctness was declining, and by logical extension, he should have concluded that the cognitive content of human beings was getting less and less true and farther and farther from the truth. But in the end, he still repeats the same old story, saying that the process of scientific development is getting closer and closer to the truth, thus causing a major logical confusion.

I will give below a definition of *science* that cannot be considered precise either. It does not appear in my book, because I do not dare to say it lightly in my book, because it is not precise or refined enough, so I only give a rough statement in my lectures. What is *science*? First, it is a logical model. Theoretically, it is presented as a narrow logic model, which is the product of the extension of the philosophical logic game, and in general, it is presented as a general logic model, which is also called empirical science. Second, it is the science of subdisciplines. Because of its high degree of abstraction and meticulous precision, it can accept the ever-expanding larger volume of information, i.e., when the volume of information expands to a certain degree, the total sum of all information cannot be rectified by any individual alone, so human beings have to study the branches of this logical knowledge system in a mode of divisions, which is the science by division. Thirdly, it is the stage of highly volatile cognition. Since it is the high-end integration of human knowledge, reaching the advanced stage of rational logic, it is by far the most destabilized model of natural induction. This is the reason for Popper's statement that any learning that can be proven wrong is called science. In short, the logical model expresses the untruth of science; the science of division expresses the crippling of science; the volatile state expresses the peril of science. Its basic features can be summed up in three phrases: the logical model comes first; the precise and meticulous form; the high degree of falsifiability; these three combined the system of knowledge called *science*.

This is a basic summary of science I made in this most abbreviated way. Since science is only a specific human phenomenon, it is not within the scope of my ultimate study. But the second volume of my *A Unified Theory of Evolution, Philosophy of Mind*, discusses how the whole affective attributes of sense-response or cognitive process unfolds compensatively, contains, of course, an account of the nature of science and its trends. I can only give a non-precise overview here.

Below we discuss the logical path of knowledge innovation.

It is only when you understand what scientific knowledge and all cultural achievements of human beings are all about, including their ideological operation and their correspondence with the world, and when you clarify these things, you can build new knowledge and you can innovate ideas. So when we come to this point in the course on philosophical epistemology, we can say something about the innovative approach to knowledge systems, mainly by pointing out its logical path. I will discuss it below in a more intuitive way.

First, do not believe that any previous scientific theory is the truth, but rather confirm that it is the furthest thing from the truth and is waiting for you to reshape it. That is, you must first confirm that science is not the truth. Imagine if you confirm that science is the truth, how can you dare to criticize and innovate in the face of past scientific dogmas that you are too afraid of? So please keep in mind that not only science, but all human learning has nothing to do with truth, which is the first and most basic requirement of background awareness for innovation.

Second, you should not expect yourself to discover any truths that are eternally rooted. Rootlessness just means that your discovery belongs to the realm of science and not to the dregs of pseudoscience. Because science is the thing that gets falsified the fastest. So when you build a theoretical model, you don't expect to build an eternal, stable system of truth. Without this extravagant hope and without setting such a high bar, innovation can become a realistic goal.

Third, avoid the Human problem. That is, the inductive method does not hold, and you should not just collect and summarize the material of the subject under study. This is because the inductive method cannot prove, only falsify, because the material that can be inducted can never be exhausted. If you keep searching for facts, keep searching for inductive elements, then it will be an infinite amount of work. That's why Hegel famously said, "erudition is never truth!" That is, any good theory, it has nothing to do with erudition, it has nothing to do with the total amount of facts you collect.

Please look at the history of science, the most significant scientific discoveries of mankind were mostly made by young people. For example, Kepler became the sky legislator in his twenties and thirties; and before he graduated from college, Newton had to take a break from school due to the Black Death epidemic, and built the inverse square law at home in his twenties. What is the inverse square law? I repeat it: the gravitational force is proportional to the product of the mass of two objects, and inversely proportional to the square of the distance between two objects. But Newton did not think that this was a major breakthrough, instead, he thought it was a very mundane and simple phenomenon, and did not take it seriously. It wasn't until he was about 40 years old, teaching at Cambridge University, that he once got drunk with a group of scholars, and an academic named Robert Hooke told Newton that he had made a major discovery, the inverse square law! Newton said, bullshit, I've known this stuff since I was in my twenties. What kind of major discovery is this?! The arguer was very annoyed and said you have to prove it for me, if you really did it. After Newton returned, he wrote his famous *Mathematical Principles of Natural Philosophy*. If there were no such an argument at dinner, Newtonian mechanics would not have appeared. This is, of course, just a popular story, we do not have to take it seriously. What do I want to say? Newton was only in his twenties when he discovered the core of his doctrine.

Similarly, Einstein was less than thirty years old when he proposed the *special theory of relativity*. He was a typical civil scientist, working as an ordinary clerk in the Bern Patent Office. When the paper on special relativity was published, almost no one could understand it. Ten years later, when Einstein was in his thirties, the *general theory of relativity* was also completed. After that, he spent the rest of his life trying to study the *unified field theory* in order to unify the four major forces in physics, but ultimately failed. As he grew older and was more knowledgeable, he achieved no more. What does it mean? Knowledge is never the truth. Kepler in his twenties to thirties, Newton in his twenties, Einstein in his twenties, how much less knowledge do they have comparing to the old professors of physics at that time? There were many university physics professors in their fifties and sixties, but did any of them create a whole new model of knowledge? So remember that erudition is never the truth, do not search infinitely for information, or summarize the material, for that is not the way to do research, that is an approach total lack of understanding of the history of human thought.

Fourth, explicitly understand Kantian problem. That is, making deductive assumptions and proofs based on basic logical premises, i.e., conjecture and modeling. Consider what I said earlier, Copernicus' theory modeling does not require facts first, it only requires courageous and rigorous conjecture, and a well-thought-out deduction of new ideas.

Fifth, stay curious. This is a mundane statement, but you must know that it is very difficult to stay in curious mind. Because as I said earlier, the sign of a person's maturity at an older age is precisely the loss of curiosity. What does it mean to stay curious? Keeping a child's mind! Because only a child will be more amazed, will be curious about everything, and will not tire of asking questions. When a person reaches middle age, he or she involuntarily loses curiosity and becomes a carrier of rigid thinking and deep stereotypes. So keep curiosity, it is easy to say, but extremely difficult to do, it will make you look a bit childish, and even some grotesque. I remember when I was in my forties, I ran into a childhood friend whom I hadn't seen for more than twenty years. We sat together drinking and chatting, and after some time he said to me, you are so old now, but why are you still talking like a young man, still a student mentality, far from mature. He was right in some sense, but this state is precisely where my brain strength lies in being able to do scholarship. Therefore, please remember that to maintain curiosity is actually to stunt mental growth or slow down mental aging, which is biologically called *juvenile persistence,* which is quite difficult.

Sixth, the power of imagination. What does it mean? What we call the world is always a model of our subjective ideas, not the true presentation of the objective world, so we have the power to create knowledge only if we have imagination, which is called *imagination*. If our perception is the true reflection of the world, what room do you have for imagination? What else do we need ideas for? The value of thought is that we do not get the truth, we must always use conjecture to simulate or virtual truth, the perception process is layers of virtual process. You know that VR virtual technology is by no means a sudden phenomenon today, the history of the universe's perception is the history of virtual iteration. Think about the electron to proton reached that electric neutrality, isn't it a virtual? Think about that salt impression reached by an acid root to a base, isn't it a virtual? Think about the light energy you transform into visual brightness, isn't it a virtual? Think about your transformation of wavelength into color or sound, isn't it a virtual? Think about the logical model you build, which is nothing but the imitation and conjecture of that cosmic case that cannot be opened, isn't it another layer of virtual?

The history of cosmic cognition is the history of virtual development, and the VR phenomenon is actually nothing more than the present-day form of virtual iteration. Since all our knowledge is virtual, what is needed for virtual? First of all, of course, imagination! Human civilization unfolds on this whimsical imagination system, so it is crucial to play and mobilize imagination in knowledge innovation. But I need to add that maintaining the ability to imagine virtual and hypothetical modeling, in no way implies whimsy; it must be followed by a strict requirement for precise logical proof. If you can't do the second half, the preceding imagination is pure nonsense, *delusion*!

Seventh, rigor must be observed. The most objectionable and taboo thing in academics and thinking is the lack of rigor, and rigor means precise logical proof.

Eighth, as long as it holds logically, or as long as the logic is self-consistent and well rounded, you generally don't have to worry about the hypothesis not being verified. That is the business of posterity, and you have accomplished much. As long as you have built a logical model that has been rigorously proven, it will be a fact in the future, even if it cannot be verified in your lifetime. Just as Apollonius proposed the conic curve, it took almost 2000 years before it was verified and implemented, which, despite Apollonius' regret, was a gain for mankind.

I call the above eight items the logical path of *intellectual innovation*. The prerequisite for understanding it is to understand the whole system of philosophical thinking and the essence of the issues covered in the two-day course.

We will end with a last question. As you listen to my class, it is easy to get the impression that I highly appreciate the Western philosophical system of thinking, while deliberately disparaging the Chinese skill culture and its sloppy logic system. Make no mistake! I repeat, I am not talking about the good and the bad, but only talk about what it is. I just want to tell you how the way of thinking created by different civilizations happens? What is the form? In what way does it unfold? In what way does it operate? In what way does it go deeper? What are the consequences of the thought that will eventually be achieved? There is no good or bad, right or wrong evaluation here. The major crises we face today are the result of the over mobilization of human intelligence potential.

Remember what I said earlier, the philosophy is called love of wisdom. What is love of wisdom? The over-mobilization of human intelligence reserves. I said at that time that any over-mobilization of functional reserves is damaging. So let me now interpret this point. When human beings have fully mobilized their philosophical thinking capacity, it has today unfolded as a great crisis for the survival of humanity as a whole, bringing great gloom to the future of humanity, and becoming a very difficult dilemma and problem that humanity must deal with as soon as possible. Therefore, I say that the thinkers, philosophers and scientists of the past are not the credit of mankind, but the calamity of mankind. Moreover, I say that the scientific era is coming to an end and the post-scientific era is coming. For science has had the following twofold effect.

First, it is increasingly difficult to penetrate the entire general logic. At the time of Einstein's article, the scientific community exclaimed that theoretical physics had become "the heaven of theory and the hell of experiment". Nowadays, it is impossible to verify the innovative theories of *superstring theory, M-theory, multiverse theory, parallel universe theory*, etc., and they have become strange theories floating in the air. This signifies that science is becoming more and more nebulous and metaphysical, and that the high-level destabilization of academic thinking has reached its extreme, and it also marks the end of science as a phenomenal discipline.

Second, mankind today can no longer bear the results of science, which has forged a huge catastrophic foundation and destructive force for mankind. Therefore, I say that the scientific age is coming to an end, and the post-scientific age will soon be here. We can therefore expect that the scientific age is the shortest-lived phase of the human paradigm of thinking. The age of theology, nearly ten thousand years; the age of philosophy, two or three thousand years; the age of science, which began with Copernicus and is now only a few hundred years old, is coming to an end. And we can imagine that in the post-scientific era, people at that time will look back on today's scientific era and think that we are extremely ridiculous - how can we believe in all that nonsense? Just like we today look at the ancient shamans who danced with the deities and find it very ridiculous. You know, back then, the shamans were equivalent to members of the Academy of Sciences today.

It must be admitted, however, that the post-scientific era must be the era of dealing with greater amounts of information. Because there is no way back for humankind, according to the law of weakening compensative evolution, the world operates in a process of compensation of information increments. The post-scientific era must therefore be an era of greater information, except that the handling of this information will be done in a completely different way than in the scientific era today. In the scientific era, any increment of information that can be rectified into a theoretical model is immediately modeled and verified. In the post-scientific era, the ability to discriminate and sift the very large amounts of information, and the ability to determine the actual cultural effects of the larger amounts of information in the long term, is something that science simply cannot do.

Since the beginning of civilization, any knowledge that can effectively deal with current problems has always been regarded as a great achievement, but what is its long-term effect? We simply have no way of determining this, because there is not enough information! The amount of information in the future will enable us to make a clear prediction of the distant effects of any kind of knowledge model, so as to reach the prevention of its harmful effects. It must therefore be a continuation of the process of incremental information, not a retrogression to the past evolutionary path. In other words, the post- scientific era must correct and eliminate the disastrous effects of today's science, and its pioneering part will still unfold and be driven by philosophical foresight, because, as I said earlier, philosophy is scientific foresight, and it explores the post-evolutionary problems in advance in the absence of sufficient information. This forward-looking function of philosophy will continue to be expressed in the post-scientific era, except that the results expressed will no longer be scientific foresight, but post-scientific foresight. This is the role of future philosophy in guiding the thinking that will continue to play a significant function in the cultural reengineering of the future post- scientific era, and this is the significance of the need for us in today's scientific era to continue the spirit of philosophical forward-looking inquiry.

Q & A After Class

Questioner: Hello, everyone! My question is just one sentence, how did you obtain your knowledge in your study? Because I found the entire class content to be very diverse in terms of various ideas, very large in terms of data, in terms of information, and the data you cited are very precise, often to one or two places of decimals. In addition, the logic was so clear and the structure was so well thought out that I had a strange worry, especially when you slowed down your speech to cite some data, some rather long names of foreigners', I would worry whether you would forget or couldn't say them out, or whether you would make up a data temporarily because there were too many data. Whenever I noticed this, I would take note of it and go back to the Internet to look it up myself, and my check online, Baidu result shows that you are right. I kept worrying for you during this process, but later it turned out to be unnecessary, which made me even more curious. What is your way of thinking? It's so accurate, so deep and so broad that you can achieve such a high level of precision. Another thing is, as the saying goes, "It's better to teach someone to fish than to give him a fish", here I might be a little greedy, that is, I want both the fish and the fishing technique, I hope you can explain it to me. Thank you!

Mr. Dongyue: My lecture in the past two days is to teach you how to fish, and I just talked about the way of thinking. I have repeatedly said that my class is useless because it only talks about the operation of the underlying ideas. As for your feeling that I have a lot of knowledge, or information, or memory, in fact I am not at all smarter than normal people, all people are equally smart. Because all of us are one species, the genetic difference between all of us is actually less than 0.1%, so the difference in intelligence of each person is minimal. It is only the direction in which each person uses his or her own intelligence, or the degree to which he or she focuses his or her entire intelligence, that differs. Most people spread their energy and intelligence over a wide range of matters, while a few will focus their intelligence and energy on a single point. It is like a palm-sized piece of sunlight on the surface of your hand, you can hardly feel the heat, but you use a palm-sized magnifying glass to focus this sunlight on a single point, and it can ignite the paper below. What does this mean? The effect of energy focused on a single point and scattered on a surface is completely different. So if you think I did lecture a lot of knowledge, you ask me how to study, then I can only give you a word: be a lonely and stupid bookworm.

Questioner: Mr. Dongyue, based on the summary you just made, I would like to make two conjectures. First conjecture is that the amount of compensation is equal to the amount of existence multiplied by the square of the speed of compensation, because it is just like mass and energy are the same thing; the second conjecture is that you just said that science may cause a lot of crises in the future, and I think human beings have no need to worry about this, even if one day human beings do not exist, it is simply a matter of their reducing to atoms. Since human beings evolved from atoms to monkeys in the primordial past, after we reduced to atoms, we can still evolve from atoms to monkeys and then to human beings, which is just equivalent to human beings sleeping for, say, 100 million years, or billion years. Thank you, sir!

Mr. Dongyue: Regarding the first question, you have to first intensively read *A Unified Theory of Evolution*, you read it really well, and then set up a model and prove it. So, you giving me the question this way now is not valid, you have to do the precision logic proof. If you can make that square proof of yours, I will highly show my respect. The second question is, from an individual point of view, life and death really doesn't matter, living longer or shorter, there is not much important difference. But please understand that all things, including human beings, have a nature to survive, which has nothing to do with whether you are willing to sacrifice yourself, so there is fear toward death in human nature. Therefore, if human survival situation is very difficult, people are afraid of death. Fear of death is not because it is good to live, but because nature dictates that all things seek to survive. Remember that it is not only human beings or anything of life that seek survival, but all things seek survival. To better understand the meaning of this statement, please read my book *A Unified Theory of Evolution*. Seeking survival is not a question of good or not, but a must, but a necessity. Therefore, the question I am exploring is not the question of life and death, but the basic theory of how to survive in the next phase of civilizational crisis.

Questioner: Hello, sir! Just now you talked about the continued pursuit of philosophy, that is, only the philosophy of the future will guide the post-scientific era, and you mentioned this morning that there is a trend in the development of philosophical thinking, that is, shallowing, moving from the very beginning of the pursuit of the origin of the world to the pursuit of the state of perception as well as the state of language, etc. The trend is obviously shallowing, so is there a contradiction in that? If we expect the future philosophy to guide the post-scientific era, will the post-scientific era be even shorter and more unstable than the scientific era? Thank you!

Mr. Dongyue: The first question you raise is based on your default that Western philosophy represents the future, while I have told you repeatedly that Western culture does not represent the future. The trend of shallowness of Western philosophy today marks the decline of Western culture. To your second question, I can give you a very clear answer that the post-scientific era must be shorter-lived and less stable than the scientific era, despite its desire to pursue stability.

Questioner: I would like to ask you, sir, is the continuation of the theory of Western philosophy that you are talking about today the starting point of your theory of weakening compensation? Or did you construct your theory from many phenomena, such as the withering of grass, or the hundred schools of thought in Pre-Qin era of China, and the changes in human society? Which aspect of these do you think might contribute more to the theory of weakening compensation? Thank you!

Mr. Dongyue: I can't quite explain this question clearly, or I am not able to understand your question well. All I can say is that any idea is not the product of induction of scattered material. The process of proving the principle of weakening compensation, in passing I explained on the problems raised and left behind by previous Eastern and Western thinkers and philosophers, but this is not the general orientation of my work, which is only to prove the principle of weakening compensation. It is difficult for me to weigh which of Eastern or Western thought has been more enlightening in this regard.

Questioner: Sir, when Newton and Einstein proposed their theories, they did so with trepidation, not with confidence. For example, Newton wanted to introduce the concept of the so-called *Ether*. But I feel that you are relatively confident when you talk about your theory, for example, you said yesterday that you could not see your theory was disproved unless you could live 800 years.

Mr. Dongyue: Yes! Let me answer your question. As I mentioned in my previous lecture, someone on the Internet once said that my work is not a philosophy book, but a science book. The origin of this claim is that my presentation contains a Cartesian coordinate schematic with a mathematical model of the coarsest and simplest function, but I can't substitute in the parameters. I specifically said that Russell said that philosophy is the foresight of science, a non-deterministic form that is explored in advance when there is not enough information, so it is said to be philosophy, and the fact that I can't introduce parameters into it proves precisely that it is philosophy. And I think the current people to introduce this parameter, I'm afraid it is still waiting for time, because the amount of information is not enough. You know Newton's gravitational constant, which could not even be introduced back then. If you look up Newton's works, the gravitational constant that he multiplied behind, was empty there, there was no data. About 70 years after the creation of Newton's doctrine, a man named Cavendish finally filled in this constant. What does this tell us? Even when science builds a relatively accurate model, it often still faces a coefficient gap with insufficient information.

As for the point that I am confident in my theories, you'll have to read my book to know whether I am confident or not so confident. When I say that Newton and Einstein were not fully confident, I do not deny that they were also confident in their doctrines. I'll give the example of another person, Darwin. After the publication of Darwin's book *the Origin of Species,* the entire European academic, civil, high society, and religious communities were all in denial, because Darwin's doctrine so severely impacted mainstream Christian culture that Darwin told his son: I will live the rest of my life in the midst of people's scorn. Darwin's son later recorded this in his memoirs, but he said that his father told him again: "My doctrine, which I firmly believe to be valid, will be universal. What does this tell us? Darwin was also confident in his doctrine, even though it was not the truth.

Questioner: Hello, sir! I would like to ask two practical questions. You suggest us to do more thinking training in terms of intellectual innovation, and the narrow sense of thinking training is running on human language. For someone like me, who has no systematic philosophical training, how to polish the conceptual rigor? The second question is, if the linguistic rigor is further compromised when translated into Chinese, do you recommend that we read some original works in foreign languages? Thank you!

Mr. Dongyue: I think the thinking training depends on what you read. Keep in mind, what is reading? Reading is a dialogue with the author. If you read printed garbage, then it is equivalent to you talking to the garbage man; if you read the classic works of the masters of thought, it is equivalent to you talking to the masters of thought. During the Italian Renaissance, a figure named Machiavelli appeared and composed the *Monarchy*. After his dismissal from office, he worked as a farmer during the day, purified himself and bathed at night, put on his formal clothes and sat upright before he began to read. Why? He felt that reading was a dialogue with the philosophers, so he was very respectful and serious, and he expressed the state of reading. Therefore, you must be selective in reading, and you must read the kind of book that makes you think deeply and even makes you feel stuck. If you read only for pleasure, if you read for quick reading, you will not achieve the effect of mind training. Reading a good book intensively is like reading a math book, and only with the help of such reading can you train your mind in precise logic. As for the text itself, whether it is English, Latin, Spanish, German or Chinese, any text is problematic in terms of its accuracy, which is why Leibniz said that common symbols must be created. How to use one's native language to reach proficiency and precision requires a long refinement of linguistics and rhetoric. The creation of any new doctrine requires new concepts, for which the original vocabulary is not sufficient, so one has to create words or change the connotation of borrowed words, which is a huge linguistic effort that also requires training. This has nothing to do with foreign languages or Chinese, but the minimum requirement is to refine and use the language you can master now.

Questioner: Hello, Mr. Dongyue! In the morning, you mentioned a concept called *truth content*, and you thought that the new theory would contain more information, so it might bring more cognitive distortion, and therefore the truth content would be lower. But then you mentioned this afternoon that the new theory would be other-consistent to the previous theory, so at least it means that the new theory would include the correctness of the previous theory. I would like to ask you to explain these two concepts in a little more detail, as I may not understand them as well as I should. Also, many of the examples you gave are in the natural sciences, but do you consider sociology or psychology, etc., to be science? Or are they somewhere between science and philosophy? Thank you!

Mr. Dongyue: You asked two questions. The first question is about the concept of *truthfulness*. Once I talk about a new theoretical model to override and negotiate with the original theory, in our past way of thinking and philosophical stereotypes, it immediately creates an illusion that it is more realistic and has a higher truth content. But you note that I may not be able to use that level of language in my lectures, but when you read my book, the "increase in information" and the "decrease in truth" are one and the same thing. The realism that you feel is only an increment of information, a coverage of the old theory, which is actually a coverage of a larger amount of information, and it does not include adding value of the *truth*, which are two concepts. What does it mean? Please read my book! Just listening to a lecture is not enough. I want this lecture to be an introduction to reading.

Furthermore, science in the strict sense is something that has a mathematical level of precise logic and can be empirically proven in the laboratory. Is sociology, psychology, etc. considered science or not? At least in the strict sense, I would hardly call it science. How do you put psychology in the lab? How do you put society in a lab, please? It is true that they can also be verified in a non-exact way, and we usually mistake the concept of science as being able to be tested practically as science, and as I said, theology can also be tested practically, which is too broad an extension. So in order to be more precise and to give more convincing examples, I will try to use the more rigorous natural sciences instead of the ambiguous so-called sciences. Although on the spot, I do not guarantee the accuracy of the expression.

Questioner: Mr. Dongyue, when you said yesterday about the origin of philosophy, narrow philosophy arose only in ancient Greece, a pure logic game played by a group of adult children. My question is: Why is this phenomenon, which seems to have arisen only in ancient Greece, an inevitable product of the cradle of early human civilization? I would like you to tell me more about why it is inevitable, please!

Mr. Dongyue: This question cannot be clarified at the intuitive level. What exactly does the concept of *necessity* mean? You have to read *A Unified Theory of Evolution*. In my lecture, I said that the necessity of philosophy in narrow sense refers to the inevitable occurrence of the compensatory gain of inductive attributes in the deep theory. At what specific point in human history it occurs or manifests by chance, you can hardly delineate a necessary structure or a necessary path at the phenomenal level. Remember, to explore all issues, intuitive level arguments are invalid, we must go into the logical depths to give meticulous proofs. So again, I emphasize that lectures are only introductory, they are not meticulous expressions.

Cultural Origin of Confucianism

Preamble

We are talking about Confucius today.

Confucius and his Confucianism have been the soul and benchmark of traditional Chinese thought and culture for more than 2,000 years. This is a situation that we can never see anywhere else in the world, except for religion.

But Confucius' doctrine, compared to Laozi's, seems shallow and straightforward. Because Confucius is concerned with real social and political issues, while Laozi is concerned with ultimate issues. Therefore, Confucius' doctrine is very bland.

Let me give you an example. The core of Confucius' doctrine is actually just eight words: "ruler rulers, subject subjects, father fathers, son sons." The first word is a noun, and the second word is a verb. It means that a ruler should be like a ruler, and a minister should be like a minister; a father should be like a father, and a son should be like a son. Confucius' doctrine is such a plain and straightforward one. He also said, "Goblet no goblet, O goblet! O goblet!" The *goblet* was a bronze wine vessel from the late Shang to early Zhou dynasties. It was originally made in a hexagonal shape, but at the end of the Spring and Autumn period, someone innovated and changed it to a round or octagonal shape. So Confucius lamented, "O goblet, O goblet, you no longer look like a goblet! " In the text of Confucius' *Analects*, we even see the statement, "Eat without speaking, sleep without speaking." It means, don't talk when you eat and don't talk when you sleep. If you listen to this, doesn't it sound like the words of an old mother disciplining her children?

It is by no means my opinion alone that Confucius' doctrine is shallow and straightforward. As you know that at the end of the Ming Dynasty and the beginning of the Qing Dynasty, the Western Jesuit missionaries came to China at that time. On the one hand, they brought in Western culture, and on the other hand, they also translated ancient Chinese texts into Western languages and introduced them to Europe. Hegel, the great European philosopher at that time, was greatly disappointed to see the text of Confucius. Let us listen to Hegel's comments on the text of Confucius. Hegel says: "What we see in the conversations between Confucius and his disciples (referring to the *Analects*) is a common sense morality, which we can find anywhere, in any nation, and perhaps even better, something that has no point of excellence can assert. It would have been better if his books had never been translated, in order to preserve the reputation of Confucius". Hegel said that Confucius' book was filled with nothing but "truism moral lessons". He even said that it would be better for his book not to be translated, as translating them would be detrimental to his glorious image.

What does this mean? In the Middle Ages, or around the modern era in Europe, the West was in a state of religious repression. At that time, Westerners knew that there was an empire in the East ruled by virtue, and its mode of governance was to establish social order by human morality, which seemed much milder than the Western Christian theocracy that suppressed human nature. Therefore, they were envious of the East, and together with some inauthentic legends of the time, they believed that the East was extremely rich. Therefore, some Western philosophers and cultural scholars at that time had regarded China as the paradise of the East. For example, Leibniz, Voltaire and other great Western philosophers after modern times used to give extremely high or even wrong evaluations to Chinese culture, which we will cover later in the course. Thus, when Hegel read the text of Confucius, he was greatly disappointed; he found it extremely shallow.

So, is Hegel right about the shallowness of Confucius' text? He is half right, at least. You may find the sociologist and orator of ancient Rome, a man named Cicero, whose *Cicero's Orations*, which you can read at your leisure, discusses politics, law, morality, human ethics, social system, etc. in such a brilliant and profound way that Confucius' doctrine cannot be compared with it at all. Cicero was not at all a great philosopher in the Western culture at that time or today, so Hegel's evaluation is justified.

So, why do we say that Hegel's evaluation of Confucius was only half right? It is because Hegel could not read Confucius! Because, as I said in the previous lesson, culture is not a fancy thing, it is a reflection of the structure of existence. Hegel couldn't understand the Eastern structure of existence and its cultural adaptation, so he couldn't understand the essence of Confucius' doctrine.

For this reason, let me make a clarification. In our lecture today, we basically do not talk about the text of Confucius. This is because the Confucian text is very straightforward and very superficial. Any middle school student today, if he finds a copy of the *Analects* with modern interpretation, literally speaking, I am sure that he can read and understand the text of Confucius. But if you want to really understand the inner spirit of Confucius' doctrine and its cultural meaning, you will never be able to do so by just staying with the text. Therefore, we will not talk about the text of Confucius in today's lecture. Our lecture today is called "The Cultural Origins of Confucius and Confucianism", which means that we will focus on the deeper things behind the doctrine of Confucius and the text of Confucius.

Confucius' doctrine was shallow and straightforward, and from a modern point of view, it consisted only of "the talk of human morality", but nothing of "the divided knowledge", that is, there was no system of knowledge, so how could he become the great sage of China's mainstream culture in the imperial era? In other words, why did Confucius last for more than 2,000 years as the chief cultural teacher of the Chinese literati and scholars? Moreover, Confucius' ambition was to "rule the country and keep peace in society", not to "study and seek knowledge", so how come the old Chinese literati of all generations could not feel the blandness and boredom of Confucianism?

Our course today is to answer these questions. That is, to examine what is the genesis of Confucius' doctrine? What is its cultural utility? What is its relevance to today's Chinese society and even to human civilization?

Background of the Times Confucius Lived

Let's first look at the context of the time in which Confucius lived.

Confucius lived in the Zhou Dynasty. As you know, the Zhou Dynasty in China took place in the 11th century B.C. and lasted until the 3rd century B.C., a total duration of about 800 years, making it one of the longest-lived dynasties in Chinese history. As I said earlier, the more primitive the social structure, the more stable it is. Then, the feudal system took place in the Zhou Dynasty of China.

We should also pay attention to one more issue. When we talk about *feudalism* today, we think that from ancient times to the present, from the Zhou Dynasty or since the unification of China by the first Emperor Yingzheng (Qin Shi Huang) to the Xinhai Revolution, the historical and educational circles collectively call it the *feudal era*, which makes a very serious mistake.

It is important to know that the feudal era in China was limited only to the 800 years during the Zhou Dynasty. The so-called *feudalism* first appeared in the first book of China, namely *Book of Shang*, what does *feudalism* mean? It only refers to the system that the highest ruler, the emperor *confers titles and feuds upon* his closed relatives or most trustable senior personnel, so that the conferred ones could help the emperor from different places to maintain the rule over the country, which is called feudal establishment. This had something to do with the actual political situation after King Wu Jifa had conquered the former dynasty of Shang. As I said earlier in Laozi's class, the Shang Dynasty was a clan and tribe confederation system, so after King Wu Jifa conquered the Shang Dynasty, he divided his blood relatives and 71 important ministers into feudal states around the Central Plains to protect him in the central government. This political system was called *feudal system*. At that time, each feudal state had its own independent power of governance, that is, it had its own internal power, diplomatic power, and even its own independent army, which was called feudal system.

By 221 B.C., the first Emperor of Qin Dynasty unified China, and his biggest political initiative was to promote the establishment of the county system. This is called a *centralized political system*, which is called a *monarchy* in political science, and it is exactly the nemesis of the feudal system. In other words, when Qin Shi Huang unified China, the feudal system in China came to an end.

So, why did such a serious historiographical error occur in modern China? It has to do with the fact that Japanese literati used to use Chinese back then. Before and after the Meiji Restoration, Japanese scholars mainly used Chinese, and they translated European history, which basically went through the clan tribal system, feudal system, and then the capitalist system. So using the Japanese translation of Western history as a reference, the Chinese students at the time, including Guo Moruo, who followed the Japanese translation at that time, copied Chinese society as a feudal system. In addition, after the Xinhai Revolution (1911) in modern China, virtually all subsequent rulers were inclined to revert to a *power centralized system*, and therefore were more willing to indulge in the mainstream culture by misrepresenting it as a feudal society. This is the main reason why Chinese historiography has been referring to the era of imperial monarchy collectively as the feudal era.

During the 800 years of the Zhou Dynasty, its feudal social form being stable and intact, occurred only in the first three centuries, known as the Western Zhou. During this period, the feudal system was regularized and the authority of the King of Zhou Dynasty was established, which was called by Confucius as "the way of the society, rituals, music and conquest came from the King". The so-called "rites, music and conquest": rites refers to the state's political law and order; music refers to the state's large-scale rituals and their major cultural activity; conquest refers to the state's sending troops to fight enemy; these three major events were decided by the King of Zhou Dynasty. The Western Zhou feudal mechanism was stable and intact, and lasted about three hundred years, and then collapsed, marked by the loss of the absolute control over the country with King You of Zhou three times scammed all vassals to rush appear only for a game to please his favored concubine, and the eastward move of King Ping of Zhou to Luoyi in Henan Province. The Western Zhou era came to an end, and the second phase of the Zhou dynasty thus started, which was called the Eastern Zhou in history.

The Eastern Zhou was divided into two periods: the first 300 years or so was called the Spring and Autumn Period, and the second 250 years or so was called the Warring States Period, which was called the Eastern Zhou. It was marked by the beginning of the decay of the feudal system and the decline of the authority of the Kings of Zhou, which was called by Confucius as "the society had no more morality, and rites, music and conquest came from the vassals".

Let's return to the topic of feudal system. The feudal system in China was eliminated at the end of the Zhou Dynasty. Then why did we consider the feudal system as the most advanced social system at that time? It was because it established a relatively unified social management system compared to the clan- tribe confederation system. Today you see the feudal system as backward, but think about it, how did the ancients establish a large regional ruling system in the first place? He could only establish it in a feudal way. This is like all entrepreneurs, when you start a business in the early days, what kind of people do you look for as your partners? You must find your own relatives and friends, because you know them best, the least effort to examine their character, and the lowest cost to reach a cooperative relationship with them. So you must have established a family company or a family and friends company in the early days, although this kind of company structure will become an obstacle as the business grows to a certain scale. But it is surely one of the lowest cost, highest trust and most stable structures in the early days, and that's where the feudal system was justified.

The feudal system had a characteristic that the whole social structure maintained a restraining power over the central power, because the feudal vassal states enjoyed complete governing power. One should note that this thing is an important breeding ground for the occurrence of modern capitalist society. What does it mean? Because China eliminated the feudal system too early in the 3rd century BC, this made it impossible for China to ever produce a bourgeois revolution or create a capitalist free market economy, even though the fact that since the Song Dynasty (roughly 1000 AD) the sprouting of industrial and commercial civilization reached the highest level in terms of the development in the world at that time. A very important reason for this impossibility was that China had eliminated the feudal social system too early.

Let me give you an example. More than four hundred years before the English bourgeois revolution in 1640, that is, in 1215 AD, a famous political movement took place in England, known as the *Magna Carta Movement of Freedom*. What is the so-called *Magna Car-*

ta Movement? In fact, the feudal lords of England joined with other social classes and signed an agreement with the King of England at that time. The agreement severely limited the king's rights, and the document consisted of sixty-three articles, which stipulated that the king only had the right to declare war and diplomacy, while all other ruling powers were basically vested in the feudal lords. Even the king's taxation rights were incomplete, and taxes had to be negotiated with the feudal lords, thus establishing the first *king under law* moral concept and political custom in the history of the world. This event eventually laid the social foundation for the development and growth of the English bourgeoisie.

Because, before the capitalist society, the bourgeoisie was equivalent to the common people, called the third class. As you know, at that time, the first nobility or the first rank of European power and nobility were monks, who controlled the spirit of people and had the right to interpret Christianity, so they had the highest social status; the second rank was the nobility, who were hereditary and took the hereditary system and held the state power; the third rank was the common people. As the bourgeoisie was the third class, the feudal lords were more concerned about their economic tax revenue, so they did not suppress the business activities of the bourgeoisie or the common people, especially the weak ruling areas between the feudal territories, which became the blank area for the third class to do business and develop class consciousness. This resulted in the gradual growth of the bourgeoisie, which eventually became the social force that launched the bourgeois revolution and established the capitalist system.

The premature elimination of the feudal system in China, the extremely powerful of imperial authority, and the dominant ideology of society that cannot be spread in a discrete shaking culture, led to the inability of modern China, or the last thousand years after the Song Dynasty, to develop and cultivate a truly modern ideological and cultural system and political structure of new strength.

By the Eastern Zhou Dynasty, the feudal system was gradually disrupted and social bonds tended to be loosened. Accordingly, historians call the Eastern Zhou period the Spring and Autumn Period and the Warring States Period, respectively. Let me explain what is meant by *Spring and Autumn*. Some scholars suggest that around the ancient times, human beings had not yet established a clear relationship between the four seasons, and thought that a year was spring and autumn. This is not the main point, rather the most important thing is that *Spring and Autumn* is the title of the history of the state of Lu, where Confucius lived. According to the legend, since Confucius had reworked the *Spring and Autumn Annals* in his later years, the book referred to the Spring and Autumn Period, which is the two hundred and fifty-five-year period from the year of Duke Lu Yin A.D. to the twenty-seventh year of Duke Lu Ai. What does this mean? As we know that in the pre-Qin era, all states had their own state history records, not just the state of Lu. For example, the book of the state history of Jin was called "乘" (*Cheng*), so if you see the character "乘" or "史乘" in ancient books, you should know that it refers to the state history of Jin. Then there is the state of Chu, which also has its own state history, and the book is called "梼杌" (*Tao Wu*). Therefore, if you see either of the characters "梼" (*Táo*) or "杌" (*Wù*) in the ancient books, you should know that it refers to the history of the state of Chu.

Then why did the period was marked with Spring and Autumn, which was the book title of the state history of Lu, where Confucius lived? It is because that Confucius used the method of "simple words of great meanings". The so-called "simple words of great meanings" is to use few words to inject significant moral and ethical meanings or value into the text, and scholars call this thing "simple words of great meanings". This is also called the Writing Style of *Spring and Autumn*. According to the legend, Confucius reworked the *Spring and Autumn Annals* with very few changes. Let me give you an example. In the original *Spring and Autumn Annals*, it is written that a minister committed regicide, that is, murdered the king of the state, and Confucius considered this a treasonous act against his superiors, so he changed the official name of the regicide in the book to call him by his first name. You know, in ancient times, the honorific title for a person is to call him by his official title, or next called by his stylish word, but if calling someone directly by his name is a disrespectful expression. So by only changing his official title to his name, Confucius expressed his indignation about this matter, which is called simple words of great meanings.

As Confucius had compiled this *Spring and Autumn Annals*, it infused his entire value system. After the Han Dynasty, Confucius' doctrine became the state religion. In ancient times, the laws were made in a rather sloppy manner, and the details of the laws were missing, so when judging cases, the officials often felt that there was not enough basis, so there actually appeared a situation of judging cases by *Spring and Autumn Annals*. That is to say, when later administrators conducted legal trials, if they could not find specific legal texts for reference, they used the values of the *Spring and Autumn Annals* as a guideline for judging cases, which shows how great the influence of the *Spring and Autumn Annals* was on later generations of China.

More importantly, the literati since then have used the Spring and Autumn Period to chronicle all the states of the world (as I mentioned earlier, in ancient times, whenever I say *states of the world,* I refer to *the states of the Central Asian. Because at that time, Chinese people only knew East Asia as a place and recognized it as the whole world*), any event that happened was chronologically dated by the Spring and Autumn Period. For example, if a certain event happened in Jin, he did not use the state of Jin's history book "乘" (*Cheng*) to chronicle it, but would say what years of Duke Zhao of Lu, and what happened in Jin. Since later generations always used the chronology of the *Spring and Autumn Annals* of Lu as the chronological mark of this period, later generations therefore called this period of about three hundred years as the *Spring and Autumn Period.*

Confucius was born in the late Spring and Autumn period, when the world was in turmoil and the dynasty had been shaken for a long time. The two major events that manifested themselves in the foreground of society during this period most fully characterize the seriousness of the disorder of the political system at that time.

First, the phenomenon of state extermination continues to occur, that is, the vassal states merge with each other. We should know that at the beginning of the Spring and Autumn Period, only the Central Plains or the Chinese region, the vassal feudal states amounted to 180 of them. King Wu of Western Zhou initially only conferred and divided 71 states, the subsequent generations of the Kings of Zhou continued to increase the number of feudal lords, so that the number of feudal lords increased as years passed by. In addition, the feudal lords of the Zhou dynasty also subdivided their feud, and the subdivided fiefs were called "采邑" (Cai Yi), which means that the feudal lords of the Zhou dynasty continue to divide their feud to their important ministers and blood relatives, later such divided fiefs of *Caiyi* were up to thousands. Just think about the land of Hua and Xia, which refers to the Central Plains and the land around it, as I said earlier, Hua refers to the Guanzhong region, marked by Mount Hua; Xia means downward, which refers to the lower land reached by the Yellow River; in such a large land, political fragmentation continued, reaching over a hundred vassal states and thousands of feudal *Caiyi*, which shows how far the geopolitical fragmentation has developed to. Under such circumstances, as the authority of the Kings of Zhou fell and the feudal lords acted on their own, the destruction and annexation of states continue to occur, which was the first social change.

Secondly, regicide happened constantly, that is, the murder of vassal state rulers happened constantly. According to ancient historical records such as the *Spring and Autumn Annals, Annals by Zuo Qiuming, Annals of States* and *Record of the Grant Historian*, there were actually about 43 cases of regicide in various states during the Spring and Autumn Period. As we know that the murder of a political head of a state is a serious political disaster. For example, the U.S. President John F. Kennedy was assassinated in 1963, and it caused several years of social and political restiveness in the United States. So it is surprising that such major political events, the murder of a state's monarch, actually occurred as many as 43 times in just over 250 years.

In recent times, some scholars found that the majority of the regicides were the sons and grandsons of feudal lords, and the ministerial officials, that is, the blood relatives of the rulers, and the hereditary ones of ministerial officials, and the hereditary ones were all nobles, that is, they were still the blood relatives of the rulers. The total of the two was as high as 77% of the murder initiators. Secondly, in terms of the motive of regicide, 51% of the regicides were committed by members of the court who usurped the throne, and 14% of the regicides were committed by the ministerial officials who competed with the rulers for power, which adds up to 65% of the total. In terms of the direct cause of the regicide, 44% were planned over a long period of time, 35% were caused by accidental events, and 21% were for unknown reasons. That is to say, the percentage of carefully planned murders was nearly half, and the percentage of unexplained unexpected events that resulted in regicide was also nearly half, which shows how easily and commonly regicide were performed at that time.

In terms of the number of regicide incidents, the first place was tied with the state of Jin and state of Qi, with eight incidents each in more than 200 years; the second place was in the state of Zheng, with five incidents; and the third place was the state of Lu, the ceremonial state of Confucius, with as many as four incidents. We can thus see how far the feudal system had collapsed by the Spring and Autumn period. It can be said that the world was in turmoil and the great powers were rising, and this was the general background of the time in which Confucius lived. Confucius was immediately invited by the state of Wei just after he was dismissed from office in the state of Lu,

The *Analects* mentions a disciple of Confucius called Yifeng Ren, who made a comment to the times in which his teacher lived. Let me start with who Yifeng Ren was. At the age of fifty-five, Confucius was dismissed from office, and as Confucius had a famous disciple Zi Lu, whose two brothers in-law, that is, two brothers of Zi Lu's wife, were high officials in the state of Wei, therefore, he was invited by the state of Wei immediately after he was dismissed from his official position in the state of Lu. Confucius traveled among the states of the time for thirteen years, and the first state he went to was the state of Wei, and also the longest state he stayed. Since Confucius had been running a school in Wei for a long time, he received many famous disciples in Wei, including this Yifeng Ren. This so-called Yifeng Ren was the lord of the fief *Caiyi* in the state of Wei. He also became a disciple of Confucius. He left a comment in the *Analects of Confucius* that sufficiently illustrates the situation of the time when Confucius lived, saying, "The world has been in chaos too long, and the heaven takes this man of moral integrity as a bell ringer". This comment says that the world has been in disorder for a long time, and Confucius would serve as a warning bell for the human world. In short, Yifeng Ren believes that his teacher Confucius will eventually become the alarm bell of the chaotic world.

We can see from this that Confucius lived in a time when the world was in chaos. Some years ago, someone in the Chinese mainstream media talked about the insights of the *Analects*, and made it into a happy life and so on, which of course was all nonsense.

SOCIAL TRANSFORMATION IN THE AGE OF CONFUCIUS

Now, let's take a look at the more in-depth content of the background of Confucius' life in the pre-Qin era.

Let me first explain what is meant by the pre-Qin era, which is a very important term in Chinese historiography. By *pre-Qin era,* I mean the period of more than 350 years before 221 B.C., when Qin Shi Huang unified China, which is collectively called the pre-Qin era. So, why is the pre-Qin era particularly important in Chinese history? Because it was the first major social transformation in the history of Chinese civilization.

Previously we went to secondary school and university, learning history to the pre-Qin era, the teacher usually said this: the pre-Qin era is the evolution of the aristocratic system of kings to the autocratic system of emperors, is the evolution of feudal slavery to private ownership of land. In this way, you can't understand what kind of socio-historical situation the pre-Qin era was. Therefore, I am here to change the expression: the pre-Qin era, is the first major social transformation since the history of Chinese civilization. You know, China's thousands of years of civilization history, there have only been two major social transformation. The second major social transformation was the Opium War in 1840, and so far, one hundred and seventy years later, the second major social transformation has not yet been completed.

Let's take a look at the situation of the second great social transformation first. So how did the second great social transformation of Chinese society take place? The transformation started from an agricultural civilization to an industrial and commercial civilization, and from an autocratic monarchy to a republican system, and it was marked by the Opium War occurred in 1840. From the Opium War to today, more than one hundred and seventy years ago, our Chinese society has been extremely chaotic and fast changing.

Let me first list the extent of social unrest and the number of major events that took place in China during these 170 years: the First Opium War in 1840; the Second Opium War from 1856 to 1860; the Taiping Heavenly Kingdom Movement from 1851 to 1864; then the Foreign Affairs Movement; then the Sino-French War in 1884;

then the Sino-Japanese War of 1894; then the Hundred Days' Reform in 1899; then, the Xinhai Revolution in 1911; then, Yuan Shikai came to power, and in 1916, Yuan Shikai died, and China entered the chaotic rule of the Northern Warlords for eleven years; from 1921 to 1927, the First Communist and Nationalist Parties Cooperation, the Northern Expedition War, known as the First Domestic Revolutionary War; then, the split between the two parties of Communist and Nationalist; then, the Anti-Japanese War, the Second Communist and Nationalist Parties Cooperation; then came the second split between the two parties of Communist and Nationalist, and then the violent Civil War in China; then entered the Mao Zedong era; and then came the Deng Xiaoping reforms .... We will find that in this short period of one hundred and seventy years, our Chinese society has been tossing and turning, tossing what? carrying out the second great social transformation! That is why I would say that this era will be the second time in Chinese history that the greatest thinkers, politicians, economists, and social activists will appear in a time of great change. I am not referring, of course, to the present time only, but to the hundreds of years that lie ahead before China will complete the second great social transformation. In other words, this second great social transformation in China has not yet been completed.

So, we now look back to the pre-Qin era, the first great social transformation of China. How did Chinese society transform in the pre-Qin era? It was a transition from a semi-mature agricultural civilization to a fully mature agricultural civilization, and even a transition in which an industrial and commercial civilization began to emerge from the agricultural civilization; it was a transition from a clan-tribe confederation system to a feudal system, followed by a transition to a monarchical dictatorship. As it was the first major transformation in Chinese social history, it led to social upheaval and many talent personnel emerged, and the entire foundation period of traditional Chinese culture was completed here, resulting in the complete shaping of China's social structure for the next two thousand years.

We now look at how the first major social transformation of the pre-Qin era actually took place from three perspectives: economic, political, and cultural.

Let's look at the economic field first. The rapid development of productivity in the pre-Qin era, farming technology has improved, agricultural civilization tends to mature, bronze tools have long been commonly used, in the farming tools iron is also gradually promoted. As we all know, although human agricultural civilization occurred 8,000 or even 10,000 years ago, in the early thousands of years of agricultural civilization in the process of exploration, hunting survival is still the main type, agricultural farming is still only an auxiliary part of the source of human living materials.

When agricultural production has developed to a certain scale, land reclamation has become larger and larger, and forest vegetation has been pushed far away, only then will mankind completely naturalize from the gathering and hunting way of life to farming civilization. Therefore, the real maturity of agricultural civilization requires large-scale development of population, large-scale land reclamation, large-scale destruction of forests, and no way to carry out hunting and gathering activities, and only at this time can agricultural civilization stabilize. Therefore, it lasted for thousands of years. It was not until the Zhou Dynasty that agricultural civilization gradually became the mainstream way of life of the Central Plains people.

Not only that, in the Spring and Autumn Period, the sprout of industrial and commercial civilization appeared in the agricultural civilization of China. As we all know, agricultural civilization developed to a certain extent, due to the diversification of agricultural production tools and the enrichment of people's life, quite a number of products tended to be made professionally. In the early days, the production of non-agricultural products was done by farmers themselves, such as building houses, such as weaving cloth, and even making pottery, but with the further development of division of labor and with the further complication of people's lives, a large number of things could not be prepared by farmers. For example, the more advanced pottery production, such as the smelting of bronze, the processing of agricultural tools, all these things, will cause the process of division of labor to gradually appear in agricultural civilization. The phenomenon of division of labor, that is, when someone stops farming and specializes only in making a certain kind of product for the use of others, we call this kind of material and product, not for our own use, but only as an exchange for each other, a commodity.

Once commodities emerged, exchange activities took place. As you can imagine, in the early days of mankind, exchange was barter, because the variety of goods was very small. Then if the variety of goods keeps increasing, the goods you can take out for exchange are not needed by the other party, and the goods needed by the other party are not in your hands. So, there is a need for a unified medium of exchange and a measure of exchange, the so-called *general equivalent,* that is, a commodity that can make a value measurement of any commodity, which is money. Therefore, the emergence of money marks the differentiation of human beings, or the division of labor in society, or the commodity economy, developed to a considerable degree before their emergence. However, we should know that in the pre-Qin era in China, money already appeared. Early on, it was shell and sword coins, which marked the large-scale maturation of the agricultural economy and the emergence of the commodity economy in China in the pre-Qin era.

Let's look at the political form below. The authority of the Zhou Emperor fell, and the bonds of the original feudal society were loosened. In addition, the vassal states grew in size, annexations occurred, state annihilation occurred, and interstates wars intensified. In addition, it triggered a major change in social class patterns.

Let me give you an example. During the Spring and Autumn Period, the feudal lord of Jin was overruled by four important ministerial officials: the famous four families of Han, Zhao, Wei, and Zhi. Later, Han, Zhao and Wei united to destroy the Zhi, and Han, Zhao and Wei dominated the state of Jin. At this time, a famous political figure named Zhao Wuxie appeared in the Zhao family, known as Zhao Xiangzi, who did one thing that shook the world. He announced the emancipation of all slaves in the land of Zhao and gave them 30mu of land. At the same time, he announced to all countries in the Central Plains that any slave who escaped from another country to the land of Zhao would be released from slavery and given land. It is important to know that this action of Zhao Xiangzi led to the rapid disintegration of the slave system in China. Why? Because the idea that "the people are the most important" was typical feudal consciousness. What does this statement mean? As we all know, Mencius famously said, "The people are the most important thing, the community is the second most important thing, and the ruler is the least important thing." Many people regard it as Mencius having democratic thoughts, which is totally wrong. Mencius never had democratic ideas, and there has never been any democratic ideas in the history of Chinese culture, and "the people are the most important" is a typical feudal idea. What does it mean? It means that for any feudal lord, his greatest interest does not lie in the size of his fief, but in the number of households and population on his fief. Because the more the number of households and population, the larger his tax base, the more generous the tax revenue, this is called "the people are the most important". Therefore, all the official systems in ancient China can be commonly referred to as the Hundred Household Marquis, Thousand Household Marquis, Ten Thousand Household Marquis, etc., all based on the number of households, that is why.

Think about this: What did Zhao Xiangzi get when he freed the slaves? He got *the people*. He thus gained two major benefits. First, labor resources, and second, soldiers. This led to the rapid disintegration of slavery in China, as all the surrounding states, who did not free their slaves at the same time, their citizens or inhabitants would flee. It is important to know that this event expresses the extreme precocity of Chinese society and the extreme intensity of its transformation process in the pre-Qin era.

Let me give you an example. We all know that in the European lands, for example, France, which had launched the bourgeois revolution in 1789, but from the seventeenth century until the eighteenth and nineteenth centuries, the European lands retained a brutal system of slavery. The slave trade, early on, was trafficked from Africa to Europe, and only later, when there was a severe labor shortage in the southern United States due to large-scale settlement and cultivation of cotton and other crops, did the slave trade shift its route from Europe to North America. When we look at Russia, by the nineteenth century, it was already called by Marx the "policeman of Europe", that is, Russia was already quite powerful and had great weight in Europe. Since Peter the Great, Russia has been learning from Europe, and its development and strength have increased so much that it was considered a formidable enemy by European countries, but Russia did not abolish serfdom until 1861. Finally, the United States, a model of an advanced country, was caught in a civil war over slavery in the middle of the 19th century.

Looking back at China, slavery in China collapsed completely as early as the sixth or seventh century B.C. You will note that by slavery we do not mean domestic servants, which continued in China until a very late date, even into the Song Dynasty. But by slavery we do not mean this section, but the retention of slavery in the sphere of production, something that disintegrated very early in China, and which expresses the dramatic changes and precociousness of the pre-Qin era in China.

Let's look at the cultural aspect below. The pre-Qin era in China was the real foundation period, or even the completion period, of traditional Chinese culture. As I mentioned earlier, after the unification of China by the first Emperor of Qin Yingzheng, (Shi Huang) in 221 B.C., China's national culture has not made any significant achievements, except for the introduction of Buddhism to China in the mid-Eastern Han Dynasty, but this event is not really considered to be its own glory.

So in what way was the foundation of traditional Chinese culture and the system of national thought laid in the pre-Qin era? First of all, it is important to know that the early culture of human beings started from the clan and tribe era. The earliest culture of mankind was called "巫"(Wu) culture. In the character "巫", the upper cross represents heaven, the lower cross represents earth, and the middle vertical represents man who communicates with heaven and earth. *Witch* is the most important cultural representative of human beings in the clan and tribe era. As I said earlier, when you look at witches today, they are all esoteric ritual dancers of unattractive figures, but they were the equivalent of today members of Academy of Sciences back then. The reason for this is that early human societies were matriarchal, and women had a very high social status. In addition, because women's instinct and intuition are far better than men's, just like men's logical thinking ability is slightly better than women's. Therefore, in men's eyes, it seems that women have a sixth sense and are able to communicate with heaven and earth, using their souls and intuition to communicate with heaven and earth. Therefore, all the witches in the early years were female witches. With the development of social history, the masculinized structure of the community occurred and male witches appeared. So you see that a big eye is drawn next to the witch, and this character is pronounced "觋" (Xi) wizard, meaning the male witch. Why do I say a big eye? Because the character for seeing is a big eye in the oracle bone script, and then a man is drawn underneath, a man carrying a big eye, and this character is to see (甲骨文 金文 小篆 见 楷体). It shows that male shamans are no longer able to communicate directly with heaven and earth with their direct senses and souls, but must see with their eyes to be counted, and male shamans are already at a much lower level than female witches.

Let's look at the gradual transformation from "巫觋" (Wu Xi) shamans to "儒" (Ru) literati. Let's look at the character "儒" in the oracle bone script. As I said earlier, the character "大" is a person with a frontal standing face, so if you draw a rain dot next to the frontal human figure, this character is "儒" in the oracle bone script. Later on, in Jin, people put the water dots scattered on the side and concentrated them on the top to form the head of the character rain, and then drew a frontal upright person at the bottom, which is the character "儒" in mold inscriptions (甲文 金文 小篆 需 楷体), which is the meaning of the character "需" (Xu) need today, and later a single upright person is added, and the character "需" is transferred to "儒" (Ru).

What can we see from the change in this character form? The so-called "儒" is actually an ancient action of a shaman to purify his body and bathe in order to show his devotion before offering sacrifices to heaven and earth and to his ancestors, which means that " 儒" (Ru) literati is a variation of "巫"(Wu) witch. The early literati were personnel who served the ritual ceremony in communication with heaven and earth, and they were considered knowledgeable, so they were called *ancient literati*. The representative figure of ancient literati is Laozi. That is why in study of Chinese ancient history, the scholarly community unanimously recognizes that the hundred schools of thought are in fact interpretations of the *ancient literati* thought of Laozi from different perspectives. Or to be more precise, it is the process of the social transformation of the pre-Qin era, as well as the complication of human life, when people focused on the ancient literati, and gradually developed a differentiated discussion and professional discourse, which is the origin of the hundred schools of thought.

We can thus see that the pre-Qin era was in fact the era when traditional Chinese culture was fully formed. For in the grand view of things, the cultural backbone of China for the next two thousand years has been nothing more than a perverted extension of antient literati.

Way of History of Civilization

I have expressed the foundational state of the first great social transformation of the pre-Qin era in three fields: economic, political, and cultural. This may not be enough for you to really feel the shaky state of the pre-Qin era, especially the direction of its changes. So let's analyze it from a more intuitive perspective.

First, external annexation wars were ongoing and getting bloodier. What does this phrase mean? We should know that humans were never at war before civilization, and all animals were never at war with each other. Fighting between the same kind of animals generally occurs only during the estrus period, that is, male animals compete for female reproductive resources. But it is only an individualized struggle and never forms a group war. And such intra-species struggle occurs in all animals, but it is always a fight of minimum possible. For example, if two male animals compete each other for female resource, once one side loses the battle, the other side won't pursue the loser, never put the loser to death. That is to say, in all animals, individual fighting of the same species is very restrained and limited. Only humans, since their civilization, intra-species group brutal killings began to occur.

Moreover, with the development of human civilization, the occurrence of such internal wars, large-scale fratricide between the same species, tends to become more and more intense and violent. At first, war appeared in the late period of clan tribes, fighting a battle to lose lives of a few people, or dozens of people is an extraordinary event. Because the early clan tribes of each social group had only a few dozen people, at most hundreds of people. But then there were tribal wars, such as the war between Yellow Emperor and Emperor Yan, Chi You three major tribes had fierce fight, which was the famous ancient Chinese Banquan Battle, Zhulu Battle of legends. Subsequently, the Shang destroyed the Xia, and Zhou destroyed the Shang, and then more than a hundred feudal states began to merge each other through wars.

You should know that wars in the Spring and Autumn period, even a death toll of few hundred people was a big war, the history books would keep a special article to record. And in the Spring and Autumn period, wars were all performed in formalities. It is recorded in the *Annales by Zuo Qiuming*, "no serious injuries, no capture of white hairs, no drums no march." What does this passage mean? It says that in the Spring and Autumn period, if the enemy army was defeated, they would never pursue them, which was called "no serious injuries", not to cause a second injury; the so-called "no capture of white hairs", that is, not to capture the opponent's elderly with white hair and white beard as prisoners; the so-called "no drums no march", refers to the ancient war, beat drums means to march, beat the gong means to withdraw; never sneak an attack before the enemy troops form an array, which is called "no drums no march". Therefore, wars in the Spring and Autumn period never used the art of cunning. Although *The Art of War* was written at the end of the Spring and Autumn Period, it was not widely used until the Warring States Period. Therefore, compared to the Warring States period, the intensity of warfare in the Spring and Autumn period was very low.

In the Warring States period, thousands and tens of thousands of people died in a battle, as recorded in history books. In the Battle of Changping between states of Qin and Zhao, Qin's general Bai Qi buried alive more than 400,000 Zhao prisoners at one time. This did not end until the last century, when mankind became highly civilized, two world wars took place. The First World War had more than 12 million direct deaths in the battlefield. Only a small town of Verdun on the German-French border, under the machine gun artillery, more than one million European youth lost their lives. In the Second World War, the number of direct deaths on the battlefield was more than 50 million, and the number of indirect deaths was 250 million. This is what happened since human civilization.

I wonder, why we humans always say the evilest man of human species bears the nature of the beast? As this is simply a slander of the nature of the beast; in fact, we should say that the worst beast of animals has human nature. We can see that the process of civilization development is the process of continuous corruption of human nature, and it is the process of increasingly intensifying of human killing each other.

Secondly, internal coups kept happening and were corrupt from top to bottom. What does it mean? I said earlier that the feudal era was coming to an end, the feudal system was getting looser and looser, and the authority of the Kings of Zhou had fallen, but it did not end here. Following that, the different vassal lords who had hollowed out the authority of Kings of Zhou, were also hollowed out by their important ministers. For example, I mentioned earlier that the ruler of state Jin was hollowed out by Han, Zhao and Wei. For example, the ruler of the state of Lu, where Confucius lived, was hollowed out by the three Huan families. Who were the three Huans? The Jisun, the Mengsun, and the Shusun. This is not the end of the story. The important ministers who had hollowed out the ruler of the state were hollowed out by their own vassals. When you read the *Analects of Confucius* you will constantly see the names of two people, one called Yang Hu, also known as Yang Huo, and the other called Gongshan Buniu. They were the two vassals of Jisun, the first of the three Huans who had hollowed out the ruler of state of Lu, and the two vassals hollowed out their master Jisun as well.

We can thus see how far the corrupt feudal society had become to the end of the Spring and Autumn period. If a political system or a social structure was shaken at the top and then infected at the bottom, and the whole society was rotten down to the grassroots level, and the administrative operation was in disorder, it marked the end of the political structure and the imminent change of a social and political form. The feudal system created in the Zhou Dynasty, was the first and most stable giant social system in the history of human civilization, and it was only established in the Spring and Autumn Period for 400 to 500 years before it was already in a state of upheavals, signifying a rapid decline in the stability of the social structure.

Third, men are not what they were in times past, and the general moral trend is declining. Notice these words I said, which were the ancient Chinese description of the moral trend of human beings. Today we all think that the higher the level of civilization of mankind, the higher people's moral standards must be. But this view is completely opposite to what the ancients said. When the ancients said "the general moral trend is declining", they meant that the moral standard of human beings is going down all the way. Who said it right? The ancients said it right! As we know, in ancient times there was no such thing as law, i.e., there was no strict law, it was called *ruling by virtue* in those days. You know that the legal society has only been created for about 3,000 years, Homo erectus existed for millions of years, or clan society existed for millions of years, antient man never used legal means to manage the community, never used violent and harsh laws to control personnel. What did they use? They used a soft, diffusible moral system to maintain social stability. What does it show? It shows that the less civilized human society is, the more stable society is, the more harmony society is, and the less violent the society manifests.

Let's look at a passage that Confucius said, "When the way of government is run by punishment, people avoid and shameless; when the way of government is run by virtue and proprieties, they have shame and order." What does this passage mean? He said that if you manage society by politics and punishment, people will avoid violating the law, and this is called "people avoid", so as to prevent from being punished by the law. However, if the law fails to prohibit something, people will dare to do it even if it is evil, which is called "people shameless". Today we are in the era of "people avoid and shameless". Confucius also said that "when the way of government is run by virtue and proprieties", that is, if you rule by virtue, by proprieties, not rule by law, then "people have shame and order". That is, people have a sense of shame, will not do things that corrupt virtue, so the whole society is in order, this is called "they have shame and order". Confucius said that the emergence of a legal society is the product of the collapse of human morality, and Confucius used the term "rituals and music deteriorate".

So I suggest that you should never praise the legal society, because the legal society is the product of human moral degradation, is the moral bond no longer effective enough to maintain social stability, so that people have to use violent way to control the progress of the human society chaos.

If this is not enough to convince you, you may want to look at the people who used to carry backpacks into the deep forests to travel, when he was tired of walking, thirsty, hungry, he asked the local mountain people to give him a bowl of water, a bowl of rice, the local people would take the best food to serve him. He had to pay people afterwards, and most mountain people were embarrassed to accept. But with the wind of civilization blowing into the remote places, they all turned the farmers' houses into small inns, and they were eager to earn your pocket money, though it is acceptable practice by both sides.

I'm talking about why human morality must tend to degenerate as civilization develops, and why human pure honesty must gradually disappear with the development of civilization? Because social life is becoming more and more complicated, more and more cunning, more and more corrupt, and it is no longer possible to maintain survival with a pure and virtuous heart. It is a sign that the process of civilization is the decaying process of human nature.

Fourth, every progress is accompanied by social unrest and tension in people's livelihood. What is the meaning of this statement? The public generally think that the more civilized a society is, the more stable it is. But in fact, as I said earlier in Laozi's class, the more society progresses and develops, the less stable the society must be. Human beings have lived stably for millions of years in the non- agricultural civilization, that is, the hunting stage of existence; agricultural civilization has survived for 10,000 years; and commercial and industrial civilization has emerged for only three or four hundred years, and today it is being replaced by information civilization or biological civilization. This is from the macroscopic point of view.

At the micro level, the stability of the social structure is also decreasing. Let me give you an example, on the September 11, 2001, the terrorists only blew up two or three buildings, the whole international political situation turned to turmoil for more than ten years, and to this day the war on terrorism is still not over. If it were in ancient times, someone destroyed or burned down hundreds of houses or palaces at a time, for example, Xiangyu, the warrior of state of Chu, burned down the huge palace city of Qin Dynasty, what impact did it have on the survival of the entire planet? Nothing! So we will find that the higher the level of human civilization, the less stable and the more turbulent the society is. Let me give you another example, today people living in towns and cities, or even people living in rural areas, if the water and electricity supply is cut off, you will immediately become worried, as the normal life is simply impossible. But in the ancient times mankind did not have electricity, all people lived along the river, and there was never a water cut. It marks the more complex and civilized human social life is, the more shakable and more fragile human social life is.

Not only that, we will also find that the tension of human social life is also increasing. For example, human in agricultural civilization was only busy for one or two months a year, because the ancient Yellow River basin only planted one crop a year, he was busy only in the sowing and harvest period of these two months, the other ten months of the year were basically non-farming time. Therefore, in ancient times, people spent forty-five days for the New Year. Today, you only have six or seven days for the New Year. Usually all the people have to rush to work every day. You know the ancients, a man worked outside farming, planting dozens of acres, nearly a hundred acres of land, rough farming, that was enough to feed seven or eight people. The ancients did not have contraceptive technology, after marriage they constantly gave birth to children, a couple of eight or ten children were common, even if half of them survived, four or five children, plus the two elderlies, a man to support seven or eight people was not a problem at all. Women were only busy at home with children, taking care of the elderlies, which would take up all her time. So in ancient times a man working outside was enough to support seven or eight people of the family, that is an indisputable fact. At that time, when having one more child it was called to "add one more pair of chopsticks", which did not constitute any burden at all. But today, not only the couple has to be busy all day, and the cost of raising a child is already a middle-income families can hardly afford. The China Business News once made a survey that it is difficult to raise a child from kindergarten to college graduation or post graduate without millions of yuan. So I'm amazed to hear people often saying that our material life is much richer today. Please note that this is not called *a rich material life,* this is called *the cost of living increased,* please don't mistake the concept!

Some people may say that the ancient people did not have cars or TVs. But you have to know that you have a car today, it is your necessities, if you do not have a car it will be a problem to go to work, and even you can not buy food home. You say you can live without a TV, yes, but your good simplicity will certainly assure you, that you won't be able to find a wife and you won't have children. So I will say it again, this is called the cost of survival increased, not called material life is rich.

Even worse, you are losing your security of survival all the way through times. Let me give you an example. The ancients had barter trade at first, and there was no inflation at all. By the time scarce metals were used as money, even in bad years of harvest, the price of food went up only two or three times. But what is the money we use today? It's paper money, pseudo money, called *banknotes*. What is the most important characteristic of such things? Inflation. In a normal year, inflation is 2% to 3% per year, which means that every fifteen years, the purchasing power decreases by half. What is worse, it is hyperinflationary at every turn. Look at the example of the end of World War I, during the Weimar Republic the defeated Germany, the Deutsche Mark inflated 80,000 times in just two or three years. During 1948 to 1949, when the Republican government of China was about to collapse, its fiat currency and banknotes inflated 30,000 times in one year. By the time when former Soviet Union collapsed in 1991, the Soviet ruble was inflated 12,000 times overnight, what was 1 ruble for 3 dollars became 4,000 rubles for 1 dollar in just a few days. Let's take the inflation 10,000 times, what does it mean? A millionaire becomes a poor man with $100 just overnight! That's why today a millionaire, a multi-millionaire, even a billionaire, he does not feel financially safe, he has to take his money to invest. Where to invest? Exchange rate, property, stock market, futures, what are these things? It is a curve that is constantly oscillating every second. Please think about it, you bind your mind on such a curve that is changing every minute every second, how can you have any happiness to speak of?

This is why, the ancients had no such a thing of happiness index. Humans must cry out for what is missing. You need to compile a happiness index nowadays because you have lost that happiness and are in extreme anxiety and unrest. Please pay attention to what I am talking about. I'm talking about an apparently opposite evaluation of the development of civilization. What is the reason that modern man gives a high opinion of the progress of civilization? It is because he does not know the state of life of the ancients, the state of living in peace and in happiness. The life of the ancients was very leisurely, very peaceful, and a sense of peace that you can never cherish when being in anxiety everywhere and all the time. As leisure is one of the three basic elements of happiness, if you lost leisure, then in no way you can speak of happiness.

The reason why we always give misjudgments about civilization today is that civilization has grown into a huge tree with flourishing leaves. When people today speak of civilization, it is the equivalent of a blind man feeling an elephant, the equivalent of a leaf that blinds eyes. What does it mean? You point to a branch or a leaf of the tree and say that is *civilization*, but no one sees the whole picture of civilization, and that is why they make the misjudgment of civilization in terms of progress. Why were the ancient sages critical of civilization, from Laozi to Confucius to Buddha Shakyamuni? Think about what Buddhism teaches. It talks about *commandment, meditation and wisdom*. What does it want to do? It is to recognize the nature of civilization, to get rid of the sufferings of civilization, and to eliminate the disturbances of civilization.

Why did the ancients have a critical attitude toward civilization? It is because the ancients were in a particular situation where they looked down on civilization. At that time, civilization was just a sapling, so they could naturally see the picture of civilization as a whole, and could see the trend of its growth. As they watched, they saw the process of civilization's progress was the process of human decay and catastrophizing human life, so they were mostly negative and wary of civilization. This was the basic social view of the Chinese sages in the pre-Qin era. We can thus see the state of cultural shaping in the pre-Qin era and the reasons why it always tends to reach a conservatism. We can also see in this way the role of the pre-Qin era in laying down and ordering the basic ideological tone of Chinese culture. It marked the survival of a profound vision in which it simultaneously laid the foundation for the stable existence of China for the next two thousand years. This is where the pre-Qin era, as the first great social transformation, had its basic constructive force on Chinese culture and social life. This is also the state of the historical background and the state of cultural emergence in which Confucius lived.

Aging Phenomenon of the Infantile Civilization

We discuss below two idiosyncrasies of traditional Chinese culture.

In our Chinese view, it is normal for a country to be unified into a large system, and it is abnormal for it to be divided into small states. Moreover, the Chinese already had a *under heaven view* more than 2000 years ago. Confucius talked about "cultivating one's moral character, managing one's family, governing the state, and policing under heaven", and Laozi also used the concept of *under heaven* (world) constantly in his books. We should know that it is very rare to have a stable system of large countries in ancient times, and it is an extraordinary state, not a normal state.

Look at Europe, which is about the same size as China and has so far been in separate dozens of small countries, and the created European Union is still wobbly. In China, a relatively stable system of great countries began to emerge as early as the eleventh century B.C., especially in the third century B.C. This is a very special and unusual phenomenon. Let me give you an example. In the region of the civilization around the Mediterranean, there was a great power system as early as the fourth century B.C., which was the Alexander Empire. But Alexander the Great lived only 32 or 33 years, and immediately after his death, Alexander's empire collapsed. There was another great power around the Mediterranean region, ancient Rome, which existed for a longer time, but it really shone as a strong and stable power for only a few hundred years, and by the fifth century A.D., the Western Roman Empire fell abruptly.

Only in East Asia, a stable system of great powers emerged early, from the Zhou dynasty over the Central Plains to the following Chinese dynastic empires, which lasted for thousands of years without falling. This is a very strange phenomenon. I call it "the aging phenomenon of an infantile civilization".

What does it mean? We all know that China is the most typical agricultural civilization system, and agricultural civilization is the first crop of human civilization, that is, the most primitive and childish form of human civilization. However, this most infantile civilization expresses the old state everywhere, which is called the old age phenomenon of infantile civilization.

Let me give you an example, macroscopically, there was a great power system 3,000 or 2,000 years ago, and unified scripts appeared in as early as the third century BC. In Europe, on the other hand, last century, there were attempts to unify European scripts, and created an *Esperanto* language, which ended in failure. In China, the imperial official examination system emerged as early as around

B.C., and largely matured by the Sui and Tang dynasties. In the early years of the Western Han Dynasty, it was called the filial piety examination or the official selection examination, and after the Sui and Tang Dynasties, it was called the imperial official examination. What is the imperial official examination? It is to select social management officials from civil ordinary level, equivalent to what we call today the civil service examination system.

In terms of the development of cultural history, you say that the imperial official examination system has a lot of problems, and that is true. It made all literati of the time read only the *Four Books and Five Classics* and only cared only about *superior learning to become an official*, and all literati were crowded on the narrow bridge of learning to become a government official, and hardly any intellectual cared about natural science, which led to a serious imbalance of neglecting natural science in Chinese culture, it is true. However, from another perspective, it is the earliest system of selection of civil officials in human history. You should know that in the ancient times, all human beings practiced the system of hereditary succession, that is, all officials at all levels of society as administrators came from hereditary succession. For example, the bourgeois revolution in France in 1789, but even half a century after the success of the revolution, the majority of official positions in France were still hereditary in 1830, and it was only after 1830 that the civil service examination and selection system was gradually implemented in France. From a macro perspective, we can find that Chinese society is extremely old and precocious.

It is not only in the macrocosm, but also in the micro details. For example, Western culture talks about *sex*, love, desire, passion, love affairs, etc. Chinese culture talks about *food*, eat, delicious dinner, nectareous, mouth water, endlessly. But we have to think carefully, who cares about sex? Young people must be more concerned about the issue of sex, if a meal is to delay his love, he would rather not eat the meal. What people care about the issue of food? Older people, seniors have not much to do in bed, so they care more about food. Food culture is the typical culture of the elderly.

Let's look deeper, talking about food culture, Chinese food is salty, spicy and sour, while Western food is sweet, slight salt and oily, it is naturally in line with the taste of children. Anyone who has ever brought up a child knows that if you cook Chinese food for the child every day at home, the child will not like the food. If you occasionally lead him to try McDonald's, KFC, the child will request you to take him there more. Why? Because Western food is naturally designed according to the taste of children. Please think about who needs salty, spicy and sour food? Older people, the taste receptors on the tongue has degenerated, not salty, spicy and sour food is not enough to make him appetite. Therefore, even Chinese food culture is biased towards the elderly.

Let's look at it further, Westerners are frank and sincere, while Chinese people have a high level of sophistication. In the West, telling lies is a big deal, and if you lie in court, it's a perjury, and you're criminally liable. In the eyes of the Chinese, Westerners are all naïve, simple-minded, and straightforward even to adulthood. On the contrary, the Chinese people tend to have a guarded-mind, in the early years of the reform and opening policy, the Western economic groups came to China to negotiate with Chinese entrepreneurs, pleasantries and flatteries two or three hours, the Westerners would not understand what the Chinese want. There is a Chinese folk proverb: "When meeting someone, you can only say a small part, but never all your heart." It means that 70% of your mind should be reserved, even the small part of what you heard are basically false words. Please think about what kind of people are honest in nature? Children, of course. Anyone who has experience of raising a child knows that a child of five or six-years old often speaks very profound words, which surprises adults. It's not profound really, but just a little bit of truth, and we've long been accustomed of not telling the truth, hence we feel a little surprise. Then what kind of people tend to have guarded-minds? Adults! Aged people! They have been through all the vicissitudes and sufferings, so they have to wrap themselves up with a guarded-mind, so the Chinese are generally old in disposition.

Then, we see that Western culture tends to be competitive, while Chinese culture emphasizes harmony. Think about it, what kind of people like competition? Children tend to like competition. You buy a small child a toy and let him play it alone, he plays with it a while and would throws it aside. If you put the child in a competitive game, he would be happy to play with others. That's why all highly competitive sports today like soccer, basketball, American football, are the largest sports industry in the world. What kind of people like harmony? Older people, they can't compete anymore, so they have to talk about harmony, so it still expresses old age state naturally.

If we look again, we will find that Western culture tends to look forward, while Chinese culture tends to look backward. It is most typical in ways of scholars doing their academic work in the East and West. We should know that Western culture is called critical scholarship, and all of us who are doing academic work today have been imbued with this Western academic style without exception. The so-called critical scholarship is to be picky at the problems you study, to be picky at the arguments of your predecessors in this field, to say that he is neither this nor that, and then to build your own theoretical model, which is the typical way of Western critical scholarship.

So what does it do in Chinese culture? We tend to look backwards; it is all about turning over stacks of paper. This is why I say that China has long since run out of masters of Chinese culture. If you meet a master of Chinese culture now, it is usually in two cases: first, you are mistaken; second, he is a fraud. For example, someone says that Ji Xianlin is a master of Chinese culture, but he himself does not admit it, because he did not study Chinese, but he is a specialist in a small language of Oriental languages. What did he study? It's an ancient language of some primitive tribes around Afghanistan and North India in antient times. So, if you meet a master of Chinese culture, he must be a fraud. Why? Because after the founding of the country and even after the Republic of China, people of the country are no longer trained in the basic norms of national culture.

So what is the basic way of doing national studies? It's all about looking backwards and turning over stacks of paper. It has three indispensable trainings.

The first is "训诂" (Xun Gu) *exegesis*. What does it mean by *exegesis*? I am not going to talk about its academic meaning, but I will make it simple, just like the first day of our lecture on the archaic script, that is, to find out the antient meaning of each Chinese character in its different eras and the flow of different eras. If you can't find the ancient meaning and the process of change of each Chinese character, you can't interpret the ancient classics. You interpret the ancient books, you use today's Chinese to interpret them, basically it is all misinterpretation. So this is called *exegesis*. What is the scholar doing? Turning over stacks of paper.

The second is "考据" (Kao Ju)*textology*. What is *textology*? Please do not understand it as archaeology. Archaeology was introduced to China from the West in modern times, and there has never been archaeology in China since ancient times, because the ancient Chinese believed that digging up the graves of ancestors was a most unethical thing to do. Therefore, in ancient China there were only tomb robbers, never archaeology. So, what is it meant by *textology*? It is a scholar who has to search all the information of previous research on the issue he wants to study, and this is called textual research. What is he doing? Looking backwards, going through stacks of old papers.

The third is "注疏" (Zhu Shu) *note*. We first look at the character "注" (Zhu), what does it mean? Not only do you have to find all the relevant information on the evidence, you also have to find the notes that previous literati made in the white space of the evidence, which is called "注". The so-called "疏" (Shu) is what a later generation of writers made note to the note that previous generation of writers left, you also have to search and gather them. What is he doing? All is looking for notes from stacks of old paper. This is the reason why there are no more masters of Chinese studies in China now, because this kind of academic training, which only looks through stacks of literatures of old books, has long been abolished in our education circle.

So what kind of people tend to look forward? Young people are always looking forward. What kind of people tend to look backward? Older and middle-aged people tend to look backwards. So, if one day you start to recall how great you were back then, it is a sign that you are getting old.

CAUSES OF *GRAND UNIFICATION* AND *RIGID AGING*

It is a very strange cultural phenomenon that traditional Chinese culture, which is the complete preservation of the first crop of the most infantile civilization in the history of mankind, yet it has shown the characteristics of old age or rigidity in the ancient times. Why did this happen? In the following, we will categorize the research on traditional Chinese culture conducted by scholars of both Chinese and the West, including the famous British historian Toynbee in the last century, the famous Harvard sinology professor John King Fairbank, and many scholars of Chinese descent, including Huang Renyu, and summarize it into six articles to give you a basic account, so that you can further understand the natural conditions and the social soil that shaped Chinese culture and Confucius' thought.

First, the loess soil is loose and fertile, the impact of the Yellow River directly formed the wide alluvial Central Plains, which was easy to carry out primitive farming. I have already talked about this part in the first day of the course, so I will not repeat it.

Second, the Central Plains is one of the only three primitive farming bases on earth, but this place has a strange climate, and almost all of its annual rainfall is concentrated in the late summer and early autumn months, resulting in frequent droughts and floods. During the Republic of China, a famous scholar named Yao Shanyou wrote a book called *Book of Integrated Drawings*, in which he examined the major droughts, floods and other natural disasters recorded in the history books for 2270 years before the Republic of China. The collected statistics show that in these 2000 plus years, there were 1392 major droughts and 1621 major floods recorded in the history books, not counting insect or locust disasters, which means that on average 1.33 disasters occurred each year. This is the reason why during the Spring and Autumn Period in China, each state borrows from or lent to other grains even though they were enemies of each other.

Let me give you an example. During the time of Duke Mu of Qin, there was a major drought in state of Jin, so the ruler of Jin borrowed grains from Qin, and Duke Mu of Qin agreed to do so with great enthusiasm. You should know that Qin and Jin have always been enemies. Because state of Jin is located in the east of Qin, the first major obstacle Qin faces is state of Jin, if it wanted to go out of the Hangu Pass to fight for the Central Plains. So now there is an idiom called "the amity between Qin and Jin", you should not to get it wrong, misinterpreting as the good relationship between Qin and Jin. It is the result of the extreme tension between the two states and the need to ease the tension by way of marriage between the royal families. Therefore, the original meaning of the phrase *amity between Qin and Jin* was a political marriage without love. A few years later, state of Qin had a huge disaster and sent messenger to Jin for help, that is, to borrow grains, but the king of Jin was replaced by Duke Hui of Jin, who was a real bastard. He not only refused to lend grains to Qin, instead he thought that the state of Qin was very weak in power, so he led his army to invade Qin. So Duke Mu of Qin led his people to fight a famous battle with Jin, known as the Battle of Han Yuan, and defeated the Jin army, and even surprisingly captured Duke Hui of Jin alive. The reason why I tell you this example is to show you that in the Central Plains, although it was an important birthplace of agricultural civilization, where there were many disasters. Being separated in small states, no one could live in peace.

Third, the Yellow River is extremely dangerous. What does this phrase mean? You should know that our ancient civilization is also called the Yellow River civilization, because the Central Plains civilization is the beginning of Chinese civilization. However, the Yellow River is one of the most dangerous rivers in the world. The vast majority of all rivers on earth generally have a sediment content of no more than about 5%. Even the second largest river on earth, the Amazon River in South America, has a sediment content of no more than 12% in the rainy season. However, the average sediment content of the Yellow River is between 42% and 63%, which is really true as the saying goes "half a bowl of sediment in a bowl of Yellow River water". Then the Yellow River flowed through the Central Plains, the river flows slower and the sediment settled, so the local civilized people were forced to constantly build embankments on both sides of the Yellow River, which resulted in the Yellow River bed being continuously raised. By the Han Dynasty, the Yellow River bed was more than seven meters above the ground level, and by the Song Dynasty, it was more than 19 to 20 meters high, becoming truly a hanging river above the ground, a hanging sword over the Chinese nation. Think about it, if the country split into small states, how can you manage the Yellow River? Anyone who attempted to do something to it alone will be totally ineffective. Because whatever you want to do to your section of the river, but the upstream state does not cooperate, not only that, they might even dig the river bank to drown you. In the book *Art of War*, it mentions the tactic of flooding the enemy. Therefore, the Yellow River has become a powerful tool to force Chinese civilization and the Chinese nation to unify.

Let me give you an example. When Emperor Qin Yingzheng (Shi Huang) was conquering to unify the country, he sent army to attack the state of Wei. His main general, Wang Ben, the son of the famous Qin general Wang Jian, led an army of 300,000 men to besiege Daliang, the capital of Wei, for three months, but the ruler of Wei refused to surrender. How did Wang Ben do? He ordered to dig the Yellow River dam and flooded the city Daliang, and so Wei surrendered immediately. What does it show? It shows that the separated small states along the Yellow River sides simply could not survive properly, not to mention any development.

Fourth, nomadic ecology and agricultural ecology are distinct and adjacent to each other. What is the meaning of this statement? We say that East Asia is a closed area, but there were two civilization forms in this East Asian land, which were agricultural civilization and nomadic civilization. Since ancient times, the nomadic civilization of the northern border always constituted a major threat to the agricultural civilization of China. First of all, remember that the Great Wall of China was never built by Emperor Qin Yingzheng, (Shi Huang). It was built during the Spring and Autumn Period and the Warring States Period by various small northern states, such as Yan, Zhao and Qin, who built the Great Wall separately. After the reign of Emperor Qin Shi Huang, the Great Wall was only built to connect these fragments. In other words, the Great Wall was not designed by anyone in a uniform way before it was built, but strangely enough, it was aligned exactly with the 15-inch isobath.

Let me explain what is 15 inches of rainfall line, or 15 inches of equal rainfall line? 15 inches of rainfall is equivalent to 380 mm to 400 mm of annual rainfall. And where the annual rainfall is less than 400 mm it is difficult to develop agriculture; where the annual rainfall is less than 250 mm, it generally can only grass grow to develop nomadic pastoralism; where the annual rainfall is less than 100 mm, it generally turns to desertification or become desert. And this dividing line of 400 mm annual rainfall actually happens to overlap with the Great Wall. What does it show? It shows that the Great Wall is a barrier line to prevent the clash of the two civilizations.

And the Great Wall is one of the most massive civil engineering projects of the ancient age of mankind worldwide, and it appeared in East Asia by chance. What does this mean? It means that the clash of two civilizations in East Asia was extremely violent! As you know, the Xiongnu nation in the pre-Qin era always infested the states in the north until the Western Han Dynasty, and then posed a major threat to the Han Dynasty. Then came the Turkic peoples of the Tang Dynasty, the Jin, Liao, Xixia, and Mongolia of the Song Dynasty, and all the way to the Nuzhen, also known as the Manchus, who later conquered the Ming Dynasty and established Qing Dynasty. So we see that China historically was constantly invaded by foreigners, all of whom were the onslaught of the nomadic peoples from the northern frontier.

We should note that the expression *whoever lags behind is beaten* is very problematic. If you take a long roll of history, except for the modern era after the 15th century AD, it was *whoever lags behind is beaten*. This is because of the emergence of a more violent civilization called the Age of Science. Thousands of years before that, mankind had always been *whoever is advanced is beaten*. For example, Zhou destroyed the Shang, who the only tribe in the Central Plains that had a written culture, and the *Book of Zhou* recorded that "only the Yin (Shang) ancestors had books and books". Zhou was the barbarian tribe without written culture, but it destroyed Shang, who was the better civilized community. In the Warring States period, the barbarian state of Qin, who had a Xiongnu style, destroyed the five better civilized states. Then look at the Tang Dynasty, which was a regime established by the Xianbei people, bearing in mind that Li Shimin had about three-quarters Xianbei blood in him, and it was the father and son who defeated the central area states and established the Great Tang Empire. Then down the timeline, the Mongols established the Yuan Dynasty in China. Remember what Lu Xun said: "Genghis Khan is not our Khan". That is, during the Song Dynasty, Mongolia was not part of China and its being part of the country was a typical foreign invasion. The Yuan Dynasty ruled for eighty-nine years, and the Chinese people obediently became slaves of a defeated country. The Yuan Dynasty divided then China society into four classes: first, Mongols; second, Central Asians with colored eyes or white Europeans; third, Han Chinese; fourth, southerners, because south China was finally occupied; all Chinese people were enslaved for a long time. Further worse, by the end of the Ming Dynasty in 1644, the Nuzhen ethnic with only a population of more than 200,000, including old, female and children, while the population of China was around 100 million at the time, they actually easily overwhelmed China, entering into the vast Central Plain area and established the Manchu regime.

This is not only true for China, but also true to the West. Think about it, who destroyed ancient Greece? By the Macedonian barbarians from its north. Then, who destroyed the Roman Empire? By the Germanic and Visigothic barbarians who came down south from Europe. As we can see, if we stretch out the long history, in ancient and even medieval times, mankind has always been *whoever is advanced is beaten*. Why? Because the people of agricultural civilization could not ride on horseback. You should know that the stirrup did not become popular all over the world until the early Eastern Han Dynasty. In ancient times, the rider's two feet on a horse were suspended in the air, and a person's main attention and strength were spent on riding the horse, with both legs clamping the horse's belly and both hands clutching the horse's mane, which was not yet securely controlled. Once the horse runs or jumps, people may immediately be thrown down, fall into a fracture, lying in bed cannot move for a hundred days. The nomadic people have been riding on horseback since they were young, with their legs clamped to the belly of the horse and their hands free to wield swords and knives, thus establishing their cavalry system.

Before modern times, cavalry has traditionally been the nemesis of infantry, because cavalry is extremely mobile. The ancient Chinese agricultural civilization did not have cavalry, only chariots. So if you read the ancient books, what words are used to describe a country's strong military power? It is described as "a country of a thousand chariots" or "a country of ten thousand chariots". The so-called *chariot*, is a chariot plus a dozen to seventy-odd foot soldiers. Three heavy armor soldiers stood on the chariot, and the rest of the light armor soldiers followed the chariot. And as I said before, the ancient vehicle was a wooden axle wearing two wheels, and the wheels on both sides always turned in the same way, so it could not move quickly and was less mobile. Cavalry thus became one of the most powerful form among infantry cluster combat.

At what point did cavalry decline? It was not until the early days of World War II, when blitzkrieg and three-dimensional warfare emerged, with planes in the sky, machine guns on the ground, and artillery everywhere, so cavalry was put down. on September 1,

1939, Hitler attacked Poland, and a Polish cavalry of over ten thousand was quickly wiped out, and cavalry tactics have since retired from the stage of history. As you can see, in ancient societies, it was only too normal for agricultural civilizations to be overwhelmed by nomadic civilizations at every turn, and were basically no match for them. This is why the clash between these two civilizations has always been regarded as a serious external problem and a basic national condition in China.

Let me give you another example. The disciples of Confucius once sat together and criticized Guan Zhong. We are all familiar with the fact that Guan Zhong was the prime minister of Duke Huan of Qi, the first of the five hegemons of the Spring and Autumn Period. So why did Confucius' disciples criticize Guan Zhong? Because they decided that Guan Zhong had serious moral defects. In ancient China, the moral concept holds that a good woman does not marry twice, and a good scholar does not serve two masters. That is, a good woman does not marry a second man in her life, and a good scholar or man does not serve a second master in his life. Before Guan Zhong assisted Duke Huan of Qi, Jiang Xiaobai, who was competing for the throne with his brother, Duke Jiu, Guan Zhong was the teacher of Duke Jiu and Bao Shuya, a friend of Guan Zhong, was the teacher of Jiang Xiaobai. During the competition for the throne, Duke Jiu failed and Jiang Xiaobai ascended to the throne. Normally Guan Zhong should have committed suicide, or at least went into exile, but he went to be the prime minister with his enemy master, Duke Huan of Qi, Jiang Xiaobai. So Confucius' disciples were right in their view that Guan Zhong had serious moral defect.

But what did Confucius say? In the *Analects of Confucius*, he left a sentence: "Minimize Guanzhong, I'll loose down my hair and wear the left". If I draw an old man with long hair, then I draw a child with an ideogram of holding the old man from below, this character is (甲文 金文 小篆 楷体)"孝" (Xiao) filial piety in oracle bone script; if I draw an old man with long hair, and I draw a hand holding a stick next to it, this character is "微" (Wei) minimize (甲文 金文 小篆 隶书 楷体). What is the original meaning of "微"? It means to hit the old man! It is the opposite of the character "孝". What is the meaning of "minimize Guanzhong"? It means to criticize him.

As you know, we have an idiom today called *quite some veiled criticism,* which means I want to complain you for something. Confucius said, if you criticize Guan Zhong, then I will loose down my hair and wear the left. What does *loose one's hair and wear the left* mean? In ancient China, it is believed that the body's hair and skin are the property of the parents and should be well taken care of. No one, including men and women, should cut their hair. If you don't cut your hair, it will grow longer and longer as you grow, so all civilized people have to tie their hair. Depending on gender and social status, the form of hair-tying is different. The barbarians wore their hair down, and today girls wear their hair down like the barbarians do. What does *wear the left* mean? The clothes we wear today are called Western-style clothes, and the buttons are in the middle, but in ancient times in East Asia, the buttons were on both sides of the clothes. And civilized men wear clothes with buttons on the right side; while barbarians' clothes button on the left. Confucius meant that if you criticize Guan Zhong, I will loose my hair down, wear the left button clothes and become a barbarian.

Why did Confucius not allow his disciples to criticize Guan Zhong? It was because Guan Zhong, as the prime minister of Duke Huan of Qi, had established a basic state policy for the state of Qi called "Respect the King and expel the barbarians". During the Spring and Autumn period, all the separate states were engaged in wars of annexation, and at this time, Qi was the most powerful state in the Spring and Autumn period and it also conquered and merged some small states. However, under the rule advised by Guan Zhong, he established the basic state policy of *respecting the King*, that is, everyone united around the King of Zhou Dynasty, united for what? To repel the barbarians! To defend against foreign invasion! Let me give you an example. When the Xiongnu attacked the state of Yan, Guan Zhong actually sent Qi troops to help state of Yan to resist the Xiongnu. As you know, state of Yan was the most important geopolitical threat to Qi, it was in the north of Qi, and the soldiers of Yan and Zhao were very powerful in fighting. During the Warring States period, Yan, under the leadership of General Yue Yi, had destroyed 72 cities of Qi, which almost led to the downfall of Qi, which led to the famous story of Tian Shan restoring Qi. This is how tense the relationship between Qi and Yan. However, Guan Zhong led his troops to help Yan to defend against Xiong Nu. When Xiong Nu attacked states of Cao and Xing, Guan Zhong not only sent troops to help them, but also helped them to restore and rebuild their states. Because Guan Zhong held an alliance with the lords nine times to unite everyone against the barbarian invasion, this led to the fact that the Xiongnu in the north did not exterminate the weak shoots of the Chinese civilization. Think about it, back then, the civilization of the Central Plains was only limited to a small area. Without Guan Zhong, Chinese civilization might have been wiped out long ago.

Let me give you an example. When I was teaching my Western Philosophy class, I laid out a map of ancient Greece for you. Ancient Greece was a large Greek confederation, including Asia Minor, including the Greek peninsula, including the Apennine peninsula which is the southern tip of the Italian peninsula. The Greek alliance was so powerful at that time that it actually twice defeated the Persian Empire, the world's first empire. Greece was twice the winner in Greek-Persian wars. Such a powerful ancient Greece was destroyed by Macedonian barbarians. If not for Guan Zhong, the Chinese nation would have been wiped out in the smoke of history like ancient Greece. This is why Confucius gave Guan Zhong a very high evaluation, actually using these eight words: "nine times unifying the states' lords and saved the world". Let me tell you that in this part of the Central Plains, separated as small states was in no way to resist the impact of nomadic civilization. This problem of clash between civilizations is tough to deal with.

Let's look at the fifth. China is a large agricultural country, but its arable land area is very small. High mountains, deserts, marshes and lakes account for nearly 90% of the country's total land area, while arable land accounts for only a little more than 10%. During the Republican era, the government department researched that China's arable land accounted for 10.4% of China's total land area; today, the Ministry of Land of the Communist Party of China researches that arable land only accounts for slightly more than 10.6% of the total land area. What is this concept? Let me give you two examples. India's land area is only about one-third of China's total land area, but its arable land area is actually 60% to 70% larger than China's. That is to say, if China can support 1.3 billion people, India can support 2 billion people. Then look at the United States, the land area and China is similar, but its arable land area accounted for more than 40% of the land area, if China can support 1.3 billion people, the United States is sufficient to support 5 billion people. But the United States said today that its only 300 million people are too much. Not only that China's arable land is extremely low, but also the Chinese have children endlessly, strong fertility, although our culture does not talk much about sex, nor does the Chinese are fond of sex, actually our biological clock matching our geological location accounts for that.

What does that mean? The ancient Chinese occupied the best part of the northern hemisphere of the earth, called the mid-latitude zone. The modern strength of the United States is also related to the fact that the United States occupies the mid-latitude zone of the Americas just across from China. The mid- latitude zone is the most suitable for biological reproduction, which is why the largest distribution of biological quality on earth are in the mid-latitude zone. The mid-latitude zone has the right amount of light and moderate temperature. It is important to know that our human physiological rhythm is regulated by the sun, which is called biological clock. In other words, our physiological operation nodes follow the sun movement. The biological clock is located roughly in the periphery of the body's visual center, which regulates the timing of the body's physiological functioning. For example, the highest blood pressure of all of us 24 hours a day occurs from 4:00 a.m. to 10:00 a.m. This is why 70 to 80 percent of cardiovascular accidents in later life occur during this time. This is because we humans evolved from 400 million years of terrestrial life as diurnal animals. We know that rats and owls are nocturnal animals, but the vast majority of animals are diurnal. We humans evolved from diurnal animals, so human physiological rhythms is adapted to the changes in the intensity of solar illumination. In the mid-latitudes, the sun rises at four or five o'clock in summer, so the ancients traditionally followed this principle of rest and work, called *sunrise to work, sunset to rest*. Four or five o'clock in the morning ancients started working, seven or eight o'clock in the evening they went to bed, a full eight hours sleep every day, the biological clock is so regulated for hundreds of millions of years. Why does blood pressure increase at the morning time? It is to increase blood supply, increase muscle explosive power, this is called the *biological clock*.

Speaking of this, we say today that science and technology is a double-edged sword, with a good side and a bad side. But I prefer to say that science and technology is a single-edged sword, only the bad side, cutting off the survival of our human longevity. I give an example, Edison invented the light bulb, and men thought there should be no side effects, but since he invented the light bulb, we humans have not been activities on time, but all live the night life. Many watches TV all night, what is TV? It is a colored light bulb after all. As a result, all people's biological clock messed up! This is one of the major underlying causes for the emergence of thousands of new diseases and the occurrence of a large number of untreatable malignant diseases. Let's go back to the topic, due to the suitable biological clock in the mid-latitude region, so the fertility of animals and plants in the mid-latitude region is very strong, efficiency of reproduction is very high, so the Chinese population since ancient times accounted for 20% to 25% of the world's total population.

Let me give you another example. An old teacher I know, a friend of his used to work as a translator and assistant to Soviet experts in the 1950s. The Soviet experts he worked for were a young couple who had been married in the Soviet Union for three years, but were unable to have a child and thought they had infertility or sterility (for women, it is called infertility and for men, it is called sterility). They came to China in 1955 and withdrew to the Soviet in 1959. Five years in China the couple had three children born in China. Before they left, he told the interpreter that China was a blessed place to have children. Think about it, China's arable land area is relatively small, and the population reproduction capacity is superb, which brings a serious trouble, is that interpersonal relations and resource relations are extraordinarily tense.

Finally, let's look at the sixth article, the closed topography of East Asia. As I have said repeatedly before, China is located in this region of East Asia, the north of which is the Siberian alpine tundra; the west is the Pamir Plateau; the southwest is the Qinghai-Tibet Plateau; the south is the Hengduan Mountains, the ancient people simply could not go over; and the east is the vast Pacific Ocean; so it is a completely closed landscape. This closed landscape led to the fact that in ancient times, when transportation and communication were not developed, it was very difficult for foreigners or foreign cultures to invade China. To some extent, it isolated the interaction between Chinese civilization and other civilizations, thus constituting a sophisticated pattern of Chinese civilization, developing and refining on its own. As I said before, culture has a masking effect, and it is only in the state of communication that culture breaks through itself.

So, let's make a brief summary: the first condition above is the reason why Chinese civilization is extraordinarily precocious, that is, the Central Plains became the only three original farming bases for human beings, so Chinese agricultural civilization developed earlier and tended to be precocious; the second, third and fourth conditions above, that is, the climate is strange and disasters are frequent; the Yellow River is dangerous and separated small states could not deal with it; the clash between nomadic and agricultural civilizations was intensive and separated states could not defend the nomadic invasions; these three factors made it necessary for China to establish a great power system at an early stage. This is the reason why China's *world view* emerged in the pre-Qin era, and why China has been a stable system of great powers since ancient times. The fifth condition above, i.e., the small size of the arable land and the high reproductive capacity of the population, led to extra tension between people and resources, which is the main reason why traditional Chinese culture paid extra attention to human and social problems and neglected natural science. The sixth condition, China's closed landscape, is the reason why Chinese culture, in the absence of communication with other civilizations, has been sculptured and refined alone for thousands of years, finally shaping a primitive and infantile civilization into a lineage of overly mature and even rigid aging culture.

Only when we understand the above general environment, background and soil can we understand the basic qualities of traditional Chinese culture and the true connotation of Confucian culture.

Three Main Elements of the Traditional Culture

We are going to talk about some topics related to Confucius personally. Before we talk about this topic, we must first establish the idea that there are three major elements that are indispensable in the ancient culture of mankind. What are these three elements?

First, the element of *seeking governance*; second, the element of *enlightenment*; and third, the element of *cannon rules*. What do all of them mean? I will explain them one by one.

First of all, we must establish the idea that human society is not created by human beings on their own, but grows out of biological society. Previously, all sociologists and philosophers, including Marx, believed that *society* was something unique to human beings, and that *society* was entirely created by human beings. This view is no longer valid today. In the second half of the last century, Western biology discovered that all living things live in social groups, and that human society grows out of biological and animal societies, which is known as *sociobiology*. We do not have time today to explain in detail the rationale for this new discipline and its content. I just want to tell you that you should not think that social systems are the product of human creation. Society is a natural structure that has existed and evolved for 3.8 billion years, and human society is merely a late derivative of biological society.

When human society happens, it immediately goes out of order. Why? Consider how biological societies are constituted. Biological society or animal society is a society whose members are differentiated and disabled at the physical level, and therefore, it must be compensated for the creation of a vital structure of complementary disabilities, which we call a biological social system or animal social structure.

Let me give you an example. Biologists study hymenopteran societies, what do they mean by hymenopteran society? Simply put, it is a society of bees and ants. Let's look at hymenopteran societies, insect societies, animal societies, how do they work? There is a queen bee in the bee community, but it is not called a queen bee, it is biologically called a female bee, and in the entire bee society, only the female bee has the ability to reproduce. Since all living organisms revolve around the central axis of sexual reproduction, humans call the female bee, the only female bee, the queen bee. The female bee is five times larger and lives ten times longer than the average bee, and she actually lays thousands of eggs per day, more than her body weight. Since it is the proliferative center of the bee society, it forms the core of the society's functioning. It is entirely a female reproductive organ, and it is so crippled that it is surprisingly incapable of any other survival.

The largest swarm in honey bee society is called the worker bee, which belongs to the category of female bees with underdeveloped female organs. They have long mouthparts, a light body and wings that are highly capable of flying, and dense leg hairs that form a special pollen basket in which the pollen can be brought back to the hive. There is also a small group of bees called drones, which mate with females during their flight, and once mating is complete, they immediately die a heroic martyrdom; they are simply a flying male reproductive organ.

In ant society there is another class called soldier ants, they have thick armor, biologically called titin, and big violent pincers on their mouths, so much so that their heads are so heavy that it is difficult to hold the balance of their body movements, they have no function and can't do anything else but play a role, guarding the door for the ant colony or participating in the war of the ant colony. What am I talking about? I am telling you that all biological societies and animal societies, whose members are physically crippled, or whose vital social system is constructed by means of physical crippling, have a social structure that is therefore forever stable. It is not possible for social stratification or structural change to occur before there has been significant mutation or variation, and therefore the social form is ultra-stable.

What is the so-called human civilization? It is the civilization of human beings to establish social structure, no longer rely on the physical level of the mutilation of the complementary, all human members are roughly equal in physical, being two shoulders carrying a head, the only difference is the two sexes. Therefore, the early years of mankind called sex structure society, called kin society, mankind gave itself another name, called clan society. Because the human body is only different in the two sexes, so once we go beyond the blood clan society and enter the civilized society, what do humans rely on for social combination? By intellectual disability. From physical disability to intellectual disability is a process, that is, by the development of intelligence to divide and differentiate, and on this basis to apply the complementarity of disability, so as to establish the subsequent late-level social structure.

Since each of us is similar and equal at the physical level, it is natural that each of us will not be willing to live in the lower class of society, and each of us will want to be in the upper class. Therefore, once the society is civilized, once the sexual structural constraints are relieved and released, human society immediately tends to be disordered. This is why the first element of the primitive culture in the early years of human civilization was the concept of *seeking governance* and the pursuit of *seeking governance*, that is, the need to achieve this demand for social governance and social stability.

The second is the element of enlightenment. As I said in the previous class, the so-called civilized society is actually the process of being expelled from the Garden of Eden, which is called Paradise Lost. In other words, nature no longer provides humans with any means of survival, and all the means of human life must be prepared by humans themselves. What we eat today, what we wear, what we use, and even the fruits we see today, are all artificially cultivated, which do not exist in nature, or exist in a primitive wild state that seems unusable now. Since all the means of survival of human beings must be prepared by human beings themselves through intellectual development, human beings have a weak qualification for social existence or natural survival. Therefore, at the beginning of human civilization, one of its primitive cultural demands must be there, called enlightenment to mobilize human intelligence. This is the reason why the second major claim of human culture was formed.

The third is the element of canon rules. What does it mean? As I said earlier, human beings are homogeneous in physical traits and equal in nature, so if each person moves according to his or her own will in society, all will tend to run in a certain direction. But the social structure has to arrange people in different structural levels, so human beings must respectively give social groups and people, the norms of positioning survival. Please think about this: Who are you to set the social rules for me to follow? Why could not I set the social norms for you to follow? In other words, since all human beings are equal, theoretically speaking, no one has the minimum conditions to establish social rules for all human beings, for all groups, i.e., there is no such qualification! Therefore, since the beginning of time, mankind had to create a master above the human world, and this is the reason why theology and religion carried so much weight in early human culture. For only a *Lord* above mankind has the qualification and condition to establish social norms on earth, which is called the element of canon law.

It is worth noting that among the primitive groups of mankind, he was either not enlightened and did not form a primitive cultural system, but wherever he was enlightened, each of these three major cultural aspirations was necessarily shared by a different person. For example, the element of seeking governance was borne by politicians and pharaohs, who were the kings of ancient Egypt; the element of enlightenment was borne by philosophers and naturalists, who were the predecessors of science; and the element of canon law was borne by bishops and priests. But only in China, these three primitive elements of culture were assumed by one person, and we call this person a sage, whose typical representative was Confucius. That is why it is said: In the West there are philosophers, but no saints; in the East there are saints, but no philosophers.

Once in the early fourteenth century, when Emperor Wen Zong of Yuan Dynasty greeted the great monks who came to China from the ancient land of Tianzhu, he asked Lu Chun, a Han Chinese minister at his side: Why do you Han Chinese follow that rustic Confucianism but stay away from such a noble Buddhism? As I said earlier, Buddhism is the most noble, philosophical, and logical religion. Then, Lu Chun gave him a very good answer. He said: *Buddhism* is gold, *Daoism* is jade, and *Confucianism* is rice and grain, and life can survive without gold and jade, but cannot momentarily lose rice and grain. This is the orientation of Confucianism. In other words, Confucianism is superficially shallow, but at its core it is in the best position to match the local culture with the structure of its existence. As I said earlier, culture is not about whether it is fancy or glamorous, but about the fact that it must be an appropriate system for the structure of survival.

Let's look at the overall structure of Confucius' *Analects* below. If you want to truly read the *Analects*, remember that three elements of primitive human culture are indispensable. First, the element of seeking governance. Therefore, the most important part of Confucius' doctrine is the search for governance, which is called "to raise the rites of the Zhou, advocate the Way of the King, dream of the Duke of Zhou, and theorize the rites of the early Zhou". As we all know, Confucius said that he often dreamed of the Duke of Zhou, and the core of his doctrine was to reform the society of the Spring and Autumn Period at that time. His political ideal was to restore the ancient system and to respect the virtuous and love the people. Therefore, he always wished to *restore the state of or-*

derly Zhou rites and *righteousness of the world* in the early years of the Western Zhou. This is called "to promote the rites of the Zhou and to advocate the way of the king". The reason why Confucius dreamed of the Duke of Zhou was that Duke Jidan was the first prime minister of the Western Zhou Dynasty who *made the rites and music,* that is, the one who established the political law of the country for the Zhou Dynasty. Therefore, the primary content of Confucius' doctrine is the part of seeking governance. He theorized the political operation of Duke Jidan of Zhou rites and music, and only after theorizing can anything be carried out in a lasting and intensive way, which is reason why Confucius' doctrine is extremely powerful in political sociology.

Confucius said in the chapter *Eight Dancers*, "Zhou has the reference of two dynasties, sufficient culture! I prefer Zhou." What does that mean? He said that the political and social culture of the Zhou Dynasty drew on the accumulation of the Xia and Shang Dynasties, therefore, its cultural heritage was extremely deep and flourishing. Therefore, I follow the culture of Zhou.

Confucius also said in the chapter of *For the Ruler*, "To rule by virtue is like the North Star in its central place and all the stars surround it." He advocated ruling the country by virtue. He said that if you have the principle of ruling the country by virtue, then it is equivalent to the North Star in the sky, around which all the stars orbit. This shows that his political aspiration was extremely high. In his book, he laid out the core political concept of ruling the country and pacifying the world and its social practical governance function, making it the legal basis and the central axis of orthodox in mainstream Chinese culture after the Qin and Han dynasties. Therefore, we say that he truly achieved the state of a man of ordinary, with the whole world in his mind, concerning the least about himself, thus he became a sage. This is the first part of his doctrine.

The second part of Confucius' doctrine is the element of enlightenment, which is "to run a private school, to educate, to teach without discrimination, to precures the style of Chinese literati." Confucius was the first to run a private school, and he did so for all the people, "to teach without discrimination", that is, to educate all people without distinction of class or hierarchy. This is what Feng Youlan said, "style of national scholarship". Note that the Chinese character "士" (Shi) scholar, has a different connotation! Chinese society emphasizes "scholar, farmer, worker, and merchant", and the social status of *scholar* is extremely high. "士" in the West refers to warriors, so if you read Cervantes' book *Don Giovanni*, what is it actually about? It is about the decline of the warrior class and its culture in Europe. But the Chinese "士" mainly refers to scholars, literati, or man of letters, the Chinese scholars were created and nurtured by Confucianism. Chinese scholars held the power of interpretation of Chinese social ideology for 2000 years, and as imperial officials from the examination system, they formed the backbone of the Chinese the bureaucracy system, and ruled the society.

Confucius' running of private schools also gradually spread the custom of going through education to the people, which served to enlighten all levels of Chinese society. Let us look at Confucius' own statement in the *Analects*: "What is there for me to cognize in silence, never tire of learning myself and teaching others what else do I expect?" He said, I silently cognize things, I am never tired of learning, and I am never tired of teaching, and having these things, what else do I require?

Yan Hui, a disciple of Confucius, once left a passage in the *Analects of Confucius*. He said, "Look up so high, study hard, look forward in the front, but as if in the back. The master is good at explaining things, teach me with literature, discipline me with manners, I want to follow him always." Please note, this is what the student said about his teacher. He said, I look at my teacher, but never see his height. There is a Chinese idiom that says, you look up at the top of a mountain but you never see its height when you're standing below it. This is what Yan Hui meant to say. He said, as for his teacher's learning, he wants to understand it, but he could not fully understand it. He said, one moment I feel that the meaning of his learning has been revealed, and the next moment I feel that the issue he discussed has another meaning; "the master is good at explaining things," he kept explaining to us; "teach me with literature", he made me know something; "discipline me with manners, " he made me see what is a man in good manners; "I could not stop", that is, I will follow my teacher all my life and would never leave him. This shows the charm of Confucius' teaching. This is why we say that "a humble scholar, teaching the common people, making it a style of education, thus he became a great master". This is the second part of Confucius' *Analects*, the element of enlightenment.

The third part is the elements of the cannon rules. The cannon rules of Confucius speak of the *Way of the Gentlemen* and the *Eight Gates*: to peruse things, to truly know things, to be sincere, to be righteous, to cultivate oneself, to well organize one's family, to rule the country, and to pacify the world. The core of them is to cultivate oneself. To understand Confucius' thought, the key is to understand the six words in Confucius' doctrine, and we will start with three words. First, "礼" (Li) ritual. As I said earlier, *rites* does not mean politeness or etiquette, but the sum of national political laws and regulations to civil etiquette. The core of Confucius' doctrine is called "restoring rites by disciplines oneself", to do one's best and restore the good old days when Duke Zhou Jidan made rites and music in the early years of the Western Zhou. This was the core of his doctrine and thought, and even his political principle.

The second word is "仁" (Ren) be good to others. The character is generally interpreted by scholars as be kind to others, which means that when two or more people are together, they should be kind to each other. Is the interpretation correct? No! Because the character "二" (Er) two here actually means "上" (Shang) upper in the oracle bone script, which we have seen in oracle bones; and we have also seen this character in the oracle bone script, means "下" (Xia) lower; so this character looks like a division symbol, and it means both "up and down", because it requires two syllables, so it was later eliminated.

Please note what is the word "仁" (Ren) be good to others? During the Eastern Han Dynasty, Xu Shen, China's first famous linguist and paleographer, said in his *Book of Exegesis* (*Shuowen Jiezi*) that "仁" (Ren) was the combined meaning "of man and of two". Xu Shen explained it wrong. Because Xu Shen could only see the oracle and bone scripts at that time, the oracle bone script was unearthed after 1899. The pattern of this character is "of man, of upper", which means "the superior person should be good be kind to the inferior person", which is called *benevolence*. Confucius speaks of *benevolence* in the *Analects of Confucius* in more than a hundred ways, but the core meaning is called "the benevolent one loves people". Therefore, we should pay special attention to the fact that Confucius' doctrine never talks about equality! The doctrine of Confucius is a typical aristocratic doctrine, called "rituals are divided for superior and inferior". In ancient times, all social officials were aristocrats, and the aristocracy was hereditary, so he believed that in order to make the world stable, the superior people must be good and kind to the inferior people, and this concept is called *benevolence*. The *gentleman* of the *way of the Gentleman* specially refers to the noblemen who have morals. Therefore, Confucius divided superior men into three classes: the first is called *sage*, which is a person in the highest position of power and has high moral virtue; the second is called *benevolent man*, that is, a person who has a certain social status and ability to govern, but also has high moral quality; the third is called *gentleman*, which is a common nobleman or a person who has the intention to pursue the moral spirit of nobility. Therefore, Confucius' *benevolence* means "the superior should be good and kind to the inferior", which is the core we should understand.

The third word of Confucius' doctrine is "恕" (Ru) *forgiveness*. Most of us understand this word in terms of the words as to forgive, excuse, pardon, but that doesn't work. You have to understand this character, which is a combination of the characters of *like*, *mind*, meaning to understand other's mind in the way you want others to understand your mind. In the original words of Confucius, "Don't do it to others what you wouldn't like others do to you," this is called *forgiveness*.

There are three other key words in Confucius' doctrine, which we will talk about later, called "孝、忠、知" (Xiao, Zhong, Zhi) filial piety, loyalty, and knowledge. The character "知" knowledge and "智" wisdom, are used interchangeably in ancient China, so it refers to intellectual enlightenment. What are the meanings of "孝" filial piety and "忠" loyalty? We will talk about them later.

Rites, *benevolence* and *forgiveness*, these three words are very important foundations to understand Confucius' doctrine. Benevolence, as I said earlier, is the core meaning of "benevolent person be good to others"; forgiveness, in the original words of Confucius, "Do not do it to others what you do not want others do to you." If you know all the religious texts, the *Bible*, the *Qur'an*, the *Buddhist scriptures*, and so on, you will see the same expression in all these religious texts, almost need no interpretation. What does it show? It shows that the third part of the text of Confucius is the canonical part.

It is important to know that Confucius was very wretched when he was alive and had no respectable status at all. For example, in *Records of the Grand Historian*, there is an allusion to the time when Confucius was traveling among the states for 13 years and once came to Zheng and lost his disciple at the east gate of the capital. His famous disciple Zi Gong went to look for his teacher, but he met a man and asked him, if the gentleman you were looking for was "a man whose forehead was like Yao, whose neck was like Gaotao, and whose shoulders were like Zichan, but from the waist down he was three inches less than Yu, and he was as tired as a homeless dog." This sentence says that the person you are looking for looks head like Yao, neck like Gaotao, shoulders like Zichan who was the first to set up a rule, and below waist is three inches shorter than Yu, and the person looks like a homeless dog. When Zi Gong returned, he told Confucius what he heard from the man. Do you know how Confucius replied? In the original text of the *Records of the Grand Historian*, it is written: "Appearance, not really, but saying like a homeless dog, it is very true!" he replied that the described looks are not necessarily like, but it is appropriate to say that I am like a homeless dog.

Why was Confucius so wretched in his life, but he was elevated to the altar, and called *King without throne* after three to four hundred years, so much so that all emperors would kneel down in front of his memorial tablet? It is because the element of cannon rule cannot be missing in the human primitive culture. So when you read the *Analects*, if you want to understand it, the key is that you have to understand the three elements that are indispensable to the primitive culture of mankind. Only after you have read and understood these things can you truly understand the overall connotation of Confucius' doctrine. The cannon of sage integrated the three elements of original culture in one doctrine, which is the high value of Confucianism. This is also the reason why Confucianism has ruled the mainstream culture of China for more than 2,000 years, like a religion, and has not collapsed.

Introduction of Confucius' Life

As I said earlier that there are no more masters of Chinese culture, therefore, it is appropriate to listen to my class not as Chinese culture, but as a branch of the overall culture of mankind or the history of human thought. I am not a scholar of Chinese culture, I am a researcher of philosophy. My lecture content is a little bit more traditional culture because it is more intimate with us and easier to penetrate our minds. In our 12-day series of classes, besides the traditional Chinese culture, there are also Western philosophy, Indian Buddhism, human body philosophy, trends and crises of human civilization, and so on. What is this class actually about? It is a different interpretation of cultural anthropology, or another kind of commentary on human cultural systems or human civilization phenomena. When you listen to my class, please make sure to develop your thoughts around this axis.

We will now talk about the life of Confucius. The birthplace and residence of Confucius was mainly in the state of Lu. Lu was the feudal state of Duke Jidan of Zhou, and the first ruler of Lu was Boqin, the eldest son of Duke Jidan of Zhou. As we mentioned earlier, Duke Jidan of Zhou, as the first prime minister of the Western Zhou, established the rituals and music, and laid down the whole state law of the Western Zhou. Therefore, in the state of Lu, the culture of rituals was extremely prosperous, and the Zhou rituals were so thickly collected that it was called "the hiding place of Zhou's rules and regulations, and the resort of Zhou's rituals and music". This is the reason why Confucius, as a native of Lu, was able to systematize and theorize the Zhou ritual culture, and finally form a unique ideological spine of Chinese agricultural civilization.

Sima Qian, in *Records of the Grand Historian · Confucius and His Family*, gives a very detailed account of the life of Confucius, amounting to more than 10,000 words, which is quite specific, compared to writing less than 700 words about Laozi, so less so that it is confusing who Laozi is, and the text pattern is quite different. Therefore, about the life of Confucius, I will speak roughly, only make a general introduction.

In fact, Confucius was not originally from the state of Lu, but his ancestors were from the state of Song. The distant ancestor of Confucius was called Fofu He, the first son of Duke Min of Song, which means that he was qualified to succeed to the throne of Song, but was unlucky not to do so. The seventh ancestor of Confucius was called Kong Fujia, who had the highest social status in the Confucian family, because he was once the Grand Secretary of the State of Song, equivalent to the Minister of National Defense, and was ranked as one of the ruling officials. The family name Kong, then, was gleaned from Kong Fujia's word, which later became the family name of the Confucian family.

During his time as Grand Secretary, Kong Fujia once led the Song army to fight a famous combat but was defeated and he was killed by the prime minister. Some historical books say that Kong Fujia was killed because his wife was very beautiful and the prime minister had long coveted his wife. This shows that it is a very dangerous thing for a man to marry a wife who is too beautiful. After Kong Fujia was killed, the status of Kong's family began to fall, and the fourth ancestor of Confucius, called Fang Shu, had already left the state of Song and moved to the land of Lu to settle. By the time Confucius' father, Kong He, also known as Shu Lianghe, was reduced to a warrior. So Confucius' family line was a ragged aristocracy, and a ragged aristocracy drifted to the state of Lu.

The *Records of the Grand Historian* records that "He and a woman surnamed Yan prayed at Niqiu and had wild union and gave birth to Confucius." This statement has been interpreted by many people, including many scholars, to mean that Confucius was an illegitimate son, which is a problematic statement. In those days, the capital of the state of Lu was near Qufu in today's Shandong Province, and there was a mountain around Qufu called Mount Niqiu. It is said that his parents gave birth to Confucius after a wild union at Mount Niqiu, so Confucius' name was Qiu and his style words was Zhongni, and Zhong means second, and the word Niqiu was included in his name and style words to commemorate this mountain. So what exactly does *wild union* mean? It never refers to illegal sex outside of marriage like today, it was a legal sexual behavior in ancient times. In ancient times, adult men and women without a spouse or widowed, in the spring, such as the second day of February or the third day of March of the lunar calendar they will go attend a temple fair, the day time is the temple prayer activities, the night can be there for wild union. You know, this custom was not only in ancient China, but also in ancient times all over the world, and even in modern China, this phenomenon is still seen in the rural hinterland. What is its moment? It is an addition to the early years of mankind's pair marriage system. Because the dyadic marriage system is a special product that occurred only after the civilization of mankind, which is not in accordance with human nature.

All living things are group marriages, and humans were group marriages before civilization. Group marriage system will never cause the waste of reproductive resources, but the pair marriage system is not. For example, young couples, soon after marriage, one of them died, a waste of reproductive resources; for example, the rich, in ancient times, can have a large number of concubines, while a large number of poor men can not find a wife, a waste of reproductive resources; for example, two of a couple stay all day long, eventually aesthetic fatigue, a waste of reproductive resources. When human beings first emerged in pair marriage system, the population growth rate was extremely slow and reproductive efficiency or reproduction number used to be a major problem. Therefore, wild union also became a legitimate act outside of marriage, and it was a necessary way to reasonably supplement sexual and reproductive resources.

Let me give you an example. It is commonly believed that the Mandarin duck among birds is strictly a pair marriage, so the most common gift given to newlyweds in ancient times was a pair of pillowcases embroidered with Mandarin ducks. But biologists have found that 51% of male mandarin ducks cheat on their wives outside the home. Think about it, male mandarin ducks can't cheat on rocks, so it's clear that female mandarin ducks are no better. What does it mean? It shows that all creatures are group marriage system, there is no real pair marriage system. In biological groups, the degree of loyalty to marriage or to a mate depends on the difficulty of its parenting, that is, the more difficult it is to raise children, the loyalty of male and female partners will be a little higher, but it is never a dyadic marriage system. And biologists study and find, a special green monkey in Africa, the size of a very small primate, because they fell more strict pair marriage system, the species soon became extinct. It can be seen that the year of the wild union, is an extra-marital legality that makes reproductive resources not wasted, which we need to clarify.

According to research, Confucius' father was already over 65 years old when he had a wild affair with his mother, Yan, while Confucius' mother was only about 17 or 18 years old, so Confucius was born only three years before his father died. Confucius grew up with his mother. Confucius' mother, Yan Zhengzai, was a poor woman, so Confucius lived with his mother all the time in the slum area. Confucius himself said "I was lowly when I was young, so I was mostly able to do despicable things" (see *Analects · Zihan*), meaning that I was lowly at birth and was mostly able to do menial jobs that others did not care to do.

When Confucius reached the age of 17, his mother died of an illness. Confucius' mother's neighbor, a playmate of Confucius when he was a child, grew up to be a carriage driver, that is, to drive a carriage for others. His mother told Confucius that the later father Kong He was a ragged aristocracy. Confucius was amazed, he knew for the first time that he was actually a noble descendant. So Confucius did two great things that shook the state of Lu in the year he was 17.

First, he went to this place of Fangdi, dug up his father's grave, and buried his mother with his father. A poor youngster actually dug an aristocracy's tomb, which was really an act defying the opinion of all others. Secondly, in this year, Jisun, who was the first of the three Huan who hollowed out the ruling lord power of Lu, held a banquet for the nobles. Why did Jisun hold a banquet for the nobles of Lu? It was because, as I said earlier, the state of Lu was the feudal state of Duke Jidan of Zhou, and all the nobles of Lu were actually descendants of Duke Jidan of Zhou, that is, they were all blood relatives. In other words, they were all blood relatives. The banquet given by Ji Sun to the nobles every year was actually a way to maintain the internal unity of the ruling class. Confucius thought he was a member of the nobility, so he went to the banquet as well, but he was humiliated by Yang Hu, the family slave of the Jisun clan I mentioned earlier, who blocked him at the door. This incident caused serious mental stimulation to Confucius for the rest of his life. Why do I tell you this part? I want to tell you that Confucius especially valued his noble status, and Confucian culture is a typical noble culture, which never talks about social equality. So you should understand this point.

Confucius aspired to learn at fifteen years old. At the age of 30, Confucius expressed himself as "able to self-support at thirty years old", why? Because when he was about 30 years old that the head of the Jisun clan, called Ji Pingzi, thought that Confucius had some ability and made him his vassal. At first, Confucius worked for Ji Pingzi as a commissioner, which was equivalent to a small official in charge of the treasury; later, he worked as a cattle keeper, which was equivalent to a horse keeper; and later, he worked as a small secretary, in charge of managing construction works on behalf of the family. Before long, he fell out with Ji Pingzi, so he resigned and traveled to state one after another, wandering through Qi, Song, Chen, Cai and other states, and finally returned to Lu. This was the first time Confucius traveled outside of Lu.

Confucius was first recognized as an extraordinary talent by the Meng Sun clan, one of the three Huan's we mentioned earlier. At this time, a man named Meng Lizi (a famous scholar in the Republic of China, Yan Ruoqu, proved that this Meng Lizi was the great ancestor of the sage Meng Ke) appeared and told his son that Confucius was a man of noble origin and not an ordinary person, and after my death, you must be humbly prostrate before Confucius and follow him as your teacher. So the youngest son of Meng Lizi, named Nangong Jingshu (some scholars believe that he might be the student named Nangong Rong among Confucius' so-called "disciples 3000 gentlemen of virtue 72"), formally and humbly requested Confucius as his teacher. Since he was from a noble background, he introduced Confucius to the then ruler of the state of Lu, Duke Zhao of Lu. Since Confucius was a good rites of Zhou dynasty, he suggested that Duke Zhao of Lu appoint Confucius to go to Luoyi, the capital of Eastern Zhou, to study the rites and music culture. So, the Duke Zhao of Lu gave Confucius a chariot, two horses and a driving slave, and accompanied by Nangong Jingshu, he came to Luo Yi in the year when Confucius was 34 years old. This is the source of that "Confucius came to the city of Zhou Dynasty and asked Laozi about the rites and learned music from Janghong" recorded in the *Records of the Grand Historian · Laozi*. According to the research, Confucius obtained the *Book of Verses*, the *Book of Shang* and the *Book of Ritual* from Laozi, who was the librarian of the royal library of Zhou, as the basic materials for his later research and teaching.

Confucius was hired by Duke Zhao of Lu and gradually began to enter the political circle. In his early days, he was actually a priest, a bridegroom who presided over funeral and ritual ceremonies, and was called ritual master, secretary of affairs, and secretary of school, that is, in charge of the ritual and academic affairs of the Lu clan. The so-called ritual master was to conduct ceremonial activities for the ruler of the state of Lu; the so-called secretary of was to run the school for the sons and daughters of the royal family of the ruler of Lu. Because of his special official status, he was able to compile the classics, study the history of Lu, teach rituals, and gather students to teach, thus beginning his career as an educator. So you may notice that Confucius' running school did not happen for no reason.

When Confucius was 35 years old, there was a civil strife in the state of Lu, that is, Ji Pingzi and Duke Zhao of Lu, had a quarrel because of a cockfight. Duke Zhao sent an army to attack the Jisun clan, so the three Huan clans of Jisun, Monsun and Shusun united and defeated Duke Zhao of Lu. Confucius followed him fled to the state of Qi, which was his second exile.

Confucius came to the state of Qi and had the possibility of being reappointed by Duke Jing of Qi, but it did not materialize later. When Duke Zhao of Lu died eventually in Qi, Confucius returned to Lu at the age of about 40. By this time, he no longer had an official status, but he had the reputation and experience of gathering students to teach, so he began to run a school for the community. The way he ran the school was called to teach without discrimination, that is, he accepted not only noble students, but also commoners' children, thus creating a pattern of private education.

It was not until he was about 50 years old that Confucius was rehired by Duke Ding of Lu, which was the beginning of his only five years of experience as an official. The reason why Confucius was recruited by Duke Ding of Lu was because Confucius had formed a strong force by running the school. Duke Ding of Lu had been hollowed out by the three Huan for a long time and hoped to use the influence of Confucius' school group to balance the suppression from the three Huan. At the same time, the three Huan was hollowed out by their vassals and needed the social power of Confucius to maintain the imbalance of power. At such Confucius entered the official circle of state Lu.

According to the *Records of the Grand Historian*, Confucius did three great things as an official in the state of Lu.

The first one was the meeting of the Narrow Valley, that is, Qi called Lu to an alliance meeting. Qi was far more powerful than Lu, and the ruler of Qi intended to take the opportunity of this alliance meeting to kidnap the ruler of Lu by the barbarians of the small nation of Cai. When Confucius found out about it, he argued with the ruler of Qi and said, "Your state once had a great man Guan Zhong in Qi, who advocated respecting the King of Zhou and expelling the barbarians, but today you are invoking the barbarians to kidnap the ruler of Lu. This is really outrageous of you. In the end, Confucius reached a diplomatic agreement with the ruler of Qi, saying that Lu was willing to befriend Qi, and that if there was a war in Qi in the future, we would send 300 troops to fight with the ruler of Qi, but subject to one condition, that Qi had to return some of the lands that Qi had occupied in Lu, which is the famous "Wenyang Three Fields". From this incident, we can see that Confucius' diplomatic ability was extraordinary.

The second is the execution of Shao Zhengmao, a court official of Lu who had disrupted the government. Shao Zhengmao was a nobleman from the state of Lu and a fellow official. This person was eloquent in talking, with a very high appeal, and he also ran a school outside, it was said that he ran the school was no less than the scale of Confucius, three times his school attracted all the students from Confucius school, and even none of the students left. During the time when Confucius was the prime minister, he took the excuse to execute Shao Zhengmao. We do not know what was going on at that time, and some scholars believe that this was a wrong case and Confucius killed Shao Zhengmao without sufficient reason to justify, but only to extinct his own rival.

The third thing is the destroy of three cities. What does it mean? It is the three Huan Ji Sun, Meng Sun, Shu Sun, they each have their own territory and city. According to what the Zhou rituals stipulate, "the ministers are prohibited to have hidden armor, nor can them own cities of over 100zhi long wall (note: a square city has four walls, each side wall is 693m or 2079ft long; each zhi is equal to 6.93m or 20.79ft)." But the ritual system has long been abolished, the actual cities area established by the three Huan were much larger than the Zhou rituals, so Confucius decided to destroy them. How come he was not obstructed by the Three Huan in doing so? It was because two of the three Huan, the Ji Sun Clan and the Shu Sun Clan, had already been occupied by their vassals, so they all supported Confucius at first, and Confucius started a battle with the vassals of the three Huan to destroy the cities. But the first battle was not favorable, and the situation became dangerous, which affected the ruler of Lu. Thanks to Confucius' calm command and good management, his men finally defeated the rebellious party of vassals and turned the danger into peace, and destroyed Feiyi. However, due to the constraints of Meng Sun's family, this project of destroying all the three private cities was finally aborted half-way. This shows that Confucius' ability to command a war was also quite outstanding.

As far as his political resume is concerned, Confucius' ability of administrative operation is considered excellent. Ancient Chinese intellects especially valued a person's practical ability, not simply academic literacy. It is important to know that Confucius' ability in socio-political practice was much higher than that of later famous Chinese literati, such as Wang Yangming and Zeng Guofan. Both the later had only the characteristics and stories of wisdom in warfare, while Confucius excelled in politics, economy, military, diplomacy, education, and many other aspects. This is why Confucius was regarded as a master of practice, and this is an important reason why Confucius was regarded as a mentor by later generations of literati and scholars.

Confucius' prestige grew and his fame was so great that it made the state of Qi feel uneasy. The ruler of Qi sent 80 beautiful women and 120 horses to Duke Ding of Lu to bribe him to dismiss Confucius. In addition, Confucius supervised Duke Ding of Lu very strictly. It is well known that Confucius had a famous saying of *four-nots*: "Don't look at things of not ritual, don't listen to things of not ritual, don't speak of things not ritual, and don't conduct oneself of not ritual", which made Duke Ding of Lu much restricted. In addition, at this time, the vassals of three Huan had been pacified, and three Huan no longer needed any help from the court, so Confucius lost his power in the political arena.

In fact, Confucius had to befriend three Huan even at the beginning of his involvement in the politics of Lu, for example, he once appointed his famous disciple Zi Lu to be a vassal of the Jisun clan. By this time, that is, in the twelfth year of the Duke Ding of Lu, the State of Lu held the Spring Festival, which was a national event. As described in *Annals by Zhuo Qiuming*, "the state big events is ritual and warfare". One is the ritual, which is an ideological declaration; the other is the warfare, which is called the military. Then, Confucius was not invited to participate in the state affairs such as the ritual at Spring Festival; after the ritual of Spring Festival, the ruler and ministers will share the meat of sacrificial offerings, and Confucius was not given the meat. Confucius was very clear in mind and realized that he was no longer appreciated by those in power, so he resigned and retired. From then on, he led his most famous disciples, Yan Hui, Zi Lu, Zi Gong, Ran You, Zi You, etc., to travel around the world and find another way out.

Since Confucius was already famous among many states, he hoped to use his reputation to persuade the lords and rulers of states to realize his political ambitions, which ended in failure. After traveling for 13 years among those feudal states, Confucius was about 68 years old when he was able to return to the state of Lu. At this time, the ruler of Lu was Ji Kangzi, the heir of the Jisun family. At first, Ji Kangzi was reluctant to have Confucius back because the ruler was worried that his high prestige would hinder the ruler from implementing the state's government. He first invited two of Confucius' disciples, Ran Qiu and Fan Xu, to return to the state, when the Qi army invaded Lu's territory, Lu was barely won the battle with the help of Ran Qiu and Fan Xu. After that Ran Qiu repeatedly requested Ji Kangzi to invite Confucius return to Lu, saying that Confucius was his teacher, and his talent and ability was far above me, so Ji Kangzi was reluctantly inviting Confucius back to Lu as counsellor of the state.

Confucius returned to Lu and did not ask about politics. Ran Qiu and Ji Kangzi were in cahoots, raising taxes and collecting money from the people, which was opposed by Confucius. Ran Qiu went to the door to convince Confucius, hoping to get support, but Confucius refuted, "If you want to do it even when the rules of Duke of Zhou is still there, why should you ask me?" That is to say, if you want to do something wrong, why do you ask me? Then he told to his disciples, (that man is) "Not my disciples! Anyone can beat the drum and attack!" that is, he openly called on his disciples to criticize and resist what Ran Qiu had done. After that, Confucius closed door to his guests and in his twilight years, he devoted himself in editing the *Book of Verses* and the *Book of Shang*, revising *the Rites* and *the Music*, correcting *the Spring and Autumn Annals*, and annotating *I-Ching of Zhou*. Around the 15th year of Duke Ai of Lu, Confucius' disciples Yan Hui, Zai Wo, Zi Lu and Confucius' son Kong Li died one after another, which caused a serious mental shock to Confucius. In the 16th year of Duke Ai of Lu, Confucius died at the age of 72 or 73.

What can you tell from my rough account of Confucius' life? Confucius was not a purely cultural person, but a pragmatist first and foremost. What we usually call literary thinkers were basically theorists, who were willing to keep lonely and work behind closed doors, and were not involved in social practice, such as Laozi, such as most philosophers in ancient Greece, Newton, Kant, Darwin, Einstein, and so on. It is because pragmatists cannot be theoretical, while theorists cannot be pragmatic. This is also one of the reasons why Confucius' doctrine seems rather pale and bland.

Throughout his life, Confucius was a young man seeking knowledge, a middle-aged man running a school, and an official in his prime, and in his later years he traveled around the states for 13 years, still trying to persuade the rulers of the vassal states to take his advice so as to enter politics, until he was 68 years old he returned Lu and devoted himself into literature study quietly, and he died at the age of 72 or 73. This shows that Confucius had very little time to concentrate on his studies, and that is why he is said to be a practical man, and a very persistent practical man.

FEATURES OF CONFUCIUS' LIFE

People only know that Confucius ran a school on a huge scale of 3000 disciples and 72 gentlemen of virtue. However, there is a contemporary old scholar, Liu Qiyu, who is a disciple of Gu Jiegang, a famous historian in the Republican era and the founder of the Doubtful Antiquity School, who believed that most of the things recorded in ancient books were arbitrary fabrications, and the more far ancient the history, the higher the degree of suspicion. So in the Republican era, Chinese historians were divided into two schools of thought: one school was called the *school of doubt*; the other school was called the *school of adopt*, that is, the insistence on sticking to the ancient Chinese historical documents and textual research. These two schools are very controversial and inconclusive, and Gu Jegang is the founder of the school of doubt. In his later years, he accepted a disciple named Liu Qiyu. Liu Qiyu said that when Confucius ran the school, it was equivalent to running a funeral technical school or a funeral company, and that business was booming. This statement sounds a bit abrupt, but it actually makes sense.

In the years when Confucius managed running school, gathered students and lectured them, he was so powerful and influential that he could be said to have had students all over the country, and among these students some disciples followed him till his last days. He was completely different from the hermit style of Laozi who had only visiting disciples. The disciples of Laozi were not allowed to follow him, they came to ask Laozi questions and left immediately afterwards. Confucius' disciples were huge in number and some remained with Confucius throughout his life. Let me give you an example: Confucius' famous disciple Yan Yuan, also called Yan Hui, whose father's name was Yan Lu, followed Confucius for two generations; and Zeng Zi (Zeng Shen), whose father's name was Zeng Cai, also followed Confucius for two generations. Think about it, Confucius continued to run the school at such a scale, which was equivalent to a large school with a huge number of students, but how he maintained its economic balance? You know, Confucius charged a very low tuition fee, which is called "with a pack of *shuxiu* as tuition fee, I never refused any student". In ancient times, the tuition fee could even be as low as a little *shuxiu*, what is *shuxiu*? It was just a pack of bacon. By paying such a small amount of tuition, Confucius said, "I have never failed to teach them."

Look at the private schools today, all are run by entrepreneurs, why? Economic balance can not be implemented. All national public universities, the local government, the central government to give them hundreds of millions, billions of funds every year, they still have to charge high tuition fees, why? it is difficult for them to maintain the economic balance of the universities. So how could Confucius school maintain its economic balance when it had a huge number of students who have been gathering for long and paying very low tuition fees, and there was no government subsidy? There is a Chinese idiom *reach the hall,* and *enter the chamber,* which has been completely changed in meaning today. The original meaning of the word *reach the hall, enter the chamber* refers to the way Confucius cultivate his disciples, there was another two words "close to door" preceded, the full content of which is *close to the door, reach the hall*, and *enter the chamber*. What does it mean? The best disciples could enter the chamber to listen to lectures and discuss with the teacher, which is called the chamber disciples; a large number of disciples stood between the hall and the corridor and waited for the chamber disciples to come out and convey their message, which was called the hall disciples. There was an even large number of students standing outside the door of the courtyard, waiting for the hall disciples to convey message, which was called door students.

With such a large group of school students, the financial expenses became a problem. At that time, the population of state of Lu was only a little more than a million, but Confucius actually had 3,000 disciples, which was equivalent to running a university with hundreds of thousands of students nowadays, how could he maintain the economic balance? Let's think about one more question: Confucius received 3000 disciples and 72 gentlemen of virtue. What does it mean by 3000 disciples? What does it mean by 72 gentlemen of virtue? The so-called 3000 disciples were the poor boys of ordinary people; the so-called 72 gentlemen of virtue were the sons of nobles. As I said earlier, in ancient times, the ruling class hereditary system was that the official positions of the ruling class could be inherited by son's generation, so disciples of the common people's boys, no matter how well they studied, they could not become officials later. The so-called "learning excellent can be an official" is only for the noble sons, this is called the 72 gentlemen of virtue. So, why should the 3000 ordinary disciples follow Confucius to study? He could not be an official even if he learned well; then what did he learn? He could learn a craft to make a living later. Then what was the craft that most needed later back then - burial, burying the dead. So Confucius once told his famous disciple Zi Xia: "You are an educated gentleman of virtue, not an educated ordinary", so we can see that Confucius clearly divided his disciples into two categories: one is the category "educated gentlemen of virtue," who were the sons of noblemen; the other is the category "educated ordinary" who were the sons of commoners. For the educated gentlemen of virtue, learn excellent could be officials later; for the educated ordinary, learn a craft to make a living later. And what was the most sought-after craft back then? To take care of the tedious funeral ceremony. You know, the average life expectancy of the ancients was less than 39 years, and death was a constant occurrence. At that time, there was a large number of births and deaths, the ancients originally made the funeral rituals extremely complex, and Confucius made the complex process of funeral culture well-arranged with methodization, gradually all ordinary families, whose member had died, would go to Confucius disciples for help, otherwise the dead body could not be buried properly. As a result, most of Confucius students had a brisk business.

In his *Daodejing,* Laozi created a phrase called "born toward death". Today, the meaning of this idiom has become the meaning of *viewing death as if returning home,* which is actually a complete mistake. Laozi said that the meaning of "born toward death" is that people run towards death as soon as they are born, which is called "born toward death". How do we know that this is the meaning? Because Laozi then added a commentary text, saying: "Birth toward death. There are three out of ten who live on; three out of ten who die at birth; three out of ten who move to the place of death." (See *Daodejing, section 50.*) He says that people start to go the land of death as soon as they are born ("born toward death"), and that only three out of ten of them are really born alive ("three out of ten who live on after birth"); then he says, "three out of ten who die after birth", that is, just after birth, three out of ten children died, because in ancient times there was no sterile concept, cutting the umbilical cord often leads to tetanus infection, three out of ten died; there were three out of then that should be able to survive, but they "move to place of death", what does it mean? The civilized people want to fight for fame in society, such as joining the army and fighting in wars, such as compete for braveness and fierce, this is called "move to the place of death". Therefore, the life expectancy of the ancient people was very short, and the accident of death was high, so the funeral activities were frequent, and the funeral process was extraordinarily complicated, so the funeral business of Confucius' disciples was booming.

Let me give you another example. If you turn to the first paragraph of the *Analects of Confucius,* there is a sentence called "Learn to practice, isn't it a pleasure". How did we explain it in the past? It explains that you study and review it from time to time, isn't a happy thing. Wrong! Who can be happy with review? Review is the most boring thing. The character "習" was misinterpreted.

Look at the oracle bone character "習" (Xi) practice,(甲骨文 小篆 楷体 简体) which has a pair of bird's wings on top and a target symbol on the bottom. What does it mean? It means that when the bird has just grown to full feathers, the parent bird will lead it to practice flying, and designate a target to practice flying, which is called "◎". What is the meaning of the word "◎"? It means to practice. Therefore, Confucius said, Learning and practicing at the same time, isn't it a happy thing? which means learning and practicing, earning money while burying the dead, isn't it a happy thing?

Besides, we have other evidence. As I mentioned earlier, when Confucius came to Qi, he was once favored by the ruler of Qi, Duke Jing of Qi. Jing thought that Confucius was a talent and wanted to appoint him as his official, but he was prevented from doing so by Yan Ying, the prime minister of the court (known in history as Yan Zi, one of the hundred famous scholars of the pre-Qin Dynasty). Why did Yan Ying block this? In the *Records of the Grand Historian,* Yan Ying said that Confucianism advocates over-formal funeral ritual accompanied with long mourning, making funeral rituals so complicated that when an ordinary people died, his family had to bury him with all they have, so it bankrupted the whole family, and if you, the ruler wanted to enrich our state and strengthen the army, while he bankrupted every family, so how could you enrich the country and strengthen the army? This was the reason why Duke Jing of Qi did not use Confucius in the end.

Let's look at one more example. An important opponent of Confucianism was Mohism. Mozi once criticized that Confucianism had four shortcomings that were "enough to impair the society", one of which was: "Elaborate burial and long mourning, double layer coffin, clothes and quilt burial, send the dead as if one migrating, three years of mourning, the concerned relative cannot get up without help, cannot walk without staff, ears not to hear, eyes not to see, this is enough to bring down the world". It means that Confucianism purposely makes funeral culture cumbersome, burying a dead for a long time, elaborate burial costs money, the coffin must be two layers, clothes and bedding accompany the burial, the process of sending a dead is like someone migrating; three years mourning, make young people unable to stand up if not helped, unable to walk without a walking stick; during the funeral, the relevant people ear not to hear, eyes not to see, care or attend nothing at all. Mozi said, "This is enough to pull down the society". Obviously, Mozi also held that Confucius had taken the funeral culture too far, and that it had spread through Lu and many other states, and produced a bad effect that was enough to impair the whole society. We can thus see that Confucius ran a school back then, which was equivalent to a funeral procedure school or a funeral company, so the criticism seems to be valid today.

I don't mean to say that Confucius was intent on getting rich; Confucius was never a profit-seeker. However, Confucius had to solve the problem of economic balance when he started a large school group. Moreover, the vast majority of his students were educated ordinaries who could not have a future as officials even if they were well educated, so why should they follow him? The purpose of this exegesis study is to prove that Liu Qiyu's statement has at least some degree of validity.

Let's look at another aspect. All scholars who study Confucius unanimously that Confucius was the first political figure in Chinese history to create an opposition party and eventually achieve a ruling position, for which there is no dispute in the academic community. Confucius once left a bold statement: "If there is someone who will use me, I need only a period of months, to achieve in three years." He said if any ruler is willing to use me, I can make his state rich and strong in just one year, and restore the order of the Eastern Zhou in three years. It can be seen that Confucius' ambition was as he said, if I can be a political figure, I will restore the Eastern Zhou, which was his goal in life.

Then Confucius ran a school, which was equivalent to running a well-organized opposition party, and he eventually achieved the ruling position, which is a very unique case in Chinese history. We should know that in ancient times, it was very common for school groups to be transformed into political groups. Because people did not have the freedom of association in ancient times, the only way to associate was to form a school group, so ancient school groups were usually transformed into political groups without notice. Let me give you an example, such as the Mohists. In our next lecture, one of the topics will be The Hundred Schools of Thought, and the content will be about Mohism, so I will only talk about a little bit of it now. To put it in perspective, one of the basic theories or important propositions of Mohism is called *non-attack*, which means that it strongly opposes war. However, since the Mohist school mainly represented the handicraftsmen, only the Mohist disciples had the ability to build siege equipment. As a result, the Mozi school was particularly a prominent warring political organization in the early and mid-Warring States. The Mozi school later formed a powerful military auxiliary force, which was described as "going to the fierce fight, never flee from danger", that is, the members of the school went to the fight in war, none of them turned their heels to run away, which was the case of the Mozi school.

As it was in the East, so it was in the West. The famous ancient Greek philosopher Pythagoras, as I mentioned earlier in my talk on Western philosophy, he and his school had presided over the ancient Greek city-state of Croton for more than 20 years, and Pythagoras is said to have died during a fierce political dispute. It is clear that in ancient times, as in China and abroad, learned societies were easily transformed into political societies.

It is worth mentioning that this political school of Confucius has its own political program, which is called *self-restrain to restore the rites of Zhou*; it also has its own values, which are *benevolence, righteousness, propriety, knowledge and faith* and *the way of the gentleman*; it even has its own organizational principle, which is called *once as teacher, forever as father*. Therefore, the power of this political group was so great that in *Han Feizi* it recorded, "Confucianism was divided into eight", which means that after Confucius' death, the Confucian school group, that is, the Confucian political group, split into eight sections, but still maintained a huge social and political power, which is one of the reasons why Emperor Qin Yingzheng (Shi Huang) wanted to burn books and bury Confucianists.

If you read carefully the *Records of the Grand Historian*, the people who cheated Emperor Qin Yingzheng (Shi Huang) were not literati of Confucianism, but all of them were necromancers, then why did Qin Shi Huang bury hundreds of weak Confucian students alive? It was because the Confucian political group system posed a threat to the political power of the Qin Empire. Let's think it further, why did the Han Dynasty establish Confucius as the state teacher and Confucianism as the state religion? It was said that Liu Bang was actually a rascal, and he actually looked down upon Confucianist literati. The history books clearly record that Liu Bang was used to humiliating Confucian students, who always wore a special-shaped hat at that time, and when Liu Bang met with any of them, he would take off his hat and grumpily urinated in it in the open, which is the well-spread saying of "urine in the Confucian hat". But it was exactly this Liu Bang, the first Emperor of Han Dynasty, when traveling to the old land of Lu, he was actually the first emperor in history to worship Confucius, and his great grandson, Emperor Wu of Han eventually established Confucianism as the state religion, why? It was because when they waved the war against Qin, Confucian political groups had been a strong potential force of anti-Qin.

Let's go back to the time of Duke Ding of Lu. As I said earlier, the ruler of Lu was hollowed out by the three Huan, and the three Huan were hollowed out by their vassals. Confucius was able to enter the ruling position because the power structure of the above rulers was tilted out of balance and had to be supported by the strong influence of Confucius' opposition party, which is the reason why Confucius was invited to the court. It is important for everyone to understand this point.

Then Confucius was ordained at the age of about 50, and in the first year he became the mayor of a city in state of Lu. It was said he did so well that history book records "officials of all other places followed suit", that is, follow his example, other officials had to learn from the management style of the mayor. Later, he was promoted to be the Minister of Works of the State of Lu, and then to be the Secretary of Justice, which was equivalent to the President of the Supreme Court today; the history book recorded that "in the 14th year of the Duke Ding of Lu, the Secretary of Justice acted as the regent of the Ministry of Justice", and he rose through ranks to become the President of the Supreme Court and the Prime Minister of the State.

So, we can make a summary on the life of Confucius below. I say that Confucius was a teacher, a businessman, and a politician, and he *killed three birds with one stone,* and he ultimately achieved his goal in all the three fields, so he could be considered to be an extraordinary great man. What does this mean? For anyone, not to mention that you do all three things, teaching, business and politics, if you can only do one of the things to the extreme, you are bound to be a great man in history. For example, if you teach, you finally become a professor in Harvard University in the United States, which is a private university that predates the founding of the United States and plays a big role in the foundation of American culture and education; if you do business, you can finally surpass Steve Jobs and Bill Gates; if you do politics, you can become the Premier of the State Council. You know, in ancient China, the highest official a literati could reach was the prime minister, you could not be the king or the emperor, because the king or the emperor was inherited through the lineage, therefore, in the antient time, Chinese literati scholars could only dream of *making oneself to become the prime minister.*

Please see, Confucius was able to run a school with 3,000 disciples and 72 gentlemen of virtue, which was equivalent to a large school with hundreds of thousands of students nowadays, considering the million population of the State of Lu, and he was able to teach the young people without discrimination, educate them with certain knowledge, cultivate them to follow rituals, and set up the moral style for scholars, so Confucius has much greater influence to Chinese culture than that of Harvard University to the American culture. His business in the antient time already developed a business group of 3000 personnel; and in politics, he reached the level of Prime Minister or Premier, under one ruler, but above all others, which was really marvelous.

In fact, traditional Chinese culture has always been relatively light on the search of theoretic learning, on the study of pure ideas and academics, but it has been very serious about practical learning, academic discipline, personal experience in practice, as Confucius himself did. What he said "raise virtue, raise merit, and raise speech", the so-called *three immortals,* the first is the *virtue,* which is not just lip service; the second is the *merit,* which is to put into practice, to do good to the world and benefit the people, and so on; the third is the *speech,* which is to write articles, to do learning. Therefore, although Confucius' thoughts and doctrines are the foundation of his ultimate legacy for later generations, he spent his life in all kinds of social practices and never tired of doing so, standing out and doing everything to the best of his ability, in this regard, he can really be considered a model and teacher of Chinese literati to apply their learning.

Therefore, I suggest that you read the *Analects of Confucius* in your spare time, it is of great reference value for you to go social practice. It is worth to know that the *Analects of Confucius* is the insight of a most competent practitioner who has accumulated a lifetime of experience. That is why Zhao Pu, the founding chancellor of the Song Dynasty, dared to say this amazing statement: "Half of the *Analects of Confucius* rules the world."

This is all we have to say about the life of Confucius.

Essence and System of Confucius' Doctrine

Earlier we talked about the whole background and soil in which the culture of Confucius or traditional Chinese culture could take place. We then very roughly covered the life of Confucius. We now move to the core of this lesson - what is the essence of Confucius' doctrine?

As soon as I started the class, I talked about the core eight words of Confucius' doctrine: "ruler rulers, subject subjects, father fathers, son sons." In fact, people did not understand what I said. What is the core of Confucius' doctrine? Where does the tenacity of Confucian culture come from? Let me summarize in one sentence: Confucius used the most primitive social bonds of human blood to rectify the super-blood and unstable social structure of civilization. This is where the core and tenacity of Confucian culture is.

What does it mean? As I have said repeatedly before, according to the principle of weakening compensation, the more primitive and low-level things are more fundamental, decisive and stable. Please keep this statement in mind and better understand it. So what is the core of Confucius' doctrine? It is to take the most primitive human blood ties, which are similar to animal social forms, and use them to rectify the disordered system and chaotic structure of super-blood civilized society. Because he used the lowest and most stable antecedent system to rectify and strengthen a slackened and destabilized later existent system, it renders his doctrine of great power that it formed the cornerstone of the conservative and stable ideology of Chinese society for more than 2000 years.

We expand on this topic below. As I said earlier, human society grew from animal blood societies. So for millions of years in prehistory, humans lived in social groups of blood clans that were no different from the structure of animal societies. Therefore, the early human subterranean culture and its association methods were closely related to blood ties.

As you know, one of the earliest cultural phenomena of mankind is called Totem. It is a word derived by a famous American scholar in the late eighteenth century, Lundgren, from an Indian phonetic translation. What is *totem*? It means that ancient humans regarded natural materials, such as animals, plants, mountains, water, thunder and lightning, as their blood ancestors, and then made them into symbols to show them to the public. Since human beings lived in a blood society in the early years, they searched for the root of their blood lineage and explored it to the natural objects beyond human beings.

Ancient China is no exception. Thinking back to Sima Qian, why did his *Records of the Grand Historian* have a great impact on Chinese culture? It was because it laid out a lineage system for the Chinese people. What is the first chapter you open in the *Records of the Grand Historian*? The *Records of the Five Emperors*. What is it about? It says that all Chinese people are descendants of the Yellow Emperor and the Yan Emperor, all Chinese people were arranged into a system of blood relatives. In *Chronicles of the Emperors*, Huangpu Mi of the Western Jin Dynasty recorded: "Shennong's family name is Jiang, mother is called Ren Si, ... traveled to Huayang, there she met a deity with dragon head, had sensation and gave birth to Yan Di." What does it mean? It says that Yandi Shennong, his mother's name is Ren Si, once traveled to the Huayang place, a chance encounter with divine dragon, so she had the feeling of pregnancy and gave birth to Yandi. This is a typical animal totem, legend of *the heir of the dragon* emerged since then.

In the *Records of the Grand Historian · Yin Family*, it is written: "Yin Qi, mother named Jandi, saw an egg fell from a black bird, Jandi took it and swallowed it. Then she gave birth to Yin Qi." Yin Qi was a founder of Yin Shang Dynasty, his mother saw a black bird called *Xuan Bird*, we do not know what this *Xuan Bird* refers to today, but some scholars thought it could be a crow. His mother found an egg fell from the bird and she picked it up and ate it, later she gave birth to Yin Qi. This era, as recorded in ancient books, is called the Totem Age. It is characterized by fictional tribal ancestry and is an important stage of far ancient human culture.

The Chinese concept of lineage culture has been preserved until modern times. During the early Zhou Dynasty, it was developed in the form of ritual culture, and then Confucius organized this ancient bloodline structure of survival. We all know that human beings started from clan alliance, which is called tribe; then they allied with each other, which is called tribal alliance; then they merged with each other, which is the prototype of state; what does this process of continuous expansion mean? It is a process in which the blood structure is gradually diluted and thinned. Because only the clan's people have blood relations, once the clan allied into a tribe, the overall blood relations within the tribe has been diluted, the tribal alliance then further allied to the higher union, blood relations will be further thinned. As blood ties become more and more diluted, and as social groups become more and more superimposed, the structural ties of civilized society become more and more lax, that is, the original internal tensions of blood kin groups will gradually disappear, and social movements will tend to become disordered. Confucius used the primitive blood ties to reinterpret and reweave the supra-blood social structure, thus resulting in the extreme stability of the institutions of agrarian civilization.

What was the situation in ancient Greece, by contrast? Ancient Greek culture, which originated from 1000 to 600 B.C., was not conducive to an agricultural civilization due to geographic and climatic conditions, but was particularly suited to commerce along the Mediterranean. Once commerce became widespread, each person had to break away from the bonds of his or her blood family and become an individual free agent, because it was impossible to travel long distances with a family. So the inherent blood structure was broken up, and they had to establish a contractual social system with gods and laws as the mediators of human relations. And what is Indian culture? It is the use of blood bond to support religion and let religion reinforce blood bond, and this is the Indian caste system.

Note the difference between the three: Indian culture is religion first, blood second, and law next; ancient Greek culture is law (contract) first, religion (polytheism) second, and blood ties nearly dissolved; Chinese culture is blood (family) first as a foundation, law (ritual) second functions as a tutor, and deities (ancestral gods) second functions as a unifier. That is why Chinese law is called the patriarchal system, and Chinese deities were all once living people.

This shows how deep the bloodline of Chinese culture is. Therefore, we say that the structure of Chinese agricultural culture and Confucian thought system is a direct continuation of the original culture of animal kinship society and human clan society. It is not like the ancient Greek culture, which had to gradually break down the animal blood structure and the human clan structure and recreate a contractual social relationship. Nor is it like the Indian culture that had to create a series of powerful deities, which is the Indian Brahminism, to solidify the caste hierarchy. China is a direct successor to the animal bloodline and the primitive human bloodline system, and then builds its own super bloodline civilizational social structure directly on top of this system, so that it is in line with the animal society without any break in it. Obviously, China is at the bottom of the primitive hierarchy.

So, how do interpersonal relationships in a blood-based society manifest themselves? Confucius accurately interpreted it as "love is differentiated". What does that mean? The sociobiology I mentioned this morning is that in the middle of the last century biologists discovered that all animals live in biosocial groups. Sociobiologists discovered that all animals have different distributions of their emotions, their love, that they are on par with their level of kinship, or kinship index. For example, parents love their children most strongly, followed by siblings. Strictly speaking, parents are only 50% genetically identical to their children because the father contributes 50% of his own genes and the mother 50%, so each child's genetic structure is only 50% genetically related to its parents. Between siblings, the genetic homozygosity is also 50%. So, why do parents love their children more than the children love their parents, and also more than the siblings love each other? It is because love can only be exerted in such an asymmetrical order of matching, that is, the species can only be passed on if the parents love their children more. For any offspring must receive extra care from its elders, or it will not survive. Thus, parents put the heaviest emotional weight on their children, followed by siblings in between, then followed by cousins in between, then followed by other distant relatives and outsiders. In such a system of emotional gradient, love is of course differentiated. That is, in the biological blood structure, or even in your genotype, your love is never equally distributed, which is called *love is differentiated*.

Then Confucius further extended *love is differentiated*, and called it "rituals are divided for superior and inferior". As I mentioned earlier, Duke Zhou Jidan made the rites and music. What does it mean by *rites*? In ancient Chinese literature, there are only five words used to describe *rites*, which are called "revere revered and love loved". Note that the first word is a verb and the second word is a noun. The so-called *revere* means "to respect those who have honorable positions"; the so-called means "to love those who are related to each other." This is the essence of the ritual system. In fact, the arrangement of these five words should be reversed and more appropriately described as "love loved and revere revered". Because all animals, including human beings, are in a blood society in their early years, they must first love their kin relatives, that is, "to love those who are related". With the evolution of species, there is an increasingly obvious difference in the sequence of the eldest and youngest; and with the development of human civilization, there also emerged class differences, so you have to show *respect* - that is, "to respect those who have an honorable position".

It is important to understand that the blood structure is immutable and insurmountable. For example, even if you are capable, you cannot turn your father into your son. You will always be a son before your father, and this relationship is ironclad and innately mated, called "revere revered" or *pecking order*. Therefore, Confucius' doctrine establishes "love is differentiated and rituals has superiority and inferiority" according to the blood structure, which is in line with human nature and biological nature. It is easy to find that Chinese ritual culture is a human version of animal blood survival structure, or a rational expression of animal blood survival structure, and we call this cultural reflection of the orderly blood structure of respect and kinship, *ritual system*. Confucius turned the ritual system of the Duke Zhou Jidan into a theoretical system, which is called Confucianism. This is the ideological core of Confucianism, so traditional Chinese culture is particularly concerned with patriarchal clan relations.

We often see the word "宗法" (Zong Fa) patriarchal law in Chinese history books, but it is completely different from *law* in the modern sense. The so-called patriarchal law is also the law of clan relations. Take a look at the oracle bone scripts of the character "宗", (甲文 金文 小篆 楷体) it draws a house first, then draw a T stand for the sacrifice, on the sacrifice stand, the offerings is dropping blood, this is the meaning of the character "宗", which refers specifically to the sacrifice to the ancestors. It is by no means a legal system in the general sense, and the orderly relationship of respect and inferiority established in the kin structure is called patriarchal law. Confucius theorized, ethicized, and systematized the ritual system of Duke Zhou Jidan, such as the *Three Principles, the Five Morals,* and *the Five Relations.* The so-called *three principles* refer to "the ruler is the principle of the subject, the father is the principle of the son, and the husband is the principle of the wife". It is all about blood relations. The so-called *five morals* refer to "benevolence, righteousness, propriety, knowledge and faith". It is also told in the patriarchal relationship, in the kin relationship. The so-called *five relations* refer to the relations between ruler and subject, father and son, brother and sibling, husband and wife, friend and friend. The first four are mostly kin relations or blood ties, and the last one is eventually incorporated into the pan-blood structure.

Let's continue to see, it is all about the blood structure, which says "father's kindness and son's filial piety, brother's kinship and sibling's respect, husband's principle and wife's obedience, ruler's grace and subject's loyalty" and so on. I talked earlier about the six most important words for understanding Confucius' doctrine: propriety, benevolence, forgiveness, knowledge, filial piety and loyalty. Why is Confucius' doctrine summarized as "ruling the society with *filial piety*"? It is because *filial piety* expresses the structure of blood relations. Since Confucius ultimately wanted to organize the whole society into a pan-blood family, *loyalty* to the ruler is equivalent to *filial piety* to the king father, so, *loyalty* and *filial piety* are linked together by the blood structure, which is the source of loyalty and filial culture. Why is *filial piety* more important than *loyalty*? It is because only when the blood structure of *filial piety* is established does the issue of *loyalty* have a basis for discussion.

Therefore, the concept of state in ancient China is very strange. Let's see the Chinese word "国家" (Guo Jia) state family. *State* is just a magnification of *family*. Note that the meaning of the word *state* in the West is completely different from our Chinese word, and there is no blood or family component in it. There are three words used in the Western language for *state, country* or *nation*: first, *nation*, which means nationality; second, *country*, which means geographical area; the third word is *state*, which means governmental and social institutions. None of the three terms used to describe the state refer to blood relations, as *nation* is a cultural concept.

And the two Chinese characters "国家" (Guo Jia), combined by *state* and *family*, but together means *state*, that is, the amplification of *family* is called *state*. So what the Chinese value is not *state* but two other things: one is called *society* and the other is called *family*. In Chinese society, there is a term called "社稷" (She Ji), what is "社"? It actually means the deity of earth and sacrifice; "稷" (Ji) actually means the deity of all grains. So the two characters represents two things: land and grain, the deities of land and grain, and the worship of these two things is called "社稷". It expresses the basis of survival of agricultural civilization, not the specific form of state government. Moreover, land and grain are more important to the family than to the state, and to anyone, family is more important than the state. This is the first point. Therefore, the Chinese use of the term "社稷" to represent the meaning of the state and the state government, which actually refers to the structure of survival of a decentralized small peasant economy, which is different from the meaning of the nation-*state* connotation as we understand it in modern times.

Secondly, Chinese people regard the family much more importantly than the state, and the family comes before the state, kin family comes before nation state, so the most important words in China are all in meaning related to the family. For example, *glorify ancestors, glorify family*, saying if you have done something that renders you great, very glorious, glorify whom? not the state, but the ancestors. This is why Chinese people attach great importance to the family, but not the state. This is why it is common in modern times to say that the Chinese nation is like a scattered piece of sand and has no concept of nationhood, because what people value most is the concept of family, so much so that there are two things in Chinese culture that carry a lot of weight, one is called *genealogy* and the other is called *patriarchal view*.

Let's look at what *genealogy* is all about. What is the most important thing for a family? *genealogy*! The study of family clan history is called *genealogy*. What Chinese people value most in life is family relations and their position in the family tree. What is the most important thing when you die? The funeral order of the five generations. It all expresses how much importance Chinese places on the structure of bloodlines. The order of blood in Chinese family is grand ancestor, great grandfather, grandfather, then father, son, grandson, further grandson, and more further offspring.

In traditional Chinese society, blood is more important than marriage for men and marriage is more important than blood for women. What does it mean? In ancient China, the most important thing for a man is his blood status in the family, and the relationship between husband and wife is not important, and his wife is just a shirt that can be changed and repudiated at any time. But for women, the marriage relationship was more important than the kin relationship. Why? Because a woman must marry someone and go to his family clan, so it is said "daughter married out is like water splashed out", so the daughter is not counted into their own family tree, and she has to follow her husband's side, follow his family tree inheritance. Therefore, in ancient China, a woman's social status was guaranteed by her marriage relationship after she got married, which is why Chinese women had to give birth to sons in ancient times, and it was a great misery to a wife if she does not to have sons. If wife did not have a son but a daughter, or if she could not have children, she won't enter the genealogy of her husband's family, and she would be a non-existent person in his family. Therefore, in ancient China, after the birth of a son, she must carry the son around the village. What for? To demonstrate and announce the establishment of her social status in the family. Why did she do so? So as to maintain her social status in the bloodline structure.

Let's look at the society outside the family, called the pyramid of power of the patriarchal structure. Notice this power structure: the highest level is the Emperor, or called son of Heaven, who is the supposed to be father of all people, so he is called the ruling father; the next level down is the Crown Prince, whose status is on par with that of the vassals; the eldest grandson of the Emperor is on par with that of the governor; the eldest grandson of the Emperor is on par with that of the scholar; the eldest grandson of the Emperor is on par with that of the common people. Try to understand the meaning of this passage, which says that the structure of noble blood is equivalent to the structure of social status and patriarchal power, that is, your position in the blood hierarchy marks your social class status. (see attached drawing)

				高祖父母				
			曾祖姑	曾祖父母	曾叔伯祖父母			
		族祖姑	祖姑	祖父母	叔伯祖父母	族叔伯祖父母		
	族姑	堂姑	姑母	父母	叔伯父母	堂叔伯父母	族叔伯父母	
族姐妹	再从姐妹	堂姐妹	姐妹	妻子	兄弟夫妇	堂兄弟夫妇	再从兄弟夫妇	族兄弟夫妇
	再从侄女	堂侄女	侄女	儿子儿媳	侄子侄媳	堂侄夫妇	再从侄夫妇	
		堂侄孙女	侄孙女	孙子孙媳	侄孙夫妇	堂侄孙夫妇		
			侄曾孙女	曾孙曾孙媳	侄曾孙夫妇			
				玄孙玄孙媳				

Look at the following sentence: The bottom social rank of the common people is equivalent to the bottom family rank of the distant relative or concubine's son. Please note that the character "◎" (Shu) *concubine* is a typical blood word. There are two Chinese blood terms, one is "◎" (Di) *first* or *formal* and the other is "◎" (She) *concubine* or *side-line*. What does it mean by *of formal wife*? The child born to the *first* or *formal* wife is called the *of formal born*. What does it mean by *of concubine*? A child born to a concubine is called a *of concubine*. In ancient China, the first heir of power and property inheritance is the first-born son, and the concubine son does not even have any inheritance rights. The so-called *direct line* means the highest blood rank, the *closest* troops to the ruler or commander is called *direct line* troops, borrowed from this blood vocabulary.

Think about what it means to call the people "庶民" (Shu Min) common people. It implies that the common people were equivalent to the children of the ruler's concubine wives, and it implies that all social and political relationships are of a blood family structure, so Chinese genealogy is very important, and it is the foundation of patriarchal relationships.

Chinese traditional culture speaks of "五服" (Wu Fu) five layers, which has a very complex meaning. It refers to both the official *five clothing styles,* and the funeral *five vests.* Let's take a look at the meaning of "五服" (Wu Fu), the *five clothing styles* of the ruling class, which reflect the relationship of peripheral circles subordinates to the ruler of the ancient state, ancient *five clothing styles* were for the emperor, vassals, ministers, senior officials, and official scholars; the term *Wu Fu* had also a meaning referring to the five peripheral regions outside the capital city of the king of the empire, it was recorded in historical books that *Wu Fu* also refers to *five circular regions,* each circular region was 250 kilometers in diameter length outward from the capital center, so totally five circular regions up to a diameter of 1250 kilometers to surround the center capital city.

The most commonly known meaning of "五服" (Wu Fu) is the funeral *five vests,* that is, relatives wearing different funeral vests, performing different funeral rituals at the funeral, show their blood relations to the dead. These five types of vests are called "*wail mourning, cry mourning, sorrow, feel sad,* and *sorry*", of which *wail mourning* is usually the son of the dead in *ragged linen vest, cry mourning* is the closest relatives in less ragged linen vests, *sorrow* is for close relatives all wearing white, some may wear a *linen string* in waist, the rest may simply wear dark plain clothes to be part of the funeral crowd. It can be seen all the participants of the funeral are arranged according to blood relations to the dead, and all activities performed at the funeral is centered on the dead, which is called *the deceased comes first.*

I believe those who have stayed in rural areas should be familiar with this system. That is, once there is a funeral event, people within the *five vests* participate in the funeral event according to different ritual procedures. The scholarly community has arranged the *five vests* into a table: look at its center, from the core of the husband and wife, upward four generations, parents, grandparents, great-grandparents, and high grandparents, plus the center point is five layers; downward, sons and daughters-in-law, grandsons and granddaughters-in-law, great-grandsons and great-grand daughter-in-law, plus the center point is also five generations; to the right, brother and wife, cousin and wife, then kin brother and wife, clan brother and wife. To the left, sisters, cousins, then kin sisters, and clan sisters. In this structural system, we assume that each square has five people, and you count all of these dozens of squares for a total it will be at least about 200 people. If each square establishes such a system of five generations, then all the people in the country could be related. Therefore, a very special notion of lineage emerged in ancient China, making the ritual pattern of bloodline based on it extremely complex, and extremely generalized as well.

Let me give you an example. In Chinese language, there are more than 300 kinds of nouns to describe relatives, and few people can figure out these nouns nowadays, while there are only about 70 kinds of nouns to describe relatives in Western languages, and at most 140 kinds. For example, the word *uncle* in English can represents the Chinese five kinds of uncle relationships, "father's elder brother, younger brother, mother's brother, father's sister's husband, mother's sister's husband", it is enough for the English speaker to use only the word *uncle*, but to express it in Chinese is very complex.

And in China, although the social structure has gradually developed beyond blood, the traditional culture has generalized all interpersonal relationships to blood. The simplest example is that when all of us take our children out and see someone your own age, we ask them to call uncle or aunt. In fact, it is neither the child's uncle nor the child's aunt; when you see someone older, you ask the child to call them grandpa or grandma, but in fact he is neither the child's grandpa nor the child's grandma; when people of the same age meet each other, they call each other brother or sister, even though there is no blood relationship between them; the way to show goodwill to others, since ancient times, is nothing more than friendship and brotherhood; all these things are the manifestation of the pan-blood culture, that is, the tendency to extend all non-blood interpersonal relationships to blood kinship in social activities.

As I said earlier, the *Records of Grand Historian* plays a role in the construction of the Chinese political and cultural moral system by describing the Chinese nation as a bloodline clan, which allows it to shine in Chinese history and Chinese culture. So you will see in the books of Confucius and Mencius all kinds of expressions in the pan-bloodline context, such as Zi Xia says, "Within the four seas we are all brothers"; and Mencius saying, "from respecting my old parents expand to respect others' old parents, and from caring my young children expands to care others' young children", meaning I take care of my own old parents and I also take care of others' old parents, and I take care of my own children and I take care of others' children, because all the people of the nation are of the same blood. By expanding and generalizing this virtual blood connection, the social relations and political structure of the entire Chinese nation is called the concept of pan-blood.

The next step is to *simulate blood relations*, that is, to extend blood relations to all things in the universe, saying that we humans are related to all things in the universe. Let me give you an example, for example, in *Mencius · All above the Mind*, it says: "Be close to your relatives and be kind to the people, be kind to the people and love things." It means that by being close to people with whom you have a blood relationship, you will then (be) benevolent to the people, because the people also have a pan-blood kinship relationship with you; "benevolent to the people and loving things", when you have a pan-blood type of benevolent heart, then you will eventually feel dear to all things in the universe, because all things also have some kind of relationship comparable to human blood relations. The love of kinship. Cheng Hao, one of the two Chengs, said, "*benevolence* is a person who takes everything in heaven and earth as one, and nothing is other than himself." He said that *benevolence* is originally used for "being kind to your relatives", but in reality, human beings are one with everything in heaven and earth, and can be treated as relatives without distinguishing this and that. He has applied the blood relationship to the whole nature. Wang Yangming said, "*benevolence* is the mind of heaven and earth. All things in heaven and earth are originally one with me. Then Zhang Zai proposed the phrase "all people are one cell with all things". What does this phrase mean? The word *same cell* is originally a blood word of biology, and then *treat things as same as part of us*. From this, we build up the whole society from the self to the family, then to the pan-blooded society, and finally to all things in heaven and earth that are like blood relations with us. This constitutes the general body of the worldview (social view) to the cosmological view (natural view), i.e., the whole worldview system is established with blood relations as the central axis.

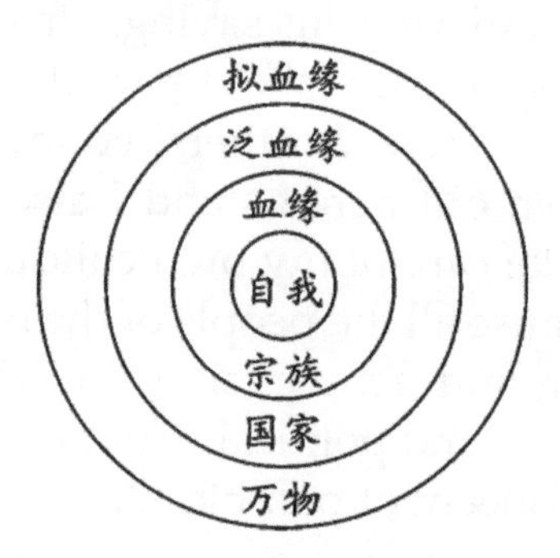

Look at this diagram, it is a general model that clearly expresses of the Chinese Confucian patriarchal worldview. The center is the *self*, then there is the *blood clan*, outer circle is the *pan-blood nation*, that is, all Chinese nationals are my blood relatives; the outmost circle is the *blood-like (of) all things*, that is, all nature is of the same kind as me; thus achieving the unification of life, social and even cosmic views.

Confucianism has thus laid the core foundation for the entire Chinese worldview. Zhu Xi once quoted a pavilion couplet: "If heaven does not give birth to Zhongni, all ages are like a long night." It says if heaven had not given birth to Confucius, mankind would have been in the darkness of uncivilization for long. Zhang Zai, a scholar of the Song Dynasty, said, "To establish my mind for heaven and earth, to establish my life for the people, to continue the teachings for the past sages, and to open up peace for all generations." The so-called "to establish my mind for heaven and earth" means that man is nothing but the mind of all things in heaven and earth, and they exist as one; then "to establish my life for the people" means that only by building up the moral lineage will the people's survival have a stable guarantee and foundation; then "to continue the teachings for the past sages," means to definitely pass down the teachings of the past sages, that is, the patriarchal ritual system, as only this structure is the most stable, the most systematic, the most gracious, and the most benevolent, so that we can say, "to open up peace for all generations."

This is where the weight of Confucian doctrine lies. In the end, Confucianism is a tight and vast system of worldviews, all-encompassing and omni-powerful. It simply does not need gods or deities; it simply does not need theology to exist. That is why Confucius said: "If one cannot do well as man, how can one do well as ghost"; "If one does not understand what life is, how can one understand what death is"; "Show respect to deities and ghosts but keep them away". Therefore, Chinese culture has nothing to do with religion, but you cannot say that Chinese culture has no religion. It does not need a supreme god that is separate from human beings' own blood relations, but only needs to set up a memorial tablet for his own blood ancestors, which is enough to construct a complete worldview and cosmology. This is the source of the unique concepts of godless culture and humanistic concern in ancient China.

The word *humanism* was used in the past as opposed to *theocracy*. Therefore, it is said that China has been a humanist culture since ancient times because its agricultural structure of survival has preserved blood ties intact, and then Confucianism has generalized and rooted these blood ties, so that *God* has no foothold at all. Moreover, it is a relationship of love and righteousness, flesh and blood, communicating deeply and endlessly, with warmth and entanglement. The Chinese Confucian doctrine is called both reasonable and emotional, but our society of rule of law today is reasonable but not emotional. Even if your relative breaks the law, even if your father or son breaks the law, you can't cover him up, otherwise you will also be punished by law. In ancient China, all interpersonal relationships were placed in the blood structure, which is the expression of your nature, your animal nature, and your animal nature is love with difference. I build the structure of inferiority and superiority according to this love with difference, because your blood structure is the structure of inferiority and superiority, your grandfather must be higher and more honorable than your father, and your father must be higher and more honorable than you (son), and your children and grandchildren are at the lower level of the blood sequence, which is inevitable. Therefore, it is reasonable and sensible, which means that it is in line with human nature and the ritual system, and therefore it is extremely stable.

The result is that Chinese society has several characteristics, first, raising children without end. As you know, even if you are a millionaire in the West, you will not care about your children after they are 18 years old, and the children will have to take out a loan to pay tuition for college. In China, even for poor families, raising children is an endless process. Not only do parents have to pay tuition for their children after they reach adulthood, but they also have to take care of the child's marriages, buying house and car, and they even have to help raise their sons' sons. In today's industrial and commercial civilization, this is obviously no longer appropriate, but it is a deep-rooted traditional custom in Chinese society. Secondly, there is no contract of exchange. In the true Chinese cultural atmosphere, there is no contractual relationship. For example, if you are in a rural area and one of your relatives borrows money from a company you run, you dare not ask him to make an IOU, otherwise he will immediately turn against you, for he thinks the contractual relationship is an insult and distrust of blood relations. Third, take the stand on relation rather than on reason. As long as there is a mutual blood relationship, the concerned man will be biased, no matter what he has done wrong, harbor him first, or you simply cannot stay in the blood group.

Moreover, Chinese society is extremely tolerant, warm, family-loving, and filial, Chinese society can be called warmly kind, and interpersonal relationships are so sticky that it is difficult for people to rationally stand clear on interpersonal relationships and blood ties. This side of it is precisely the source of the other side, which is cowardice, servility, selfishness, hypocrisy. Think about it, in primordial ancient societies, or in medieval societies, everyone lived in their own blood group, a village was a family. How dare a young man has any derailment? You do not have the slightest room to move, because the whole family group is restraining you, conditioning you, oppressing you, which makes the individual confined in it so much so that you could only be extremely cowardly, extremely tolerant, and over time, servility has developed, you can not object at all to what the elders say, let alone resist, because "love is differentiated, rituals are divided for superior and interior". Therefore, Chinese people have private virtue but not public virtue, the so-called private virtue is the virtue of blood relatives, someone is a very disciplined person in the blood group, but once he gets out of the circle, he may be unstrained and unbridled in society, and may do anything. So we often see such criminals, you go back to his village to investigate, all the village people say he is a good boy, but out of the village he becomes lawless, because China since ancient times, only emphasize on blood morality, but no super blood morality. If we see it with today's eyes, it is only private morality, nothing of the public morality. Because people are under the strong oppression of the blood structure, there is no way to express any super blood sentiment, any super kinship community feeling, and all criticism and rebellion are suppressed and destroyed in the budding state, resulting in nowadays people having to cope with various social situations inside and outside in an extremely hypocritical way.

It thus also creates the rule of man, centralization of power, self-containment and internal struggle. Do you dare to talk about equality before the law in a blood-based structure? Do you dare to talk about freedom and democracy? Do you dare to say that your father is a tyrant? Do you dare to say that your father's imperial power is not benevolent? Therefore, it must be a structure of human rule, and then generalized, it must only establish a totalitarian structure of the whole society also. Listen to Lu Xun's sarcasm: "The father's words are always right, but the son's words are wrong long before they are said." In other words, the totalitarian state is the inevitable expression of blood culture. Then it is not difficult to understand the quality of its self-containment and its expertise in internal struggle, because all its social behaviors are based on blood or pan-blood structure, so any struggle process is closed, which is called "family shame cannot be disclosed", thus forming an extremely bizarre relationship of interpersonal attachment and interpersonal harm.

Chinese society is based on a Confucian bloodline culture of rituals, with so much red tape and so much constraints that even the emperor was often hollowed out by the scholarly class. The Chinese bureaucracy, below the Chancellor, was recruited through the imperial examination system, and because Confucianism was so complex that the emperor did not have the ability to fully understand it, he had to learn it through lifetime with timely interpretation from scholars, and even through a group of scholars to interpret some critical points, so the Chinese bureaucracy formed a strong consensus group with irreplaceable say, just as the Western cardinalate had the right to interpret God's holy doctrine. This is where the extraordinarily complex entanglement between the emperor and the bureaucrats comes from. It shows how complex and heavy the Chinese culture of ritual and Confucianism is.

Historical Reasonableness of Confucius' Thought

As for the core of Confucian culture mentioned earlier, I will not tire of repeating it again: the Confucian doctrine is to use the most primitive, lowest and most stable human blood structure to maintain and reorganize the order of the disordered structure of the super blood society, thus forming a rigid and fixed system of ideological maintenance and stability and social structural ties. Since the more primitive something is, the more fundamental, decisive and stable it is, Confucius' doctrine, in its most primitive blood form, constitutes the strongest doctrinal system of human ethics and achieves a super-stable social effectiveness that is rare in the world. This is the core of Confucius' doctrine, so please be sure to understand it.

We make some comments on the doctrine of Confucius below.

Consider why Chinese society has become one of the strongest and longest- lasting examples of bloodline structure in the world. Why is it the only one that has developed a distinctive Confucian patriarchal and ritualistic culture? It is because Chinese society, as I said in my previous lecture, is the most typical, pure and sophisticated agricultural civilization system. The agricultural civilization of human beings occurred in the era of clan and tribe, in the era of blood society. And on each acre of land, we must work together, intensive farming, in order to get food and clothing. This is the basic characteristic of agricultural civilization. The blood group structure is the most ready-made and favorable way to constitute this stable collaboration. This, coupled with the closed pattern of geography and agroecology, has resulted in a continuous lineage of blood culture with no break in the middle.

In ancient Greece, as I said in the first lesson on the origins of human culture, because its natural physical conditions were not sufficient to sustain the community in an agricultural civilization at a time of population explosion, and it could exchange goods with the help of the narrow sea lanes along the coast of Mediterranean Sea, and could exchange food in the Nile basin of North Africa and the two river basins of the Middle East, commercial activity occurred prematurely on the basis that the agricultural structure could not be sustained. And the commercial structure could not be fulfilled in a blood-community manner, so its blood-personal ties were broken up long before the time of Homer, the 10th century B.C. By the 6th century B.C., its blood-community structure had nearly disappeared. 70% to 80% of the people had left their original Greek settlements and were scattered throughout the Mediterranean rim. As a result, each of them became free singletons, with no blood ties between them. Thus, they had to create *gods* to serve as intermediaries for human beings to maintain their social relations. As a result, their theology developed, their juridical contracts developed, their philosophical ideas developed, and their city-state political structure was transformed accordingly.

The most typical example is the *Thoreau Change* that took place in Athens in the 6th century BC. Thoreau was the chief consul, and he made significant reforms. In his capacity as consul, he acted as an arbiter, finding a balance between the interests of the nobility and the common people. With the new law, he abolished the hereditary political privileges of the nobility and established the cultural concepts of *citizenship* and *civil rights*. Then he established the political system of *citizens' assembly*. It was not entirely fair, dividing citizens into four classes according to the amount of their property, and their rights were not equal. However, for the first time, he balanced the interests of the various factions, so that all free people had room for negotiation and concessions in their interests. This led to the establishment of a contract society, or an unwritten rule of law society. This was later inherited by ancient Rome, and by the 5th century B.C., the *Twelve Bronze Tables* had emerged.

The law-making process of the *Twelve Bronze Tables* was not monopolized by the consuls, but by a ten-member constituent assembly composed of five representatives from the nobility and five representatives from the commoners. In the Ninth Schedule, *Public Law*, there is a provision that "no special law shall be made for the benefit of any individual". This established the basic concept of "equality before the law". That is, man is not equal to God; but under God, all men are equal.

Why did they establish this structure of checks and balances with *God* as the supreme intermediary and *law* as the social bond? It is because blood ties have disappeared and interpersonal relationships cannot be maintained without contractual negotiation. Therefore, we must pay attention to the fact that the Western ideological system, cultural system, legal system, and democratic social system are the products of the structure of existence, just like the Chinese blood family patriarchal system and the system of loyalty and filial piety, which are not the cultural concepts created by someone on a whim. As a result, two completely different concepts of *people* emerged, and this is the difference between *family member* and *citizen*.

In China, the concept of *citizenship* has not existed since ancient times. All of us are just members of *family, clan or nation*, you are just a member of the family or the blood ties of the community as nation. Confucius said to Zengzi, "think about it, my way is consistent." That is to say, my whole theory is actually a basic core and a thread of consistence, which is called "one thread of consistence". When Zengzi came out, the other students asked him what the teacher meant by this statement. Zengzi made a summary and said, "The way of teacher's theory is only *loyalty* and *forgiveness*." The teacher's doctrine is nothing but the summation of *loyalty* and *forgiveness*. What does it mean? In the context of interpersonal relations among the common people, it means to be loyal and forgiving to others; in the context of social and political structure, it means to be loyal and forgiving to the ruler, and to forgive and tolerate any mistakes made by the ruler. Thus, from the family to the whole society, all of things is carried out as one, that is, the social structure is still the family structure, which is called the *sentiment of family country*.

What is the difference between *member of family* and *citizen*? *Member of family* is not about equality, because there is a difference in love and a difference in ritual. But it also has another consequence, it does not allow competition, it suppresses it. Because within the structure of blood, inequality is ironclad and is a biological imperative. In this structure, you can never compete. You can't turn a father into a son by competition, right? Then what is *citizen*? It is an interpersonal relationship of mutual equality under God, under the divine. And once everyone is equal, the social system will be divided. How to divide? By competition! So a structure of equal competition is formed. The two are totally different, and it has a significant difference in its sociological connotation.

So, let's now talk about the competitive structure. Bio community structure faces two kinds of competition. The first is *interspecific competition* and the second is *intraspecific competition*. Interspecific competition is the competitive relationship between different species, which needs no further explanation. Why did Darwin give special thanks to Malthus in the introduction of his book *Origin of Species*? It is because Malthus' theory of population revealed for the first time the structure of competition within humans of the same species, which inspired Darwin to realize that competition between species is not only *interspecific competition*, but also *intraspecific competition* in particular. The so-called *interspecific competition* is the kind of competition in which wolves eat sheep; the so-called *intraspecific competition* is the competition between wolves and wolves. Then interspecific competition is a natural evolutionary sequence that no one can overcome. Moreover, interspecific competition does not pose any fundamental harm to species, but is a natural system for the balance of ecological food chain of species.

But *intraspecies competition* is very different! Because everyone is of the same species, each with the same competitiveness, endowed with the same sharp claws, once in competition, it will appear as a lasting, fierce battlefield of life and death, no way in any corner to hide, forming the greatest pressure of biological survival. And this kind of internal struggle is inevitable, it also originated from the nature of survival, which constitutes the biggest crisis within any species. This is why the lower the ability of primitive species, the more stable its survival, the slower the rate of extinction, because its ability is low, the intensity of intra-species competition is low also; the higher the top of the food chain, the faster the extinction rate, because the species ability is too strong, it seems to have an advantage in interspecies competition, but in the intraspecies competition, it is also causing very serious damage, thus constituting their survival crisis greatly aggravated. The higher the species, the faster it becomes extinct.

The reason Confucius raised his doctrine systematically in ancient times, was that he unconsciously discovered that the most important problem facing mankind was intra-species competition. With the development of modern science, we can see that Confucius repeatedly emphasized the importance of *harmony is superior*, which is equivalent to advocating *intra-species harmony*. Humans are a very powerful species, if they cannot resolve their own intra-species competition, and if they cannot solve intra-species competition, if they cannot form intra-species harmony, then they will cause great trouble for themselves. Because among all living things human is already at the top of the food chain, and they do not have much interspecies competition, so all the disasters they have to face come from intraspecies competition. This is why we find that in the history of human civilization, "man-made disasters gradually replace natural disasters" is an ironclad! Because the continuous improvement of human capabilities will inevitably lead to the deterioration of human intra-species competition, thus posing a great threat to the overall human survival.

The core of Confucius' doctrine is *restoring rituals through self-discipline*. He was actually standing at the end of the Eastern Zhou Dynasty, but wanted to go back to the early years of the Western Zhou Dynasty when Duke Zhou Jidan made rites and music, which was obviously reactionary and intended to maintain the feudal system. As I said earlier, the unification of China by Emperor Yingzheng of Qin Dynasty established a monarchical dictatorship, which completely destroyed the feudal system, but why was Confucius' doctrine elevated to the status of state religion after that? It was because even though Confucius originally intended to preserve feudal society, his doctrine of restraining intra-species competition was so strong that it was able to establish a stable and orderly system of superiority and inferiority in the age of monarchy, thus effectively suppressing the social competition of East Asian agricultural civilization. This is the reason why Confucius' doctrine, although it was completely distorted and became the deform system by the Qin and Han Dynasties, and was in no way inherent in Confucius' concept of "I follow the Zhou", has been the cornerstone of Chinese culture for 2000 years. This is what we should pay special attention to understand.

But you must also understand that the Confucian approach of the order of superiority and inferiority and social inequality, which seeks to reintegrate the internal competition of human beings today, is obviously obsolete. Therefore, the doctrine of Confucius has declined, and the slogan *Down with Confucianism* has been heard in modern times. However, the grassroots issues with which Confucius' doctrine is concerned are an increasingly serious dilemma that the whole humanity faces today. The doctrine of Confucius thus constitutes the base-level reference system for today and even for the re-creation of human civilization in future.

We will discuss another issue below, the historical rationality of Confucius' thought. Confucius used the primitive blood structure to maintain the solid development of the super blood farming civilization society. Today, as the world enters the era of industrial and commercial civilization, Confucian doctrine is obsolete. We have been justified in criticizing the Confucian doctrine violently since the beginning of the last century. But the prerequisite for you to really criticize and clarify the Confucian doctrine effectively is that you understand it first. It is important to know that Confucius' thought, his doctrine back then, was an effective system for maintaining the social structure of East Asian agricultural civilizations, which is called the historical justification of Confucian culture.

Let me give you an example. Confucian culture advocates a custom of three-year mourning, which means that when a parent dies, the son has to observe mourning at the grave side for three years. This system seems absurd to us today. The average life expectancy in ancient times was about 39 years, and people did not know much things until they were 16 or 17 years old, and they only live for about 20 years after that. Parents seldom die on the same day, the father died, the son set up a grass hut at the grave side, and mourning for three years; then mother died, he tied up a grass hut again, and mourning for another three years. So he has to spend six years mourning at side of the graves, this is a thing that seems really absurd. But why it was an important, prevailing, and the most humane practice in patriarchal system in ancient China? It is because the event of parent's death makes human feelings deeply bruised and it needs to take three years to heal.

What is the most serious emotional setback suffered by modern people in general? Only one, be disappointed in love! Love is a strange thing, if it goes smoothly, the two won't see it so much vital; if there is a little obstacle in the middle, such as parental disapproval, the two will love each other desperately. Then, someone breaks it off when two people are in hot love, this is called a disappointed love, the consequences can be terrible. Each or two of them will be emotionally bruised so profoundly that martyrdom may occur, that is, someone will commit suicide over it. Even if not suicide, at least three years he won't find another one in replace, this is called *the lost one is unmatched*.

The ancient people had a very close relationship with their parents; it was completely different from the relationship a child has with its parents today. Nowadays the child is only two or three years old and you send it to the nursery, or you leave it to its grandparents. Except the child sleeping time, all its awake time the child is basically not with the parents. Nursery school, elementary school, high school, college. Not only that, most of the parents actually act as accomplices to the teacher. The teacher forced the child to study, and the child is hard enough, it is normal that the child does not like to read, you have seen any monkey holding a book reading on a tree? But parents are more vicious than teachers in forcing the child to read, so it is your good luck today if the child does not see his parents as enemy.

But in ancient times, children were with their parents every minute. Parents not only raise their children, but also teach them, which is called *upbringing*. Parents and children were never separated. Look at the character *teach*. In the oracle bone scripts, two forbidden symbols are drawn on the top, a child is drawn on at the bottom, and a hand is drawn next to it, holding a small wooden stick. (甲文 金文 小篆 教 楷体) What is *teach*? To tell a child what not to do! To teach a child what is dangerous to do! So *teaching* in ancient times was never the full of lectures and formulas that we have today, which make you dizzy, feel sick and rather to die. The ancient *teaching* was to hold the child's hand and tell him the things not to do, because the ancient people lived in the jungle full of crisis, all kinds of wild animals may attack the child. Therefore, the ancient *teaching* was very soft and was for the protection of the child only.

Please think about it, the ancient people lived with their parents since they were born, eat, drink, pull up, taken care of everything, taught softly for decades, and deep love developed in between like flesh and blood. Suddenly, the parent died one day, the child suffered a psychological and emotional setback, it was far more serious than today's young man disappointed in love. Therefore, he fell a chaotic-mind for three years, nothing he could do well, so it was better for him to set up a grass hut to mourn at the grave site. So, back then it was the most humane ritual custom.

You know in times of dynasties, the Chinese political science has a term called *deprived mourning*, what is *deprived mourning*? When the emperor's minister, his parents died, the emperor should give the minister leave of three years of mourning, but the emperor could not leave this important minister, so only give him two or three months, he asked him to come back to work, this is called *deprived mourning*. In other words, even as the emperor, he could not easily do such things against human nature as depriving subject's period of mourning, this was called *ritual custom of three years mourning*.

In fact, it was not a rule of Confucius to mourn at the graves of parents for three years. It was a direct manifestation of the relationship between the ancient people and their parents, a custom that had existed for a long time among the nobles and folk, but it was Confucius who organized and normalized it. It was the most humane rule back then. If you don't understand this, you can't understand the culture of Confucius. What seems to be a serious paradox today was in fact the most humane flow of warmth back then.

Let me give you another example. Confucius preached the *separation of men and women*. Mencius expressed it as *intercourse are prohibited between men and women*. In recent times, we have been desperately criticizing this article of Confucius and Mencius, saying that it has seriously hindered the freedom of love between young men and women and caused a series of love tragedies, for example, Liang Shanbo and Zhu Yingtai and so on. But you have to think about why the ancients spoke of *the separation of men and women*? It is important to know that not only the Chinese did so, it was no exception all over the world. Westerners in the Medieval Ages, measures of separation for men and women were very strict, so much so that the legs of the table are wrapped up, so that you did not see the legs of the table which may lead you to fancy women's thighs. Some even gave women, adult unmarried girls or wives whose husbands were away chastity locks, a triangle of pants made of iron, to lock up her pubic area.

Why were they so nervous about such a trivial thing as sex?

Why did the ancients have to be so strict about the separation of men and women? It was because at that time human beings were living in their own blood group. Please think about it, in a blood group, if you could love freely, what would be the result? You might love your sister, brother, cousin, nice, or even uncle, aunt, it must be an incest! This was why since ancient times, *matchmaker's words and parents' decisions* were authoritative on issue of children's marriage, because only matchmakers and parents could tell which person was not related to your son or daughter, and the marriage union would not be incestuous.

Why is the issue of incest particularly important and must be strictly prevented? It is because all animals must be banned from incest. You may have seen some years ago an American movie *The Lion King*, surprisingly, it played the plot as Hamlet. The scenario was that the lion king's brother, the lion cub's uncle, in order to usurp the throne, killed the lion king, and then expelled the lion cub out of the group. But some biologists pointed out that even if the lion cub's father, the Lion King, were alive, it must have driven the male lion cubs out of the clan group on the days of their sexual maturity. What for? To prevent incest! We must know that in all animals, when its offspring grow to sexual maturity, one of the two sexes must be driven out of the community by the father. For example, the lion society, monkey society, when the male offspring grow sexual maturity, they must be driven away. For example, in the wild horse society, when the female pony grows to sexual maturity, the father will bite it bloody to drive it out of the herd.

Why do all animals need to be protected from incest? I invite you to look at the genetic structure of biological systems. The majority of our human diseases are genetic, even the flu has a 14% heritability. On the surface, colds are caused by viral infections, but when a flu comes, why do some people suffer it and others are unharmed? Why are some people seriously ill and others slightly ill? It is because the innate immune quality of each person is different, so the heritability of the flu is 14%. However, the heritability of most diseases is as high as 60% to 70%, which means that heredity is the main factor. In clinical practice, we often see that a disease appears in your generation, trace the family history, but not in your parents' generation, then go up to find the same case in your grandparents' generation, which is called intergenerational inheritance.

Why is this so? Let's look at the DNA double helix structure of living things. It is such a combination, this side of the long chain is called the dominant gene, the other side is called the opposite gene, together called *allele*. The two genes are lined up in a long chain and twisted together to form the double helix structure of a gene.

First of all, we must understand that all higher species in the biological world are genetically predisposed to aberrant diseases (we will discuss more on this topic in the *Philosophy of the Human Body* class). Why is there intergenerational inheritance? It is because all the evolved genes are disease genes. If the opposite gene is identical to the dominant gene at this moment (AA or aa), it is called purely heterozygous; if the opposite gene is not identical to the dominant gene (Aa or aA), it is called heterozygous; only when the disease gene remains purely heterozygous, the disease will be manifested, which is clinically called *hidden genetic disease*. If any of the parents has the disease gene, but their genetic structure is heterozygous, then although the disease gene will be inherited, they themselves will not develop the disease, which is called a *recessive carrier*. This is the reason why intergenerational inheritance occurs.

Why do all animals forbid incest and restrain themselves from incest behavior? It is because if you marry someone whom you are related by blood, the chances of a purely congenic histocyte occurring are greatly increased due to the high rate of genetic homozygosity between blood relatives, which means that the probability of mobilizing hidden genetic diseases is greatly increased. During the long period of biological evolution, any species that did not have the instinctive quality of incest taboos would rapidly become extinct due to the massive outbreak of all hidden family blood line diseases and dominant genetic diseases in the population. It can be seen that the Confucian doctrine back then proposed the separation of men and women, in fact, unconsciously maintained the security of the Chinese nation's lineage.

Why are you free to choose your love today? It's because today's society is highly super blood, the probability of you meeting your immediate blood relatives in nursery, primary, secondary and university is not even 1%, so you can decide your love freely and even be sexually liberated, it will never cause incest, or at least the chance of causing such incest is very low.

Please think again, if free love was allowed in ancient society, what a situation it would be? A state of widespread incest would have occurred. What am I talking about? I am telling you that if you want to understand the doctrine of Confucius, you have to go back to his time, and his doctrine was very reasonable at that time, and it was a cultural adaptation system to maintain human survival.

Confucius' doctrine was benevolent and kind, or at least that was his original intention. Confucius was also very refined and was described by his disciples as "gentle, kind, respectful, frugal and modest". In the text of Confucius, we find the only foul-mouthed scolding of Confucius: "The one who initiated the stone figures for the tomb will have no offspring". What does that mean? In those days, the nobles treated the common people, especially the slaves, not as human beings, and at the end of the Spring and Autumn Period, there was still a system of slaughter and burial in the states of the Central Plain. Confucius was extremely disgusted by this. He not only opposed slaves buried alive with their deceased masters, but was also angry when he saw people making clay figurines into human figures for burial, which he thought was disrespectful to human beings and a reminder of the institution of burying the living with the dead. Therefore, he said, those who create human figurines at the beginning should have no descendants. Confucius, who was gentle and kind-hearted, made such a foul-mouthed remark, which shows his kindness and benevolence of heart. Therefore, we must understand that Confucius' culture, in his every word and deed back then, had the goodwill and effectiveness to maintain the survival of human beings.

Meaning of the Culture of *Virtue Oriented*

What is the core of Confucius' culture? Observe virtue! "To cultivate oneself, to well organize one's family, to rule one's country, and to pacify the world". To *cultivate oneself*, that is, cultivate one's moral character, is in the first place. The second is to *well-organize family*, as I said earlier, in the traditional concept, the family comes before the state, after the family is well organized, then one could have the chance to think about ruling the country, *to rule the country* (refers to the vassal feudal state) is not the purpose, but *to pacify the world* is, so there is a *view of the world* (the pursuit of *the great road for the public, the great common world*). Why did he put *cultivating oneself* at the bottom? Because the culture of observing virtue is a system of survival and maintenance, the basis for the sustaining of society. To what extent Confucius valued virtue, he said, "When I see a virtuous man, I think of how can I learn from him and align myself with him, and when I see an unworthy man, I introspect my mind to see how I can avoid myself that way." What does that mean? He said that when I see a person who is very virtuous, I immediately want to learn from him and align myself with him; he said that when I see a person who has done something corrupt, I immediately reflect on whether I have this kind of inferiority in me. To what extent did Confucius observe virtue? He observed virtue to the extent of *being prudent in solitude*. In other words, when he was alone, he could still strictly restrain his mind and adhere to the moral bottom line. Of course, there are many ways to interpret the term *being prudent in solitude*.

Today's human beings are morally bankrupt and human nature is corrupt. As I said earlier, today is the era of *people avoid and shameless*, they don't touch anything that is prohibited by law so as to avoid being prosecuted, but they dare to do anything that is not prohibited by law. The reason why human beings still follow morality today is that they use it as a kind of decoration, as a kind of adornment, this is the first; secondly, they use it as a strategy. What does it mean by strategy? It is that the reason why I abide by morality in this occasion is because if I don't, it will bring me more damage. If such a strategy is use by people, then it also means that if they do not observe morality in a certain occasion, they can gain more benefits, they will immediately abandon morality. This is the human condition today, and this is why a society of law must emerge.

Why did Confucius place extra importance on morality? We will explore this question below. As I have said repeatedly before, traditional Chinese culture is the most primitive first crop of human civilization, that is, a refined and well-preserved cultural system of agricultural civilization, therefore it represents the lowest level of human thinking. And I add that the more fundamental something is, the more foundational, decisive and stable it is. When we explore the most basic qualities of traditional Chinese culture, it is particularly important to understand that it must have the most significant connotation among the elements of the culture of survival. What is morality? It is the *rule of survival*, or the *rule of maintaining survival*. What is law? It is *the bond of society*, or *the bond of maintaining social order*, and the weight of these two is completely different.

Let me first explain why it is a requirement for survival that Confucius was much concerned for reverence and observance of virtue. Anthropologists did fieldwork in the early part of the last century. At that time, a large number of primitive clan social groups still existed in Yunnan of China, Africa and Indonesia. Fieldwork is a method of anthropology, which is to establish a close relationship with the people in the society they are investigating for a long time, so that they can conduct in-depth academic research. In the early 1900s, anthropologists went to primitive clan societies to do fieldwork and lived with them for several years, and found that the primitive clan societies followed only two morals. First, the incest taboo, that is, no incest. As I said earlier, the incest taboo is a rule of survival, any species violates the incest taboo, the species will quickly become extinct; second, not to eat the same kind, that is, not to eat humans.

You have been seeing reports of primitive cannibalism on various websites lately. Please note, that is only a gimmick on the Internet for the attraction of the public. Cannibalism is very rare in primitive human clan societies. In primitive human societies, two of the most important morals were not to commit incest and not to eat humans. Why shall not eat humans? It is because all biological species do not eat their own kind. In the biological species, the phenomenon of eating the same kind is very rare. For example, when the praying mantis mates, the female will eat the male mantis, this situation is rare, it is just a special way to reproduce. This topic is a bit complicated, so we will not discuss it today.

As far as organisms in general are concerned, 99% of organisms do not engage in cannibalism. Why? It is because any disease-causing microorganisms, viruses or pathogenic bacteria, do not cross-infect different species as hosts. What does this statement mean? Let me give you an example. Human TB bacteria do not infect cattle, and cattle TB bacteria do not infect humans, so the medical community extracts TB bacteria from humans, cultures them, and later injects them into cattle. Since the bovine host is not susceptible to human TB, it is cultured in the bovine body for more than 260 generations. The virulence of the microorganism decreases generation by generation in hosts that are not susceptible, and then the human TB bacterium is extracted from cattle and injected directly into humans, which is called *live attenuated vaccine*.

What am I talking about? I'm telling you that disease-causing microorganisms do not cross species as hosts, that is, they do not infect different species at the same time. What we see today with swine flu and bird flu is due to a severe mutation of this type of virus, which starts to invade other species, for example, humans, but its pathogenicity to pigs and birds immediately decreases. Well, I have here explained why all creatures do not eat their own kind. Because eating meat of the same kind species, it causes a massive infection of a certain type of virus or bacteria within its own population, resulting in a persistent plague. That is, the species that constantly eats its own kind, it will quickly become extinct in the long-term biological development process due to the continuous outbreak of plague. Therefore, natural selection must only keep the kind of species that feel sick when they meet the flesh of their own kind, and will eliminate species that crave the same kind of food.

Am I made myself understood? what is morality? the provision of survival! This is the weight of morality. As I said earlier, the process of human civilization is the process of gradual moral failure. When I say this, there may be many people who disagree with me. They feel that it is obvious that the more civilizationally advanced countries are, the higher the moral standards of their populations usually are. Please note that this is a floating opinion! Our general evaluation of society and reality is what I call situational evaluation. I say that your life is becoming more and more unstable, your anxiety is increasing, and you are not getting happier, but more and more unhappy. You think I am saying the opposite because you are caught in the limitations of situational evaluation and cannot extricate yourself. You stand in the structure of survival that you cannot transcend today, and you stand in the situation of survival that you have highly adapted to now, and you look back at the poverty and scarcity of the ancient mundane life, and you look back at the social disaster that has been magnified by historical prejudice, and you think that you cannot appreciate it and adapt to it, and you think that the state of survival then was worse and eviler than now, and this kind of view is hanging on one thing, and this kind of evaluation is meaningless. Because your own narrow subjective situation becomes your illusionary evaluation scale. So, what is a valid evaluation? Finding the *ultimate measure* and giving the *ultimate evaluation*! That is to say, to go beyond the obscurity of your own subjective situation, to the bottom of the rules of survival, which is called the ultimate evaluation of a large scale.

Why is that the higher the species, the faster the extinction rate? Why is that the more civilization develops, the more stressful the overall human existence and the more serious the social crisis becomes? Only when you have drawn a large scale, analyzed the whole sequence of evolution, and compared the evolution of all organisms, can you complete this ultimate evaluation, and only then can you say whether the development of ancient and modern societies is fortunate or unfortunate. In other words, to find the scale of ultimate evaluation is the most fundamental point in constructing human culture and human scholarship. Let me give you an example. From the surface details, it seems that we human beings have become very gentle and friendly nowadays. But we should know that in terms of overall cultural tendencies, our civilization and culture have actually become more and more vicious. For example, modern history reviews often regard those who destroyed the world as the heroes of history-making. But in ancient China, people like Shang Yang, Qin Shi Huang, and Cao Cao were poorly evaluated in mainstream culture, because they were vicious and brutal and wrecked the lives of the people. In today's political evaluation, they have actually become positive historical figures worthy of recognition and emulation.

I will give another example; the ancient human wealth disparity was extremely low. In agricultural civilization, all of the people could not get rich, everyone was equal physical strength, the total population of society was very small, with their own physical strength to cultivate the land, a family could plant about a hundred acres, rough farming, no one could be richer than others. At that time, people were not motivated by greed and did not pursue excessive wealth. But in the age of capitalism, however, those who could amass great wealth were envied by all, even though it inevitably crushed the vast majority of people into abject poverty, which was the great calamity of human economic life, its basic state tended to deteriorate more and more.

The ancient human weapon maker was ashamed of himself. In his text, Laozi said something to the effect that he who kills on behalf of the slaughterer will mutilate himself. He said that only the Way of Heaven and Earth has the power to destroy, and man does not have the power to kill others. It can be seen that human beings naturally have the intuition of protect lives. Therefore, the ancient weapon maker was ashamed of himself, and he did not dare to proclaim his profession as an honor. But we all know that today, in all countries of the world, those who make atomic bombs, hydrogen bombs and missiles are hailed as national heroes. That is, we will see in the large scale, the development of human civilization is a process of increasingly thinning moral values and increasingly being violent in the inner. This is the value of Confucius' culture of benevolence as well as focus on morality, which fundamentally upholds human existence, while humanity today is gradually moving away from it.

The ancient Chinese culture has become the only one of all ancient civilizations that has continued to this day. The important reason for this is, of course, is the closed landscape of East Asia, where disturbances of different nations were difficult to enter. However, the underlying force of Confucius' doctrine, the force of the bloodline structure, cannot but be an important reason why Chinese civilization has been able to "stagnate without dying". In other words, social development seems to have stagnated, but the basic survival security of Chinese civilization and the Chinese nation has been maintained for more than 2000 years without dying or falling.

Confucian culture appears to be a low-intelligence state, but it is a low- intelligence restrained state that fundamentally maintains intraspecific calm and resists or restrains intraspecific competition, thus leading to the relatively peaceful survival of the entire civilization of the Chinese nation. The fact that mankind has turned away from it today portends the collapse of the edifice of human civilization.

Look at humans today, whatever they do, they have to make a name for it. Even if they want to fight a war, they have to find an excuse. What excuse? Moral excuse, which is called moral high ground. Why does man have to find the moral high ground for anything he does, even if it is an evil thing? It is because only from the moral high ground that it has the most touching appeal, or the most inspirational power. Why is morality the most touching? Why does morality connect with the soul of human beings? It is because morality upholds the lowest rules of human existence. That is why the figures who have had the greatest influence on humanity are not politicians, not military men, and not economists, but three supreme framers of moral norms. The first one is the Buddhist Siddhartha Gautama, who, as a prince, actually asked his monastic or sangha organization to step into humble homes to ask for meals for himself. What was he doing? Seeking the equal identity of the poor people with nobles. Because of its extremely high moral standing, it has so far influenced more than one billion people in Southeast Asian and East Asian societies. The strength of its charisma and the beauty of its image is unmatchable by anyone.

The second one is Jesus. He was the founder of Christianity and openly claimed to be the Son of God. Christianity was born out of Judaism, which only recognizes God, Jehovah, and denies Christ's descent into the world, saying how could God be incarnated into human? How could the Virgin Mary give birth to her son? That is why they do not recognize Jesus and say that Mary was a prostitute. This is the reason why European Christian civilization has long been anti-Semitic culture. You should know that Hitler's massacre of 6 million Jews during World War II was never a sudden catastrophe; it was the accumulation and continuation of more than 2,000 years of anti-Semitic culture in European Christian civilization. If you read Shakespeare, his plays contain a lot of slander and mockery of Jews. Then Jesus proclaims himself the Son of God, which is too bizarre as a physical mortal, no matter how he justifies it. But why is Jesus revered by billions of people today? It is because he gave his flesh and blood for the redemption of mankind from original sin. The power of his holy virtue conquered the whole Christian world.

Finally, let's look at Confucius. As I said earlier, the entire core of Confucius' doctrine lies in the establishment of virtue, and he thus became the patriarch of Confucian culture covering hundreds of millions of people in East Asia. What am I talking about? Morality is the provision of survival, which has the highest surface appeal and at the same time the most profound effect of maintaining survival. This is where the value of ancient traditional culture lies. For example, when I talk about Laozi, I say that his conservatism, not progressivism, is his most important cultural value; when I talk about Confucius, I say that his concept of the importance of virtue is the lowest cultural frame of reference. Because all these things already disappeared today, they even became counter-arguments or extravagant talk. Progressivism has replaced conservatism, and the rule of law has replaced morality. And what is it that humanity has lost? It is a very important question to think about.

In my Western philosophy class, I talked about a topic in which I said that there were three major categories of ancient human culture: first, *virtue oriented*; second, *faith in God;* and third, *love of wisdom*. I said that in ancient Greece, its culture tended to be *love of wisdom*, and the culture of *love of wisdom* is to mobilize human intellectual potential and intellectual reserves. Then what is a culture of *virtue-oriented*? To put it in perspective, there are only two intellectual forms of human civilization-making: one is to extend the scope of inward cooperation or solidarity; the other is to expand the scope of outward exploration or depth of knowledge. The former extends the *fictional story* into *virtue oriented* or *faith in the Lord*, while the latter extends the *virtual state of mind* into the *love of wisdom* of precise logic, that is, into the philosophical thinking of *hypothesis and proof*. Both must be developed simultaneously, but each has a different focus.

Please understand this paragraph. The intellectual activity of mankind develops in two directions, one direction of human civilization, which is based on hypothesis and fiction, seeks to establish an expanded scope of cooperation within humanity; the other is the outward search for deepening knowledge and intellect. So, what is more important of the two? When I lectured on Western philosophy, you all think that the culture of love of intellect is so wonderful, but don't misunderstand, the culture of love of intellect is the extreme mobilization of human intellectual ability, while the culture of virtue oriented is the stable guarantee of human inward cooperation. These two directions are opposite to each other: if your statute of inward cooperation is too harsh, the intelligence of individuals will be suppressed; on the contrary, if your inward cooperation is out of harmony, the more the ability of individuals is enhanced, the more serious the overall crisis humanity will face.

What, then, is more important for the survival of humanity? The harmonization of interhuman relations for all of humanity! The avoidance of excessively vicious intra-species competition is far more important than the promotion of competence! That is, a culture of emphasizing virtue, is far more important in terms of its effectiveness in preserving survival than the ancient Greek culture of loving wisdom, which led to the mobilization and unleashing of the immense technological capabilities of humanity today. What does the increase in capacity bring to us? The higher the capacity, the more sinister the future of human self- destruction if intra-species competition grows and internal cooperative and symbiotic community relations cannot be reconciled.

On the surface, Chinese *virtue-oriented* culture is the shallowest culture in terms of intellectual mobilization. Compared to the *faith in God* cultures, such as ancient Egypt and ancient Babylon, which believed in God, it did not lead to the development of a philosophical culture and did not achieve a deeper mobilization of intellectual potential, but it had to fictionalize a god, and then it had to seek to prove the existence of this god. Although its mobilization of intelligence is not as thorough as that of the ancient Greek philosophical *love of wisdom* culture, it is higher than that of the Chinese culture of emphasis on virtue. It is almost a direct extension of animal society, a civilized interpretation and rationalization of the social structure of animal blood, so it mobilizes intelligence to the shallowest extent, and is expressed as a culture of the lowest intelligence.

But it is precisely this lowest intelligence, the most basic state of culture, that most effectively deals with and extends the important virtuous element of cooperation within the human being, revealing it as the *rule of survival*. And what is the result of the constant mobilization of human intelligence by the culture of *love of wisdom*? It is the intensification of competition within the human race.

As I said earlier, citizens and family members are each endowed with a completely different personality. What is the essential difference between a citizen under the authority of a deity and a family member in a blood network? Citizens speak of equality, but at the same time openly mobilize competition; family members speak of superiority and inferiority, but unintentionally suppress competition. Intraspecific competition is becoming more and more brutal and inescapable, which in itself is very frightening, and what would be the result if it is equipped with a significant increase in intelligence? Consider what would happen to two male monkeys if they had guns in their hands while competing for female reproductive resources. Please think again, if these monkeys then hold the atomic bomb in their hands, the entire monkey group will face what results? It can be seen that the mere improvement of ability will not only not help to balance and resolve the intra-species competition, but will eventually put the fighters to death, which is the gloomy prospect faced by human beings. This is why when I taught a class on Western philosophy, I said that the culture of love of wisdom may seem colorful, but it may not be worthy of praise, while the culture of emphasis on virtue by Confucius may be more profound, although it seems dull and plain.

I will explain the frame of reference specifically below. I keep saying in my classes that traditional Chinese culture is the preservation of the most primitive civilizational thoughts of mankind. I say that the lower something is, the more it has the role of a frame of reference. What does this mean? Please pay attention to the term *a frame of reference*, which is a term in physics. Newtonian mechanics, for example, is divided into inertial frame of reference and non-inertial frame of reference. I will just give you an example and not talk about complicated concepts. For example, if you are standing on the ground, the earth is moving at high speed, you do not feel, this is called inertial frame of reference; if you are sitting in a car, also with the ground as a frame of reference, you can feel the high-speed movement, this is called non-inertial frame of reference. Physics is the study of the displacement of objects in space-time, and what is my philosophy research? The study of the evolutionary movement of matter. Please note that physical motion and evolutionary movement are two concepts, physical motion is the external motion or spacetime motion of matter, and evolutionary movement is the internal movement or endomorphic movement of matter.

What, then, is the philosophical or humanistic frame of reference? To put it simply, the humanist-historical movement can be divided into two similar frames of reference: one is always trapped in a self-conscious progressive situation, unaware of the deteriorating trend of human civilization, which is the inertial frame of reference; the other is to look deeply into the differences between ancient and modern thought and culture, so as to judge the current critical situation of human existence, which is the non-inertial frame of reference. In other words, the lower the level of culture, the more closely and more importantly the issues it seeks and discusses are related to the basic survival of human beings. Therefore, it has a more important reference role in the path of civilization development.

Its reference perspective is twofold: one involves the roots and foundations of the genesis; the other refers directly to the superposition and intensification of the development axis. Chinese traditional culture is the lowest level of human society's roots and foundations, and by referring it to the superposition and intensification of human history on the development axis, it constitutes the best comparative material for the ultimate review of human civilization. This is what I mean when I repeatedly say that traditional Chinese culture is an important fundamental frame of reference for human beings to construct the next phase of civilization's stable continuation and safe survival.

If you stand in this perspective and think back to what I just said about Confucius' virtue oriented culture actually discussing the problem of overcoming intra-species human competition and the problem of coordination, then you will be able to understand a quote that Confucius once said that you would find too absurd today, "Don't worry about scarcity but about uneven, and don't worry about poverty but about unrest." He said that the stability of human society need not worry about the scarcity of goods, but about the uneven distribution; he also said that the survival of human society need not worry about being poor and plain, but about living in an increasingly shaking and uneasy way of life. What does it mean by restlessness? It is the growing uneasiness, anxiety, instability, and crisis. It is the opposite concept of industrial and commercial civilization, which pursues wealth and encourages competition.

Returning to the maintenance of basic human survival, what Confucius' doctrine discusses and proposes are the most fundamental and the most relevant issues to survival stability. This is why we find that the more capable species in biological history, the faster they become extinct, because their intraspecific competition becomes more and more intense. This is why the Chinese culture of low intelligence and emphasis on virtue existed steadily for 2,000 to 3,000 years without ever being interrupted, while ancient Greece was surprisingly wiped out abruptly in the fourth century B.C. This is why the more developed our civilization is today, the more we are today far removed from agricultural civilization, our wealth is enormous, our capabilities are high, but humanity faces a heavy fundamental crisis, to the point of facing an existential crisis of humanity as a whole. Obviously, from the perspective of this frame of reference, the future survival of mankind is faced with such a dilemma: the dilemma of how to choose between rapid development and stable maintenance.

We're going to summarize this lesson below. Please understand what I am talking about when I explain Confucius. The reason why I gave Confucius' culture a very high evaluation is that human culture is nothing but a product of the structure of survival, which I repeatedly emphasized in the first class. This is the reason why I said that Hegel could not read Confucius and gave him such a low opinion. This is because the industrial and commercial structure of survival in the West is completely different from the purely agricultural structure of survival in China.

And I have repeatedly emphasized that the structure of survival that I am talking about is never the concepts of productivity and relations of production. Because, using this theory of matching productive capability with relations of production, we clearly see that it is problematic. China, for example, and most of the Eastern countries in the world now, for example, which are currently tens of thousands or hundreds of thousands of times more productive than they were in ancient Greek times, have not established the ancient Greek system, the Roman republican system, or the constitutional system or superstructure that the West has today. It shows clearly that this doctrine is a major paradox.

The structure of survival refers to the sum of natural survival dynamics and spontaneous derivative elements, and the system of adaptation of the degrees of existence and compensation. There is a relationship between this and the social and cultural development of human beings. As for what I mean by "the sum of natural survival dynamics and spontaneous derivative elements", what really is its meaning, you will have to read *A Unified Theory of Evolution*. Here I just want to tell you that to understand Confucian culture, you have to understand the general elements of the provisions of the ancient Chinese agricultural survival and its historical rationality, which is a basis and a model for you to understand Chinese culture, human civilization, and all these connotations of the frame of reference of the changes in the human world.

And you also have to remember that any culture is a temporal category, and the evolution of human civilization is a natural process or spontaneous process, and I said this in my first class. Human civilization is not the result of human choice. You don't have a choice, you can't stop it even if you want to. For this reason, all great human cultures will eventually fail, they must be effective only within a time frame, they must initially maintain survival, and later they must impair survival. Why did Chinese culture decline in modern times? It was because it seriously hindered the Chinese people's transition from an agricultural civilization to an industrial and commercial civilization, so it was eventually abandoned.

Why, at the beginning of the lecture, I talked about the group of scholars of the New Culture Movement, the group of scholars of the Republic of China who brought down Confucius' doctrine, whom we have to highly respect if we stand on the progressivist position, is because they cleaned up the old traditional Chinese culture and made it possible for the transformation of Chinese society to be realized relatively smoothly. Let me give you an example. The ancient civilizations of India, of Egypt, of the two rivers, they are much more in decline today than China. India was ruled by the British for a long time, one of the official languages in India today is English, India is also a country of democracy, but it has all kinds of problems with its social development, why? The ancient civilization of Egypt, the earliest ancient civilization, its social situation today is disordered and its development is confused, why? They did not thoroughly clean up its traditional culture. The Chinese, by constantly reflecting on and cleaning up their traditional culture in the early part of the last century, have to some extent removed the ideological and cultural obstacles to social transformation, which led to the modern revolutionary movement and the rapid progress of reform and opening up in China, which we should pay attention to and understand. So when we talk about the high value of traditional culture, please remember that it is a temporal category in the evolutionary development of human society, not an eternal value.

At the same time, we should never underestimate its role in becoming the "basic reference system of human civilization and culture". In recent times, two terms *dross* and *essence* have been used constantly in discussing traditional Chinese culture. But no scholar can really say which parts of traditional Chinese culture are the *essence* and which things are the *dross*. In fact, the dross and the essence can only be viewed in this way: whenever you take ancient culture and apply it directly, what it expresses is dross; but whenever you take its underlying ideas and use them as a humanistic reference system, its bits and pieces are the essence.

Let me give you an example. If you take the *separation of men and women* and use it today, isn't that a joke? Isn't it dross? You take *rule by virtue* and use it today to oppose *rule by law*, is it not dross? Isn't it a joke? However, if you look at it in the opposite way, with a frame of reference, it is all the essence. The failure to maintain the culture of emphasis on virtue, which is the base of human survival, marks the overall crisis of human civilization in the ideological and cultural form. Therefore, I repeat, at the level of social operation, if we copy the ancient culture and apply it directly without discrimination, the best culture will be the dross; at the level of ideological reference system, the bits and pieces of traditional culture are the base level reference system for the ultimate evaluation on a large scale, so that it appears to be all the essence. This is how we see and evaluate traditional culture.

The way I talk about Confucius today, first of all, the general context of the time in which Confucius lived; the first great social transformation of the pre-Qin era in China; the three basic elements of Confucianism that combined the original human culture; the hotbed and soil of the East Asian existential structure in which Confucian culture took place; a brief biography of Confucius and an evaluation of his practical merits; the blood kernel and old-fashioned strength of Confucian doctrine; the historical rationality of Confucian thought; and, finally, the significance of the foundational reference system of culture of emphasizing virtue is discussed.

If you have listened to this lesson on this series, you have a better understanding of what kind of spiritual underpinnings Confucius and Confucian doctrine really are, and what a rich system of cultural connotations it is. From now on you have a basic understanding of Confucianism and Confucian texts and an orientation to reading them.

Okay, we'll leave time for questions and answers.

Q & A After Class

Questioner: If Confucian culture is so powerful, why has it not ensured that Chinese society is not in turmoil? Why has the Confucian culture not been shaken even though Chinese society has been in turmoil?

Mr. Dongyue: Social unrest is the constant state, because *society* is the weakest natural structure (see *A Unified Theory of Evolution*, Volume 3). What I call social unrest in my class is that the more advanced the social form, the more fragile and volatile, it is compared to historical development, and the more primitive the social form, the less volatile it is, so there is no such thing as an unshakable society. Chinese society has also been volatile and progressive, but why it has not been able to shake Confucian culture for thousands of years, only shows the primitive stability of Confucianism and its strong stabilizing effect. I will focus on this issue in my class on Legalism tomorrow.

Questioner: Hello, Mr. Dongyue! Through your lectures on Western philosophy, I learned that a large part of your *A Unified Theory of Evolution* is based on the logic of Western philosophy, and then an argument is made. But our course is just the opposite, we have four classes to learn about our own Chinese culture while we learn about the West and the East, but only one class to learn about Western philosophy, I am curious why we should have spent more time to learn about our own culture.

Mr. Dongyue: You should never take my class as a class on Chinese culture, I am not a master of Chinese culture, and I am not a professional scholar who studies Chinese culture. As I said, I only study philosophy and the history of human thought, taking traditional Chinese culture as one of the branches. You listen to this class, a total of 12 days of lectures, and listen to it as cultural anthropology. The reason why I am biased in the part of Chinese culture is that people are closer to it, and it is easier to communicate with its lineage of thought, so using Chinese traditional culture to sort out human civilization will make people feel easier and understand it more plainly and transparently. I said on the back cover of the third edition of *A Unified Theory of Evolution*, which is not printed in the current fourth edition, that my philosophical system is constructed by applying the Chinese concept of *the unity of heaven and man* and the Western method of logic and discernment. As I said earlier that the principle of weakening compensation, that is, my philosophical system, seems to me to be very simple, so when I first finished my work, I thought that this theory should have been discovered in the West long ago. However, I have not found any similar literature after a long search. It is because Westerners do not have the conservative thinking that characterizes the East. My work is not only a product of Western philosophy, but also a product of Eastern culture. It is only because the presentation is a Western academic hypothetical proof system, a philosophical discursive system, that you can read it and feel that it is mainly a Western philosophical state. The reason why I give less lectures on Western philosophy, only two days, and more courses on Chinese culture is that the thinking of Western philosophy does not easily fit with ours, so I only give a basic account. If you are interested in it, you have to go and build your own deep study after the class in the future. If I systematically conduct a class on Western philosophy, the major part of class will doze off, and the lecture will be unsustainable. As long as you listen to this class with such a goal in mind, you are not studying Chinese culture, you are not studying Western philosophy, and even the philosophy of the human body and Indian Buddhism that I will talk about later, are not the focus of these courses, but you have to look at it as cultural anthropology, to see what is going on in human civilization? What exactly are the trends and orientations? If you look at this lecturess series with such a vision and mindset, you can really understand what each lesson is actually about.

QUESTIONER: Hello, Mr. Dongyue! You said that we are in the midst of the second great social transformation, can you talk about what the future direction of the second great transformation might look like?

MR. DONGYUE: I say that the second great transformation of Chinese society has not been completed so far. Because the Opium War was only 170 years ago, and the first social transformation took 300 to 500 years, the second social transformation has not been completely completed. What is the second social transformation?

The transition from an agricultural civilization to an industrial and commercial civilization, from an autocratic monarchy to a republican and democratic system, and from a traditional culture to a future culture, is very complex and turbulent. So what are its prospects? Simply put, China is today undergoing a high rate of commercialization and free-marketization. Although the state economy still dominates, and although marketization is not deep, it is not easy to have made such a turnaround through a hundred years of revolution and thirty or forty years of reform. The political system, the democratic system, has obviously not been established, and the system of parliament and elected government has not really been established, so I said that this transformation has not yet completed.

But we should note that the development of human civilization is accelerated, the transformation of agricultural civilization to industrial and commercial civilization, human beings took thousands of years to complete, or to have these two transformations. Since China was very stubborn in guarding its agricultural civilization, it was not until the West opened the doors of China with its firm ships and cannons that China began to transform in modern times, a very painful transformation, even the ideology and culture, the national character and the personality of the country had to be transformed, so this transformation was very painful and the Chinese tossed and turned for 170 years. But since this progress is accelerated, we can imagine, or predict, that the transition of mankind from industrial and commercial civilization to post-industrial and commercial civilization, which is the next phase of civilization as I have repeatedly said in class, will be very fast, because we have seen today the undermining effect of the culture of industrial and commercial civilization. As I have said time and again before, any culture is a time domain, maintaining survival in the early stage and undermining it in the late stage. Western industrial and commercial civilization and industrial and commercial culture have already brought deep disasters to mankind today, so I doubt if the development of industrial and commercial civilization today will give the Chinese people a few hundred years to transform steadily. It is very likely that before the transformation of Chinese industrial and commercial civilization is completed, the next post-modern transformation will be forced to occur and surge into the tide. So I hope you will understand my lecture, as I am more concerned with the ideological construction of the third social transformation of human beings in the future.

Questioner: Hello, Mr. Dongyue! As you said, morality is the basic provision that sustains human survival, and human evolution is an irreversible process of human social development, so if we want to delay the extinction of humanity, then with the largest scale of human survival, should it be the evolution of civilization, the moral compensation is also progressive? The moral provision of the first agricultural civilization of mankind was based on family, clan, tribe, and state under these organizational ties that human beings did not eat human beings, and members of clan groups did not conduct incest, then the moral provision of the second industrial and commercial civilization should be replaced by law. I wonder if the morality for the future third technological civilization that mankind needs to build should be a larger scale based on the morality that every man does not commit crimes and benevolent to others across races and regions?

Mr. Dongyue: Okay, first of all, let me say that *weakening evolution* has two meanings: first, the process of progress is the process of catastrophizing the intensification of crisis; second, the process of progress is unstoppable; these two meanings are both contained in it. Therefore, we can be sure that the culture of emphasis on virtue is a culture with a low degree of compensation; the culture of science and technology is a culture with a high degree of compensation, and the degree of compensation will only get higher. Then if mankind still wants to seek full stability of survival in the future, if it still wants not to be wiped out by its own civilization, then mankind must take the ancient culture as the original reference system, and reconstruct the structure of human culture and civilization, although this process is by no means to retrogress. That is, I said that Laozi's doctrine had serious shortcomings, and he thought that there was a way to go back. But my theory of weakening evolution makes it clear that there is no way to go back, as the evolution is one way movement. So, it is impossible for human beings to retreat from industrial and commercial civilization to agricultural civilization. It is impossible to replace commercial and industrial civilization with agricultural civilization to sustain mankind, which will always be an illusion. But mankind can overcome the inherent drawbacks of its own culture according to the problems exposed by industrial and commercial civilization, and seek the next phase of survival without blocking the generational gain of compensation and without rapidly pushing itself to extinction, which is obviously the most significant issue facing mankind in the future, and it is much more important than the science, politics, and economy that concern mankind today. This is why I said in *The Decline of Humankind* that a post-state, post-capital and post-scientific era is coming.

Questioner: Mr. Dongyue, I heard you mainly elaborate on geographical condition, agricultural civilization and moral ethics, which is more like a compass and a measure of moral ethics. I have a question that between blood and bloodline, the *heritage of filial piety* has been neglected in such an explanation system.

Mr. Dongyue: Listen to my lecture, I talk about the core of the whole Confucian culture, which is the bloodline culture, that is, the construction of bloodline culture, that is, to reorganize the bonds of the super bloodline social structure with the bloodline culture. The strength of Confucian culture is most importantly expressed in the bloodline culture, which I should say has been emphasized very heavily. It is very obvious that the development of industrial and commercial civilization today is a deconstruction of the social and cultural structure of the bloodline. Who today would still confine their social life to blood relations? Who else still speaks of filial culture? If an adult today raises a child and wants the child to help him in his old age, I say he must be out of his mind, he simply can't do it. Not only he can't do it, but what are we seeing today? Not only is the old ethnic culture disintegrating, the family system disintegrating, but even the core family is gradually disintegrating. Divorce rates are increasing, the number of dinks who don't have children is growing, and celibacy is prevalent. The process of blood dilution and blood fading in human society is very obvious. And blood ties are an animal ties structure that actually expresses the safest and most serene structure of social existence. But I hope that you will not be influenced by this course, that you will not end up going home to a culture of filial piety, that you will not expect your sons and daughters to provide for your old age. In industrial and commercial civilization, parents only raise up their children, and children only raise up their grandchildren, never the parents. If you still expect your children to take care of you when you're old, and still try to seek practical survival benefits in your bloodline, you are bound to have trouble later. It is important for you to listen to my class and understand the reason why the flux of human thought occurs. In my Confucius class, I've talked enough about the inner meaning of bloodline patriarchal ritual culture. To hear and understand it is not to manipulate it retrospectively, but to understand the meaning of its base layer of reference system.

Questioner: Einstein once said that in the future field of knowledge, Newtonian mechanics, relativity and quantum mechanics will be revised, and the laws of statistical mechanics are eternal, which is now said to be statistical physics, to supplement this information, when reading the book, *A Unified Theory of Evolution*, what do you think?

Mr. Dongyue: I am relatively new to the statistical physics you mentioned, and I cannot answer this question. Humankind is highly concerned about the development of science today; can we think that the development of science has come to an end? The survival problem facing humanity in the future will never be the problem of insufficient development of science, but the problem of excessive development of science. Therefore, I say that the post-scientific era is coming. I cannot comment on the question you raised, because I am not familiar with the subject you mentioned, and if you have researched in this area, then I hope you will write it down and use your article to make me understand your question.

Questioner: In the context of the second great civilizational transition, how should we as an integrative human race seek for internal consolidation and external adaptation of individuals, communities, organizations, and especially families? Thank you!

Mr. Dongyue: As I said in my lecture, a theorist cannot be practical, and a pragmatist cannot be theoretical. As a theorist, I am actually clueless when anyone looks to me for answers in their personal social behavior. I just want to make one point here: most of the outstanding men in human history, or the heroes in history, were people who mastered new ideas. I have given many examples of this, and my doctrine, as a new system of thought in modern society, may become a logical signpost for you in your social life if you are familiar with it. As for how it can provoke your thinking and become a guide in your life and behavior, it is up to you to digest it according to your actual situation, and I really have nothing to say about it. My doctrine is completely contrary to today's mainstream culture, which speaks of competition and development, and is all about progressivism, and the direction of operation of human society today is completely consistent with the dynamic that I want to criticize in my doctrine. I am at a loss as to how people living in today's social and cultural tide should understand and practice my doctrine. Therefore, I say in my book that my book is written for posterity, and that people of today reading it may instead get themselves into some trouble, and for that I apologize to my students!

Questioner: After listening to your lecture today, I have a feeling that the scientific era will lead humanity to a rapid demise. But I wonder now if it is possible to alleviate this extinction in the next era, and to solve this relationship within the human race through the traditional Chinese culture. We are now rapidly dividing, but isn't it possible that the traditional Chinese culture can find a frame of reference within it that can solve, or at least slow down, that decline and destruction? Is this a direction?

Mr. Dongyue: You are very right. This is what I mean when I speak of Chinese culture as having declined long ago, and I speak at the same time of Chinese culture as an important frame of reference for the future of human thought and the re-creation of future civilization. So, Chinese culture has its value, but not on a superficial operational level. I have elaborated on this point at the end of this lesson, and I hope that in the course of your study you will make sure that you understand where the two concepts of dross and essence are implemented.

Questioner: Hello, Mr. Dongyue! The current family situation in China is mostly one-child, which is very similar to the fragmentation of blood ties in the West that you talked about earlier. For example, children from the mainland may go to the coast to work, and in fact, parents and children are separated from each other. So after such a fragmented humanistic structure like that of the West, what are the things that can be tapped to inherit and develop the doctrine of Confucius that will be more suitable for this future evolution? Thank you.

Mr. Dongyue: I really can't answer that. I can only say that Chinese society is undergoing the transformation of industrial and commercial civilization today, and Confucian doctrine or traditional Chinese culture is a typical cultural system of agricultural civilization, and you can't copy it directly at the application level. Many students ask me a question: How should I educate my children? Which aspect should be emphasized, Chinese or Western studies? In terms of social survival security and social adaptability of your children, I have to advise you that Western studies should be the main focus and Chinese studies should be secondary. Because your children will be competing for survival in the structure of industrial and commercial civilization, Chinese culture is an agricultural civilization system, which is very poorly adapted to the current survival structure, so I am afraid that learning Chinese studies and traditional Chinese culture should not be the main course for your children. But if your child knows some of the essence of Chinese culture, it may be beneficial to the future development of future generations, making him characteristically heavier and more profound, and it will play a complementary role, that's all I can say.

Questioner: I would like to ask if there is any possibility for mankind to save itself after embarking on the path of no return in scientific development. Is there any possibility of religious beliefs in this regard? I don't know which religion Mr. Dongyue advocates.

Mr. Dongyue: On the issue of religious beliefs, I will discuss it in my Buddhism class. I declare now that I am not religious, and any religion to me is just a research material for the original human culture, and will not constitute my faith. Whether religion can save the world or not, we will talk about this topic in the Buddhism class.

Questioner: Mr. Dongyue, let me ask a question. As a student of Mr. Dongyue, we all have studied the formula of weakening compensation, is it possible to have a precise and simple formula like $E=mc^2$ or $F=ma$ to describe the trend of weakening compensation of human and biological evolution, so as to draw the curve of weakening compensation into a relatively standard and scientific coordinate system.

Mr. Dongyue: As I have said repeatedly in my lectures, that my doctrine is a philosophical system, why is it a philosophy and not a science? It is because there is not enough information to bring in the parameters, it is a forward-looking study of an uncertain problem. And I have also said that this parameter will definitely appear in the future as the amount of information increases, and when this parameter gradually appears, the mathematical model that I have given will definitely have a more accurate correction. If these parameters are obtained, and if the mathematical model can be implemented precisely, it should be able to calculate not only the degree of existence and the degree of compensation of each biological species and human beings, as well as their respective masses in the universe and their prospects, and it should also be able to calculate the degree of existence of all matter, including all kinds of inorganic substances, and their entire mass distribution. But I can hardly call it a science anymore, because I think the emergence of my doctrine marks the end of the scientific era. I repeat, the future will be a post-scientific culture, but I cannot say now what the future post-scientific culture will look like. Therefore, even if my doctrine were to be substituted with the parameters one day, I believe it would not be a continuation or supplement of scientific culture.

Questioner: The question I would like to ask is, in what way will the post-state, post-capital, and post-science era that you predict come? In this process, what role can each of us play as subjects of human society?

Mr. Dongyue: If you read my *A Unified Theory of Evolution*, you should know that the margin of mankind to operate in the future is very narrow, that is to say, if the law of weakening compensation is a natural law, the possibility of mankind to modify this natural law is extremely low, or even impossible, and this is the great problem faced by future generations. But if we insist on advancing our own rapid development, according to this natural law, it will bring major disasters to human beings, so what should we do? On this topic, I expressed it in a less confident way in the book *The Decline of Humankind*, which you can find and read if you are interested. It is very difficult to publish now, and only the old editions of the past are still available in *Fuzhou Useless Space*. I just want to emphasize one point here: all civilizational forms and social behaviors of human beings, including ideological trends and cultural effects, you have to equally consider it as a product of this natural law. That is to say, mankind's review of modern civilization is also a result of natural evolution. In this sense, mankind will certainly deal with this problem in the future, but in what way and with what effectiveness he will deal with it, we cannot say now, we can only provide a basic theory for future reference and exploration.

Questioner: I have a small question after reading the third volume of your book *A Unified Theory of Evolution*, but it is the most important question for me. In your book, you mentioned that the social structure will become more and more complex and intensive in the future, and in the section of *Great Common*, you mentioned that after the gradual differentiation of autonomous attributes, they will be divided into each individual, and the efficiency or substitutability between individuals will become higher and higher. Is there a contradiction between the system and the individual? Or maybe there is some mistake in my understanding. Thank you, sir.

Mr. Dongyue: The key here is that you have to understand the concept of *degree of structure*. In my book, I said that human society is only the final compensatory form of the natural structuring process. Particle structure, atomic structure, molecular structure, cellular structure, organism structure, social structure, it evolves, layers upon layers, showing a trend of increasing complexity; at the same time, as the rate of differentiation increases, the structural system becomes more and more fragile and shaky; these two are not contradictory at all. The problem can be solved by clarifying the concept of structure degree and the relationship between structure degree and differentiation degree. I can't say now in which chapter I have specifically discussed the relationship between structural degree and differentiation degree, that is, the leftward and rightward leaning of structural differentiation degree, find out these chapters and read them, it may help to understand this problem.

Questioner: I have a question here. Mr. Dongyue said at the beginning of this lesson that the emergence of the legal system is a step backward in human development, and there is no need to envy the West, some developed countries in terms of legal system. But I have a doubt, we often go to some developed countries, see people and nature, people and animals live in harmony, there are quite high costs of breaking the law, so we can see the green mountains and water there. In the ancient countries of our eastern civilization, an air, water, food problems are becoming more and more serious, there is an anxiety in my heart, though we proposed the rule of law, what can we expect the future of the road in the end? In the future development of human beings, is it morality that upholds human beings? Or is it the law that protects human beings? Can the emergence of the rule of law promote the progress of human beings, or is it a regression, as you said? I am a little confused. Thank you, Mr. Dongyue!

Mr. Dongyue: I think you have misunderstood this part. I have repeatedly said that the legal society is a product of progress, not regression, so it is inevitable that human beings will move towards the legal society. I am just saying that the legal society is the same process of moral degradation of human beings, the time when *people avoid and shameless* as described by Confucius, and I am not wrong at all. Think about it yourself, is it a product of progress or a product of regression? So I also said in the end, today's rule by virtue is pure fantasy, you can only enter the legal society today, the legal system in future will become more and more detailed, but you will never get the survival advantage. How did the West get green mountains and green water? It is the result of transferring polluting industries to newly developing countries. If China wants to control the environment today, polluting enterprises have to be pressed, where? It must move to more backward countries and regions. Therefore, it is crucial not to do situational evaluation, not to limit to a small scale, but to do the ultimate evaluation on a large scale. Please note that in my lectures, there is absolutely no reactionary meaning, my doctrine is precisely talking about why you can not be reactionary even if you want to! Please do understand this point.

Questioner: I have a question regarding the book *A Unified Theory of Evolution*. You once said that any philosopher's theory has some implicit assumptions in addition to his axioms, for example, Euclid's geometry implies that the world is flat. Are there some important implicit assumptions in *A Unified Theory of Evolution*, besides the finite range of sustaining, and the assumption that existence is imperfect to begin with and that it is not nothing in any case, is there any other important implicit assumption? Or what is the case of the logical poles in *A Unified Theory of Evolution*?

Mr. Dongyue: I gave a hypothetical proof system, and I tried to be logically rigorous, so I said that, mathematically and logically, the highest degree of existence can only converge to one, and the lowest degree of existence can only converge to zero. This statement may imply some deeper underpinning elements, which may be deeper than the existing scientific concepts such as the law of entropy increase, mass-energy equation, evolutionary theory, etc. I cannot say this issue is clearly now. I only say that everything in the universe is in process of weakening evolution and exists only in a finite interval of non-spatial and temporal sustaining, and human is a species on the right side of the critical line of non-existence. As for how humans exist and survive on this critical line, I cannot give a detailed description of this topic without the substitution of specific parameters. This may be something that can be studied clearly by future generations.

Questioner: My question is: From the perspective of human civilization, how do you see the seemingly contradictory issue I am going to talk about? The first aspect of this contradiction is that Confucian civilization in China is not essentially supportive of industrial and commercial civilization, that is, the Confucian culture of the so-called agricultural civilization, which is actually anti-industrial and commercial civilization, and industrial and commercial civilization is the other extreme. But on the other hand, in the past 40 years, China's industry and commerce, or at least the progress of its material civilization, has achieved almost nothing in the history of mankind in the past 40 years. From the perspective of human civilization, what do you think about these two seemingly contradictory things? Thank you!

Mr. Dongyue: No contradiction! I think China is now undergoing a rapid transformation of its industrial and commercial civilization, and therefore its material and wealth creation is very large, and it is the result of this rapid transformation of its industrial and commercial civilization. At the end of the course, I said that in the early 1900s, China cleaned up its traditional culture by "knocking down Confucius' doctrine", which is the reason why China's modern social transformation is relatively successful among the traditional ancient countries. In fact, China has abandoned its traditional culture long ago, but there are some root things that it could not get rid of even if it wanted to. Please note that China's development today does not rely on traditional culture, but is oriented towards learning from the West, though not thoroughly, but with a vigor that is more Western than the West, more radical than the West, in such a way that it is undergoing transformation. The so-called forty years of rapid development, even faster than the West, there is a misunderstanding that needs to be clarified, that you are not a pioneer, you are a learner, you are a follower. The difficulty of learning from others, and exploring the path at the forefront, is completely different, hence China's rapid breakthrough in imitating and learning from the West. The Chinese must not be proud of this thing, because you are taking what others have readily available and applying it. That is why I said in *The Decline of Humankind* that China's social transformation today comes at a time when industrial and commercial civilization is moving from an ascending period to a descending period, that is, when industrial and commercial civilization is going to bring negative effects to mankind, and China is following it. In the long run, it may not be a blessing for China. In the immediate term, we gain certain benefits, and in the long term, what damage it will bring us is yet to be reassessed in the future. I suggest you read *The Decline of Humankind*.

Well, that concludes our Confucius lesson for today.

Legalism and Social Implementation of National Culture

Preamble

We are talking about Legalists today.

Since among the hundred schools of thought of the pre-Qin era, those who had the greatest influence later on the survival and development of Chinese society were Laozi, Confucius and Han Feizi, we set up a special lecture on Legalists. The process of Legalism occurred as a political operation in the early days, and was not summarized as a theoretical system by Han Feizi until the end of the Warring States period. Therefore, we discuss today's class on Legalists in two parts, the first half on the political operation of Legalists, and the second half on Han Feizi's legalism theory system.

The emergence of Legalism marks the retreat of Confucianism into the background, just as the emergence of Confucianism marks the retreat of Laozi's doctrine into the background. What does this phrase mean?

As we mentioned earlier in the Laozi class, Laozi's doctrine advocates a return to small states with less population, to the primitive clan society of mankind, to the state of existence before civilization occurred. This had obviously become a cliff by the Spring and Autumn period, and everyone knew that this path was not feasible. Therefore, although Laozi's doctrine is the closest to the ultimate inquiry, it could only be used as a conceptual background, laying at the bottom of the doctrines of the hundred schools of thought in Chinese society.

Confucius' doctrine explicitly states that *I prefer Zhou*, and he was highly affirmative of the civilized society of East Asia and its feudal political system, and he was actively involved in the social transformation movement of the Eastern Zhou states. Although he also advocated a return to the early days of the Western Zhou Dynasty when Duke Zhou Jidan made rituals and music, he recognized the *fait accompli* of civilizational development after all.

As I said, the doctrine of Confucius is a theoretical rectification of the *rites and music* of Duke Zhou Jidan in the early years of the Western Zhou Dynasty. I also said that the so-called *ritual* refers to the social law of revere revered and love loved; the so-called *music* is said in the original ancient texts to mean music is also a general ethics, that is to say, *music* is not just simple music, but refers to large social rituals and their music, which expresses the ideological declaration. Confucius systematized the ritual culture, and the core of his doctrine is *revere revered and love loved*. This seemingly artificial rational system is in fact a direct continuation and transmission of the animal blood society. What does it mean? Think about the primate society, the apes and monkeys also have to deal with the blood relations within the community to make it stable and harmonious, how do they deal with it? First of all, it is *love loved*, that is, be close to those who are related to each other. In primate societies, monkeys groom each other's fur and help catch lice, why? It is just to show affection to the kinship. The next step is *revere revered*, that is, respecting those who have honorable positions. Monkey society, ape society, as a rule, also obey and respect the power of the blood clan leader, which is the monkey king. It can be seen that "revere revered and love loved" is typical of the spontaneous pattern or natural order of animal blood kin society. The ritual culture was expressed as *revere revered and love loved*, obviously inheriting the inherent, moderate structure of this animal society and later rationalized into the old structure of *rule by virtue*. It was also characterized by the same moderate and orderliness of superiority and inferiority, aiming at smoothing out competition by means of this intra-group repressive relationship.

However, with the high development of agricultural civilization, in the pre-Qin and Spring and Autumn Periods, the population developed on a large scale, the class hierarchy was divided, interpersonal and resource relations gradually became more and more tense, and the competition in human society became more and more fierce, or even worse, so legalism began to emerge and forcefully put up the banner of *rule by law*. So Confucianism, which advocates *ruling by virtue*, receded into the background because it is too soft.

Since the doctrine of legalism fundamentally reveals an extremely dark reference system at the base of human nature, it reveals the great inferiority of human nature. Therefore, it is necessary for us to study it, examine it, and understand it, so that we can have a more profound outlook on the internal state of human civilization itself and its development prospects.

The core of the doctrine of Legalism lies in "jurisprudence of centralized power", that is, the axis of the centralized power system lies in "the rule of kings or lords". Let me first explain the character "王" (Wang) *King* in the oracle bones inscriptions. "Confucius once made a commentary on the character "王", saying that the upper horizontal stroke represents heaven, the lower horizontal stroke represents earth, and the middle horizontal stroke represents the man who communicates with heaven and earth, and that the vertical stroke represents the communication between heaven and earth. However, we cannot find this symbol in the oracle bone inscriptions, so obviously Confucius was wrong. The earliest form of the character "王" that we see in the oracle bone inscriptions is like this (甲文 金文 小篆 楷体). What does this figure depict? What does an axe mean? It means the right to kill one's own people internally, and the one who has this power is called *king*. It can be seen that when human civilization entered the era of the Three Emperors and the Five Sovereigns, as well as Yao, Shun and Yu, the kings alike, violence control has gradually become an important tool in the internal structure of human society.

Note also that the original concept of the word *Fascist* (Latin for fasces), which was never the term of the popularized meaning in World War II; it was originally derived from the name of the scepter of the ancient Roman magistrate. The scepter with an axe head in the middle of a bundle of sticks appeared in ancient Rome and was called the *fasces*. This scepter was called *fascism,* and it marked the emergence of the idea of violent control of mankind in both the East and the West. The original meaning of *fascism* expresses or symbolizes the supremacy of the sovereign, of the state, of power, of violence, and it is the product of such a civilizational structure. Thus, the system of kings, the fascist system, expresses the new stage of human beings moving from *rule by virtue* to *rule by law*, that is, the control of society by harsh laws.

The Origin and History of Legalism

The first Chinese legalism occurred in the late Spring and Autumn period, roughly the same time as Confucius. The reason why Confucius emphasized *ruling by virtue* was to counter the first signs of *ruling by law*. There is a sentence in the *Annals by Zuo Qiuming*: "In the past, the previous kings' system was to deliberate things, not by means of punishment". In the early days of human civilization, or even earlier before that, there were no strict laws in human bloodline social groups, and the social management model was like this: the bloodline patriarch, i.e., the old mother and grandmother in matrilineal society, and the old father and grandfather in patrilineal society, was the administrator of the group. When the clan encounters any problem, the patriarch will bring all the adults together to discuss and deal with the social problems together. There was no violent control and no harsh laws. This is called "previous kings' system was to deliberate things, not by means of punishment". By the middle of the Spring and Autumn period, this situation was already clearly unsustainable.

At this time, private ownership had already emerged, and privatization of land was widespread, as the history books say, "The public field boundaries were canceled, and the land was redivided." In Laozi's class, I talked about "井田" (Jing Tian), *井-shaped public land system*, which was actually the remnant of the original clan society, and by the Zhou Dynasty, at least one-ninth of the *井- shaped public land* was still preserved. By the middle and end of the Spring and Autumn period, the *井-shaped* public field system had almost completely collapsed. The so-called "开阡陌" meant that the public land was divided into private land using land ditch as the boundary. This led to the emergence of the landowning class and the tension between different classes, while the political landscape of each state was also complicated, the social transformation of "punishment to senior scholar officials" occurred. According to *Annals of Zuo Qiuming*, in the 6th year of the reign of Duke Zhao, "Zheng people cast the written law of punishment." The so-called "Zheng people cast the written law of punishment" refers to the first time that Zichan, the prime minister of state Zheng, established the written law of punishment by casting inscriptions on bronze vessels, which is called "cast the written law of punishment". The content of Zichan's legislation, his "law of Punishment" has been lost.

So let's look at the earliest legislation of Zichan in the state of Zheng, what was the reaction of the society? In the early Qin Dynasty, there was a collection of folk songs *public recitation*, we see such a recitation: "take my clothes as property tax, take my field as land tax, who kills Zichan, I will follow him". What is the meaning of this folk song? It says, Zichan deprived me of my family property by legislation of the property tax, deprived me of my real estate by legislation of the land tax, if anyone can kill Zichan, I am willing to give up everything to help him to follow him. This shows that the initial entry into the grim era of ruling the people by law, suddenly destroyed the gentle ecology of millions of years of ruling the people by virtue, and was inevitably met with strong resentment from the people at the bottom. However, later in the collection of folk songs *public recitation*, we find another song, which is supposed to be within a few years after the previous one, but the situation has changed. It reads: "I have young boys and sons, and Zichan taught them; I have fields, and Zichan cultivated them; when Zichan dies, who will inherit him". It says, I have young boys and sons, I want Zichan to teach them; I have fields, I want to be instructed by Zichan on what to plant, and if Zichan dies, who will inherit his business. We find that at this time in the same collection of folk song *public recitation*, the evaluation of Zichan's legislation produces a clear mood of embracing. It shows that the emergence of a legal society was a necessity and an appropriate and effective way to regulate social tensions after they occurred.

The *Annals of Zuo Qiuming* also records that in the 29th year of the reign of Duke Zhao, the Jin people cast the penal tripod. That is, 23 years after the Zheng cast the written law of Punishment, the state of Jin also began to legislate. As we all know, the maximum number of words cast on a bronze vessel is usually no more than three to five hundred. It can be seen that the legal provisions in the early years of mankind were very simple, only programmatic norms. The legal system of mankind became more and more complicated with the process of social structure or moral degradation, and eventually came to bind every detail of life of every person. The Jin legislation marked the beginning of the widespread implementation of the legal system in the Central Plains, and the full-scale destabilization and disorder of civilized society. Confucius thus lamented, "Jin is dying, having lost its propriety." He said that Jin was going to fall because it had lost the proper limits in the way it manages society. It was clear that Confucius resisted a society based on the rule of law and believed that the violent control of harsh laws was a damage to human civilization.

Is Confucius right in this statement? Half wrong, half right. First of all, the subsequent fall of Jin was not directly causally related to Jin's legislation, and from this point of view, Confucius' statement was incorrect. However, since human beings entered the society of the rule of law, the stability of the society has been reduced, the tension of the society has been increased, the internal contradictions and internal competition of the society have been fully erupted, and all civilized order has entered into a state of violent upsets and imbalance since then. From this point of view, Confucius' statement and lament can be regarded as true.

Although Legalism emerged at the end of the Spring and Autumn Period, it was not until the Warring States Period that Legalism as a politically practical system was really involved in depth in social management on a large scale. As you know, the so-called Warring States period refers to the final division of the state of Jin by Han, Zhao, and Wei, who hollowed out the king of state of Jin, and then established the three states of Han, Zhao, and Wei, which was confirmed by the then Emperor of Zhou Dynasty in 403 B.C. Thus, the Warring States period came. The state of Wei was thus a new state in the Warring States period, and its first ruler was named Wei Si, the famous Marquis of Wei, who appointed an important legal figure as his important minister, Li Kui, who sometimes was written in history books as Li Ke.

According to historical records, both Li Kui and Wei Si were probably disciples of Zi Xia's Xihe school. Zi Xia was a disciple of Confucius, and after the death of Confucius, Zi Xia established the Xihe school, which was the first to express the merge of the *ritual system* and the *legal system*, that is, the germ of the idea of legal system in the culture of ritual system, and finally grew matured in the doctrine of Xunzi. Li Kui thus became the first man who practiced legalism and built the theory of legalism during the Warring States period in China. As a result of Li Kui's emphasis on agriculture and law, and his reward for farming and warfare, Wei became the most powerful of all the vassal states in the early Warring States period. Li Kui was the first to change the law in the state of Wei, and he wrote the *Book of Laws*, which was the first legal book to reach a theoretical framework and detailed entries in the form of a canon. This book was later lost, and we only know a little about it indirectly through the *Book of Shang Jun* and some articles of *Han Feizi*, as well as other relevant historical materials.

Li Kui, who first changed the law in Wei, implemented some efficient policies. First of all, it was called "exhaust land and buy-sell good price", what does it mean? This is to promote the development of agriculture, to adopt the policy of agriculturalism, to encourage the reclamation of wasteland, to encourage intensive farming, this is called "exhausting the land"; the so-called "buy-sell average price", What does it mean by "average price"? It was the policy of the Legalist to protect agriculture, in good harvest years the price of grains was low, the government would buy in grains from farmers at a fair price; in bad years the price of grains soaring up in market, the government would sell grains at a fair price. The first man who established this policy to balance the fluctuation of agricultural production was Li Kui, who effectively protected the agricultural production system.

Then he established a clear system of rewards and punishments, and abolished the system of hereditary officials, and selected the best and the brightest. As I mentioned earlier, in the early days of mankind, the system was hereditary officials, and only the nobles could participate in the management of society and become officials. In the state of Wei, Li Kui was the first to abolish the hereditary system and to select and promote talents according to their abilities, which made Wei rapidly powerful. Li Kui took quite a number of specific approaches back then, and we don't have time to go into details here. I will just give you an example to see how detailed he did it. He set up a strange rule that whenever a lawsuit was tangled between the defendant and the plaintiff in the court, what should be done? The two sides held an archery contest, whoever won the archery contest, won the lawsuit. What was he doing? Encouraging civilians to train themselves to become soldiers for war. For this reason, Wei was the most powerful state among the vassal states of the Central Plains in the early Warring States period, and could be considered the first of the seven superpowers. During the period when Li Kui was the minister, he employed another important person, Wu Qi. When talking of Wu Qi, you will first think of him as a war commander, but in fact Wu Qi was an important legalist figure. Let me briefly introduce Wu Qi below.

Wu Qi was originally from the state of Wei and fled to the state of Lu after committing a murder in Wei. He was a man who liked to talk about war, so he was valued by the ruler of Lu and wanted to appoint him as a general. However, a minister advised against it, saying that Wu Qi's wife was from Qi, the enemy of Lu, and it was difficult to guarantee that he would not have different intentions. When Wu Qi heard this, he went home and killed his wife, and was finally appointed general of Lu, which is the famous story of killing his wife to seek his generalship. Wu Qi led the weak army of Lu defeated the attack of Qi, showing his strong ability to lead the army in battle. Therefore, in ancient Chinese books, whenever mentioned Sun Wu school, Sun refers to Sunzi and Wu refers to Wu Qi, and Sun Wu school refers to the military science.

Since Lu was a ritual state where Confucianism was upheld, Wu Qi was rejected later by the Lu people due to his past of killing his wife for his generalship. So he went into exile in Wei, where he was recruited by Li Kui. Together with Li Kui, Wu Qi started the earliest selection system of *Wei military men* in the state of Wei, and established a powerful military machine. Wu Qi was a very strategic general and loved his soldiers like his son, which made Wei's military power invincible. Wu Qi led the Wei army to attack state of Qin, Qin army was no rival at all. He led the Wei army break the Hangu Pass, then conquered the Tongguan Pass, all the way to the Guanzhong Plain, and finally forced Qin to cede the entire West River land to Wei, which is the famous West River County. This lost land was not regained until nine to ten years after Shang Yang's Change of Law, when Qin became stronger and Shang Yang led the Qin army finally defeated the Wei army. The Duke of Qin Xiaogong gave the land of Shangluo to Shang Yang (also known as

Wei Yang), who was then called Shang Jun. This shows how strong Wu Qi's military ability was.

Wu Qi led his soldiers and loved them as his son. There was an account in the history books that Wu Qi saw a soldier wounded and his wound festered and turned into pus, so the general leaned down and sucked the pus for the wounded soldier. When the wounded soldier's mother heard about this, she began to wail sadly. When others asked her why she wailed so sadly, the mother said that her son's father had fought in the war, and after he was wounded, Wu Qi sucked the pus for him personally with his mouth, and since then he had fought for the general regardless of his own death, and eventually he died in a battle. From this incident, we can see how deep of Wu Qi's heart in leading his troops.

Wu Qi had made great achievements in Wei. After the death of Li Kui, Wu Qi thought that he was the most qualified to succeed the ministerial post, but in vain, the next chancellor was Tian Wen, and Wu Qi argued with Tian Wen about this. After Tian Wen, Wu Qi's turn again did not come, and the third chancellor of Wei was the famous Gong Shucuo. When Gong Shucuo became the chancellor, he was a bit uneasy, so he accepted the advice of one of his disciples and met with the king of Wei, saying that Wu Qi was not originally from Wei, and that if he was not of our Wei people, he would have a different heart. If the king wanted to continue hiring him, he should give the princess to Wu Qi so as to win his heart, and if Wu Qi accepted her, it would prove that he was usable, otherwise, he should be watched with a wary eye. At this time, Wu Qi was celibate because he had previously killed his wife to win his generalship, and he was a bachelor since then. The king of Wei accepted Gong Shucuo's suggestion, but as soon as he left the palace, Gong Shucuo invited Wu Qi to be his guest, and he secretly instructed his wife to humiliate himself in front of his guest at the banquet. Gong Shucuo's wife was the princess of the Wei royal family, and as a result, Wu Qi was left with an extremely bad impression that the princess was arrogant and unworthy of a wife. Therefore, when the king of Wei later talked to Wu Qi about marrying the princess, Wu Qi flatly refused. With this despicable tactic, Gong Shucuo drove Wu Qi out of the state of Wei.

Having said this, I have to mention a historical fact. Since Wei was the earliest state to change the law and became the most powerful state in the early Warring States period, it used to have a great attraction to scholars from various states in the Central Plains at that time. The famous talents Wei concentrated at the time, including the later Shang Yang, Zhang Yi and Fan Sui, all of whom were originally hanging about in Wei but eventually left the state. I am afraid that the decline of Wei was not unrelated to its cynicism and jealousy and the loss of many talents.

Wu Qi went into exile in the state of Chu and was reappointed by the king of Chu. He first served as the governor of the county of Wan in Chu, and after a year he was promoted to the post of magistrate, the chancellor of Chu. Wu Qi then began to change the law of Chu, turning himself into a political figure of legalism rather than just a military figure. He began to establish a legal system by "clarifying the law and implementing the orders" and "reducing the titles and the wealth of the nobles" by suppressing the status and property of the original nobility. Because the noblemen would resist the new laws in the state, Wu Qi had to first weaken the power of the vested interests. How did he do it? He adopted the strategy of "returning the land after three generations". The land held by the nobles could only be inherited for three generations, and after three generations, the land has to be returned to the state, thus weakening the force of the nobles. There was another measure called "degrade ministers", that is, to exile important hereditary ministers and move them to the remote areas of Chu to prevent them from disturbing the new government. It was obvious to everyone that Wu Qi's change of law must have aroused strong opposition from the aristocratic power of Chu. He went on to "rectify the official system" and "block the private door", that is, to organize the official system of the state, not to allow the use of the inherited system, not to allow private sales of official posts; "remove the useless" and "appoint the wise", that is, to implement the system of human resources, recruiting the wise and capable; "encourage fine farming" and "support military training", like Li Kui, to develop farming in the state of Chu, and at the same time reward the military and warfare, and use the surplus to build a larger military force.

The state of Chu was located in the middle and lower reaches of the Yangtze River, and it was considered a large state during the Spring and Autumn Period because it was vast and arguably the largest in area among all the vassal states. But during the Spring and Autumn period and the early Warring States period, it rarely became a consistently strong state. The reason for this, as I mentioned in the first lesson, was that the natural weather conditions were initially not conducive to the development of agricultural civilization. Therefore, despite its vast territory, the state of Chu had a small population and was still basically a tribal state, with a weak economic base and weak mobilization power in wartime.

Wu Qi started to implement the change of law in Chu, which made the state of Chu became strong rapidly. *The Records of the Grand Historian* records that Wu Qi's change of law was only a year old, and it became so strong that Sima Qian described it in the original text: "So he pacified Baiyue in the south, merged with Chen and Cai in the north, defeated three Jin, and attacked Qin in the west. All the lords were troubled by the strength of Chu". In other words, Chu destroyed Baiyue in the south, including a large number of barbarian tribes in Lingnan region, and annexed Chen and Cai in the north, defeated the allied forces of Wei, and conquered Qin in the west.

However, Wu Qi was unlucky, for he was in Chu for less than six years when the king Dao of Chu suddenly became violently ill and died. As soon as the king died, the noble group of Chu immediately revolted and brought troops to storm the Chu palace and shot Wu Qi with arrows indiscriminately. The history books record that Wu Qi was able to destroy his political enemies even after his death. This incident refers to the fact that the rebels broke into the Chu palace and Wu Qi had nowhere to escape, so he bent over the corpse of the king Dao of Chu. The rebels shot arrows indiscriminately, killing Wu Qi and injured the corpse of the king of Chu. According to the law of Chu, anyone who wounded the king's body should be beheaded with all his clan family. Later, King Su, the next king of Chu and son of King Dao, had all the seventy-two noble families who led the rebellion beheaded, which was the story of how Wu Qi was able to destroy his political enemies even after his death.

Wu Qi's change of law in Chu was interrupted at this point. That being said, Chu was a vast country, and if the change of law was successful, then Chu was the country most qualified to eventually unify China. It is important to know that although the doctrine of Legalism took place in the five civilized states of the Central

Plain, its real implementation was limited to the relatively backward barbarian states. Because its legal theory was too harsh, the practice was too cruel, the five civilized countries of the Central Plains simply could not be implemented. This is just like Marxism happened in Germany and England in the core region of Europe, but the European and American countries could never adopt it, and as a result, it ran to the backward countries of the East and became widespread, the reason was the same. If Wu Qi had succeeded in changing the law back then, the state of Chu, as a southern barbarian, would have been expected to carry out this law change movement very thoroughly. Wu Qi's change of law was earlier than Shang Yang's change of law in Qin, so Chu's strength also came earlier than Qin's. If Wu Qi was lucky and the change of law could be sustained, then Chu was likely to replace Qin and become the first vassal state to unify China.

Even though Wu Qi's change of law failed, it was recorded in the history books that "if there are three families left in Chu, Qin will be knocked down by Chu". This means that even if only three families were left in Chu, it would be Chu people that eventually destroy the Qin Dynasty. As you know, soon after the reign of Qin Shi Huang, the war against Qin broke out and the Qin Dynasty was finally destroyed, by whom? By the Chu! Xiang Yu and Liu Bang were both Chu people. So technically speaking, the Han Dynasty was actually a dynasty established by the Chu people. That's all we have to say about Wu Qi.

Brief Introduction of Shang Yang

We will focus on Shang Yang's Change of Law.

Shang Yang's original name was Wei Yang, also known as Gong Sun Yang. It should be obvious from these two names that Shang Yang was originally from the State of Wei, and was a son of the family of the Duke Wei. I will talk a little about the State of Wei in passing. It can be said that Song and Wei were the two states with the greatest literary talent in the Spring and Autumn and Warring States period. Why I want to mention these two states in particular, because most of the heavyweight thinkers, literati and famous scholars and heroes in the hundred schools of thought of the pre-Qin dynasty in China came from these two states.

Let's look at state of Song first, as I mentioned earlier, the *Book of Zhou* records that "only the previous Yin people had books in volumes", which means that only the people of Yin Shang were literate back then. After King Wu destroyed the Shang Dynasty, he established a fiefdom for the Yin people in the land of Chao Ge, which was the state of Yin. He also appointed Wu Geng, son of King Zhou of former Yin Shang Dynasty, as the head of the state of Yin. As soon as King Wu died, Wu Geng joined forces with Guan Shu, Cai Shu and Huo Shu, the three brothers of King Wu who were stationed in the Central Plains to supervise the administration, to start a rebellion, known as the "Three Supervisors' Rebellion". Duke Zhou Jidan led his troops to put down the rebellion, killed Wu Geng, imprisoned Guan Cai, and then moved the remnants of the Yin Shang nobles to another place, which is today Shangqiu in Henan Province, and established a new state, Song. Because Song was a feudal state of the Yin Shang noblemen, it had a flourishing literary culture. The most important thinker of the pre-Qin era, Laozi, as I mentioned in my previous lesson, was probably an immigrant from Yin Shang, not from the state of Chu; Confucius, as I also mentioned, was from Song; Mozi, who was a great official of Song, is considered by most scholars to be from Song; and Zhuangzi, who was undoubtedly from Song. As you can see, most of the most important academic and intellectual talents came from the state of Song.

The second one deserves special mention is the state of Wei. Wei was one of the first feudal states after King Wu had conquered Shang. King Wu initially established a feudal system with 71 states, divided into two parts, one called the feudal state and the other called the service state. The so-called feudal states were the feudal states of King Wu's blood relatives and important ministers, mostly Ji and Jiang in family names; the so-called service states were the original large tribes of the Xia and Shang Dynasties, which were preserved and served the Zhou royal family, such as the state of Chen, which was the descendant of Shun, and the state of Qi, which was the descendant of Xia. When King Wu first divided the kingdom, he gave the most important pivotal place of Yin Shang, which is the area around Anyang today, to his dearest little brother, Kang Shu, who therefore had a great influence on the later state of Wei, and he insisted on adhering to the feudal system created by King Wu and never allowed any changes. Secondly, as I mentioned earlier, Confucius was dismissed at the age of fifty-five, and since one of his important students Zi Lu, who's two brothers were senior officials in Song, Confucius traveled around all then states and was the first to enter state of Wei, and stayed the longest in Wei, entering and leaving the state three times and running a school there for a long time, so he took in a group of important followers, including Zi Xia, in the state of Wei. This led to the overlapping of a second crop of literary lines in Wei, and thus created a unique practical talent in Wei. Some scholars believe that Guigu Zi may also be a native of Wei, while Sun Bin, Pang Juan, Su Qin and Zhang Yi were all students of Guigu Zi. We will find that Wei was truly a land of talent. However, because Kang Shu and his descendants were overly conservative, which led to Wei's steadfast refusal to change, these outstanding talents were unable to stretch in Wei, so they went away to find another stage. This is the reason why Wei Yang left Wei, through other state finally came to Qin.

Wei Yang, also known as Gongsun Yang, was a son of the Duke Wei family, that is, the noble blood of the king of Wei, but he put himself in a very low position, actually came to Wei to do a guest under the door of the chancellor Gong Shucuo. As you know, during the Warring States period, the nobility of various states had the habit of keeping guests, the most famous were the four princes of the Warring States – Plain Jun, Xinling Jun, Mengchang Jun, Chunshen Jun, they kept up to three thousand guests. A large number of idioms we have today, like imitating chicken and dog to steal, cunning rabbit have more outlets, are from the stories of these diners. Then Wei Yang put himself in a very low position. He went so far as to become a guest under Gong Shucuo, and was appointed as a minor official in the ministerial office, named Zhong Shuzi. Before going to court, Gong Shucuo would discuss the state affairs with the most capable and knowledgeable of his disciples, so that he could have a basis for his opinions in the court. He later found that Wei Yang, the youngest of his disciples, had a different opinion from the others every time, and he was the only one who could prove afterwards that his opinion was profound and true, which made Gong Shucuo a deep impression of him.

However, the powerful Gong Shucuo never recommended Wei Yang to the king of Wei. It was only when Gong Shucuo was dying of old age that the king of Wei came to see him, and Wei Yang's fate was revealed. This king of Wei was the famous King Hui of Wei, later also called King Hui of Liang. I will first briefly talk about King Hui of Wei, this person was too famous in history, although he was really a dim king, the reason why he was later called King Hui of Liang, because after the loss of Wei Yang, Qin change of law, Wei army lost the battle and lost the West River County, threatening the former capital of Wei, An Yi, forcing Wei to move the capital to Daliang, which is today's Kaifeng area, since then King Hui of Wei was also called King Hui of Liang. Why was King Hui of Wei so famous? It was all due to his act of attaching himself to the most talent men! If you read the book of Mencius, you will find a lot of chapters about the conversations between Mencius and King Hui of Wei. If you read Zhuangzi's book, there are also interviews with King Hui of Wei. King Hui of Wei even hired the famous talent gentleman Huishi as the prime minister of the state, who was a close friend of Zhuangzi. All such reasons or records made King Hui of Wei became famous in history, so we can see that attaching oneself to the talent gentlemen may also make one's name far-reaching. When King Hui of Wei came to see his prime minister Gong Suncuo, he asked, "Who will succeed you when you are 100 years old? " Gong Shucuo replied, "Wei Yang!" King Hui of Wei was shocked, as at that time, Wei Yang's name was not known outside of the ministerial office, and the state of Wei did not know who Wei Yang was. Gong Shucuo suddenly proposed to let this person succeed himself as the head of the state, the king Hui of Wei decided that Gong Shucuo was old and mind confused, so he ignored it. Then Gong Shucuo seriously said, "If you do not want to use this person I recommend to you, please kill him and do not let him leave the state." As soon as the king Hui of Wei left, he called Wei Yang to his bed and said, "I recommended you to the king Hui of Wei, but it seems that the king Hui of Wei has no intention to use you, so I have advised the king Hui of Wei to kill you. Please leave this state as soon as possible."

He had said all that he should say for the sake of the public and the state, and he also had said all that he should say for the sake of the private and friend; the rest was up to their own fate.

However, Wei Yang did not move to go, but as usual. After Gong Shucuo's death, other disciples asked Wei Yang, "Why didn't you leave when your lord told you to escape before he died? " What he replied really showed that he was talent with insight. He said, "if the king Hui of Wei despised me and did not appoint me, he would not bother to kill me, so there was no question of my personal safety." As a matter of fact, King Hui of Wei forgot who Wei Yang was next minute, so Wei Yang came to Qin easily.

Let's take a look at the situation of the state of Qin. At the time, Qin was in a state of decline and its new ruler was the Duke Xiao of Qin, whose father, the Duke Xian of Qin, probably died of injuries sustained during the war between the lords. The situation was not optimistic as Qin was severely squeezed by the Central Plains states. As I mentioned earlier, during the Spring and Autumn Period, Duke Mu of Qin was almost the hegemon of the Spring and Autumn Period, but after Duke Mu of Qin, the *Records of the Grand Historian* explicitly records that 14 successive kings fell into disarray, in the words of Sima Qian was, "the ruler and his subjects were in disarray." So by the beginning of the Warring States period, the state of Qin was already in jeopardy.

At the age of twenty-one, the Duke Xiao of Qin succeeded to the throne and he faced severe pressure of competition from the great powers. History records that in the first year of Duke Xiao became ruler of Qin, the six states held an alliance meeting, that is, the five states of the Central Plains plus Chu were present, but Qin was not invited. The history books did not record what issues were discussed at the alliance meeting, but the whole Qin state was in a panic, thinking that the meeting was to discuss how to divide the state of Qin, which shows how critical the state of Qin was at that time. Under this pressure, the Duke Xiao of Qin issued the famous Order of Recruiting Talents with the intention of recruiting talents from all states of the time. *The Records of the Grand Historian ·Annal of Qin* recorded a fragment of it: "If any of the guests and ministers can come up with a marvelous plan to strengthen Qin, I will honor him as senior official and share the land with them". This means that anyone who can come up with a miraculous plan to make Qin strong, I will appoint him to a high official position and share the land with him.

It was under this order that Wei Yang came to Qin. There were many scholars from all over the land who went to Qin, Wei Yang was only one of the unknown ones, so how could he get the favor of Duke Xiao of Qin? History records that Shang Yang went through the back door of one of Duke Xiao's courtiers. The so-called *favorite courtier* refers to either a eunuch or a minister who made fun of the king. Shang Yang went through such a humble doorway and made sure to meet with Duke Xiao. The first time meeting was not an attracting one, and Duke Xiao dozed off; the second time Duke Xiao could barely listen to him; he repeatedly asked to see him, and the third time they had a good talk; after that, they worked closely together, and thus Shang Yang's change of law began.

BRIEF DESCRIPTION OF SHANG YANG'S CHANGE OF LAW (I)

Shang Yang was capable to manipulate the change of law in Qin, the main credit should of course go to the Duke Xiao, who was only a guest minister and had no political power in Qin, and any change in law would have touched the interests of the noble group of Qin, which would cause a backlash from the noble group, all because Duke Xiao of Qin stood against it himself alone that allowed Shang Yang to safely continue the change in law, obviously Duke Xiao bore extremely great political danger and pressure.

We should know that political cooperation is very difficult, because both the benefit and risk are great. For example, the relatives or friends of ordinary people have very good relations, but once you do business and run a company, your relations with most of the friends and relatives involved in it will eventually collapse. Why? The interests are huge, and the stakes are also sensitive, so the concerned relationships are particularly prone to break down. If you look at political cooperation, the interests are even more important, so it has always been difficult to last. However, Wei Yang was really lucky, he and Duke Xiao so closely cooperated that they worked together for decades. Although Duke Xiao was under tremendous pressure and died at the age of 44, he accompanied Shang Yang to change the law for more than 20 years. As soon as Duke Xiao died, Shang Yang was revenged to death by the nobles group. The next ruler, King Huiwen of Qin, cracked Shang Yang, but the changed law already carried out in the state and it was difficult to return. King Huaiwen of Qin knew the effectiveness and value of Shang Yang's Law Change, and continued his policy without any damage, and it was continually implemented by the next six kings until King Yingzheng finally unified all the states and he named himself the First Emperor. Therefore, we can say that King Yingzheng unified the six states, put an end to the Warring States period, and established the Qin Empire, but the initial groundbreaking work was actually founded on the Change of Law by Shang Yang.

There were two characteristics of Shang Yang's actions. First, he was determined to change the law without considering his personal safety and security. Second, do not take care of personnel. As we know, a general politician should first of all be good at interpersonal relations and clever in deal with all aspects, that is, he should be able to smooth out the opponents, but Shang Yang was an exception and had no scruples. Let me give you an example. In the early days of Shang Yang's law change, he immediately ran afoul of the nobles. The nobles did not dare to resist him openly, so they urged the only son of the Duke Xiao of Qin, Prince Qin Si, who later became King Huiwen of Qin, to break the law. Shang Yang immediately pursued the matter, and since the crown prince was too young to be punished, he turned to pursue the responsibility of the crown prince's tutor and the crown prince's teacher who had failed to teach him well. The two were both quite powerful figures, one of them, Gong Ziqian was said to be the half-brother of Duke Xiao of Qin, and also the noble leader and military head of Qin. When the prince broke the law, Shang Yang pursued the case relentlessly and punished his teachers, Gong Ziqian was not convinced and acted accordingly in defiance, and Shang Yang proceeded to impose additional punishment, actually imposing cutting-off the nose. Think about it, Duke Xiao won't live a hundred years, and after Duke Xiao's death, the crown prince was to succeed the throne. The crown prince's teachers were definitely his closest staffs, Shang Yang openly tortured and humiliated the crown prince's men, which was definitely an act to end his future. This was Shang Yang's style of action, showing him determined to change the law without regard for others!

However, as I said this, you must not think that Shang Yang was a reckless person. Liang Qichao, a famous scholar during the

Republican period, once said that there were only six men in Chinese history who could be called statesmen, in other words, anyone else could only be called politicians, and Shang Yang was one of these six statesmen. It is important to know that after the establishment of the imperial system by Qin Yingzheng, (Shi Huang), only emperors alone were more than 300 in China history, plus thousands of famous ministers in the past, and if we count those vassal kings and political scholars in the pre-Qin era, where talents flourished and the stars were brilliant, the number of political figures in the history of the country should be no less than ten thousand. But Liang Qichao thought that only six men in Chinese history could be born the title of statesman, and among them was Shang Yang, which shows that Shang Yang was definitely no ordinary person.

Let me give you an example, at the beginning of Shang Yang's change of law, he set up a rafter at the south gate of Qin's capital, Liyang, that is, he set up a big log there. Let me first talk about Liyang, the original capital of Qin was in the place of Yong, which is in the area of Baoji Fengxiang in the west of Guanzhong, Shaanxi Province today. Since the Qin state was under attack from the east by the Central Plains, including the Wei army, and from the west by the barbarians, the Duke Xian of Qin, the father of Duke Xiao, had to move his wartime capital to the east of central Guanzhong, not far from today's Lishan in Lintong, and build a small city as a temporary capital. As for Xianyang, the huge capital of Qin, it was not built until after the success of Shang Yang's change of law. Then, at the south gate of Liyang, Shang Yang ordered a rafter to be erected, and then announced to the surrounded people that anyone who carried this wood to the north gate would be rewarded with ten gold. The gold in the pre-Qin era was not gold but bronze, but the amount of such one gold was equivalent to the total harvest of a farming family in a year, and ten gold was equivalent to the total harvest of a farming family in ten years, which was a rare opportunity to get rich. However, all the people gathered to watch and talked each other, but they were not moved, because it was too bizarre, and it also showed that the credibility of the Qin government was in question. Shang Yang immediately raised the reward amount to 50 gold, then a young man came out and said, "I will carry this rafter to the north gate," even if the government cheated me, there is no important loss, he thought it to himself, so he carried the rafter to the north gate along with the laughter of the crowd, Shang Yang immediately cash the reward, this person instantly became rich. This is the famous story of "setting up a rafter to establish credibility". What was Shang Yang doing? He was telling the Qin people, "I, Shang Yang, will act what I say, and I will keep my promise, so please follow the law from now on." We can see the wisdom of Shang Yang from this very small event.

When Shang Yang first came to Qin, what he saw was an uncivilized scene. In *The Records of the Grand Historian* records this: "At the time I came to Qin, it was a scene of the Western Rong uncivilized life style, father and sons lived together. I set up ritual of separation between men and women, build houses like those in Lu and Wei." This was a piece of words from *Book of Shang Jun*, that is, the book of Shang Yang, and Si Maqian believed it was true description and put it in his historical book record. What does it said? It says when I, Shang Yang, came to Qin, there was no distinction between fathers and sons as they lived in the same room, that is, they had not yet established a pair marriage system, to some extent, it was still a group marriage system. But now I have made a new system to teach the difference between men and women, and I have to bring the civilized culture of the Central Plain states into the Qin state, so that it could establish a family system of pair marriage with a difference between men and women. The Qin people used to live in dens or kilns, and I led them to build houses and palaces as the most advanced states of Lu and Wei. We can see from this passage how backward Qin was at the time of Shang Yang's arrival.

Shang Yang's change of law in Qin was very profound, knowing that more than a hundred years before Emperor Qin Yingzheng (Shi Huang) unified China, Shang Yang's change of law had already given the basic model of the entire Qin system, it was recorded in books of history: "In the beginning of the 12th year, a small feudal place was divided into 31 counties", that is, the establishment of the prefecture and county system; "flattening buckets, weighing and measuring" that is, the establishment of unified measuring system; "encourage people to reclaim new land, and men start paying tax at 14 years old," that is, the establishment of encouraging farming and new tax system; "burn poetry books and make the law clear to people," the state was governed by a new law from then on; all these were state policies that Shang Yang already adopted. After you hear this, you should understand that many of the decrees implemented by Emperor Qin Yingzheng, (Shi Huang) after he unified the country, which we used to believe it as the great achievements of Emperor Qin Yingzheng, were actually what he extended the old policies of Shang Yang's Law Change to the whole country.

We will focus on the details of Shang Yang's change of law. First, the people were forced to learn a minimum level of etiquette. This etiquette did not refer only to Confucianism, but also to free the people from barbarism and establish a civilized way of life and social organization that was advanced at that time.

Secondly, every national was forced to have a proper occupation, and no one should be idle. What to do? To take measures to emphasize agriculture, that is, to develop all the wasteland in Qin. In ancient times, the sons of noblemen and rich merchants were not engaged in farming, and spent all their time in socializing and sex. The sons of the nobility only had to inherit a rank in the army, and then slightly trained to inherit the title, just like the British princes nowadays have to serve in the army to go through the process. Shang Yang stipulated that anyone, including the sons of nobles and rich merchants, who was found to be idle would be deported to the frontier to reclaim the land. We can thus see that Shang Yang's change of law was similar to Wu Qi's. As long as he wanted to change the state government, he had to deal with the laziness of the noblemen and restructure the interests of all social classes. All these measures were certainly severe offences to the noble system.

Thirdly, he also stipulated that a family with two adult males should be forced to live separately, what does that mean? In ancient China, a large family system was practiced, and the descendants of a grandfather or even a great-grandfather had many children and grandchildren, and there were many side branches, but they never divided their families, and they all gathered together to share a big pot of rice. This was what Confucius said "organize the family well." A large family has dozens of hundreds of people, and it was difficult to satisfy all of their mouths, it was not easy if you could manage to make a family quiet no dispute. We all know Chen Ping, one who aided in forming the Han Dynasty. It was said that when he was a young man, his clan slaughtered pigs for the New Year and shared the meat, but the patriarch was unable to calm the crowd, he let Chen Ping to take care of it. Chen Ping handled the matter to the satisfaction of everyone, which is called the capability of well organizing the family. However, there was a problem with the clan system, because the implementation of communism within the family, each could do their best, but the distribution was done according to the needs of each and every one, it was not counted no matter how hard one worked, so most of the clan members soon became not motivated to work hard; in addition, at the time when Shang Yang changed the law, Qin was financial constrained, expanding tax revenue was a priority. But the tax system was to take the family as a unit tax base, so if the family was not divided, the tax base would be very thin; for these two reasons, the new law requires any man once he reaches adulthood marriage must be separated from the family. Shang Yang new law had two benefits for the state in one act.

Fourth, reward farming. As I have said repeatedly before, the simplest summary of the so-called law change was: reward farming and reward military warfare. The way Shang Yang rewarded farming was very interesting. First of all, he destroyed the limits of previous [illegible]*-shaped* public fields, plus newly reclaimed land, and the state divided all the land to individuals for private. Theoretically, the land could be bought and sold freely, but in practice, no one dared to sell it, because if you sold it, you had nothing to live on. Because all the professional walks of life other than farming, including medicine, hunting, logging, business, etc., were basically banned. This greatly motivated people to focus on farming. The new law stipulated that the Qin nationals were not allowed to engage in commerce, but only in agriculture. As I said in the first lesson, the profit of commercial activities was much higher than that of agriculture, so China had adopted the state policy of emphasizing agriculture and suppressing commerce since ancient times. Shang Yang clearly implemented this policy, all non-agriculture walks of life were considered not legal, thus the policy greatly maintained Qin's economic foundation and basic strength of the state.

However, the social function of commerce is to deploy resources across local boundaries, and Qin would have had a serious resource imbalance if commerce had been banned. For example, Qin was an agrarian society, and in ancient times armor needed cowhide or animal skins, which Qin did not have, or at least not enough of. Moreover, the material of weapons in that era was still mainly bronze, the so-called bronze is an alloy of copper and tin. Tin should account for 8% to 10%, because pure copper is too soft to be used as a tool or weapon. But there were no tin mines in Qin, and even copper mines were few, so where could the state get such shortage of materials if he categorically banned commerce? Therefore, Shang Yang opened his policy to merchants of other states and gave many preferential policies to merchants from all other states if they came to Qin to do business. This created a charming pattern of Qin people doing farming and merchants of other states doing business, which established a solid and reasonable national economic foundation for Qin. By the way, this is very much like the situation in the early days of Deng Xiaoping's reform and opening up policy, in modern times, it can no longer be considered a superb move, but only shows that the management dilemma of Chinese agricultural society continued until a few decades ago.

One more special feature was the inverted progressive tax. What does it mean? According to Shang Yang, among all farmers who plowed and wove cloth, the highest output was exempted from taxation, and the lower the output, the higher the tax rate. As we all know, the personal income tax and corporate income tax we have today are formulated in such a way that the higher your output or income is, the higher the relative tax rate is and the higher the absolute tax value is. Shang Yang did the opposite, the higher your output, the lower my tax rate, and the lower your output, the higher my tax rate, until you are forced to quit. What was he doing? He was forcing the people to work diligently in agriculture. According to historical records, when this policy was first implemented by Shang Yang, many Qin people were indeed bankrupt and had to flee into the wilderness because of the low output and heavy taxes. We could see how severe Shang Yang's change of law was, even the way to promote farming was so outrageous.

Brief Description of Shang Yang's Change of Law (II)

The fifth item of the law change is that Shang Yang made generous conditions to invite immigrants from other states. There is a famous chapter in *The Book of Shang Jun* called *Immigrants*, which is a policy of introducing immigrants. It says immigrants come to Qin will get a land over hundred acres and nine years tax exempted. Why he gave so favorable conditions to attract immigrants from other states? It was just like the aforementioned Zhao Xiangzi's emancipation of slaves to increase the number of soldiers and labor resources. Shang Yang's policy of recruiting immigrants was implemented to an amazing extent in the later Qin Dynasty. By the time of King Yingzheng, Qin had only four to five million citizens, but his army was nearly a million. Think about it, the average national would have one out of every four or five people as a soldier, where did he get so many soldiers? All the young and strong people were conscripted, who would do the agricultural production? All relied on immigrants, and almost all agricultural producers were immigrants. All the young and strong people of Qin were conscripted, and they could not unify the country without this. This shows how important the policy of immigrants was to the subsequent economic development and military struggle of Qin.

A question of course arises here, where did Qin get so many lands to grant? This brings us back to the time of Duke Mu of Qin in the Spring and Autumn Period. The Duke Mu of Qin used a man from the state of Yu, Baili Xi, also known as a five-ram scholar, who was a slave that Duke Mu of Qin traded for five black ram skins, and he used this Baili Xi as the state minister. The Duke Mu of Qin used a number of foreign talents, including Baili Xi, Qian Shu, You Yu and so on. We should mention here that state of Qin was broad-minded in employing foreign talents. Since Duke Mu of Qin set an example, Qin often used foreigners as prime ministers, from Duke Xiao of Qin to use Shang Yang, from King Huiwen of Qin to use Zhang Yi of Wei, and from then on to use Fan Sui, Lu Buwei and Li Si, all of them were talents from other states. Imagine how you would feel if the Premier of the State Council was always a foreigner. This expresses Qin's unconventional broad-mind of hiring foreign talents, which is the opposite of Wei's narrow-mindedness of constantly losing talents.

Back then, Baili Xi, You Yu and others adjusted the state policy for Duke Mu of Qin. Before that, the basic national policy of Qin was to defend to the west and aggressive to the east, that is, to go out of the Hangu Pass and compete with the other rivals in the Central Plains. However, Qin was weak at that time, so they formulated a new strategy, changing it to defense to the east and aggressive to the west. During the time of Duke Mu of Qin, Qin gradually encroached on the vast barbarian region in the northwest, which made Qin's land area increase greatly. The western region was sparsely populated, which left room for the reclamation of land resources for the later policy of immigrants in Shang Yang's Change of Law.

Sixth, establish social grassroots organizations. First of all, implement the household registration system. In the early years of the Western Zhou Dynasty, China had something similar to the household registration system, called the policy of numbering people, but it was not really implemented in place. The first person to implement a household registration system in Chinese history was Shang Yang's Change of Law. The so-called household registration system means that every citizen is registered with the government, and the government manages every head. This policy was recognized as a human rights violation by the United Nations Human Rights Organization in the latter half of the last century, and only a very few countries in the world, such as China, North Korea and Benin in Africa, still have a household registration system. It was started with the Change of Law by Shang Yang.

Not only that, Shang Yang also divided people into groups, every five or ten households into one group, thus established the system of investigating and tying up together. Later in China, it was called the linked-up system, which means that if one of the ten families made offence of the law, the other nine families must report it, otherwise they would be tying up together and be punished together, thus establishing the world's earliest system of whistleblower and secret informers. This is how Shang Yang established the system of state rule.

Seventh, the establishment of local governments and the implementation of the prefecture and county system. As I said earlier, the early years of mankind were a clan and tribe system, the Shang Dynasty was a tribal confederation system, the Zhou Dynasty entered the feudal system, and the Spring and Autumn Period was a time when the feudal system was relaxed but remained largely unchanged. What does the *prefecture and county system* mean? It broke off the clan, tribal system, the feudal system, and all places were directly administrated under the centralized government, and a political prefecture system of monarchy was thus established. Why is it called the prefecture county system? A Chinese historian named Tang Degang once gave it an explanation. Look at the traditional Chinese character "縣" (Xian) county, which is written like this, and its origin is "懸" (悬 hanging). What does "懸" mean? It means that when the feudal system was established in the early years of the Western Zhou Dynasty, a part of the land territory was reserved and left in suspense for the time being, so that the future kings and lords could make a backup, which was called "懸" (悬 hanging) or *county*. This remaining part of land was directly managed by the central emperor of Zhou, which later evolved into the county system in state of Qin.

The *county system* was the natural nemesis of the *feudal system*. By the 4th century B.C., the feudal system was first eliminated in Qin through the Change of Law by Shang Yang, a far-reaching political reform initiative. As I said in my Confucius class, the feudal system was the cradle of the modern capitalist social system. Because China eliminated the feudal system prematurely, there has never been a bourgeois revolution in the true sense of the word in Chinese history. The difficulties, obstacles and humiliations of the social transformation of modern China are not unrelated to this, so it is hard to say that this change is a fortunate event worthy of praise.

Eighth, the unification of weights and measures, forcing the whole country to use the same standard of size, liters and kilograms. The earliest person to implement the unification of weights and measures was Shang Yang. This had two advantages: first, it made trading fairer; second, it made taxation more uniform. Shang Yang not only set out the specific standards for the unification of weights and measures in a very strict manner, he also required local officials at all levels to come to the central government offices to have their weights and measures checked every year. The implementation of a law change policy to such a detailed degree was unprecedented.

Ninth, interpersonal disputes must be adjudicated in court, and private duels are not allowed. What does this mean? Not to mention the ancient times in China, in the Medieval Ages, and even in modern era in the West, the government only cared about state affairs. In civil disputes, the parties concerned had to coordinate and settle their own disputes, and if they failed to do so, they had to fight. Until the 17th and 18th centuries, the West still retained the legacy of aristocratic dueling. Pushkin, the famous Russian poet, died at the age of thirty-two in a duel. More than 2,000 years ago, when Shang Yang changed the law, he already made it clear that all civil disputes should be brought to court and no private fights were allowed. What was he doing? To avoid internal strife and depletion among the people. You know that back then, private fights were common, and they often turned into group fights. A tribe or a village often fought over unclear boundaries or over irrigation water in the summer, causing a lot of damage. In the Qin Dynasty, there was a court of law where all matters of all sizes had to be adjudicated by the court, and no private disputes were allowed. As you know, after the Han Dynasty, there were no more courts and no more judges in China. It is not entirely true to say that "Han inherited the Qin system". You should know that after the change of law by Shang Yang, there were independent judges in the Qin state and even in the Qin dynasty later. After the Han Dynasty, the magistrate is the administrative officer, the county magistrate, the state governor directly appeared in court to judge the case, the judge position disappeared without a trace. However, in the Qin Dynasty, there were independent judges, and they were under the vertical leadership of the central government and not under the control of local governors. The judge had the authority to decide on civil and criminal cases, and on the other hand, any decree issued by a magistrate had to be submitted to the judge for review to see if it complied with Qin law, which meant that he also had the role of supervising the lawful administration of the magistrate. This shows another aspect of how advanced the rule of law was in the Qin Dynasty.

Shang Yang implemented the law and carried out every detail very thoroughly. It is recorded in the *Records of the Grand Historian* that in the early days of the Reformation, a large execution site was built on the Wei River and more than 700 people were executed at one time. Sima Qian described the bloodshed as "the Wei River was red", which means that the water of the Wei River, the largest tributary of the Yellow River, was dyed red. According to some scholars, the massacre was probably caused by the villagers' armed struggle. The cruelty of the massacre shook the court and almost shook the state of Qin and the implementation of the law change. From this we can see how the determination and cruelty of Shang Yang was.

Tenth, fighting against the enemy is the first-class merit and receives the first-class reward. Eleventh, one must be successful in battle to be promoted to a higher rank. Let's combine these two paragraphs together. What is it? Rewarding soldiers for warfare. In the early days of the ancient times, the warriors were the fighters in order to monopolize the force; later, when the military expanded, the noble warriors became only generals and lieutenants, and the soldiers were the sons and young men of the common people. They fought bravely, then had a record, and even they got injuries, they were never promoted to officers, at most get a little money reward. The reason was that all official titles and all military ranks were hereditary. Shang Yang went so far as to change the title system, that is, he abolished the original five levels of titles and turned them into a false honor. Then he created another 20 grades of titles and rewarded soldier fighters according to their military merits.

Let's talk about the traditional knighthood system. In ancient China, titles were divided into five levels: Gong, Hou, Bo, Zi and Nan, i.e. Duke, Marquis, Earl, Viscount and Baron. Why is the social status called title? It is because at the beginning of class differentiation in ancient times, the powerful and noble people used different drinking utensils when they attended noble banquets according to their position in the patriarchal system, so that they could determine their social status, so they called social status as *knighthood.* In ancient times, there were five types of drinking utensils and five levels of titles. The first level of the highest knighthood with tass, the second level with chalice, the third level with goblet, the fourth level with mug, the fifth level with cup.

Just look at how important titles were in ancient times! Not only did it define your social status, not only did it determine which level of official you could be, which rank you could receive in the army, but it even determined what kind of life you could enjoy. For example, the size of your compound, the magnificence of your house, the height of your gatehouse, the kind of carriage you drive, and even the kind of clothes you wear, are all defined by the title. Therefore, in ancient China, merchants were rich but not noble, and without this title, you could not enjoy this standard of living. The title was so important that Shang Yang turned it into an honorary title, abolished its connotation, and established another 20 levels of titles for merit reward. Basically, military merit was used for rewarding and military merit was used for ranking.

Think about it, in ancient times, soldiers fought in the bloody battlefield, either died, fatally injured, or disabled, no matter how brave and hard fighting, you could never become an officer, but today you could actually be promoted to the highest rank. Even if your ability could not do the prime minister, at least you can enjoy the treatment of the title of the phase, think about what kind of change this was? So, the Qin army was suddenly turned into an army of beast. The soldiers fought bravely and desperately for the enemy's head. According to *Strategies of the Warring States*, after Shang Yang changed the military ranking system, the soldiers of other six states had cramps in their legs before the battle started. The soldiers of the state of Qin were rewarded with additional rank for each head of the enemy they killed, so that all of them fought desperately for the enemy's head as soon as they entered the battlefield, regardless of whether they were dead or alive.

I suggest that you visit the Terracotta Warriors and Horses in Lintong when you have time, there shows the terracotta warriors of an army formation of the Qin Dynasty, in which there were only low and middle-ranking officers, a hundred chief was equivalent to a company commander, a thousand chief was equivalent to a regimental commander. From officers to soldiers, all wearing light armor, without helmets, hanging only a towel on their heads. You should know that after the middle of the Warring States period, all countries provided their armies with heavy armor. The so-called heavy armor, divided into three layers, inside a layer of mesh armor, outside a layer of animal skin armor or cowhide armor, and then the chest and back and then bronze pieces and iron pieces to add protection, head heavy helmet, holding a large shield, only the defense wear was more than forty to sixty pounds. It seriously affected the soldiers' offensive capabilities; Qin also provided their own army with heavy armor, but the soldiers did not want to wear it, preferring to wear light armor, no helmets to reduce the defensive load, so as to improve offensive mobility, desperately chasing the head of the enemies, so much so that history books contain incidents where Qin soldiers fought for the heads occasionally. Think of the impact, warriors waist wrapped around the bloody heads of the enemies, all the way forwards, blood shed along the way behind, what a horrible picture!

It was obvious that this would not work, as hanging a head around the waist was certainly not conducive to continuing the attack, so Shang Yang reverted to the ancient system. In the oracle bone script, there is a character that starts with a very figurative ear and a hand next to it. Which character is this? "取" (Qv) take. What is the meaning of the character "取"?( ) In the late clan system of ancient times, when there were wars between clans, how did they reward the warriors for fighting in the early days? They cut off the enemy's left ear! The soldiers were rewarded by counting the ears of the enemies. Shang Yang reverted to the old practice and demanded that the soldiers be rewarded with titles by counting the left ears of the enemies that the soldiers cut off and brought back.

During the Sui and Tang dynasties, Japan sent students to learn from China and they even took this trick back. By the Warring States period in Japan, there was a famous shogun Toyotomi Hideyoshi who eventually unified Japan and then he raised an army to attack Korea. The Japanese army killed a lot in Korea, cut off the ears of Korean soldiers and people, and brought them back to Japan for reward. The amount of ears were piled up like a hill, and they made a special grave called *ear grave,* which is still well kept in Japan. This is why today's South and North Koreans, mentioning the Japanese, they would gnash their teeth in hatred, showing more bitterness and deeper hatred toward the Japanese than the Chinese do. The credit should first be given to Shang Yang.

By rewarding farming and military warfare, Shang Yang made the state of Qin economically rich and its military machine powerful. In just about ten years after the change of law, Qin suddenly became strong and became a formidable enemy of the civilized states in the Central Plains. In the *Book of Shang Jun,* there is a passage that reads, "When the people see war, they are like hungry wolves seeing meat; fathers send their sons, old brothers send their younger brothers, and wives send their husbands, all saying, no gain, no return." It says that fathers contributed their sons, old brother contributed their younger brothers, and wives contributed their husbands, encouraging them to enlist in the army, and told them that if they could not capture the enemies and cut off their heads, they would not get the reward title and would no need to return home. This shows how deep and brutal the Shang Yang's Law Change was.

Twelfth, the formulation of legal texts. Shang Yang established the *Six Laws* with reference to Li Kui's *Book of Laws*, which are the famous *Law on robbery, Law on theft, Law on prisoners, Law on prosecution, Law on violation of bans,* and *Law on criterion of imposing penalty,* which are recorded in the *Book of Shang Jun* and the unearthed Qin tablets, so we will not go into details. As you can see from the lesson, Shang Yang's change of law was a complete system for the complete transformation of Qin society at that time.

Review of Shang Yang's Change of Law

The following are some comments on the Shang Yang's Chang of Law.

First of all, let's discuss whether Shang Yang's Change of Law was a tyrannical rule and how it should be evaluated. Shang Yang's law change was very cruel. It was recorded in the *Records of the Grand Historian* that "those who dropped garbage on public road would be face-branded", that is, if you dumped garbage on the public road, you would be punished by face-branded. It was recorded in the *Records of the Grand Historian*: "Those who do not report the violation will be cut off at waist", that is, ten households were organized into a group and a system of tie-up together was established, if one person violated the law, the other nine families had to report, and those who did not report the violation, the law was very clear, "be cut off at the waist"! Some people think that this record was unreasonable, saying that the person who directly violated the law, the punishment may not be cut off at waist, how could the other nine families be punished so cruelly simply because they did not report, which could not be justified legally. We have no way to determine its authenticity, but we cannot exclude that there were cases in which those who did not report were cut off at waist. The *Records of the Grand Historian* also contains: "the law stipulates that those missed the deadline will be beheaded". In ancient times, there were two types of taxes: one was the collected food, cloth or money as taxes; the other type was called corvée, which meant that all men had to participate in the construction of the state as stipulated without pay, with various kinds of public labor as legal obligations. For example, twenty-five days a year, it was stipulated that you must report to work at the scheduled time, and if you are late, you will be beheaded, which is called "beheaded if fail to report". As you know, it was because of this article that eventually led to the collapse of the Qin dynasty. Why Chen Sheng, Wu Guang had the uprising? When Chen and Wu led a group of people to serve in a distant place, they encountered heavy rain and the roads were flooded, so they could not arrive on time. As they were afraid of being beheaded, they started uprising against the Qin tyranny, so the state of Qin began to collapse.

The *Records of the Grand Historian* also records: "The road was blocked with men in ochre clothes, and those with noses ugly." The *ochre clothes* were worn by the prisoners, and the number of prisoners was so many that the road was blocked by their procession. What does it mean by "those with noses ugly"? There were too many men who had been punished with their noses cut off, and people were used to seeing men with their noses cut off, so anyone had a good nose was looked different. Of course, this is a little bit too much, but it shows how harsh Shang Yang's change of law was. The *Records of the Grand Historian* is pretty fair in its records. On the one hand, it records the harshness of Shang Yang's law change, saying that "Shang Yang was a man of mean nature"; but on the other hand, it also says that "after ten years of implementing the law, the Qin people were very happy, there was no more scavenger on road, and no more bandits hiding in the mountains, and the families were rich." It means that after ten years of the law change, the people of Qin were happy to support the law, people on the road did not scavenge for money, bandits in the mountains were not found, and families had enough food and clothing. This shows that Sima Qian was fair in recording history and he stated facts in all aspects.

However, in traditional Chinese culture and among traditional literati, most of the comments about Shang Yang's Law Change were extremely bad. Let me cite an example. Su Shi once wrote an article entitled *On Shang Yang*. In it, there is this passage: "The names of two men in the world are like maggots and flies in dung and filth, and if speak of them, they will defile the mouths and tongues, and if write them, they will defile the writing material." This refers to Shang Yang and Sang Hongyang. Sang Hongyang was an important minister of Emperor Wu of Han Dynasty, and the policy of official management of salt and iron, which was the first monopolistic state enterprise in China, was the product of Sang Hongyang's proposal, which was traditionally regarded in ancient Chinese culture as a bad policy of competing with the people for profits. This was why Su Shi (Dongpo) said that the names of Shang Yang and Sang Hongyang were as filthy as maggots, flies, feces and garbage, and when I mentioned them, I feel they defile my mouth and tongue, and when I wrote about them, I feel they defile my writing material. It can be seen that traditional Chinese scholars or literati generally had a very bad opinion of such tyrannical figures who practiced tyranny to the people.

However, Confucius once had another comment on this kind of issue, of course, it could not be directed at Shang Yang, but at the ancient law, which was related to Confucius' sentiment of "good feeling toward ancient ritual". Once his disciple Zi Gong mentioned about the severe penalty of antient law, for example, in the early Zhou Dynasty, there was a precedent penalty that "if you dumped garbage on the public road, your hand would be cut off". What did Confucius say? He said, "this is the way to rule the society", which is a manifestation of his deep understanding of the way of governing the society. He went on to say: "If one abandons garbage in the street, it will make the street filthy and stenchy, and make other people angry, and if other people angry, they will quarrel with you and fight, and if they fight, it will involve three tribes that may lead to mutilate each other. This would even lead to the destroy of the three tribes, therefore penalty could be severe". He said that if you dump the garbage on the street, it will lead to the stench, so that others are very uncomfortable, so people will be angry fight, and eventually cause personal injury. Since it may bring out serious consequences, it is okay to control it with severe punishment. Confucius also said, "people tend to avoid heavy punishment, and it is easy not to throw off garbage in the street, so that such injury can be avoided, and this is the way of governance." He said that people will avoid heavy punishment, and not littering was an easy thing to do, so that neither side would cause harm, and therefore it was considered an effective means of governing the society. This was Confucius' comment.

In fact, in ancient societies, penalties were generally heavy. Unlike today's laws, which break down the severity of punishment according to the degree of harm done to society, the ancient system was simple and rough, with broad regulations. This was not only true in China, but also true in the West. For example, in the *Twelve Bronze Tables Law* of ancient Rome, there was a clause in the *Eighth Table of Private Offenders*: "Anyone who slanders another person with words or sings lyrics that insult another person in public shall be punished by death". It was a song that was not sung well, you would be killed. It shows that this severe law practice was common in ancient times.

But you should note that there was a major difference between the Law of the Twelve Bronze Tables in ancient Rome and the Law of Shang Yang in China. As I said in my last Confucius class, the Law of the Twelve Bronze Tables was legislated by five nobles and five commoners. And it has a provision in its ninth table, the Public Law, that "no special law shall be made for the benefit of any individual." That is to say, no one can enjoy privileges and everyone is equal before the law. The people legislate and the law is uniformly enforced. The rule of law by the Chinese legalist and Shang Yang style was that the king and a few important ministers legislate and only for others to follow, not for themselves. Therefore, they have privileges outside the rule of law, and the king is above the rule of law, and the king is above the law, which is the exact opposite of the concept of "the king is under the law" after the *Magna Carta* movement in England, as I mentioned earlier. This serious flaw in Chinese legalism, and this fatal loophole in Shang Yang's Law Reform, eventually led to the downfall of Qin.

We have examples to prove it. The rule of law in Qin did not apply to the privileged class. For example, King Ying Zheng once happened to see Chancellor Li Si's brilliant parade and was displeased and muttered a few words to himself. As a result, some time later, it was found that Li Si's ceremonial parade soon became minimalist, which made the king realize that his private criticism had been heard by Li Si. Ying Zheng went so far as he decapitated all the palace attendants who were serving him at that time, without asking any questions. According to the Qin law, killing anyone and inflicting punishment on anyone should be done according to the law, but this was invalid for Ying Zheng.

The second emperor of Qin, Hu Hai, conspired with Zhao Gao

to usurp the throne. He was the companion and teacher of Hu Hai when he was young. In order to maintain his power, Zhao Gao colluded with Hu Hai upon the death of emperor Qin Yingzheng (Shi Huang), closed the news of Shi Huang's death and issued a false edict to make the eldest son, Fusu, suicided, and even eventually killed more than 20 of his own siblings. But Hu Hai was a half-witted, brain-damaged master who took over the second reign of the Qin dynasty, which eventually led to the collapse of the Qin empire.

We can see from here that the law of the Legalist was severe, but in the ancient society it was still justifiable. However, Shang Yang's Qin law, which was implemented step by step, was very different from the ancient law, which was harsh but difficult to implement, and thus Qin law was extremely harmful, and could be called a tyranny of evil laws. The fact that his law was a privileged one, which left room for a few people to do whatever they wanted, was a huge flaw and a scourge.

Let's look at the second item. Some years ago, a series of important Qin law documents were unearthed at the Sleeping Tiger Land in Yunmeng, Hubei, China, the famous Sleeping Tiger Land site and the Sleeping Tiger Land Qin jian. In this site, surprisingly, more than 1,100 pieces of Qin Dynasty bamboo slips were unearthed. As we all know, in archaeology, a tomb with more things may not be as important as a few pieces of bamboo slips or a few bronzes with inscriptions, because the written records make it possible to decide the specifics of the site and to give more definite information about the escapades. This site is the tomb of a judge named "喜" (Xi) in the Qin Dynasty during the time of King Yingzheng or the First Emperor of Qin. After the excavation of this site, the Chinese archaeological community was shaken by the fact that for the first time, Chinese people and Chinese academics knew that such a comprehensive legal system existed in Qin after Shang Yang's Change of Law. In the past, only a few words could be found in the *Book of Shang Jun*, but there was no documentary evidence of how the laws were set up and how detailed they were. The unearthing of the Sleeping Tiger site Qin bamboo slips made the scholarly community realize the completeness of the Qin Dynasty's legal system, which not only had a major state law and criminal law, but also had an independent civil law system.

It is important to note that the Roman Empire did not establish the first civil law code in the West, known as the *Roman Code,* until the sixth century AD. The Qin bamboo slips from the Sleeping Tiger site indicate that a whole system of civil law was created in Qin around the third century B.C. through the Change of Law by Shang Yang. For example, there was the land Law, which was the agricultural law; the craftsmen Law, which was the artisan law; the storage Law; the corvée Law; the market Law, which was the trade law; and the measurement Law, which was the law of weights and measures; all of these belonged to the civil law. It even contains the Law of the Household, which is somewhat similar to our marriage law today; the Law of the Golden Cloth, which is somewhat similar to our property inheritance law today; the Law of the Placement of Officials and the Law of the Removal of Officials, which is the law of the selection of officials and the law of the removal of officials. It has all these laws. It even has a Law of Closed Investigation, the content of which is similar to the modern procedural law. When we see these things, we marvel at the greatness of the system that was used when Shang Yang changed the law and established a rule of law society for Qin.

Paradox and Dilemma of Reform

We finally explore the paradox of the change of law.

In the history of human civilization, it has always been a very difficult thing to transform or change the political structure of society and the configuration of social institutions. Because, since the class division, changing any kind of social system will inevitably touch or damage the vested interests of the original social ruling class. And they are the most organized and powerful people in the society at that time, how can you change the social system? Therefore, throughout the history of mankind, whenever there was a need to deeply change a social system, basically only by revolution.

There are two terms in political science that are worth perusing: one is called *reform* and the other is called *revolution*. We now say *reform, change* and the ancient *change of law* and so on, in political science are all under *improvement*. By *improvement,* we mean changing the state system without violent war. A *revolution* is a violent overthrow of the original ruling class and establishment of a new configuration of the social system. Please note that not all violent movements can be called revolutions. For example, in China, dynasties change every two or three centuries, and peasant uprisings overthrow the imperial power, which is not called a revolution, but a riot. Why? The new regime they established was still a replica of the original social form without any institutional innovation or change in the socio-economic and political system.

There are very few events in human history that can be called *revolutions*. For example, *King Wu overthrew the Shang* is called a revolution, and the earliest use of this word in China comes from the chapter of the *Book of Shang* that describes this event, because he changed the clan-tribe confederation system of the Shang Dynasty into a feudal system. The 1911 *Wuchang Uprising*, for example, eventually transformed the monarchical system into a republic, so it was also called the *Xinhai Revolution*, while the Hundred Days' Reformation, which took place some years before it, was completely different. There was also the British and French bourgeois revolutions, which changed the feudal system and monarchy into a capitalist social system unique to modern times, which is called a revolution.

Generally speaking, it is easy to understand that people can really change the social structure only through violent revolution. This is why in human history and in Chinese history, reform, improvement and law change have always failed. Why? Because the force you use to improve, reform or change the law is exactly the object you want to reform. Think about it, isn't it? With what power do you rely on to carry out social reform? You are relying on the existing social ruling class, the existing bureaucracy at all levels, the existing upper aristocracy, and through them, you are revolutionizing their lives, making them give up their vested interests in order to reorganize a new pattern and a new system of resource distribution. This is called the reform paradox.

Moreover, for all reformers, they are always focusing on the most serious social problems, the most concentrated point to start the reform passionately. And this part is precisely the sensitive point that the existing vested interests would never allow to touch. Therefore, when the forces of two sides collide, it must cause a fierce backlash. Since the target of the reform is the most powerful people in the society, how can the reform be carried out? How can the reform be successful? This is the crux of the *reform paradox*. Therefore, in the history of mankind, all movements of reform, law change or improvement have mostly ended in failure.

Let me give you an example. In the middle of the Tang Dynasty, the empire was in a state of turmoil. Since the An-Shi Rebellion subsided, the Tang Dynasty did not actually solve the problem, and the dispersion of the military governors in control of outlying prefectures intensified. From a few rebellious military governors of the prefectures during the An-Shi Rebellion expanded to 48 rebellious military governors of the prefectures, splitting the country. During the Yongzhen period of Emperor Shunzong of Tang Dynasty, the *Two Kings* and *Eight Secretaries of State* changed the law, among which were Liu Yuxi and Liu Zongyuan, famous scholars of Tang Dynasty. They only did minor reform of the official rule, and the change of law failed. The *two kings* were killed, and all the *eight secretaries of state* were exiled.

During the Northern Song Dynasty, the society was extremely vulnerable due to the enormous pressure from the Northern nomadic civilizations including Jin, Liao, Western Xia and Mongolia, and there were constant demands and calls for reforms. During the reign of Song Emperor Renzong, the *Qingli New Deal*, or the *Qingli Reform*, took place. Fan Zhongyan, a famous scholar, was the leader of the reform, his so-called New Deal was only a minor economic reform and an overhaul of the government, which ended in failure, and he was put in exile. His most famous essay, *Notes of Yueyang Tower*, was written during his exile. In the years of Song Shenzong, the Northern Song Dynasty carried out a second reform, the famous *Xining Reform*, or Wang Anshi's Change of Law. Wang Anshi also carried out only a little bit of economic and official reforms that was not deep to the bones, but still ended in failure, and he himself was relegated twice.

Likewise, the *Hundred Days Reform* in 1899 was a failure. Why did the *Hundred Days Reform* happen? It was because Japan opened its doors in 1853, followed by the Meiji Restoration, while China was invaded by the Great Powers in 1840, followed by the foreign affairs movement, it was actually that China was in the first to learn from the West, Japan was in the second, why in the end China was surpassed, and then in 1894 in the Sino-Japanese naval war China was beaten, and finally had to change the law to strengthen it? This requires an understanding of the different ways in which China and Japan reacted to the impact of the Western civilization.

The so-called Foreign affairs movement refers to learning the technology of western application level of strong ships and powerful guns, but China's deeper culture, social concept and political system were never allowed to be shaken. In Zhang Zhidong's words, it was called "based on China's culture as the body to learn Western technology for our purpose", which is the essence of the foreign affairs movement. In Japan, the Meiji Restoration was started in 1868. But the slogan they put forward was "to get out of Asia and enter Europe", to learn the West comprehensively, to transform Japanese society, to abandon Tang culture, and to accept Western culture.

During the Sui and Tang dynasties, Japan sent envoys to Sui and Tang to study Chinese culture, and they called Chinese culture *Tang learning,* which means that traditional Chinese culture had been popular in Japan for thousands of years. After the Meiji Restoration, they immediately realized that Western culture was superior to traditional Chinese culture. They immediately abandoned all the Tang culture and studied the West from the root. Japan sent students, sent envoys to several Western countries to study their culture deeply, and they brought back all they could learn from Western countries, even including the congress system, and the false emperor system. From 1868 to 1894, just a short period of 26 years, in the famous Sino-Japanese naval war, Japan actually defeated China, the first power in East Asia, and cultural mentor it had been looking up to for a thousand years. There were many scholars in Japan at that time kneeling in the street and howling, looking toward China from afar and crying, tearing their hearts out for their teacher to be so vulnerable and sagging, so unbeatable. You can imagine how strong the stimulus of this battle at the time to the Chinese literati, how deep the pain! So, with the Sino-Japanese War as the line, the late Qing Dynasty officially announced the end of the Foreign affairs movement, China began to carry out social reform, launched a constitutional reform movement, which is the *Hundred Days Reform Movement* in 1899. Even under such a crisis situation, Kang, Liang's effort to change law, its new policy went on about a hundred days, but it eventually came to failure, the six gentlemen were beheaded by the Empress Dowager Cixi in Beijing Cai Shi Kou, which led to China to carry out a revolution, Sun Yatsen led the *Xinhai Revolution* thus triggered.

The failure of the *Hundred Days' Reform* is still being discussed in the academic circles today, and what a far-reaching national calamity it created. The *Xinhai Revolution* was unsuccessful, and instead of establishing a constitutional government, China ended up in a chaotic situation that lasted for decades. If the Hundred Days Reform had gone as smoothly as the Meiji Restoration in Japan, how fortunate the Chinese nation would have been. What am I talking about? The paradox of reform is difficult to solve.

Now we look back at Shang Yang's Change of Law. You will note that Shang Yang's Change of Law was by no means less profound than any revolution. It carried out reforms not only in the economic field, but also in the political field, and it even changed the state system, which was previously a feudal system and thereafter a monarchical dictatorship. It was not simply a general political and economic reform, but a fundamental change of the state system. Such things can usually only be achieved through revolution, and Shang Yang's change of law basically took a bloodless and non-violent approach to accomplish this revolutionary change of law and improvement. This is very rare in history, which is why Liang Qichao said that Shang Yang is one of the only six great statesmen in China since ancient times.

Here, let us recap the process of Shang Yang's Law Change. Shang Yang was a nobleman of Wei, why did he initially put himself in such a low position that he went to Wei's prime minister's office as a retainer? It was because he knew very well that he could only see the documents of Li Kui's *Book of Laws* in the ministerial residence of Wei. So he gave up his vanity and went to work for Gong Shucuo as a guest, during which time he studied Li Kui's *Book of Law* and well prepared his theoretical ideas for the future practice of law change.

He went to the state of Qin to see the Duke of Xiao and went through the door by a favorite minister named Jing Jian. The reason why he put himself so low again, to the point of insulting his reputation, was that he had to examine the king. It is generally believed that only the king examines his subjects, not the subjects examine the king. However, Shang Yang knew in his mind that if he wanted to carry out a comprehensive law change, he had to examine whether his political partner had the power to take charge. So he went through the back door and the lower doorway, and made sure to meet the king, Duke Xiao himself. He talked with Duke Xiao three times, and the *Records of the Grand Historian* records that the first time, he talked about the imperial way; the second time, he talked about the king's way; and the third time, he talked about the hegemony. This conclusion to his talks is not good, it is not clear what the talks were, let me change to a clearer way.

In Chinese political science, there are two very important terms: one is called the way of the King and the other is called the way of the Hegemon. The so-called *king's way* is the way of "internal sainthood and external kingdom". It is the way of cultivating virtue internally and ruling the country with virtue externally. When Shang Yang first met with Duke Xiao, he first talked about the king's way, which was a model of ruling by virtue in the ancient times. In the middle of the Warring States period, the era of great rivalry had already begun, with intense intra-species and inter states competition. In such an era, he still talked about the king's way to Duke Xiao. Therefore, Duke Xiao was so drowsy that he came out and criticized Jing, saying, "How could you introduce me such a pedantic and empty talker! " What was Shang Yang doing? He was examining the king.

The second time he met with Duke Xiao, he talked about the way of hegemony, the way to enrich the country and strengthen the army to fight for hegemony. We all know that in the Spring and Autumn Period, the way of hegemony had already emerged, this was neither a new doctrine, nor was it a new initiative, but after all, he came to touch the painful point, so Duke Xiao finally listened. He did not talk about the change of law until his third meeting with Duke Xiao. Because he knew that the change of law was a very harsh and radical process, which would shake the foundation of the state and hurt the nobles, and was beyond the reach of ordinary politicians. The results of his first two visits revealed that Duke Xiaog was not interested in those relatively soft reform initiatives, so this is how he got into the subject. The two men talked with each other for three days and nights.

According to the *Records of the Grand Historian*, they met three times in the first year of Duke Xiao, but Shang Yang's Law Change was officially launched only in the third year of Duke Xiao, with a gap of two years in the middle. What was Shang Yang doing in these two years? What was Duke Xiao doing? We can imagine that they were making comprehensive legal, personnel and political preparations, all the preparatory work before the actual operation, never fighting an unsure battle, and making it a very secure starting base before they began to implement the change.

In the first nine years of Shang Yang's Change of Law, only economic reforms were made. If political reform was carried out too early, the whole noble system simply could not accept it. And in the face of economic reform, the nobles were a little uneasy, but they benefited from it. Because the peasants were motivated to work harder and paid more rents and taxes to the nobles, the nobles had an increased income instead, so the nobles simply could not unite to resist the change of law.

Nine years later, when the nobility became disorganized and the forces of the reform grew, Shang Yang started political changes, abolishing the old title system and establishing the county system, etc. The whole process was extremely structured, and the political operation was brought to a rhythmic and artistic level. With such a smooth implementation, Shang Yang's Change of Law finally changed the state system and achieved a social change movement that could only be accomplished by revolution, which is a rare improvement in human history. This is a rare achievement of improvement in human history. We can thus see Shang Yang was really an ambitious hero.

China's contemporary Deng Xiaoping's reform is also considered quite successful, and we have benefited from its rapid development and national strength in these four decades. However, compared with Shang Yang's reform, there is still a big gap between the two. First of all, Deng Xiaoping's reform escaped the dilemma of reform paradox out of an extremely special historical fortune, what does it mean? The reform took place after the turmoil of the Ten-Year Cultural Revolution, when Mao Zedong and the Gang of Four acted too much out of line and what they did hurt the entire bureaucratic class. Their programmatic slogan of the Cultural Revolution was to overhaul all the party officials in power who wanted to go way of capitalism. As a result, almost all cadres at all levels were beaten up and all officials were humiliated, and because they went too far, they wiped out all the powerful and noble who could be the possible oppositions to the subsequent reform, and pushed all bureaucrats to the state of expecting reform. Isn't that so? So Deng Xiaoping's reform was a chance made by history, a lucky break from the reform paradox! Therefore, at least half of the credit for the reform should be given to the Gang of Four.

Moreover, Deng Xiaoping's reform was called "crossing the river by treading the stones" in his own words, without prior top-level design, and only economic reform. Crossing the river by treading the stones would face a problem, when came to deep water, treading stones became impossible, then the reform would be stalled. If Deng Xiaoping had made sufficient preparations before the reform, including systematic top-level design, even if it was only imitating Shang Yang's Change of Law, and started political reform nine years after the economic reform, such as the minimum one, the establishment of a public disclosure system of officials' property, which happened to be before 1989, why would it be so bad that the student movement in all over the cities against government officials' corruption? Even till today the authorities still do not dare to carry out a public disclosure system for officials' assets, because the scope of corruption is too wide, the impact is too large, the regime could not afford the consequences of lawfully judging and punishing nearly all officials of the whole bureaucracy. I am telling you this because I want you to further appreciate the thorough depth of Shang Yang's change of law in contrast.

I'm not trying to give blanket praise to Shang Yang's Change of Law, I'm trying to show you where the social significance and operational difficulties of the Change of Law itself lie. For you listeners, it's revealing in that as long as you're an organizational leader, whether you're doing administrative work or business management, you're faced with this paradox of reform. Because any organization, it must tend to decay over time. By decay, I don't just mean corruption and bribery, but that any organization will definitely become disorganized, lazy, or even go completely out of order, which is called *law of de-organization*.

For any organizer or leader, you need to constantly refresh and reform your organization as the situation evolves. But you must face a reform paradox. You are either the general representative of vested interests, so you will by and large refuse to reform, or you will do superficial reforms and not at all to touch in substance; or you face the reform paradox, that is, the object of your reform is precisely the force you need to rely upon. You can't escape one of these two. But if you fail to refresh your organizational system, the organization itself must tend to become disorganized and corrupted, which is a huge problem for all social practitioners, social organizers, and social leaders. If necessary, you can refer to Shang Yang's change of law.

Theoretical Framework of the Doctrine of Legalism

We have talked about the political practice of Legalism, and we will talk about Han Feizi's integration of the theory of Legalism below.

Before I talk about Han Feizi's theoretical doctrine, let me briefly talk about Shen Buhai, a person who may not be known to you.

The reason for mentioning Shen Buhai is that Han Feizi's thoery of law consists of three parts, namely, *law, tactics,* and *power*. The so-called *law* is to make the law public, so that the people know what the legislation is, so that the people can follow it; the so-called *tactics* is the king's hidden tactics to deal with and control the ministers, the founder of this thing was Shen Buhai; the so-called *power* is the king's sovereignty above, forming an oppressive pressure on anyone below, only this *power* of sovereignty can be established, the *law*, the *tactics* can be expected to be implemented. The theoretical origin of *power* comes from the Jixia school of state Qi in the early Warring States, where it was first proposed by the famous scholar Shen Dao. We will not go detail about it here.

Shen Buhai was almost the same generation as Shang Yang, who was the prime minister of state Han and also practiced law change. But as I said earlier, the degree of law change in the five civilized states of the Central Plains was hardly thorough. In the case of Shen Buhai, who was the steady prime minister of the state Han, the change of law was mainly limited to the reform of the official system, and the method used was the power games.

Shen Buhai assisted Marquis Zhao of Han. Marquis Zhao was

a small-minded political figure in his own right. According to the history books, the Marquis Zhao of Han often played smart. For example, in one temple festival, he thought that the sacrificial pig brought up by the minister of ceremony was too small and felt that it was not solemn enough, so he asked for a replacement. After the minister went down, it was too late to adjust the pig, so the minister probably just pulled the body sides and changed the shape, and sent it up again as before. As a result, Marquis Zhao, who was well aware of the details, judged that his subordinate had played smart on the pig sacrifice based on its ear image alone, and severely reprimanded him. For this reason, Shen Buhai criticized Marquis Zhao: "The eye, ear and mind are not enough to rely on". It means that you should hide deeply and not show your intelligence, which will make the courtiers more and more alert and disguised.

Marquis Zhao of Han was such a cunning and obscene monarch, and he and Shen Buhai, who was passionate about power games, were really a natural pair. Shen Buhai specialized in this way and invented a large set of power theory. We won't go into the details here, but I'll just tell another story. Once, Wei invaded Zhao and surrounded the capital of Zhao, Handan. Zhao sent an envoy to Han to seek assistance from the prime minister Shen Buhai. However, he could not understand the mind of Marquis Zhao, so he went to his subordinates Zhao Zhuo and Han Chao secretly and told them: "You are all the eloquent scholars of the state, and ministers also, raise your proposal to the king when necessary, even if the king does not accept your words, at least it shows your loyalty." Then, he asked these two men to persuade the Marquis Zhao of Han to support state Zhao, while he was watching the situation aside and found that Marquis Zhao of Han was disgusted with this matter. When these two ministers left, he began to changed his tone and gave the Marquis Zhao of Han various reasons why he did not need to save Zhao.

This is Shen Buhai's personality, which was evident in his conduct and his end in the Han's reform. I am telling you this just to let you know about Shen Buhai, who was the founder of the Chinese Legalism *Tactics*. If you see the term *Shen-Han's theory* in ancient books, *Shen* refers to Shen Buhai, *Han* refers to Han Feizi, and *Shen-Han's theory* refers to the theory of legalism.

We will discuss Han Feizi next. Han Feizi is a great master of legalism theory. Han Feizi was born in 280 BC and died in 233 BC, only 12 years before the reign of King Yingzheng of Qin, which means that the theory of legalism in China finally took shape at the end of the Warring States period.

Han Feizi and Li Si studied together under Xun Kuang, or Xunzi, a great Confucian of the mid-Warring States period. As I mentioned earlier, Xun Kuang, on the one hand, revered the ritual system and advocated benevolence, righteousness, propriety, knowledge, and faith, but on the other hand, he also advocated the rule of law and severe punishment. Here, we should note that in the past, it was easy to misunderstand that Confucianism respected the ritual system, so Confucius opposed the rule of law, it was assumed that Chinese legalism had nothing to do with Confucianism. But in fact, the origin of legalism was closely related to Confucianism. Even Sima Qian was wrong about this, so Sima Qian arranged the biographies of Shen Buhai, Han Feizi, Laozi and Zhuangzi together in his *Records of the Grand Historian*, called *Biography of Lao Zhuang Shen Han*. Even Sima Qian thought that Legalism was a *school of post-Daoism*, but in reality, Legalism was a reformation or variation of Confucianism. The most important figures of Legalism, such as Li Kui and Wei Wenhou, were students of the *Xi He school of Zi Xia*, and the heavyweights of Legalism, such as Han Feizi and Li Si, were disciples of the great Confucianist Xun Kuang. Then, after Han Feizi and Li Si left their teacher Xunzi, Li Si went to state Qin to engage in political practice and eventually became the court minister and later the prime minister of King Yingzheng of Qin. Han Feizi returned to his homeland and he theoretically did his studies indoors.

In fact, Han Feizi initially tried to persuade the king of state Han to implement the change of law, but the king did not listen to him, so Han Feizi had to sit in his study and write down his ideas of law. Han Feizi was a brilliant writer, and his essay on the law happened to reach the Qin state. According to the *Records of the Grand Historian*, the king of Qin sighed and said, "If I could meet this man and talk with him leisurely, I would have no regret before my death." So, he sent his troops to attack the state of Han.

By this time, Qin was so powerful that Han was no match for it, so the king of Han had to hand over Han Feizi at Qin's request and appointed him as Han's envoy to Qin, and so Han Feizi came to Qin. Han Feizi was a famous scholar of law, and his political views were in line with those of the king of Qin, and he was treated with extraordinary courtesy, so we can imagine what a joyful scene they would meet. However, it was the opposite. After meeting with the king of Qin, Han Feizi had a disagreement with him, which caused strong dislike to the king of Qin. When Han Feizi met with the king of Qin, he was not interested in discussing legalism with him, but kept requesting the king not to attack Han. This matter annoyed the king of Qin, because the former prime minister of Qin, Fan Sui, had left Qin a great military and political plan, which was called *far diplomacy and near attack*. The king of Qin had a plan to establish diplomatic relations with distant states, and attack the neighboring states first, so that the neighboring states could be taken and the distant states would become new neighboring states, and then all states could be gradually swallowed up. Han was close to Qin, and was the target of Qin's early attacks. Then, Han Feizi, as an envoy of Han, asked the king of Qin not to invade Han, which was just like blocking Qin's military and political strategy.

We can see from this that although Han Feizi's theory was very harsh, Han Feizi himself was a benign and useless scholar. We know that the literati of that era were usually not responsible for their own state, because the prevailing social concept at that time was "ruling the state and pacifying the world", and no matter who ruled the country, as long as there was an opportunity to pacify the world, even if one's own homeland was wiped out, he would not hesitate to do so. Therefore, people like Wei Yang and Wu Qi did not serve their own state, but worked for other states to realize their lifelong ambitions.

Han Feizi, on the other hand, was bent on fulfilling his duties as a Han's envoy to Qin. As I have said before, A pragmatist cannot be theoretical, no can a theoretician be practical. Han Feizi, as a theoretician, was obviously very poor in political practice. You are all familiar with a story that Newton, although he was extremely intelligent, established the classical mechanics, creating the entire industrial era, but the legend says that he had two cats at home, he actually carved two holes in the door, he could not understand how the two sizes of the two cats could use one hole in the door. This of course may be a made-up joke, but it shows that the thinking of most theoreticians is out of bounds and the unique line of "theoreticians can not be practical".

Han Feizi thus annoyed the king of Qin, and Li Si took the opportunity to bad-mouth him, and the king of Qin put Han Feizi into prison in anger. Soon after Han Feizi was imprisoned, Li Si instructed the head of the prison to quietly poison Han Feizi's food, and Han Feizi died. The king later realized that he had done something wrong and wanted to free Han Feizi out of the prison, but it was too late.

Having said that, we need to mention that among the hundred schools of pre-Qin, the most tragic fate was those of the Legalist figures. Wu Qi was shot as a hedgehog, Shang Yang was cut as pizza, Han Feizi was poisoned by his former classmate Li Si, and Li Si himself was cut off at waist by Zhao Gao along with his young son. So, why were the most tragic fates of those legalist figures among the hundred schools of thought in the pre-Qin era? It was because the doctrines of the Legalists were so cruel and decisive that their political opponents had to use corresponding means to deal with them; furthermore, the Legalists were prone to psychological perverted, with unusual and perverted behaviors due to their ruthless legalism doctrines, which inevitably led to misfortunes.

After Han Feizi's death, someone recorded Han Feizi's legal writings, totaling more than 100,000 words, into fifty-five literary treatises, which have survived in twenty volumes. Han Feizi's book is a brilliant work that expresses the highest level of scholarship among the hundred schools of scholars of the pre-Qin dynasty in China. Han Feizi's legal treatises were filled with so many allegorical allusions that it is difficult to figure out the central line of thought in Han Feizi's legal system without careful exploration.

We are talking about Han Feizi today, mainly based on the commentary on Legalism in Guo Moruo's *Ten Criticisms*. In passing, I would like to say a few words about Guo Moruo. When he was young, Guo Moruo was a man of great talent, and during the Republican period, he made many important studies in history, literature, theater, oracle bone inscriptions, etc., reaching considerable heights. But after the founding of the country, he suddenly fell into the imperial literati, talk timid, extremely good at flattering, the early days of the Cultural Revolution, even he was the first to advocate the burning of his own books, thus setting off a national book-burning frenzy, so literarily disgusting.

We move on to the text of *Han Feizi*. Han Feizi boasts in the *Law Evaluation* that "Shenzi has not exhausted the tactic, and Shang Yang has not exhausted the law." What he means was that Shen Buhai has not yet played with *tactics of the power games* to the extreme, and Shang Yang has not yet achieved the depths of *law* either. If anyone wants to find the essence of law and magic, he has to come to me, Han Feizi.

There are four basic features of Han Feizi's thought. First, the distortion of Laozi. As we all know, Laozi's theory of *Dao* is that *Dao* is the basis for the evolution of all things, but Han Feizi changed Laozi's *Dao* to *Law* and thought that *law* and *tactic* is the Way of Heaven. He said, "There is no duality in the *Dao*, so it is said as one, so that the bright ruler is worthy of the unique *Dao* of tolerance." The *Dao* he talked about here is not Laozi's *Dao*, but the way of *law* and *tactics*. Moreover, he explicitly criticized Laozi because Laozi talked about retreat and trance, and advocated to be indifferent to the world and follow the nature, which is called *tranquility*; he thought that the way of heaven and earth could not be known by the general way of direct feeling, which is called *trance*. But Han Feizi said: "Tranquility is the teaching of uselessness; trance is the word of lawlessness. A person who serves the ruler and raises his relatives, cannot serve the ruler and raise his relatives in a tranquil way, but serve in his speech, faith, law and tactics; and his speech, faith, law and tactics cannot be in a trance. The words of trance, the study of tranquility, is the confusing art to the world." That is, all obedience to the sovereign power, obedience to the law and tactics, is the only *truth* and the important thing in the world, so as to reorganize the basic connotation and external form of Laozi's *Daoism*.

The second characteristic of Han Feizi's doctrine is called non-Confucianism, that is, he opposes the doctrine of Confucianism in general. Han Feizi was a disciple of Xunzi, the great Confucianist, and he was a Confucianist by birth. However, he advocated "relying on law and tactic, but not on faith", that is, you should rely on law and power, but not on benevolence, righteousness, propriety, knowledge and reliance; he advocated "upholding the law but not the virtues", that is, you should respect the law but not the virtues. He used the tiger and the leopard as a metaphor for the ruler, and the stocks and the fowls as a comparison for the imperial minister. He has a very famous article called *The Eight Traitors*. He has this passage in the article: "First is in bed together, second is next to each other, and third is father and brother." In this article, he listed eight kinds of traitors that threatened the king. The first is called the same bed together, that is, person of sleeping in the same bed with the king, that is, the queen and prince, he said this is the first threat to the king; second is person at side, the so-called person at side, is the king's important minister, the ancient king's important ministers, most were the king's blood relatives; third is father and brother, the third danger to the king came from his father and brother.

Han Feizi has a good reason for saying so. You may recall that in my Confucius class yesterday, there were 43 regicides during the Spring and Autumn Period (255 years), and more than 70 to 80 percent of them were committed by these three types of people. Han Feizi's insight was sharp.

The third characteristic of *Han Feizi* is that he tampered with the Mohist doctrine to serve his doctrine of law. The Mohism spoke on behalf of the interests of the low-class craftsmen, but at the same time they advocated the *dictatorship of the brilliant ruler*, a topic that we will expand on in the next class when we talk about the series of the Hundred Schools of Thought. Then, Han Feizi draws on these Mohist views and proposes a further in-depth discussion. In his *Law Evaluation,* he explicitly stated that "a nation should see with one eye and hear with one ear", which means that a state should have only one head, and the king should decide everything, and all other subjects should only have the obligation to blindly obey. This is why the Chinese later had the name the *school of Moh-Legalism, Moh* refers to the Mohists, *Legalism* refers to the Legalist, the so-called *school of Moh-Legalism* is an alias of the *school of Legalism*.

The fourth characteristic of Han Feizi's theory is his criticism of Xunzi. As I mentioned earlier, Xunzi was Han Feizi's teacher, but since Xunzi, as I mentioned earlier, advocated benevolence, righteousness, propriety, knowledge and faith on the one hand, and harshness of law on the other, Han Feizi criticized his teacher for his confused thinking and denounced his doctrine as "the study of foolishness and contradiction." Here we can see how thorough Han Feizi's legalistic spirit was.

Basic Orientation of Han Feizi's Doctrine

Let's skim some of the original text of *Han Feizi* below to sort out the main line of Han Feizi's legal theory.

Han Feizi said in the chapter of *The Out Upper Left*: "Those who admire benevolence and righteousness but weak and chaotic are the three Jins; those who do not admire but strong is the Qin. But why not yet become emperor? The rule of law is not yet completed." What he meant by this passage was that all the civilized countries in the Central Plains that insisted on benevolence, righteousness, propriety, knowledge and faith were in a state of weakness and chaos, while Qin, which did not believe in Confucius' rituals, was very strong. Then why has Qin not yet unified the country and become emperor? His answer was that "the rule of law has not yet been completed", that is, the Qin state has not yet thoroughly implemented the rule of law.

Please note that by this time, the system of Shang Yang's Law Change had already continued for six generations of kings, and Han Feizi still criticized that the implementation of Qin's law was not thorough enough. Han Feizi said in the *Suppression of Rebellions*, "A sage's governance is the way to make people to love me, but not to rely on people loving me". He said that the wisest ruler who governs a state must not make the people to love him, but must make them dare not to not love him. The difference here is that he believed that the benevolent rule of loving the people was undesirable, and that only violence, cruelty, and fear were the only resources for political power and social administration, which is an important foundation of Han Feizi's legal theory.

Han Feizi said in the *Eight Arguments*, "The way of efficient management is not to seek clean officials, but to make sure that one knows the law and tactics." What he meant was that the most important way to govern a country was not to use clean officials, but to use officials who knew the art of law. Since Han Feizi rejected clean officials, the practice of bribery and corruption has become a political tradition in China throughout its history. Therefore, we should not think that there exist corrupt officials in China only now, or in the Republic of China, but in fact, the history of Chinese politics for more than 2,000 years is the history of Chinese corrupt officials for more than 2,000 years. No wonder there has been a saying in China since ancient times that "a clean governor has at least a hundred thousand snowflakes silver". Let me tell a story. During the Northern-Southern Dynasties, the founder of the Western Wei Dynasty, Yu Wentai, who had won the kingdom, had an appointment with Su Zhuo, a famous literary figure at the time. He asked Su Zhuo: "How can the country be managed?" Su Zhuo gave him the answer: "Find the capable officials". He also asked, "How to find capable officials"? The latter part was not recorded in the history books, and it may be a fabrication of the overheard history, but this fabrication can illustrate the characteristics of Chinese corrupt politics - Su Zhuo replied: "Use corrupt officials, kill corrupt officials". Yu Wentai was greatly puzzled and said, why use corrupt officials? Su Zhuo told him, using corrupt officials you get three benefits: first, a corrupt official who follows you can reap huge benefits, so he must be the most loyal to you; second, because he is a corrupt official, you have evidence of his corruption in your hands, so you can most easily control him, if he is a little unruly, you intimidate him to become good; third, you can also kill a few corrupt officials when needed, so that you can win the people hail for the sovereign wisdom. This is what China has been doing since ancient times to combat corruption, isn't it? All these things are the legacy of Han Feizi's legalistic thinking.

Han Feizi said in the *Beware of Internal*, "If you trust your son too much as a ruler, then treacherous officials will take the advantage of your son to get what they desire". He said that as a ruler you can never too much trust your son, otherwise, some selfish officials will gather around him and become a threat to you. He also said, "If you trust your wife too much as a ruler, then treacherous officials will take the advantage of your wife to get what they desire." He said that as a king, you must not love your wife too much either, because if you favor the queen, then treacherous officials will gather around her and eventually pose a threat to you as well. He even gives strict inferences to prove that the greatest threat to the king is the queen who shares your bed. Let's see how he proves it. He says: "A husband of fifty years old is still lust for beautiful women, and a woman of thirty years old is declining in her beauty, so if a woman of declining beauty to serve a lustful husband, she will be estranged, and her son will be implicated and cannot be a successor." What does this passage mean? He said that a man of fifty years old is still strong and lustful, but a woman of thirty years old has no more color. We look at a woman today at the age of thirty still beautiful, but you should know that the average life expectancy of the ancients was only about thirty-nine years old, girls at the age of 14 or 15 years old married and gave birth to children, 30 years old has been a woman pretty old. He said, when the queen is old and no more attractive, the king will turn to lust for other women, and eventually estrange the queen or even send her into the cold palace, so that the queen and the king's son can no longer inherit the throne.

He went on to say, "If only the mother is the empress dowager and the son is the ruler, then she will be able to do whatever pleased, and her pleasure with man will be no less than that of the previous king." He said that only when the queen became the express dowager, and her son, the crown prince, ascend to the throne and becomes the king, could she ensure that her power remains. Although at this time, the queen no longer has a husband, but her pleasure with men can even be better than the former. How did she solve her problem of sexual hunger? Find male prostitutes, just like Empress Wu Zetian did. Han Feizi concluded, "That is why poisoned food or choke is used". He says, monarch, you have to beware of your wife, this is the reason why the queen especially wants to kill you. He even listed the specific methods in detail: first, hemlock poisoning, that is, quietly put poison into the king's meals to kill him unnoticed; second, strangulation, while the king is asleep, with a pillow to cover him to death. Look at Han Feizi's consideration for the preservation of the king!

Han Feizi said in *Famous Schools*, "A strict family has no shameful children, but a loving mother has prodigal sons, and this is how I know that the power of authority can prohibit rebellion, but the virtue of generosity is not enough to stop turmoil." He said that if there is a strict father in a family, then the children will be more prosperous and seldom have any problems; while if there is only a loving mother in a family, there will be prodigal sons here. In this way, he said, I know that severe power and authority are the resources for management, while virtue and kindness are not enough to get rid of turmoil.

This statement by Han Feizi seems to make sense at first glance, but in fact he is intentionally confusing the concepts. Modern psychological research has found that if a child's father is too violent when the child is young, then such a child will be psychologically perverted, and when he grows up, he will have a low level of human stretching, but a probable high crime rate. A child who lives in a loving atmosphere will have a fuller humanity in the future and will have a relatively more expansive life. Of course, if a mother loves her child too much, she will indeed spoil her child, but that is a very small rate, not the norm. For example, if your father wears a blue hat, you cannot say that those who wear blue hats are your father. Han Feizi uses this confusion of concepts here to prove that violence and cruelty are the only resources for management.

So he said the following paragraph: "The mother loves the son twice as much as the father does, but the son follows his father's orders ten times than to his mother's. An official has no love for the people, but the people follow official's order ten thousand times than they do with parents. Parents accumulate love but their children listen to their orders poorly, officials give orders to the people with authority and the people have to follow, the policy of severity or love can be decided." He said that the mother loves her children, more than the father's love, but the children listen to the father ten times than they do to the mother. He said that the officials had no love for the people, but the people listened to the government and were far more obedient than they do to their parents. Parents love but cannot discipline their children, while officials are loveless but can rule the people with authority. It is clear which is more effective, love or severity. He again emphasizes that brutality and harshness are the essence of ruling power.

In his *The Tactics*, Han Feizi said, "The tactic is invisible, and the use of them is unknowable. Nothing should be done apparently, watch defects in darkness; seeing as if not to see, hearing as if not to hear, knowing as if not to know." What is this passage about? It is about power games! He means exactly the same thing as Shen Buhai preached. He said, as ruler you must not operate in open, you must play games in the dark. You must hide in the shadows, observe every move of the ministers, but do not let your subordinates find out what you are doing. He said that even if you find a problem with a minister, you should not accuse him openly, you have to find another opportunity to punish him, do not let him know that you have been informed of his corruption, this is called "seeing as if not to see, hearing as if not to hear, knowing as if not to know".

The book of *Han Feizi* is full of such sinister theories. I just cite just one example above to demonstrate Han Feizi's subtle talk about the *tactic* of the *law, tactic, and power*. Han Feizi said in *The Tactics*:

"If there is achievement, the king will have his virtue in it, and if there is fault, the minister will have his sin." As we know, the way the king manages his rulings is that the front-line officials make specific suggestions to the king, and the king decides to adopt them or not, depending on the situation. Han Feizi warned the king that if his policy was effective, the credit would go to the king; and if his advice was adopted but not effective, the blame would fall on the minister. He said that was the relationship between the king and his subjects.

Han Feizi said an interesting passage in *Eight Advices ·Troubles*. He said, "An official who advances step by step the official ladders to a highest position is a wise man." Meaning, if an official, who started from the grassroots and rose to a high position by promotion, then the king you have to beware of, because this kind of person is especially wise. He then said, for this kind of men of capability and ambition, the king must use three methods to restrain them, what are the three methods? One is *hostage,* the second is *reward,* the third is *fault-finding*. What is *hostage*? The original text reads "relatives and wives, can be hostage;" that is, you have to hold his wife and children in the capital, as hostages, once the official rebels, you will kill his family, this is called hostage; two is *reward*. What is *reward*? "to promote in ranks, or to confer titles of nobility, which are the rewards;" that is, you have to give him a high official rank, let him get rich, including allowing him to accept bribes to satisfy his greed. What is *fault-finding*? "to find and blame or punish at trifle faults," what does it mean? It means that you have to nit-pick, to find the possible fault with which to punish or threaten him, such as imprisoning him or hanging him to death and so on. He said for officials who have the capability and ambition and have raised all the way from the grassroots to the top, you can use these three methods to temper them.

He then said: "for virtuous officials, hostage is enough to hold them; for greedy officials, reward is enough to constrain them; and for treacherous officials, fault-finding is enough to intimidate them". That is, for the virtuous minister, you just hold his wife and children as hostage, he will not do anything improper; for greedy, corrupt officials, you just let him get rich, you will be able to control them; for the competent and cunning minister, you have to be fault-finding, and threaten him from time to time. Then he said: "If you cannot bear to kill him, then he will probably offend you later; if you cannot get rid of him as small problem, you will have big trouble." He said that you need to act first to get rid of officials who are not obedient to you, so as to avoid trouble in future.

He also provides the method of punishment: "if you can find proper accusation or excuse, just sentence him to death; if a minister makes you upset, but you cannot find any fault or excuse, killing him will harm your reputation, then you may poison him to death with food or drink; this is called to remove potential traitors." Meaning, if you can find a proper crime or excuse, you can simply kill him; if the minister makes you very upset, but you really cannot find his fault, then what to do? You can quietly poison this minister's meals and poison him to death; he said this is a good way to eliminate those who pose a potential threat to you. Listen to what a lovely this Han Feizi was!

Han Feizi said in *Dictatorship*: "The power of the ruler is dictatorship. Rule the people with severe law, so severe that the people would be content if they are not punished, and nobody dare to ask for reward from you." What does that mean? He says that the power of the king cannot be divided. As you know, modern political democracy is about the division of power, checks and balances, which is completely opposite to the view of Chinese legalism; he also said that you must impose strict laws, and the laws must be so strict that the people are satisfied with just not being sanctioned by the law, and no one dares to ask for rewards from you.

He also said a famous quote that expresses the relationship between the people and the king in Han Feizi's mind. The original saying goes like this: "the relationship of ruler and his people should be, when the king is in trouble, use the people to die for him; when the king is at peace, use the people to work the best for him". It means to say, the relationship of the ruler and the people should be when the state is in turmoil, or in war with others, you let the people to die in the battlefield for you; when the state is in peace, you let the people work hard to produce wealth for you.

Han Feizi said in *Out Upper Right*: "If a minister becomes some kind of force that you cannot handle it, then remove him immediately. If a minister is not moved when you reward him or praise him, he is not afraid of when you punish him or defame him, these four methods have no effect on him, you should kill him." He said if a minister has formed some kind of power and you can't dissolve it, then get rid of him immediately; he also said that in the face of a minister, you reward him, praise him, he is not moved; you punish him, denigrate him, he is also fearless; add these four ways to him, he does not change, what to do? Destroy him quickly.

Han Feizi said in his *Eight Comments*: "If there is difficulty in enacting laws, then you should consider which is better, enacting the law or drop it; if you decide enacting the law is right, you should do it, even though there is the opposing force. There is no law without difficulty, no work without harm, and there is nothing only one side good under the sun." He said that legislation is a difficult thing, the force of opposition must be very large, you discern which is the less evil for you, then you should still choose to legislate. He further explained that anything you do, it is impossible only good without harm, law punishment is inevitably brutal, the side effect is indeed very large, but compared to the higher gains, you have to make up your mind to start it; if you want to have no harm, no difficulties and easily legislate, there is no such good thing in the world as the implementation of laws. We can see that Han Feizi even directly explained for the king in advance how to weigh things and how to consider and decide it.

Han Feizi also said in *Means of Control*: "The good way to rule state, the priority is to stop the evil doing, but what is the method of eliminating the slightest evil thing? It is necessary to make the people to watch each other and inform each other." What does it mean? He said that when you govern a country, how do you know the small but widespread wrongdoings in the society and among your subjects? He said that there is only one way for you to do this, and that is to establish a system of linked-in investigation and punishment. Let the people spy on each other and inform each other, and improve the system of secret agents and informers, so that you can eliminate all the evil seeds of lawlessness from the imperial court to the people.

He said in *Human Master*: "The reason why the tiger and the leopard can win over people and deter all other beasts, is due to its claws and teeth. When the tiger and leopard lose their claws and teeth, then man will be able to control them". He said that the reason why the tiger and leopard became the king of all beasts, even man is not its rival, because it has sharp teeth and claws; if its sharp teeth and claws were removed, then the tiger and leopard will inevitably lose its prestige and be controlled by man; he then went on to say: "Nowadays, those who are powerful are the claws and teeth of the ruler, and if the ruler loses his claws and teeth, so he would be like the tiger and leopard". He said that for the king, who are your sharp claws and teeth? If you are not good at employing black-hearted men as powerful ministers, you are like a tiger and a leopard who have lost their claws and teeth. Please note the meaning of this passage from Han Feizi, he actually advocates the use of brutal officials by the ruler.

As we know, all Chinese rulers used brutal officials, such as Wu Zetian's Lai Junchen, the famous brutal official who created the allusion *Please try the jar you suggested against others*. In fact, not only Empress Wu Zetian, Chinese kings of all generations have used brutal officials, because brutal officials were their minions, until Mao Zedong, who was Mao's minion? Kang Sheng. From the time of Yan'an rectification to the end of the Cultural Revolution, Kang Sheng looked at Mao Zedong's eyes and acted according to Mao's indication, whoever made Mao unhappy, Kang immediately fabricated charges and framed him. Eventually Kang Sheng became one of the rare high officials around Mao Zedong who did not suffer any before his death.

Han Feizi said in *Out Upper Right*: "The wise ruler harnesses his subjects, like the hunter tames his eagles. Hunter who tames falcons first breaks its lower plume, then it will rely on master for food, of course it will be tamed. The same is true for a wise ruler with his subjects, makes the subjects to rely on master for benefits, make them obedient to master, of course they will be in harness." He said that a wise master harnesses his ministers, just like a hunter trains a falcon; how does a hunter train a falcon? He shot off a falcon in the wild, captured a chick back alive, then plucked its plumes on the wings, so that it cannot fly, it will rely on the hunter for food, until it is tamed completely dependent on human. During this period, it gradually grew full of feathers, and then released it to catch prey, such as rabbits and so on. Before the hunter releases the falcon, he took a thin rope to tie up the neck of the falcon so that it could not swallow, and after it caught the hare and it had to bring it to the master, who loosened the tied knot around its neck to feed it. He said that a wise king should control his ministers as a hunter controls his falcons. Han Fei was so sincere in teaching the king how to control his ministers.

In the *Fault-Finding* Han Feizi says: "for the minister who proposed on a specific matter, the king listens to what the minister proposed, then decides to grant him in charge of the matter. If the minister completed the matter as what he said previously, you may reward him for his work and his words; if what the minister completed is different from what he said previously, you will punish him for the difference between the matter and his words. Therefore, for all your ministers, whose words small and accomplishment large is punished, not punish his large accomplishment, but his improper words, for improper words is worse than his accomplishment, so punish him." What does this passage mean? Usually, when a monarch governs the state, the minister who is involved in the specific work must first give his opinion and provide the monarch with a few solutions or strategies, and then the monarch will give the minister the corresponding authorization according to the minister's proposal, and only after that will the minister implement the work according to the monarch's authorization. He said what should you do if a minister says well and does not do well? This we all understand, you should punish him; Han Feizi also asked, if the minister does better than what he said, what should you do? We would think, of course you should praise the minister. Wrong! Han Feizi suggests the monarch to punish him as usual. He said if you don't punish him, then in the future all the ministers will give you a speech, he can do ten points, he only speaks to five points, and then he only has to do six points, seven points, you still have to reward him. It is obviously that you are waiting for others to cheat you? So Han Feizi went on to say: "When a wise lord has a minister, the minister must not overstep his official position and be meritorious, and must not say anything inappropriate. If he goes beyond his official position, he will be punished to die, and if he said anything inappropriate, he will also be punished". He said that a minister must fulfill whatever he says, and he must never act beyond the authority of the king, or he will be punished immediately. Even in such details we see how Han Feizi made careful calculations for the kings.

Speaking of this, we have to mention Machiavelli, a political scientist who appeared in Italy in the late Renaissance period of the 15th and 16th centuries in Europe. As we all know, before and after the Renaissance, Italy was not a unified country, it was divided into several small duchies, such as the Duchy of Venice, the Duchy of

Milan, the Duchy of Florence and so on. At that time, a political figure named Machiavelli was active in Florence. He used to hold an official position in the Florentine Republic, but after the restoration of the Medici family, he was dismissed and imprisoned, and after his release, he lived in seclusion in the countryside. During that time, he wrote a famous book called *The Prince*.

In this thin book, Machiavelli made an amazing point when he said that human nature always turns to evil and not to good, therefore kings ruling the world must not follow civil morality. The king must be as fierce as a lion and as cunning as a fox, which is why the emblem of the Paris School of Administration is still a lion and a fox today. He then said that kings do not have to be moral, they have to do everything, conspiracy, assassination, lies, fraud, threats, treachery, talking to people, as well as talking to ghosts, in short, everything, as long as the goal is right, they can do whatever they want. This is the tone of Machiavelli's *The Prince*, which, for the first time in European history, freed political science from theology and ethics, and which is said to have been the first book in which modern Western political science was established. So, we can see that the word *modern political science* itself has a malicious and insidious meaning. If you have time, read the book *The Prince*, as its Chinese translation is available today. Comparing with *Han Feizi*, the content of *The Prince* is really a small dish, as *Han Feizi* is much more detailed, profound and brilliant than it, though Han Feizi was more than 1,700 years earlier than Machiavelli, his book reflects the darkness of Chinese legalism.

Outline of Legalism: *Support the Ruler and Degrade the People*

Han Feizi said in *The Five Harms*: "all the state people talk about governance, and when ordinary people have the law books of Guan-Shang, the state is poorer: more people talk about farming, less people really go farming. When more people talk about war, ordinary household has books of Sun-Wu, the state military is weaker: more people talk about war, less people take arms to fight. Therefore, a wise lord uses the force of people instead of listening to their words, reward things of real value and prohibit things of useless." What does it mean? He said that all books should be burned, except for a few agricultural books, medical books; legal books, military books are reserved for the kings and his important ministers to read, most of the private collection of books should be burned and banned. Why? He said that if the people of your land all talk about the rule of law, and talk about the law of Guan-Shang, Guan refers to Guan Zhong, Shang refers to Shang Yang, *the law of Guan-Shang* refers to the legal literature. He said that if more people read books on law, then more people would talk about farming and fewer people actually carry hoes to do farm work; he said the same is true with books on warfare, because if the people read books on warfare, the number of people who talk about warfare increase, then the number of people who carry guns to fight for you will reduce. He finally added that a wise king would only let the people work hard and not allow them to talk too much, and for this reason he must reward things of real benefits and forbid imaginary thoughts. This is a typical policy of fooling the people, keeping the people in ignorance.

Note that the Legalists first implemented the policy of fooling the people in the land of Qin. Many scholars say that the policy of fooling the people in China actually began with Laozi. Don't be mistaken! Though Laozi advocates abandon knowledge and drop all learning, he did not advocate fooling the people. He hoped that no one, from up the patriarchs and rulers, down to the common people, all would not develop intellectually, not involved in civilization, which would be the gospel of humanity. Therefore, Laozi advocates being *a foolish man*, not a *policy of fooling the people*. The character *people* in antient refers to *inferior people*. In oracle bone scripts, an eye is drawn with below a straight-out symbol, (甲骨文 金文 小篆 民 楷体) which earlier meant a slave with downcast gaze, who dared not raise his eyes to look at others.

Han Feizi said again in *Explanations*: "The law of forbidding evil things: the top level is to prohibit man's mind, the middle level is to prohibit his words, and the lower level is to prohibit his deeds. What does it mean? We all know that in modern law, people are free to think, free to speak, and the law only prosecutes a person's illegal deeds, and he is sentenced according to the actual damage he has caused to society. Han Feizi, on the contrary, said, the best law is to forbid a man's mind; so that he does not dare to have the idea of evil; the second-best law is to forbid him to speak freely, that is, to make him dare not to speak freely. The lowest law is the one that makes him dare not to do bad things. Because of Han Feizi's idea, there has been no freedom of speech in China since ancient times, and not only that, there is something called *crime of written*. We are all familiar with it, the most typical *crime of written* occurred in the Qing Dynasty, but in fact, China has been a crime of written since ancient times, but the Qing Dynasty did it more thoroughly. A story circulated in the Qing Dynasty, said that a literatus once in the outdoor reading, the breeze blew his book pages scraped, so he said a limerick: "the wind does not know the words, why it turns the book pages", and was overheard by someone, who informed it to the authority. The official in charge of this case, saying that this limerick implies irony that the Manchu people of the Qing Dynasty were illiterate, so he was beheaded for this, this is called *crime of written*.

In fact, freedom of speech has never existed in China, especially in the second half of the last century, when it was even more intensified. During the Cultural Revolution, everyone was intimidated into silence, and if you kept a manuscript, or even a private diary, you had better burn it before it was too late, in case someone found out that there was something wrong with it, it would put your life at risk. So no one dared to write a diary at that time, except to follow an official style of writing, that is, the Lei Feng diary.

There is another crime in ancient China, which happened in the time of Emperor Wu of Han Dynasty, and it sounds strange, called *the crime of evil-thought*. What does it mean? You slandered me in your mind, so I have to kill you! This is called *forbidding his mind*. You see, this is Han Feizi's law, which is the sum of Chinese legalist theory.

Han Feizi's ideology advocates *legislate law for autocracy*. His entire theory of law consists of only five words, the original words of which are *respect the king power uninfringed*, that is, to respect the king and his sovereign is not to be infringed, and this is the primary outline of his legislation. As you know, the modern law of mankind is that the people elect the members of the parliament, who make the law in the legislative body of the congress, which is specifically used to limit the powers of the government, political parties and the military, this thing is called *constitution*. I have heard some scholars say that Chinese legalism is the precursor of the modern rule of law, which is totally nonsense. In fact, they are two fundamentally different legal systems, namely, the legal system of agricultural civilization, and the legal system of industrial and commercial civilization that eventually emerged from the Greco-Roman system, with no inheritance between them. They are two separate legal systems, which are completely opposite in terms of the basic connotative intentions or the terms and conditions. So the traditional Chinese law of legalism is not at all the same thing as the modern legal system of the West.

Han Feizi advocated *the law stifles humanity*. The purpose of his legislation was to stifle human nature without any regard for human rights. He said in his *The Five Harms* that "parents treat their children with a calculating mind" and "the people are submissive to power only, but never to benevolence and righteousness", saying that parents have to use a calculating mind to discipline their children, let alone kings and officials to rule the people. He said that the people would only submit to power, but never to benevolence and righteousness. He suggests to severely restrict personal freedom and bring the social life of the people into the regulated channel of the tyrannical government.

Han Feizi advocated *Replace culture with law*. He proposed to take law as education and let officials to be the teachers. He said that if education is to be carried out, it must be based on the law; then who can be the teacher? Only officials who knew the law could be teachers. He said in the *Famous Schools*: "The people's wisdom is not available, only the hearts of infants. Therefore, to seek wisdom or talent when needed, and to do politics and look for the right persons, are not good for the state." It means that the people's wisdom is not available, and the education is not developed, talent and capable people are scarce, only when upper full of wisdom and lower in foolishness, the state can be peaceful.

Han Feizi advocated *the use of both the law and the tactics*. He said in the *Beware of Internal*, "As ministers never rest a moment to spy on the mind of the king." That is, your ministers are always looking at you with evil intentions, so the king should always be on guard. He says bluntly in the *Law Evaluation*, "If you have no tactics to rule over treachery, then you only help your subjects with your power and strength." He says that if a ruler does not have the tricks of heart, he will lose his power and resources to others. He then says, "The tricks is hidden in the mind, to make disputes between the ministers, so as to use hidden tactics to control the ministers." What does that mean? The art of power is something that must be hidden in the heart and not exposed. He said, King, think about it, you are just a single person, how can you deal with hundreds of ministers, the power of two sides is not equal. You only have one way, use the hidden tactics, use the power games, constantly divide them, make them contradict each other and quarrel with each other, so that you can keep your power balance in the middle.

Han Feizi advocated *the severity of the law*. He said in the *Punishment Reward*: "Do not avoid ministers when punish someone, and do not leave out the lower man in reward for good deeds". He also said, "relatives and nobles are not exempted from law, and law covers your closest relations". When many scholars see such words, they say that Han Feizi advocated equality before the law. Obviously not. Because Han Feizi thought that the greatest harm to the king was his relatives and nobles and loved ones, so this does not mean that Han Feizi's theory of law advocates equal rights in law.

Han Feizi's ideal of the rule of law is fully expressed in the following passage: "The wise king examines the truth of what is right and wrong, and observes the situation of order and chaos. Therefore, when he governs the state, he corrects the laws and presents strict punishments, so as to save the masses out of chaos, and remove the scourge of the world, so that the forceful will not bully the weak, the many will not push around the few, the old will be satisfied, the young and orphaned will grow, the borders will not be invaded, the ruler and his subjects will be close to each other, the father and the son will protect each other, and there will be no danger of death and captivity." (See *Han Feizi ·Suppression of Rebellion*) What does this passage mean? He said that a wise king, as the supreme legislator and judiciary, must be aware of what is right and wrong, and understand the situation of governance and turmoil. Based on this, he must establish strict laws and make them public. Only in this way can you save the people from turmoil and remove the scourge of the world, so that the strong will not bully the weak, the many will not intimidate the few, the old will be supported, the children will be raised, the borders will not be invaded, and the ruler and subjects, father and sons will be close to each other and protect each other, avoid becoming unjust souls, captives or slaves under the sword of others. In other words, is Han Feizi right in thinking that this system of his law is responsible for the whole society? Yes! What do you mean? In the social structure of agrarian civilization, only this simple and brutal legal system is the cheapest, easiest to operate and most effective in control, because the law itself is the inevitable product of this structure of existence.

As I said earlier, the Chinese legalists were by no means good to the people. They were so vicious in their legal theories, in their governance and political conduct that it is hard to appreciate. For example, Shang Yang once put forward a *theory of weak people,* and his *Book of Shang Jun* originally said, "If the government does what the people hate, the people will be weakened; if the government does what the people like, the people will be strengthened." What does this passage mean? He says if you make policies and decrees that the people like, that's bad, the people will become strong because of that; if you make policies and decrees that the people hate, he says that's good, because the people will become weak; that is, politics is always against the people. He immediately followed with the very famous eight words called "if the people weak and the state is strong; if the people strong and the state is weak". He said that the state would be strong only when the people were weak, and if the people were strong, then the state would not be able to control the people, and the state would be weakened, and this is his famous *weak people theory.*

What is politics? Chinese legalistic politics was dedicated to bully the people and destroy their vitality and dignity. Only when the people were weak and shrinking could the power of the state be consolidated and the authority of the king be manifested, which was called the *theory of weak people,* also known as *weak people and strong state.* Regarding the implementation of the strategy of governing the weak people, he provided three methods: First, the policy of fooling the people. Shang Yang directly said: "If the farmers do not know and are not good at learning, then they will be diligently farming". He said that the peasants would be ignorant and uninterested in learning, so that they would work diligently. Therefore, he advocated burning books and banning them, outlawing the people's freedom of moving to other states, and stipulating that the

Qin people should not associate with foreigners. In short, cut off all your sources of information, so that the people are closed and dumb, this is the first way to weaken the people; the second policy called humiliating the people, that is, to constantly downgrade the people, so that the people feel that he is worse than a dog or a pig, only then will the people respect the officials. He originally said this: "if the people have private glory, then they will themselves no different with the humble officials", he said that if you make the people feel very glorious and self-respecting, then people will despise officials and defy the government; you only make the people feel very humble and lowly, then the officials will have authority; his third policy called impoverishing people, the original text said "If the people are rich, they will not look at the officials' rewards, and the officials will have no power to hold the people obedient; he went on to say, "If they were humiliated, they will value the nobles, if they were weak, they will respect officials, and if they were poor, they will be eager for reward," and he said that if you leave the people no dignity, they will respect nobles; If you make the people weak and powerless, the officials will look strong and honorable; if you make the people poor, they will be eager for official rewards. This is the key to the internal rule of Shang Yang's change of law, and this is the basic attitude of Chinese legalists towards the people.

So we must understand that Chinese legalism and its jurisprudence are incompatible with the modern legal system, which is all about the supremacy of the state, or *statism*, and the people are merely the instruments of state power. The state is supposed to be an institution that serves the people, but in Chinese rule of law culture and political science the opposite is true: the people are merely livestock to be herded and driven by the state. That is why Guo Moruo said, "In the society under Han Feizi, there are only hounds (informers), wolves (minions) and cattle and horses (the oppressed), where is the breath and dignity of man!" Lu Xun said in his essay that there are only *two eras* in China, one is "the era when slaves are temporarily secured" and the other is "the era when slaves are not allowed to be slaves". The former refers to the era of being exploited and oppressed, while the latter refers to the era when even the condition of being exploited and oppressed is lost, so that one has to rebel, and so on, in a cycle of repeated rule and turmoil. Therefore, in traditional Chinese society and the Chinese doctrine of legalism is the typical doctrine of state supremacy and statism, a violent way of ruling, and that everything serves the state power, and the people are extremely lowly, only serving as the fish or meat on the chopping block of the state politics. The best resource to maintain state political power and its system of rule of law is power of oppression and brutality, which is the basic theoretical framework of Chinese legalism.

Comparison and Exploration of the Political Wisdom in East and West

We have talked about the outline of Han Feizi's legal theory earlier, and now we discuss some issues related to it below.

Since the establishment of legalistic theory, China gradually entered the mature stage of the monarchical dictatorship. Because of the highly repressive nature of the Chinese political legalistic system, the development of Chinese culture has since entered a dark and stifling era. Since the Qin Dynasty and the establishment of the monarchy, there was no significant development of Chinese national culture and its ideas, which was the inevitable consequence of Han Feizi's *take law as culture*.

In China society of dynasties, cultural and military achievements were something being proudly mentioned by later generations. In fact, in all dynasties, all official governance was a wanton distortion and castration of academia. For example, Emperor Zhu Di, the Great of Yongle, compiled the *Yongle Compilation* under the imperial authority. Some say it was a model of official governance in the Ming Dynasty, but what actually was the *Yongle Compilation*? The official government forcibly collected all the books from the people, forbade private collection of lost books, and then brought all the books over to be reviewed by the government-organized propaganda agency, and burned all those that did not conform to the mainstream ideology, and finally only those that could please and assist the autocratic system were gathered into a book, which was the *Yongle Compilation*. As for the Qing Dynasty's *Siku Quanshu (General Catalogue of the Four Categories)*, some say it was the glory of the Qing Dynasty's cultural achievement, but what actually was it? All the folk books were collected, and anything that did not conform to the Manchu rule, including the traditional Chinese "distinction between Han people and the northern nomadic barbarian" content, was deleted or extinguished, and then things of officially approved, or even falsified things were edited, which is the so-called *Siku Quanshu (General Catalogue of the Four Categories).*

Therefore, all the official academia under Chinese governance can basically be said to be an organized destruction of true cultural scholarship. The Chinese scholars, the traditional Chinese culture, have focused all their attention on the social problems of human nature, so much so that natural science has been completely abandoned. So it is logically thought that Chinese political science, jurisprudence, human ethics, etc., should have reached an extremely high level. But on the contrary, all the wise men concentrated all their efforts on the social and political problems of human nature, and what they created was a simple and crude legalistic political system as mentioned above. Therefore, it is said that the Chinese have very poor political wisdom, and there is some truth in this statement.

You see, from ancient Greek culture to Western civilization, they have used their primary intellect to look at the stars, to investigate the field of nature, which led to philosophical thinking and the establishment of a whole system of natural sciences. It is amazing that they have used only a little bit of their wisdom in humanities, sociology, law and legal system, and yet they created a very complex and systematic system of democratic constitutional government.

We should know that the Western democratic legal system, it is an exquisite and complex system of checks and balances, it is never as simple as the minority obeying the majority and only using the votes to speak. During the Cultural Revolution, China was also in a state of the minority obeying the majority. At that time, it was called "uniting 95% of the people and imposing dictatorship on the 5% of the landlord, the rich, the rebels, the evil and the rightist", but this was not *democracy*, it was a typical *tyranny of the majority*.

The so-called democracy is a complete institutional structure, first of all, it is a *horizontal separation of powers*, called *the separation of legislative power, the executive power and the judicial power*, which are independent and check each other. The legislator has the highest status, the Congress, which has the power to make laws, and all state institutions, all associations and organizations, including any individual, must act under the legal statutes it establishes, but the Congress and its members have no executive power and no judicial power; the government has executive power, and it obtains the ruling position through the legal competition of multiple parties, but it has no legislative power and no judicial power. The government has executive power and has come to power through legitimate multiparty competition, but it has no legislative power and no judicial power; the judiciary, the body that decides cases, has the power to exercise the law, but it has no legislative power and no executive power. This creates a system of mutual checks and balances of power, which are horizontal checks and balances.

As if this were not enough, it then establishes a *vertical separation of powers* system. Instead of a system of officials appointed by superiors to subordinates, each locality had its own local legislature, and local voters elected local councils and local chief executives, thus creating a lower-level separation of powers structure, which is called federalism. Its system of local decentralization is independent at every level, and lower officials, state and county leaders are not appointed from above, but are accountable to the people of their own region and to their local councils. It can even be done that a neighborhood express its public opinion unimpeded, if the people of that neighborhood form some kind of common agreement, for example, there should be no building at the corner of an intersection, otherwise the view is blocked when cars go to this place to turn around, so the people of that community, the people of a small street area make a decision that is valid when it is filed and approved in the court, this is a further separation of powers on the vertical line.

This is not the end of it. It has another layer of external power called *the public opinion*. In Western countries, including the United States, the government is explicitly prohibited by law from running public opinion organizations, such as newspapers, radio stations, television stations, magazines, publishing houses, and so on. Except for foreign propaganda organizations, which the government can establish only with the authorization of Congress, the government is not allowed to intervene in these internal public opinion organizations and can only leave them to the private sector, and any individual or association has the right to get involved in the above-mentioned industries, thus forming a pattern in which public opinion is independent of the government's power to monitor the government's exercise of power. Therefore, the public opinion sector is also called the fourth power system. This situation is just the opposite of China, where all public opinion institutions in China are only allowed to be run by the government and not by the private sector.

It does not end here, it draws another line, called *natural human rights*. Under this line, people's basic rights and individual rights are not infringed by any public power. For example, the right to personal reputation, the right to portrait, the right to property, the right to freedom of speech and association, etc. cannot be infringed by anyone, including all public powers.

It doesn't end there; it also provides for a provision called *unconstitutional review*. That is, the Supreme Court has the power to *unconstitutionally review* the actions of the President and specific initiatives of the executive branch, and to independently rule on the constitutionality of government, political parties, and the military, which are organized and powerful groups that operate outside the scope of the constitution established by the legislature.

Such a system of checks and balances constitutes the complex legal system of a democratic and constitutional society. Notice the word *law* in the West, which is also known as *law* in natural science, and the two meanings are combined into one word. What does it mean? It means that *rationalism* and *humanism* are the same, and *natural laws* and *humanistic rules* are the same. They believe that the law is a product of pure reason, just as you find the laws of nature, a purely rational, purely logical derivation. It is not based on someone's special needs, but on the maximization of the overall social interest, using reason to arrange a legal system of equal rights. It is like a traffic law, where traffic lights are not set up to serve any private interests, and the way it is designed, and even the arrangement of the number of seconds read, is adjusted according to the traffic flow, and all people must strictly comply with it. It is a very systematic and thorough rational structure, a purely rational structure, which Kant called "the moral command of pure reason", that is, all morality and law should be unfolded on this system. This is a very different concept from the Chinese legalistic theory, which only serves the political control of the authorities.

And we should also note that the rule of law in the West was never formed suddenly, it took more than 2,000 years of reforming and refining to gradually form a perfect system. You should know that scholars in ancient Greece, such as Plato and Aristotle, had made special studies on different political systems. For example, monarchy and tyranny, aristocracy and oligarchy, republicanism and democracy ......, they constantly analyze and compare, and examine in detail the advantages and disadvantages of each political form.

In ancient Greece, the Athenian city-state practiced democracy, which was once actually quite naive, even absurd. For example, Socrates, the famous ancient Greek philosopher and teacher of Plato, was actually given death by a vote of Athenian citizens. Why is the Peloponnesian War constantly explored in Western historiography? The Peloponnesian War was a war between two groups of ancient Greek city-states, one led by the Athenian democracy and the other led by the Spartan dictatorship in the Peloponnese, known as the Peloponnesian War. In both wars, democratic Athens were defeated, so what did Westerners explore in the Peloponnesian War? The flaws of democracy. During the wars, the citizens of Athens dismissed and exiled any general who was a good fighter, had a high record of success, and showed a great deal of prestige while the war was going on, by tile vote. Why? Fear that they would become dictators one day because they had too much power and prestige, which resulted in the continuous defeat of the Athenian League in the Peloponnesian War. It is clear that Western democracy has gone through more than 2,000 years, and the refinement from roughness to refinement is not a one-day process; it is a product that has taken thousands of years to process.

When we talk about laws and political systems, these things seem to be very important on the surface, but in fact, "culture precedes system". What does this mean? As I said earlier, democracy and the rule of law are composed of a complete system of theories and concepts, and it requires a permeable social and cultural pavement as a prerequisite. For example, in China's 1911 *Xinhai Revolution,* Sun Yat-sen's ideal was to establish a democratic constitutional system. More than a hundred years have passed since then, and the successive leaders of modern China, from Yuan Shikai to

Chiang Kai-shek to Mao Zedong, have never really established a democratic society. Why? During Yuan Shikai's time, during the warlord era, it had a parliament, it practiced party politics and had opposition parties. But what was the point? The parliament was either dissolved under pressure or there were only useless parliament members, party leaders could be assassinated, party activities could be restricted by the power, and Yuan Shikai finally claimed to be the emperor. Chiang Kai-shek's proposal of "one doctrine, one party, one leader" is the total opposite of constitutional democracy. What does it show? It shows that even if you have this system, if you do not have the corresponding cultural foundation, the system will be deformed, and eventually be abandoned.

This is why the realization of a democratic system can never be accomplished by merely establishing an institutional framework, which is why the Western constitutional democratic system has never been able to replicate outside of Europe and the United States, or at least not implemented in its original form, and has always been degenerated. Even Japan, which proposed to *leave Asia and enter Europe* and once studied the West comprehensively, returned to its old form in the Showa era, and the emperor became the *real ruler* from a *false ruler* and militarism returned. After World War II, MacArthur ruled Japan, and he established a constitution based on the American legal system and imposed it on Japan, with the result that Japan is still dominated by one party, the LDP. So Japan is the best extraterritorial democracy or the best imitation of it, but it is not yet fully aligned with Western democracies. All other non-European and American democracies have largely failed to reach maturity. Why? Because culture precedes the system! Please do understand this point.

I will say one more small thing in passing. Some people say that the United States has no culture, and there is some truth to that. The United States was founded only 240 years ago, and when you travel to the United States, it is difficult to see those European style lofty churches, exquisite sculptures, and all kinds of paintings and art exhibitions after the Renaissance, which are indeed rare in the United States. But if you say that the United States has no culture, that is your lack of understanding of American society, which is actually the product of inheriting and carrying forward the advanced ideas of modern Europe. You know that American society is actually the purest experimental ground for the implementation or enforcement of the most advanced ideas of a group of modern European thinkers. It includes Locke's "Sovereignty in the People" in his *Treatise on Government*, Montesquieu's "Separation of Powers" in *The Spirit of the Laws*, Rousseau's "Natural Human Rights" in *The Social Contract*, and John Mueller proposed "representative democratic legislative structure", Adam Smith proposed "invisible hand" and advocated "free market economic theory".……. It is the purest implementation of the entire ideological system of this group of modern European thinkers in the New World of North America. What does that mean? It means that these European thinkers, their new ideas, when they were still subject to the constraints of the old traditions in the European continent, even if they could be implemented later, they were inevitably accommodated to some extent, but only in the United States, a brand-new experimental field, was it really fully implemented, which is the basic spirit of the American *Declaration of Independence* and the American *Constitution*. It was the purest implementation and practice of this new idea that created the advanced pattern of the American superpower for nearly a century.

What am I saying? I am telling you that, regardless of whether democracy is good or bad, at least it does not happen overnight, it is the product of thousands of years of social and cultural sculpting, and it has to be nurtured by the soil of the corresponding structure of existence for the system to emerge and grow.

As for the saying that the Chinese have extremely poor political wisdom, which is valid on the surface, but not valid in the depths. Why? Because the traditional Chinese agricultural civilization itself will not produce some of the most basic ideas such as individual rights, democratic checks and balances, this kind of culture simply does not have the soil to develop. Therefore, in the world, without exception, as long as the ancient great river civilization, agricultural civilization of the regional countries, never produced a democratic system of thought and culture of the rule of law. What does this mean? Once again, it shows that any culture is only a product of a certain local structure of survival, and can never happen without a reason. Under the institutional structure of China's purely agrarian civilization, you can't even ask basic questions about *democracy* and *civil rights*. It only talks about social power and state power, but never about individual rights. Democracy is based on the rights of the individual, and public power is only a limited delegation of individual rights. This kind of culture can never be produced in agricultural civilization, so you can't see the democratic rule of law system in any agricultural civilization in the world, including *the Code of Hammurabi* in 1776 B.C. in ancient Babylon, all the way to *Han Feizi* in the third century B.C. in China, this system is exactly the same, it simply can't produce the kind of system of thought of Western industrial and commercial civilization from the budding state of the circum-Mediterranean to the modern tendency to mature state.

Therefore, the evaluation of the Chinese people's lack of political wisdom is in fact a manifestation of the lack of understanding of the conditions in which culture is born. In a particular social situation, such questions or problems do not arise, so how can conclusions be pursued and subsequent answers be generated? In an agricultural civilization, there was no individual freedom, and individual freedom was not advocated, because collective collaboration was the easiest and most effective way to survive in farming. Therefore, in its ancient culture, there were no individual rights, no notion of equality, no demand for freedom, but rather "love is differentiated" and "ritual are divided for superior and interior", and it used such a system, though simple, but very effective, though rough, but very low cost, to form an effective system of social control. Therefore, a culture, including a political-legal culture, must be the matching state and matching product of a certain structure of survival, and it can never happen for no reason, which is called *culture precedes system*.

Legalism may sound like the opposite of Confucianism, but in fact, their starting point and the most fundamental basis are the same thing, that is, the thought system of blood society. Confucius' doctrine is "interpreting rituals with benevolence", Han Feizi's doctrine is "interpreting rituals with law", both of which are derived from and regressed to *rituals*. As I said before, what are *rituals*? *Revere the revered and love the loved*, that is, the social blood structure or blood foundation is the common basis of Confucius' theory of benevolence and love and Han Feizi's theory of law. On the surface, they appear to be opposed to each other, but in essence they are unified and connected in their bones. Since they are both patriarchal by blood, this is why the Confucian parent is like a loving mother and advocates a benevolent system; the Legalist parent is like a strict father and advocates a legal system; both ultimately fall into the same *rule of human* system and *authoritarian* structure. Because of the interplay and complementarity between them, Confucianism and Legalism merged after the two Han dynasties, which is known in history as "Confucianism at the outside and Legalism at the inside" and "Confucianism on the surface and Legalism in the internal". These two things were so well integrated that they finally constituted the multi-aspect fulcrum for the stable existence of Chinese society.

If you look closely at the Chinese culture of the hundred schools in pre-Qin era, its entire traditional system is actually built on this same foundation. Laozi stands in the foremost, he advocates to return to the natural society of primitive blood clan; Confucius accepts feudal civilization system, but reorganized the civilized social structure with the blood ritual relationship; later, as social tensions increased, Han Feizi advocated the use of law to interpret rituals, and the use of severe punishment to consolidate and strengthen the pyramid of blood patriarchal social structure; and the Mohists stood at the high point of transcending reality, speaking out on behalf of the industrial and commercial civilization and launching a deconstructive challenge to the Confucian bloodline social system, but in the end they failed to penetrate the maze of history.

With regard to the different arguments of the hundred schools of pre-Qin era, you can only clarify the reasons for the occurrence of these ideas if you look deeper into the foundation of agricultural civilization on the basis of blood groups, and you can also understand why the extension of individual rights is impossible in the social structure of agricultural civilization. While without the extension and protection of individual rights, there can be no conditions for democracy and contract society to occur, and this is where the differences and special features of the political cultures between the East and the West.

REVIEW OF HAN FEI ACADEMIC IMPACT

Let's discuss one more issue below. Democracy looks wonderful and Han Feizi's legalism sounds very cruel, but you cannot say that the human nature under democracy is benign and the human nature under Han Feizi's legalistic system is cruel. In fact, human nature is the same thing, but different cultures make it flow in different ways. You should know that after the democratization of the West in modern times, they did a lot of evil, they talked about human rights and fairness internally, but looted and killed externally, and did nothing but evil. Chinese society behaves in the opposite way, they were brutal and tightly controlled internally, but benevolent externally.

Look at the event of Zheng He several times sailed to the West with a huge fleet, never to conquer other countries, but to establish a tribute system. As long as you recognize China as the central heavenly dynasty among all nations, you give me one piece of tribute, I will give you ten times of your tribute back, this is called the *tribute system*. It was very benevolent externally, but it was extremely harsh internally, what was the reason? As I said earlier, China's unique closed landscape was the only place in East Asia at that time where agriculture was produced, surrounded by deserts, mountains or oceans, so it had no way to obtain the wealth of the agricultural era externally, and no way to exchange it for food like city states around the Mediterranean Rim, and it had no place to loot externally. And all the struggle for wealth, all the interests entangled, were happened internally. Because of the fierce competition within the region, it was extremely harsh in the way it controlled itself internally. It was benevolent externally because it has no way to gain benefits externally. The West, on the contrary, has to loot externally, but internally it has to talk about human rights and fairness, forming an inward cohesion. But its overall culture, including its democratic system and the basic state of its industrial and commercial civilization, all exposed its evil side of human nature thoroughly.

For example, Columbus discovered the New World, the white men actually exterminated more than ninety percent of the local Indians, though the vast majority was caused by viruses and bacteria brought over, it is indisputable that the white men used to wipe out the Indians by means of armies and muskets; then there is the East India Company, the earliest Dutch bourgeois revolution and the establishment of the Dutch East India Company, referring to today's Indonesia; the British established the East India Company, in today's India; their companies actually had government shares, with the government ceding part of public power as shares, and so these companies could build armies and have some diplomatic power. They were in the East India Company, whether it was the Dutch East India Company or the British East India Company, they were equally extremely brutal in the way they ruled over the natives.

In India under British rule, there was a disaster one year, a region of India rich in grain production, all the output was forcibly collected by the East India Company, which caused millions of people to die of hunger in the region at one time, and this is just one of the countless evils done by the East India Company. Another example is the slave trade, you know that the slave trade, the total population of Africa is only about 90 million to 120 million, but actually 60 to 70 million people were sold into slavery, across the ocean, sick and hungry, 70% were dumped in the ocean, the rest arrived at the destination. The white men treated the black Africans like cattle, open their teeth to see their age, and then they bargain the price of the sale with local plantations' owners, the slaves did not have any human rights. Such a cruel slaveholding system did not disappear in the United States until the middle of the nineteenth century. Something as brutal as this could not be done by the Chinese to the outside world. It was not until World War II that Hitler used the industrial assembly line to exterminate the Jews by about six million, something China never did. Instead, China took in a large number of Jews during World War II, and until now, Israel has been grateful to China for this matter.

What am I talking about? I am talking about human nature is the same, human beings are the same kind of species. It's just that the state in which the evil of human nature manifests itself, expressing itself in different ways and flowing in different directions, depending on how the culture is shaped, that's all. China's internal political structure is extremely cruel, and it has a very bad side. Let me give you two examples. Emperor Cheng, Zhu Di, of the Ming Dynasty, who usurped the throne of his nephew, demanded that all his subjects loyal to the former Emperor Jianwen change their positions. At the time Fang Xiaoru, a famous scholar refused him, Zhu Di then threatened to exterminate his nine clan relatives, What does extermination of nine clans mean? Just say exterminate three clans, it includes your own family, the father's family, mother's family and wife's family, if all the members of the three families were killed, this was called to exterminate three clans. Think about the number of people involved in the extermination of the nine clans! Fang Xiaoru said that even if my ten clans were exterminated, there was no compromise, so Zhu Di brutally ordered the real extermination of the ten clans. What was the tenth tribe? Your students and friends were among those exterminated. In other words, if a teacher commits a crime, all of his students would be beheaded. Such an execution, once killing thousands of people, was horrifyingly bloody.

Let me give you another example. Still this Emperor Zhu Di of Ming Dynasty, he once had a love consort who was a Korean, sent over to the Emperor of China as a tribute, surnamed Kwon. Zhu Di doted on her so much, that he took her with him even when he was leading troops to war, marching to the northern frontier, but Kwon was physically weak, once suffered a wind chill and soon died. Zhu Di was heartbroken and could not forget her. After some years, concubines in his palace, due to disputing each other, rumored that Kwon was poisoned to death by some palace girls. On hearing that, Zhu Di did not even distinguish, ordered all concubines and palace girls, who were there when the concubine was alive, nearly 1,000 people, be lynched. Zhu Di himself, every day took a chair to sit there watching the torture, his own women were cutting by knives, with horrible howls. He was actually watching it! simply unconscionable! And he was actually the highest leader of the country! So, I say that human nature is of the same. East and West civilization, East and West political structure, East and West social legal system, it does not express who is good and who is evil, it is just a platform shaped by different cultures to show different human nature. This is a point I have repeatedly stressed.

Han Feizi's scholarship was based on the principle of *undermining morality and concentrating power*, which was exactly the same as Machiavelli's view that all morality was only a constraint and a fetter for the monarch to exercise power. The two men were totally the same opinion. Han Feizi said in *Cautions*, "the king and his subjects have a hundred battles a day", a phrase that sounds familiar to us. What he said was that the subordinates of the king were spying on the king every day, thinking of how to subvert you, which is the meaning of "a hundred battles a day." It is very similar to the saying of Mao Zedong before the Cultural Revolution: "Class struggle should be talked about every year, every month, every day". Han Feizi's doctrine matches very well with the structure of internal struggle in Chinese society, so its way of internal control was also very brutal. Guo Moruo made seven summaries on him: first, power cannot be shared, that is, power must be concentrated in the hands of the king himself, never to share power; second, deep concealment, not to intrigue in the open; third, beware of others as evil-minded; fourth, do not abide by any ethical values; fifth, implement the policy of fooling the people; sixth, the law must be severe, the reward must be prudent; seventh, when necessary, by any means; in the final analysis, it is the word *guile*.

Once upon a time, Chinese society was known as a state of etiquette. Confucius' culture of etiquette has indeed created a state of etiquette. In ancient times, there was a township gathering of archery ritual. It was a regular annual archery competition held in the countryside, and it had all kinds of rules and regulations. Before the competition, the participants need to toast to the elders, then to salute each other, then start the archery competition. The participants salute each other after the competition, and the winners get their rewards from the elders with bows in return, finally all young people salute the elders before they left, then the young people leave with good wishes saying to each other, etc. It was very complicated. It is important to know that to this day, the Japanese ninety-degree bow and many other rituals, and the Korean obsequious and considerate behavior, are actually the spread of the ancient Chinese rituals in East Asia.

However, since the rise of the doctrine of Legalism, the moral decay of Chinese society has been the result of the unscrupulous and corrupt way of behavior practiced by the upper class. Since ancient times, the traditional Chinese culture has been popular with a series of underhanded, poisonous, power-wielding, mutilating others for personal gain. In the years of Republic of China actually appeared a monograph called *unscrupulous science,* that is, how a shameless face with a selfish evil mind could play scams around, even forming a discipline, which might be unique in the world. And according to statistics, this book from the Republican era until today, has long been in the top of best-selling books. We can see to what extent the Chinese folk culture has declined, which is sure the dark product of the Chinese legal theory and law system.

When I talk about this legalism, it may give you the illusion that the Legalists were taking the credit for the stability of Chinese society that has survived for thousands of years. You should know that the doctrine of Legalism was popular only in the upper class, the government system, and the royal system in China, which has been developed a state or a pattern called "accompanying the king is like accompanying the tiger." While there has been also formed a phenomenon popular among the Chinese lower class, called "the sky is high and the emperor is far away", that is, the entire Chinese society at the grassroots level, in fact, is under the cover of the doctrine of Confucianism, which is the mainstream of culture in Chinese society.

As you know in ancient China, the government structure was made of three levels only: central court level, state and county level, and county level. There was no government agency under the county, that is, there was no government agency at the township and village levels. It was not the same as it is now, a township government, under which there is still a village cadres system, in the ancient times there was none. And 99.99 percent of the people live at the township and village levels, so what did they rely on to manage the people at the bottom? There were only a few court officials worked at county government office, the other dozen people were actually temporary workers, like constables, jailers, servants, and even the master secretary were temporary workers. It was quite different from today's a county government. Now if you go to a county, see the tallest, most imposing building must be the county government, which is stuffed with hundreds of thousands of people, all are county officials or public workers. So how did a county with a population of tens of thousands or hundreds of thousands manage with a few appointed court officials? It was managed by the township, village level gentry, gentry to manage.

In the past, all Chinese villages had ancestral halls. The so-called ancestral halls had several functions: first, ancestor worship; second, education and deliberation; and third, as a place to enforce family law. Who would enforce the family law? Who would educate and deliberate? The village gentries! Who were these village gentries? They were intellectuals, or elders, armed with Confucianism. They used Confucianism, the spirit of Confucianism, and Confucian theory to manage the grassroots of society, and were respectful and benevolent in their affair-dealings. Therefore, in ancient China, the general civil disputes, all within the scope of the township community to solve by their own, unless unusual and vicious events, such as murders or arsons, would be referred to the county government offices to deal with. Therefore, Chinese civil society, in general, was nourished and survived under the atmosphere of Confucianism, which was the cornerstone of Chinese social stability.

Hayek, a famous sociologist and economist, discussed a problem. He said that Western scholars once studied two villages in Europe and found that each of them had its own characteristics. One village is very rational, a child fell into the pond, the mother wanted to jump in the water to save the child, but she could not swim, the villagers and neighbors would stop the mother, saying that you could not save the child, but would be drowned, you might as well save your life, you could have more children in the future; the other village was simple and irrational, if a child fell into the water, the mother would jump into the water to save her child, the result was often the death of both mother and child. The culture of these two villages was completely different. European scholars followed up the research and found that after several decades, the extremely rational village where the mother did not save the child from drowning was scattered, while the warm affectionate but not rational village thrived and survived. We can use this to give an evaluation: muddled warmth is more beneficial than cold rationality! This is where the difference between Confucianism and Legalism lies. The doctrine of Legalism was extremely rational, and the system of legal theory woven into it was quite elaborate, reaching the highest level of Chinese pre-Qin scholarship, but it only created a rigid super-stable and super-oscillating structure of Chinese society, with the cycling of dynasties coming and going.

A famous scholar named Jin Guantao once proposed that Chinese society is a super-stable and super-oscillating structure. Chinese society is extremely stable, with no social or institutional changes for thousands of years, which Marx called *social fossil*, and the monarchical system of more than 2,000 years has been well maintained, and the imperial power system has not changed at all, this is called a super-stable state; however, there have been violent turmoil with farmers uprising, warriors troops attacking and conquering, killing and destroying, and finally dynasties collapses every 200 or 300 years, this is called super-oscillating structure. So you can see that in China, the ancient relics of the past generations were long gone. When you go to Greece, Rome, Spain and France today, most of their ancient buildings were preserved, which is of course related to the fact that Chinese ancient buildings were of civil and wooden structure, unlike the stone buildings in Europe, but it was also related to the super shaking structure of Chinese society. Every two or three centuries, the society fell in turmoil, destroying all the wealth and culture, and then building a model of the previous one and operated as before, which is called super-stable, super-oscillating structure. It actually stems from the inherent quality of the agricultural civilization itself, and the cultural atmosphere and political structure that this quality inevitably leads to. Of course, its super-stable state has much to do with the Confucian doctrine.

As I said in my Confucius class, Confucius used the most primitive and lowest blood ties to reorganize the social disorder of the super blood civilized society, thus constituting an extremely stable sequence of social structures, which is the cultural origin of the super stable society. Where did its super-shock character come from? From legalism. Of course, this super-stable structure itself, its cultural foundation itself, its survival structure itself cannot be super-stable forever. But the excessive repression, the excessive brutality, and the excessive social damage brought about by the legalistic system was one of the major reasons for the constant and violent shocks in this society. In a time when slaves were not allowed to be slaves, the only way for the people to survive was through rebellion, and Chinese society was thus super-stable and super-shocked.

The system of legalism and its political construction, we call it the *blood family society*, the imperial power is the product of the blood family, the whole society was the power's prey, this is called *family society*. In order to maintain the interests of the family, they would not hesitate to rule the society by tyranny, using an extremely cruel legal system, controlling society in a way that advocates violence and cruelty, thus constituting a strange mentality of the Chinese people, who, instead of being patriotic, have often held a mentality of hating the state since ancient times - hating the state, because the state is not my state, it is someone else's state. During the anti-Japanese war, Mao Zedong could not help but exclaimed in his speech to the tomb of the Yellow Emperor that "there are many traitors of the nation"! At that time, the China pseudo-army who followed the Japanese order to fight domestically, amounted to more than two million people, which was the evil result and definitely related to the long-established political system and the law system of legalism.

We summarize the lesson below. The doctrine of legalism is rife with the worship of violence and cruelty, expressing the underlying inferiority of human nature. What does that mean? Think about intra-species competition among living things, and in what way? By competing with the most powerful fists and the strongest muscles. How does lion king and monkey king become kings? By fighting, just through competing with others in violence. Therefore, in the biological world, their billions of years of evolution, the social status of the middle and higher animals are obtained by virtue of violence, thus laying a reference to the darkness of human nature. Human nature is endowed with a basal reverence for violence, whether interspecies or intra-species competition, the most basic means used by all animals is violence and cruelty. When it comes to humans, he can use reason to weave a complete set of brutal law network to control the whole group, thus shaping the extremely dark structure of human civilization.

That is why Goethe famously said, "If a man wants to use his reason, he aims only at becoming more bestial than a beast." This is the result of human use of reason in intra-species competition, that is, human use of reason only makes biological intra-species competition in human society more intense, more brutal, but this is the underlying provisions of human nature, bestiality, biological nature. For this reason, psychologists found a very strange phenomenon, they do statistics found that the most powerful, the most competitive kind of personality in human society, the temperament state usually presents depressive manic type. It is a man who is manic, inclined to violence, depressed at every turn, and then suddenly extremely excited, this kind of person is very successful, why? Because his depressive state is his acute perception of unfavorable occasions and appropriate avoidance, his manic excitement state is his effective mobilization and full play of his biological energy in favorable occasions, so this character of the person is very socially competitive, although you will find it very uncomfortable with him in close contact. So for a woman, if your husband is bad-tempered, I'm afraid you have to praise him and not just spill your grievances, because this character of your husband expresses his human or animal nature more powerful to participate in intra-species competition.

What am I talking about? the bottom reference system. It signifies that there is a prescribed level of viciousness beneath human nature, human animal nature, human social nature, and even human social institutions, and it is the most basal part and the most difficult to overcome. The doctrine of legalism was actually to have mobilized this part, replaced it with a rational form, and made it into nothing more than a potential mobilization and rapacious tension for civilized social control.

Nevertheless, as civilization developed till date, the state of human society is rapidly developing in two directions: on the one hand, intra-species competition is becoming more and more intense, we can constantly see competitions going on between individuals, between companies, between groups, and between countries, all of which are the same species of human beings, which, out of different interests, have formed different associations and are engaged in intra-species struggles at different levels. This sequence of struggles is becoming more and more brutal and larger in scale, and the international pattern of the world today is the same as the inter states pattern of the Central Plains in the Spring and Autumn era, Warring States period in China. All juridical coordination exists only within the state domestically, international provocations, internationaldisputes actually have no rules and regulations to follow, and the so-called international law is actually just an empty shelf. Once people compete at the international level, there would not be any means of restraint, just like entering a jungle to compete. And the human species today has reached an extreme level of deterioration in competition at the international level. On the other hand, the human race today has increased its capabilities, whether it is technological, violent or destructive, all of which have increased significantly. The collision of the two will lead to the danger of human extinction. If, at this time, mankind still insists on playing smart, seeking various competitive advantages, domestic class struggle, international hot and cold war, strengthening competitive ability in various ways, and taking pride in this, as a symbol of civilization manifestation and national strength, then mankind will be in a dying state with no future.

In any other species, there is necessarily a limit to intraspecific competition because it is limited by its own innate endowment of physical intelligence. Even when a primate monkey fights with another monkey, it is difficult to kill the other monkey. It is too difficult for it to kill another monkey. There is no big difference between the ability and physical state of the two sides, so it is not easy to defeat each other, and it is difficult to kill each other. But humans do not have this limit, with the continuous improvement of their own technological capabilities, the human race can reach the level of intra-species competition to destroy the species. Therefore, mankind is facing a future of self-destruction, which has never occurred before in the 3.8 billion years of biological history, and today mankind is approaching such a major crisis. Therefore, the major issue facing mankind today is how to dissolve the "competition of separate national groups" and establish a new universal value of "non-competition, powerlessness, and non-violence", which is a matter of life and death for mankind.

Remember, human nature is paved with violence and cruelty at the bottom, which is a very frightening human element that will constitute a destructive prospect for the future of humanity in an uncontrolled manner. Therefore, humanity today needs to mobilize its great wisdom to recreate a community of human destiny, which, in the words of China's hundred schools in pre-Qin era, is called a *globalized view of the world*. As I said earlier, China had a *world view* instead of a *national view* as early as the pre-Qin era, and humanity today urgently needs such a *world view* in the era of globalization. Only if we care about the future of the entire human species on a higher level than the national level can we call it *community of human destiny*. How to build a future unified human society that eliminates national borders and group competition on the level of bestiality-based humanity is obviously the first major challenge facing humanity. The Chinese doctrine of legalism, as a negative reference system for the construction of the future civilization of mankind, presents a major problem that needs to be solved urgently.

Well, that concludes our lecture for today. We set aside time below for our discussion.

Q & A After Class

Questioner: Hello, Mr. Dongyue! Since China and the United States has been in trade disputes, how can we look at the trade war between China and the United States from the perspective of the cultural differences between the East and the West? Thank you!

Mr. Dongyue: I really can't talk about such a specific issue, and I'm afraid you'll have to find the Minister of Commerce to discuss it. You will find that human competition at the national level is getting more and more intense, more and more competitive projects, and stronger and stronger competitive will. And in any national system, class differentiation, group differentiation, and company differentiation all constitute competitive relationships. We do not discuss specific issues, we just look at this competition process is obviously not a process of dissolution, but a process of intensification, and all aspects, and all the details. Therefore, as I said earlier, *culture precedes system*, if human beings want to deal with this problem, according to the natural flow of human nature, it will not make this problem easily dissolved, but will make this problem more and more serious. Because this is a trend of 3.8 billion years of biological evolution, how difficult it is for human beings to overcome their own natural properties. So this issue is of great significance in cultural reconstruction and becomes a big issue for the future survival of human beings.

Questioner: Hello, Sir! My name is Li Peng, and yesterday's class we talked about how China is still in the process of transforming from an agricultural to an industrial and commercial civilization, and that this transformation is not yet completed. Today's class also mentioned that culture precedes systems, and the obscurity of culture gives us reason to believe that this process of transformation will continue for a long time yet. And how do you see the third transformation that China is likely to enter? Is it possible for China to go straight to the next transformation without the second one being finished? Thank you!

Mr. Dongyue: This is a very good question. Since natural evolution, biological evolution and even the evolution of human civilization has always been an accelerating process, the second great social transformation that China faces is likely before its completion when the third social transformation and civilizational transformation is already imminent. It is only that the third social transformation must not take place within the national sphere, that is, it must be the subject not only of China but of all mankind. Because it is impossible to solve the fundamental problem of intra-species competition within the state group, the state is the highest expression of intra-species competition. Therefore, as long as the state exists, human intra-species competition cannot be weakened, but only strengthened. This is the reason why I say that the next phase of human civilization will be a post-state, post-science, and post-capital era. Therefore, if China wants to lead the future civilization of mankind, it has to seek a way out to lead the future survival and development of mankind on a new ideological and cultural concept, a cultural concept that transcends national interests.

QUESTIONER: Hello, sir! I think it should be very difficult for people today to imagine the post-scientific era in today's scientific era. I think it is very difficult for people today to imagine the post-scientific era, just like how to imagine the scientific era in the age of religion and agriculture, which is a very big obstacle. I would like to ask you about the scenario, the way of thinking, and the value system of the post-scientific era that you envision, and what it might be like. What role will science and technology play in that era? How will its culture be placed? Thank you!

MR. DONGYUE: What you said earlier is very true, that is, if human beings are in a certain state covered by mainstream culture, it is very difficult for alien culture and new ideas to emerge, because it does not match your current survival structure or survival situation at all. For example, if I talk about the post-scientific era today, it will seem awkward. Today is the scientific era, if you act against science, if you ignore science and technology, if you let your children out of science education, you and your children will inevitably face a huge existential crisis. But this is exactly how new ideas happen, it is to produce the seeds of alien ideas when traditionally the original mainstream culture is still prevailing. This is why Li Bai's poem contains the line: "All sages were silent since antient", that is, the occurrence of new ideas must initially be a very weak voice, but it represents the future. As I said earlier, any culture that does not have a maintenance effect on its carrier is a sign that the culture is in decline. So we can logically and theoretically foresee that the scientific era is coming to an end. But we can't describe the specific state of the post-scientific era, which is very difficult to do, but we can only explore theoretically the basic situation and the basic direction of the post-scientific era that will happen. If you are interested in this issue, please find the book *The Decline of Humankind* and read it.

Questioner: Hello, Mr. Dongyue! Is it because of the ugliness of human nature that Han Feizi developed his legalism independently from Confucianism? Or was it inevitable based on the extension of the Confucian theory of lineage? Then, I am also concerned about a question: You concluded that a theoretician cannot be pragmatic and a pragmatist cannot be theoretician. Why did you come to such a conclusion? Thank you!

Mr. Dongyue: First of all, as I said earlier, I said that Han Feizi was a virtuous scholar. Han Feizi's doctrine was very harsh and very vicious, but he himself was not lacking in goodness. What does it show? The theory of Legalism, the thought of Legalism, and the political structure of Chinese society were in no way related to the virtue of any one person. Even if there were no Han Feizi, a Li Feizi would have created such a culture, and he could not have created any other legal system, so human culture is a product of a certain structure and situation. The difference between the Chinese and the Westerners in terms of intelligence is minimal, not because the Chinese were not intelligent enough to create a democratic social structure, but because the soil and environment in which they live simply make it impossible for them to raise this question.

I will answer your second question. I said that "those who are theoreticians cannot be pragmatical, those who are pragmatic cannot be theoreticians", we do not need either induction or deduction, it is an obvious fact in history. Just think about one thing: "Is it difficult to know" or "is it difficult to do"? In ancient China, it is said that "knowledge and action are united, knowledge is difficult and action is easy", while some people say that "knowledge is easy and action is difficult". Think about any new idea, new culture, how does it happen? Biologically speaking, there is basically no difference between the intelligence of each person, the difference is minimal. The practice of measuring IQ is actually very problematic, all people are equally intelligent. So what makes a person who creates a new culture or a new idea? Newton and Einstein, who we think of as geniuses, were actually as smart as all of us. The reason why they created such complex systems of thought is related to their individual intelligence, but it is not the most important. Rather, it is because he focused his life's energy and intellect on a single point of use. The way we generally use our intellect is to seek survival with our intellect, and in order to survive in society, our intellect is spread out, we have to deal with problems in all directions, and we seek to balance our personality. But how is it possible for a person to be innovative and creative in academic, theoretical and ideological terms? All people have the same intelligence, what makes you do it? There is only one possibility: you have focused your life's energy and intellect on this one thing. Even so, only one or two out of millions of scholars have really made a difference, which is called theoretician cannot be pragmatical. It is not that he is not capable of doing real work, but once he disperses his energy and intellect to be pragmatic, he will never be able to make the theoretical and intellectual achievements that others cannot. And pragmatist cannot be theoretician, since his energy has been scattered, he can't focus back the escaped energy. The complex structure of a survival system that has taken shape in adulthood has bound you. People in doing academics, learning, or even in doing anything, need to start work from a child. The so-called child's work, that is, you have to start training in this area since childhood, you will be able to eventually stand out, into the outstanding generation, which is the reason why the theoreticians cannot be pragmatical, the pragmatist cannot be theoretician. There are too much of information we need to face and deal with today, and human beings have to face too many things if they want to survive. This is why in this day and age, we keep talking about a word called *specialization*, which means that anyone who spreads his or her energy to deal with survival issues and cultural issues, you must have a balanced survival and a balanced personality. But you can never be really deep in any one field. If you want to develop deeply in any field, you must sacrifice the energy and intelligence invested in other fields, and this must be the case, which is called the *era of specialization*. So we analyze from this perspective, we can conclude that the theoretician must be unable to do the real things, and the pragmatist must also be unable to do the theoretical things, in any personal ability, the two cannot be balanced, unless you are superhuman.

Questioner: When you talked about political wisdom, you mentioned that the political wisdom of the East is relatively low-end compared to the democratic and liberal political wisdom of the West. Nowadays, we often hear a saying on the Internet that Chinese political wisdom has a clear superiority that the West does not have. This includes the fact that many of China's rulers and administrators are elites selected from the grassroots, so they certainly make decisions with a higher level of vision that the Western electoral system cannot. China's non-democratic system is relatively more efficient than the West's, so both of these points ensure the superiority of Eastern political wisdom. Does it mean that it is more suitable for the structure of China's survival at the time when the people's wisdom is not fully enlightened?

Mr. Dongyue: I'm very familiar with this voice you're talking about, and it's the official word in mainstream culture and mainstream politics today. Listen to it, what is the saying that elites coming up from the grassroots rule society? The typical theory of human rule. He says he is the most efficient. How is efficiency expressed in the thousands of years of autocratic rule of mankind since ancient times? It all depends on whether the king is enlightened or not. Efficiency is indeed high, high efficiency in doing good things, but also high efficiency in doing wrong things and bad things, there is no constraint structure, so high efficiency can be expressed in any field, the end result cancels each other out, and even more mischief, this is the difference between a democratic system and an autocratic system of human rule. It is not at all surprising that we hear such voices in the mainstream today, but we do need to think deeply about this issue, to consider the origins of this problem, to think about the thousands of years of human political history, what issues have been summarized and discussed. The issue should be very clear in its conclusion after centuries of discussion in the humanities of modern Western society, thousands of years of discussion from the time of Plato and Aristotle. More importantly, is efficiency that important? What do you ultimately seek for a country, a nation, a group? It is survival. As I said earlier, the increase in efficiency and capacity is precisely the source of human disasters, so the constant pursuit of high efficiency by human beings today must be a negative concept in the future structure of civilization, I am afraid. So I think this issue is very clear to me, and it is very normal to have different voices in the society.

Questioner: Hello, Mr. Dongyue! Nowadays, both the political and academic circles are shouting the slogan of reviving Confucianism, which reminds me of Mr. Yu Yingshi's saying "the kiss of death". The more the government promotes Confucianism and affirms Confucianism, the faster Confucianism will die. There are also some scholars who strongly advocate Confucianism as a national religion, what do you think, Mr. Dongyue?

Mr. Dongyue: I think my point is very clear. What does Confucianism mean? Confucianism is the backbone of traditional Chinese culture, and what is traditional Chinese culture? It is the cultural integration of the most refined and typical agricultural civilization system in the world, and this is called Confucianism. In fact, it has been called *religion of Confucianism* since ancient China, so there is a saying of *unity of three religions* in China since ancient times, that is, Confucianism, Daoism and Buddhism. As I said earlier, the ancient culture of mankind must have the elements of *governance*, *enlightenment,* and *rule,* so Confucianism has long been a religion. However, I have been saying in my classes that there is no way back for human beings, that the world is evolving in one direction, and that although the civilization process is in a deteriorating process, there is no way back for you. I talk about the historical rationality of Confucian doctrine, saying that it was a cultural maintenance effect back then, but then I say later in the discussion about the dross and the essence that you can't retreat, you just take it and use it, and you immediately fall into an absurd and ridiculous situation. So Confucianism is only the base reference system for human beings to construct future civilization, and this is where its essence lies. Taking it directly as the mainstream culture today is equivalent to returning human beings to agricultural civilization. Because culture must match the structure of survival, if we take Confucianism as our present culture, how can it form an effective cultural maintenance effect? So those claims are not valid at all. We study Confucianism as a ladder to understand the process of human culture or the history of human thought, as a method and a way of thinking to find the future reference system of human culture. To say that Confucianism can save China and the world, is the same absurdity as saying that retreating to agricultural civilization is the future and gospel of humanity.

QUESTIONER: Hello, Mr. Dongyue! The world today is a bit like the Warring States period in China, where there was a lot of strife and warfare, and nationalism and statism are getting stronger, so I quite agree to what you mentioned transformation from nationalism to humanism, from statism to globalism in *The Decline of Humankind*, But in the past, China was eventually unified by the Qin state in the Warring States. Is it possible for the whole world to become unified in the future? If it is possible, will it be China to do the unification? If it never gets unified, will it be because aliens invade the earth and then have to unite to fight the aliens? Thanks!

MR. DONGYUE: For the issue of aliens, I'll put it in the last session of Day 12 for a slight discussion. Let's start now with your first topic, will human globalization proceed in the same way as the state Qin conquered and wiped out the other six states, is it possible? You should know that human capabilities of today, including those of nations, have reached devastating heights, and if the world is unified today by the powerful and violent way of the Warring States period, as I said in my book *The Decline of Humankind,* the path would have been a precipice long ago! Just ask, who would dare to conquer China by force? Who dares to conquer Russia by force? Who dares to use force to unify the United States? It is for sure that he will use atomic bomb to fight with you. So today there is no possibility of global unification by military violence. And if it is a violent unification, then it must also be a violent rule, just like what was established after Qin swept the six states, the tyrannical system of the Qin Dynasty. Can all of humanity today accept a violent regime system? Can a violent United Nations be accepted by all mankind? This is also hopeless. Therefore, the future community of destiny and post-state era of humanity will be based on a new ideology and culture, and progress will be made by means of common human consultation. But it has one prerequisite, that is, all mankind must have this cultural consciousness, because culture precedes system.

QUESTIONER: Hello, Mr. Dongyue! Zhang Juzheng of the Ming dynasty, as a teacher of the emperor, was given a very good platform to practice Confucianism, but in the process of doing so, his students found that his words and actions were not consistent, and took extreme actions against Confucianism. Or is it that Confucianism itself is like a flashlight, shining on others but not on oneself? Thank you, teacher!

MR. DONGYUE: As I said in my lecture on Confucius, Confucian doctrine tends to be corrupted during its cultural development. Confucius' own sincerity, righteousness, and cultivation may not be false, but Confucian doctrine necessarily tends to corrupt. It is because the process of human civilization is the process of the continuous corruption of human nature, or the process of the continuous extension of the inferiority of human nature, so Confucianism itself must eventually meet such an end. If Chinese Confucianism had collapsed at this time, and new ideas had emerged and formed a cultural trend, then China's national fate today and its recent humiliating national fate would have ceased to occur. But what emerged in the Song Dynasty? It was the Cheng brothers, Zhu Xi, Wang Yangming, the group of people who recreated and strengthened the Confucian doctrine. What does this mean? It shows that the survival structure of Chinese agricultural civilization was stable and the cultural soil of Confucianism was still rich, so it was inevitable that Confucianism would come back and even solidify into *theories of science*. Although Chinese society declined all the way to the Opium War afterwards, it shows that the soil of Chinese agricultural civilization was exceptionally fertile for more than two thousand years. Building a new culture was difficult, despite the deterioration of Confucianism, and despite the gradual causticization of Confucianism. We will discuss this issue in depth in our next class on the collection of the hundred schools of Confucianism and the changes in Confucianism.

QUESTIONER: Hello, teacher! Today, I argued with a post-2000-year kid who was listening to the class with me, because I couldn't convince him. He said why the law was created because morality is corrupted? Morality does not fall, but in my mind, I think morality falls because people's hearts are corrupted, so I can't explain this. Please you give me an explanation.

Mr. Dongyue: In my class, I said that in the early years, human beings were *ruled by virtue*, I said that in ancient China, someone already commented that people's minds were not as good as in ancient time and the morality was deteriorating, I said that you can only do "situational evaluation" on the surface, that is, on the surface, the moral standard of human beings is improving, behavior is being refined, but from the bones of human culture it is becoming more and more violent, I have talked about these issues, you have to do the "ultimate evaluation". The emergence of the legal system in human society is itself detrimental to morality. Because it is not moral to maintain social bonds, "the law cannot be prohibited", this is the basic rule of law society. Therefore, it is no longer the time to use moral framework to restrain human behavior, and *rule by morality* is no longer possible in this era. In this era, the complexity of society and the heightened social tensions make moral bonds simply insufficient to sustain them. So even if morality does not collapse, moral drift, moral wavering, moral dilution from a distance is inevitable. So I don't think you need to convince him, because I'm afraid it's an illusion for any new idea to gain the approval of a larger number of people in a dominant cultural environment. It needs the times to continue to evolve for certain doctrines themselves to be able to gradually flourish. Therefore, I have followed three principles in my academic career: first, do not argue; second, do not convince; and third, do not agree. I suggest that you do not have to argue with anyone either. If you accept an idea, you should seek to prove it and see if it is true, or if it is correct and consistent with the facts. If you see people who don't accept it, take it for granted, because the fact that most people don't accept it is what makes it a new idea. If most people accept it at the moment, it means that your new idea is no different from the old one.

Questioner: Hello, Mr. Dongyue! I would like to ask how you evaluate the study of the West in Taiwan. We know that there was a perfect fusion of Chinese traditional culture and Indian Buddhism. How do you comment on that fusion, Thank you.

Mr. Dongyue: This is a bit complicated, because we have to discuss multiple factors on a specific issue, and it is impossible to discuss with a single factor. Taiwan has two characteristics: on the one hand, its traditional culture is well preserved, and on the other hand, its Western culture is more fully accepted, which is related to the New Culture Movement in the early part of the last century; in 1916, the New Culture Movement, with Chen Duxiu and Lu Xun as its banners, proposed to overthrow Confucianism. The Communist Party was an active supporter of the New Culture Movement and the Down with Confucius Movement, while the Nationalist Party held a reserved, neutral attitude. Chiang Kai-shek spoke of propriety, righteousness and honesty, and he respected the revered Zeng Wenzheng, and held a certain degree of respect for traditional Chinese culture. But at the same time, you should note that the Nationalist Party platform is fully Westernized, it is called the Constitutional Party platform, which means that its political goal back then was to establish Sun Yat-sen's constitutional republican system. Only because Sun Yat- sen was frustrated, he divided the political process into three steps, called the military period, the training period and the constitutional period. That is, the country was first run in an army maintained and militarized way, then the nation was trained to be familiar with constitutional government, and finally it entered the constitutional system. Since the goal of its party platform is to establish a constitutional government, it is somehow logical that it will eventually move toward a democratic system in Taiwan. What is the CCP's party platform? The dictatorship of the proletariat. So this is completely different. On the surface, the KMT appears to be compatible with both traditional Chinese culture and Western constitutional culture. In fact, the influence of traditional Chinese culture on contemporary times has been minimal, it is only a superficial color, and has long since been shattered by the ongoing century-long process of cleaning up the old culture, which does not constitute realistic ideological resistance or cultural binding force at all, and this is what causes the KMT to seem to exhibit cultural contradictions.

Your second question will be discussed not now, but in my class on Buddhism later as one of the 12-day courses.

Questioner: Hello, sir! I would like to ask a question. You talked about the stability of China's culture and social structure, is because the whole East Asia is a single closed structure in terms of geography. In today's globalization, our whole world, although we seem to be in constant communication, as well as global trade and the Internet, some scholars are already discussing the "end of history" and the "end of art", does it mean that we are now in a rigid structure that seems to be very active in terms of communication, but is also a single closed structure? Because the cultural exchange between us is no longer able to cause the kind of refinement that we had at the beginning. Thank you, sir!

Mr. Dongyue: Today it is no longer possible to form a communication barrier in the geographic landscape; the information flow barrier today is created by the state power. The strength of this barrier is completely different from that of geographic closure. Therefore, it is impossible for any government to close off external information, external communication and external cultural impact for a long time; it is only a transient phenomenon. It is only a matter of time before Chinese society is integrated into the international community. Today, China is fully integrated into the world economically, and Chinese society has actually been fully westernized culturally, except for a slight gap in political awareness and reality. Isn't the entire curriculum we have today, from elementary school, secondary school to university, and even what we wear on our feet and heads today, all Western things? Therefore, the barriers of communication today, including the artificial barriers of communication, must be very weak, and it is impossible to form as effective a barrier as in ancient times or the Middle Ages of several hundred years back, so the convergence of human cultures will become higher and higher. But the general direction of the spontaneous flow of Western culture, as well as other national cultures around the world, is not the future of humanity today. Humanity must seek new ideas in the dominant cultures of the modern world, and this will expand the future of human existence. My implication of this statement is that even if Chinese culture is not shielded, Western culture does not represent the future, even though Chinese culture has long been in decline and I do not admit that Chinese culture can save the world, nor do I admit that Western culture represents the future. It needs a whole new cultural reinvention. As to whether today's global communication is not sufficient, whether it has formed some kind of interstellar closure, whether it has hindered the development of the people of the earth, my view is the opposite, not that the development is too slow, not that the development is not sophisticated enough, but that the development is too fast, so fast that it is too close to the cliff to brake, and this is the most worrying thing at the moment.

Questioner: When we talked about the Meiji Restoration of Japan, we mentioned that Japan studied China for a thousand years, but after the Meiji Restoration, it was able to break away from Asia and enter Europe in a very short time, within thirty years, and then became one of the world powers. Since it had studied China for so long, why could it have such a rapid transformation? Japan is an island nation, its land area is small and its population is small, does it have something to do with this special structure of existence? Or does it have something to do with other factors? The second question is that Japan, especially in ancient times, was known for its *sword* culture, was it related to Japan's worse environment of survival, so they were more upheld violence? Okay, thank you!

Mr. Dongyue: The exploration of Japanese culture is indeed a rather complex issue, and Western scholars have also specially studied it, writing works such as *The Chrysanthemum and the Sword*. Then I will answer briefly why Japan abandoned traditional Chinese culture so easily. It is because it received Tang studies in the Sui and Tang dynasties, and Tang studies was originally a foreign transplanted culture for it, not its native culture, and did not fundamentally connected to it. In addition, the culture of island countries is usually very special. Look at the Britain, the British culture is of same with that of the whole Europe, fully merged, so that the British scholars had great contributions in the shaping of modern system of thought in Europe. I mentioned earlier that Locke, Newton, Hume, Adam Smith, John Mueller, and so on, were all British, but there is still a difference between British and continental European culture. Continental Europe developed a strong monarchy in the Medieval Ages, while England remained largely feudal until the bourgeois revolution. If you look back at Japan, Japanese history by and large did not establish a really solid centralized power, but was always a feudal state, so Japan does have some similarities with England in terms of social structure and historical process. From this point of view, on the one hand, Tang study was not an inherent culture of Japan, and on the other hand, Japan's feudal social structure is slightly similar to that of Britain, so we can certainly imagine that it would be easier and smoother for Japan to accept the social doctrine and social philosophy of the post-feudal era, that is, to carry out the transformation of capitalist society. I am afraid that this is the reason why the Meiji Restoration process in Japan appeared to be relatively simple, while the social transformation in China was extremely difficult, just as the bourgeois revolutions in continental Europe were relatively slow and difficult to produce. As for the many other details of the cultural characteristics of Japanese society, I am not sure what to say about them, and you might need a professional scholar to discuss them.

CPSIA information can be obtained
at www.ICGtesting.com
Printed in the USA
BVHW040248080223
658118BV00004B/104